De Valera

DE VALERA

Rise 1882-1932

David McCullagh

Gill Books

Gill Books
Hume Avenue
Park West
Dublin 12
www.gillbooks.ie

Gill Books is an imprint of M.H. Gill & Co.

978 07171 55866

Print origination by Carole Lynch
Edited by Ruairí Ó Brógáin
Proofread by Neil Burkey
Indexed by Adam Pozner
Printed by CPI Group (UK) Ltd, Croydon, CR0 4YY
This book is typeset in Adobe Caslon.

The paper used in this book comes from the wood
pulp of managed forests. For every tree felled, at least
one tree is planted, thereby renewing natural resources.

A CIP catalogue record for this book is available
from the British Library.

5 4 3 2

ACKNOWLEDGEMENTS

This book began with a casual conversation on Dublin's Molesworth Street in 2011. Fergal Tobin, then the Publishing Director of Gill Books, suggested Éamon de Valera as my next subject. I was dubious, given the number of times the ground had been covered: surely there was nothing new to say?

Fergal, who can be very persuasive, convinced me that it was both possible and worthwhile to go back to the source material and try to produce a comprehensive, even-handed study which could illuminate the real Éamon de Valera, the man behind the mask he habitually wore in public. How far the finished product meets that aim is, of course, for others to judge.

If the book wouldn't have been started without Fergal, it wouldn't have been finished without Commissioning Editor Conor Nagle, who inherited the project on Fergal's retirement. Conor has somehow managed to maintain his sunny optimism and positive attitude despite my best, or worst, efforts to ignore deadlines and expand the text. Crucially, he agreed that two volumes would be required to do the subject justice – the present one, *Rise*, looking at the events which shaped Éamon de Valera; the second, *Rule*, examining how he in turn shaped Ireland in the period after 1932.

Also at Gill, I'd like to thank Managing Editor Sheila Armstrong, whose task in overseeing the production process was made considerably more difficult by the author; copy editor Ruairí Ó Brógáin; Marketing and Communications Manager Teresa Daly; and picture researcher Jen Patton.

I owe a debt of gratitude to various friends and colleagues: Franc Myles and Ed Mulhall read sections of the manuscript and offered invaluable advice; Ray Burke of RTÉ and Dr Mark O'Brien of DCU pointed me in productive directions relating to the *Irish Press*, a subject both have written books on; Dr Stephen Kelly of Liverpool Hope University kindly allowed me access to a memoir by Gerry Boland; Francesca Walsh was a generous supplier of books; Joe Ó Muircheartaigh pointed me towards a Clare quotation; Senan Molony of the *Irish Daily Mail* shared some inherited rugby anecdotes which gave great background (though they didn't make it into the final text); Bethan Kilfoil clarified an issue in Welsh; and at various times Joe Mag Raollaigh, Brídóg Ni Bhuachalla and Rónán Ó Domhnaill translated documents in Irish for me.

Much of this book is based on the de Valera papers in the UCD Archives, as well as on other collections in that invaluable institution: my thanks to the staff there, particularly Principal Archivist Kate Manning, and Orna Somerville, and to the staff of other archives in which I have researched: the National Archives of Ireland, the National Library of Ireland, the Public Record Office of Northern Ireland, and the National Archives of the United Kingdom. My thanks too to Fianna Fáil General Secretary Seán Dorgan for granting access to his party's records in UCD. Tracy Lenihan of the de Valera Museum in Bruree very helpfully gave me a tour of the museum, located in the former national school, and of the house de Valera grew up in.

Recent years have seen an explosion in the amount of material available online. I would particularly like to thank the Bureau of Military History, whose collection of Witness Statements and Military Pension applications are a treasure trove of information (as well as a source of endless fascinating distractions!); the indispensable *Dictionary of Irish Biography*; the fascinating *Century Ireland* website; and Dr Michael Kennedy and Dr Kate O'Malley at *Documents on Irish Foreign Policy* – the volumes quoted in this book are all now available online, but really there is no substitute for the printed version.

Finally, and most importantly, to the two women in my life, my wife Anne-Marie Smyth and our daughter Rosie, who have both had to put up with de Valera for longer than seems reasonable, and who still have Volume 2 to look forward to. Their encouragement and support was constant. I really couldn't have done it without you – my love and my thanks to you both.

David McCullagh,
July 2017

CONTENTS

CHAPTER 01

SLÁN LEAT, DEV

As the great white gates of Áras an Uachtaráin swung open, the waiting crowd surged forward, impatient for a glimpse of the man in the back of the presidential Rolls-Royce. Some had been waiting for hours, and the 85 stewards were having difficulty keeping the roadway clear as enthusiasm mounted.[1]

It was June 1973 and Éamon de Valera was finally leaving public life, which he had dominated for more than half a century. The last surviving commandant of Easter Week, the undisputed leader of Irish nationalism during the War of Independence, commander of the 'legion of the rearguard' during and after the Civil War, head of government for 21 years, President for two terms, de Valera had an unrivalled position in Irish public life – though a deeply controversial one.

Estimates of the size of the crowd varied: 6,000 according to the *Irish Times*; double that, said the *Irish Independent*; 50,000 in de Valera's own *Irish Press*. Whatever its size, there was no doubting the crowd's enthusiasm. There were spectators on car roofs, sitting in trees, and clinging to the Phoenix Monument, and others crowded six-deep along the road. There were also – according to the *Irish Press* – 'many elderly women . . . weeping and waving white handkerchiefs'.

The emotion was real, though it was far from the 'spontaneous tribute' suggested by the Fianna Fáil leader, Jack Lynch. In fact, the party had carefully prepared the ceremony. Banners were made for each of the 26 counties, with the county name and party logo prominently displayed. The National Executive had also organised special trains and buses to bring members from around the country to Dublin.[2]

Lynch was determined to make the most of whatever glory reflected on him from the founder of Fianna Fáil. As the navy-blue Rolls-Royce nosed out of the gates, Lynch stepped forward and opened the door, shaking hands with the President for the benefit of the cameras and welcoming him 'back among us' again, after his 14 years above politics.

When the cluster of photographers and camera crews blocking the road finally parted, the car moved off. The honour guard of Old IRA veterans saluted, and the crowd broke into patriotic song: 'A Nation Once Again', then 'Wrap the Green Flag Round Me, Boys'. The President's senior aide-de-camp, Colonel Seán Brennan, sat beside the driver, while Frank Aiken, dapper as always, with a crisply ironed handkerchief in the breast pocket of his suit, sat in the back beside his Chief.

Cheering crowds lined the route out of the Phoenix Park, along the south quays and through the city centre to the venue for de Valera's final public speech. The choice of location was instructive. There were many potential backdrops: the Department of the Taoiseach, where he had presided for so long; the Dáil, which he had dominated for decades; the head office in Burgh Quay of the Irish Press Group, which he had established; or even, of course, the gates of the Áras itself.

Instead, de Valera returned to the scene of his first appearance on the national stage, where his enduring myth began: Boland's Bakery, an otherwise obscure building by the Grand Canal, where he commanded the garrison during the Easter Rising.[3] This choice underlined the fact that, without 1916, de Valera – born in New York with question marks over his paternity, sent across the ocean by his mother to grow up in a humble home in Bruree, in rural Co. Limerick – would hardly be ending his days as perhaps the most famous man in Ireland.

The five thousand people waiting at Boland's gave him an enthusiastic reception. Helped out of his car by Aiken, de Valera, somewhat hampered by the furled black umbrella he was holding, raised his trademark black homburg hat to acknowledge the crowd. Guided by Aiken and Brennan, he slowly made his way to the platform. Many of the signs held by the crowd were in Irish, including one simply saying, *Slán leat, Dev*.

After the national anthem, Lynch made a lengthy speech, paying tribute to his former leader, 'the greatest Irishman of this century', for his years of service, beginning with the Easter Rising. He was followed by speakers representing the four provinces: Máire Geoghegan, a 22-year-old teacher from Co. Galway, later a TD, minister and European Commissioner; Seán Ó Ceallaigh, a former Clare TD; Cathal Brugha, grandson and namesake of one of de Valera's greatest friends; and Seán MacEntee, a former minister whose sometimes turbulent relationship with de Valera had dimmed none of his admiration for the man he now referred to as 'Ireland's George Washington'.

Then it was time for the outgoing President to make his final speech, which he delivered in a firm voice, speaking throughout in Irish. He told the crowd that, while he had once thought he wouldn't see Ireland free and united in his lifetime, he now believed he would – a somewhat rash prediction for a man in his tenth decade. He urged the crowd to have faith in the country, and in the language, and thanked them for their loyalty over the years. Then he left the platform, pausing as an afterthought to pay tribute to Erskine Childers, who was to be sworn in as President the following day. De Valera was then driven to the nursing home in Blackrock where he and his wife, Sinéad, would spend their final days.

Comment on his departure was mixed: all agreed he was the dominant political figure of the previous half-century, though it was recognised that his record was not unblemished. There were, of course, many achievements: his welding together of the disparate elements of advanced nationalism in 1917; his grit and determination in coming back from the devastating defeat of the Civil War; his skill in drafting a new constitution, introduced in 1937, to solidify independence; and his leadership in asserting that independence during the Second World War. He had founded the most successful political party in the country – out of office now, but sure to be back in government soon – as well as a hugely successful newspaper group.

But even in 1973 there were plenty of people prepared to say that de Valera's record was a dismal one. He was blamed by some for instilling in the country a narrow cultural nationalism that made Ireland a grey place; to others he was at fault for the economic failure that almost submerged the state in its third decade; to many more, he was responsible for the Civil War.

In the decades since his death, in 1975, the negative parts of de Valera's legacy have been stressed. His reputation has taken a battering, his stature diminished in comparison with others who have risen in public estimation – principally his greatest rival, Michael Collins, and his closest lieutenant, Seán Lemass.

But even his harshest critics have to acknowledge his dominance. For good or ill, it was his vision that set the tone of Irish society, his leadership that set the pace and direction of the march towards independence, albeit for only 26 of the 32 counties. This dominance is all the more remarkable given the barriers to his rise to power: his unusual background, his upbringing in rural poverty, his obscure career as a teacher of mathematics. And yet he became the leader of nationalist Ireland, obeyed without question at home and revered abroad. And then, just as rapidly, it was all snatched away after the signing of the Treaty. He became a pariah, hated, harried and imprisoned by his political opponents. But from the nadir of

1923 he managed to claw his way back to prominence, shattering one political movement and founding another, launching a hugely successful newspaper, and winning the trust of the Irish people.

It was an extraordinary rise – and it is this rise that explains the person he had become by 1932, when the time came for him to rule. It was this rise that forged his character, formed his views and fostered his self-belief. The story of his rise begins with the most fundamental of questions: who was he, and where did he really come from?

CHAPTER 02

THE QUESTION OF FAMILY HISTORY

In International Law am I a Spaniard or an American?
Éamon de Valera, 1916[1]

As I was less than two years of age when my father died I do not remember him, and have only such slight information as my mother had.
Éamon de Valera, 1950[2]

. . . the question became of importance some forty odd years ago, and I would like to have it answered.
Éamon de Valera, 1962[3]

A missing piece of paper troubled Éamon de Valera throughout his long life: his parents' marriage certificate. He was bothered enough by its absence to seek it – or any other evidence of their wedding – over many years, using many different agents: his half-brother, his cousin, ecclesiastical authorities in America and Spain, even the Irish minister in Madrid during the Spanish Civil War. Proof of the marriage would silence persistent whispers about his legitimacy, as well as proving to the world – and to himself – that his mother had been telling the truth about his parentage.

But no proof would be found, despite the efforts of de Valera and his legion of helpers, and of future biographers and genealogists. Neither would any proof be found of the supposed death of his father, Vivion de Valera, in Denver, or perhaps New Mexico, unless it was in Minnesota. Indeed, there is little evidence that Vivion ever existed.

Of course, an individual's paternity should not affect our opinion of them. But the point is that the questions about his father and about his parents' marriage affected Éamon de Valera. Did his own doubts about his ancestry lead him to take a more extreme approach in politics, to try to become, in effect, 'more Irish than the Irish themselves'? And what was the effect of the repeated slurs de Valera had to suffer as he climbed to prominence? He was sometimes referred to as 'that Spanish-American bastard' or as an 'illegitimate Dago'.[4] In fact, there is very little evidence of any Spanish connection.

The official story is easily told. Catherine (Kate) Coll emigrated to the United States in 1879. There she met a young Spanish man, Vivion de Valera, a former sculptor who had become a music teacher after his eye was damaged by a chip of marble. They were married in 1881, and the following year their son, Edward, was born. Vivion, because of ill-health, travelled west, where he died, in Denver, Colorado. Kate, forced to work full time, then arranged for her son to return to her home place to be cared for by his grandmother.

To believe Kate Coll's story is to believe that no record survives of her marriage; that all written evidence of her husband's existence was lost; and that no credible Spanish connection would emerge after her son became world famous. Any one of these things is believable; to believe all of them requires a leap of faith. On the other hand, there is a birth certificate and baptismal certificate which bear his father's (misspelled) name. And when Catherine Coll de Valera remarried, the officiating priest accepted both that she had been married before and that her first husband was dead.

The only evidence for the first marriage is Kate Coll's word, and she was a notably unreliable witness. She appeared to be confused – or evasive – about many details: where she met her husband, where they were married, where he died. As she put it herself in a letter to her son, in relation to her accounts of his father, 'Please excuse me if . . . I contradict anything I have told you. It is because I forget or was not really sure of it.'[5] Even a dutiful son with a pressing need to believe her story must have found this less than convincing.

Kate Coll arrived in New York on 2 October 1879, aboard the *Nevada* from Queenstown (Cobh).[6] New York had a population of 1.2 million,[7] and the sheer scale of the place must have been a shock to a young woman from rural Ireland, although she had the benefit of an aunt in Brooklyn with whom she could stay until she found a job.[8]

When the 1880 census was taken in the following June, Kate was living as a servant at 98 Lawrence Street, Brooklyn. The household was made up of Frank Giraud; his wife, Martha; their children, 17-year-old Edgar and 4-year-old Ella; Frank's sister Lillie, who was 24; and the 22-year-old Irish servant girl, Catherine Coll (she was actually 23). Giraud was described on the census form as an 'artist' – in fact, he was a vaudeville performer. Born in 1840, he trained as a blacksmith before becoming a minstrel and cannonball juggler in a circus. He served in the Union Navy during the Civil War, before returning to show business. In 1866, while on his way to New Orleans, he was one of a handful of survivors when the *Evening Star* sank off the coast of Georgia.[9] Rescued after five days in the water, his injured leg was nearly amputated, until a surgeon saved it after recognising a Masonic signal he gave.[10] In later life he gave up the stage for a career in real estate. He died in 1900.[11] Giraud was moderately successful on the stage – but the family were hardly 'members of New York high society of that period', as one biography of de Valera later claimed.[12]

And it was here, in Lawrence Street, that Juan Vivion de Valera enters the story – probably. For on the question of when she first met the father of her eldest child, as on so much else, Kate Coll changed her story. On one occasion she told her son that she met his father at Greenville in New Jersey; on others she said she met him at the Giraud home, where he used to call to see Frank's sister Lillie.[13] The latter is the more widely accepted version.

Mary Bromage, an early and sympathetic de Valera biographer, noted Kate's conflicting claims about her husband.

> Those who heard about Vivion through Kate were to recall him variously as a sculptor, a professor, an actor, a linguist, a doctor, a singer, a raconteur, but always as a gifted, educated and entertaining individual . . . Some were under the impression that he had come from South America, others from Cuba . . .[14]

David Dwane, who wrote the first, highly unreliable, biography of de Valera made the improbable claim that Vivion de Valera learnt Irish following his marriage, with Dwane even purporting to quote Kate on the subject. 'It was amusing to hear him trying to talk Irish.'[15]

In a letter to her son, Kate also described Vivion as improbably multi-talented. He liked to write poetry, she said, and was 'a great mimic'. His favourite musical instrument was the mandolin, and his favourite pastimes were drawing and writing. 'I must say I never saw any person that could write as perfect as he did, and his Capital letters were a wonder,' she wrote. But were any examples of this penmanship to be found? They were not.

> I have been looking through all my treasures to see if I could find any of his letters, but somehow I can't find them . . . Where I put them I can't remember. I was very ill for some time and having strangers around they got mislaid.

She then moved on to Vivion's appearance.

> 5 ft 8 in height, weight over 160 lbs, medium dark complexion, dark brown eyes, and dark brown curly hair, small hands and feet, always ready to play a trick or a joke . . .[16]

Kate said that in 1880, after they first met, Vivion went west to Denver for the sake of his health. When he returned she had left the Girauds and was working in Greenville, New Jersey, for a family named Armstrong. The relationship resumed, and in September 1881 they were married.

Her story was that she and Vivion were married on 19 September 1881 by Father Hennessey, at St Patrick's Church in Greenville, Jersey City. The witnesses were Fred Hamilton, a friend of Vivion's, and Lily Brady. In 1931, as her son was close to winning power in the Irish Free State, she would swear a deposition to this effect,[17] presumably in response to political charges about her son's legitimacy. She added that the church was near Bayview Cemetery, on the right-hand side heading from Jersey City to Greenville.[18]

However, there is no record of the wedding in the records of St Patrick's Church. In 1935, three years after Kate's death, a priest friendly with de Valera made enquiries of the parish priest at St Patrick's. He regretfully replied that there was no record of the marriage, though he suggested that the wedding might have been performed by Father Hennessey in another parish in New Jersey or New York.[19]

In 1956 de Valera asked a visiting New Jersey judge to look for a copy of his parents' marriage certificate. The judge enlisted the help of the then parish priest of St Patrick's, Monsignor James Hamilton, who searched the records from 1875 to 1900 without success.[20] In response, de Valera speculated that he could have been wrong in associating Father Hennessey with the church in which his parents were married.[21] However, Kate quite frequently claimed to have been married in Father Hennessey's church, including in a sworn deposition.

But could she have been mistaken? St Patrick's is on the *left-hand* side going from Jersey City to Greenville, and is a good half-hour walk from Bayview Cemetery. Hamilton suggested an alternative: St Paul's Church in Old Bergen Road.[22] This is closer to the cemetery – only a 13-minute walk – and is on the right-hand side of the road. Despite the name and the lack of a connection to Father Hennessey, it matches the rest of Kate's description. But, again, there is no record of the marriage. Hamilton was evidently not one to give up easily: he went on to check all the old churches in Jersey City and those established in New York City before 1880, again without success.[23]

In 1961 Father John Furniss got involved, contacting Hamilton, who described his efforts: personally inspecting the records of the older churches in Hudson County (which includes Jersey City); writing to the older churches in New York to see if any of them had a record of the marriage; and checking every church in the diocese to which Father Hennessey was attached. 'I spent one whole year in a fruitless investigation but let not my efforts discourage you.'[24]

De Valera, by now President of Ireland, wrote to Hamilton to thank him for his efforts and asking 'if you can give me any reason why my mother's marriage should not have been entered' in the parish register.[25] Hamilton replied, perhaps diplomatically, that the only reason he could think of was neglect of entry, which happened sometimes, for instance if the priest was called away urgently. However, he wrote that

> after a lapse of more than eighty years the task of ascertaining the facts of marriage either by legal or ecclesiastical records seems well-nigh impossible.[26]

A clearly disappointed de Valera thanked him once again.

> I am afraid we must leave the matter where it now stands. It is rather unfortunate that it must remain like this, but there seems to be no help for it.[27]

There was, however, another twist in this story. Kate Coll was always very definite about where she was married – except once. In an interview with the *New York Evening Journal* on 1 August 1924 she stated that she and Vivion were married in New York. Her grandson, Terry de Valera, seized on this discrepancy to get around the awkward absence of a record of the wedding at St Patrick's. He implied that the hypothesis of a New York wedding is made more credible by the fact that this 'recently discovered information' was 'supplied by Kate de Valera herself'.[28] The American genealogist Joseph Silinonte was similarly impressed by this development.

> In the bride's own words, she was married in New York City and not in Jersey City as we have been told for years. Why has this erroneous information been printed and stated over and over again?'[29]

The answer, of course, is that the Jersey City story came from Kate herself; her reference in the *Evening Journal* interview to getting married in New York may have been an error on the part of the journalist, or a mistake by her, possibly mixing up her first and second marriages. Such a mistake, however, hardly increases her credibility. And it remains the fact that the churches of New York were also searched for a marriage record – without success.[30]

Absence of evidence is not, of course, evidence of absence. It is quite possible that the marriage, wherever it took place, was not recorded properly. The problem is that the marriage certificate is not the only missing piece of evidence.

Six years of research by a team of four genealogists failed to unearth a single mention of Vivion de Valera, or any variant of that name, in the entire 1880 United States census. The only person with a similar name recorded in New York was a Cuban-born student, Claudio Valera, then a patient in a mental hospital. Vivion is not recorded in any city directory for New York, Brooklyn, Jersey City or Newark, or in the list of thousands of artists kept in the New York Public Library's Division of Art. Nor is there any record of his death. The only documentary records of his existence are his son's birth and baptismal certificates.[31]

Vivion de Valera does, however, appear in legal documents sworn in 1931. The deposition sworn by Catherine Wheelwright, as she then was, in April of that year states that she married Vivion de Valera in 1881, and that 'the sole issue of said marriage was one son named Edward de Valera . . . the legitimate son of deponent and the aforesaid Vivion De Valera'.[32] This document is supported by two further sworn depositions, by Patrick J. Hennessy and Catherine Daly, both of 76 Granite Street, Brooklyn, who said that they were 'well acquainted' with Catherine Wheelwright, 'and knew her in the year 1882, at which time she introduced her husband,

Vivion de Valera', to them, and that they had 'various other friends who knew the said Catherine de Valera and the said Vivion de Valera to be wife and husband'. However, in both depositions the surname was first spelt 'de Valero' before being corrected to 'de Valera'.[33] This is a simple enough mistake – though, curiously, it was one also made on both the birth and the baptismal certificates of his son, and on the hospital admission record of his wife.

Edward de Valera was born on 14 October 1882 at the New York Nursery and Child's Hospital in Lexington Avenue; he was baptised seven weeks later, on 3 December, at the Church of St Agnes, 141 East 43rd Street. His mother's address was given as 61 East 41st Street, a short walk from the church, and less than a mile from the hospital.[34] The Nursery and Child's Hospital was 'an institution for the destitute, unwed and working mothers.'[35] Joseph Silinonte traced the hospital records of de Valera's mother. She is recorded as 'Mrs Kate De Valero' and as having been referred by 'Mrs Abraham', of 61 East 41st Street. Whether Kate was living in an apartment in the same building, or lodging with Mrs Abraham (actually Jennie Crager Abrahams[36]) is not clear. Another oddity of the hospital record is that the address of Kate's brother Edward, then living in Rahway, New Jersey, is given under 'parent's residence', apparently because the hospital needed an address for the next of kin.[37] It seems odd that Kate gave her brother's address, rather than her husband's, who is not mentioned on the admission form. According to Terry de Valera, the explanation lay in Vivion's state of health: he was 'ill about the time of Father's birth and away from home.'[38]

Whether or not he was present at the birth, Vivion de Valera was named on the birth certificate – though the original gives his surname as 'de Valero'. It also gives his son's name as 'George'. After the Easter Rising, when she was trying to prove that her son was born in America, Kate produced an affidavit confirming that she told the doctor, Charles Murray, that the child was to be named George, but that by the time of the baptism she had changed her mind and named him Edward.[39] In any event, Murray seems to have been in no doubt that Vivion was the child's father.

The birth certificate does not explicitly state that the parents were married, but strongly implies that they were, as it gives Kate's name as 'de Valero' and her maiden name as 'Coll'. There is no ambiguity about the baptismal certificate, which names 'Vivian De Valero' as the father and Kate Coll as his 'lawful wife'. The Rector of St Agnes's, the Rev H. C. MacDowell, baptised Edward on 3 December 1882.[40] Many years later,

Vivion de Valera, Éamon de Valera's eldest son, was given permission to alter the record in St Agnes's so that the name he shared with his grandfather was spelt correctly.[41]

It would appear, then, that both Dr Murray and Father MacDowell believed Vivion to be the father, and he and Kate to be married. Their signatures on the birth and baptismal certificates are, however, the only official recognition of Vivion de Valera's existence. Even his death is shrouded in mystery.

According to Kate, her husband was forced by poor health to travel west again in the summer of 1884, when his son was 20 months old. She gave the uncharacteristically exact date of 30 June for his departure. The following spring she was informed by Vivion's friend Fred Hamilton that he had died. This information was verified by a friend of Kate's, Pat Regan, a Bruree man on the New York police force. According to the notes that Éamon de Valera meticulously kept in a Bible he won at school, his father died in November 1884, in Denver – or Minneapolis.[42]

Again, there are more questions than answers. Where did Vivion die? Given that there is no record anywhere of his death, how did Pat Regan confirm it? When exactly did Kate hear of the death, and why did she decide so quickly to send her son to Ireland? These were questions that troubled Éamon de Valera in later life, and he made concerted efforts to find answers.

In 1944 the publication of a biography by M. J. MacManus 'brought up the question of family history again', and, de Valera told his half-brother Tom Wheelwright, he was 'anxious to get all the facts I can'.[43] Tom made enquiries in Denver, which led to coverage of de Valera's search for his father in the newspapers in that city, to no avail.[44]

A more thorough search was carried out two decades later by de Valera's cousin Ed Coll. Now President of Ireland, de Valera eagerly supplied what information he could – which wasn't much.

> I would say my father went west either in 1883, 1884 or 1885. He was certainly dead before I came to Ireland in April 1885, possibly a year before that date. My mother understood that he died at Denver, but I had also heard mention of Minneapolis. Later I was told that many others who were . . . going to Denver with lung trouble passed on to Santa Fe, where many of them died . . . If you succeed in finding anything it would, of course, give me the greatest pleasure.[45]

But Ed's search of burial grounds and churches in Colorado, Minnesota and New Mexico found no trace of Vivion.

There may have been no record of Vivion de Valera's entry into the United States, of his life there, of his marriage or of his death. But there was still the Spanish connection to investigate, and this Éamon de Valera did for more than half a century, though without satisfying himself that he had found the link he was seeking. Once again the problem was the vague and sometimes contradictory story told by his mother.

In 1922 Kate told one Irish visitor that she had no clear knowledge of any relatives in Spain. She gave the names of her husband's parents as Antonio de Valera and Emilia Costa, and was quite definite that Vivion was an only child.[46] And yet she also told Éamon that his father had a brother and a sister, Leon and Charlotte.[47] These names are typically French, adding further to the confusion.[48] And she named Vivion's father as Juan on other occasions.[49] Given the confusion over such basic facts, it is hardly surprising that a solid connection with family in Spain was never established.

While several branches of Valeras or de Valeras in Spain did claim kinship, Éamon de Valera was never able to prove the link, as 'such information as they sent me did not correspond to the information given to me by my mother'.[50] Both Maire O'Brien, while Republican representative in Madrid in the 1920s, and Leopold Kerney, while Irish minister to Spain in the 1930s, made extensive efforts to uncover the Spanish side of the family tree. Kerney believed de Valera was a relative of the Marqués de Aunon, whose family name was Valera, a grandson of the writer and diplomat Juan Valera. However, the names and dates did not support this theory, and de Valera himself did not accept it.[51]

On a visit to the Sanctuary of Loyola in the Basque Country in 1953, de Valera, then Taoiseach, came across the name of the sculptor of a statue of St Ignatius – Lorenzo Coullaut Valera. Thinking of the story that his father had been a sculptor, he had the Spanish embassy in Dublin and the Irish embassy in Madrid make contact with the sculptor's family. The result was a very detailed family tree, which again failed to positively prove a link with Vivion de Valera.[52]

The issue became active again after de Valera was elected President in 1959 and was seeking his coat of arms. This proved difficult without names and dates and places of birth of his ancestors, even of his father and grandfather.[53] The aid of the Spanish Jesuits was enlisted,[54] as were the services of a Spanish genealogist, who was unable to do more than produce a highly speculative family tree. Again and again, the missing wedding certificate was mentioned as the vital clue that could unlock the mystery of Vivion de Valera's origins.[55] Eventually – five years after the first request – the Spanish heraldic authorities produced a coat of arms,[56] but whether it corresponded to the correct branch of the family must be open to question.

De Valera's exotic name helped him to stand out in later life. But it also led to suggestions that he was Jewish (the Fenian John Devoy referred to him as 'a Jewish bastard'[57]). After the Nazis came to power, the Irish Legation in Berlin was instructed to protest after a German paper alleged that de Valera was Jewish.[58] While de Valera was not anti-Semitic, several of his contemporaries were. These included Count George Noble Plunkett, whose odious views on the subject were set out at length in a letter to de Valera in July 1921.[59] De Valera's response does not appear to have survived, but he may have mentioned the rumours about his own background, because Plunkett took it upon himself to do some research on the matter in the British Museum Library, concluding that 'the story of the Jewish de Valera is a *myth*'.[60]

Vivion de Valera remains a shadowy figure. As Joseph Silinonte concluded after six years of research, 'No substantial trace . . . has been found . . . Two questions remain: who was Vivion de Valera and did he marry Kate Coll?'[61] Answers to those questions may of course emerge; proof may yet be found both of Vivion's existence and of his marriage. That, however, is irrelevant to a consideration of the character of Éamon de Valera. As far as he was concerned, there were no concrete answers, and the uncertainty about his father and about his own status must have had an emotional cost. That cost, however, was minor in comparison to that exacted by his relationship with his mother.

CHAPTER 03

MORE OR LESS AN ORPHAN

. . . every time I hear others talking of their mothers I feel more or less an orphan.
Edward de Valera to his mother, 1905[1]

The first fifteen years of my life that formed my character were lived amongst the Irish people down in Limerick . . .
Éamon de Valera, 1922[2]

To be a labourer was what was before me.
Éamon de Valera[3]

Éamon de Valera's earliest memory was of lying or kneeling on a floor, aged about two, gazing up at a woman in black who was looking down at him. 'I think of the figure always as that of a rather slim woman, pale face, with a handbag . . .'[4] The woman was his mother, paying him a visit. Kate Coll de Valera had had to go back to work after her husband left in the middle of 1884, and had no option but to have her son cared for by others. He keenly felt the separation, particularly when he was sent back across the Atlantic to Ireland. Those feelings were compounded by her failure to reunite the family after she remarried. That sense of loss may explain much about his personality.

While Kate took a job as a nursemaid to a doctor's family in Fifth Avenue in New York, her son was consigned to the care of a fellow Co. Limerick woman, Mrs Doyle, in Manhattan.[5] This was not an ideal arrangement, but it appeared to be working. Why, then, did Kate send her son back to Ireland?

The immediate cause may have been her husband's death. Kate claimed to have heard the news in the spring of 1885, not long before she

sent her son away on 9 April. By coincidence her brother Edward happened to be going back to Ireland, giving her the chance to send her own
Eddie home to be cared for by her mother. This left her free to pursue her
career in New York – and, as it transpired, to build a new life and a new
family. It would also change the course of her son's life. Discussing the
matter decades later with the poet John Montague, also a native New
Yorker, de Valera said he had little feeling for the city of his birth, and he
speculated on what he would have become had he stayed in the city.
'Cardinal or chief of police?'[6]

Edward Coll was 18 months younger than his sister Kate and had
followed her to the United States. Given that his name and address were
on her hospital admission form, the two were obviously close, and he used
to meet her in New York every Sunday to attend Mass and share the latest
gossip from home.[7] (Oddly, given this close relationship, he was unable
in later life to offer any detail about Kate's husband Vivion.[8]) After
contracting malaria in the swamps of New Jersey, he was advised to take a
long sea voyage as a cure. He went to New York to say goodbye to his
sister, and ended up taking his nephew, at the age of two-and-a-half, with
him back to Ireland.[9] The *City of Chicago* left New York for the ten-day
voyage on 9 April 1885.[10]

Kate instructed her brother to give the child porridge every morning
and to put him in his velvet suit on arrival in Ireland so he would look his
best when he met his grandmother. The first night out, two-and-a-half-
year-old Eddie wept uncontrollably, to the distress of his uncle. 'Half the
night I was kept awake with his crying that tore at the very heart of me.'[11]
However, the child cheered up over the coming days, playing with a toy
violin he had been given. 'The ship passengers loved to watch the boy as
he tucked the small instrument under his chin and pretended to play.'[12]

Arriving in Queenstown on 18 April[13] was Éamon de Valera's second
memory.

> I was with my Uncle leaving the ship . . . I saw in front of me an
> expanse of blue green water. That, and the rail of the ship, are the
> things that are most deeply impressed upon my memory . . .[14]

The two Edwards then headed for the Coll family home in Bruree, Co.
Limerick.

Within three years, Kate Coll de Valera was to marry again – but not
before a visit home, arriving on the day after St Patrick's Day, 1888.[15]
Recalling her visit many years later, Éamon de Valera said he 'remembered

her black bag. It was a big black bag with a pocket on it under a flap'.[16] Why his mother's handbag made such an impression on the boy is not clear – it is about the only detail he seems to have recalled from their encounter. Kate could presumably have taken the five-year-old Eddie back with her to America. One of his American cousins later claimed that the family in Bruree 'pleaded to keep him there'.[17] Whether or not this was the case, Kate returned to New York alone. This is perhaps understandable given that the boy was just about to start school – and in the light of an impending change in her own circumstances.

On 8 May 1888 she was married at the Church of St Francis Xavier in Manhattan to an Englishman, Charles Wheelwright. The officiating priest had no doubts about her previous marital status, using her married name, de Valera, followed by her maiden name, Coll, on the marriage certificate.[18]

Kate had met her new husband while working as a governess for a family in Lenox, Massachusetts, where Wheelwright was a coachman. They later settled in Rochester in New York State and had two children: Annie, born in 1889, who died in 1897, and Tom, born in 1890, who was to become a Redemptorist priest. Curiously, in several census entries Kate is listed as having been married only once and as having had only two children, one of whom was living.[19] It was as if her first child was not just out of sight, but out of mind.

There are hints about how young de Valera felt about this in the surviving letters he wrote to his mother and to other relatives. In 1889 the seven-year-old Eddie wrote to his aunt Hannie, who had recently joined her sister Kate in America. 'Tell Mamma I am angry to her for not writing. Tell her also I will write her a long letter soon.'[20] This note perfectly illustrates de Valera's mixed emotions about his mother, combining resentment with a sense of filial duty. In 1896 he enlisted Hannie's help – significantly, not his mother's – in an attempt to escape from Bruree. Carefully waiting until his uncle Pat was out of the house, and advising his aunt to reply care of a friend so their correspondence would remain secret, he wrote: 'I am going to school regularly and Uncle is as kind as ever, still I am not content here I would by far rather to be over, as I have no one to be with . . .'[21]

His complicated feelings about his situation are teased out in two further revealing letters. In 1902, a week before his twentieth birthday, he wrote to his half-brother Tom, now twelve, who had just started on his road to the priesthood at a Redemptorist college. De Valera was responding to an earlier letter in which Tom complained of being homesick. This was too much for de Valera, who couldn't help contrasting their situations.

> You have had a privilege heretofore which numbers have not had. You have been always near a loving mother, others who may have almost as much love as yours have to live separated by the ocean from her they love. You can see mother on your vacations, I must be content with the hope to see her one day. So then try and be happy.

He then gave some advice about study, before circling back to the most important topic, their mother.

> Remember the sacrifices she is making for us. Every mother loves her child and we are exceptionally blessed with a mother's love, yet she is willing to sacrifice our company, to sacrifice the joy of having us by her side – all for the service of God.[22]

That was certainly one way of putting it.

In a letter to his mother three years later de Valera again gingerly mentioned his feelings about their separation.

> Mother you will think it strange but every time I hear others talking of their mothers I feel more or less an orphan. Fate has been rather hard on us. I know how much better I would be had I been under your softening influence, and perhaps I too could have made your path less difficult had I been with you.[23]

The summer of 1907 saw something of a family reunion, when Kate came home again on a visit with Tom. As well as visiting the Coll home in Bruree, they spent time in Dublin, Bray, Howth and Lisdoonvarna.[24] According to de Valera's later account, his mother suggested that he come to America with her. The suggestion was, however, a decade too late. The boy who had yearned to escape from Bruree was now 24, was beginning to make progress in life and felt he belonged in Ireland. And it was too late to change whatever effect a sense of abandonment had had on his character.

So de Valera's formative years were spent in Bruree, in the care of his grandmother. Elizabeth Carroll had been born to Irish parents in London in 1836.[25] Her father, Edward, was involved in building work, possibly as a stonemason. After a fall from scaffolding left him seriously injured the family returned to Ireland,[26] where Elizabeth married Patrick Coll, a labourer. They had four children – de Valera's mother Catherine, Edward, Patrick and Johanna (known as Hannie). In December 1870 Kate, just about to turn 14, left Bruree National School to take up full-time work.[27] She worked for various families in the area as a domestic servant, before emigrating to the United States in 1879.[28]

Patrick Coll, senior, died in 1874,[29] which worsened the family's already difficult financial situation. The family lived in a single-roomed thatched cottage with mud walls on a quarter-acre of land about a mile outside Bruree village on the Athlacca road. Later, just as her grandson came to live with her, Elizabeth Coll was given a labourer's cottage, and her holding doubled to half an acre.

The interior of the 22-foot-by-16-foot slate-roofed cottage is surprisingly spacious. Inside the half door is the stone flagged kitchen, with two rooms to the right; when de Valera lived in the cottage there was just a single attic room, over the downstairs bedrooms – the kitchen was open to the roof. The attic room or loft was reached with a ladder which hung on a peg near the door during the day.[30] All cooking was done on the open fireplace.[31]

The acquisition of the new cottage was a significant step up in the world for the Coll family – but it was also the cause of serious distress to its newest member. When Eddie woke up in the old house on the morning after his arrival, he found himself alone in his strange surroundings. His screams of terror attracted his 15-year-old Aunt Hannie, who explained that the adults were up in the new house.[32] In the main, his new home held happy memories for him. In later life he recalled combing his grandmother's long auburn hair in the kitchen and plucking out the occasional silver thread. 'I don't think the sun shone so beautifully through any window or any door as it shone in that kitchen.' He added, however, with a hint of an unhappier side to his life: 'I was very often alone in it.'[33]

His grandmother doted on him, refusing to have his long blond curly hair cut, and dressing him in his velvet suit – and, much to his annoyance, in his aunt's button boots – for a photograph to be sent to his mother in America.[34] When he finally got rid of his curls, he felt he was 'at last a real boy', no longer 'a bit of a sissy'.[35]

His grandmother also seemed reluctant to send him to school: when the neighbour who was supposed to walk him to school on his first day forgot to, she took this as reason enough to keep him at home for another year.[36] He finally started at Bruree Boys' National School on 7 May 1888, aged five-and-a-half. On hearing his name the principal was unable to spell it; his uncle had to write it on his book so the teacher could make it out.[37] But de Valera was still known to his classmates by the more familiar surname of his grandmother – to them he was Eddie Coll, or as it was pronounced in rural Limerick, 'Naddy Cull'.[38] Eighty-five years later he claimed to have

> a perfect recollection of the school . . . There were nine desks all told, each seating four pupils. Half the boys would be seated and the remainder used stand around the walls.[39]

Those at the desks would be writing or working on maths, while the boys standing at the wall were being taught directly by the teachers.[40]

De Valera early on demonstrated a competitive streak that would become more pronounced in later years. This was directed towards a boy of his own age, Jack Potter, and seems to have been started by his uncle Pat, who invited Jack into the house to read aloud and then made unflattering comparisons with his nephew's abilities. De Valera came down with measles on the day a school inspector was due to visit and Potter was sent to the house to see where he was. De Valera overheard his rival agreeing with his grandmother that it would be better to keep him in bed. The patient concluded that this was an attempt by Potter to prevent him progressing to the next class, and so when his grandmother wasn't looking he got dressed and ran to the school, where he duly passed the examination.[41]

De Valera's memories of his childhood were unexceptional but give a strong impression of solitude. His grandmother sometimes left him in Bruree church as she ran errands in the village; when she collected him he complained about being lonely. 'Lonely?' she said. 'How could you be lonely in God's house? Why didn't you talk to him?'[42] The potential comfort of religion was thus highlighted early.

He was, in effect, an only child, and while he was friendly with a neighbour, Tom Mortell, as well as with a number of boys in school, he spent a lot of time alone. One biographer wrote that

> Eddie, learning quickly to read and being inclined to stay by himself, was soon living in a world populated by the old heroes in Ireland's story-books . . . Sent early in the morning to the creamery, he would read as he waited . . . The other boys would congregate round the warmth of the boiler in the creamery yard to pitch pennies, but Eddie did not join in, only raising his eyes from his page to see who might be winning.[43]

Even more suggestive of loneliness was his recollection of a favourite book and a favourite game.

> What I liked best was playing Robinson Crusoe. I remember reading the book while I minded cows . . . What I liked best was to go away and play in the stream. It had an island in it. I could get away from everybody. I used to play Robinson Crusoe there . . . I had no-one to play with. I was alone a good deal. In the river I had a little island and I used to shape it and make plans about it. This was Ireland and I was the ruler of it.[44]

Bruree, a twenty-minute walk from the Coll home, is a picturesque village, with a stone bridge crossing the River Maigue, a tributary of the Shannon. As well as two flour mills, the village boasted a small factory for making cloth.[45] It was a bustling community, and decades later de Valera recalled its evocative sounds.

> The sound of the mill wheel . . . the sounds of the cooper, particularly them twisting the firkins or barrels around on the floor . . . At the smithy, I particularly liked to see the two men with heavy sledges battering down the iron . . . The sound of the shoemaker as he beat the sole when he had cut it out of the leather . . . The sound of the carts and the trucks and the trot of the horse and of the whistle of the train . . .[46]

Despite its small size, Bruree had notions of grandeur, amplified by parish priest Father Eugene Sheehy who frequently spoke of its 'great and glorious past'.[47] The name of the village comes from the Irish Brú Rí, 'meaning the palace, or residence, of kings'[48] – there had been forts of local chieftains there, as well as two castles of more recent vintage.

In the social hierarchy of rural Ireland, land ownership was everything, and the Colls were near the bottom of the heap with their labourer's cottage and their half-acre of land. Indications of their status were plentiful, particularly to one of de Valera's sensitivity. Decades later, he would recall his rival, Jack Potter, coming to school on a donkey 'with a beautiful leather saddle. I used to envy him.'[49] De Valera had to make do with a sack for a saddle on his donkey, and a piece of cord for stirrups.[50]

Life on a smallholding involved plenty of work, as de Valera later told the Dáil.

From my earliest days I participated in every operation that takes place on a farm. One thing I did not learn – how to plough . . . I cleaned out the cowhouses. I followed the tumbler rake . . . I took my place on the cart and filled the load of hay . . . I took milk to the creamery. I harnessed the donkey, the jennet, and the horse . . .[51]

The exception in this list – ploughing – is, as Ronan Fanning has argued, 'revealing of the Colls' poverty: a tiny holding of half an acre required little ploughing.'[52] To earn extra money, Pat Coll sold eggs and kept pigs, as well as fattening cattle for sale at Charleville Fair. The cattle fed on the 'long acre', the grassy roadside verges. This was illegal, so young de Valera had to keep watch for the local RIC men on patrol. If he spotted them, he would either drive the animals off their route or pretend he was moving them from place to place.[53] Like most of the rural poor, de Valera had no reason to love the RIC.

While relatively poor, the Colls were politically conscious – something passed on to young Eddie, from the *Freeman's Journal* cartoons his uncle posted on the walls of his attic bedroom,[54] and from listening to Pat reading to his grandmother from the newspapers. He was particularly struck by the 'Mitchelstown Massacre' of September 1887,[55] when the RIC fired into a crowd of protesters, killing three men. He also remembered the controversy over the forged Parnell letters and the later split in the Irish Party over Parnell's relationship with Katherine O'Shea, and even the 1892 heavyweight championship fight in New Orleans between John L. Sullivan and 'Gentleman Jim' Corbett.[56]

The people of Bruree were 'strongly nationalistic'.[57] Survivors of the Fenian attack on the nearby Kilmallock police barracks in 1867 were 'highly thought of'.[58] And the young de Valera was exposed to a national-ist view of history from his uncle Pat, who used to read aloud from Abbé James MacGeoghegan's massive *History of Ireland*.[59] The boy himself read A. M. Sullivan's *The Story of Ireland*, as well as novels – his favourite, *Robinson Crusoe*, and *Ivanhoe*, one of the first books he remembered reading at National School. He and his uncle also tried to learn Irish from the lessons by Father Eugene O'Growney in the *Weekly Freeman* in 1893, though when Pat gave up, de Valera did too.[60]

Pat was also active in politics, though his election to Kilmallock Rural District Council came in 1899,[61] after de Valera had left Bruree. But the boy was still in the house when his uncle attended the founding meeting of the Irish Land and Labour Association at Limerick Junction in August 1894.[62] Organised mainly in Cos. Cork, Limerick and Tipperary, it campaigned for cottages, rent reductions and employment on road works.[63] Pat described himself on the 1901 census form as a 'general labourer and district councillor';[64] given his modest circumstances, his election was presumably a testament to the regard in which he was held by his neighbours.

One important political influence in the village was Father Sheehy, a leading nationalist figure and member of the IRB.[65] As a curate in Kilmallock, he had been jailed for four months in 1881 for Land League activities. In 1884 he was appointed administrator of Bruree parish, when the parish priest was ill, and became parish priest himself in 1886.[66] As an altar boy, de Valera listened intently to his sermons, regarding him as 'one of the great Land League priests, very much on the side of the tenants'.[67] Fr Sheehy was centrally involved in a row over evictions with a local landlord in 1886 – a protest meeting in the village was the first political event attended by de Valera.[68] However, Fr Sheehy's time in the parish was cut short as he went to the United States to collect funds for a new church. Typically, de Valera missed the communal send-off the parish gave him – he was minding cows by the roadside, reading *Robinson Crusoe* while the celebrations were going on.[69]

Eddie de Valera's life in Bruree was marked by a steady reduction in his emotional support. First Uncle Ed, who brought him there, returned to America; then, in 1887, when the boy was five, Aunt Hannie also went to America. He was very fond of her, as 'she had been very kind and apparently understood children well'. Touchingly, he remembered her final morning in the Coll house, helping him on with his boots and lacing them, telling him he would have to put them on himself from then on. 'My grandmother sobbed bitterly as she was saying goodbye . . .'[70] His grandmother's death in July 1895 was the most significant and wrenching change to his circumstances, 'a definite milestone in my life'. Mrs Coll had high hopes for her grandson: 'She had, of course, at times wished that I could become a priest, but that seemed out of the question . . . She had planned that I should be apprenticed to a trade if she could afford it.' He, however, doubted that this would be possible.[71]

In later years, de Valera loved to reminisce about his youth in Bruree; any letter from a former neighbour was sure of a response, and his papers contain lengthy recollections of the village and of the sights and sounds he experienced as a boy. He spoke at great length to interviewers and biographers about the village and his place in it. In fact, the further removed he was from Bruree, both in time and space, the more he idealised it. But when he actually lived there, he couldn't wait to get out of the place. Just like his mother, he escaped as soon as he possibly could; just like her, he had absolutely no intention of ever going back. Her escape was through the timeworn route of emigration; his would be through education.

But to do so, he would have to convince his uncle. Pat was a big man – 6 feet 3 and ¾ inches in height[72] – and de Valera remembered being frightened as a small child of how high he lifted him in play.[73] As de Valera got older, his impression was that his uncle was severe:

> he was a wonderfully good parent in his way [but] he had very high standards. I gave trouble. I remember staying out all day when I knew I shouldn't. All the boys of the school stayed larking about. I remember saying to myself that I would be beaten in any case so I might as well see what there was too.[74]

This is not the only reference to corporal punishment in de Valera's reminiscences – for instance, he 'got a whacking from my uncle for staying out late in the evening after school to see the cranes lifting the wreck of the train at Bruree station';[75] on another occasion he was 'reported for a thrashing' by his grandmother, presumably to his uncle, after a domestic misdeed.[76]

These incidents raise the question of the warmth of their relationship. Corporal punishment was, of course, accepted practice at the time, and de Valera's reminiscences do not imply any resentment at being beaten – in fact he readily admits that he gave trouble. Pat asked him to be godfather to his first child, Elizabeth, in February 1897, which implies he was fond of the boy.[77] And when Pat was later applying for a parcel of land, his nephew wrote a letter of support to the Land Commission: 'I am considerably indebted to him for my upbringing and I am anxious to assist him'.[78] On the other hand, it is noticeable that de Valera didn't name any of his children after members of the Coll family – the only family names passed on were his own Gaelicised version of Edward, and the name of his father, Vivion.[79]

When his mother died, Pat Coll inherited the cottage and the half acre of land, and his changed circumstances allowed him to marry Kate Dillane the following April. Marriage brought the possibility of a family, which made Eddie's future status at Knockmore uncertain. Meanwhile, his school attendance suffered as he faced an increase in his domestic chores after his grandmother's death[80] – including making the wedding breakfast after his uncle's marriage.[81]

Pat wanted his nephew to become a monitor in Bruree National School – a kind of paid teaching assistant, which might lead to a career as a teacher. It would in any case have brought some income into the household, as well as leaving de Valera free to perform jobs after school. And this is where de Valera showed the stubborn determination that would serve him so well in his political career, for he clearly regarded this suggestion not as an opportunity but as a trap.

Bruree's attractiveness had already been lessened by the departure of his friend Tom Mortell. Many years later, asked if there was any unhappiness in his boyhood, de Valera mentioned Tom's departure.

> I had heard that he was going to Limerick to learn the grocery business and that meant my nearest companion going from me . . . I remember saying to myself, I suppose I have to keep on digging potatoes for the rest of my life![82]

He would tell the historian Dorothy Macardle that Tom had entered

> a big world from which I was forever shut out. To be a labourer was what was before me . . . Though I dreamed a great deal, I had no ambitions or expectations . . .[83]

Fortunately, another local boy provided an example. Paddy Shea was a couple of years ahead of de Valera at school; he subsequently attended the Christian Brothers' school in Charleville, Co. Cork, and there won an exhibition (a prize for performing well in an exam), which led to his being accepted at St Munchin's College in Limerick, the diocesan college run by the Jesuits. 'I said to myself that what Pat Shea could do, I could do.'[84] His first hurdle was to persuade his uncle.

Not unreasonably, Pat Coll expected his nephew to help with the farm work and contribute to the family income. By going to Charleville, de Valera would instead continue to be a drain on the family finances and would have less time for chores. But de Valera delivered what he later called 'my ultimatum': he wouldn't become a monitor – the options were 'Charleville or America'.[85]

This last suggestion may have been an empty threat. He had already written, in secret, to his aunt Hannie, bemoaning his situation and claiming that he would far rather be in America. He wanted her to get his mother to write to Pat, asking him to send the boy over to her, 'and perhaps he might let me go'.[86] There is no evidence of what action, if any,

Kate took on this plea, though she did provide some financial support – de Valera wrote to thank her for a money order she sent for Christmas, 1897, which 'helped to get me a portion of the books which I required at the reopening of school'.[87] But perhaps the mere threat of his nephew going to America and his losing help on the farm was enough to change Pat's mind.

In the summer or autumn of 1896 de Valera was taken by his uncle to see the headmaster of Charleville, Brother Prendeville. The headmaster was dismissive when Paddy Shea's name was mentioned: he was exceptional, and not everyone could expect to do so well. At this, Pat went overboard in extolling his nephew's virtues. De Valera remembered that he was

> foolish enough . . . to praise me excessively, telling him that I knew, not merely arithmetic, but that I knew some algebra and geometry. How little that was he was not aware at the time, nor indeed was I fully aware of it myself.

He was made aware very quickly when Brother Prendeville asked him an algebra question he was unable to answer.

> So my reputation was immediately shattered. However, when I went home and looked at the factors I did not forget them in a hurry again.[88]

Despite this embarrassing setback, de Valera was accepted into Charleville, starting on 2 November 1896. His day began at 6.30 when he lit the fire and made his breakfast, before walking a mile to Bruree station to catch the train at 7.40; on hard uncushioned seats in third class, he would try to catch up on his homework during the 20-minute journey; then another walk to school itself, which started at 9 a.m. Then in the afternoon the seven-mile trek home, as he had agreed his uncle would only have to pay one train fare a day.[89] On one of his long walks home, he claimed to have come up with an ingenious solution to a difficult problem. He was sometimes told to buy bread in Charleville and bring it home – without eating any of it. So was another boy who sometimes walked home with him. It occurred to de Valera that there was a way to have some bread without breaking his orders. 'I have been told not to touch my loaf, but I could eat a bit of yours, and you a bit from mine so that, coming home, each of us can truthfully say "I have not eaten from this bread".'[90] Though probably apocryphal, it was the type of story he loved to tell about himself – or, even better, have others tell – demonstrating his crafty ingenuity.

De Valera's aim in Charleville was to obtain an exhibition, which would allow him to continue on to a more prestigious college. The state examination, the Intermediate, was divided into junior, middle and senior grades, the latter corresponding to the Leaving Certificate, which was introduced in 1924.[91] De Valera was preparing for the junior grade and was advised by Brother Prendeville to take English, French, Greek, Latin and mathematics, the latter divided into algebra, arithmetic and Euclid (geometry). In June 1897, after seven months at the school, and aged only fourteen, he sat the junior grade. He did well enough, passing Latin, English and algebra, and receiving honours in Greek, arithmetic and Euclid.[92] Given the circumstances, this was a good result for a trial run – but the pressure was on to raise the bar the following year.

He wrote to his mother in January 1898, apologising that he had been unable to write before. 'I have very little leisure time, on account of having to study pretty hard'. He enclosed his Christmas exam results, hoping his mother would be pleased with them. But he would have to work hard, as 'there is very keen competition between us boys, though the most of them are better circumstanced then I am, as they stay in town'.[93]

De Valera triumphed in the junior grade at his second attempt, in June 1898, aged fifteen, securing honours in all seven subjects.[94] He was first of the three exhibitioners in the school, winning £20 a year for three years.[95] He later claimed to have been in the top 40 candidates in the country[96] – in fact, he was 45th among the male candidates; for some reason, girls were listed separately, and five of them had higher aggregate marks than de Valera, leaving him in 50th place overall.[97] Nonetheless, when he was

> informed that I had secured an exhibition I felt that my life's ambition had been realised. I was now, I felt, on the road to success. In those days there was a great deal of competition between the various schools and colleges, and those who secured exhibitions were fairly certain of being given a place in one of these schools, on the payment to the school of the money received by way of exhibition.[98]

Things were not quite so straightforward, however. He first tried to follow, once again, in the footsteps of Pat Shea from Bruree by applying to St Munchin's, 'but for some reason my letter was either unanswered or not accepted'. He then applied to the Jesuit Mungret College, near Limerick, with the same result.

This was worrying, and de Valera discussed it with the curate in Bruree, Father James Liston – who, while on holiday in Lisdoonvarna, would have one of the most crucial conversations of de Valera's young life. He met a fellow priest there, Father Larry Healy, who happened to be the president of Blackrock College, an exclusive school in Co. Dublin run by the Holy Ghost Fathers. Liston sang the praises of his young parishioner, so much so that Healy agreed to take de Valera as a boarder.[99]

At the end of August, Healy wrote to Liston advising him that his 'young friend' should study the prospectus for the Scholasticate (for trainee members of the order) and for the lay college. If he 'feels drawn to the work of sacrifice which the Missions entail' he could write to Father Kearney at the college; but because the Scholasticate was very crowded at the time a better option might be for him to enter the lay college for a year and consider his vocation. Healy would accept the £20 exhibition in lieu of fees, and

> our arrangements for subsequent years would be as favourable for the boy. If his application is equal to his proved talents he ought to have a pretty brilliant career both in the Intermediate and at the Royal University.[100]

This was a generous offer – the normal annual fee in Blackrock was £40 – but it was not generous enough for Pat Coll, who sought £5 for himself from the £20 exhibition (which, in fairness, would have been used to offset the cost of sending his nephew to Blackrock). Father Healy got over this problem by ignoring the request.[101]

De Valera later described himself as 'walking on air' when he received confirmation that he was going to Blackrock.

> No more long trudges over the interminable distance . . . from Charleville to Knockmore. No more chopping of turnips for the cows, or the drawing of water, or the attempts to do my lessons in the intervals . . .[102]

There was more expense to properly outfit him for Blackrock: he had to acquire sheets, night attire, a couple of suits (one cost 16 shillings), and a tin trunk to hold everything – all of it paid for by Pat Coll.[103] Having outfitted his nephew appropriately for his new position in life, Pat drove him to Kilmallock Station in the donkey and cart, and saw him onto the train.[104] And with that, Eddie de Valera escaped from Bruree.

CHAPTER 04

I HOPE TO DO SOMETHING

I am studying hard and hope to do something this year.
Edward de Valera, 1901[1]

*I love study so much that if it were taken from me, I would feel
for the loss of my best friend.*
Edward de Valera, 1902[2]

*It is heartless cruelty . . . to bring a youth up from a low station
. . . and when he has learned to form ideas beyond his class . . .
then only to disillusion him and place him . . . where to advance
is impossible and to go back out of the question.*
Edward de Valera, 1903[3]

A month shy of his 16th birthday, Eddie de Valera was on his way
from Bruree to Blackrock, Co. Dublin: a journey taking him
much further than the 200 kilometres separating those places. As
he sat on the train, his tin trunk beside him, de Valera counted the
telegraph poles to estimate the train's speed[4] – the speed at which he was
leaving his old life behind.

It was the beginning of one of the most important relationships of de
Valera's life. Blackrock College seemed to meet the emotional needs that
had been left unfulfilled by his absent father, by his mother across the
Atlantic, and by his tough upbringing in Co. Limerick. While he would
always display a dutiful respect for the memory of his father, a somewhat
stiff devotion to his mother, and a taste for romanticised reminiscences of
his Bruree boyhood, he became and would remain a 'Rock boy' – though
the relationship wasn't always as close as he liked to suggest. His loyalty to
the College in later years was evident not just in the tradition of his sons

following him to Blackrock but in his own reluctance to leave the College, even after he was no longer studying or teaching there, and in his devoted attendance at sports days, plays and any other events the College put on. He chose to live and die in the vicinity – most of his family homes were there, and his final address was the Linden Nursing Home, two kilometres from the College.

Blackrock College was established in 1860 by Holy Ghost Fathers from France, with the aims of training personnel for missionary service and providing 'a first-class Catholic education for Irish boys'.[5] It was an exclusive school, with a competitive record in examinations: in 1898 it had the highest number of exhibitions of any boarding school.[6] However, its political atmosphere was a far cry from the nationalism of the Christian Brothers: the prospectus promised students 'a sound English education',[7] and when Queen Victoria drove by the college in April 1900 the vast majority of students had no problem in saluting her (de Valera was not among the recalcitrant minority).[8]

On arrival, young Eddie de Valera was given something to eat in the refectory and was then shown around by another boy, the tour concluding with his new bed in the dormitory at the top of the school building.

> I remember well how happy I was on that night . . . I could not understand why boys coming to such a place should be weeping. I had heard some sobbing: but to me this coming was really the entry into Heaven.[9]

The boys he heard crying were homesick; there was little danger of de Valera feeling homesick for Bruree. As he later recalled, he felt he was there as an equal, with the same chance of studying as the other boys[10] – it was now up to him to make the most of his opportunity.

However, his path was not a smooth one. For one thing, because of the delay in getting accepted, he arrived a week after the start of term; for another, many of the other boys had been in the school for years and were familiar with Blackrock and its ways.[11] While his classmates came from all over Ireland – and some from further afield – few had emerged from the rural labouring class. His curiosity value would have been increased by advance advertising: at the start of term the Dean of Studies, Father Thomas O'Hanlon, warned the other students that they would have to pull up their socks. 'There is a prodigy arriving from Charleville who will set the pace.'[12] And then, of course, there was his exotic name; some of his classmates told their English teacher that the new arrival was foreign. 'We

Irish', the teacher told a puzzled de Valera, 'are known to be a courteous people to strangers, so will you please sit up at the top of the class.'[13]

Far worse came from the notoriously strict Father James Keawell in Latin class. 'Hard on himself and demanding on others, he had an excessive idea of a boy's capacity for learning.'[14] De Valera found that Keawell 'gave enough work each day for the week. There were written compositions, exercises, grammar, Latin idioms and so on to learn.' Keawell felt the new boy's work was not up to scratch, and was continuously sending him to Dean O'Hanlon. De Valera was

> miserable and disappointed. I asked to get into another class – a lower class – but that was not permitted . . . Had I been punished by the Dean I doubt if I would have remained on in the College, I would have sought to get away.[15]

Luckily, O'Hanlon was understanding. 'De Valera, are you really doing your best?' 'I am, Father,' he protested, on the verge of tears. 'Then go back to class; keep doing your best; and don't mind what anybody else thinks.'[16]

Days in Blackrock were packed, with students up at 6 (5.45 in summer) and into the study hall 15 minutes later for prayers and study. Breakfast was not until 8.20, while classes began at 9.15. There was a half-hour lunch break at 11.30, with dinner at 3.30 and supper at 8, and prayers in the dormitories at 8.30. This was followed by yet more study until half nine or ten, followed by some time in the library until half past ten.

This was hard work, though the hours were no longer than those de Valera put in during his Charleville years; but now he was devoting himself full time to his own work, rather than spending hours on the farm.

There were new subjects to get used to, such as elocution lessons with Abraham McHardy-Flint. Shortly after de Valera started at Blackrock he went to this class for the first time, where another boy was asked to recite a piece. 'Being quite unaccustomed to anything of this sort', de Valera's reaction to the performance was to think his fellow-student 'mad'. The following week, to his horror, he was called on to recite something. The only poem he could think of was 'The Downfall of Poland', which had been in one of his school readers.

> I shut my eyes tightly before what I felt to be a mocking throng and recited it; as it affected me very much I recited it with great feeling, and when I had finished it McHardy-Flint said, 'I didn't think we had

an O'Connell here.' I am certain that I recited it without any actions of any kind, and with my eyes tightly closed.[17]

The poem, by Thomas Campbell, had a theme of sacrifice in the cause of country which appealed to nationalist youth.

> Our country yet remains!
> By that dread name, we wave the sword on high
> And swear for her to live! – and with her to die![18]

Although he had been put off joining the scholastics when he went to Blackrock, he asked the president of the college to be allowed stay with them during the Christmas recess in 1898. The scholastics were allowed home only during the summer, so they had no choice but to stay on; but, to de Valera, Blackrock was preferable to Bruree. He befriended two of the prefects (Holy Ghost seminarians acting as teachers), Ned Shea and Jim Burke, and volunteered to help them in their secretarial work, sending out reports.[19]

His own Christmas report was reasonable, placing him sixth out of a class of 18, winning first place in religious instruction and arithmetic, with honours also in Greek, English, algebra and Euclid, but passes in French and Latin (an indication of his difficulties with Father Keawell).[20] He had done well in mathematics in Charleville, but it was at Blackrock that his love of the subject really blossomed. He later remembered his two 'splendid' teachers, Father Kearney, who took him for algebra and geometry, and Tim Sullivan, who taught arithmetic. 'In the latter's class I first became interested in mathematics [and] found I could beat the others easily in arithmetical problems.'[21] Top of the class that Christmas was John D'Alton, the future cardinal, who later recalled de Valera as 'a good, very serious student, good at mathematics but not outstanding otherwise'.[22]

During that same Christmas break de Valera's new friend Jim Burke was responsible for his first – disastrous – experience of rugby, getting him to play for the prefects against the scholastics. Improvising a tackle, the inexperienced Bruree boy got down on his knees and stuck his head between the opposing player's legs; his ear was badly torn by a stud, leading to several stitches. His first rugby game having literally left its mark on him, de Valera opted to be a spectator for the time being.[23]

Throughout the early part of 1899 de Valera continued to work hard, gradually improving his standing in the class: in the early-summer house examinations he had moved up to fourth place.[24] And then came his first great test in Blackrock, the middle grade of the Intermediate examinations. Not only did he get honours in all seven subjects – Greek, Latin, English, French, arithmetic, Euclid and algebra[25] – but he came first in overall marks in the school and was in eighth place nationally.[26] While three of his fellow students won gold medals for coming first in their subject in the country, de Valera had won what was more important for him: a new exhibition of £30 for two years. And coming first in the school 'was regarded as a very great achievement . . . This made me hope . . . the following year . . . to do something better in the senior grade.'[27]

De Valera, then, began his senior year in Blackrock in good spirits. As the leading student from the previous year, he read prayers in church and in the study hall, and also in the dining-room during retreats. Seán Farragher, who researched de Valera's time in Blackrock in great detail, has noted that de Valera 'highly appreciated' this task, which would not necessarily have been welcomed by every student. 'Until then he was somewhat of an outsider among his peers, being a newcomer and otherwise undistinguished . . . He tended to look back on it with a certain satisfaction.'[28] However, he was less pleased by another result of his new position – a nickname based on the similarity between his surname and one of the prayers he had to recite which began 'Deliver us, O Lord'. 'Had I a nick name? Indeed I had! And I hated it! I was "Deliver-us".'[29]

Life was, as de Valera later recalled, 'pleasant', despite the hard work.[30] It was so pleasant, in fact, that he again declined to go home to Bruree for Christmas, as his uncle wished:

> as my vacation was so short and the expense so great, I thought it would not be worth my while to go home. I like this College and some of my companions are very nice.[31]

However, there were signs that he was not performing as well in his studies as he would have hoped. In the Christmas tests, two students who were repeating the year took first and second place; but John D'Alton came third, dropping de Valera into fourth place. A letter to his mother in March 1900 hinted of unease. He blamed his failure to write more regularly on

> stress of work. This year especially I have more than I can do. I . . . felt poorly during winter and spring . . . Just imagine we have but three months more to prepare for the summer examinations.[32]

As he later recalled, his hopes of a good result were 'completely dis-appointed'.[33] While he got honours in six of his subjects, he achieved only a pass in trigonometry. This gave him joint second place in Blackrock College, but he was only in 40th place nationally. There was no new exhibition for de Valera, just a £2 book prize.[34]

Two months shy of his 18th birthday, de Valera now faced a decision about his future. He had confessed to his mother some months before that he had 'scarcely an idea' about what he should do next. 'I suppose this year's results and whatever the president [of the College] thinks best for me, will shape my course next year.'[35] He decided to remain at Blackrock – despite his setback in the senior grade, he still had a second year of the £30 exhibition he had won in the middle grade. This, along with an hour's teaching per day,[36] was enough to pay for him to progress to the next level in Blackrock: the University College.

Known as 'the Castle' because it was housed in Williamstown Castle beside the school, this prepared students for the examinations of the Royal University of Ireland. De Valera hoped to secure a scholarship each year to pay his board and tuition. The BA course was spread over four years, starting with a full year to prepare for the matriculation examination, followed by three years of the arts degree proper. He opted to concentrate on mathematical science, despite his disappointing trigonometry result the previous year. This was due partly to personal preference; partly to the fact that fewer students took the subject, leading to less competition for scholarships; and partly to his knowledge that such a degree would be more help in securing a teaching job. The drawback was that he would have to do much of the work on his own, the maths and science teachers at Blackrock not being of the highest standard.[37]

Students at the University College were supposed to be housed in Williamstown Castle, but it couldn't accommodate the 32 students recorded in the 1901 census[38] so De Valera ended up in overflow accom-modation known as 'the Piggery', a popular spot with students, being freer from supervision. Early in his stay there he was woken by four students who lifted him out of bed, warned him to keep quiet and retrieved wine bottles they had hidden under the floorboards.[39] This lack of discipline wasn't to his taste. When another student left a room in a better location vacant, de Valera occupied it without permission[40] – another instance of his determination to better his situation.

De Valera's aim was still the priesthood. In March 1901 he wrote to his mother informing her that he supposed he would go to Holy Cross College, Clonliffe, the Dublin diocesan seminary, to become a priest (as

John D'Alton would do) either that summer or the summer after. 'Do you see any objection to it? I would like to have your opinion.' He again complained of ill-health over Christmas and stated his determination to improve on the previous year's results. 'I am studying hard and hope to do something this year.'[41]

This time he was not to be disappointed, taking a first-class exhibition in the matriculation exam, with a first in natural philosophy and second class honours in English and mathematics.[42] His exhibition was worth £24, which, along with teaching, would pay his way the following year.[43] His first attempt at teaching had also been a success: the two students he tutored passed all their subjects in their solicitors' apprentice examination. They showed their appreciation by presenting de Valera with a ticket for the March 1902 Rugby international between Ireland and Wales.[44]

Needless to say, life in the Castle wasn't all work; many enjoyed the occasional illicit trip 'over the wall' to one of the nearby pubs, the closest and most popular being Keegan's. Buying a round in Keegan's was the standard penalty for losing a wager, which was a problem for the cash-strapped de Valera. He recalled one occasion when the last one over the wall that night was to stand a round. He took the precaution of researching the hand and footholds on the wall, which got him over before some of the others.[45] Surprising as it may seem given his later image, de Valera also frequently strolled around Blackrock Park with friends, listening to the band, but mainly looking at the girls – what he later referred to, in a piece of Rockwell slang, as 'totty twigging'. He and a friend came to grief when they tried to progress to the next level by gate-crashing a party in one of the large houses in Blackrock. Perhaps unwisely, they attempted to make themselves look older by wearing false moustaches. The disguises got them past the door, but the heat of the room soon melted the glue holding them in place, and they were unceremoniously ejected.[46]

Although de Valera did not play rugby at this stage, he enthusiastically participated in a wide range of sports, including boxing, cycling, cricket and athletics. He went to bed early and got up early, had a drink of milk and then ran around the field before breakfast.[47] His sporting escapades in Blackrock provided him with a rich fund of stories displaying him in a positive light which he relayed to various biographers and others likely to repeat them. For instance, he told a story about a race in which he felt exhausted and ready to give up, until he realised that his opponent must be feeling the same way; he got his second wind and won. This victory brought him a wooden biscuit barrel as a prize,[48] and an allegory for his political career, as recounted by his faithful acolyte Frank Gallagher: 'When in after life he was in charge of the nation's affairs and things seemed hopeless for Ireland de Valera recalled that race – and held on.'[49] Then there was the race he lost because he stopped to help another competitor who was taken ill: 'his chivalry lost him a possible prize'.[50] There was also a story he told against himself; determined to keep pace in a cycling race with the eventual winner, he spotted his singlet and kept right behind him, only to realise too late that he was trailing the wrong man, a slower competitor wearing the same colour.[51] There was probably a political parable there too for those wishing to see one.

A Saint Vincent de Paul Conference (branch) was formed in Blackrock College at Christmas, 1900; de Valera was elected secretary and then president, a post he held until he left the Castle. According to another member of the Conference, some of the more cynical students regarded the SVP with derision.

> The President continued his way imperturbably and light-heartedly – to all appearances unconscious or oblivious of smiles . . . He was earnest about the work in a degree beyond his fellow worker . . .[52]

His role brought him into contact with such public figures as the Irish Party MP William Field and the curate of Blackrock parish, Edward Byrne, later Archbishop of Dublin. One of the places he visited as part of his charitable work was Linden Convalescent Home, where he would spend his final days 70 years later. He also visited the houses of the poor. One family he visited contracted smallpox, so he had to be vaccinated. He was severely ill afterwards, and he noticed from that time a deterioration in his eyesight, which he suspected had been brought on by the vaccine.[53]

In the Castle, de Valera was refused admission to one student club, known as the Coptic Society, whose members had a 'secret language' using reversed syllables. This exclusion evidently rankled as he recalled it half a century later.[54] He was, however, able to secure a number of positions of semi-authority at the Castle, which involved tedious tasks unattractive to other students. He was made secretary of the library, which gave him the power to search other students' rooms to find missing magazines; he appears to have performed this task with a zeal that made him unpopular.[55] He was also on the committee of the University College Debating Society, as well as taking part in the debates.

In one he argued that the culture of Greece had made a greater contribution to civilisation than the conquests of Rome (an appropriate argument for the future supporter of the Irish language against that of the conquerer); in another he praised Napoleon for saving France 'from scenes of Anarchy'. He also displayed an equivocal attitude towards free trade and protection (he was 'in favour of a little of both'), and preferred constitutional monarchy over Republicanism, because 'constant elections disturb a nation' – he also argued that 'there is no rule so tyrannical as that of them all'.[56]

He delivered a paper to the society on 18 February 1903, on the university question. The establishment of the Royal University had not satisfied the demand of Catholics for a university of their own; the topic was a controversial one and would not be resolved until the National University of Ireland was established in 1908. The views of the 20-year-old de Valera are interesting not just because it was a major political issue at the time, but because 18 years later he would become chancellor of the NUI.

He proposed using the structure of Dublin University, of which Trinity College was the only constituent college. Another college, acceptable to Catholics, should be established and endowed with similar funds and buildings. In due course, another college could be set up for Presbyterians. All would form part of the single Dublin University. While autonomous, they would be subject to the supervision of a University Senate. This would mean that the future politicians of the country

> would have the exceptional advantage of knowing each other thoroughly . . . They would have common sympathies and interests for which they would be ready to sacrifice their individual prejudices and inclinations and would be the embodiment of such a public spirit as raises patriots and constitutes stability.

Particularly significant was his positive view of Trinity – a view that would not have been shared by many Catholics at the time.

In his address he referred to the clergy as 'the natural leaders of the people', which some have taken as an indication of his clericalist instincts. This may be true, though the comment was made in the context of the clergy having 'no real education which would suit them for that office'. He was also critical of the lack of university education among the new politicians (such as his Uncle Pat) serving on various local authorities. These were the views of a rather conservative young man.

Perhaps the most significant insight into his personality came in a passage which has not been widely quoted, but which may disclose his feelings about his uncertain future.

It is heartless cruelty, worthy of some devilish ingenuity, to bring a youth up from a low station, as the Intermediate often does, and when he has learned to form ideas beyond his class, when he has learned enough to develop . . . taste, and to be fired it may be with noble ambitions, then only to disillusion him and place him . . . where to advance is impossible and to go back out of the question.[57]

The insecurity expressed in this address was due in part to his mixed academic fortunes. In his First Arts exam in the summer of 1902 he got only a pass, earning him a second-class exhibition worth £15[58] (although he was still well within the top 10 per cent of students at the Royal). Again, he supplemented the proceeds of his exams with teaching.[59]

Luckily, he had also hedged his bets by entering for a mathematical scholarship, which he sat on his 20th birthday, on 14 October 1902. As he told his half-brother Tom, if he got the scholarship 'it will enable me to begin and complete my studies for the priesthood. If I fail to get it I will have to remain here teaching some time longer.'[60] De Valera's high hopes were to be disappointed yet again: he came fourth,[61] which secured a second-class scholarship worth £24 – useful, but not enough to make him a priest.

Throughout his life, de Valera had a tendency to fall asleep while reading. One of the prefects in the Castle study hall attempted to catch him napping several times without success, but eventually managed to sneak up to the snoozing de Valera, turn the book he was reading upside down, and then wake him. De Valera's attempt to claim he had been awake was scuppered by his inability to read upside down. The school doctor was unable to find a way to help him, so he finally attempted to solve the problem by studying in a tree, where failing to stay awake would have fairly immediate consequences.[62]

Falling asleep wasn't the only difficulty de Valera faced. It appears that this studious young man feared that academic success made him vain and ambitious – qualities he deemed unseemly in a potential priest. In a letter to Tom in October 1902 he went into considerable detail about this problem. The letter was prompted by Tom's starting his studies at a Redemptorist college in the United States. De Valera was enthusiastic, telling him to 'pray for perseverance' when he found the going tough. He warned against those moments when 'the world will offer you its choicest pleasures, honours, etc. for the purpose of ensnaring you', adding that he had himself had such moments, and that the only way to triumph was 'by aid from above'.

Be on your guard against day dreaming, imagining yourself in very glorious positions. It seems a very innocent pleasure but in my case, it has been the chief method Satan has employed to disturb my peace of soul and make me waver.

He observed, somewhat immodestly, that he had been successful in almost everything he had undertaken, 'brilliantly successful, more successful I fear than is good for my salvation'. It was clear, as de Valera himself acknowledged, that this 'preaching' would be better directed at himself than at Tom, but he concluded that it could do no harm to share his own experience. He also enthused about the fact that Tom would find the work hard at first but that 'it will soon be loveable in itself. I love study so much that if it were taken from me, I would feel for the loss of my best friend'. He urged his brother never to be content with second best, but always strive to be first – before adding, obviously remembering his earlier advice, that he should do so 'as a matter of duty . . . towards God and never to gratify your own pride'.[63]

As well as disclosing his guilt over his pride, the letter also suggests some disenchantment with his position in Blackrock, which perhaps explains an attempt the following June, just before his second-year exams, to plot a change of scene. His job application to St Wilfred's College in England displays striking similarities to the letter he wrote seven years before to his aunt Hannie, seeking her aid in getting him out of Bruree. In particular, he pointed out that he had not yet informed the Blackrock College authorities that he was planning to leave and asked that any reply be kept confidential. 'Secrecy would be gained by its being sent in a plain envelope'. He was 'desirous of seeing a little of England and English character' and therefore wanted to find a position at St Wilfred's similar to the one he had in Blackrock. He then recounted in minute detail his academic achievements – 'One cannot be very modest in a case like this!' – and the subjects he was best suited to teach.[64] For whatever reason, de Valera now wanted to put some distance between himself and the place which had been home and emotional support for five years. Nothing came of this approach to St Wilfred's; but an even better opportunity was about to arise.

First, of course, there was the small matter of his Second Arts exam, where again he was disappointed to get a pass, with a second-class exhibition. He was among 11 students awarded this grade of exhibition, out of the 330 candidates for Second Arts in the Royal University in 1903.[65] Again, he was in the top tenth of candidates – but he was not achieving the type of marks he hoped for. His future depended on getting a good degree, so his final year would be crucial. And his final year was not to be spent in Blackrock.

There is no doubt that Blackrock College had been extraordinarily good to de Valera; in return, de Valera would be extraordinarily good to Blackrock through the years, remaining loyal to it and its traditions, sending his sons there, attending its events almost obsessively. It was also during his Blackrock years that people first noticed the trait that would serve him so well in politics: his great personal charm. Seán Farragher, who interviewed many of his contemporaries, wrote that in all these interviews, 'his character comes through as that of one remarkably upright, honest and of truly noble cast, but by no means a plaster cast, as he had a remarkable sense of humour'. One contemporary thought he was the last boy he would have imagined becoming a politician, because he was incapable of telling a lie. On hearing this, de Valera laughed and suggested that the comment couldn't be used in his official biography, as many people wouldn't believe it.[66]

Despite his emotional attachment to Blackrock College, the letter to St Wilfred's shows that he was growing a little tired of it after five years. There is also a sense in which he didn't really fit in. Farragher caught this: 'Whereas he was a good mixer and was readily accepted in all company he was never immersed in the crowd . . . he held himself consciously or otherwise in some way apart'.[67] But that was about to change.

CHAPTER 05

A HARD BATTLE TO FIGHT

It was in Rockwell that I became healthy and strong.
Éamon de Valera[1]

I have a hard battle to fight just now . . .
Edward de Valera, 1905[2]

A man of your vigour and ability is sure to get on sooner or later.
Professor Edmund Whitaker to Éamon de Valera, 1912[3]

Rockwell College, Blackrock College's sister institution, is just outside Cashel, Co. Tipperary, and in the summer of 1903 it was looking for a maths teacher. There was constant staff movement between the colleges: the vacancy in Rockwell was created by a teacher deciding it was time 'to improve himself' by returning to study at Williamstown Castle in Blackrock.[4] This should have given de Valera pause for thought, as he was facing his final exams that year, but the forces in favour of change were stronger. Rockwell had the advantage of being familiar, with many faces he knew already; it was in his native Munster, around 60 kilometres from Bruree; and it offered a steady income – his salary was £25, rising to £60 per annum in 1904 after he had his degree.[5]

The move to Rockwell College in September 1903 was a turning-point for de Valera. In his new environment he made many more friends, acquired the nickname – 'Dev' – that stayed with him ever after, developed into a decent rugby player, and even changed his appearance: he went to Rockwell weighing 10½ stone, but within six weeks he weighed 12, thanks to 'stout, claret, and good Tipperary beef'.[6] De Valera always spoke of his time in the college with fondness. 'It was in Rockwell that I became healthy and strong.'[7] Because he lived in the college he was quickly accepted by the staff 'in a way he would not have been at Blackrock, where he still had the status of a student'.[8]

De Valera was one of a handful of lay teachers at the college, becoming part of their close-knit group. One, Jack Barrett, was 'one of my very best friends . . . His very name always brings back to me some of the happiest days of my life.'[9] Another was Tom O'Donnell, later a TD, and the first person to contract his name to 'Dev'.[10]

Through the Rockwell rugby team, de Valera also became close to two local men, Jack and Mick Ryan, Triple Crown-winning Irish internationals: Mick was one of only three people he wrote to when awaiting execution in 1916.[11] The Ryan brothers were frequent visitors to the college, and in return the teachers, including de Valera, played cards in Mick's house, went to the races with them, and joined them fishing and shooting. These rural pursuits must have reminded de Valera of his boyhood in Bruree, though he was now far removed in status from the labourer's cottage – his gun licence, issued in November 1904, described him as 'Edward de Valera, Professor, of Rockwell College'[12]. On one of these excursions Jack Ryan advised de Valera to 'aim at the thistle and you'll hit the rabbit', which sounds like a slur on the future Volunteer's marksmanship; de Valera later blamed his difficulty in hitting a target on his eyesight, which was then beginning to deteriorate, although he didn't realise it.[13]

There was also romance. Mary Stewart, whose family owned a hotel in Cashel, had her eye on de Valera, and it seems he was interested too: he came up with a cipher so their postcards couldn't be read by the postman. Frustrated by his inability to make out what they were saying, the postman eventually wrote on one of the cards, 'What is all this "sigh for"?'[14] This episode prompted a colleague to write a poem lampooning the young lover:

The sigh is for a valiant knight
(the k-night was dark and long!)
Who to his lady-love would write,
(now, was that writ – or wrong!)
So he the letters twenty-six
Shook up with philtre gay,
The potion then with sighs did mix,
And marked it: 'Once a day!'[15]

The relationship probably did de Valera's reputation no harm, but it didn't develop – after all, he remained uncertain whether he might still become a priest.

Rugby rather than romance took up most of his spare time. The college team was made up of students, teachers and others, like the Ryan brothers who helped Rockwell College to several Munster Senior Cup finals, though they never won.[16] The arrival of a new teacher from Blackrock naturally led the rugby community at Rockwell to ask the all-important question: could he play?

> The first day he togged out we appraised him critically. It was doubtful if his slight build would stand up to the strenuous type of Munster play, but he had courage and determination. We felt that he would make the grade, and he did . . .[17]

As usual with anything he put his mind to, he took nothing for granted, training conscientiously either alone or with Jack Barrett, and hounding the Rockwell cobbler to add bits of leather to his boots as he modified them in order to 'balance the pressure'.[18]

After just five months of playing seriously, he was called for a Munster trial, with the north of the province playing the south. De Valera's team was narrowly beaten, and his opposite number went on to be capped for Munster and later Ireland, indicating a missed opportunity.[19] De Valera continued to be an important player on the Rockwell team,[20] most memorably in the college's victory over Garryowen in March 1905.[21] Although he failed to convert the two Rockwell tries that were the only scores in the match,[22] his performance was long remembered for a spectacular kick to clear his lines from a Garryowen attack.[23] There was another outcome of that match: as he cryptically noted, 'Drank some whiskey and bad results . . .'[24] He later explained that, instead of his usual couple of bottles of stout after the match, he had had eight whiskeys – partly because of the victory, partly because of the intense cold. He became argumentative on the train home and then vomited in the jaunting car bringing them back to the college, though 'luckily nothing but the ground got it'.[25]

It wasn't the only example of uncharacteristic behaviour. He had a stand-off with the college president over the provision of cocoa, which was part of his contract. The president withdrew cocoa from all staff because it was so expensive; de Valera threatened to move to a hotel and charge the college; the president offered to resume his cocoa supply if he agreed not to drink it in front of the other teachers; de Valera refused; and eventually all the staff got cocoa again. He defied the college authorities again when they locked the door on a group of teachers – including de Valera – returning late from dances in Cashel. On the first occasion, de Valera climbed through a window and let his friends in; on the second, they removed the lock from the door and threw it in a lake.[26] One might wonder how much time this convivial life left for study. The answer was, not enough.

On 20 June 1904 de Valera returned to Blackrock to prepare for his degree examination, which he sat in October. While waiting for the results he again explored the question of his future, and specifically whether he should enter the priesthood. He took a weekend retreat with the Jesuits in Rathfarnham Castle, where he discussed the matter in depth with his confessor. The priest avoided the question for some time, before de Valera impatiently broke in, 'But what about my vocation?' 'Oh! Your vocation. You have what is known as an incipient vocation.' Seeing that all he had after all his years considering the issue was an *incipient* vocation, he decided to forget about it, whistling merrily as he cycled back to Blackrock.[27] There the matter rested for the time being, with de Valera clearly expecting a career as a lay teacher, armed with his new degree.

But when the results were published, he suffered a bitter dis-appointment. There were six candidates for the BA in mathematical sciences: four received first-class honours; de Valera and one other student had to be content with pass degrees.[28] It must have been a huge blow to his ego; more importantly, it reawakened his fears for his future, because a permanent university appointment appeared out of reach, and even a decent teaching job would be hard to find. The battle to convince his uncle to send him to Charleville, the hard grind of his years there, his escape to Blackrock, all the endless hours of study – had it all been in vain?

The results were part of a pattern: while he was an assiduous student with a genuine love for mathematics, he frequently found exams difficult. The question is whether he wasn't very good under pressure or whether he just wasn't very good at maths. A later mentor, Professor Arthur Conway of UCD, suggested it was the pressure, observing that, while 'his mathematical abilities are of a high order and he is possessed of great brilliancy and originality', he was 'adapted to excel in research work rather than to do himself justice in examinations'.[29]

This assessment is borne out by his results in Blackrock. While maths subjects were his best in his brilliant middle-grade result in 1899, they were among his worst in the senior grade the following year, with his worst result, a pass, being in trigonometry.[30] In his matriculation examination in

1901, maths was his worst subject, as it was again in his much poorer First Arts results; maths was his best result in Second Arts in 1903, mainly because he did badly in his other subjects – but mathematical physics was his worst result.[31] It is then surprising that de Valera chose to take maths and mathematical physics for his final degree. He might have fared better with other subjects, perhaps taking his career in a different direction.

He did at least still have a job, but teaching at Rockwell was not enough; he felt he had to repair the damage done by his pass degree through further study. He wrote to Professor T. J. Bromwich of Queen's College, Galway, enquiring about the MA there, which he wanted to complete while continuing to teach at Rockwell. Bromwich advised him that 'you will find the MA course worse than the BA for private study'. The college did offer senior scholarships, but these required two academic sessions in Galway to qualify. The junior scholarships hadn't got this requirement, but, as Bromwich gently put it, 'I fear that your degree would disqualify you for them'.[32] Galway was clearly impossible, but he considered other possibilities, including writing a book on elementary algebra,[33] which seems quite ambitious given his recent disappointment.

De Valera never lacked ambition, but the idea of writing a book, or even studying for a master's degree, while at Rockwell was a pipe dream. He came to realise that 'if I stayed further in Rockwell I would vegetate there'.[34] The life was comfortable, the work congenial, but it was a dead end: to make progress he must leave. And even before he formally resigned his post at the end of the summer term in June 1905, he had moved on in a somewhat surprising direction.

He had been considering studying at Trinity College, Dublin, for some time. As early as August 1902 he had written seeking details of courses,[35] and in February 1904, some six months before his final BA exam, he had enquired about a sizarship (a scholarship offering lower fees, cheap rooms and free dinners), which he intended to compete for. He may have been put off this plan by the advice he received that expenses would come to £60 for the year at the very least, even with the sizarship.[36] But now, in January 1905 – six months before he left Rockwell – he took the plunge, paying the £15 entrance fee.[37]

He was one of only 34 Catholics out of that year's intake of 320 students, and he was consigned to the care of Stephen Kelleher, the only Catholic fellow of the college.[38] De Valera aimed to compete for a scholarship, which would cover two thirds of his fees for five years, as well as entitling him to cheap rooms and free dinners. Kelleher advised him that the course 'is not very difficult. An Honours graduate of the Royal

University has more than covered the ground'.[39] He didn't mention how someone with a pass degree might get on, and when de Valera sat the scholarship examination in mathematics on 29 May 1905 he came last out of 13 candidates.[40] While this was something of a disaster, he did much better in a junior freshman exam on 30 June, coming first out of 80 candidates. This excellent result – not surprising given that he was 22 and already had a BA – allowed him to continue in Trinity for another year, and to have another go at the scholarship examination. But in the meantime he had to earn a living.

On leaving Rockwell he had expected to find his way back into Blackrock, as a part-time teacher at the very least.[41] But, to his intense disappointment, there was nothing for him, which is surprising in the light of his popularity with the staff at the college. One biographer suggests that this may have been due to his occasional defiance of the rules and clashes with authority in Rockwell,[42] though Father Nicholas Brennan, who was president of Rockwell in de Valera's time, later wrote him a glowing reference. 'He was devoted to learning, was extremely popular both in the class-room and the athletic field, and in every way deserves the highest praise that I can give.'[43] Be that as it may, de Valera never worked at Blackrock or Rockwell again.

A possible option was Liverpool, where the Christian Brothers were looking for a maths teacher. De Valera thought he could teach during the day and study engineering at Liverpool University at night. He took the night boat to Liverpool, arriving at 4 a.m. and walking the streets until the school opened; but having met the headmaster and taken a look at the school, he decided he 'wouldn't stay for love or money'. To compound his misery, on the journey home he had his first brush with a recurring problem: seasickness. When he finally saw Howth on the horizon he 'thought it stood still and was never coming nearer'.[44]

He finally managed to secure a part-time post, at Belvedere College, the Jesuit school in Dublin. He supplemented this by teaching at Holy Cross College, Clonliffe, and at the Eccles Street Dominican school for girls. He lived in a succession of digs,[45] being so short of funds that at one point he not only had to share a room with his Rockwell companion Jack Barrett but even had to share a bed.[46] It was an unsettled, and unsettling, existence. He wrote to his mother four days before Christmas, 1905, explaining how busy he was, teaching all day and working for himself in the evening.

I am trying to get a scholarship in TCD . . . but the Exam is very hard and the disadvantages for work and proper instruction are altogether against me. I am at that stage when advancement without opportunities is nearly impossible . . . I have a hard battle to fight just now.[47]

Meanwhile, the question of his 'incipient' vocation had not gone away. Quite apart from his own wishes, both his grandmother and his mother had favoured his becoming a priest.[48] There was encouragement too from former school friends, such as John Keogh, who in October 1905, after finally deciding to join the Church himself, urged de Valera to do likewise.

Why stay out any longer? Would it not be better for you to come in at once and begin your life work? You have a very high idea of the Priesthood. So much the better . . .[49]

Perhaps prompted by this advice, de Valera broached the question some months later with the president of Clonliffe College, who took three days to think about it and then discouraged him. 'Advised him not to come in now. To give up Trinity scholarship, to read for th. [theology] and RNI [religious knowledge instruction] and to read what may be useful to begin Th. study next year.'[50]

This was the third time (at least) that he had been discouraged from starting on the path to the priesthood. Ronan Fanning suggests these rejections might be explained by his inability to provide a copy of his mother's marriage certificate, which was then required of every candidate for the priesthood.[51] However, it's not clear how the clerics would have been aware of this problem, and there is no indication that de Valera himself was aware of any difficulty about his parents' marriage certificate at this time; when he sought it out later, he was surprised not to find it. It may simply be that there was something in his character that was regarded as potentially unsuitable for the priesthood. But despite this apparent rebuff by the Church, de Valera would remain true to his faith his entire life.

Against the advice of the president of Clonliffe, de Valera sat the Trinity scholarship examination again, on 21 May 1906. While he improved, he was still ninth out of ten candidates, and failed to win a scholarship,[52] marking the end of his attendance at Trinity College.[53] But his luck was about to change.

During the summer months, when there was no rugby, de Valera occasionally played cricket at Blackrock. One of the regular players was Father Joseph Baldwin, confessor to the Sisters of Mercy at their teacher-training college in Carysfort Avenue, just a mile from Blackrock College. Baldwin told de Valera of an opening there for a maths teacher and urged him to apply.[54] The one fly in the ointment was that the post had been held by Mattie Conran, who had given de Valera grinds. Conran, later professor of mathematics at University College, Cork, approached mathematics as a science, a viewpoint de Valera appreciated. The nuns at Carysfort, however, did not: their students needed to pass exams and were regularly being failed, so they felt a more straightforward approach was required.[55] De Valera went to see Conran, receiving his blessing to apply for the job.[56]

On 19 September 1906 de Valera signed on as professor of mathematics at Carysfort, with a salary of £125 per annum, to increase by yearly increments of £10 until it reached £150.[57] He was clearly delighted with his new job and status as a professor. His teaching was kept strictly practical: if he had any notions of trying a scientific approach, he had the example of Conran, and the presence of a nun sitting in on his class, to keep him on the straight and narrow.[58] The principal, Sister Keenan, later said de Valera gave

> the most perfect satisfaction in every sense of the word. He was perfect master of his subject, and made it so clear and so interesting that he arrested the attention of one hundred students with the greatest ease. He was painstaking, devoted, very punctual and full of energy.[59]

When he reached the top of his pay scale a further agreement was made to increase his salary to £200 over three years.[60] While in Carysfort he even got to write the book he had contemplated in Rockwell, a slim volume entitled *Examples in Arithmetic and Mensuration,* by E. de Valera, BA (Professor of Mathematics).[61]

Part of the attraction of the job was that he was back in his old Blackrock stomping-grounds. He moved to digs in Carysfort Avenue, near the training college[62] and then, in September 1907, back into the Castle in Blackrock College for a year. It was unprecedented for someone not studying or teaching in Blackrock to live there, but Father Downey, the dean of the Castle, made an exception for him, because he 'knew that he would be an asset to the place'.[63]

In 1908 he moved to Merrion View Avenue in Ballsbridge. His new landlady, Mrs Russell, was a native Irish-speaker, and he was then beginning to learn the language. His final address before his marriage was nearer to Blackrock, in Vernon Terrace, Booterstown, where he lived from October 1909 to September the following year.

Another attraction of the Carysfort job was that it required him to teach for only two hours, from 9 to 11 a.m. This left him plenty of time to pick up extra teaching work and to pursue his own studies. To his classes in Clonliffe College and Eccles Street he added St Mary's College in Rathmines and Loreto College on St Stephen's Green.[64] But these involved teaching students sitting Royal University examinations – and the days of the Royal were numbered. The university question which he had discussed in the Blackrock College debating society was finally resolved with the establishment of the National University of Ireland in 1908.[65] From then on, if he wanted to teach at university level he would have to get a job in one of the constituent colleges of the NUI, or at Trinity.[66]

But he remained determined to progress, spending his summer holidays at courses on experimental science in Belfast, on physics in 1906 and 1908, and on chemistry in 1907.[67] Back in Dublin he attended lectures in Trinity by Professor Edmund Whittaker, the Royal Astronomer of Ireland. Whittaker was impressed by de Valera, telling him in 1912 that 'a man of your vigour and ability is sure to get on sooner or later'.[68]

De Valera also attended lectures in UCD on the metaphysical aspects of mathematics, given by William Magennis; on mathematics, by Henry McWeeney; and, most importantly, on mathematical physics, by Arthur Conway.[69] Conway introduced him to the work of William Rowan Hamilton and his concept of 'quaternions', a number system for describing three-dimensional space. Hamilton had been working on the problem for more than a decade when, in October 1843, as he was walking along the banks of the Royal Canal near Broome Bridge in Cabra, he had a moment of inspiration. 'I then and there felt the galvanic circuit of thought close; and the sparks which fell from it were the fundamental equations . . .'[70] He was so excited that he carved the equation into the stone of Broome Bridge. De Valera regarded the bridge as 'a holy place' and searched in vain for traces of the inscription.[71]

De Valera did some serious research on quaternions. Conway, writing a testimonial for him in 1912, said de Valera had gone deeply into the subject, and was 'at present prosecuting an important original research in them which promises to be of considerable interest'.[72] The research was never finished, and he never got the MA he had hoped for. But mathematics – and quaternions in particular – remained an abiding interest. He wrote to Conway from Lewes jail after the Easter Rising, discussing mathematical topics including quaternions; in Arbour Hill after the Civil War he attempted to master the theory of relativity; and during his presidency he would refuse to take the walk ordered by his doctor until his secretary read him a maths problem he could ponder as he walked.[73]

Of course, life wasn't just about work and study. In Belvedere College he renewed his acquaintance with his elocution teacher, Abraham McHardy-Flint, who had written a play for the Abbey, *A Christmas Hamper*, which was due to open on 28 November 1905.[74] Having been let down by one of his actors, he pressed de Valera into service to play the character of Dr Kelly. De Valera had only two short rehearsals, and as he went on stage he worried about the audience's being able to hear him; as a result, he declaimed his lines so loudly that he could be heard out on the street.[75] In his diary the critic Joseph Holloway observed that 'the tall thin appearance of Mr E de Valeria [*sic*] as he made his entrance as Dr Kelly at the end of act 2 caused many to laugh, especially as Mrs Flint was over-acting very much at the time. He fitted in better in the picture during the death-scene'.[76] The play closed after its second night.

He also continued playing rugby, joining Blackrock College Rugby Football Club, eventually captaining the second team (as well as becoming club secretary). Oddly, in his reminiscences about this time he mentions being captain of the seconds, but not his frequent appearances for the firsts,[77] almost as if being the chief counted for more than playing at a higher level. In 1908 de Valera led the seconds to the Leinster Junior League final at Lansdowne Road, where they were beaten 6–3 by Dublin University Seconds.[78] Seán Farragher recorded that some blamed him for the defeat, because of what they saw as 'almost a fixation he had about his ability to take penalties and place kicks'.[79] A hand-drawn postcard in de Valera's papers, addressed to 'E. Develara [sic], Captain Blackrock Rugby Team', seems to support this allegation: in it, a figure who is presumably meant to be de Valera is shown about to kick a ball (although the ball looks round rather than oval), and beside the picture is written: 'Alas!! Alas!! Alas!! For our blighted hopes; but I told you so.'[80] However, according to newspaper reports of the match, a player called Connolly failed to convert Blackrock's only try; there is no mention of any other missed kicks.[81] Despite this significant question mark over the idea that Blackrock lost the match because of de Valera's insistence on taking the kicks, the story has been given much prominence in interpreting his character. Like many other stories about him, it appears it is too much in tune with perceptions of his character to leave out, even if unsubstantiated.

While he enjoyed his work at Carysfort, he still hungered after some-thing better. As well as his continuing mathematical studies, he completed a postgraduate diploma in education in 1910, coming third of the three UCD candidates in the final exams.[82] And he continued applying for jobs. He was beaten twice in the competition for school inspector by candidates he considered inferior but better connected. He was particularly resentful of his second defeat.

> Felt outraged at this, as I felt he had neither the academic qualifications or experience I had. Resolved never to go up again.[83]

This theme – that if he was beaten it must be because of cheating by the other side – was to recur throughout his life. He also applied for the chair of mathematics at UCG in 1912 (though he withdrew from that competition).[84]

That year he had a stroke of luck that finally made him a university lecturer. Daniel Mannix, president of St Patrick's College, Maynooth, the national seminary, wrote inviting him to apply for a position as lecturer in mathematics and physics. Mannix made it clear it would be only a temporary position, 'as the Bishops look forward to having a resident Professor in the near future'.[85] Needless to say, the professor would not be a layman, and would certainly not be the holder of a pass degree. In fact, the post would go to Father Pádraig de Brún – de Valera's former pupil in Rockwell and Clonliffe – who was by then both a priest and a brilliantly qualified mathematician. De Brún was conducting post-graduate studies in Germany, which he would extend by another year in 1913, to the benefit of his former teacher, who continued in his temporary post.[86]

Bolstered by this new position, in May 1913 de Valera launched an audacious and persistent bid to become professor of mathematical physics at UCC.[87] He assembled a formidable battery of testimonials and had them printed: 'Qualifications and Testimonials of Edward de Valera, Professor of Mathematics in the Training College, Blackrock'. They paid tribute to his ability as a teacher, his brilliance at mathematics, his aptitude for research – from Sister Keenan, principal of Carysfort; from Father Brennan, president of Blackrock College; from the UCD professors Conway, Corcoran and Magennis. The latter delicately raised the sore point of his pass degree. 'He gave me the impression of being a keen thinker and a steady worker – a student whose many and varied attainments are not adequately represented by his academic distinctions.'[88]

While somebody with a pass degree and no further qualification shouldn't have been in the running for an academic post of this kind, the initial decision was in the hands of the governing body of the college, where canvassing could overcome such difficulties.

That May, J. J. Horgan – a Cork solicitor, Irish Party activist and Gaelic League enthusiast – received an unexpected visitor,

> a tall, lanky young man about my own age. His dark hair and sallow complexion suggested a foreign origin which his name justified, but his rich Limerick accent seemed to belie.

De Valera bore a letter of introduction from Professor Corcoran, who had taught Horgan in Clongowes Wood College. A subsequent interview

> confirmed Father Corcoran's eulogy. My visitor, whose modesty was only equalled by his charm of manner, was equally acceptable on other grounds, for it appeared that he was not only an active member of the Gaelic League but also, like most young Irishmen at that time, a supporter of John Redmond's home rule policy.[89]

Notwithstanding de Valera's lack of academic qualifications, Horgan set to with a will to have him selected. In this effort, Horgan's main opponent was his own father-in-law.

Sir Bertram Windle, president of UCC, was rather more concerned with academic excellence than was his son-in-law, and he was impressed by the report of the academic council, which stated that, of the eight applicants, E. H. Harper, a graduate of TCD then teaching at the University of Bangor, was 'incomparably the best candidate'; he was followed by a Mr Riddell, who was followed by a Mr Bowen; there was no mention of a Mr de Valera. However, that was not necessarily decisive for the governing body, made up of councillors, clerics and representatives of teaching orders. They were susceptible to persuasion, and they were persuaded of the virtues of the young man with the strange name and the lacklustre degree.[90] An ebullient Horgan telegraphed de Valera: 'You tied for first place, congratulations.'[91] But the final choice rested with the senate of the NUI, which proved less susceptible to the charm de Valera had used so effectively in Cork, appointing Harper professor without opposition.[92]

So de Valera was to remain an anonymous employee of a minor college. In the meantime, teaching had introduced him to a consuming new interest – one that would lead him to his future wife and supply him with a new name and even a new identity.

CHAPTER 06

I NEED A KISS, URGENTLY

In small things, Dev is very much given to weighing things; he sees all the difficulties and takes all the precautions. On the other hand, when a big matter is at stake, he will go boldly forward.
                                                            Sinéad de Valera[1]

I need a kiss, urgently . . . Can you sleep without those long limbs wrapped around you?
                                        Éamon de Valera to Sinéad de Valera, 1911[2]

That man will go far.
                                        Bulmer Hobson on Éamon de Valera, 1913[3]

In later life Éamon de Valera claimed to have had a long-standing interest in Irish, and to have been 'always anxious to learn the language'.[4] This was a considerable exaggeration: he had ignored opportunities to learn it, and he only bothered himself about it when it affected his career prospects. What is striking, however, is how completely his attitude changed once he had taken it up. He became a zealous convert, using Irish at home and, when he could, in public, changing his first name to Éamon and at times converting his surname into de Bailéara or de Buileára.[5] In later years the language became a central part of his identity and of his concept of Irish nationalism. 'Were the choice therefore given to us at this moment to secure our territory but to lose the language, or to lose the territory but save the language, we should unhesitatingly choose the latter'.[6] For him, as for others in the Gaelic League, Ireland without its own language was no nation at all.

Irish became such a central part of his identity that he tried to disguise the fact that his own proficiency was limited. Although his 1937

Constitution was drafted in English and then translated into Irish, article 25.5.4 states that, 'in case of conflict between the texts . . . the text in the national language shall prevail'. De Valera followed a similar approach on less important documents – a letter to an Irish language expert about the dialect spoken in Bruree, for instance, was written in English, with 'to be translated into Irish' at the top.[7] His speech for the installation of Douglas Hyde as President of Ireland in June 1938 was drafted by hand in English; then a typed Irish version was produced, as well as a typed version of the original English text with 'translation' written at the top.[8] De Valera's commitment to the language was sincere, but such subterfuges would be seen by many as entirely in keeping with the state's approach, paying lip service to revival without giving much effective help.

His own first encounter with Irish was in Bruree, where his grandmother used it occasionally. She did not, however, encourage him to learn it. Many of her generation regarded it as being of little value, particularly when so many young people emigrated. When Father Eugene O'Growney published Irish lessons in the *Weekly Freeman,* de Valera and his Uncle Pat talked about following them, but didn't; de Valera blamed this on his uncle's lack of enthusiasm, but he was well capable of studying alone when he wanted. There was an Irish class in Blackrock College, but he made no effort to join it, explaining lamely that he was doing all the subjects he needed for the Intermediate, and 'to take up a new subject would . . . have been a handicap'. Another opportunity presented itself in Rockwell, where one of his students gave him several lessons, but they were discontinued 'for some reason or other that I do not now remember'.[9] Until his mid-20s, then, de Valera had shown no more than a passing interest. So what changed?

The short answer is that Irish had become essential to his career. This was largely due to the Gaelic League, established in 1893 by O'Growney, Douglas Hyde and Eoin MacNeill. It organised classes to spread knowledge of the language and, more importantly, built up political pressure for it to be used in schools and universities. The number of children being taught Irish in national schools rose from 1,825 in 1899 to 180,000 in 1911,[10] and a campaign to make Irish a compulsory subject for matriculation to the NUI finally succeeded in 1910, when it was made mandatory from 1913.[11] This made knowledge of Irish vital for teachers – and for those who trained them.

In October 1908 de Valera joined a beginners' class at Leinster College in Dublin and shortly afterwards the Ard-Chraobh (central branch) of the Gaelic League, housed in the same building in Parnell Square. 'Now I meant to apply myself seriously to the learning of the language.'[12]

The Gaelic League had a well-developed organisational structure, with a network of cumainn (branches), a coiste gnótha (executive) and an ard-fheis (annual convention), and de Valera quickly became deeply involved in this structure, once again being elected to (or more likely volunteering for) some of the jobs that other members may not have been eager to undertake – a delegate to the ard-fheis, a member of the Leinster College Committee, and a collector of funds at church gates.[13]

More importantly, he met his future wife in the Leinster College classroom. Sinéad Ní Fhlannagáin (christened Jane Flanagan) was born in Balbriggan, Co. Dublin, in 1878.[14] Sinéad went to school at St Francis Xavier's in Drumcondra, becoming a monitor in 1890; six years later she entered Baggot Street Training College, and in 1898 she got a teaching job in Edenderry, Co. Offaly, where she first heard of the Gaelic League.[15] She returned to Drumcondra to teach in St Francis Xavier's from 1899 until her marriage in 1910.

Sinéad joined the Gaelic League in November 1899, learning and then teaching Irish to students, including another future president, Seán T. O'Kelly. She also became involved in amateur dramatics, most famously in a play by Douglas Hyde, *The Tinker and the Fairy*, in which she and Hyde were the principal actors. The play was staged in May 1902 in the back garden of George Moore's house in Ely Place.[16] Sinéad was delighted with the praise she received from the likes of W. B. Yeats and the dramatist Edward Martyn. Significantly, none of her family was there, and she went home for tea with her parents rather than to the after-show dinner, 'for I would not feel at home in such high society'.[17]

She was also politically engaged – in contrast to her future husband. She wept as a 13-year-old as she followed Parnell's funeral cortege to Glasnevin Cemetery,[18] and in 1900 became a member of Inghinidhe na Éireann ('Daughters of Ireland'), a radical nationalist group founded by Maude Gonne, which later merged with Cumann na mBan.[19] On an excursion to Tara with some fellow Irish-language enthusiasts, a toast was proposed 'that we may soon have a King in Ireland'. Sinéad responded, 'Oh, no, a Republic.' Another woman in the company added, 'May you be the president's wife.'[20]

There was no suggestion that she herself might play a public role, and that was the way she liked it. Sinéad devoted herself to home and family, to the exclusion of any public activity, apart from what she was reluctantly persuaded to undertake at her husband's side. This devotion, of course, allowed de Valera to apply all his energy to his political career; and when it came to a conflict between that career and Sinéad's wishes, the career won. Yet Sinéad's inner strength should not be underestimated. Many who met her recalled her charm – she particularly enchanted President John F. Kennedy – but she could also be tough. Indeed, from Easter 1916 on, she had to be, as she coped with her husband's lengthy absences, with family illnesses and with harassment from pro-Treaty forces during the Civil War.

Politically aware and accomplished, yet also more interested in home life than in 'high society', Sinéad was a very good and enthusiastic teacher,[21] and her classes on Tuesday nights were popular.[22] While small in stature (especially compared to her future husband) she was good looking and she had attracted the interest of both Seán O'Casey and Ernest Blythe.[23] But it was another young man who caught her attention, 'an exacting pupil, fond of giving posers'. At Christmas, 1908, she received

> a nice plant with a card on which was inscribed 'Ó Chara' [from a friend]. I thought it must be Dev who sent it, but as I was not sure, I was afraid to thank him.[24]

Over the next six months the two must have got over their shyness, because they were engaged on 6 June 1909.[25]

This was fast work, especially for de Valera, whose only known previous romantic relationship was with Mary Stewart four or five years earlier in Rockwell. Even though Éamon and Sinéad hardly knew each other until they were engaged, he wanted to get married that August. Jack Barrett, his Rockwell colleague, cautioned against rushing so quickly into matrimony, though they delayed for only another five months. Sinéad later recalled that his impetuosity was characteristic.

> In small things, Dev is very much given to weighing things; he sees all the difficulties and takes all the precautions. On the other hand, when a big matter is at stake, he will go boldly forward.[26]

Her young admirer, Ernest Blythe, who had moved to Bangor, Co. Down, to work as a journalist, claimed to have received a letter from her shortly before her engagement suggesting doubts on her part. She had written, 'without indicating any details, that she was in a state of indecision and very troubled in her mind'.[27] This sounds very much like sour grapes, which would have been entirely characteristic of Blythe: when asked who Sinéad was to marry, he replied, 'Ah, some class of a mulatto called Demerara'.[28]

Sinéad was to teach Irish that summer in Tourmakeady, on the shores of Lough Mask in Co. Mayo, and her fiancé went with her. On the way, they stopped off in Claremorris, where de Valera had arranged to meet a close friend from Blackrock College, Frank Hughes. Spotting Hughes on the platform, de Valera asked Sinéad to wait while he had a word with him; Hughes began a great flow of conversation, before de Valera interrupted to ask, indicating Sinéad: 'What do you think of that girl?' He expected Hughes to share his enthusiasm, but his friend simply replied: 'Not much' and carried on talking. He changed his attitude, of course, once the situation was explained.[29] Despite the embarrassment he caused his friend and the thoughtless way he treated his fiance, de Valera evidently thought this incident amusing, as he told Seán Farragher about it.

During their engagement the couple occasionally went to the theatre, and more often for walks at Howth,[30] possibly the inspiration for an undated poem in de Valera's papers.

> My head rests on the bosom of her I love, the soft pulsing of her heart soothes like the breaking of the waves o'er the beach, her hair freed from confining bows blows on my cheek . . . The voice of my love is a sweet treble to the deep bass of the waves . . .[31]

While possibly not de Valera's finest piece of writing, it did capture his euphoric mood. However, his mother was less enthusiastic when he finally broke the news. Kate Wheelwright complained that it was 'a great surprise to me as I always hoped to see you here unmarried' (not that she had done very much to achieve that). She expressed the hope that her future daughter-in-law was a Catholic, that she could cook and sew, and that 'she is of a lively disposition as if she is not, I fear you will be sad'. With the experience of two marriages behind her, she advised her son that

> there are three jewels in married life . . . fidelity, to be ready to share each other's joy and sorrow, and fear and love of the Lord. The demons are jealousy, covetousness, and pleasure seeking.[32]

Éamon de Valera and Sinéad Ní Fhlannagáin were married on the morning of 8 January 1910. According to Sinéad, the priest was very nervous, having had to learn the Irish for the ceremony: 'He married us two or three times before he got the words right.'[33]

Frank Hughes, despite his faux pas at Claremorris, was best man; Sinéad's sister Bee was the bridesmaid. They honeymooned in Woodenbridge,

Co. Wicklow, but de Valera was back to teach in Carysfort within a week. His class welcomed him back with an ovation; one of the students, Nora Ashe (sister of Tom), wrote a blessing in Irish on the board for him, which he misunderstood. Even worse was a misunderstanding with Sineád when she was ill before their marriage. She used a phrase in Irish meaning 'It's hard to kill a bad thing'; his reply can be translated as 'It certainly is'.[34]

After briefly living in de Valera's digs at Vernon Terrace, they moved into their first, rented, house at 33 Morehampton Terrace in Donnybrook. Soon after they moved in, Sinéad sent her husband to buy some household necessities. He arrived home with a chandelier that almost touched the floor, a patched cello and two copper plates depicting rural scenes. 'He thought he had got marvellous bargains'.[35]

He had more success in his Irish studies, perhaps because he now had an in-house tutor. He proudly recalled getting first place in his final exams in Leinster College in May 1910[36] – in fact he was second of the seven candidates.[37] Nevertheless, he was now a qualified teacher of Irish and would teach classes in the Ard-Chraobh from that autumn.

In the meantime, he was to spend the summer at an Irish college in Co. Galway. This indicates how his priorities had changed: from 1906 to 1908 his holidays involved courses in experimental physics and chemistry; from 1909 to 1911 he went to Irish college, first as pupil and then as teacher. Tamhain, an island at the head of Galway Bay, was in those days Irish-speaking. The challenge of keeping it that way was demonstrated to de Valera when he asked a question in his painstaking Irish of an old man wearing a traditional báinín jacket. Insulted, the old man replied 'Do you think I do not know English?'[38] It was here that the former British diplomat and Irish nationalist Sir Roger Casement was funding an Irish-language school (one of several colleges and nationalist groups he was supporting).[39]

De Valera was left to run the school as he saw fit, with the occasional missive from Casement. 'I know of no-one who could so well superintend matters'.[40] A later letter was generous in its praise of de Valera. 'I must congratulate you on the success that has presided over your efforts'.[41] But de Valera had to tell Casement that the college was a failure: there weren't enough students; the ones who did come didn't stay long enough; and, worst of all, the college didn't offer the certificates National School teachers required. The contrast with the successful school in An Spidéal was stark. He suggested improvements: the villagers could provide better accommodation, advertising should be improved, and they should specialise in advanced students.[42] But with only about 20 students each year, the school was uneconomic and closed after three years.[43]

Being in Tamhain for all of August meant being away from Sinéad, an absence he found difficult. Their marriage was evidently a close one, with three children born in quick succession: Vivion in December 1910, Máirín in April 1912 and Eamonn in October 1913. In August 1911, with Sinéad at home caring for the infant Vivion, de Valera expressed his loneliness in a letter.

> I need a kiss, urgently . . . I want to press my wife to my heart, but we are 150 miles apart. Darling, do you think of me at all? – can you sleep without those long limbs wrapped around you? – those same limbs are longing to be wrapped around you again – two weeks – fourteen days – how can I endure it? You do not know how sorrowful I am . . .[44]

The following year Sinéad had two babies to mind, and her husband was once again lovelorn.

> I am always thinking of you darling – yet I don't wish you here for want of proper accommodation . . . I feel empty, joyless without you.

He went on to include some lines from an erotic poem in Irish. He explained that

> we had it in class today, I couldn't go into the meaning with the mixed class but I wished you were with me till we discuss it . . .[45]

Meanwhile, de Valera was continuing his progress through the ranks of the Gaelic League. He later proudly recounted that Dr McHenry, principal of Leinster College, always used to propose him as a teller for votes, as he 'thought I would play fair'.[46] But de Valera suspected others were not playing fair when he failed to be elected to the coiste gnótha at the ard-fheis; he rightly suspected a conspiracy, but wrongly believed it was being conducted by Sinn Féin, the political party established by Arthur Griffith in 1905. Returning home after his defeat, he threw the ard-fheis programme on the kitchen table and told Sinéad he would 'never have anything to do with Sinn Féin'.[47]

His mistake was understandable, as at this time all nationalist opponents of the Irish Party tended to be referred to as 'Sinn Féiners'[48] – a fact that would be of inestimable value to that party when the 1916 Rising was wrongly referred in the press as the 'Sinn Féin Rebellion'. But the election had in fact been rigged by members of the Irish Republican Brotherhood.

The IRB was to play an important part in de Valera's life for the next decade, but he seemed then unaware of its existence; it was, after all, a secret society. The IRB had declined substantially, from a reputed 35,000 members in 1879 to just 1,660 by 1912. Despite this, it had managed to remain in existence, promoting complete separation from Britain and maintaining the idea that freedom could be won through physical force.[49] The Gaelic League (like the Gaelic Athletic Association) was an excellent cover for the IRB. One Brother who infiltrated the League was Thomas Ashe, a Kerry schoolteacher living in Co. Dublin. He was a leading member of the GAA and a piper of some repute, charismatic and handsome, described by one admirer as 'a Viking chief in appearance'.[50] At the Gaelic League's ard-fheis in Galway in July 1913, Douglas Hyde denounced Ashe and his associates as 'disrupters' and tried to have them removed from the leadership. One of Hyde's allies proposed the reduction of the executive to 25 members to make it more difficult for the radicals to retain their seats; Ashe suggested 35. De Valera proposed a compromise, 30, which was accepted. Ashe and his allies were duly re-elected.[51] De Valera was regarded as independent and, not for the last time, capable of producing an acceptable compromise.

The IRB finally staged a takeover of the Gaelic League at the Dundalk ard-fheis in 1915, at which its constitution was amended to include a commitment to seek 'a free Irish nation'. The apolitical Hyde resigned as president, and Eoin MacNeill was elected in his place.[52] Though not a member of the IRB, MacNeill supported the Gaelic League taking a more political line, as part of what might be termed a pan-nationalist front. He later admitted that the decision had damaged the League.[53] In a speech in August 1917 (by which time he was considerably more radical than he had been in 1915) de Valera rejected the notion that the Gaelic League could be non-political, because 'the language . . . stands in the way of absolute union between this country and England'. The Gaelic League might not side with any particular party, but it was certainly opposed to what he called imperialism.[54]

By the time he turned 30, in October 1912, de Valera had achieved much. He was established as a minor academic, with a permanent job in Carsyfort as well as a temporary appointment at Maynooth. The emotional void left by his upbringing had been filled with a happy marriage and two small children, with a third soon to follow. He had developed a consuming interest in the revival of the language which occupied much of his spare time and gave him a cause to pursue. Yet he remained relatively unknown and politically uninvolved. While the Gaelic League may have radicalised him, in the sense that he became preoccupied with national identity, it had not politicised him. Membership of it might be regarded as a necessary condition for future republicanism, but hardly as a sufficient one.[55]

And while the Gaelic League was a fertile recruiting-ground for the IRB, it appears that no-one tried to recruit de Valera. He later claimed that the first person he heard advocating an Irish republic was Patrick McCartan, speaking at a public meeting at Beresford Place in Dublin opposing the visit of King George in 1911. De Valera told McCartan years later that he thought 'it was a fine ideal but one not likely to be attained'.[56] He was dismissive of the radical nationalists in Sinn Féin and almost certainly remained what he had always been: a nationalist, of course; a home-ruler, certainly; but not a Republican or a revolutionary.

And yet there was potential there, if opportunity arose. He had displayed some political skill in the Gaelic League, managing to rise through the ranks by taking the jobs no-one else wanted. And he had a formidable charm. In April 1913 Ernest Blythe returned briefly to Dublin after four years in Bangor. There he stayed with the radical nationalist and IRB member Bulmer Hobson, who accompanied him when he decided to call on Sinéad. To Blythe's disgust, she assumed they were there to see her husband and brought them up to his study. But while Blythe fumed, Hobson became increasingly impressed by de Valera. As they left, Hobson remarked, 'That man will go far.'[57] The question was, how – and where to?

CHAPTER 07

THOSE WHO SIDE WITH IRELAND

They have rights who dare maintain them.
Manifesto of the Irish Volunteers, 1913[1]

Those who side with Ireland will go to that side of the hall, and those who would like to support the British Empire will take the other.
Éamon de Valera, 1914[2]

The 3rd battalion is much the weakest in the matter of command.
Commandant J. J. 'Ginger' O'Connell,
chief of inspection, Irish Volunteers, 1916[3]

Half a century later, Éamon de Valera would date the beginning of his active political life to November 1913, when he joined the Irish Volunteers. 'This,' he declared, 'was the casting of the die.'[4] While rather pompous, the observation was accurate: in only four years, this decision would lead an obscure maths teacher to a position of national leadership.

The formation of the Volunteers was part of an unfolding crisis over home rule. In 1912, John Redmond, leader of the Irish Party, appeared to have achieved what had eluded Daniel O'Connell, Isaac Butt and Charles Stewart Parnell: home rule for Ireland. Holding the balance of power in Westminster, Redmond had induced the Liberal government of Herbert Asquith to sponsor a home-rule bill giving Ireland self-government. And this bill would actually become law, as the Liberals had removed the veto from the House of Lords. All the peers could do was delay home rule for three parliamentary sessions, until 1914.

There were two major problems with this victory. The first was the very limited nature of what was on offer, far removed from the Dominion status that would finally be achieved under the Treaty. The Home Rule parliament would be subordinate to Westminster, which could reverse any act of which it disapproved (though given the reluctance of Westminster to interfere in Northern Ireland during the half century of Stormont rule this may have been a moot point). Advanced nationalists viewed the proposal as 'a mild milk-and-water effort . . . a third-rate debating society masquerading as a National Parliament'.[5]

The other difficulty was the north-east, where Protestant unionists formed a compact local majority with no wish to be ruled by Dublin. Unionists in the rest of Ireland had used this local majority to frustrate W. E. Gladstone's attempts to introduce home rule in 1886 and 1893. By 1912 Ulster unionists had decided that, whatever happened in the rest of Ireland, home rule would not apply to them. On 28 September 1912 an estimated half a million men and women signed Ulster's Solemn League and Covenant, promising to use 'all means which may be found necessary to defeat the present conspiracy to set up a Home Rule Parliament in Ireland'.[6]

These pledges would be backed by violence, or at least the threat of it, through the Ulster Volunteer Force, established in January 1913. The Conservative Party backed their Unionist allies, even in the threat of force against the elected British government. The Conservative Party leader, Andrew Bonar Law, a Canadian of Ulster extraction, declared:

> There are things stronger than parliamentary majorities . . . I can imagine no length of resistance to which Ulster can go in which I should not be prepared to support it.

Lord Alington said in September 1913 that if unionists suffered violence

> the people of this country will be so enraged that they will require some blood of the members of the Cabinet . . . If an Irishman is killed he could hardly be spared. But if it was a couple of Cabinet Ministers we should say, 'Good riddance.'[7]

De Valera was later criticised for inflammatory remarks made in the period before the Civil War; but his were mild compared with what was being said by His Majesty's Loyal Opposition between 1912 and 1914.

The threat of violence worked. Asquith and his colleagues began to openly discuss some way of excluding Ulster, or part of it, from home rule. It was only a matter of time before nationalists concluded that the only effective response was to threaten force themselves. On 1 November 1913 Eoin MacNeill published an article entitled 'The North began' in the Gaelic League's newspaper, *An Claidheamh Soluis*.[8] He claimed that the establishment of the Ulster Volunteers was 'the most decisive move towards Irish autonomy that has been made since O'Connell invented constitutional agitation.' The point, he claimed, was not *for* whom Ireland was held, but *by* whom Ireland was held – and the Ulster Volunteers were saying they would hold it. 'There is nothing to prevent the other twenty-eight counties from calling into existence citizen forces to hold Ireland "for the Empire".'

MacNeill's article was eagerly read by IRB members, who were anxious to see a nationalist counterpart to the Ulster Volunteers but who were equally anxious to hide their own involvement. What they needed was a respectable figurehead, and MacNeill was perfect. Bulmer Hobson, the leading IRB conspirator who was so impressed with de Valera, along with his fellow-member Michael O'Rahilly (who had given himself the title 'the O'Rahilly'), called on MacNeill to discuss how to start a volunteer force, and to encourage him to lead it.[9]

The Irish Volunteers were formed at a public meeting in the Rotunda in Parnell Square, Dublin, on 25 November 1913. The excitement was so intense that, two days beforehand, Hobson risked booking the Rotunda Rink, the largest hall in Dublin, for the meeting.[10] The *Freeman's Journal* reported 'animated scenes', with thousands of young men trying to get into the Rink. Even after the Rotunda's Large Concert Hall was opened as an overflow, hundreds remained outside.[11]

Among the crowd was Éamon de Valera. Immediately in front of him in the hall was his former parish priest, Father Eugene Sheehy, along with a star of Bruree's hurling club, Larry Roche. De Valera didn't feel confident enough to make himself known to these luminaries.[12] While de Valera was too timid to say a word to his former priest, his future second-in-command, Seán T. O'Kelly, had been given charge of the overflow meeting, which he chaired 'with that cocky self-assurance which always endeared him to an audience'.[13]

Inside the Rink the meeting 'pulsated with an intensity of national feeling'.[14] As MacNeill finished speaking, the band struck up 'A Nation Once Again', an unofficial anthem of Irish nationalism, which the audience sang enthusiastically. As they concluded, stewards (members of the IRB) appeared with enrolment forms.[15] Three thousand signed on the spot,[16] including de Valera, though not before he gave the matter some thought, as befitted a man of 31 with the responsibilities of a growing family. He realised that volunteering might mean fighting, but he persuaded himself that there were not enough unmarried men to fill the ranks, and 'made that an excuse for myself to join'.[17]

His original membership card was made out to 'Emin Dilvara'.[18] Volunteer 'Dilvara' was ordered to report to 41 York Street, off St Stephen's Green, where he was taught 'to stand at ease, attention, turn left and about; taught to form fours, etc'.[19] Given the large pool of Irishmen who had served in the British army, Volunteers were told to 'follow exactly the drill set out in the *British Infantry Manual, 1911*'. [20]

De Valera progressed through the ranks. The Volunteers in Dublin were divided into four battalions, allocated to four quadrants of the city. Each battalion was headed by a commandant and was divided into a number of companies, each under a captain. De Valera was successively a corporal in charge of a squad and a sergeant in charge of a section, before being elected second lieutenant. Laurence Kettle was elected captain, and another man, William Condron, became first lieutenant. Characteristically, de Valera suspected underhand methods. He felt there was some 'wrangling', as he thought Condron 'not as good at work as I was'.[21]

The company was at this time drilling in Sandymount Castle, and Lieutenant de Valera used to walk home with a neighbour, Batt O'Connor. O'Connor was an IRB member as well as a Volunteer, and on one of their walks he asked de Valera if he would join 'the physical force boys'. De Valera declined. 'I hated to bind myself to obey orders given by people whom I did not know.'[22] Although he didn't mention it, he may also have had religious scruples about secret organisations – scruples that for some formed a 'stone wall' preventing them from joining the brotherhood.[23]

Sandymount Castle was owned by the Plunkett family, and its use had been secured by Joseph Plunkett, later one of the leaders of the Rising. Another Plunkett family property, Larkfield in Kimmage, was used for battalion exercises on weekends. De Valera recalled the drills overseen by a retired British army sergeant-major, Merry, who

> used to get us to perform evolutions such as getting a battalion of four or five companies of about a hundred, drawn up in column of companies, in line, to change direction 'right'.[24]

De Valera himself made an impression on some of the Volunteers, one of whom remembered him at the Kimmage exercises.

We regarded him as a kind of remote figure. We couldn't afford to buy a uniform, but the officers could . . . De Valera always came in uniform . . . We thought he looked rather funny. He was a very tall man riding on a bicycle in a uniform and we had a sense of class distinction over these differences.[25]

His seriousness of manner was much in evidence at this time. The personal charm, so effective in private, and in the classroom, was still there, of course. But his image was now that of an austere, aloof authority figure.

That image helped his ascent up the Volunteer hierarchy – an ascent that took another leap forward in May 1914 when a new unit, E Company of the 3rd Battalion, was formed at a meeting in Donnybrook at which 250 new members were enrolled. Among the speakers was the O'Rahilly, who claimed that Volunteers were being enrolled at the rate of 2,000 a day; the force was now 90,000-strong, and in due course they hoped to have a standing army of 300,000. To cheers, he said, 'When that army is fully trained and equipped we will like to see the man or country that will dare take from us our rights and liberties.'[26]

De Valera was detailed to take charge of the new company, using a hall belonging to the Ancient Order of Hibernians (an organisation closely linked to the Irish Party), at 17A Main Street, Donnybrook. He evidently impressed his new charges, being unanimously elected captain of the company on 3 August 1914.[27] Within two months it had about 130 men on the rolls.[28]

The spectacular growth of the Volunteers could not be ignored by the Irish Party, especially as the home-rule crisis loomed. In June 1914 Redmond had issued an ultimatum to the Volunteer Executive: they could either accept a large bloc of his nominees (who would hold a majority on the Executive) or face his denunciation.

Many of the hard-line IRB members opposed the move; Hobson did not, arguing that Redmond's opposition would destroy the movement.[29] His voice was decisive in swaying MacNeill towards accepting the ultimatum, earning Hobson the undying opposition of such former allies as Tom Clarke and Seán Mac Diarmada. These two, as treasurer and secretary, respectively, were in effect in control of the IRB.[30] Clarke and Mac Diarmada were busy infiltrating the senior ranks of the Volunteers with their own men, leaving MacNeill in office but placing IRB loyalists in positions of command;[31] now Hobson was side-lined too.

Hobson had good reason for wanting to avoid a split: he was planning a crucial importation of arms.[32] On 4 December 1913, only nine days after the establishment of the Irish Volunteers, a royal proclamation had prohibited the importation of arms into Ireland.[33] Given that the Ulster Volunteers had been arming themselves for months, this seemed directed at nationalists. That suspicion was reinforced when the Ulster Volunteers, with no interference from the authorities, brought 25,000 rifles and millions of rounds of ammunition into Larne, Donaghadee and Bangor in a meticulously planned operation in April 1914.

The response of the Irish Volunteers came on 26 July, when guns were run into Howth aboard the *Asgard*, a yacht owned by Erskine Childers, then still a moderate Liberal supporter of home rule. De Valera was almost involved in a gun-running episode the day before, during a separate attempt to bring arms into Kilcoole, Co. Wicklow. He was asked by Seán Mac Diarmada to use his motorcycle and sidecar to collect Liam Mellows and bring him out to the Scalp, near Enniskerry. Mellows handed him a revolver and told him they were going to collect guns at Kilcoole. However, a message arrived telling them the mission was off.[34] The IRB must have regarded de Valera as trustworthy, even though he was not himself a member.

The following morning, 26 July, E Company assembled at Belmont Avenue, outside Donnybrook, and proceeded to march to Howth. When they got there de Valera was ordered to form a cordon across the end of the pier as the arms were being unloaded from the *Asgard*. This led to considerable grumbling among his men, who worried they would miss the opportunity to get guns themselves. Eventually he persuaded another unit, which had already been armed, to take over cordon duty while he and his men obtained some of the last rifles to be distributed.[35] Jubilant, the Volunteers marched back into Dublin, feeling like real soldiers at last.

At Clontarf an effort was made by the Dublin Metropolitan Police to disarm the Volunteers. Nineteen guns, of the 900 landed, were seized,[36] but they later had to be returned, as their confiscation was illegal.[37] De Valera sent two-thirds of his own men home, leaving each remaining man with three rifles. He then collected his motorbike and sidecar, which he used to transport his remaining men and their cargo, finishing the job just before dawn.[38] After Howth and Kilcoole, the Volunteers had secured 1,500 rifles, which Pearse admitted were 'much inferior to the British service rifle and even to those which [the Unionist leader Edward] Carson's men have'. His other problem was that the Redmondites were keen to have as many as possible transferred north, which made sense if they were to be used for defensive purposes, but did not sit well with Pearse's plans for offensive action.[39]

However, the crisis over Home Rule was about to be transformed by events elsewhere. On his way to Howth, as his company swung down Westland Row, de Valera had noticed newspaper placards warning of the threat of war in Europe.[40] Two days later Austria-Hungary declared war on Serbia, a month after the assassination of Archduke Franz Ferdinand in Sarajevo. The United Kingdom – including Ireland – would be at war within days.

There was a geo-political dimension to the worsening situation in Ireland. With Europe divided between two military alliances – Germany and Austria-Hungary on one side, Britain, France and Russia on the other – the Germans eagerly took advantage of the Irish troubles, supplying arms to both the Ulster and the Irish Volunteers.[41] Meanwhile, the British uneasily realised that, while they might have the troops to pacify Ireland, or to intervene on the Continent, they lacked the resources to do both. Sir Henry Wilson, Director of Military Operations at the War Office, told the Cabinet at the end of June 1914 that the entire British Expeditionary Force would be required to impose home rule and restore order in Ireland. Enforcing the government's will in Ireland would prevent it meeting its treaty obligations in Europe.[42]

The outbreak of war meant that, to the relief of British politicians, the Irish crisis could be put on the back burner. The home-rule bill was passed for the third time by the House of Commons – but it was suspended for the duration of hostilities, with a proviso that some arrangement would be made for Ulster before it was brought into force. And here John Redmond made his fatal mistake, telling a parade of Irish Volunteers in Woodenbridge, Co. Wicklow, on 20 September that they should serve not just in Ireland, as he had previously suggested, but 'wherever the firing-line extends, in defence of right, of freedom, and of religion in this war'.[43] This commitment to the British cause might have paid off, if the war was to be a short one; unfortunately for Redmond, and for those who answered his call, it was not.

The original Volunteer leadership was already deeply disillusioned by the Redmondite faction on the Executive, which they deemed 'quite impossible' as they prevented 'any effective work towards arming or organising the Volunteers'.[44] On 24 September the original members of the provisional committee said that after his Woodenbridge speech Redmond was 'no longer entitled, through his nominees, to any place in the administration and guidance of the Irish Volunteers organisation'.[45] Redmond, however, retained the loyalty of the vast majority of Volunteers. By late October, 158,360 had followed him into a new organisation, the National Volunteers; a mere 12,306 stayed with MacNeill.[46]

The split came to Donnybrook on the night of 28 September. De Valera recorded what transpired, because he got involved in a controversy over the split, after an inaccurate report of proceedings in the *Evening Telegraph*.[47] The paper had claimed that a meeting chaired by J. R. Donnelly had passed a motion of loyalty to Redmond, after which about 20 dissenting Volunteers walked out. De Valera indignantly wrote to the paper, pointing out that the meeting was the normal Monday-evening Volunteer parade, not a special one for considering the split; that no motions were passed; and that he was the commander of the company, and there was no 'chairman' of the meeting.[48]

After a further article giving the views of the Redmondite loyalists, de Valera wrote a detailed account of the evening. He arrived at the AOH hall as usual at 7:30 p.m. As the regular drill was about to begin, Donnelly, an Irish Party activist, approached him and asked what attitude was going to be taken on the split. De Valera did not see

> any immediate necessity for splitting into two parties men who had worked cordially together. But it was evident that Mr Donnelly . . . [was] not to be denied. What my own attitude would be was well known. I decided then in the interests of discipline to address the men. I told them that the time for division had evidently come. I explained my own views and permitted Mr Donnelly to speak . . .

Finally, deciding that the 'farce' had gone on long enough, de Valera told 'the men who intended to remain faithful to their signed declarations to fall in', and they proceeded outside to drill. He further claimed that there were 50 with him, not 20.[49] De Valera's version accords reasonably well with the later recollection of one of the Volunteers present, Liam Tannam.

> Éamon de Valera put the matter bluntly that the parting of the ways had come, and . . . then said, 'Those who side with Ireland will go to that side of the hall, and those who would like to support the British Empire will take the other.'[50]

There was a majority, albeit a slim one, in favour of de Valera's support for MacNeill – an outcome very much out of line with other units, presumably because of de Valera's influence over his men. Despite this result, and because the hall belonged to the AOH, the Redmondites remained in possession, and de Valera's side had to continue their drill outside.

In his response to the split, de Valera displayed a distaste for politics and politicians, referring to the Irish Party men left behind as 'politician boys' in a 'practice parliament' and lampooning their excessive loyalty to Redmond. In addition, he laid stress on staying faithful to signed declarations – a matter that would arise again in other splits. The question of finance, also to arise later, was an issue here too – de Valera wanted to keep the name of the Irish Volunteers, as well as 'a big sum of hard cash collected in that name'.[51] As he left the hall – at least according to his later account – he said: 'You will need us before you get Home Rule'.[52] Even though he took the more advanced nationalist position, he was apparently still thinking in terms of home rule as the eventual outcome, not a republic or anything like it.

De Valera would feel that the split had come at the right time, and on an issue that was plain to the people (participation in the First World War), and that this justified the Executive's acceptance of the Redmondite nominees in June,[53] when a split would have been more damaging. But in the autumn of 1914 he was hard pressed to cope with the dwindling numbers in his company. Having lost the use of the AOH hall, he was reduced to drilling in a field in Eglinton Road, opposite Donnybrook Church. He unsuccessfully attempted to secure Sandymount Castle for 'all the Donnybrook men who intend to remain true to their pledges', telling Joseph Plunkett that if they could have the grounds and hall on Thursday evenings, 'we would, in a very short time, have a splendid Company there. A hall will be absolutely necessary if we are to keep the men together during the winter.'[54]

Many of those who initially sided with de Valera were young and drifted away under parental pressure, leaving only 25 Volunteers at the next parade, and just seven within a few weeks. One of them recalled that, 'even with that small number', de Valera carried on 'as if he had a full Company and solemnly issued orders to form fours with the seven men'. De Valera remained optimistic, telling each of his followers to 'be a recruiting sergeant'. The numbers gradually built up again to 25, at which point members of the Dundrum Company joined, swelling the ranks further.[55] Those who stayed with the Volunteers, according to one member of the 3rd Battalion, tended to be 'working class or lower middle class . . . The men for the most part were in steady employment, were serious and many of them were given to reading'.[56]

Early in 1915 a new hall was secured, at McGinn's grocery in Beaver Row, on the banks of the Dodder. Just before de Valera was promoted to commandant of the 3rd Battalion, the company moved again, to the former site of Pearse's school, Cullenswood House in Oakley Road in Ranelagh.[57] After being promoted, de Valera retained a keen interest in E Company, encouraging Liam Tannam to stand for election as captain in his place and tutoring him for four weeks in how to run the company and in what military books he should study.[58]

When the Volunteers reorganised after the split, Headquarters took a closer interest in the appointment of officers. Company commanders were still to be elected by the members, but they had to be ratified by Headquarters. Battalion officers were to be appointed by HQ.[59]

On 10 March 1915 the Volunteer Executive appointed de Valera commandant of the 3rd Battalion, whose area was the south-east quadrant of the city. Seán Fitzgibbon, a member of the Executive, was to be vice-commandant.[60] De Valera's appointment was significant in that he was not a member of the IRB – the only battalion commander in Dublin who wasn't. However, Pearse had sounded out his attitude towards a possible rising; de Valera said that, as a soldier, he would obey his superiors.[61] Pearse then handed him his letter of appointment, which also invited him to a meeting the following Saturday, as 'there are several important matters that the Headquarters staff wants to discuss with the Commandants'.[62]

This meeting, on 13 March 1915, was the first time the newly promoted de Valera was formally made aware of plans for a Rising. He and the other city commandants – Thomas MacDonagh, Ned Daly and Éamonn Ceannt – were told action could come as early as September, and Pearse showed them the letter that was to be sent to them as a signal. The messenger would use the password 'Howth', and each commandant chose his own response; de Valera chose 'Bruree'. The news must have been electrifying, though de Valera's later recollection was distinctly downbeat. 'I was only one at that meeting who did not expect to survive.'[63]

Shortly afterwards de Valera summoned his battalion to a meeting at 41 York Street, where he said that there was a possibility they would have to fight, that he would be unable to give them notice, and that they should always be ready. 'Those who did not want to be in the Battalion on these terms should leave it without delay'.[64] This may have been the occasion when a young member of the battalion, Seán Lemass, got his first look at his future Chief. He had mixed feelings.

My impression of him was of a long, thin fellow with knee breeches and a tweed hat. But he had, of course, enormous personal magnetism and the capacity to hold that crowd of Volunteers there while he addressed them at inordinate length as he always did. There was not a movement among the crowd until he had finished. It impressed me enormously, notwithstanding what I thought was his rather queer-looking appearance.[65]

Joseph Plunkett was responsible for drawing up the military plans for the Rising as a member of the IRB's Military Council. The other original members were Pearse and Ceannt, both known to de Valera through the Gaelic League. In September they were joined by Tom Clarke and Seán Mac Diarmada. The Labour leader James Connolly was invited onto the council in January 1916 to ensure he didn't start a premature insurrection with the Irish Citizen Army, and he was made commandant-general of Dublin. Thomas MacDonagh was added at the beginning of April, partly because of his role as commander of the Dublin Brigade, partly because of his close relationship with Eoin MacNeill, a fellow lecturer at UCD.

This small group planned the Rising, without the knowledge of the IRB's Supreme Council, and ignoring its constitution, which required the IRB to await the majority decision of the Irish people as to when war with England should begin (an unworkable provision which was removed from the constitution in 1917).[66]

In May 1915 Plunkett joined de Valera's former benefactor Roger Casement in Berlin. Casement had been ineffectually negotiating with the German government for arms, as well as failing to raise an Irish Brigade from prisoners of war. Plunkett related the Military Council's plans in an effort to persuade the Germans that the supply of arms – and, crucially, troops – could lead to a successful insurrection. Because the Rising that actually took place had no realistic chance of success (Connolly said they were 'going out to be slaughtered'),[67] it is sometimes assumed that the Military Council was always intent on a 'blood sacrifice' – a glorious failure that would redeem Ireland's nationhood. But in fact the leaders believed victory was possible if the circumstances were right – if they got German support and if Volunteers throughout the country took part.[68] When both preconditions for success were removed in the days before Easter, the leaders went ahead anyway – because they were certain they were about to be arrested, and because even a failed Rising could lead the people away from their commitment to constitutionalism and limited home rule.[69]

MacNeill took a different view, believing that the use of violence by the Volunteers would be justified only if it had popular support, and if it was used in self-defence (to prevent the British disarming them, for instance, or in opposition to conscription). This was in line with the Volunteer manifesto: 'Their duties will be defensive and protective, and they will not contemplate either aggression or domination.'[70]

In public, Pearse stuck to the line favoured by MacNeill: action would be taken only if the Volunteers were

> justified to their consciences in taking definite military action . . . We do not anticipate such a moment in the very near future; but we live at a time when it may come swiftly and terribly. What if Conscription be forced upon Ireland? What if a Unionist or a Coalition British Ministry repudiate the Home Rule Act? What if it be determined to dismember Ireland? What if it be attempted to disarm Ireland? The future is big with these and other possibilities.'[71]

Meanwhile, training continued, and the new commandant, de Valera, was soon leading his troops in simulated battle. There were regular manoeuvres involving other battalions, such as an attack by the 3rd and 4th Battalions on Stepaside village, held by the 2nd Battalion. One of de Valera's officers recalled seeing Pearse 'with a contented and happy smile on his face as he saw the lines of armed men descending the mountains'.[72]

It didn't always end so well, of course. On one occasion, a company of the 1st Battalion managed to capture the 3rd Battalion staff.[73] Marching home afterwards, the commandant 'was in very bad humour' as a result.[74] On another occasion manoeuvres had to be abandoned in an attempt to recapture the battalion transport, a donkey named 'Kaiser', who had escaped after his owner was scolded by de Valera for allowing the animal to drink from a stream needed as a water supply.[75]

While these large-scale manoeuvres were conducted in open country, most of the lectures delivered to junior officers at Headquarters, at 2 Dawson Street, concentrated on street fighting, as did company-level training.[76] De Valera delivered some of these lectures, covering 'Scouting and Communications, including signalling, field telegraphs, map making and reading, compass, despatch carrying, etc.'[77] When he was brought into the Rising planning, Connolly lectured on street fighting, to which 'he seemed to attach great importance'.[78] He at least had some military experience, as a former British soldier – de Valera's expertise came from his voracious reading of military manuals.

Lectures were all very well, but the practical experience of handling firearms was more important. One group of 3rd Battalion officers fired off a few rounds from their revolvers one Sunday morning; looking at the results, the O'Rahilly mordantly observed that the British were perfectly safe.[79] De Valera bought himself a carbine for £5, as well as a clip-fed semi-automatic pistol (named 'Peter the Painter,' after the famous anarchist) that could be fitted with a shoulder stock to convert it into a carbine.[80] On the firing range he was told by one of his instructors to aim with his left eye[81] – an echo of the long-ago advice in Rockwell to aim for the thistle to hit the rabbit.

The Dublin Brigade was the best trained and most active in the country, and on Whit Sunday, 23 May, it was ordered to parade through Limerick, where the Volunteers had been having a tough time. The Dubliners discovered what their Limerick comrades had been dealing with as they marched through the Irishtown district, 'greeted by cabbage stumps' thrown by women whose husbands were off fighting in the British army.[82] One Volunteer officer recalled that 'some women ran in and tried to tear the uniforms off the men, some spat in their faces.'[83] When the march was over, the Dublin Volunteers broke into small groups to get something to eat before catching the train home. They soon discovered that the trouble was not over, as 'bands of intoxicated rowdies of both sexes roamed through the city attacking and maltreating not only the Volunteers but lady visitors'.[84] De Valera, left in charge by Pearse, had to send a squad with pikes to rescue 'some men attacked in pub'; eventually the threat of rifle butts and fixed bayonets cleared a way for the Dublin Volunteers to their train.[85]

However, the Dublin Brigade's next major public display was a triumph: the funeral of Jeremiah O'Donovan Rossa. When the fierce old Fenian died in the United States his body was brought home for burial. The funeral procession in Dublin on 1 August 1915, from City Hall to Glasnevin Cemetery, was a triumph of IRB and Volunteer organisation. De Valera, probably because of his new position as adjutant to the Dublin Brigade, was on the organising committee. In a famous photograph of the committee he is clearly identifiable in his Volunteer uniform at the back of the 50-strong group – still peripheral, but getting close to the centre of power. The committee ranged from the relatively pacific wing of advanced nationalism – represented by Arthur Griffith, founder of Sinn Féin, and Thomas Farren, president of the Dublin Council of Trade Unions – to the radical IRB faction, led by Tom Clarke, who sat in the centre. Also prominent in the picture are two other men executed after 1916; Major John MacBride and Thomas MacDonagh, chief marshal of the parade.

The Volunteers put on an impressive display, capped by Pearse's graveside oration:

. . . the fools, the fools, the fools! – they have left us our Fenian dead, and while Ireland holds these graves, Ireland unfree shall never be at peace.

As one of de Valera's subordinate officers recalled, 'This may have sounded a bit strange to the ordinary person, but to those of us who knew the things that were likely to happen it was sweet music indeed.'[86] De Valera's daughter Máirín, then three years old, later recalled watching the parade and 'feeling very proud as my father marched by in his green volunteer uniform'.[87]

De Valera's appointment as brigade adjutant was not a promotion, as he was already a commandant, the rank that went with the post.[88] It mainly involved the kind of mundane administrative tasks that most officers probably wouldn't welcome. De Valera appears to have been good at it, however, thanks to the meticulous (some would say pedantic) attention to detail for which he was renowned. His tasks included over-seeing training classes, advising on instructors, arranging rooms, and putting applicants for membership in touch with their nearest Volunteer unit.[89] His work greatly impressed MacDonagh, the brigade commander.

MacDonagh was four years older than de Valera, and while they shared some similarities in background, their differences – especially in personality – seemed more pronounced. MacDonagh was far more sociable than de Valera, with a wide circle of friends and a reputation for being talkative (far too talkative, in the eyes of some in the IRB).

De Valera remained extremely loyal to, and fond of, MacDonagh. After MacDonagh's death he reminisced about how 'Tommie' had the worst writing he ever saw: de Valera 'used to pray he would never get a military order in writing from him, and he asked him once, if ever he was sending him an order, to type it'.[90] Orders from MacDonagh were to be vital to de Valera's role in the Rising: he declined to follow orders from MacNeill or Pearse unless they were countersigned by his direct superior.

In October 1915 MacDonagh urged de Valera to seek election to the Volunteer Executive. De Valera refused, as he had been in rapid succession appointed company captain, battalion commandant and brigade adjutant. 'I felt that I was being moved before any of the work which had been given was really well done'. Being on the Executive would inevitably distract him from his existing tasks. One day when they were leaving Headquarters together,

Tommie MacDonagh continued to press me as he was mounting his tram. I still continued to refuse as the tram moved off. He indicated – nodding his head – that I ought to accept. I shook my head as a final gesture of refusal.

MacDonagh didn't take this refusal as final: when the convention opened in the Abbey Theatre on Sunday 31 October he signalled to de Valera in the gallery that he would nominate him; but again de Valera refused.[91]

Although he declined further advancement, he was certainly very aware of his status as commandant – a status that was potentially threatened by his second-in-command, Seán Fitzgibbon, who was a member of the Volunteer Executive. This anomalous situation bothered de Valera greatly: by virtue of his position on the Executive, Fitzgibbon might be held to outrank him. De Valera was not a man who took challenges to his authority lightly, and it wasn't clear what would happen if the two men disagreed. The matter came to a head on St Patrick's Day, 1916, at a major mobilisation of the Irish Volunteers in Dublin city centre.

After a church parade,[92] Eoin MacNeill took the salute from the entire Dublin Brigade at College Green,[93] a significant site, associated as it was with the original Volunteers of 1782.[94] Many Volunteers recalled an incident involving de Valera, who was in charge of a cordon across Dame Street, between the Bank of Ireland and the corner of George's Street. A British officer approached this cordon, demanding to be let through, but he was refused by de Valera, who ordered three files of Volunteers to overturn his car if it attempted to move. Eventually a policeman advised the officer to retreat, which he did, to the cheers of the crowd.[95] It is striking how many Volunteers later recalled de Valera's determination to hold the line in their statements to the Bureau of Military History.[96]

But perhaps de Valera's most significant confrontation that day was with his own subordinate. Seán Fitzgibbon, on his authority as a member of the Executive, suggested a compromise with the British officer. De Valera not unreasonably regarded this as 'interference', and ordered his vice-commandant back to his place. This was the final straw, as far as de Valera was concerned, and he insisted that 'there should not be in my Battalion, under me as officers, any members of the National Executive'.[97] This account was frequently related by de Valera, presumably to demonstrate both his principled stand and his influence with his superiors; and most biographers have accepted that Fitzgibbon's removal from the 3rd Battalion was as a result of this complaint. In fact, Fitzgibbon remained attached to the 3rd Battalion until ordered to Co. Kerry by Pearse on the Monday of Holy Week, in order to help with the planned landing of arms there.[98] The following Wednesday, de Valera informed the battalion staff that Fitzgibbon would not be with them, as he had other duties to perform, and the battalion adjutant, Patrick Begley, was appointed in his place.[99]

But de Valera had a more serious challenge to his chain of command: at least two of his officers, Simon Donnelly and Liam Tannam, were members of the IRB and thereby privy to more information about the planned Rising than he was. Crucially, Tannam was instructed that 'in the event of conflicting orders I was to take the orders of my next superior officer who was a member of the IRB as against the orders of any other officer'[100] – which could have put his commandant in an awkward position. When de Valera complained to MacDonagh about this situation, he was told that it was because he was not in the IRB. De Valera said that he was subject to the Executive of the Volunteers, and that one could not serve two masters. MacDonagh cheerfully replied that this wasn't a problem, as the Executive was controlled by the IRB. De Valera then reluctantly agreed to be sworn in to the IRB – on the understanding that the oath would require him to follow only the orders of the Volunteer Executive, and that he would attend no IRB meetings or know any of the personnel, 'or share any secrets except those that were essential for the proper exercise of my command in the Volunteers'.[101]

De Valera thus took the IRB oath but satisfied himself that he wasn't *really* taking it – perhaps a precedent for a different kind of oath he was to take in 1927.

Though far from belonging to the IRB's inner circle, de Valera was to be carried along by those who did. As Easter, 1916, approached, Connolly told him the position his battalion was to occupy: the Boland's Bakery area, where he was to cut the route into the city from Dún Laoghaire and the south-east, and to neutralise Beggars Bush Barracks in Haddington Road. The two men walked together to the bridge at Grand Canal Street, where they surveyed the buildings surrounding Grand Canal Basin. The imposing structure of Boland's Mill was particularly noted; Connolly suggested it contained plenty of food and could be reduced only with field artillery. According to de Valera, Connolly breezily predicted that, once the barricades were up, 'thousands would flock' to join the rebels; de Valera thought differently. He also disagreed with Connolly's proposed line of retreat to the north of the city; he burnt the map with the suggested route, as he believed the only chance of escape was to the south.[102]

De Valera continued to study his area of operations, taking his five-year-old son, Vivion, as cover as he walked to Baggot Street Bridge and then on to Grand Canal Basin.[103] He also travelled on the train from Lansdowne Road to Westland Row several times.[104]

As Easter approached, the tension heightened. On Saturday 15 April all officers of the Dublin Brigade were summoned to a lecture at

Headquarters. The speakers, including de Valera, MacDonagh and Ceannt, gave 'the impression that in a very short time' the Volunteers would be 'going into action'. After some time, Pearse

> rose amidst dead silence, stared over the heads of the volunteers assembled in the room, and paused for almost one minute before he spoke. The first words he uttered sent a thrill through the persons present . . . 'I know that you have been preparing your bodies for the great struggle that lies before us, but have you also been preparing your souls?' . . . Most of us left that meeting . . . with the impression that in a short time we would find ourselves in action in the field.[105]

On the following Wednesday there was a dramatic development. At a meeting of Dublin Corporation the Sinn Féin alderman Tom Kelly read out the so-called 'Castle Document', a purported plan by the authorities for the rounding up of Volunteer leaders. There has been controversy over whether this document was a fake, but even if it was it closely resembled contingency plans that had been drawn up in the Castle.[106] The week before Kelly made the document public, Major Ivon Price, chief intelligence officer of Irish Command of the British army, had suggested that the time might be ripe 'for the proclamation and disarmament of this hostile anti-British organisation before it is given an opportunity to do more serious injury'.[107] Whether or not the Military Council of the IRB really believed the contents of the document, it was the perfect cue for their next move: formal notification that the Rising was imminent.

De Valera was cycling home from Dawson Street on that Wednesday when he passed Pearse's courier, Joe Sweeney, who was cycling in the opposite direction. Sweeney

> jumped off his bicycle and ran across the street to me. He gave me a note and said 'Howth'. I answered 'Bruree' and took it. It was the instruction agreed on.[108]

De Valera's preparatory work now paid off as he instructed his company commanders on their duties. His notes set out the general object to be attained; the necessity of following instructions and avoiding being surprised; the need to ensure that each squad had the tools required, as well as adequate supplies of water; and the need to maintain secrecy.[109] He ordered them to have an armed guard, day and night, from the Thursday on.[110] On Holy Thursday he slept at home, fully clothed, his automatic by his side,[111] and on the Friday and Saturday he slept at the house of Lieutenant Mick Malone to avoid arrest; he felt the battalion needed him to lead them into position.[112]

On Good Friday at Battalion Headquarters, at 144 Great Brunswick Street (Pearse Street), he told his officers what positions were to be occupied. Joseph O'Connor's A Company was to hold the railway line from Grand Canal Quay to Dún Laoghaire, occupying all the level crossings, the railway workshops in Upper Grand Canal Street, and positions overlooking Beggars Bush Barracks. B Company, under Seán McMahon, was to take over Westland Row Railway Station (Pearse Station) and link up with the 2nd Battalion, which would be in control of Amiens Street Station (Connolly Station). C Company, under Eddie Byrne, would be in Boland's Bakery, the Dispensary Building at Grand Canal Street, and Roberts' builders' yard; a section under Malone would occupy a number of premises in Northumberland Road. D Company, under Joseph O'Byrne, would use Boland's Mill as a base while holding a line from the Merrion level crossing along the coast to the Liffey. E Company, under Liam Tannam, was detailed to form part of the headquarters garrison at the GPO, while other Volunteers were to occupy Kingstown Railway Station (Dún Laoghaire) and the pier.[113] It was an ambitious plan – one that would stretch the battalion severely even with a full mobilisation.

De Valera was able to give detailed explanations of the positions, telling Joseph O'Byrne exactly where to place his men in Boland's Mill and accompanying him there on the Saturday to ensure he understood exactly what was required.[114] Joseph O'Connor was

> amazed at the amount of information our Commandant had accumulated . . . He was able to discuss every detail even to the places where it would be possible to procure an alternative water supply, where we could definitely find tools for such things as loopholing walls and making communications . . . I cannot remember a query put to him that he was not able to answer immediately, and there was not a solitary suggestion to improve the dispositions made.[115]

This description has frequently been given as evidence of de Valera's military acumen. Given the importance of the Rising to his subsequent political career, his admirers liked to stress his ability as an officer. Some of this praise was merited, but on the eve of going into action all was not well with the 3rd Battalion. On 14 March the chief of inspection, J. J.

'Ginger' O'Connell, wrote a report on the Dublin Brigade, commending the 2nd Battalion as having the highest standard of command, while the 1st and 4th had a good level. But the 3rd was

> much the weakest in the matter of command. The number of officers is now down to a minimum and the quality of the NCOs is not good. If new officers are to be appointed it will not be at all easy to find them within the battalion.

His damning assessment recommended amalgamating D and E Companies in order to get over the shortage of suitable officers. This report must have been a serious blow to de Valera, though O'Connell was careful to spare the commandant from personal blame.

> It is to be understood that the unfortunate state of command in the 3rd Batt is – as far as can be seen – to be traced to unavoidable circumstances, and by no means to any fault of individuals.[116]

Whoever was at fault, it was not comfortable reading on the eve of battle.

While Commandant de Valera informed his officers of what was to come, he continued to leave his wife in the dark. By Sinéad's own account, 'one could not but feel that there was something coming, but I never realised that a rising was contemplated.'[117] De Valera went to say goodbye to his family, without indicating that it might be a final farewell, taking a 'peep at the children who were sleeping'.[118] He also made out a soldier's will and went to Confession at the University Church in St Stephen's Green.[119] He may not have taken his wife into his confidence, but she was much on his mind. When he met Joseph O'Connor in Camden Row on Holy Saturday he remarked, 'We'll be alright, it's the women who will suffer. The worst they can do to us is kill us, but the women will have to remain behind to rear the children.'[120] Sinéad only realised what was afoot on Easter Monday, when their maid informed her that the Volunteers were digging trenches in St Stephen's Green. 'Then I understood all.'[121]

MacNeill had also been kept in the dark until the last moment, but was persuaded by Pearse, Plunkett and MacDonagh to approve action on the basis of the landing of German arms in Co. Kerry and of the threat of a government round-up revealed in the Castle Document. But he changed his mind when news arrived that the arms ship, the *Aud,* had been intercepted by the Royal Navy and scuttled. Finally, at 1:30 in the morning of Easter Sunday, MacNeill went to the offices of the *Sunday*

Independent and arranged to have an order printed cancelling all planned operations.[122]

The order caused consternation and confusion in the 3rd Battalion. Simon Donnelly was shown the *Sunday Independent* by a stranger in church, but his company mobilised as planned at Camden Row, with the officers telling the men to ignore the paper, it being 'an enemy press'.[123] Joseph O'Connor found the order 'a great shock' but decided it would be wrong to obey it. He contacted de Valera at Battalion Headquarters 'and let him know my feelings. It was decided that the Battalion would mobilise as ordered'.[124] Meanwhile, the Military Council met at Liberty Hall. Tom Clarke wanted to go ahead with the Rising that day, but the other members felt that MacNeill's countermanding order would cause too much confusion, and that they should act the following day instead. Clarke was right: far more Volunteers mobilised on the Sunday than would turn out on Monday.[125]

While debating what action to take, the Military Council apparently received word that the 3rd Battalion might act unilaterally. Michael Staines, quartermaster-general of the Volunteers (outranking de Valera), was at Liberty Hall, where Connolly, Pearse and MacDonagh 'appeared to be worried that de Valera was going out with the 3rd Battalion in spite of the cancellation'. He was ordered to make sure de Valera understood the new orders and was sent over to Great Brunswick Street with Seán Heuston. De Valera, apparently believing them to be acting on behalf of MacNeill and Hobson, threatened to arrest them. Heuston was on the point of drawing his revolver, but the more emollient Staines persuaded de Valera that he would be on his own if he went out. De Valera 'gave me no indication whether or not he was prepared to obey the order'.[126]

Meanwhile, MacNeill had been unable to reach MacDonagh to confirm that the Rising was off. He therefore wrote to de Valera, as brigade adjutant, at 1:20 p.m. on Easter Sunday.

> As Chief of Staff, I have ordered and hereby order that no movement whatsoever of Irish Volunteers is to be made today. You will carry out this order in your command and make it known to other commands.[127]

De Valera was by now desperately trying to contact either MacDonagh or Pearse. Having failed to do so, he sent his orderly, Michael Hayes, to find Pearse at St Enda's in Rathfarnham. By the time Hayes returned from this fruitless mission, MacDonagh had turned up. 'He seemed in high spirits, was in uniform with high laced boots and a cloak.'[128]

MacDonagh was accompanied on his visit to Great Brunswick Street by W. J. Brennan-Whitmore, a Volunteer officer who had just joined his staff. Meeting de Valera for the first time, Brennan-Whitmore encountered 'a sallow-complexioned man, wearing glasses and dressed in full officer's Volunteer uniform . . . I thought him dour and aloof, even unfriendly.' He was surprised at de Valera's insistence to MacDonagh that he would not act on any order he received unless it was signed, counter-signed, timed and dated (given the prevailing confusion, this seems sensible enough). After leaving, Brennan-Whitmore remarked to MacDonagh that they would have trouble with that officer, to which MacDonagh replied with a smile, 'Oh, he's all right. A bit of a stickler for the book of rules. But he is all right.'[129]

Having received whatever confirmation he required directly from MacDonagh, de Valera now replied to MacNeill:

I have ordered demobilisation – the Dublin Brigade as a whole has been demobilised. E de Valera, Cath. Club, B[runswick] Street. 3.20 p.m.[130]

His own men were ordered to demobilise but to hold themselves ready for further instructions.[131] That evening, on Joseph O'Connor's suggestion, de Valera attended a concert for the A Company arms fund in Parnell Square, where he explained the reason for the cancellation of that day's operations, adding that he expected all Volunteers to turn out if called on to do so.[132] But at least two of his officers were pessimistic. Simon Donnelly said MacNeill's countermanding order that day had had a 'very bad effect . . . a state of general demoralisation prevailed throughout the ranks'.[133] O'Connor was even more downbeat, warning that at least six months' hard work would be needed to restore morale, and that only a fraction of the men would turn out the following day if ordered to do so. De Valera tried to look on the bright side, suggesting that things weren't as bad as O'Connor claimed.[134] He would find out how wrong he was the following morning.

CHAPTER 08

IRISHMEN WHO WOULD DARE

We showed that there were Irishmen who, in face of great odds, would dare what they said.

Éamon de Valera, 1916[1]

Commandant de Valera had been a real live wire . . . for ever on the move, ignoring danger, and as a matter of fact, to my mind, taking unnecessary risks.

Capt. Simon Donnelly[2]

The leader in Boland's was a fine looking man called the Mexican, he is educated and speaks like a gentleman.

Miss L. Stokes, 1916[3]

D
e Valera spent the night of Easter Sunday, 1916, at the Battalion Headquarters in Great Brunswick Street (now Pearse Street). Although he knew from the previous evening that action was scheduled for noon, he didn't send the mobilisation order to his officers until shortly before ten o'clock in the morning on Easter Monday. While this may have been in line with his own instructions, the delay added greatly to the prevailing confusion. Liam Tannam of E Company was woken at 10:30 by a Volunteer delivering the order to mobilise by 10. Pointing out the time, the Volunteer was told: 'It can't be helped, you are to do the best you can'.[4] Joseph O'Byrne of D Company, who had stayed up most of the night awaiting orders, found he could contact only 15 of his men; the rest had gone off to enjoy the Bank Holiday.[5]

Joseph O'Connor, having issued orders to his men to mobilise, called in to Battalion Headquarters. De Valera told him they were going into action at noon.

I asked him were they mad. His reply was: 'I am a soldier and I know you are a soldier also' . . . He shook hands with me and said: 'We may never meet again.'[6]

Once the decision to launch an insurrection was announced, some thought better of joining it. When O'Connor explained to his men that a republic had been proclaimed and that they were about to go into action, two Volunteers took the opportunity to withdraw and were allowed go home after surrendering their weapons.[7]

De Valera later put the nominal strength of the 3rd Battalion at about 500, with just 130 turning out on Easter Monday.[8] The number fluctuated during the week, as some men joined up late, and some left. Years later, Simon Donnelly put the total number available at between 120 and 130, while the Boland's Garrison Committee had 172 on the rolls – which Donnelly took as an indication of 'the number of contradictory statements that are being furnished' about participation in the Rising.[9] Whatever the precise figure, it was a disaster. De Valera expressed his frustration later in the week to Sinéad.

> Had MacNeill let things go the day before Sunday we'd hold this position for months. My force here would have been *exactly* five times its present strength.[10]

This shortage prevented the 3rd Battalion from carrying out its original orders: there was no prospect of holding positions in Dún Laoghaire, or even the line of the canal as far as Leeson Street, as Plunkett and Connolly had envisaged.

De Valera deliberately reduced the size of his garrison by refusing the help of Cumann na mBan – the only garrison commandant to do so. A unit of Cumann na mBan, the women's auxiliary of the Volunteers, had been detailed to co-operate with him and had mobilised on his instructions on Easter Sunday. They had never received the counter-manding order issued to Volunteers that day, being left to disperse after a long afternoon of uncertainty.[11] On Easter Monday the unit assembled at Merrion Square, but eventually a messenger from the Boland's garrison told them they would not be needed and could return to their homes.[12] O'Connor later claimed that the Cumann na mBan unit had 'unfor-tunately' been forgotten in the rush to occupy positions on Easter Monday,[13] though if a messenger sent them home, they could have been summoned to the Boland's. It appears de Valera believed that women should be spared witnessing the horrors of war.[14] His action deprived the garrison of useful assistance – even if he didn't want women in the firing line, they could at the very least have released Volunteers by carrying out various medical and catering tasks. And the locking of the gates of the garrison against women provided a striking metaphor for their treatment in the Ireland he would rule.

De Valera wasn't just down on numbers: he also lost several crucial officers, including Vice Commandant Patrick Begley, Adjutant George Murphy, Quartermaster James Byrne, and C Company's Captain, Eddie Byrne. This must have further undermined de Valera's confidence in his subordinates, already shaken by Ginger O'Connell's damning inspection report. In the circumstances, it is understandable that he was reluctant to delegate and took on too much work himself.

As noon approached, de Valera inspected the men of D Company before they moved off to occupy Boland's Mill, the massive building overlooking the approach to the city from Ringsend. Painfully under-strength, Captain Joseph O'Byrne did the best he could: four men occupied the distillery opposite the mill; two each were sent to the draw-bridge leading to Ringsend and a nearby granary; and a grand total of five took over the massive mill building itself. O'Byrne felt 'it was impossible to fortify the building as I would have liked'.[15]

Meanwhile, the rest of the battalion headed off, led by an ass and cart and a commandeered motor van carrying stores including rifles, shotguns and ammunition.[16] They headed towards the centre of operations at Boland's Bakery, on the corner of Grand Canal Street and Great Clarence Street (Macken Street), less than a ten-minute march, where de Valera was to establish his headquarters (despite the popular misconception that he was in the entirely separate Boland's Mill).[17] On the way, 19 men under Lieutenant Mick Malone peeled away down Lower Mount Street and Northumberland Road, where they would occupy important positions. The bakery was central to the 3rd Battalion's area of operations, about half way between Malone's unit, covering Mount Street Bridge to the right, and O'Byrne's men in Boland's Mill on the left.

As soon as C Company entered the bakery, Donnelly set them to work loopholing and sandbagging the walls at the junction of Lower Grand Canal Street and Grand Canal Quay, a position overlooking the canal bridge which was itself barricaded with overturned bread vans.[18]

A Company occupied positions along the railway line as far as the Lansdowne Road level crossing. Sections of the railway were dismantled and trenches dug – a heavy task for a reduced force.[19] Visiting the positions on Monday evening, de Valera was critical of the trench parapet, claiming that a bullet could go through it. As he was ordering the trench to be strengthened, some military were seen approaching the gates of Beggars Bush Barracks. 'There they are, come on, fire,' de Valera was reported to have said, leading to a few shots being fired,[20] fatally wounding a corporal.[21] These men were reservists, many of them too elderly to join the army. They wore armbands with the letters *GR*, for 'Georgius Rex', and were inevitably known in Dublin as the 'Gorgeous Wrecks'. Returning to Dublin from exercises, the reservists split into two columns. One, making its way to barracks down Shelbourne Road, was attacked on de Valera's orders; the other had the misfortune to pass Malone's positions in Northumberland Road, where four of them were killed. This action is controversial, because the reservists were either unarmed or carrying rifles with no ammunition,[22] although they were combatants – those who got inside the barracks were soon firing at the Volunteers. The garrison of the barracks, until the arrival of members of the Sherwood Foresters on Wednesday, was only about 20, with little food or ammunition. According to one of the officers inside, it was ripe for seizure by the Volunteers 'if only they had rushed it'.[23]

B Company under Captain Seán MacMahon occupied Westland Row railway station, ordering passengers to go home before locking and barricading the station, while further down the line wires and signal connections were destroyed.[24] One citizen stranded on a stopped train at Sandymount walked as far as Westland Row, observing Volunteers with picks and shovels ripping up the tracks, and an old lady at the station abusing an armed Volunteer: 'Before turning away in disgust she yelled that she would like to "bate" him herself, he with his "tupence ha'penny rifle".'[25] This was just one example of how the Rising disrupted ordinary life in the city, leading most Dubliners to view the Volunteers with irritation – at best.

De Valera and MacMahon planned to occupy positions between Westland Row and St Stephen's Green, including Oriel House, at the junction of Westland Row and Fenian Street, as well as the houses on the corners of Merrion Square with Clare Street and Merrion Street.[26] But as the party was preparing to enter Oriel House they were ordered back to the railway station: the operation had been cancelled, because the enemy had occupied the Shelbourne Hotel, cutting off access to the garrison in St Stephen's Green.[27] It wasn't the last time de Valera would alter plans at the last minute.

The failure to occupy Dún Laoghaire weighed on de Valera's mind. At midnight on Easter Monday he ordered Simon Donnelly to lead four

Volunteers to scout along the Rock Road towards Dún Laoghaire and to challenge anything they met. Donnelly was not keen.

> I didn't altogether like the job as I knew it was rather ticklish and the men fairly nervy, however, orders were orders and we were just about to start off when the Commandant changed his mind, much to the relief of those going on the expedition.[28]

Two nights later, all available men were lined up on the railway line in preparation for an advance to Dún Laoghaire. After two hours and another change of mind, they were ordered to return to their original positions. 'The Commandant then instructed the men to have a sleep, the first they had for the week, and he took over patrolling the railway line himself.'[29]

One sortie that did go ahead disabled the nearby gasworks. About a dozen men took part, led by de Valera and Donnelly. The latter marked each of their backs with flour so that they could make out the man in front in the dark. They then crawled up a gangway that gave access through a hole in the bakery wall to the railway line and walked along as far as the bridge over South Lotts Road. As they climbed down, Volunteer Andy McDonnell dropped the crowbar he was carrying onto the roadway, where it made an extremely loud clatter.

> I was much more afraid of the Commandant than I was of the British troops and, without thinking, I . . . dropped on to the road, grabbed the crowbar [and] climbed over a wall . . . before I was missed.

De Valera roused the watchman and, gun in hand, had the gates to the gasworks opened. Confidently claiming that he would have a garrison of 'a few hundred men' in the works within an hour, he sent the workers home, removed some pieces of machinery, which put a stop to the gas supply for most of Dublin, and then departed, having locked the gates. 'The idea was to let it be known that the Gas works were held, when in actual fact we did not leave a man in it.'[30]

The newly promoted battalion quartermaster, Michael Tannam, was in charge of feeding the men. Supplies of bacon, sugar, tea and Oxo cubes had been brought in, while the bakery supplied bread and the men boiled water for tea on open fires. Electricity and gas had been cut off (by de Valera), but the water supply operated throughout.[31]

While the garrison never actually ran out of ammunition, it was in very short supply, and it had to be used sparingly.[32] Rest was hard to come by, especially when British snipers got the range of the various outposts. 'Sleep we got in fits and starts, and if you managed to remove your boots once in a while you were lucky.'[33] Sentry duty was constant, with de Valera insistent that anyone failing to give the password should be shot – and killed. He nearly fell victim to his own instruction one evening, when he used the previous day's password.[34]

Not surprisingly, given the perils of active service, there was a certain amount of religious fervour. De Valera had to reprimand some of his men when he found their posts deserted as the sentries joined in the Rosary, their rifles stacked in a corner. 'There is a time for prayer, and a time for duty,' he told them sternly.[35] A priest heard Confessions behind a van in the bakery, the men leaving their posts one by one, 'hat in one hand and . . . gun in the other'.[36]

A story told about the treatment of a prisoner, backed by two independent sources, is troubling. A cadet in the Royal Artillery, G.F. Mackay, had been captured in Westland Row Railway Station, and kept prisoner in Boland's Bakery all week. After British soldiers were reported to have fired on the garrison from the roof of Sir Patrick Dun's hospital across the road, de Valera drew up a document saying if they continued using hospitals for military purposes, he would have no alternative but to shoot the prisoner.[37] According to the battalion's first aid officer, Seán Byrne, he, de Valera and Mackay all signed the document; Mackay asked Byrne if he thought the commandant would carry through with his threat, getting the not very reassuring reply, 'It all depends upon your people'. In later life Mackay claimed to have believed that de Valera would never carry through his threat;[38] but it represented a ruthless disregard for the rules of war even to think of shooting a prisoner as a reprisal.

The most famous episode of de Valera's Rising took place on Wednesday: the Battle of Mount Street Bridge. The guiding light here for the Volunteers was Lieutenant Mick Malone, who had been chosen for his leadership and his ability as a marksman, both of which were to be vital. De Valera presumably chose or at least approved Malone's dispositions, but that was the last direct involvement he had in the 3rd Battalion's most important engagement of the week. Perhaps the greatest influence de Valera had on the battle was purely fortuitous. Malone had complained that his unit's rifles were inadequate; in response, de Valera gave him his 'Peter the Painter' automatic pistol.[39] It was this weapon Malone used to such deadly effect.

Malone and three others occupied 25 Northumberland Road, a substantial three-storey-over-basement house on the city side of the

Haddington Road junction, on the left as the British troops approached. Further back on the same side of the road, another five Volunteers occupied the Parochial Hall, and on the other side, closer to the canal, five more were in the school buildings. Finally, a section of five men under George Reynolds held Clanwilliam House, which gave a clear view down Northumberland Road. As the hours passed and the time for action approached, Malone sent two of his tiny garrison in no. 25 back to the bakery, feeling they were too young for the job, which left just himself and James Grace in the house. The Volunteers in the school sandbagged windows and doors but quickly realised that the building was set too far back from the road to have any military value. Malone agreed, and the five men returned to Boland's Bakery.[40] Crucially, though, the British forces believed the school to be the main rebel stronghold and concentrated on attacking it.

Having landed in Dún Laoghaire on the Wednesday morning, a brigade of the Sherwood Foresters marched towards the city centre via Ballsbridge. The troops hadn't finished their training, and were without grenades and heavy machine guns. They had been ordered to destroy or capture any rebel positions they encountered, rather than by-passing them.[41] Given their lack of the necessary weapons, this order was tantamount to a death sentence.

The British advance guard, a single file of troops on either side of the street, was allowed past before Malone and Grace opened fire. The British began taking heavy casualties, their situation made worse by not being sure where the firing was coming from. Eventually, the long-delayed arrival of grenades around five o'clock, as well as a supply of fresh troops, allowed 25 Northumberland Road to be subdued.[42] Malone died in a hail of bullets after the British finally got inside; Grace managed to hide in the kitchen before fleeing the house. Unable to make it back to the main garrison, he hid in gardens before eventually being arrested on Saturday morning.[43]

Having dealt with Malone's position, the British then had to cross Mount Street Bridge under the fire of the rebels in Clanwilliam House. One of them, Thomas Walsh, described the soldiers as 'sitting ducks for amateur rifle men'.[44] Some of the more experienced British officers claimed 'it was worse than anything they had been through in France'.[45]

Finally, superior numbers told, but the cost of victory was high: a total of 162 British casualties, 30 of them dead,[46] compared with only five dead Volunteers.

The flames from Clanwilliam House were visible from Boland's Bakery, where de Valera was now expecting a direct assault on his main positions.

It was this expectation that explains his failure to reinforce Malone. A contrast could be drawn with Commandant Ned Daly of the 1st Battalion, who reinforced and resupplied his own outposts at Reilly's Fort and North Brunswick Street near the Four Courts, thus keeping them in action.[47] When de Valera was criticised for this perceived failure during the 50th anniversary of the Rising, his loyal officers leapt to his defence. Joseph O'Byrne said he had been ordered by de Valera to fire on the British troops attacking Clanwilliam House; his men climbed onto the roof of Boland's Mill to do so.[48] And Simon Donnelly made the point that there simply *were* no reserves to throw into the battle at Mount Street – the garrison was already severely stretched holding what it had in the Bakery and on the railway line, and in any event, once Clanwilliam House was under suppressing fire there was little point putting more men into it.[49]

The perceived need to reinforce the main position led to the four men in Roberts' Yard being ordered to return to the bakery even before Clanwilliam House fell.[50] The positions in Mount Street did not get the extra support their importance warranted because de Valera (and his officers) were expecting the main assault to be launched on their central positions. This was the same reasoning that led the quartermaster in the GPO, Desmond FitzGerald, to ration food supplies so they could last several weeks – a decision that made him extremely unpopular with the garrison.[51]

In the Boland's garrison de Valera expected an attack during Wednesday night. He had his troops man the trenches – or, rather, the area just behind the trenches, his idea being that they would lie a few yards back, and as the British tried to find them in the trenches they would fire on them.

> De Valera passed along the lines exhorting the men to remain steady in their positions to receive bayonet charges. He gave thrilling pictures of how we were going to have a glorious victory or a still more glorious death.[52]

Fortunately this 'encouragement' was not required, as no night attack was made.

Worried about the threat of a full-scale assault, de Valera sought to consolidate his garrison. On Thursday he withdrew the few men in the old distillery and came up with a brilliant trick to prevent the British occupying it. He had a party, led by Captain Mick Cullen, climb the distillery tower and place a green flag on top. This attracted the attention of the gunship *Helga* on the River Liffey.[53] From Boland's Mill, Joseph

O'Byrne saw the shelling which left 'the top turret a mere skeleton (with its flag flying, though at an angle) and . . . [smashed] the slates of the roofs of some of the adjoining out-buildings'.[54] This not only made the distillery useless to the British but it also diverted fire from positions that were actually occupied.[55] Cullen, who had also sent out bogus semaphore signals from the top of the tower, returned from his terrifying experience 'with his nerves rather shattered', and had to be taken off duty.[56] De Valera was delighted with his strategem, and has rightly been praised for it. Curiously, though, when retelling the story to his children, de Valera felt the need to embellish it considerably, claiming that he personally led the mission to hang the flag. According to his son Terry, he would relate how he was exposed in silhouette to sniper fire, and how he had difficulty seeing the rungs of the ladder, because of his poor eyesight and fear of heights.[57] He appears to have told the same tale to his official biographers[58] – perhaps hinting at a lack of self-confidence about his performance during 1916.

This brings up the most controversial question about de Valera's role in the Rising: did he have a breakdown? Given that his subsequent political career was entirely built on his 1916 reputation, this was a matter of some importance and sensitivity. As he ruefully wrote many years later,

> none of the accusations made against me by certain members of B Company were made prior to the signing of the Treaty in 1921. The members who made the accusations were those who took the Treaty side.[59]

This is true – up to a point. While the rumours were assiduously peddled by de Valera's pro-Treaty enemies, there is enough corroborating evidence from others to raise serious question marks.

The first extensive written criticism of de Valera's performance in the Boland's garrison appeared in *An tÓglach,* the official journal of the Free State army, in April 1926. De Valera would hardly have expected a complimentary account from that source, but in fact the series of articles by George Lyons, formerly of B Company of the 3rd Battalion, did pay tribute to his qualities. The articles acknowledged that his absence would have meant 'disaster for the command', that 'the rank and file would probably have lost confidence and dispersed', as they saw him 'as a man suddenly and providentially sent us for the occasion, different from the rest of us . . . and likely to do something that nobody else could possibly think of'.[60] However, this praise was given in the context of a claim that other officers were thinking of removing de Valera from command because of his erratic behaviour.[61]

Much of the problem, Lyons felt, was due to de Valera's overwork, which in turn was the result of his lack of support. He was

> up and down the lines with restless feverish anxiety . . . insistent upon keeping himself and us all 'on the go'. Many appeals were made to him to conserve his energy and take rest. 'If I could only trust the men to stay at their posts and keep a sharp look-out,' he would reply.[62]

Lyons went on to describe de Valera 'rushing about in his old restless fashion', with 'scarlet flannel puttees blazing beneath his green uniform'. He claimed to have advised de Valera to get some rest, as the men were worried about the officers overworking themselves.[63]

Lyons stated that Simon Donnelly 'came very nearly to supplanting' de Valera at this point[64] – a claim to which Donnelly took strong exception, calling Lyons's account 'prejudiced and inaccurate'.[65] Unfortunately for de Valera's reputation, many of the claims were rehashed in *The Easter Rebellion* (1964) by the British journalist Max Caulfield. Much of Caulfield's critique of de Valera's performance appears to be based on Lyons's articles in *An tÓglach*. He did interview a number of survivors, including Donnelly, but who said what is not clear, as the book is not footnoted.[66] After criticism from old republicans, Caulfield insisted that he had portrayed de Valera as 'a gallant, courageous, intelligent man . . . under enormous stress'.[67] A rebuttal by Donnelly, published in the *Sunday Press*, denied that the men had lost faith in their commandant, or that de Valera had not trusted the men. Donnelly rejected any suggestion that he or anyone else had tried to replace him. He concluded with a reference to their political parting of the ways after the Civil War. 'While I differed strongly in later years with our President, Commandant de Valera of Easter Week is an officer I will always salute.'[68]

The problem is that Donnelly's own account also suggests that de Valera was indeed close to, if not actually suffering, some kind of a breakdown. Unlike Lyons's, Donnelly's account is that of someone with no Civil War axe to grind.

> Commandant de Valera had been a real live wire from the first moment we entered the position: he was for ever on the move, ignoring danger, and as a matter of fact, to my mind, taking unnecessary risks. On the Friday he presented a very worn and tired out appearance, and in spite of several requests from different officers for him to take some rest, he declined to do so. However he was prevailed on eventually and he

retired to an office he was using in the dispensary. I placed a guard over his office with strict orders that under no consideration whatever was he to be disturbed and any message arriving for him was to be sent to me. However, he was not resting very long and after a few hours he was on the move again, anxious about a hundred and one different things.[69]

Joseph O'Connor, who had been promoted to second-in-command of the battalion, was another important witness who rejected the claims made about de Valera by 'privates in our Garrison, men who could not possibly have known anything of the amount of work the officers had to perform'. However, he went on to hint obliquely that things changed over the course of the week.

> At no time *up to Thursday* did I receive any order or hold any discussion with the Commandant that was not in perfect order and clear with precise instructions as to what he required to be done.[70]

Both O'Connor and Donnelly were critical of de Valera's decision early on Friday morning to withdraw the garrison from the bakery to the Guinness Malt Store on Grand Canal Quay. O'Connor thought that, while the store was a strong building, it would be easy for the British to surround; Donnelly thought its position was too isolated for their headquarters. After a couple of hours de Valera agreed, and the men returned to their original positions.[71] But that night de Valera had a further brainwave, according to Donnelly's account.

> Late on Friday night the Commandant for some reason known to himself . . . ordered me to withdraw from the bakery and take my men on to the Railway. I did not understand why this order was issued, but my duty was to obey and the order was carried out.[72]

On the railway line, which was about 15 feet higher than the bakery, the men had a depressing view of the city centre in flames.

> After some time, however, the Commandant apparently altered his plans and we were ordered to reoccupy the Bakery.[73]

Luckily, the men were able to return to their previous positions without British interference, but the incident raises serious question marks over de Valera's judgement at this stage.

On Saturday the noise of battle from the city centre died down – an 'ominous silence', according to George Lyons.[74] Other Volunteers scoffed at the rumours that Pearse had surrendered. 'We were holding our own, so fight on'.[75] In fact, Pearse had indeed surrendered unconditionally at 3:45 on Saturday 29 April 'to prevent the further slaughter of Dublin citizens, and in the hope of saving the lives of our followers'.[76]

De Valera, of course, knew nothing of this on the Saturday. He and O'Connor discussed their options, deciding they should make towards the Dublin Mountains when they were sure they could offer no further help to the garrisons in the rest of the city.[77]

But on Sunday morning, word came of a messenger. Elizabeth O'Farrell, who had served in the GPO garrison and brought Pearse's offer of surrender to the British there, had been asked to bring the surrender order to each garrison. De Valera was suspicious, as he didn't know her.

> Reasonable caution demanded that I should assure myself that the note was genuine and that it was being obeyed by the other units of the Dublin Brigade. To surrender without this assurance could be equivalent to desertion of comrades in the face of the enemy.[78]

He insisted on having the order confirmed by MacDonagh, and O'Farrell left to meet her British army escort, who took her towards Jacob's.[79]

In the meantime, a number of his officers having vouched for O'Farrell, de Valera accepted that the order was genuine.[80] Instructing O'Connor to gather the men together, de Valera prepared to meet the British. It may have been at this point that he wrote a note to Sinéad.

> To my darling wife: If I die, pray for me. Kiss our children for me, tell them their father died doing his duty . . . We showed that there were Irishmen who, in face of great odds, would dare what they said.[81]

He also wrote to outlying posts, advising them of the surrender order,[82] as well as a note for the British taking over the Bakery:

> Sir, in the Bakery (Boland's) which my men occupied there were some ninety van horses. We endeavoured to give them food and drink – would you communicate with the manager of the mill and give him permission to get them food and drink. It would be a pity that so many animals should unnecessarily be destroyed. E de Valera.[83]

He then instructed Seán Byrne, the first-aid officer, to prepare a white flag, which he did by taking a sheet from the dispensary and tying it to a walking stick. De Valera told Byrne, 'I know what is going to happen to me, but I will do my best for you and the men'.[84] Accompanied by their prisoner, Cadet Mackay, they crossed the road to Sir Patrick Dun's Hospital, where de Valera formally surrendered, to Captain E. J. Hitzen. Byrne was sent back to collect the rest of the garrison.[85]

O'Connor, meanwhile, had broken news of the surrender to the men. 'The excitement in Boland's was terrible. What did we want to surrender for? This was the main topic. Volunteers were shouting themselves hoarse denouncing everyone who had surrendered; others were singing songs and some were openly crying.'[86] When it was explained that the order came from Pearse and was aimed at saving innocent lives, 'the temper of the men cooled down, and discipline was fully restored'.[87]

Finally, at about one o'clock (several hours before the garrisons in Jacob's and the South Dublin Union surrendered), O'Connor marched the 3rd Battalion out of Boland's garrison, Byrne with the white flag by his side. In Grattan Street, were de Valera was waiting for them with some British officers, O'Connor handed over command, and de Valera ordered the men to ground arms. An onlooker later recalled that they

> looked exhausted, bedraggled . . . I remember seeing President de Valera marching at their head. He was pale, tired, thinner, and more gaunt than when I had previously seen him; but, as usual, he carried himself erect and had the appearance of one still in command of his men . . .[88]

De Valera, 'clearly suffering deeply under the tragedy of the occasion', and 'with tears in his eyes', shook hands with each man before they formed up and marched, hands over their heads, into Mount Street.[89] A British soldier asked what their commander's name was; on being told, he replied: 'He was a Devilero alright'.[90]

Some residents cheered the Volunteers as they marched off. De Valera somewhat bitterly observed that they could have come out to support them, even if they were armed only with hay forks.[91] Spotting Cadet Mackay on the footpath, de Valera shook his hand and wished him well; the luckless Mackay was immediately arrested and marched to the RDS with his former captors.[92] The column, still led by Byrne with the white flag, followed by de Valera and Captain Hitzen, moved off towards Ballsbridge, passing the remains of Clanwilliam House and 25 Northumberland Road.[93] One onlooker recorded that the Volunteers were fine looking fellows, swinging along in good step. Of course they looked shabby and dirty, they had been fighting for seven days . . . The leader in Boland's was a fine looking man called the Mexican, he is educated and speaks like a gentleman . . .[94]

In Ballsbridge, de Valera was taken to the town hall, while his men were accommodated in cattle stalls in the RDS Showgrounds.[95]

De Valera's Rising was over, and he would build his political career on the legend that grew around his role. Supporters tended to make three claims about de Valera in 1916: that his was the last garrison to surrender; that he was the senior surviving officer of the Rising; and that he had been a splendidly effective commander. The first two claims were false, the third debatable. The Boland's garrison surrendered several hours before MacDonagh and Ceannt did, and de Valera was conscious of the incorrect claims later made about this. In his papers is a draft speech to be delivered by the chairman of the organising committee for the garrison's 50th anniversary. Several references to Boland's garrison being the last to surrender have been crossed out, presumably on de Valera's instructions, and replaced with such phrases as 'held their post to the end' and 'surrendered only when they were ordered to do so'.[96] Neither was he the senior surviving officer of the Rising: Thomas Ashe, commandant of the Fingal Battalion, held the same rank; Tom Hunter also held the rank of commandant, though he didn't command a garrison; and Michael Staines had been appointed quartermaster-general of the Headquarters Staff in March 1916.

And what of the claims about his success in Easter Week? He was very well prepared to take over Boland's garrison, but the battalion had serious problems identified by Ginger O'Connell. De Valera was certainly an encouraging presence to his men for most of the week, but he overdid things, refused to delegate, and ended up burning himself out and teetering on the brink of a breakdown. He had good ideas, but he was also indecisive, and did little to support the positions at Mount Street Bridge, scene of the battalion's greatest success. But, after all, he was an amateur, and his failure to reinforce success was a minor error compared to those of the professionals, the British generals who insisted on reinforcing failure by sending unprotected troops into the killing zone of Northumberland Road.

Even if de Valera wasn't the great commander his acolytes later claimed, he was about to discover that he possessed the military virtue Napoleon prized above all others: he was lucky.

CHAPTER 09

Q95

Tomorrow I am to be shot – so pray for me – an old sport who unselfishly played the game.

Éamon de Valera, May 1916[1]

De Valera . . . is a real firebrand and fanatic . . . He is decidedly a 'personality' and the others seem to look up to him as their leader . . .

Governor of Dartmoor Prison, October 1916[2]

Remember it is not for paltry concessions for yourselves you are fighting, it is for Ireland's honour . . . It must be death rather than surrender.

Éamon de Valera, May 1917[3]

The men of the 3rd Battalion began to worry about their commandant amid rumours that he had been shot,[4] or that he was likely to be. At least two schemes were hatched to help him escape, one involving a tall Volunteer named Malone who was to swap uniforms with him,[5] another involving the firemen in Ballsbridge station, who offered to spirit de Valera away while pretending to answer an alarm.[6] De Valera refused both offers, partly because he wished to stay with his men but also because he suspected a British trap.[7] On the morning of 2 May 1916, after two nights in the RDS Showgrounds in Ballsbridge in Dublin, the 3rd Battalion was marched to Richmond Barracks in Inchicore, where the rest of the prisoners were being kept. Little interest was taken in them except in High Street, where a crowd threw missiles at them.[8]

The new arrivals were a source of interest as they marched into the barracks square, with de Valera at their head, leading them 'like a conqueror',[9] with 'his height and stature making him conspicuous among his captors'.[10] The two-day delay in reaching Richmond Barracks almost certainly saved de Valera's life by delaying his court-martial. The prisoners already in the Barracks had been screened, those to be tried had been assigned numbers, and there was a long queue ahead of de Valera.[11] De Valera was kept in a detention cell for three days before being transferred to the barracks gymnasium on Friday.[12]

The men were hungry for information: de Valera closely questioned a Volunteer from Galway about the course of the Rising in that county,[13] and the prisoners persuaded a guard to give them his newspaper when he had finished with it. It contained the disturbing news that Major John MacBride had been executed.[14] DMP detectives were constantly moving about the room, identifying leading figures, and it wasn't long before de Valera was moved to a smaller room.

In room 4 of L Block, de Valera found himself in the company of Count Plunkett, father of Joseph, military planner of the Rising. Count Plunkett, a rather eccentric figure, would play an important role in the coming years thanks to the prominence of his son; at this stage he was unaware that Joseph had already been executed. Also there was the alderman Laurence O'Neill, who would be elected Lord Mayor of Dublin in 1917. Though an Independent, he would prove a crucial ally for de Valera and Sinn Féin. De Valera's Volunteer colleague Batt O'Connor was there, as was Seán T. O'Kelly.

In an attempt to lift their spirits, the prisoners put on a mock drama – 'The Pretender to the King of Dalkey Island' – in which de Valera was the defendant and Plunkett the judge. De Valera's buttons were cut off and distributed as souvenirs, while O'Kelly got his fountain pen.[15] De Valera told one biographer that the game got on his nerves, so he put it to an end and took up his copy of St Augustine's *Confessions* instead.[16]

It was hardly surprising that de Valera failed to appreciate the joke; he was facing a death sentence. On the day he arrived in Richmond Barracks, 2 May, Patrick Pearse, Thomas MacDonagh and Tom Clarke were court-martialled; all three were executed the following morning. They were followed on 4 May by Ned Daly, William Pearse, Michael O'Hanrahan and Joseph Plunkett. On the 5th, Major John MacBride was executed, and on the morning of 8 May, Éamonn Ceannt, Seán Heuston, Con Colbert and Michael Mallin were shot. De Valera was court-martialled later that same morning, and the omens were not good. Of the men already shot, Patrick Pearse, MacDonagh, Clarke, Plunkett and Ceannt had been signatories of the Proclamation, and therefore in British eyes more guilty than de Valera; but Daly and Mallin were of similar stature, having commanded garrisons; and William Pearse, MacBride, O'Hanrahan, Heuston and Colbert were of lower rank.

The courts-martial and executions were taking place at bewildering speed and with questionable legality. The British commander, General Sir John Maxwell had elected to try the rebels at Field General Courts-Martial as he believed speed was of the essence. The trials were held in secret, with no defence counsel permitted – in stark contrast to the four British soldiers who were tried for murders committed during the Rising.[17] There was no representative from the Office of the Judge Advocate General, either, which normally 'provided a significant check on the power of the Generals'.[18]

For the prosecution, the most significant problem was evidence. Maxwell's advisor was Second Lieutenant Alfred Bucknill, a barrister who worried about the lack of proof 'to pin any particular offence against any particular person'. Apart from the Proclamation, they had a couple of signed orders and the proof of officers who had taken the surrender at various outposts.[19] But the death penalty could be imposed only if it could be proved that the accused had been assisting the enemy.[20] And here Pearse came to the aid of the authorities, with a postscript to a letter to his mother. 'I have reason to believe that the German expedition on which I counted actually set sail but was defeated by the British fleet.'[21] As Bucknill later acknowledged, the prosecution 'would have been in some difficulty without this postscript'.[22]

One of the prosecutors was an Irish King's Counsel, William Wylie. He would go on to claim that de Valera was not prosecuted at all in 1916 – thanks to him. According to his account, Maxwell asked who was next on the list for court-martial; he replied that it was Connolly, and Maxwell insisted that he should be tried, despite his injuries. De Valera was next, and Maxwell asked if he was likely to make trouble in the future. Wylie said he didn't think so, as he wasn't important enough and wasn't one of the leaders.[23] Therefore, according to Wylie, de Valera's life was spared. In 1964 President de Valera would ask Wylie what he remembered of his court-martial, to which he replied, 'You were not prosecuted at that time and there is nothing to remember.'[24]

The claim that de Valera was not tried at all is flatly contradicted by the trial register, which lists his court-martial on 8 May, along with Thomas Ashe, Richard Hayes, and the Lawless brothers, Frank and Jim.[25] To de Valera the room in which he was court-martialled looked like a schoolroom, and he recalled that the process felt rather like an examination.[26] The prosecution relied on an order signed by Connolly identifying de Valera as a commander.[27] The court-martial apparently also heard evidence from Captain Hitzen that de Valera had surrendered to him, and from Cadet Mackay that he had been in command in Boland's Bakery.[28] It was an open-and-shut case, and de Valera was transferred to cell 59 in Kilmainham Jail to await his fate.[29]

If Wylie really did discuss de Valera's case with Maxwell, it is probable that it was at this point, when the General was considering whether to confirm or commute the death sentence. But even then, Wylie's opinion of de Valera's importance was hardly conclusive, given some of the lesser figures already sent to the firing squad. Two other factors were far more likely to have had an effect: the American connection and the political backlash caused by the executions.

The idea that de Valera was spared simply because he was born in America is surprisingly widely accepted, despite the lack of evidence to support it. For one thing, being an American citizen didn't save Tom Clarke;[30] and, although he was born in New York, de Valera hadn't applied for citizenship on reaching the age of 21 and so was not legally under US protection.

However, his wife and friends were determined to use any weapon they could find to save his life, and this seemed the best available. Sinéad had four young children and was three months pregnant. She was lucky to have her sister Brigid (Bee) with her, who advised her to get her husband's birth certificate to the American consul as quickly as possible.[31]

The work of the consul, Edward Adams, had been severely interrupted by the Rising. When he finally made it in to the office, on 4 May, he found that no post had been delivered and that the telephone and telegraph were under military control, so he went home again.[32] However, events in Washington on the same day encouraged a more active approach as Britain's treatment of the prisoners was raised in the Senate; over the following weeks a number of resolutions called for them to be treated as prisoners of war.[33]

These developments encouraged the US government – and the consul – to look as if they were doing something. Adams was requested to intervene on behalf of a number of prisoners with American links, including Diarmuid Lynch and Liam Pedlar. He later claimed to have been instrumental in having Lynch's death sentence commuted, even though he had not, as he claimed in his official report, attended his court-martial.[34] Similarly with de Valera: Sinéad had made contact and produced a copy of her husband's birth certificate; Adams wrote to Sir Mathew Nathan, Under-Secretary for Ireland, to point out the fact of de Valera's American birth. That was the sum total of his 'intervention'.[35] Others made similar moves: from Blackrock College, de Valera's old mentor Father Downey contacted a number of past pupils in influential government posts to inform them of his American origins.[36]

Sinéad was convinced that she had saved her husband's life, writing to his mother in July: 'Of course it was the American influence here that got Ed's sentence commuted.'[37] However, Bucknill insisted that de Valera's American birth 'had nothing whatever to do with it':[38] de Valera was saved because of the political backlash against the executions. De Valera agreed, dictating a memorandum in 1969 discounting the American factor in his reprieve: 'I know of nothing in international law which could be cited in my defence or made an excuse for American intervention, except, perhaps, to see that I got a fair trial.'[39]

While it was in line with de Valera's self-image to reject suggestions that he had received special treatment, it is likely that he was correct. Of the 14 men executed in Dublin,[40] all but two were court-martialled before de Valera. Only Connolly and Mac Diarmada were tried after him.[41] And as de Valera never tired of pointing out, Thomas Ashe, his fellow commandant, who had inflicted significant casualties in north Co. Dublin, was court-martialled on the same day and also escaped execution.

By the time de Valera came to be sentenced, Maxwell was under increasing political pressure to stop the executions. As early as 30 April 1916, the day of de Valera's surrender, John Dillon warned John Redmond of the danger of a public backlash if prisoners were shot.[42] Redmond took this up with Asquith on 3 May, the day of the first three executions. Asquith said that he was 'shocked' when he heard that Pearse, Clarke and MacDonagh had been shot, and that it was his intention that there would be no more executions 'except in some very special cases'.[43]

Redmond raised the matter in the House of Commons on 8 May – the day of de Valera's court-martial. Asquith wrote to assure him. 'I sent a telegram to Maxwell yesterday, and I hope that the shootings – unless in some quite exceptional case – will cease.'[44] Maxwell told the Prime Minister that 'Connolly and MacDermott still remain to be tried today and if convicted must suffer extreme penalty. As far as I can state these will be last to suffer capital punishment.'[45]

Maxwell is generally held accountable for turning the tide of public opinion in Ireland with the executions, though he insisted that he had 'done nothing vindictive' and that the number of casualties during the Rising justified his actions.[46] And it could have been far worse: there were rumours of mass graves being prepared for those shot, and 35 blindfolds and white-card targets were prepared for executions.[47]

De Valera, of course, was unaware of all this as he sat in his cell in Kilmainham, awaiting death. He wrote some letters, though not to his wife – possibly because he expected to be allowed see her before his execution – or to his mother. To his rugby-playing friend from Rockwell, Mick Ryan, he adopted a slightly jocular tone.

> Just a line to say I played my last match last week and lost. Tomorrow I am to be shot – so pray for me – an old sport who unselfishly played the game.[48]

To Mother Gonzaga in Carysfort he said he had just been told he was to be shot; he thanked her for her kindness and asked her 'to pray for my soul and for my poor wife and little children whom I leave unprovided for behind'.[49] Similar sentiments were expressed in a letter to his Rockwell teaching colleague Jack Barrett.

> I am to be shot for my part in the Rebellion. It would be easy to die but for the poor wife left with her helpless little ones. Should you find it possible in later years to advise her as to what she should do with the children I know you will do it . . .[50]

But on 10 May he was told that his sentence had been commuted. In the relief of knowing he was to live, he poured his heart out in a letter to Sinéad.

> My darling wife: I know the agonies you must have endured during the past few weeks. The suspense at any rate is now over – the sentence of death passed on me has been commuted to penal servitude for life – so you have now only to cope with a certainty . . . I needn't tell you I am counting the minutes till I see you. As all letters are read by the prison authorities I cannot write to you, love, the kind of letter I would like, or tell you how, through it all, you were ever present in my thoughts.[51]

Sinéad brought her two eldest children, Vivion and Máirín, to see their father in Mountjoy Prison, where he had been transferred. A warder was present and told them they were forbidden to speak Irish. At one point de Valera said he was sorry he had not been able to keep his pistol for Vivion, at which point his five-year-old son pulled his toy gun out of his pocket. His father advised him to 'keep it and use it when the time comes'. Sinéad promised to be father and mother to their children – a promise she would more than fulfil in the years ahead.[52] Short of money, she moved back in with her parents in Munster Street and sold her husband's motorbike for £30.[53]

But how long would she be on her own? On being told that his death sentence was being commuted to life imprisonment, de Valera assumed it literally meant 'life'; another prisoner surprised him by accurately predicting that he would be out in a year.[54] As far as he and his colleagues knew, they were facing into long years in prison, almost certainly under the same atrocious conditions endured by Fenians like O'Donovan Rossa and Tom Clarke. It was no wonder that de Valera looked 'morose' in Mountjoy, where the senior IRB members Thomas Ashe and Harry Boland pointed him out to Robert Brennan, a Wexford Republican and journalist, who described him as 'serious for his years, with extraordinary long legs and a head that was small for his large frame'.[55]

On 17 May these three, along with de Valera, formed part of a small group of prisoners that left Mountjoy for an unknown destination. The next day their train arrived in Princetown in Devon, from where they were marched under heavy military guard to their new home – Dartmoor Prison.[56]

Many of the new inmates would have been familiar with its forbidding reputation from novels and detective stories.[57] They were greeted by warders armed with batons, ordered to strip, and then subjected to a 'most revolting personal search'.[58] After this ordeal they were given their convict uniform: 'tunic, breeches, long stockings and forage cap, all stamped with the broad arrow'. They were also closely shaved and each was given a number: de Valera became convict Q95.[59]

Each prisoner was in a single cell and was issued with a thin mattress and two blankets (an extra blanket was distributed in winter); the heating system was antiquated, and no heat reached the cells.[60] There was a strict ban on communicating with fellow prisoners. At exercise time, warders were stationed at intervals to enforce silence, though the convicts grew adept at talking out of the sides of their mouths.[61] During work – sewing mailbags in the central hall – no talking was allowed. In 'the icy silence and gloom of Dartmoor . . . there was gloom and downheartedness amongst the prisoners.'[62]

And that should have been the last anyone heard of Éamon de Valera for quite some time. Instead, prison was the making of him, paving his way to national leadership. His supporters liked to depict his leadership in prison as the natural result of his status and his character: a role thrust onto his somewhat unwilling shoulders. This is highly misleading. His status was not quite as Olympian as his admirers later claimed: while he was recognised as a leader early on, he was part of a leadership group, not in sole charge. And he did not have command thrust upon him: he seized it by elbowing rivals out of the way. Having tasted leadership during the Rising, de Valera discovered both that he was good at it and that he liked it.

On 29 May, Captain Eardley-Wilmot of the Prison Commission visited the prisoners. He was impressed by

> the mathematician, de Valera, son of a Spanish father . . . He was anxious to impress upon me the fact that there was no military reason for his surrender, but that as his superior officers had sent word that he was to lay down his arms, of course he had to obey.[63]

De Valera's days of obeying others were, however, numbered. On 30 May, Eoin MacNeill arrived in Dartmoor, and the following morning he made his appearance in the main hall.[64] As MacNeill came down the stairs to join the rest of the convicts, de Valera stepped out of line, called the men to attention, and instructed them to salute their former chief of staff by giving the order 'Eyes left'.[65] There were a number of reasons for de Valera's action: he always said it was to show due respect to MacNeill, who would naturally be apprehensive of his reception after his counter-manding order; it would also serve to restore the prisoners' self-respect by asserting military discipline; this in turn would have the not incon-sequential effect of demonstrating that de Valera was a leading – if not *the* leading – figure among the convicts. There was another consideration: a show of respect for MacNeill carried an implied criticism of the IRB[66] (which was represented in Dartmoor by de Valera's only possible rival, Thomas Ashe).

De Valera later recalled his order being 'obeyed as if on a ceremonial parade'.[67] This recollection was endorsed by many of those present. Robert Brennan said it was obeyed with 'military precision',[68] while MacNeill himself recalled 'all the other prisoners' obeying de Valera's order.[69]

But the incident may not have been quite that triumphant. De Valera told Frank Gallagher in 1928 that the men were not expecting his command 'and did not answer smartly';[70] an even less flattering British account claimed that the prisoners 'paid no attention' to de Valera's order.[71] In any case, what was important was that de Valera gave it, thus staking a claim to leadership.

His action was also courageous: incitement to mutiny was punishable by flogging. De Valera was brought before the governor, Major E. R. Reade but he was 'let off with a severe caution and twenty-four hours confinement to his cell'.[72] The reason for Reade's lenience may have been de Valera's less than defiant attitude: he explained that he acted on the spur of the moment in an attempt to make amends for his disagreements with MacNeill. 'He was very sorry and prepared to undergo any punishment the governor thought proper.'[73]

The prisoners settled down to a long, boring summer. Despite constant surveillance, the prisoners managed limited conversation. In this way de Valera met a new arrival, Seán MacEntee, later to be one of his senior ministers. On his first day, MacEntee was placed at the bench immediately in front of de Valera, who 'looked up at me in friendly curiosity, giving me an assuring nod and letting me know that I was among friends'. Characteristically, despite the difficulty of communicating, MacEntee managed to have a disagreement with de Valera on the question of Northern politicians.

> He was surprised indeed that I had so much that was good to tell about 'wee' Joe Devlin. Though his views mellowed later, he was then firm in the conviction that the trouble there was due to British guile and nothing else. It was a view with which I did not agree.[74]

Their disagreement on the North would continue for the rest of their political careers.

But such snatched conversations couldn't overcome the enforced isolation of prison life. At first, de Valera told a visiting priest, he feared he would go mad, being saved only by the availability of books.[75] The books in Dartmoor were, however, of limited interest to him. In June he petitioned the authorities for the use of his fountain pen and writing paper in order

> to continue certain researches in higher applied mathematics . . . I could then spend with profit the spare time which at present the Prison Regulations permit me to spend in, for the most part, desultory reading.

Despite a list of distinguished referees, including Professor Conway of NUI and Professor Whitaker of Edinburgh University, the request was rejected.[76] The Prison Commissioners took the view that de Valera – and Bob Brennan, who had requested pen and paper to pursue literary work – should be turned down, because ordinary convicts were not allowed these privileges; if the rules were to be changed for the Irish prisoners they should be taken out of convict prisons and treated as prisoners of war under military control.[77] De Valera was, however, allowed to receive a number of mathematical books.[78] His was one of many such applications from the Dartmoor prisoners: there were 'extremely numerous' applications for 'concessions such as books, drawing instruments, books on Irish language, and so on'. By contrast, the Republican prisoners at Portland in Dorset did not make a single such application. The Prison Commissioners were baffled at the difference, as the two groups of prisoners were selected at random and were both of mixed social status and education.[79]

Solace could come unexpectedly. One summer evening, after a long afternoon sewing mailbags in the warm and stuffy workshop, de Valera was feeling 'unusually tired and weary in spirit' as he mounted the stairs up to the cells. Suddenly a Latin phrase flashed across his mind, '*Forsan et haec olim meminisse juvabit*' ('Perhaps this will be a pleasure to look back on one day'). He was at a loss to understand why he thought of this fragment of Virgil, but he described the effect as 'magical'.

> Before I reached the top of the stairs it was as if I had been changed into another person. I was completely renewed in energy and spirit. Looking back I have always regarded this experience as one of the most extraordinary happenings in my life.[80]

Perhaps this incident prompted a relatively upbeat letter to his mother assuring her he was 'in good health and as you see not in bad spirits', and telling her not to worry about him. Were it not for his wife and children, he observed, the cloister of his recently ordained half-brother, Tom, 'would not be so very different to mine – except the surroundings and the free will'.[81]

Far from being cloistered, Tom had been conducting a vigorous campaign to interest the US State Department in his brother's case; he also enlisted a number of priestly allies to lobby their congressmen and senators to aid the effort.[82] The American embassy in London took the case up, first with the War Office and then with the Home Office, mainly to find out if de Valera was claiming to be an American citizen and if so on what grounds.[83] However, the State Department believed that, although de Valera 'may be' an American citizen, it was no reason for him to get clemency, and there was no reason for the American government to intervene.[84]

Kate Wheelwright was also determined to play her part. 'Although I am frail now Almighty God has given me nerves of steel.' She was convinced her son had been badly treated and collected documents to prove his American birth.[85] De Valera began asking questions about his father which proved difficult for her to answer. 'In International Law am I a Spaniard or an American? . . . Send me an account of all you know about my father and his people.'[86] He told the prison authorities that, depending on the answer to this question, he was either Spanish or American. The governor recorded that de Valera 'further states that he did not become a British citizen, but he would have become an Irish citizen if that had been possible'.[87] However, de Valera eventually concluded that his American birth would not lead to special treatment, and he advised his family in the United States not to go to any further trouble or expense. 'I cannot see on what grounds America can interfere.'[88]

There was no shortcut out of Dartmoor, and this may have prompted de Valera to adopt a newly defiant approach in the middle of October, some five months after his arrival. On the morning of 16 October, he was caught throwing a loaf of bread across the landing to another prisoner, John McArdle. According to Brennan, de Valera was caught by a particularly observant and officious warder[89] – an unfortunate accident, in other words. But the official report suggests it was a deliberate attempt to cause trouble. When challenged, he not alone admitted the charge but said he had other loaves in his cell, which he intended to distribute in the same way.[90] He tried to save McArdle from punishment, saying he had simply caught the loaf 'as he would an orchard fall'. De Valera added that 'he knew he would soon be caught' throwing bread but 'felt quite justified as the Medical Officer had refused McArdle extra diet'. As punishment de Valera was given two days' solitary confinement on no. 2 diet (bread and gruel), and he lost marks for remission.[91] According to Governor Reade, de Valera was 'defiant in his attitude' and refused to eat or do the work prescribed in solitary confinement: 'picking oakum'.[92] Reade advised the Prison Commissioners that if de Valera continued to refuse food he would have to be forcibly fed. He was also uneasily aware that punishing de Valera could have wider consequences. 'The RC Priest has informed me that there is a decided undercurrent of unrest amongst the Irish prisoners and there are hints of a sympathetic strike (labour) on Valera's behalf'.[93]

Reade believed that most of the prisoners would be led by de Valera and by two other prisoners he identified as 'agitators', Desmond FitzGerald and Richard Hayes.[94] The Prison Commissioners suggested moving all three to Maidstone Convict Prison in Kent, where they would be 'out of their Irish environment'.[95] Reade wasn't convinced about the other two but was anxious to get rid of de Valera, who was 'a real firebrand and fanatic . . . He is decidedly a "personality" and the others seem to look up to him as their leader'.[96]

Dartmoor's medical officer indignantly rejected the rationale for de Valera's throwing of the bread, pointing out that the allegedly hungry McArdle had never requested extra food (although many of his companions had complained about the amount they were getting). The doctor insisted that the Irish prisoners were thriving on the prison diet.[97] This may have been true for most, but some certainly suffered in prison. Seán Etchingham (known as 'Patsy', because of his 'Patsy Patrick' column in the *Enniscorthy Echo*) couldn't eat the food and, according to Brennan, 'nearly died of starvation'.[98]

But a medical examination of de Valera after his two-day hunger strike suggested he wasn't exactly fading away. Although he was of 'spare physique', his weight had increased during his time in the prison from 163 pounds to 171. His general health was good and seemingly unaffected by two days without food. The doctor considered him 'sane'. De Valera was 'civil and pleasant', but he insisted that he was a prisoner of war and should be treated as one, and he threatened to repeat his hunger strike if put under punishment again. If he resumed the strike it would be 'war to the bitter end'. The doctor concluded:

> I consider Prisoner to be of a determined and fanatical temperament, and I fully believe he will carry out his threats re hunger striking, at any rate for a long period.[99]

Before hearing that de Valera had given up his hunger strike, the Prison Commissioners ordered his transfer to Maidstone Prison, along with Hayes and FitzGerald, on 27 October.[100] In a petition to the Home Secretary, de Valera bitterly complained that they were chained together for the 12-hour journey, 'so that when one of us had to perform the natural functions he had to drag his two companions with him and violate every law of common decency.' He also complained of the 'indignity' and 'personal degradation' of having to associate intimately with ordinary convicts.[101] This petition was part of the propaganda war now being waged over the treatment of the prisoners, with questions being raised in the House of Commons by Irish MPs.

In Maidstone Prison, the three exiles were put to work in the printing and binding department. De Valera stitched copy-books and wished he could be promoted to the more interesting job of stitching and binding pages of books.[102] He took exception to being forced to associate with the other prisoners. As he later recalled, they were chiefly wife murderers in large numbers and other cut-throats, criminal abortionists, sodomists (a share from navy), men guilty of incest, swindlers of all types, counterfeiters etc. . . . we had to use the closets, baths etc. used by these men, many of whom were known to be suffering from venereal diseases.[103]

While the three prisoners were subject to the same regime as the ordinary convicts, the rules were bent in a number of ways. De Valera was allowed to keep eight volumes of the *Proceedings of the Royal Irish Academy*, which he had received in Dartmoor without permission.[104] When Sinéad wrote to tell him of the birth of their fifth child, Ruaidhrí, he was allowed to write a special letter dealing only with the birth; even though he strayed from that subject, the letter was sent, with the offending portion excised.[105] And when he received a cheque for £1 6s 3d from the Royal College of Physicians of Ireland (a fee for setting an exam), he was allowed to send it to his mother-in-law.[106] It was used to buy the Flanagan's Christmas turkey, which was traditionally supplied by de Valera.[107]

The Prison Commissioners were determined to maintain discipline by refusing special treatment to the Irish prisoners. If the government wanted to relax the conditions, they would have to transfer the prisoners to War Office administration. It had already been decided to release the unsentenced prisoners interned in Frongoch army camp as a conciliatory gesture; now the government decided to ease the conditions of the sentenced prisoners, gathering them together in Lewes Prison in Sussex so that ordinary convicts wouldn't see their treatment.[108] The Prison Commissioners were reluctant to allow de Valera, FitzGerald and Hayes to join their comrades, but the Home Secretary, Herbert Samuel, favoured 'giving these three men a fresh chance at Lewes'.[109] The Prison Commissioners then insisted that in Lewes, the three should not be allowed to talk during association, 'until they shall have proved themselves fit for it by a period of good conduct'.[110] Again, Samuel over-ruled them, 'on the clear understanding that, if they misconduct themselves, they will go back to Maidstone'.[111] In a further concession, all the prisoners were transferred without chains.[112]

Their new home at Lewes Prison seemed

to be a beautiful place after the experience of Dartmoor. The cell floors were of wood and there were hot-water pipes and, though they were never hot, they looked good. The lighting of the cells, too, was infinitely better.[113]

The prisoners were put to work weaving hearthrugs on a loom and making brushes of coir fibre. They were allowed to talk during work, which was 'a very distinct improvement', and the governor, Major Marriott, was 'respected by all'.[114] Just before Christmas, de Valera wrote to his mother noting that 'our position has now been considerably improved' and that he was in good health and spirits – and had not yet despaired of serving Mass for Tom 'some time'.[115]

The prisoners devoted most of their spare time to study, reading in their cells and discussing their subjects of interest during exercise, Desmond FitzGerald on literature, W. T. Cosgrave on housing, while 'de Valera enjoys scientific matters'.[116] MacNeill asked his wife to send a Spanish dictionary, as there was only one in the prison and it was in great demand. He wrote that there was 'a general desire among the prisoners here to acquire or improve a knowledge of Irish and I am often engaged during exercise time in giving oral lessons'.[117] De Valera was one of those working on his Irish,[118] though mathematics remained his great interest.

According to de Valera, he took 'command as senior officer of prisoners at Lewes'.[119] His acolyte Robert Brennan attributed his ascension to leadership to his personality.

> It is curious to recall now how easily and naturally de Valera stepped into the leadership . . . In Lewes he became the leader of us all, without any consultation, debate or election – there was an election later, but long before that he had become 'the chief'. Whenever any proposal was made or discussed, the first question everyone asked was: 'What does Dev think of it?' Even at that early stage, there was the contradiction that though we found him tantalisingly conservative, we were all looking to him for a lead.[120]

In fact, he was *not* the senior officer in Lewes: Thomas Ashe was also a battalion commandant, and Tom Hunter too held the rank of commandant.[121] For that matter, MacNeill was still in theory senior to them all as chief of staff. Several accounts suggest his election was not unanimous – Frank Lawless claimed that Ashe disputed de Valera's seniority, and sought election himself.[122]

Brennan recalled that Ashe 'and a few others' opposed de Valera,[123] and Piaras Béaslaí claimed that de Valera was chosen as commandant in order to avoid a divisive election, with Ashe and Hunter agreeing to act as his deputies.[124] Peadar Clancy stated that the leadership was a triumvirate of de Valera, Ashe and Hunter.[125] De Valera appears to have had an ambivalent attitude towards Ashe: he nominated Hunter to succeed him in command if he was transferred from Lewes, with Ashe as second substitute.[126] He may well have been wary of him as a senior figure in the IRB, and he would most likely have seen him, rightly, as his main rival for leadership.

De Valera's style of leadership was described by Brennan as that of a 'constitutional autocrat'. There was plenty of time for discussion, which usually allowed de Valera to persuade others to follow his preferred course. But if the decision went against him he was prepared to threaten resignation; if they didn't agree with him, they would have to find another leader.[127] In another account, Brennan said de Valera 'bitterly' resented questioning of his leadership. 'He held that since authority had been freely bestowed on him by his comrades, every man was bound in duty and in honour to recognise it.'[128]

Years later, in conversation with Dorothy Macardle, de Valera admitted that he usually found it difficult to reach decisions, as he always tried to see all sides of the question. But in prison he had 'enforced my own will on people without listening to opposition'.[129] Perhaps this was because the prisoners still regarded themselves as under military discipline; perhaps it was because de Valera felt the need to dominate, as his leadership was new and therefore precarious.

A major disagreement with Ashe concerned political activity, to which de Valera was opposed. While the convicts served their time in Lewes, there had been a sea-change in Ireland away from military activity and towards politics, and there had been a swing in public opinion against the Irish Party. Three by-elections since the Rising – two in safe Unionist seats in the north, one in West Cork – had been uncontested by advanced nationalists. But now, with IRB encouragement, it was decided to contest North Roscommon. Count Plunkett was the candidate, and he won with 3,022 votes (compared with 1,708 for the Irish Party candidate). As with all the by-elections, of course, North Roscommon was fought on the basis of the old register and not the new and much wider one that would be in force for the 1918 general election.

It was only after his election, under pressure from such supporters as Michael Collins, that Plunkett announced he would abstain from the House of Commons.[130] Plunkett was self-important and tactless, managing to alienate many advanced nationalists, who resented his 'dictatorial attitude', especially as many of them had served the 'cause' much longer than he had.[131] He was, however, the best figurehead they had, and in April he held a conference bringing together the disparate elements of advanced nationalism. Despite some disagreement, the conference eventually elected a committee to draft a policy, which included Plunkett, Arthur Griffith, Cathal Brugha, the union leader William O'Brien and a number of others. This committee would preserve a precarious unity of purpose until the new Sinn Féin was established at a convention in November.[132]

In Lewes the prisoners were suspicious of the turn towards politics. At first they feared that Count Plunkett would be beaten, and even when he won, they drew up a statement warning of the dangers of electoral contests, 'but we decided not to send it as those who were working at home knew best what tactics the situation demanded'.[133] The matter became more pressing when another seat became vacant, in South Longford, and those outside wanted to nominate the Lewes prisoner Joseph McGuinness, a Longford native. De Valera complained that it was impossible for them to get a clear picture of what was going on at home. 'The information we are able to get is very meagre and often most contradictory. We are in a regular fog.' He explained that the prisoners regarded themselves as specially identified with 'last Easter's sacrifice', and they were worried that contesting elections could 'create a wrong impression as to the ideals, principles and opinions which prompted' the Rising. While they supported Plunkett's plan of appealing to the post-war peace conference, they were unsure of the rest of his policies, suspecting that they might be 'a reversion to the old Sinn Féin *political* movement'. De Valera wrote that

> we are not willing to risk that which has been purchased by our comrade's blood . . . on a throw with the dice loaded against us . . . The safest course for us and in the long run the wisest is to continue as soldiers.

To that end, he expressed the hope that the arming, organising and training of the Volunteers was continuing in their absence.

> The Irish Volunteers . . . must be kept a permanent force at the country's back. That it seems to us is our mission . . . and we must allow nothing to make us forget it.[134]

This view was accepted by the prisoners – with the notable exceptions of the senior IRB members Harry Boland and Thomas Ashe. The latter suggested leaving the decision in the hands of those outside, as they were better informed,[135] and he claimed that standing for election was 'not giving recognition to the British parliament but giving the people an opportunity to support Irish freedom'.[136] Ashe had the advantage over his colleagues of better information, thanks to coded messages from Collins in Dublin explaining the changes at home.[137]

But on Easter Sunday, 8 April, McGuinness wrote to Plunkett declining the nomination.[138] De Valera wrote a memorandum explaining the decision and demostrating cautious conservatism.

> It would be a great satisfaction to win but to lose would mean bankruptcy . . . I for one would have to be almost *certain* of success before I would risk such a stake . . . When I can avoid it I am averse to letting *other people*, no matter how wise they are *commit me* to such a risk.[139]

The reasoning was sound, and the risk was real. But those on the outside simply ignored McGuinness's refusal and carried on with the campaign. Some of the prisoners were so angry that they wanted to repudiate the campaign, but the majority decided to say nothing so as not to harm

> the Cause which is the only thing we all have at heart. Nobody should think however that contesting elections is the policy which the men here would advocate if they had a say in the matter.[140]

However, their suspicion turned to joy when the result was announced on 10 May. After a recount, McGuinness was elected by a margin of 37 votes, and

> there was nearly a riot in the Prison when we got the news, discipline broke and we chaired Joe in the Prison Hall and put him up on a table to make a speech. Joe obliged and the Prison rang with the cheers of 130 Irish convicts.[141]

For de Valera, despite political success on the outside, the main theatre of action remained Lewes. The first major clash with the governor occurred at the beginning of March, when Thomas Peppard and Richard Kelly were reported for talking in the workshop. The governor ordered that Kelly be punished, at which point the prisoners as a body refused to do any work. MacNeill, Ashe and then de Valera spoke up for Kelly; the governor said he had intended Kelly to have only one meal of bread and water as punishment, and that he would now be released.[142] Some of the Irishmen were surprised that de Valera, their recognised leader, was not the first to speak out.[143] De Valera, however, seemed pleased with developments, writing to a colleague in Ireland that 'by united action we have emancipated ourselves somewhat from being punished for such offences as talking during work'. He believed, however, that a crackdown was imminent. 'The governor here seems inclined to be reasonable and to treat us properly . . . but the screw is evidently being put on *from the top.*'[144]

He was right. The Prison Commissioners in London were disturbed by the governor's appeasement of the prisoners, and they sent an inspector to read a warning to them: if they didn't stop talking they would be confined to their cells for work. This time de Valera did speak up, complaining that this was a breach of the terms given to them when they arrived in Lewes. The inspector then had a private meeting with de Valera, in which de Valera admitted 'a difficulty he had in expressing himself by speech'. Their discussion went nowhere until Eoin MacNeill and Éamonn Duggan were brought in. 'MacNeill spoke with an eloquence foreign to de Valera, protesting that the Home Secretary had broken his promises of free conversation and a less rigorous discipline.' The inspector suggested that each of them should send a petition to the Home Secretary.[145]

De Valera advised his contacts in Ireland that the authorities would either accept the previous situation in Lewes, which would be a victory, or else split the prisoners up and send them to different prisons, in which case none of them would work, which would mean solitary confinement and punishment diet. He suggested a number of questions that could be asked in the House of Commons by Laurence Ginnell, the independent nationalist MP who had championed the cause of the prisoners for months. De Valera wanted a confrontation with the authorities: he said the inspector at Lewes had decided not to take severe disciplinary action against the prisoners on the advice of the Catholic chaplain. 'I did swear when he did not try it on and especially at his reverence for not letting him do it.'[146]

In his petition to the Home Secretary (the Conservative Sir George Cave), de Valera complained that they were still being treated as 'criminals' rather than as a 'class apart', as they had been led to expect when they arrived in Lewes. He denied that they were unwilling to work, but admitted that they did not take kindly to the debasing and soul-killing labour associated with prison – such as picking oakum, which he had refused to do in Dartmoor. He then noted particular complaints: morning exercise was too short for all the men who wanted to use the toilet facilities; the machines used for cutting hair and shaving were 'almost instruments of torture'; and letters were long delayed.[147]

Having written his petition, de Valera warned his fellow prisoners that he might be moved from Lewes. He advised them that their guiding principles should be to obey their chosen leaders, to never allow themselves to be beaten – 'If you feel that *in the long run* you can be beaten then *don't begin*' – and to avoid personal squabbles with officials. He appointed Tom Hunter as his deputy, followed by Thomas Ashe, Piaras Béaslaí, Éamonn Duggan, Richard Hayes and Austin Stack. He advised them to always consult MacNeill – 'He will be an ideal spokesman for you and think twice before you undertake anything to which his judgement is opposed' – and ordered them not to make any protest if he was removed.

> If I am shifted they will have their preparations made to deal with you. If you keep quiet they will be more nonplussed than ever . . . You may be tempted to hunger-strike, as a body do not attempt it whilst the war lasts unless you were assured from outside that the death of two or three of you would help the cause – as soldiers I know you would not shirk from the sacrifice – but remember how precious a human life is.[148]

Such drastic action was not necessary. The inspector at Lewes advised the Prison Commissioners that any attempt to enforce silence during work would provoke a violent reaction. The Prison Commissioners reluctantly advised the Home Secretary to relax the rule, which he did, telling the governor that the prisoners could talk during work 'within proper and reasonable limits'.[149] De Valera triumphantly reported that they had won the battle. 'We talk fifty times as much now as ever before but we are into a new struggle again'. This time it was about food: along with the rest of Britain, the prisoners were having their rations cut. De Valera said they would 'kick up a row' if the diet wasn't changed back.[150] Again, the authorities appear to have backed down, as the 'row' didn't materialise. And, again, appeasement of the prisoners led to further confrontation.

De Valera had apparently sought approval from home before intensifying the prison war. Confirmation arrived in a telegram to Harry Boland claiming that his uncle had died, which led to some embarrassing condolences from the authorities.[151] The 'triumvirate' of de Valera, Hunter and Ashe were apparently divided on the wisdom of going ahead with the attempt to gain the status of prisoners-of-war. According to one account, Ashe rejected the idea of the other two of postponement; he insisted on going ahead on the appointed date.[152] In his final order, de Valera betrayed no doubt about the course of action they were about to take.

> The Irish people demand that we be given the status of prisoners of war ... *We have the express approval of our friends at home* ... Remember it is not for paltry concessions for yourselves you are fighting, it is for Ireland's honour ... To fail – to be weak – would mean dishonour to the dead – to Ireland ... It must be death rather than surrender.[153]

And so, on Monday 28 May, the strike began. At morning parade de Valera handed the chief warder an ultimatum stating that they were refusing to work until they were granted prisoner-of-war status. The prisoners, on cue, lifted their caps and cheered for Ireland. The governor scurried down to the parade ground, where de Valera repeated their demands. Marriott said he would forward the document to the Home Office, and 'on this promise Dev stepped back into our ranks and we returned to our cells, where we remained for some days in solitary confinement'.[154]

On Wednesday an order from de Valera was discovered in a prison bathroom. It stated that, if they were allowed go to Mass on Sunday, 'no man is to go to his cell again ... The idea is to compel them to bring in the military if we can'.[155] Not surprisingly, Mass was cancelled. The prisoners compensated by saying the Rosary on Sunday morning.[156]

With no progress made after a week, de Valera ordered the men to begin breaking up their cells.[157] The authorities responded by removing the furniture the prisoners had been using to cause the damage, leaving them to eat their food sitting on the floor.[158] With nothing left to smash, the prisoners turned their attention to taking the walls apart – 'a slow job for the first brick but easy after that'.[159] The prison was 'literally pulled to pieces, brick by brick, holes were bored in the walls and in the floors'.[160] The aim of this mutiny was to provoke the authorities into bringing in the military, which would be a propaganda victory; but the fire brigade was brought in instead to hose them out of their cells before they were split up and dispersed to other prisons.[161]

By this time, de Valera had already been transferred back to Maidstone Prison, once again in restraints and in convict uniform. The authorities were determined that discipline be restored, but they were faced with a difficulty: the penalty for mutiny was flogging, which was politically impossible to implement. The best the authorities could do was to put recalcitrant prisoners on punishment diets and keep them in solitary confinement, with the inevitable effect on their health, which would lead to more political fallout. There was also the danger of hunger strike (the authorities were not aware that de Valera had forbidden this).[162] Harry Boland wrote a letter explaining what had happened to the prisoners and threw it into the street as he was being transferred; a passer-by found it and posted it to Boland's mother, as requested. When the letter was read out at a protest meeting in Beresford Place in Dublin, a riot ensued, during which the DMP inspector John Mills was struck on the head by a hurley and killed – the first fatality among Crown forces since the Rising.[163]

The governor of Maidstone tried to assert his authority, telling his new charge that he would impose discipline. De Valera refused to stand to attention or button his uniform; the following day he refused to stand up when the governor entered his cell. He also attempted to break up his punishment cell, being defeated by the thick glass in the window.[164] When more prisoners from Lewes arrived, they found their leader on a bread-and-water diet. They refused to exercise with criminal convicts, being denied Mass as a result. The following day they were all given three days' solitary confinement; when they refused to work they were put on bread and water.[165] It was clear that the prisoners were heading for yet another confrontation; luckily for them, and for the prison authorities, the government decided to release them.

On 15 June, Bonar Law informed the House of Commons that all the prisoners were to be amnestied. The ostensible reason was the coming opening of the Irish Convention in Dublin, established to reach agreement among the various Irish parties on the introduction of home rule. 'Nothing could be more regrettable than that the work of the Convention should be prejudiced at the outset by embittered associations,' Bonar Law told MPs.[166]

De Valera ordered the prisoners to show no signs of elation when the governor informed them of their release. To his satisfaction, the men's reaction was 'magnificent . . . complete silence'.[167] The following day the Irish prisoners were brought to Pentonville Prison in London, described by Eoin MacNeill as 'the dirtiest prison in all our experience'. De Valera was bitten so badly by fleas that he 'looked as if he had had an outbreak of measles'.[168] On Sunday evening they were brought to Euston Station and put on the train to Holyhead.[169]

There they were met by Patrick McCartan, sent to consult fellow members of the IRB about sending a message to American President Woodrow Wilson. A fortnight before, Wilson had declared that 'no people must be forced under a sovereignty under which it does not wish to live'. McCartan sought Ashe's opinion; Ashe deferred to de Valera, advising McCartan to discuss it with him and with MacNeill. The result was an appeal to President Wilson, signed by all the Volunteer officers the following day, which McCartan brought to the United States.[170]

The prisoners had been given third-class tickets for the mail boat, but, 'feeling in a first class mood, Éamon de Valera decided that we should all travel 1st Class, and we just brushed the ticket checkers aside'. De Valera later recalled that, when the hills of Co. Wicklow came into view, 'the happiness of the boys and the beautiful picture presented by the approaches to our country can never be forgotten'.[171] He called for three cheers for Ireland, 'which were lustily given'.[172]

The ship docked at Dún Laoghaire just before 8 a.m. Under de Valera's orders, the men waited patiently for the other passengers to disembark, before marching down the gangway in military formation. Only about a hundred people were there to greet them, as most of their supporters had expected them to come into Dublin Port. They had spent the night at the North Wall – 3,000 of them, according to the pro-unionist *Irish Times*, which was unlikely to exaggerate the number.[173] When the crowd heard that the men were arriving by train, 'there was a general stampede to Westland Row'.[174]

When the train arrived, just after nine o'clock, the crowd went wild. The released prisoners couldn't get out of the carriages at first, such was the crush of people. When the Volunteer stewards finally extricated them and they emerged into the street, 'the scene beggars description. The people of Dublin appeared to have crowded themselves into one street, and we were actually carried and placed out on the wagonettes.'[175] Another observer recalled the deafening cheers. 'All Dublin went wild with delight and was left to herself to do so, the forces of "Law and Order" being conspicuous by their absence.'[176] The climax, according to one of the former prisoners, came when de Valera, Ashe, Stack, Boland and Shouldice emerged from the station. 'On seeing them, the crowd simply went mad. Rounds and rounds of cheers rent the sky.'[177]

One of the problems for all observers was identifying which of the shaven-headed former prisoners was which. 'It was known that Mr John MacNeill, Mr de Valera, Councillor William Cosgrave, and other prominent Sinn Féiners were amongst them, but very few were able to pick them out'.[178] Whether they could recognise de Valera or not, many in the crowd now knew his name. His 1916 record and his leadership of the prisoners 'united to make this hitherto unknown man the most famous and most sought after individual in Dublin on this historic occasion'.[179]

Journalists seeking statements from the prisoners were firmly told that any statement would come through their leader, de Valera – but de Valera declined to talk.[180]

The massive, enthusiastic crowd paraded the prisoners around the main streets of Dublin, waving Republican flags and banners. In O'Connell Street 'the cheering was unabated, and the sight of the gaunt ruins of the GPO appeared to infuse fresh enthusiasm'.[181] The prisoners were then brought for breakfast at a hotel in Gardiner Street, before having a group photograph taken in the grounds of the Mansion House.

Eventually, de Valera managed to break away, his Dartmoor visitor Father Tom Roche having arranged a cab to take him to Munster Street, where Sinéad was waiting anxiously. De Valera had endured a tough time in prison; but his wife had arguably had an even more difficult year at home. Her three eldest children – Vivion, Máirín and Eamonn – went to live with her aunt Kate Byrne in Balbriggan, while she kept Brian with her in Phibsborough. She had nursed her sister Mary, who died in August 1916; her fifth child, Ruaidhrí, was born in November; her mother died in January 1917; and her father was becoming senile.[182]

But now the couple had a joyful reunion. Sinéad noticed the flea bites on her husband's hands and how 'odd' he looked in his prison-issue clothes.[183] She soon had him back 'in great spirits and very good health', and both were busy but happy.[184] But as a friend had once predicted, 'a humdrum home circle will hardly . . . satisfy his eager straining spirit',[185] and domestic bliss would not hold him long. He was already plotting a new course. His vice-commandant, Joseph O'Connor, offered to hand back command of the 3rd Battalion, but de Valera declined, explaining that 'his activity would be in the political line from thenceforward'.[186] Opportunity had come knocking once again for Éamon de Valera, and once again he was prepared to seize his chance.

CHAPTER 10

THE COMING PARNELL OF IRELAND

We congratulate Commandant de Valera – the coming Parnell of Ireland – on his triumphant return.
Corrofin Rural District Council, July 1917[1]

... a man of great ability with considerable influence going down to the country for the express purpose of stirring the people to rebellion against the authorities ...
David Lloyd George on de Valera, October 1917[2]

I hope de Valera will keep straight ... He is getting enough adulation to turn an older and more experienced man's head.
Kathleen Clarke, October 1917[3]

D e Valera's opportunity came as a result of the bad luck of the MP for East Clare, Willie Redmond, brother of the leader of the Irish Party. Willie had followed his brother's call and joined up, becoming a captain in the 16th (Irish) Division. At 56 he was far too old for front-line service, but he left his staff position to join the assault at Wytschaete, Belgium, in June 1917, and was killed.

Three groups had to be convinced that de Valera was the right candidate for the resulting by-election: Count Plunkett's national committee, representing advanced nationalism;[4] local activists; and the released prisoners. The initial idea for his candidacy came from the national committee, as he 'was looked upon as the leader of the men in prison'. There was some doubt about whether de Valera would accept the nomination, so a formal decision was deferred to a future meeting. Crucially, though, the veteran Sinn Féin activist Seán Milroy was sent to Co. Clare to prepare the ground.[5]

This turned out to be fortunate, because the people there had their own ideas. An initial meeting of advanced nationalists in the constituency backed a local man, Peadar Clancy. From Cranny, in west Co. Clare, Clancy had fought in the Rising and been sentenced to death, his sentence being commuted to life imprisonment.[6] This tentative decision was reported in the papers, which noted that 'the name of Edward de Valera, who is also in jail, has also been mentioned'.[7]

On 14 June a much bigger meeting of about 200 delegates was held in the Old Ground Hotel in Ennis. In advance, there had been lobbying in favour of Eoin MacNeill, particularly by priests, but he was strongly opposed by local Volunteers.[8] Father Alfred Moloney proposed de Valera, citing his record during the Rising.[9] In total, five candidates were nominated, but after Milroy 'addressed the meeting at some length' the others withdrew and de Valera was formally adopted as candidate.[10] Clearly, the support of the Volunteers was crucial, as without them MacNeill might well have been chosen, as was Milroy's advocacy – the delegates were left in no doubt that 'Dublin wanted only de Valera'.[11] That evening the national election committee formally ratified de Valera and sent Dan McCarthy to Co. Clare to start organising the campaign.[12]

The effort to elect de Valera was proceeding well; all it needed now was the candidate's agreement – not a foregone conclusion, given his opposition to Joe McGuinness's selection for South Longford. The secretaries of the convention in Ennis sent him a telegram: 'You are Sinn Féin's selection for Clare.'[13] (The use of the label 'Sinn Féin' was rather elastic: he was the candidate of a wider coalition than the party of that name, though Sinn Féin raised funds for him and all its leading figures campaigned for him.[14]) He received this news somewhere between leaving Pentonville Prison and boarding the ship at Holyhead. During the voyage, he confided to Patrick McCartan that 'he knew nothing about politics and did not like them'; he would prefer to stick to his work with the Volunteers. McCartan advised him not to make a decision until he had spent a week at home to witness 'the new spirit in the land'.[15]

That new spirit was certainly evident in the reception for the prisoners on their arrival, and it may well have swayed de Valera. That day a group of senior former prisoners met and discussed East Clare. Some – possibly a majority – wanted Thomas Ashe to be the candidate, but he declined to go forward, telling his cousin Pádraig that 'a small but solid group is supporting de Valera with great persistence. If I accept I believe it may cause disunity in our ranks'.[16] When Ashe declined to seek the candidacy, de Valera was unanimously selected.[17]

Ashe's comments suggest that de Valera was not so reluctant a candidate as he let on, though some believed that his reluctance was genuine. Michael Staines recalled the meeting at which 'we got de Valera's consent to stand as a candidate' – hardly the language he would have used if he suspected that his candidacy was the result of intrigue. But the candidate would stand on his own terms, only agreeing

> to go to Clare on condition that John McNeill [*sic*] would accompany him. A few objected, but finally agreed if John McNeill would declare in favour of an Irish Republic. He did so.[18]

During lengthy conversations with de Valera, MacNeill gathered from him

> that he was no more than I was myself a doctrinaire republican . . . He urged on me, however, that the demand for an Irish Republic would present a stronger appeal to the electorate and the public than anything else less definite . . .[19]

So MacNeill went to Co. Clare with de Valera, drafting his first letter to the press and helping him compose his first speech.[20]

The help was evidently needed. On 22 June, on his way to Co. Clare, de Valera stopped off in Bruree for a triumphant homecoming.

> Outside the village Mr de Valera was met by a large concourse of people, who greeted him in the most enthusiastic manner . . . The horse was taken from under the car on which Mr de Valera was seated, and it was drawn by a number of men.[21]

The reception by his former neighbours must have been gratifying for de Valera, though opinions on his lengthy speech were mixed. One observer said it was 'passionate and determined as, with blazing eyes, he sent home every argument with telling effect'.[22] Another considered that 'his speech was halting'.[23] A third said it was all about Easter Week, adding that de Valera's uncle Pat, the former councillor, 'sat on the wagonette and, pulling his nephew's coat tail every now and then, said repeatedly in a loud whisper "State your policy." The attempts appear to have been unnoticed by de Valera.'[24]

The following day de Valera arrived in Co. Clare. Although the county boundary was only 40 kilometres from Bruree, de Valera was unknown there, and exotic. 'Some unkindly comments were made about the people who were responsible for selecting the man who bore such a name.'[25] By contrast, one local priest felt the 'romantic foreign name was a great asset: if he had been plain "Michael Murphy" he would not have had half the appeal to the Irish people'.[26] In Ennis, de Valera was met by 'an immense crowd, displaying Sinn Féin flags and with blazing tar barrels'.[27] In his speech he firmly committed himself to complete independence, and he justified the Rising while assuring his potential constituents that there would be no repetition. He subscribed to every word of the Proclamation,

> and to assert it in arms, were there a fair chance of military success, I would consider a sacred duty . . . At the moment a military assertion of it is not feasible – but you men of Clare can assert it by your votes . . .[28]

De Valera's Irish Party opponent, Paddy Lynch, had already been campaigning for a week, though given that there hadn't been a contested election in 22 years, the Irish Party machinery in Co. Clare was rusty. Lynch, a King's Counsel, had the advantage of being from the county – 'Clare for a Clareman' was the motto on many banners[29] – but the disadvantage of being the Crown prosecutor for Co. Kerry, which provided plenty of ammunition for attack, especially when contrasted with a man sentenced to death after the Rising. He was also accused of being 'a Castle Place Hunter' in handbills[30] and in song: 'Now you're getting old, man, you want to be MP, to grab some English gold, man, Cute Paddy Lynch KC.'[31] De Valera claimed, in contrast, to be restoring honesty to politics. 'The depths to which the party machine has dragged public life is almost inconceivable.'[32]

According to a local Volunteer, Lynch was 'the strongest candidate' the Irish Party could have found, being 'extremely well liked', with 'innumerable family connections in the constituency'.[33] As one Sinn Féin member was heard to say, 'He has defended one half of the murderers in Clare and is related to the other half'.[34] Perhaps his main problem was a lack of support from the Irish Party.[35] John Redmond showed little interest: he was ill and was grief-stricken by the death of his daughter as well as his brother, and his attention was moving from the Irish Party – which he realised 'was finished . . . as an instrument for achieving self-government' – to the faint hope of reaching agreement at the Irish Convention.[36] The RIC were not optimistic about Lynch's chances. 'Such is the impetus gained by Sinn Féin from the victories at Roscommon and Longford that his success is not probable'.[37]

That impetus was most obvious in the uniformed presence of Volunteers from all over the country. They were highly visible, parading in uniform, drilling with hurleys, canvassing votes, raising money and, on polling day, bringing people to vote.[38] They also protected meetings, trying in particular to ensure de Valera's safety. Michael Brennan, hearing rumours that the candidate would be shot, spent several nights guarding roads along which he was to travel.[39] There was certainly a need for policing: the RIC were ineffectual, the County Inspector lamely (and wrongly) claiming that 'almost every young man carries a revolver'.[40]

Despite the implication that the Volunteers were the source of all trouble, in many cases they were the victims. The recollections of Volunteers are replete with complaints about 'separation women' and former British soldiers attacking them.[41]

From the start, de Valera's campaign was far better organised. When the candidates lodged their nomination papers on 2 July, he had 42, each signed by ten constituents, to Lynch's 26.[42] In the Old Ground Hotel in Ennis, the director of elections, Dan McCarthy, insisted on the entire team (many of whom worked until three or four in the morning[43]) being up for breakfast at eight, when speakers would be given a programme for the day, and canvassers handed a list of people to see. Cars – crucial in a county with a poor rail network and many isolated villages – would be waiting for them as soon as breakfast was over.[44]

The hotel was packed to capacity, with election workers from all over the country, some of them sleeping on mattresses out on the lawn,[45] as there was literally no room at the inn. Liam de Róiste recorded those he met in Ennis, including Count Plunkett, Darrell Figgis, Joe McGuinness, Laurence Ginnell and Constance Markievicz. Griffith told de Róiste that de Valera was to be 'the future leader of the Sinn Féin organisation'.[46] There were plenty of younger men destined for future fame there too, including Michael Collins and 19-year old Frank Aiken, who ran despatches for Austin Stack.[47]

De Valera made as many as five speeches a day – a punishing schedule for a political neophyte.[48] Before his first major speech in Ennis, Dan McCarthy worried that he would not have the voice for outdoor public speaking; he advised a 'fiery speech' and a loud voice. McCarthy was satisfied with the result, telling the candidate he was now convinced of victory.[49] De Valera managed to turn his inexperience to his advantage, contrasting his own bluff soldier image with that of his opponent, telling one crowd that he lacked the eloquence of a King's Counsel. They would 'have to take him as one who did his duty and one who was willing to do it again'.[50] He also first demonstrated his habit of interrupting the next speaker to say something he had forgotten in his original speech.[51]

The threat of conscription was a huge issue – 'probably the strongest . . . of the many motives impelling the population towards Sinn Féinism', according to the RIC.[52] De Valera claimed that 'Easter week stopped Conscription', and he warned voters of the danger of their sons being enlisted 'in a service much more risky than the setting up of an Irish Republic'.[53] Lynch pointed out, correctly, that it was actually the opposition of the Irish Party at Westminster that had prevented conscription, and that it had done so since May 1915, a full year before the Rising.[54]

Lynch warned that de Valera wanted 'to establish an Irish Republic by revolutionary means', and he emphasised 'the terrible loss of life and destruction to property that a revolution would mean and without the faintest hope of success'.[55] He made the most of clerical supporters, such as the parish priest of Feakle, Father Hayes, who claimed that 'Sinn Féin was a party of Socialism and Anarchy and bloodshed which struck at the roots of society'.[56]

Part of the reason for bringing Eoin MacNeill to Co. Clare was his ability to neutralise such attacks. His knack for appealing to the clergy was demonstrated when his speech in the main square of Ennis was interrupted by the Angelus. He immediately removed his hat and invited a priest to lead the crowd in prayer.[57] De Valera was no slouch at appeasing religious sentiment either, remarking that 'they regarded their first duty as to God and their second to their country'.[58] De Valera deliberately surrounded himself with as many priests as possible: at a huge meeting in O'Connell Square in Ennis on 29 June there were 16 prominent clerics on the platform or nearby in the crowd.[59]

De Valera had to carry out a balancing act: constantly appealing to the legacy of Easter Week but allaying fears of further violence. But he made it clear that he stood for a Republic – a clarity that had been absent in North Roscommon and South Longford.[60] The *Cork Examiner*, which supported Lynch and the Irish Party, believed that both candidates had been clear on what divided them. Lynch stood for constitutional methods at Westminster, de Valera for a Republic completely independent of Britain.[61]

On the eve of polling, de Valera demonstrated his eye for detail, noting the need for local guides in the cars transporting voters on polling day and for armed guards to accompany the ballot boxes to Ennis after the close of polls. He also specified 'No drink',[62] ordering the bar in the Old Ground Hotel to close on polling night, which generated considerable resentment among thirsty election workers.[63]

The *Irish Independent* cautiously predicted a de Valera victory, though it noted the Lynch camp's claim that 'many who wore the tricolour shed the sentiment . . . when they reached the secrecy of the ballot box'.[64] This sounded like clutching at straws: it was. Lynch got only 2,035 votes, to de Valera's 5,010, a margin of victory double the most optimistic forecast.[65] The *Cork Examiner* said the vote 'marked the passing of the old order'.[66] The 'crushing character' of de Valera's victory was also gloomily noted by the *Irish Times,* which said East Clare had 'voted for a programme of revolution'.[67]

The playwright Lennox Robinson was in the crowd in front of Ennis courthouse as the results were announced.

> De Valera is in, the Volunteers cheer again and again . . . The hero of the day, in Volunteer uniform, comes forward. Young, dark, eager, vivid, the very counterpart of these young men around us . . .'[68]

De Valera told the excited crowd: 'Here is John Bull's answer . . . It is a victory for the independence of Ireland, and for an Irish Republic.'[69] He then marched through the main streets of Ennis at the head of 700 young men in military formation.

Addressing supporters from the window of his committee rooms in Westmoreland Street in Dublin the following evening, de Valera said the only flag to which they owed allegiance was the Tricolour – 'and when it came to fighting for that flag Irishmen would not be found wanting'. To cheers, he pointed out that in order to be heard at the post-war peace conference they must first claim absolute independence, and in doing so they would be voicing the wishes of the people of Ireland. He added a threat to Ulster unionists on their day of celebration, 12 July: 'if Ulster stands in the way of the attainment of Irish freedom, Ulster should be coerced. Why should she not be?' Their programme, he explained, was abstention from Parliament, coupled with arming and equipping themselves to maintain their rights, which would be won 'whenever they got the chance'.[70]

His words were of particular importance because de Valera was now, in many eyes, the leader of advanced nationalism. 'The Banner County speaks for all Ireland,' said one message; Easter Week was vindicated, said another; de Valera was 'the coming Parnell of Ireland' according to a third.[71] His name was suddenly everywhere, from the Sinn Féin club in Bruree to an Irish dancing class in Dublin.[72] Invitations to speak flooded in from all over the country. W. J. Brennan-Whitmore, who had not been impressed when he met de Valera the day before the Rising, now pleaded for a visit to Co. Wexford, which 'would absolutely ensure our complete success'.[73] His prison companion Austin Stack offered a few weeks of rest 'in the wild Gaelic west' as an inducement to attend a Casement commemoration in Kerry.[74]

The British army noted with dismay that the election result 'has given an enormous impetus to the disloyal movement', with demonstrations throughout the country – some 'harmless enough', some featuring 'violent seditious oratory', with at least one, at Ballybunnion, Co. Kerry, leading to an attack on the local RIC barracks.[75] Having paraded illegally with Tricolours and drilled with hurleys in Co. Clare, the Volunteers returned to their home districts and did the same: the authorities responded with a ban on drilling in July.[76] This led to confrontation, arrests and the imprisonment of activists and a further ratcheting up of tension.[77]

In advance of a by-election in Kilkenny City, Michael Collins wrote to de Valera about the need to find 'a candidate . . . that we could all agree to'.[78] The Dublin alderman W. T. Cosgrave, a veteran of the Rising, was the choice, and his election on 10 August was Sinn Féin's fourth victory in a row in contested by-elections. The party seemed unstoppable – though, as it turned out, Sinn Féin would not win another contested election for ten months.

De Valera's new prominence was recognised on 18 July, when he was, rather belatedly, co-opted onto the National Council of Sinn Féin.[79] At the same time he was also co-opted onto the Executive of the Irish Volunteers[80] – the body he had refused to seek election to two years before. He was also still regarded as a leader of the released prisoners. Collins, in his role as secretary of the Irish National Aid and Volunteer Dependants' Fund, sought a meeting with de Valera, Thomas Ashe and Tom Hunter to discuss how the released men could be helped.[81]

According to the records of grants, de Valera received the very substantial sum of £740 from the fund, and Sinéad was offered 'all necessary financial assistance' in setting up 'an Irish Kindergarten' – the records show a grant to her of £50.[82] In September 1917 de Valera found a new home for his family, in Kinlen Road in Greystones, Co. Wicklow. It had an unsuitably English name – 'Howbury'[83] – but he immediately renamed it 'Cragh Liath' after a mountain in Clare.[84] The three eldest children – Vivion, Máirín and Eamonn – who had been living in Balbriggan, were reunited with their parents. To Sinéad's dismay, they had forgotten Irish in their year away, and she had to teach them the language again.[85]

Sinéad was presumably expecting better times now that her husband was home. In January 1917 he had written from Lewes Prison promising that he would

> make you far happier than we have ever been before . . . I hope, am certain indeed, that I will not in the future be guilty of so many acts of unconscious selfishness as I was in the past . . .

It was a promise he was not to fulfil, as events swept him away from home for long periods. In November he wrote that he was sorry to be away so often, adding, 'When I cannot talk to you, I have so much to say to you, but when we are together I am dumb. Can you understand?'[86]

On 25 September, Thomas Ashe, on hunger strike in Mountjoy Prison after being convicted of making a seditious speech, died following force-feeding. His funeral, on Sunday the 30th, was the biggest demonstration in Dublin since the O'Donovan Rossa funeral two years before. It was possibly bigger, with a cortege stretching for at least five kilometres and, significantly, a heavy clerical presence, led by the Archbishop of Dublin, Dr William Walsh.[87] The funeral culminated with a brief oration delivered by Michael Collins after shots were fired over the grave.

> Nothing additional remains to be said. That volley which we have just heard is the only speech which it is proper to make above the grave of a dead Fenian.

These succinct words, such a contrast to Pearse's eulogy for Rossa, propelled Collins into the limelight. The funeral was also important in the rise of Collins's close colleague Richard Mulcahy, who was given charge of the reconstituted Dublin Brigade in recognition of his work organising the parade.[88] Everyone who was anyone in advanced nationalism was there – except Éamon de Valera.

He had had a prior commitment in his constituency, and on the day of the funeral he was addressing a massive meeting of up to 25,000 people in O'Connell Square in Ennis. Again wearing his Volunteer uniform, he told the crowd that he was following Ashe's hearse 'in spirit' and that no other engagement could have kept him from the funeral. But, he added, 'perhaps after all his place were there, side by side with the living, to carry on the cause for which Tom Ashe died'.[89] De Valera had certainly come under strong pressure to attend the meeting; he preserved in his papers a telegram from Ennis, pleading with Griffith to

> get de Valera to keep his appointment here Sunday otherwise we are down and out. Huge county demonstration arranged can't put off.[90]

But it still seems extraordinary that he would miss such a crucial moment in the revival of the movement – and the suspicion must remain that he was at least in part prompted by his sometimes strained relationship with Ashe.

In July, Henry Duke, the Chief Secretary for Ireland, briefed the War Cabinet, complaining that, since their release, de Valera and others had moved from a claim for representation at the peace conference to 'an avowed advocacy of physical force'. Duke wanted there to be no tolerance for drilling, the wearing of uniforms or the bearing of weapons, but the War Cabinet worried that a crack-down would force the Irish Party to defend Sinn Féin, thus scuppering the Irish Convention. The result was a rather muddled instruction to Duke to prevent drilling and the wearing of uniforms 'where it was obviously used in connection with active steps in revolutionary organisation' and to take prompt action against 'any direct incitements to violence'.[91]

The army commander in Ireland, General Sir Bryan Mahon, had mixed views on whether or not to arrest de Valera. He pointed out to Duke that a speech by de Valera in Tullamore on 29 July – in which he said they were 'out to organise, arm and equip the Irish Volunteers for defensive and offensive action' – was 'clearly an incentive to violence'. However, Mahon hesitated to act

> if, by so doing, he might become a martyr when there appears to be a chance of his being discredited among his followers owing to his doubtful parentage.[92]

Finally, on 10 August, Duke decided it was time to act,[93] and Mahon issued instructions for de Valera's arrest on the 14th.[94] However, one of the detectives ordered to carry out the arrest was Éamonn 'Ned' Broy, a Sinn Féin sympathiser; he warned de Valera, who promptly disappeared.[95] Broy's superior, Superintendent Brien, had to report that 'no trace can be found' of their target.[96] Journalists started asking awkward questions at the Castle about whether a warrant had been issued.[97] More importantly,

Sir Horace Plunkett, chairman of the Irish Convention, warned that de Valera's arrest would lead the nationalist side to withdraw from that body.[98] In view of this, and of the unwanted publicity, Duke cancelled the attempted arrest.[99]

The vacillation of the authorities had handed another victory to Sinn Féin, and to de Valera. After this lucky escape, he ramped up his rhetoric even further, telling a feis in Tipperary how to break the Defence of the Realm Regulations: each man should carry a hurley wherever he went, and wear uniform. 'When every nationalist wore uniform all could not be put to gaol together'.[100] He told a meeting at Factory Cross, Co. Clare, on 4 October that 'the time for speech making was now past, and the hour for action arrived'. The following day at Inagh, Co. Clare, he said, 'Get all the arms you can – any kind of arms'.[101]

Mahon again pointed out that it was impossible to move against minor figures for drilling and wearing uniform if de Valera was not prosecuted; Duke, dithering once more, brought the question back to the War Cabinet.[102] He outlined a statement he intended to make in the House of Commons, including extracts from de Valera's speeches, adding that he would conclude that 'firm action was necessary and would be taken'. This would involve the immediate arrest of de Valera and between 50 and 100 others. The response was hesitant, with some ministers saying action should not be taken unless the government was prepared to see the policy through. And there were hints that Duke's colleagues were getting fed up with him, and with Irish problems.

> A view was expressed that the Irish question was so small a matter in relation to the vast problems with which the Government was confronted . . . that it might be undesirable to pay too much attention to it, particularly if it would involve this country in serious difficulties.

But Duke was given approval to arrest de Valera, and perhaps others, at a time of his own choosing.[103]

Thus fortified, Duke made his statement to the House of Commons, noting the dangers of the situation – which apparently came as a surprise to most of the English members. David Lloyd George, Prime Minister since the previous December, also weighed in, saying he had read de Valera's speeches.

> I say that they are calm, deliberate and, I might say, cold-blooded incitement to rebellion . . . That was not the speech of a violent,

excitable man. It was the case of a man of great ability with considerable influence going down to the country for the express purpose of stirring the people to rebellion against the authorities . . .[104]

However, the government was attacked by John Redmond, Joseph Devlin and other nationalists, who claimed that 'provocative' actions would derail the Irish Convention,[105] and Duke backed down. De Valera had escaped again – thanks to Redmond and Devlin – and was free to continue his quest for the leadership of advanced nationalism.

This was to come to a head at the Sinn Féin ard-fheis on 25 October, which in effect established a completely new party, owing little more than its name to Arthur Griffith's old organisation. There had been increasing tension between the moderate followers of Griffith – still wedded to non-violence and prepared to accept less than full independence if necessary – and those, such as Cathal Brugha, who were committed to the Republic, and to the use of violence to achieve it. Further complicating matters was Count Plunkett, still under the erroneous impression that he was a potential leader of the movement.

For the various factions to work together, two things had to be agreed: policy and leadership. In effect, the policy split came down to whether or not the movement should seek a republic. IRB members were obviously committed to doing so; so too were many non-IRB members who had fought in the Rising. This faction insisted they would not back down from the Proclamation. The 'old' Sinn Féin – headed by Griffith and including Seán Milroy and Darrell Figgis – opposed committing Sinn Féin to a republic, either from conviction or because they thought the people would not support it. Collision seemed inevitable.[106]

However, de Valera had a potential compromise formula, which he had tested at a public meeting in Rathfarnham a full month before the ard-fheis. He argued that, in order to have their case heard at the peace conference, they must proclaim Ireland a republic – which would be understood in America, France and Russia. But then, he suggested, 'once freedom was attained the Irish people could choose a Monarchy or a Republic'.[107] The confrontation came a fortnight before the ard-fheis, at a meeting in Cathal Brugha's house in Rathmines. There was

a hot dispute . . . A split would have been inevitable only for de Valera. When people got up and walked out he brought them back again. We remained until about one or two in the morning.[108]

The resulting agreement was signed by Brugha, Griffith and de Valera.[109] By agreeing to seek recognition of an Irish republic, but leaving the ultimate form of government for later decision, both sides could argue they had achieved something – though in reality it was a victory for the radicals.

Brokering this compromise was undoubtedly a significant achievement – all the more impressive given that de Valera had little practical experience of politics. Despite this acceptance of a Republican policy, the IRB was still suspicious, and tried to repeat its takeover of the Gaelic League in 1915 in order to ensure not just a Republican constitution for the new Sinn Féin but also a leadership 'which could be relied on to uphold it'.[110] Here de Valera's political nous came to the fore again. Both he and Cathal Brugha had left the IRB after the Rising, but in characteristically different manners. Brugha argued with the IRB and left with bad blood on both sides; de Valera politely requested to be relieved of his oath in August 1917, 'as he had conscientious scruples' and had 'never slept easily' since he took it. De Valera's resignation was accomplished without any ill-feeling and, in fact, Collins 'declared his belief that de Valera would never hurt the IRB'.[111] Although he regarded de Valera as *'distant,* strange, stand offish',[112] Collins was one of the first to suggest him for party leader,[113] and IRB men were instructed to get themselves selected as delegates to the Sinn Féin ard-fheis and vote for de Valera.[114] His name headed the 'ticket' to be voted for, handed out to Sinn Féin delegates who were members of the IRB by Collins. A rival list drawn up by Darrell Figgis was headed by Griffith.[115]

Behind the scenes, de Valera was actively canvassing for votes – not that he would have admitted it. He told Dr Kathleen Lynn and Helena Molony, trade union activists who had served with the Citizen Army during the Rising, that he was being proposed 'as a kind of compromise between Count Plunkett, Griffith and MacNeill.' According to Molony, he said that 'he himself was not anxious for it – he was very modest and retiring – but that that was the decision of the boys'.[116] Despite his 'modesty', he secured the promise of their votes.

But while everyone expected a contest for the leadership, Griffith was not convinced that he should fight to retain the presidency of the party he had founded. Griffith was aware of his own defects: he was shy, lacked the personal touch and was in any case happier concentrating on journalism.[117] When the party secretary, Páidín O'Keeffe, pressed him to fight for the presidency, Griffith replied, 'You know very well, Paddy, that I am not a leader'.[118] And if he was not to lead himself, there was really only one alternative. In the DBC café in O'Connell Street the two men had a frank talk. De Valera told him that his name was going to be put up as the unanimous selection of the Volunteers. He bluntly told Griffith:

> You shouldn't go forward. If there is a vote taken you will be beaten. You won't get the backing or the loyalty of the Volunteer section.

Griffith agreed 'that there was only one way unity could be preserved': by having de Valera as president.[119]

Queues began to gather outside the Mansion House in Dublin for the opening of the ard-fheis at six o'clock in the morning of 25 October – there were hundreds waiting at the door an hour later, with the crowds and traffic being marshalled by Volunteers in civilian clothes.[120] There were 1,700 delegates in the packed Round Room, representing more than a thousand Sinn Féin clubs throughout the country.[121] The young Waterford delegate Rosamund Jacob had been sent with clear instructions: to vote against any attempt to stick to Griffith's old Sinn Féin policy. Despite that, she was impressed by Griffith's opening speech.

> Very good, with his usual quiet restrained power and effect of saying less than he could, but you'd imagine from him that he and the old Sinn Féin crew had done everything, and no credit to Easter Week at all.[122]

Sitting beside her, Kathleen Clarke took a similar view, describing Griffith as attempting 'to rob the dead of the fruits of their honest labour', and feeling herself to be 'in a foreign element'.[123]

The most important business was the election of president. Plunkett withdrew 'in favour of Mr de Valera, the man who fought for us in Easter Week'.[124] Griffith did the same,

> to the astonishment of all, including his closest friends . . . The applause that broke out and lasted for some minutes at this wholly unexpected announcement reflected the assembly's relief at the solution and the removal of the severe tension.[125]

Griffith then paid a lengthy tribute to the coming man.

> Mr de Valera is twelve years younger than I am . . . He is a man whose sincerity and courage and determination you all know; but I know more

about him than that from recent experience. I know that he is a man of cool judgement, in whose judgement I have absolute confidence . . .[126]

While the radicals had secured the leader they wanted, things didn't go so well for them in the other elections. After being denounced from the floor, the competing tickets were strongly condemned by de Valera ('The motives were probably the best, but in beginning a new Ireland it will not be necessary to resort to such methods any more') and by Griffith. When the results of the voting were announced the following day, Griffith and Fr Michael O'Flanagan were elected vice-presidents of the party (Plunkett came a poor third); W. T. Cosgrave and Laurence Ginnell were honorary treasurers; and Austin Stack and Darrell Figgis were honorary secretaries. Of the 24 members of the Executive Council, MacNeill came first, with 888 votes, and Michael Collins scraped in with 340, in joint last place with Ernest Blythe.[127] Controlling less than 400 votes at the ard-fheis, the IRB still 'needed to conspire to acquire power'[128] – not that that would be a problem for Collins.

An inordinate amount of time over the two days of the ard-fheis was spent discussing two rival schemes for party organisation, one promoted by de Valera, the other by Brugha. The differences were trivial, but that didn't stop de Valera expounding the virtues of his version, at length, several times. One delegate remembered him 'jumping up every minute to set right somebody's erroneous idea of it'.[129] Father Pat Gaynor, who was elected to the Executive, said de Valera dominated the convention.

> On his feet at every turn to justify and insist on his own formula, and he had his way. I liked the leader who knew his own mind and was firm in upholding decisions . . .[130]

De Valera explained to the delegates that the reason his scheme was so complicated was that it would

> show the country that this is a democratic organisation run by the people themselves. The people themselves have power over this organisation and those they elect will not be able to machine them.[131]

If de Valera's rambling, complicated explanation was a foretaste of his style of party leadership, so was the result – he received practically unanimous backing from the loyal ard-fheis. Brugha's rival scheme was backed by only one other delegate, his future bitter rival, Michael Collins.

The proposed new constitution committed the party to 'make use of any and every means available to render impotent the power of England to hold Ireland in subjection by military force or otherwise'. Father O'Meehan of Kilbana pointed out that, as worded, the clause 'might cover anything from pitch and toss to manslaughter', and wanted to add the phrase 'which in the judgement of the National Council are deemed legitimate and effective'. But de Valera rejected his amendment, arguing that 'available means' meant 'justly available', and O'Meehan withdrew his amendment.[132]

The most dramatic moment of the ard-fheis centred on Eoin MacNeill. De Valera had insisted on having him on his platform in East Clare, and he continued to view him as useful. He told Robert Brennan not to forget that 'the clergy are with MacNeill and they are a powerful force'.[133] Just as the IRB needed MacNeill to launch the Volunteers, now de Valera needed him to put a respectable stamp on the new Sinn Féin.[134] But not everyone was convinced.

When the nominees for the Executive were announced, Constance Markievicz bitterly attacked MacNeill, invoking Connolly's claim that he had cut the ground from under them when they were going out to fight for Ireland. 'To put our lives in the hands of such a man is a dangerous thing,' she told them. Griffith strongly defended MacNeill. So did de Valera, who said that, while 'we may find fault perhaps with his judgement', he was convinced 'that there is no first-hand evidence that shows MacNeill acted otherwise than as a good Irishman'.[135] This was too much for Kathleen Clarke: 'my heart felt like bursting with indignation and rage'. While Griffith's support for MacNeill was to be expected, 'de Valera doing so was an outrage'.[136] She rose to speak, claiming that her husband told her that MacNeill had signed the Proclamation but later repudiated it, and that he had 'played a dishonourable part'. Once again de Valera intervened. 'I know from the statement of one of the men who died that John MacNeill did not sign the proclamation.'[137] From previous conversations, Kathleen Clarke knew he was talking about Thomas MacDonagh; later that evening, 'disgusted' at the proceedings, she noted that, even if MacDonagh had known what was going on, he would not have been free to tell anyone about it. 'As a matter of fact,' she wrote, 'de Valera knew just what any officer in the Irish Volunteers knew and no more'.[138]

Clarke's contribution had an effect. 'She did not speak at length but she shed tears and aroused the sympathy of the meeting.'[139] But she and Markievicz were not supported – the silence of the IRB faction being particularly conspicuous[140] – and de Valera's intervention was probably crucial. Some delegates may have felt sorry for MacNeill after his being 'so violently attacked . . . and decided to vote for him when the time for voting came'.[141]

De Valera began his presidential address by stressing that the new constitution committed Sinn Féin to securing international recognition of an independent Irish republic. This was the policy he had stood for in East Clare and the reason he had been elected to lead the party. He said his election was 'a monument to the brave dead and . . . proof that they were right'. He rejected criticisms of the Rising from

> the theologians of the *Irish Times* and the *Freeman* . . . with a pipe in their mouth and a glass of grog by their side, with their feet planked up on the mantelpiece in the Editorial Chair.

He said physical force could be used in certain circumstances: if they were sure it would succeed,

> resistance to the British Government in arms would not be merely a legitimate thing, but we would be a lot of cowards unworthy of our liberty if we refuse to take advantage of it.[142]

His rhetorical support for further violence was far stronger than is sometimes suggested.[143]

He went on to deal with his own compromise clause to the new constitution, allowing for a referendum on the future form of government once the Republic was recognised.

> There is no contemplation in it of having a Monarchy in which the Monarch would be of the House of Windsor . . . If there is a monarch in this land, he will be an Irish monarch.

He concluded by urging all to unite under the flag of the Irish Republic. 'We have nailed that Flag to the Mast; we shall never lower it.'[144]

There were mixed views of de Valera's Presidential address: Rising veteran Frank Shouldice thought it 'glorious',[145] while for Rosamund Jacob it was 'not half as good a speech as Griffith's the day before'.[146] The important thing was unity: Joseph McGuinness rejoiced that the newspapers had been deprived of the 'trouble they were looking for'.[147] But in Dublin Castle, Duke still expected that 'disagreements between the de Valera section and the Griffith and MacNeill section... will rapidly develop'.[148]

The day after the ard-fheis, a Volunteer Convention was held in Croke Park. De Valera presided, with delegates from all registered companies sitting around on the hay which filled part of the Pavillion; ranged behind de Valera were the other members of the interim Executive, including Brugha, Collins, Stack, Diarmuid Lynch, Michael Staines and Éamonn Duggan.[149]

Before the convention, Seán McGarry (now president of the IRB and secretary to the Volunteer Executive) had written to MacNeill seeking the return of any documents, property and money belonging to the Volunteers.

> I am also instructed to state that any statement which a member of the old committee might wish to make should be placed on the Irish Volunteer records.[150]

Feeling that a written statement would not suffice, MacNeill appealed to de Valera to be allowed attend the convention 'so that we may give and receive an account of our stewardship as well as the circumstances permit'.[151] Despite the fact that the existing constitution of the Volunteers gave them the right to attend, 'Mr de Valera flatly refused to have us admitted'.[152]

Seán Fitzgibbon, a member of the old Executive, and former vice-commandant of the 3rd Battalion, asked his successor in that position, Joseph O'Connor, to seek a hearing at the convention for himself and MacNeill. But de Valera argued that only a court of inquiry could get to the bottom of matters, and that this could lead to arguments and do more harm than good.[153] Given de Valera's spirited defence of MacNeill at the ard-fheis, his refusal to allow him even a hearing before the convention is striking. De Valera needed MacNeill in Sinn Féin; he did not need him in front of the IRB-dominated Volunteers. His decision was logical, if rather ruthless.

But while MacNeill was repudiated personally, his policy was not. The Volunteers rejected the notion of a small group being able to stage-manage a Rising, with de Valera prominent among those arguing for broad agreement before physical force was to be employed.[154] It was decided that a majority of the 19-member Executive (not just a majority of those attending a particular meeting) would be required before such matters as peace and war were decided.[155]

De Valera now combined leadership of Sinn Féin and the Volunteers. Although his position in the Volunteers was mainly symbolic, the military and the political sides of the movement were now in lockstep, the efforts of each supporting the other, and de Valera was the undisputed leader of advanced nationalism.

De Valera's twin elections by acclamation had come just four years after he sat as a non-entity in the crowd in the Rotunda Rink. Thanks to the Rising, to the execution of so many of its leaders, to the discrediting of others who had not taken part, and to his own thirst for responsibility, he was now a full-time politician, enabled by his annual salary of £500 as Sinn Féin president to forget his teaching career.[156] Father Pat Gaynor came to know him well and to like and admire him.

> I have heard, truly or falsely, that de Valera became very autocratic later in life, but in 1917–21 he was always courteous, always reasonable and calm in debate (though decisive in his own views), always a perfect gentleman.[157]

Above all he displayed dexterity in bringing the factions together. As Cathal Brugha said of him: 'Who else but Éamon de Valera could have kept Arthur Griffith and myself together?'[158]

Crucial to his rise was his 1916 record, and the sense that 'something heroic and noble in his behaviour had marked him out and had focused public attention on him'.[159] This assessment, by P. S. O'Hegarty, is notable because it was written by a man with little sympathy for the new leader. O'Hegarty also described him as being

> in those pre-American days . . . a slow-moving, painfully uncouth, massive, speaker, with a disarming habit of pouring forth as new dis-coveries things which had been for twenty years the commonplaces of separatist thought. His great value to the country was his honesty and his simplicity and his singlemindedness.[160]

But doubts remained about his ability to actually lead the movement, and the country. William O'Brien, the maverick nationalist MP, remarked to his colleague Tim Healy shortly after de Valera's accession that Sinn Féin 'have the game wholly in their hands if they could only develop a leader of capacity. Unluckily there is no such person on the horizon.'[161] Doubts were also expressed by someone much closer to the new leader, Kathleen Clarke.

> I hope de Valera will keep straight, at times I fear he is too easily influenced and he lacks experience, perhaps it is that he is young, he is a lovable character, light-hearted and boyish and he is getting enough adulation to turn an older and more experienced man's head. I wish I could feel more sure of him.[162]

Those doubts – and de Valera's leadership – were about to be put to the test.

CHAPTER 11

THE MOST EFFECTIVE MEANS AT OUR DISPOSAL

It is a question whether you would rather be killed in France or at home fighting for your country.

Éamon de Valera, April 1918[1]

I for one shall never whittle down the Irish demand.

Éamon de Valera, November 1918[2]

. . . de Valera and others of the more moderate views, are acting as a brake.

British Intelligence assessment, May 1919[3]

Now that he was in charge of Sinn Féin, de Valera set about 'tightening up' the organisation. He was in the head office every weekday, while weekends were devoted to speaking engagements throughout the country.[4] He was also anxious to get his own people in place, such as the Wexford journalist Bob Brennan. De Valera explained that he didn't want 'them' – Griffith and Darrell Figgis – to control Sinn Féin publicity; he wanted his own man in charge. When he wrote his first press release, Brennan discovered that de Valera's idea of control was to painstakingly correct it. 'I was to learn that he never saw a draft submitted by anybody but he must alter it.' Brennan eventually got around de Valera's pedantry and need for control by sending the material for publication without letting him see it.[5]

He was now indisputably a man of importance, as his constant police tail indicated. The DMP carefully noted his appearance.

6ft 1ins, slight active make, oval features, sallow complexion, long nose, clean shaven, brown hair, walks with a long stride. Dresses well in grey tweed suit, fawn overcoat and trilby hat. Wears pince-nez . . .[6]

His admirers gave less prosaic descriptions. 'He looked whiter than before and as thin as ever, but very nice. He has lovely curly hair.'[7]

In the wake of the ard-fheis some in authority wanted to take a tougher line with Sinn Féin. General Sir Bryan Mahon warned the Chief Secretary, Henry Duke, that 'present methods . . . will not stop drilling or wearing of uniform', and he called for the arrest and deportation of the leaders. 'Clemency has been given a good trial and without satisfactory results.' The Under-Secretary, William Byrne, backed him, warning that things were only going to get worse 'after the formal declaration of disloyalty' adopted by Sinn Féin at the ard-fheis. Duke, however, once again dodged the decision, pointing out that the Lord Lieutenant, the Attorney-General, the Solicitor-General and the Assistant Under-Secretary disagreed with Mahon and Byrne.[8]

De Valera had the ability to draw a crowd. There was 'intense excitement' about his visit to Tullamore;[9] his reception in Bantry created 'a strong sense of confidence in the Nationalist movement';[10] Liam Lynch expected 'a big demonstration' when de Valera came to Fermoy.[11] The meeting there also demonstrated de Valera's determination – an accident disabled his car in Ballyhooley, so he borrowed a bicycle and cycled the ten kilometres to Fermoy, with the 'strong detachment' of police who were following him tagging along behind.[12]

But Henry Duke assured his Cabinet colleagues that the 'outlook is less threatening' in Ireland than it had been a year, or even three months, before. He predicted a continued reduction in support for Sinn Féin – unless conscription was introduced.[13]

De Valera's first visit to the Redmondite stronghold of Waterford saw his public meeting proclaimed by the authorities due to the potential for violence between rival groups. The meeting was moved to Ballinaneegh,[14] where de Valera taunted John Redmond, the local MP, by drawing attention to his former supporters on the platform. 'These men would still be true to Mr Redmond if Mr Redmond were true to Ireland.' He stressed the importance of the Volunteers: 'without physical force backing, their words would be vain and empty talk'. But, he said, force would not necessarily be used, as 'no man, unless a fool, would fight for what he could get without fighting for'.[15]

At tea afterwards in a supporter's house, de Valera was 'hoarse' and 'evidently tired'; Rosamund Jacob took him to task for referring only to men and not to women in his speech; he tried to pass it off, wishing he always had someone to prompt him on this point; she tartly responded that he hardly required prompting at his stage of life.[16] De Valera remained traditional in his views on gender. When he found Una Brennan in her husband Bob's office in Sinn Féin headquarters, thinking her one of the women staff, he scolded her for being alone with a married man; she explained and he 'laughed heartily',[17] but it is noticeable that he immediately found fault with the woman, not the man, who after all was the one he knew to be married.

The next test of Sinn Féin's appeal – and the first since de Valera became leader – was in the South Armagh by-election. The Irish Party was strong locally and backed by the muscle of the AOH. John Dillon believed it was 'almost the most favourable seat for us in Ireland'.[18] As the campaign got under way, their candidate, Patrick Donnelly, warned that if Republicans tried to use aggressive tactics 'they would most assuredly be met by their own weapons'.[19] De Valera sent for reinforcements, and more than a hundred Volunteers were despatched from the Dublin Brigade to protect meetings.[20] The southerners were taken aback by the harsh sectarian reality of northern politics and by drunken loyalists from Belfast. 'The blasphemous, filthy epithets hurled at the Pope were particularly offensive to Catholic ears'.[21]

While Donnelly was a prominent local solicitor, Sinn Féin's candidate was Patrick McCartan, who suffered from two drawbacks: he was from Co. Tyrone, which might make him a local in Dublin eyes, but not to voters in Co. Armagh; and he was in the United States and unaware of his selection. Given the weakness of Republicanism in Co. Armagh, the Sinn Féin campaign was inevitably dominated by outsiders, and local people resented their sometimes high-handed actions – including the establishment of an election headquarters in Dundalk, outside the constituency.[22] It is debatable how many votes were won by Constance Markievicz's telling voters they wanted the kind of liberty 'won by the Bolsheviks in Russia',[23] and the mention of de Valera's name at an election meeting provoked a shout of 'We'll have no Spaniards.'[24]

As Seán MacEntee had discovered in conversations with him in Dartmoor Prison, de Valera had little clue about Ulster, and his attempts to appeal to its voters were somewhat clumsy. In notes written in the

Imperial Hotel in Dundalk he claimed that 'next to their own province all [Irishmen] love Ulster best'.[25] More significant were his pronouncements on unionism, which he described as 'a rock in the path' of nationalism.

> They must if necessary blast it out of their path . . . If the choice offered to them was the choice of Solomon they would reject it . . . The child was theirs; this was their land.[26]

Twelve months after the breakthrough in North Roscommon, Sinn Féin went down to ignominious defeat, winning only 1,305 votes to Donnelly's 2,324 (the Unionist candidate got 40, indicating large-scale tactical voting by the Protestant community).[27] De Valera tried to put a positive gloss on the result. He wrote to McCartan that South Armagh

> has not daunted us. Unionists and Redmondites are now together but we will beat them both. Sinn Féin is stronger than ever. So are the Volunteers.[28]

It is true that the election helped spread both the Volunteers and Sinn Féin into new territory, but the result had dented the party's aura of invincibility.[29]

De Valera attempted to mend his hand in Ulster with a 12-day organising trip, accompanied by MacEntee.[30] It was far from plain sailing. When a meeting in Raphoe, Co. Donegal, was threatened by gangs of Orangemen and Irish Party supporters, an urgent call was sent to Letterkenny for Volunteers. They arrived, armed with slash hooks, pick handles and lengths of lead piping. Their opponents quickly withdrew, but when the Volunteers made to follow de Valera stopped them: they were there to ensure free speech, not start unnecessary fights.[31] He drew a crowd of 2,800 in Derry, though the RIC claimed that 'no persons of any importance were present'.[32] It was probably around this time that, passing a small cottage in the countryside, de Valera wistfully told his travelling companion that he wished the campaign for independence were over so he could settle in such a house to study mathematics for the rest of his life.[33]

More by-election woes had meanwhile overtaken Sinn Féin. The death of John Redmond left a vacancy in Waterford; his son, Captain William Redmond, resigned his seat in East Tyrone to contest the by-election. Once again, the Irish Party had been lucky: the Redmond name meant a lot in Waterford, and the British army was also more popular than in other parts of Ireland, thanks to the booming local munitions industry.[34] Redmond's supporters were also quite prepared to use violence. 'No man could walk out singly carrying a Sinn Féin emblem without being almost beaten to death.'[35] De Valera discovered the truth of this observation while canvassing in the business district of Waterford. He refused a bodyguard, insisting he had no need of one in any part of the country. The local commander, better attuned to Waterford realities, sent four Volunteers after him, telling them to hang back so de Valera wouldn't realise he was being followed. Some minutes later, the staff in election headquarters 'saw Mr de Valera, his hat crushed and dirty, walking in a square formed by the four Volunteers. Behind him was a yelling mob of about one hundred men and women.'[36]

The Volunteers from around the country who helped with the by-election campaign were obviously vital. However, de Valera worried that some who were wanted by the authorities risked arrest. This came to a head on the eve of polling, when armed RIC men sealed off the Volunteer Headquarters in Thomas Street. As tension mounted, de Valera arrived, telling the men that, 'at times of excitement, the thing is to be calm'. Anxious to avoid a confrontation that could quickly get out of hand, given that some of the Volunteers were armed, he got the county inspector to withdraw his men, on the promise that the Volunteers would leave the city by the first train.[37]

De Valera's action probably prevented a confrontation and certainly prevented a number of arrests. His pacific approach was in stark contrast to his bellicose rhetoric. So were his private comments on his opponents: he told a small group of Sinn Féin canvassers that the Redmondites were not their enemies, as they 'really want the same as we do ourselves only they don't believe we can get it'.[38] Whatever about that, the Redmondites got the Waterford seat, winning by 1,242 votes to 764. The by-election in East Tyrone was quieter, but had the same result: defeat for Sinn Féin, 1,802 votes to 1,222.[39]

Sinn Féin could argue that these three by-elections were not representative – elections in Ulster were no guide to what would happen in the other provinces, and Waterford was far from typical either. This was proved in April when the Irish Party didn't contest the Tullamore by-election, allowing Patrick McCartan to be elected unopposed. But the fact remained that the Sinn Féin bubble, if not quite burst, had been deflated; the party that seemed impossible to beat had been beaten three times, and in fact had not won an election since de Valera assumed the presidency. But once again British intervention restored his fortunes.

The Irish Party had managed to prevent the extension of conscription to Ireland. Even Lloyd George admitted that conscription in Ireland could lead to a rupture with America, that only 160,000 men would be conscripted (and they would have to be rounded up at the point of a bayonet), and that their removal from Ireland would disrupt vital food production.[40] But all that changed on 21 March 1918, when the Germans launched their Spring Offensive on the Western Front. Bolstered by a million troops released from the Eastern Front after the Bolsheviks ended Russia's war, the Germans made major advances.

Suddenly, the difficulties of conscription in Ireland seemed less important than the need to plug the gaping holes in the Western Front, and it was clear that no more men could be squeezed out of the UK if Ireland wasn't included. So on 28 March the Cabinet agreed in principle to extend conscription to Ireland, along with the introduction of a form of home rule based on the report of the Irish Convention. This was despite the warnings of the inspector-general of the RIC, Joseph Byrne, of the army's commander in Ireland, Sir Bryan Mahon, and of the Chief Secretary, Henry Duke, who said, 'We might almost as well recruit Germans.'[41]

As the clamour rose in Britain for extending conscription to Ireland,[42] de Valera's speeches became increasingly inflammatory. On 6 April, at Edenderry, Co. Offaly, he said

> you are morally justified in shooting every one of an escort if conscription is enforced . . . It is a question whether you would rather be killed in France or at home fighting for your country.[43]

On 9 April, the Catholic Hierarchy publicly warned the government against introducing conscription, 'a policy so disastrous to the public interest and to all order, public or private'.[44] Duke once again warned his colleagues of the threat of resistance, but the Cabinet decided that the army could deal with it.[45] According to the Deputy Cabinet Secretary, Tom Jones, the discussion on this issue took only two minutes.[46] If it seems bizarre that such a vital decision – one that did more than anything to produce Sinn Féin's victory in 1918 – was taken so casually, it merely illustrates a truth about Anglo-Irish relations: those relations are far more important to Ireland than to Britain. Lloyd George 'was simply too busy with the war to accept the impossibility of conscripting Ireland'.[47] In the House of Commons, the Home Secretary, Sir George Cave, blithely said 'he was advised and believed that the application of the Bill to Ireland would yield a large number of men'.[48] Duke quickly disabused his colleagues, warning of a 'grave crisis'. He suggested two possible courses of action: immediate, rigorous coercion, with widespread arrests (which he considered 'impossible as a practical policy'); or the securing of a home-rule settlement in return for Ireland's co-operation in the war. If his colleagues decided on the former course, 'the Chief Secretary or other Minister to be entrusted with the task should be appointed without delay' – in other words, he would not implement such a policy himself.[49]

When the House of Commons passed the conscription bill, the Irish Party withdrew, returning to Ireland to lead the fight there – a tacit endorsement of Sinn Féin's abstention policy. It sought nationalist unity against the measure, and de Valera displayed considerable cunning in his preparation for meetings with the Irish Party. On Friday 12 April he went to Archbishop's House in Drumcondra to try to get Archbishop Walsh on side. Although Walsh was unavailable, de Valera persuaded his secretary, Michael Curran, of the need for a strong episcopal statement.[50]

Curran encouraged the Lord Mayor of Dublin, Laurence O'Neill, to convene at the Mansion House a meeting of the Irish Party, Sinn Féin, Labour and independents. It was arranged that O'Neill would telephone at lunchtime the following day to ask that a delegation from the conference be received at the Hierarchy's meeting in Maynooth. Finally, at nine o'clock on the morning of 18 April, de Valera called again to Drumcondra to clear with Walsh his proposed statement.[51]

At the Mansion House conference, chaired by O'Neill, de Valera and Griffith represented Sinn Féin; John Dillon (Redmond's successor) and Joseph Devlin the Irish Party; William O'Brien and Tim Healy the independents; and Tom Johnson, (the other) William O'Brien and Michael Egan were there for Labour. De Valera put forward his anti-conscription pledge.

> Denying the right of the British government to enforce compulsory service in the country, we pledge ourselves solemnly to one another to resist conscription by the most effective means at our disposal.

This wording he refused to change in any way, without telling the others that this was because he had already agreed it with Archbishop Walsh.[52] According to the independent MP William O'Brien, de Valera's

> transparent sincerity, his gentleness and equability captured the hearts of us all . . . Even the obstinacy (and it was sometimes trying) with

which he would defend a thesis . . . became tolerable enough when, with a boyish smile, he would say: 'You will bear with me, won't you? You know I am an old schoolmaster.'[53]

Once the wording was agreed, a delegation of de Valera, Dillon, Healy and O'Brien (Labour) was chosen to meet the bishops at Maynooth. The bishops agreed to issue their own statement, although at Cardinal Logue's insistence they added an important qualifier to the means of resistance to be used: these should be 'consonant with the law of God'.[54] But de Valera discovered that even the cardinal's commitment to peaceful means was not unlimited. When de Valera discussed the matter with him, Logue said, 'Well, now, Mr de Valera, when I talk about passive resistance, I don't mean we are to lie down and let people walk over us.'[55]

The Hierarchy agreed to order a special Mass in every Catholic church in the country the following Sunday, with an anti-conscription pledge to be taken outside afterwards, along with a collection to fund the campaign.[56] The crowd outside the Mansion House that mobbed the delegation returning from Maynooth agreed on who was most responsible: when de Valera emerged

> he was caught in the surging mass and hailed as Ireland's deliverer . . . Thousands followed De Valera to the depot where he was to take his train for Greystones.[57]

The MP William O'Brien thought de Valera was 'too good for this rough world of old Parliamentary hands, and will no doubt subside into a meek instrument of Dillon's'.[58] Nothing could have been further from the truth, and O'Brien's misjudgement perhaps shows how effective de Valera was at disguising both his abilities and his intentions.

De Valera, as president of the Volunteers, joined the GHQ Staff in a meeting to discuss the threat of conscription. They decided that Volunteers should take all precautions to avoid arrest – including avoiding confrontations that might lead to violence – unless there was an attempt to seize arms, in which case they were authorised to use them. If arrested they were to be defiant.[59]

The British policy was an abject failure. Edward Shortt, a Liberal, had replaced Duke as Chief Secretary, but the real power lay with the new Lord Lieutenant, Lord French. Though born in England, he was of Irish descent, wrongly believing this gave him an insight into Irish thinking. He planned to subdue resistance to conscription with air power, which 'ought to put the fear of God into these playful young Sinn Féiners'.[60] By June, French had 100,000 troops tied down in Ireland (up from 25,000 in March), conscription had not been introduced, and the number of volunteer recruits was tiny: the government launched an appeal in June for 50,000 volunteers by October, but got only a fifth of that target.[61]

Dillon bitterly noted that Lloyd George threatened conscription

> hot-foot on our three successive victories over S.F. at the last three elections . . . It is hard to escape from the conviction that he deliberately adopted the policy of destroying the constitutional party in Ireland . . .[62]

The change could be seen in a by-election in East Cavan, a constituency the Irish Party considered eminently winnable: on 20 June, Arthur Griffith won the seat by 3,785 votes to 2,581. If the tide had been turning against Sinn Féin in the previous few months, it had now turned back. Apart from conscription, Griffith's campaign benefited greatly from another British initiative, which de Valera considered decisive. 'Whether Griffith would have won Cavan was very doubtful before he was arrested in the German plot'.[63]

On 9 May 1918 the Cabinet had decided that, before proceeding with either conscription or home rule, it would have to 'restore respect for government, enforce the law and, above all, put down with a stern hand the Irish-German conspiracy which appears to be widespread in Ireland'.[64] The belief in a 'German plot' was partly prompted by the rhetoric of Sinn Féin leaders, and partly by the arrest of a member of Roger Casement's Irish Brigade, who was landed on the coast of Co. Clare by a German submarine.[65] In fact, de Valera had contradicted suggestions that an independent Ireland would allow Germany to use its ports against Britain in an interview with the *Christian Science Monitor*.

> If England took away her troops and our independence were acknowledged, we would fight to the last man to maintain that independence. It is not a change of masters we want, though I do not know that the change would be for the worse.[66]

There was plenty of warning of what was coming. Ned Broy, a Republican sympathiser within the DMP's detective division, passed to his contacts a list of those to be arrested, as well as the exact day of the swoop.[67] Seán T. O'Kelly had been separately warned by another Dublin Castle detective. He personally informed de Valera, who said he was sick and tired of getting such warnings.[68] This supports the view that de Valera's arrest was due to carelessness. However, others have suggested that the party leadership allowed themselves to be arrested because it would generate useful propaganda.[69] As Liam de Róiste in Cork noted:

> As a political measure, it is excellent – for Sinn Féin: a fool's act for the British Government, as everyone knows it is based on a lie.[70]

As de Valera left Harcourt Street Train Station for his home in Greystones, DMP detectives kept watch and alerted the RIC that he was on his way.[71] He was offered a further chance to escape when, at Bray, the train driver warned him that two detectives were a couple of carriages behind. The driver offered to slow the train on the approach to Greystones so de Valera could jump off. He declined and was arrested on the platform.[72] He had been at liberty for only 11 months.

Michael Collins was later critical of de Valera, both for allowing himself to be arrested and for carrying documents that were used against him. 'He should not keep that blasted memorandum on organisation in his pocket'.[73] But Collins prospered in the absence of de Valera and other leading figures, with the help of another fugitive from arrest, Harry Boland. Between them they very capably took the reins of the Sinn Féin organisation.

The RIC delivered de Valera to Dún Laoghaire, where he was put on a British ship along with those arrested by the DMP. The prisoners' book reads like a who's who of the revolutionary movement. Richard Hayes, Joe McGrath, Tom Hunter, Arthur Griffith, Joe McGuinness, Darrell Figgis, W. T. Cosgrave, Constance Markievicz and Count Plunkett are among the names.[74] The prisoners were brought to Gloucester Prison, with smaller parties then being sent to Usk in Wales and to Lincoln, with de Valera in the latter group.

The War Cabinet now began to consider how they could justify the arrests to the public. A meeting on 22 May was not terribly reassuring. Shortt outlined the evidence, which consisted largely of speeches by de Valera and other leaders, dating as far back as the previous October. There was evidence from informers, he claimed, that Figgis and Stack were communicating with German submarines through fishermen on the west coast; and there were documents found on de Valera 'dealing with general organisation and the arrangements for the rising'. General Jan Smuts of the War Cabinet pointed out that this evidence was considerably weaker than the published statement claiming that there was proof of a German plot. Lord Curzon said if the evidence included speeches that were a year old the government might be asked why it had waited so long before arresting those responsible. Lloyd George brushed this aside, saying the government had 'taken the risks in the interests of conciliation'. It was agreed that the 'evidence' justified the arrests, but that it would require 'most careful presentation to the public'.[75]

The following day the War Cabinet approved a lengthy public statement purporting to prove links between Germany and Sinn Féin. This statement leaned heavily on the pre-1916 contacts between Berlin and the organisers of the Rising. Evidence of continuing contacts in the post-Rising period, it said, could only be summarised, as giving full details could endanger the sources of the information. Great stress was laid on captured documents. 'According to documents found on his person, de Valera had worked out in great detail the constitution of his rebel army, and hoped to be able to muster 500,000 trained men.'[76] This exciting-sounding document, hand-written by de Valera, was titled 'Memorandum on Irish Army organisation' and went into great – indeed, excruciating – detail on how a future independent Ireland could defend itself, and on how its army should be organised, trained and funded.[77] The key word is 'future': the document had absolutely nothing to do with another Rising, as the War Cabinet could have found out by consulting the intelligence officer of Irish Command. Major Ivon Price concluded that it related to an independent Ireland. 'I do not think that it in any way relates to any army which he hoped at present to raise to assist the Germans.'[78] Admitting this, of course, would have been decidedly embarrassing, so the expert's opinion was allowed to gather dust.[79]

In the wake of the arrests, Tim Healy and his wife called on Sinéad de Valera in Greystones. He thought her

a lovely woman . . . very pious too. She said sadly 'up to this I prayed for both sides in the War, but . . .' They have 5 small bairns and soon may have six, I think.[80]

Sinéad was at the time six months pregnant; her second daughter, Emer, would be born on 15 August, the second of their children to be born while de Valera was in prison. Sinéad coped admirably with the birth and with six small children. From prison, de Valera replied to a letter saying his family was well: 'It is very reassuring . . . Women suffer so much uncomplainingly. What agonies women are enduring today . . .'[81] Two months later, Sinéad's suffering was intensified as one by one the children (and the maid) succumbed to flu, the deadly epidemic which killed more people worldwide than the First World War, including more than 20,000 in Ireland.[82] Sinéad nursed them all with no medical help, as doctors and nurses were unavailable.[83]

As internees, rather than convicts, the prisoners in Lincoln enjoyed a significantly more relaxed regime than in Lewes or Dartmoor. The prisoners pooled their food parcels for an extra meal at 8 in the evening, as Terence MacSwiney explained.

> We have a sort of communistic life and everything is common property . . . All of the fellows are interested in something or other. Irish classes are of course the rule. There is also a Spanish Class . . . For amusement there is hand ball and rounders.[84]

De Valera was not short of little luxuries either, managing to get himself both a typewriter and a gramophone for his cell.[85]

Outside, preparations for the election continued. The Standing Committee approved de Valera's selection as a candidate in East Clare, as well as in South Down and the Falls division of Belfast, the constituency of Joseph Devlin.[86] His name was later withdrawn from Down after a pact in the north was reached with the Irish Party,[87] but he was also put forward in the Mayo constituency of John Dillon. In a message to the Standing Committee, de Valera said the prisoners believed 'that it is no slave status that Irish heroes have fought and died for but the securing for their beloved country her rightful place in the family of Nations'.[88] In handwritten notes from this time he wrote that 'I for one shall never whittle down the Irish demand . . . During my period of popularity be it long or short, I shall always endeavour that I may be the mouthpiece of truth and justice and liberty'.[89] Prison certainly hadn't dented his self-belief.

The Sinn Féin election machine was being put into operation by Dan McCarthy and James O'Mara, a successful businessman and former Irish Party MP. Each constituency had its own director of elections, who reported directly to O'Mara; the constituency director then appointed sub-directors to look after finance, organisation, canvassing, publicity and transport.

> The responsibility was placed on an individual and the old vexatious committee system, with its divided responsibility and endless talk, was eliminated.[90]

In an apparent attempt to dampen Griffithite enthusiasm for boycotting Westminster, de Valera wrote to O'Mara: 'Try to get the election issue kept close to the real point – abstention is only a corollary.'[91]

De Valera was clearly determined to make complete independence the sole election issue. But how far did he succeed? What did the people who voted for Sinn Féin in 1918 think they were voting for? And did their vote imply support for an armed campaign? It is of course impossible to be sure, but the interpretation of the 1918 electoral mandate would be of considerable importance in future arguments over the War of Independence and the Treaty. Even Mary MacSwiney was later to admit that the result in 1918 'was rather a vote against the [Irish] Party than for a Republic definitely'.[92] After the election Father Michael O'Flanagan said, 'The people have voted Sinn Féin. What we have to do now is to explain to them what Sinn Féin is.'[93] The 'Republic' was certainly used by many as shorthand for a rather vaguely defined independence – hence the commitment in the Sinn Féin constitution that the final form of government would be decided after independence.

De Valera frequently adverted to the possibility of violence if it could be effective or if there was no other route to independence. The manifesto committed the party to using 'any and every means available to render impotent the power of England to hold Ireland in subjection by military force or otherwise'. Ronan Fanning considers that 'this explicit threat of physical force reflected the IRB's influence, which the imprisoned de Valera was unable to counteract'.[94] However, the phrase was lifted directly from clause 3 of the Sinn Féin constitution adopted the previous year, which de Valera had defended against suggested amendment.

With the vote now given to all men over 21, and to women over 30 who were householders or married to householders, the electorate was vastly expanded, from 698,000 to 1.9 million. It was eight years since the last election, so only an estimated 360,000 had ever voted before, giving far more scope for a new party to make inroads.[95] Labour's decision to stand aside also helped: while Labour leaders had agreed a pact with Sinn Féin that would allow them to run a number of candidates unopposed, they came to the conclusion that the few seats they were likely to win were not worth the risk of alienating Protestant workers in the north.[96]

Sinn Féin won 73 seats (five candidates were elected in two constituencies, leaving the number of MPs at 68), Unionists won 26, and the once-mighty Irish Party was reduced to only six seats. Four in the north were uncontested by Sinn Féin as the result of a nationalist pact to prevent a split vote. Only Joseph Devlin in Belfast Falls and Captain

William Redmond in Waterford City defeated Sinn Féin opponents. The Irish Party's collapse was undoubtedly magnified by the 'first past the post' electoral system: it won 21.7 per cent of the vote throughout the country, compared with 46.9 for Sinn Féin and 25.3 for Unionists.[97] But these figures underestimate support for Sinn Féin, which won 25 seats without a contest; these were presumably abandoned by the Irish Party because Sinn Féin support was higher than average there.[98] In the six counties of what was to become Northern Ireland, Sinn Féin won three seats, the Irish Party four – and Unionists 22. This awkward prefiguring of partition was simply ignored by de Valera in his later references to Sinn Féin's triumph in the country as a whole.[99]

In Britain, meanwhile, Lloyd George led his coalition to a sweeping victory. But he was now more than ever the prisoner of the Conservatives, and to allay their suspicions of his approach to Ireland he had been forced to include in the manifesto a commitment to the exclusion of the six north-eastern counties from a future home-rule settlement.[100]

The Irish Party's decision not to contest East Clare was sensible: having won the by-election on the old register, there was no chance of de Valera losing it on the new one. But the decision allowed de Valera's supporters there to move *en masse* to East Mayo to support his campaign against John Dillon.[101] On the eve of polling, Dillon told his son James never to expect gratitude in politics. 'I have just yesterday returned the last evicted tenant in this area to his holding, but tomorrow he and many others in this county whom I have helped will vote to end my political career.'[102] He was routed, losing by 4,514 to de Valera's 8,875.[103] Proving once again that the north was different, Joseph Devlin more than reversed that margin in Belfast Falls, defeating de Valera 8,438 to 3,045.

Of course, while all this was happening, de Valera was still stuck in Lincoln Prison. But his thoughts increasingly turned to ways of getting out. Towards the end of 1918 he read of plans by Sir Horace Plunkett, chairman of the Irish Convention, to go to the United States on a propaganda visit. Such a visit would see Plunkett pressing the case for dominion home rule.

> It was tantalising to be in within prison walls when there was work to be done to inform American opinion aright as to the true state of Irish feeling. I made up my mind to try to escape . . .[104]

At about this time he told his mother of one of the ways in which he was passing his time behind bars.

I know you will be glad that I have served all our masses here. I feel like a little boy again and I pray that my childish faith may ever remain with me.[105]

If his new career as an altar boy helped his faith, it also helped his escape plans. The prison chaplain was rather careless with his keys, which allowed de Valera to take a wax impression of the master key for all the doors in the prison. Now all he needed was someone to make a replica for him.[106]

A remembered music-hall performance of a comedian pretending to be drunk provided inspiration. A Christmas card was sent to Seán McGarry's wife, showing an inebriated McGarry holding a large key corresponding to the wax impression of the master key, with the slogan *1917: He can't get in!* along with a picture of him in his cell, with a large keyhole, again with the exact dimensions of the locks in Lincoln, with the caption *1918: He can't get out!*[107]

Once the meaning was deciphered in Dublin, efforts were made to spring the Chief. A number of attempts were made to smuggle a key to him inside a cake, but none worked, so finally a cake was sent with a blank key. A fellow prisoner, Peter de Loughrey, a locksmith, then managed to fashion a key that opened every door in the prison. For de Loughrey the process was

> trying and at times exasperating. I had to be as noiseless as I could . . . With the file and two stout pen-knives I made a key. It wasn't exactly artistic.[108]

De Loughrey's role is instructive: his was in the end the most vital part of the operation. And yet he is not mentioned in de Valera's official biography.[109] The approved version of the story highlighted de Valera's ingenuity in securing an impression of the key, and in designing the cartoon Christmas card, and in devising various codes to communicate with those outside: he escaped, according to the faithful Dorothy Macardle, 'by means of a plan which he had long been preparing'.[110] But all his ingenuity would have come to nothing if de Loughrey hadn't been able to make the final key.

The whole escape was, of course, for propaganda purposes: de Valera later admitted that his main fear was that the government might decide to release him before he could escape.[111] There was some worry when, on 21 January 1919, four prisoners – Joe McGrath, Frank Shouldice, Barney

Mellows and George Geraghty – managed to escape from Usk Prison in Wales. Those planning de Valera's escape were furious, fearing it might lead the authorities to tighten security,[112] but in fact the governor of Lincoln Prison took no action after Usk.[113]

On the night of 3 February, Michael Collins and Harry Boland waited outside Lincoln Prison for de Valera to appear. He had with him the president of the IRB, Seán McGarry, and the Sinn Féin veteran Seán Milroy. As Peter Hart has noted, 'even in his prison breaks, de Valera made sure he brought his left and right wings along with him.'[114] A relay of taxis took the fugitives to Manchester.

And then the rumours began to pour in: he was spotted in a Catholic church in Scotland;[115] he was on a train in France, dressed as a priest;[116] he was on his way to Spain;[117] he was even reported to be dead.[118] In a forerunner of the popular Where's Wally? puzzles of later years, *The Shamrock* magazine invited readers to find de Valera amidst the squiggles on a map of the British Isles and France.[119] In fact, de Valera spent a fortnight in various houses in Manchester. On the Friday after his escape, Cathal Brugha came to see him. While de Valera's official biography implies that Brugha was there to update him on what had been happening in Ireland in his absence,[120] he in fact went to Manchester to make sure de Valera came back to Ireland rather than going directly to America, as he wished.[121]

Once the manhunt had subsided a week later, he was brought to Liverpool and smuggled aboard a ship, arriving back in Dublin at 1 a.m. on 20 February.[122]

In de Valera's absence, two important events had taken place on the same day that illustrated the tension between peaceful and violent tendencies in Ireland. On 21 January 1919 the Sinn Féin MPs elected in December who weren't in prison assembled in the Mansion House as Dáil Éireann. Cathal Brugha was elected chairperson, and then the deputies adopted a constitution for the Dáil; a Declaration of Independence; a Message to the Free Nations of the World; and a Democratic Programme (a sop to the Labour Party in recognition of its decision to stand aside in the general election). A committee of experts on Irish established to decide the proper names for the new body, its committees and its principal officers agreed the correct translation of the word 'republic', rejecting Collins's suggestion of 'poblacht' in favour of 'saor-stát'.[123]

De Valera, Count Plunkett and Arthur Griffith were appointed delegates to the Paris Peace Conference. The following day Brugha was elected temporary President of the Dáil Ministry (government), and he appointed four ministers: Eoin MacNeill in Finance, Michael Collins in Home Affairs, Count Plunkett in Foreign Affairs and Richard Mulcahy (chief of staff of the Volunteers) in National Defence.[124] All of this was in accordance with the manifesto put before the people in the previous month's election. What had happened earlier that day in Co. Tipperary was not.

The shooting of two policemen during the robbery of gelignite at Soloheadbeg is often seen as the start of the War of Independence. The action was on a small scale and locally driven, not being sanctioned by Volunteer GHQ. It was therefore like many other operations up to the Truce in 1921. However, it did not signal the beginning of open hostilities: its significance was only apparent with hindsight. The leaders of the ambush – Seán Treacy, Dan Breen and Séamus Robinson – had decided to take action because they were worried that the political side of the movement was overshadowing the military: 'we wanted to start a war, so we intended to kill some of the police'.[125] In some people's minds, Soloheadbeg would assume an importance equal to or greater than that of the meeting of the first Dáil; and Constables James McDonnell and Patrick O'Connell would be forgotten by history, as Breen, Treacy and Robinson were lauded.[126] Mulcahy took a different view: 'the Soloheadbeg incident was as near murder as anything that had taken place during that time'.[127]

On de Valera's return to Ireland his first hiding-place was in the home of his friend Dr Robert Farnan in Merrion Square, where he gave his first interview since his escape, to Ralph Couch of the *United Press*. Fearing misquotation, and perhaps nervous of his ability to express his thoughts verbally, he insisted on writing out his answer to Couch's question, a practice he would follow for years to come. He stressed the importance of the principles set out by Woodrow Wilson, and of Ireland's appeal to the peace conference.

> We ask the world to listen and to judge between Ireland and England . . . If Ireland's claim is still flouted . . . she must only find refuge once more in her own indomitable spirit . . . If England wants still to rule here she must do so with a never sheathed sword.

This last sentiment led to such headlines as 'Violence is the only alternative'. In a statement Sinn Féin insisted de Valera was responsible only for his own words, not for the interpretation given to them by newspapers.[128]

While Merrion Square was convenient for meeting journalists, it was not considered safe. Archbishop Walsh's secretary, Michael Curran, agreed to hide de Valera in the grounds of the Archbishop's House in Drumcondra, provided that Walsh could be kept out of it. A room at the Gate Lodge in Drumcondra Road was prepared, and on 24 February, de Valera arrived. He spent his days working on a document, 'Ireland's claim to independence', that was to be submitted to the Paris Peace Conference. After dark he walked the grounds with Curran, who was under the impression that de Valera's departure to America was imminent – he had overheard him asking Harry Boland to get him a fountain pen for the voyage.[129] He left Drumcondra on 3 March and by the 11th was in Liverpool awaiting passage to America.[130] It is not clear if he had managed to see his wife or family in the interim, but in any event the transatlantic trip was postponed, because of the release of all the German Plot prisoners.

Even the bellicose Lord French had come to the conclusion early in February 1919 that the time had come to release them. In a memorandum for the Cabinet on 7 February, four days after de Valera's escape from Lincoln Prison, French pointed out that their internment had been justified by the threat of a German invasion – a justification that obviously no longer existed. He believed that moderates within Sinn Féin were being driven to more extreme positions by their continued detention, and that the shooting of the RIC men at Soloheadbeg was due to 'the withdrawal of de Valera from his position of responsibility'.[131]

His suggestion was rejected, but a month later Pierce McCan, MP for East Tipperary, died of influenza in Gloucester Prison. Fearing further deaths, the new Chief Secretary, Ian McPherson, announced that all interned prisoners would now be released. Some escapees took the general amnesty as a signal that it was safe to come out in public. The four men who escaped from Usk, as well as McGarry and Milroy, attended a service in the Pro-Cathedral in Dublin in memory of McCan.[132] De Valera was more cautious, even avoiding the funeral of his father-in-law, Laurence Flanagan, in mid-March.[133] In reality he was perfectly safe. In April, replying to a parliamentary question, the Home Secretary confirmed that 'it is not proposed to take any steps for his re-arrest'.[134]

Just as his escape from Lincoln had been a propaganda coup, Collins wanted to make de Valera's return to Dublin a public spectacle. He organised a 'national welcome' for 26 March, with the Lord Mayor, Laurence O'Neill, to 'receive him at the gates of the City and . . . escort him to the Mansion House, where he will deliver a message to the Irish people'.[135] The location for the planned reception, Mount Street Bridge, was highly symbolic – and highly offensive to the British. So was the reception by the Lord Mayor, usually reserved for royalty. The Chief Secretary severely criticised O'Neill for planning 'to receive, as His Majesty alone should be received . . . a man who claims unlawfully to be the President of an Irish Republic'.[136] The Cabinet agreed to a request from Dublin Castle to ban the reception.[137]

De Valera now faced the choice of going ahead and risking bloodshed or backing down and risking humiliation. Some, like P. S. O'Hegarty, felt that the latter course was 'clearly impossible' and that a withdrawal 'would be as fatal to the morale, and I believe to the success, of Sinn Féin as was the Clontarf withdrawal to O'Connell's Repeal Movement.'[138] However, when Collins argued a similar case before the Sinn Féin Executive, he found himself 'in a practical minority of one'. He too cited the example of Daniel O'Connell's decision in 1843 to cancel a monster meeting after it was banned by the British. 'We are having our Clontarf today. It may not be as bad but it is bad and very bad.' He laid the blame squarely at de Valera's door. 'The chief actor was very firm on the withdrawal'.[139] De Valera felt that 'an orgy of blood under the pretext of quelling a riot' would suit British purposes.[140]

With bloodshed avoided, De Valera now felt safe to appear in public, meeting the Lord Mayor in the Mansion House the next day and speaking to reporters (though saying nothing of substance).[141] That afternoon he went home to his family in Greystones, his arrival being noted by neighbours and reported to the RIC sergeant.[142] He was driven home by Robert Brennan and Cathal Brugha, despite his protests that he could take the train. According to Brennan, this was

> another trait of Dev's which then, and later, irritated his colleagues very much. It was his Spartan hatred of spending a penny of public money needlessly.[143]

At about this time de Valera had a revealing conversation with Mulcahy, in which de Valera informed him, 'You are a young man now going in for politics. I'll give you two pieces of advice, study economics and read *The Prince*.'[144] Mulcahy, always ready to see the worst in de Valera, would later blame him for introducing Machiavellianism into Ireland, contrasting it with the Christian faith he felt informed Griffith's world view.

> What I call the de Valera spirit . . . is based on a conception of man's nature that . . . for purposes of seeking power . . . tangles men up by trickery and deception . . . Untold damage has been caused politically and economically to the country by whatever philosophy of this particular kind dominated de Valera.[145]

At the beginning of April the Dáil met in private session in the Oak Room of the Mansion House over three days. Brugha resigned as Príomh-Aire (Prime Minister), to be replaced by de Valera (who was referred to in the minutes as both Príomh-Aire and as President of the Dáil); salaries were set at £600 for the President and £350 for ministers. The Ministry was expanded to a maximum of nine members, and de Valera appointed Griffith (Home Affairs), Brugha (Defence), Collins (Finance), Plunkett (Foreign Affairs), Markievicz (Labour), MacNeill (Industry) and Cosgrave (Local Government). Three more 'heads of department' were appointed: Laurence Ginnell (Propaganda), Robert Barton (Agriculture) and Ernest Blythe (Trade and Commerce).[146] This selection – wider and more balanced than the Brugha Ministry – showed the shifting power within the movement. With MacNeill demoted to a sinecure, Collins moved into the role that would make his name. It also included, in Markievicz, the first woman government minister in western Europe.[147]

On 8 and 9 April 1919 an extraordinary Sinn Féin ard-fheis was held in the Mansion House. After thanking delegates for their support, de Valera asked Father Michael O'Flanagan to take the chair so that he, de Valera, could contribute to the discussion on proposed changes to the party constitution.[148] This should have come as a warning to those familiar with the party president's style. Sure enough, in the words of the *Daily Mail*, he 'made a speech every few minutes . . . on the principle that "explanation saved discussion"'.[149] The constitutional changes were designed to make a clear distinction between Sinn Féin and the Dáil, to ensure that the party could not dictate to the assembly, and that prominent members of the assembly could not dominate the party organisation. No member of the Ministry (except the President and the Minister for Home Affairs) was to be allowed serve on the Sinn Féin Standing Committee, only a third of whose members could be TDs.[150]

In his presidential address to the ard-fheis, de Valera stressed the need for Woodrow Wilson to deliver on the principles he had laid out during the war; if he did so, Ireland's desire for independence would be recognised. But Ireland would stand by those principles even if Wilson did not. De Valera said he was 'very near to being an American himself,' and if he had gone to America he 'would have gone not to the Irish people, but to the Americans themselves.' He then said he would never renounce the Irish Volunteers, 'their last reserve', but stated that they were a national force at the disposal of the government of the Republic. 'They will obey that Government, and do exactly as that Government demands'[151] – a very doubtful claim, as Soloheadbeg had already demonstrated.

The following day the Dáil met in public session, with de Valera stating in brief their programme: an appeal to the Paris Peace Conference, envoys to other countries, non-cooperation with English law, and the raising of a loan, £250,000 at home and the same amount abroad. Interestingly, given his comments the previous day, he said that Brugha, as Minister for Defence, 'is, of course, *in close association* with the voluntary military forces which are the foundation of the National Army'.[152] One might wonder who exactly was in charge in that relationship. Brugha certainly wondered, because in August he persuaded the members of the Dáil that they, along with all Volunteers, should swear an oath to the Irish Republic and to the Dáil, arguing that this was necessary to 'regularise the situation': under their existing constitution the Volunteers owed loyalty to their own Executive.[153]

De Valera's most significant contribution to the April session of the Dáil was his proposal that members of the police forces – the RIC and DMP – should be

> ostracised socially by the people of Ireland . . . The people of Ireland ought not to fraternise, as they often do, with the forces which are the main instruments in keeping them in subjection . . . They are the eyes and ears of the enemy.

He accused the police of 'brutal treason against their own people', adding that they 'must not be tolerated socially as if they were clean healthy members of our organised life'. His motion was passed unanimously.[154] Many policemen resigned as a result of this boycott.[155] It also made it easier for them to become targets of violence in the coming months. De Valera attributed his incendiary statement to recent police behaviour; perhaps, even unconsciously, it had its roots in the country roads around Bruree, where he had evaded RIC patrols in his youth.

But if there were signs of de Valera's militancy, there were signs too of moderation. Replying to a question from Alderman Tom Kelly about social policy, de Valera made it clear that he had no intention of pursuing the radical reorganisation of society suggested by the Democratic Programme adopted while he was still in Lincoln. Such matters must await the removal of the foreign occupier. A motion by the Sligo deputy Alec McCabe, seconded by Markievicz, committing the Dáil 'to a fair and full redistribution of the vacant lands and ranches of Ireland among the uneconomic holders and landless men', was withdrawn after discussion and referred to a committee instead.[156] The British certainly seemed convinced that de Valera was a moderating influence. Basil Thomson, the Home Office Director of Intelligence, believed that 'while some members of the Sinn Féin Executive are urging a policy of violence, de Valera and others of the more moderate views are acting as a brake'.[157]

While the spectre of renewed violence remained in the background, Sinn Féin trumpeted the possibilities of reaching independence through Paris. De Valera employed his usual painstaking approach to drafting the submission. Collins observed that 'the damned Peace Conference will be over before he's satisfied'.[158] The strategy at the peace conference seemed of the moment, as new states were being established throughout Europe. But these were emerging from the ruins of the collapsed empires – not from the territory of the victorious Allies. French President Clemenceau put it bluntly: intervention in the affairs of the Allies 'seems to me a question which the present Peace Conference can in no way consider under any circumstances whatever'.[159]

But de Valera staked his hopes on the attitude of President Wilson. A delegation of prominent Irish-Americans, the American Commission on Irish Independence, followed Wilson to Paris. Lloyd George was persuaded to give the Commission permission to go to Ireland, and he seemed open to allowing the Irish delegation of de Valera, Griffith and Plunkett to travel to Paris (though not to address the conference). However, this all changed when the American Commission members made a series of provocative Republican statements while in Ireland. Lloyd George and Wilson were happy to use it as an excuse to drop the Irish issue.[160]

De Valera toyed with the idea of going to Paris himself, but was advised by Seán T. O'Kelly and George Gavan Duffy, Republican envoys to Paris, that there was no point, as he would not be allowed appear before the peace conference.

> Our American friends are satisfied the fight must be transferred to the United States . . . We are of opinion that it would be useful if you could go to the States . . .[161]

American Commission member Michael J. Ryan, a Philadelphia banker, had told de Valera that if he wanted a loan raised in the United States he would have to go there himself to raise it.[162]

On 1 June – Sinéad's birthday[163] – after word came through that passage had been arranged, he left their home in Greystones. He was observed by the DMP boarding the mail boat, having bought a return ticket to Manchester.[164] In fact, he was heading for the land of his birth; he would not return for 18 months.

CHAPTER 12

REACHING FOR THE STARS

We are reaching for the stars in the hope of obtaining the mountain tops.

Éamon de Valera, 1919[1]

I spend most of my time shaking hands. I'll have the biceps of a blacksmith before I'm finished.

Éamon de Valera, 1919[2]

His head is turned to a greater extent than any man I have met.

John Devoy, 1920[3]

On 16 May 1919 Harry Boland, envoy of the government of the Irish Republic and senior figure in the IRB, arrived in New York after 12 days 'sweating over a coal shovel' in a ship's engine room.[4] Boland – 'a pleasant looking young man with black hair and a brick red face and a very cheerful and frequent grin'[5] – immediately got to work on his appointed task of bringing the argumentative Irish-American factions together and getting them to send urgently needed money to Ireland. As he explained in a letter to de Valera in Dublin, he had 'a *very very* stiff fight to get any money for home . . . I applied "the oil can" and got the disputants together'.[6] Boland's ability to get on with people made him an ideal choice for the job of smoothing over difficulties with his 'oil can' charm. But his time as an independent envoy came to a sudden stop after less than a month. On 12 June, to his consternation, he received a handwritten note from de Valera, announcing his own arrival in New York: 'Rather unexpected this! Will tell you idea when we meet.'[7]

De Valera's own transatlantic journey had begun in Liverpool, where he was kitted out in sailor's gear by Neil Kerr, the local IRB 'centre' (head of the local 'circle'). Kerr regretfully concluded that 'he did not look the part'.[8] Needs must, however, and de Valera was handed over to Barney Downes, bosun of the *Lapland,* bound for New York via Halifax. Downes hid his guest in the bottom of the ship, where he was undisturbed by police, but did have a cheese sandwich in his pocket eaten by rats. For the rest of the voyage de Valera was concealed in a small store room. His main problem was seasickness, which was so bad that Downes feared he would die. A couple of drops of brandy revived him, and a steady diet of Bovril kept him going all the way to New York.[9]

Once the *Lapland* docked in New York on 11 June, Downes went ashore to find Boland, who 'nearly had a fit when he found whom we had on board.'[10] Despite his American birth, de Valera had been put on the passport refusal list three months before by the State Department, at the request of the American embassy in London.[11] But landing in America proved to be simplicity itself: dressed in Downes's jacket, 'the Chief just walked off that boat as a sailor, with a heaving line in his hand'. He was brought to a bar on Tenth Avenue, where he was greeted by Boland,[12] who had just come from a meeting of the National Council of the Friends of Irish Freedom (a front organisation for the IRB's sister organisation, Clan na Gael). Boland had brought with him Joe McGarrity, a prosperous Philadelphia publican, hotelier and spirit merchant who would be an important ally in the faction-fighting to come.[13]

That first evening de Valera also met John Devoy – veteran Fenian, editor of the *Gaelic American*, leading figure in Clan na Gael, and soon to become his most bitter opponent in the United States.[14]

De Valera had made clear his priorities in his note to Boland before he even stepped ashore. 'Am anxious to travel to Rochester tonight. Hope it can be managed.'[15] Thirty-four years after his exile to Ireland, and 12 years after her last visit to Ireland, de Valera wanted above all to see his mother. This was perhaps natural given the length of time since he had seen her, though his urgency also suggested a deep need to secure her approval for his new-found status.[16] His time in Rochester was relatively brief; Boland recorded that they had to leave the city 'hurriedly, to escape news men'.[17]

De Valera also stayed for a few days with McGarrity in Philadelphia. The businessman was keen that his guest should look the part, fitting him out with suits, expensive luggage and some good advice. De Valera's official title was President of the Ministry of Dáil Éireann,[18] but he needed something snappier and more easily understood by the local people: 'President of the Irish Republic' would fit the bill admirably, he thought.[19] De Valera later recorded that 'I was popularly referred to as President of the Republic almost from the beginning, and much more so from the time I went to the United States'.[20] The reason, of course, was that he had appropriated the title.

De Valera later claimed that one of his reasons for travelling to the United States was to help bring the Clan na Gael factions together, as Boland 'apparently was not succeeding' in doing so.[21] Given that Boland had been in America for only a fortnight when de Valera began his journey, this was clearly nonsense. In fact, Boland had reached an agreement on the very night de Valera arrived that a quarter of the Friends of Irish Freedom's Victory Fund would be sent to Ireland.

The Friends of Irish Freedom, established in 1916, was controlled by Clan na Gael: 15 of the 17 members of the first FOIF Executive were Clan members. The organisation was relatively quiet during the First World War, when anti-British sentiment was unpopular, but it expanded rapidly after the February 1919 Irish Race Convention in Philadelphia, which was attended by more than 5,000 delegates.[22] Diarmuid Lynch, born in Ireland but a naturalised American citizen, was its national secretary. After serving in the GPO during the Rising, his death sentence had been commuted; but in 1918 he was deported to the United States.[23]

While in America, Lynch had been elected to the Dáil, and he was one of a number of TDs in the United States. Patrick McCartan had been sent to America as a Republican envoy in 1917, and Liam Mellows had escaped there after leading the small-scale 1916 operations in Co. Galway. Mellows, McCartan and Boland had a difficult relationship with the FOIF leaders John Devoy and Judge Daniel Cohalan; by contrast, Lynch became their ally. For Cohalan (and therefore for Devoy), the most important issue was the prevention of an alliance between the US and Britain; their opposition to the League of Nations was an extension of this aim. To them, it was entirely logical to use funds raised by the FOIF to fight the League of Nations, rather than sending it back to Ireland. They believed that defeating the League of Nations would in turn help Irish independence.[24]

Devoy was an isolated figure. Living alone and devoting all his time to his newspaper, he was deaf and had outlived most of his friends.[25] He relied greatly on his closest associate, Judge Cohalan. According to McCartan, Cohalan 'was a masterful man, at the height of his power, and was by far the most adroit American politician in Irish circles'.[26] Boland agreed that Cohalan was 'a very able man and a sincere lover of Ireland'; but he also had 'a wonderful opinion of his own ability and . . . an intolerance for the opinions or ability of others, and to put it bluntly he is a little envious of de Valera'.[27]

De Valera is frequently blamed for the split with Cohalan and Devoy. While he certainly contributed to it, this is rather unfair. Even before he stepped off the *Lapland* the FOIF leaders were in dispute with Boland, Mellows and McCartan. Besides, feuding American factions were nothing new – and those feuds frequently involved Devoy. In 1897 Maude Gonne found Clan na Gael 'split into two warring sections', with Devoy accusing another leading figure of organising the murder of a third.[28] Hanna Sheehy-Skeffington also found Devoy difficult to deal with during her American tour.[29]

But these tensions lay in the future as de Valera prepared for his first public appearance in America, at the Waldorf-Astoria Hotel. The Fifth Avenue hotel was one of New York's most prestigious (it has since moved – the original address is now the site of the Empire State Building). It would become de Valera's permanent base for the next 18 months – a rather expensive address, but arguably worth the money if its lustre rubbed off on the Irish delegation.[30]

In a written statement de Valera said he was in America 'as the official head of the Republic established by the will of the Irish people, in accordance with the principle of self-determination' – thus blending the demand for recognition of the Republic with Wilson's promise of self-determination. He claimed that he was entitled to speak for the Irish people 'with an authority democratically as sound and as well based as that with which President Wilson speaks for the United States'. He also claimed that Ireland would have been better off 'under a Kaiser, Emperor or Czar' than under the British Crown,[31] a reference picked up by the *New York Times*.

> It is six months since the fighting ceased, but the Kaiser is not yet a popular hero in this country. Our distinguished visitor has hitched his wagon to a fallen star.[32]

De Valera would discover that the image of being pro-German was a serious problem in the United States; bringing it up in his first statement to the press was unwise.

He later spoke at a reception attended by more than 1,500 people, presided over by Cohalan, who asked the audience to file past de Valera one by one so they might shake hands with him.

As soon as news of de Valera's arrival in America reached the Lord Lieutenant, Lord French, he sought an order under the Defence of the

Realm Regulations prohibiting him from re-entering or residing in Ireland.[33] After some discussion of the legal difficulties – de Valera was, after all, an MP and arguably entitled to return to his constituents[34] – the Home Secretary issued an order in October 1919 excluding de Valera from the United Kingdom under the Aliens Act.[35] However, Collins assured de Valera that 'when the time comes you need not fear that there will be the slightest difficulty in out-manoeuvring them'.[36]

After de Valera's public appearance, his uncle Ed wrote with

> a hearty welcome to you back to the land of your birth. You have made a good deal of history since the day I took you home to your grandmother . . . It is a sublime step from an English prison to the Waldorf Astoria![37]

Later, Ed's children met their famous cousin on his trips to Rochester. They found him 'a serious-faced man with penetrating eyes, tall and dignified and thin to a painful degree. He was gentle but not soft.'[38] His cousin Edward Patrick Coll, who had served as a captain with the US Army, asked him how he hoped to free Ireland against the might of the British war machine he had seen in France. De Valera's reported reply was significant. 'We are reaching for the stars in the hope of obtaining the mountain tops.'[39] This chimes with Devoy's opinion of de Valera as a moderate.

> I arrived at the conclusion long ago that he is not a sincere Republican, but wants to keep Ireland in the British Empire. He asked me the night he landed what I thought of Colonial Home Rule . . .[40]

The issue that provoked the beginning of the split with the American leaders was money. De Valera explained his plan to raise a loan of $10 million, which Cohalan and his allies regarded as preposterous and probably illegal. They argued instead that the FOIF should continue raising its Victory Fund, from which a significant proportion would be given to de Valera. This didn't suit his purposes: apart from the question of money, the floating of a bond would help the concurrent propaganda campaign in favour of recognition of the Republic.

If he wanted to float his bond, he was going to be on his own – unless he could wrest control of the FOIF from Cohalan and Devoy. Boland was characteristically optimistic about the prospects for the bond and the chances of having the Republic officially recognised. He had reason for this view after the first big public meeting of de Valera's American mission, at Fenway Park in Boston – 'the largest ever accorded to any individual in the history of America,' according to Boland. And there were indications of similar enthusiasm elsewhere, with invitations for de Valera to speak pouring in from all over the country.[41] At least one offer of matrimony – to 'an Irish bride of royal descent' – also arrived at the Waldorf.[42]

The audience in Boston was estimated at 60,000 by the local press, and de Valera had to apologise at the start because his 'voice will not carry to the limits of this meeting'. He said the size of the crowd proved that during the war Ireland had not lost the support of Irish-Americans, who still supported 'the struggles of a people fighting against a tyrant far greater than Germany'.[43] According to the *Boston Globe*,

> It was electric . . . In the thoughtful, militant, clean-cut face and gaunt personality of de Valera, there is somehow also personified that new spirit which had come to Irishmen everywhere . . .[44]

Three days later de Valera spoke at a meeting at Cubs Park (Wrigley Field) in Chicago, and

> appeared to be almost awed by the reception he got . . . Pandemonium reigned when de Valera rose to speak. For thirty-one minutes the crowd cheered. Amid shouting, flag-waving, de Valera was lifted shoulder high by some of his confreres on the platform, and the crowd yelled itself hoarse.

While the enthusiastic reception could not be denied, a British official in New York was critical of de Valera's platform performances: 'De Valera lacks personality . . . and even his friends say that his voice and hesitating speech disappoint many who expect a fluent orator. De Valera at present is reading most of his speeches which is undoubtedly because he fears being misquoted in the newspapers.'[45]

De Valera continued his triumphal progress on this first sweep of the country: San Francisco, Salt Lake City, as well as cities in Montana, Maryland, Pennsylvania, Rhode Island and New Jersey. In San Francisco his visit included banquets of Irish county associations, reception by the mayor, dinner with the archbishop, the unveiling of a statue of Robert Emmet in Golden Gate Park, receptions, interviews, meetings – even a cinema screening of film of his arrival.

All of the spare time of the President between the hours and on the times not mentioned as officially scheduled above, were completely taken by receiving those who desired to be introduced and those who desired conference with him on the question of Ireland . . .[46]

He wryly complained to Collins

I spend most of my time shaking hands. I'll have the biceps of a blacksmith before I'm finished – had I time I'd get articles into all the newspapers. Am out today in private house lent by a friend. May get some work done now – Lord as I write here comes another visitor . . .[47]

De Valera began making plans for a new organisation to run the bond drive in place of the FOIF. He secured the help of Frank Walsh, chairman of the American Commission on Irish Independence, who was a more willing collaborator than Cohalan.[48]

There were, however, legal issues to be dealt with, so de Valera consulted a New York lawyer and former politician who was later to play a role in his career: Franklin D. Roosevelt.[49] The legal worries were very real: the State Department advocated a firm line against the sale of the bonds, in order 'to prevent our territory being used to further rebellion against a friendly state'.[50] The wording of the bond certificates was finally approved by the lawyers, though at least one batch of thousands of application forms had to be destroyed after de Valera insisted on changing 'a word and a comma or two . . . to ensure greater definition of its purpose'.[51] The original idea was to launch the bond drive in October 1919, at the same time as his national tour began – an utterly unrealistic plan that soon proved impossible. Eventually, de Valera sent word that he needed the help of Sinn Féin's acknowledged financial expert, James O'Mara.

Demanding and strict, O'Mara could be difficult to get on with, though these were qualities that would greatly benefit the meticulous work of the bond drive. By the end of his time in America he came to detest de Valera. Perhaps they were too alike, a view held by O'Mara's wife, who noted that 'when two autocrats get together they very seldom get on well'.[52]

In preparation for de Valera's first proper tour of the United States, he set out his typically detailed suggestions, specifying that at least one city in every state should be covered; that 'great care should be taken to see that correspondence is not mixed up through the fact that there are several towns of the same name in the different States'; that entry into important towns should be in the evening, 'so as to facilitate demonstrations'; and that efforts should be made to travel by aeroplane or airship, as 'the advantages of the air are beyond question'.[53]

The tour was designed to circle the entire United States, though due to de Valera's exhaustion it eventually ended in California rather than continuing through Texas and New Orleans and back up the eastern coast. It was a massive undertaking, and de Valera recalled with pride that 'it was said that no man's constitution could stand it, that [the Democratic Party orator] William Jennings Bryan was the only person who attempted anything like it, that he had a special car or coach with masseurs, etc., doctor . . .'[54]

Liam Mellows was the advance man, investigating each city and the committee in charge of receiving de Valera, smoothing out difficulties and ensuring the best possible reception for the Chief. Mellows was 'energetic and dedicated'[55] and 'a most charming man . . . with a power of oratory that made you see the things he had experienced, and dream the same great dreams'.[56] Boland travelled with de Valera, troubleshooting, co-ordinating various groups and acting as an extra speaker when necessary. Seán Nunan, a 1916 veteran and former Dáil clerk, was de Valera's personal secretary and 'a kind of aide-de-camp'.[57]

The tour began in Philadelphia on 1 October, de Valera speaking in front of the Liberty Bell in Independence Hall. The following evening he spoke before an estimated 3,000 people at the Metropolitan Opera House. His departure on the 3rd was delayed by an enthusiastic crowd, 10,000-strong according to his own account.[58] At their next stop, Pittsburgh, they were met by another 10,000 people. As Boland wearily noted, 'If cheers and parades mean anything we have won. Wish we could translate cheers etc. into deeds'.[59]

At the University of Notre Dame in Indiana, 1,500 students 'and every member of the faculty, lay and clerical' listened as de Valera, 'presenting argument after argument for the case of Ireland, held his audience enthusiastically for an hour and thirty minutes'.[60]

Boland's diary conveys the wild enthusiasm of the crowds, as well as the wearying grind of making the same speeches over and over again and putting up with the sometimes slipshod local arrangements. 'Boys at home more capable to organise than any I have met here so far,'[61] he complained. But there were compensations, as indicated by his colourful description of Louisville, Kentucky: 'Dark and bloody soil, lovely women, fast horses, strong whiskey'.[62]

An idyllic day was spent on an Indian reservation in Wisconsin, where de Valera was made a Chief of the Chippewa Nation, only the second non-Indian to receive this honour.[63] He was given the Indian name 'Nay nay ong a ba', meaning 'the Dressing Feather'. De Valera later recalled that the honour 'meant more to me than all the freedoms of all the cities I was ever given . . . It is not an "honorary chieftain" they made me! I am a real Chief'.[64]

The latter end of the trip was overshadowed by his increasing concern over the financial aspect of the mission. 'Not pleased with affairs in New York and Washington . . . I fear the Bond Drive has not been properly organised.'[65] Eventually, Boland was sent back to New York to take up the reins, while James O'Mara, fresh from Ireland, joined the tour in Portland, Oregon.

The tour of the west coast saw increasing tension with such patriotic bodies as the American Legion, who were critical of de Valera's perceived pro-German stance during the war. He was heckled during a speech in Seattle, and a Tricolour was ripped off his car by American Legion members in Portland. A speech that night in the city auditorium was almost cancelled when city officials banned the display of Irish flags.[66]

He still received an enthusiastic welcome in San Francisco, though he was reported to have collapsed from fatigue. Despite doctors' orders to rest, he insisted on continuing to Los Angeles. There, a huge crowd attempting to get into his speech at the Shrine Auditorium found the doors locked, after the owners bowed to pressure from the American Legion to cancel the event; the speech had to be rescheduled.[67]

A critical statement in the newspapers by Devoy was seen by de Valera in Denver some days later. De Valera later recalled that

> our opponents were out to sow suspicion at home and bring about a situation which would necessitate my recall. They were setting the Prairie on fire behind us.[68]

Meanwhile, back in Ireland, violence was becoming more and more pronounced.[69] Up to the autumn of 1919, Volunteer activity was mainly defensive; but a series of shootings of policemen, and particularly the shooting of a soldier in an arms raid on a military patrol in Fermoy, led to the banning in September of the Volunteers, Sinn Féin, Cumann na mBan, the Gaelic League and the Dáil itself.[70] This led the Minister for Defence, Cathal Brugha, and the Volunteer chief of staff, Richard Mulcahy, to sanction 'an active, aggressive policy', which saw its first fruits

in a raid on the RIC barracks in Carrigtohill, Co. Cork, on 4 January 1920
– the first of many raids throughout the country.[71] De Valera had left
Arthur Griffith in charge in his absence as President Substitute,[72] but as
he had no role in the Volunteers his authority was limited in practice to
the civil side of the movement.

Volunteer units throughout the country burnt down RIC barracks and
in some areas began actively ambushing; reprisals forced some of them to
go on the run, which led to the formation of the flying columns that
further drove the intensification of violence. And the underground Dáil
government attempted to establish a civil administration, the Republican
courts being particularly effective.

Military reinforcements poured into the country, as did new recruits
for the RIC – the infamous Black and Tans and Auxiliaries. It is hardly
surprising that those at home had little sympathy with the travails facing
their compatriots in the United States. In March 1920 Collins wrote to
Nunan, who had complained of some difficulty.

> Oh yes, I am fully aware of all the little troubles you have had in the
> New World, but the little troubles here are so absorbing that one is
> inclined to forget them.[73]

De Valera returned to New York on 29 November, where Boland
reported him to be 'in great form, bursting with energy and determined to
carry out loan come weal or woe'.[74]

De Valera claimed it was 'heart-breaking' to have to go on speaking
tours when, if he had time to prepare a few newspaper articles, 'it would
be much more effective'.[75] But the tour, with its massive, cheering crowds,
putting de Valera centre stage, must have been a significant boost and a
reassurance that his leadership was secure.

The opposition of Devoy and Cohalan had the reverse effect. Mellows
recorded de Valera's reaction to the perceived disloyalty of Devoy and
Cohalan. 'Never saw a sicker man. Disillusionment isn't the word.'[76] This
was the first time that de Valera's leadership had been contested in any
way. To suddenly be challenged must have come as an unwelcome shock,
and it goes some way to explain the somewhat irrational lengths to which
he went to try to best Cohalan in particular.[77]

Of course, de Valera's own personality contributed to the problem. In
August he jauntily told Griffith that he had 'got a bad reputation here as
being "a very stubborn man"'.[78] He evidently found the charge slightly
ridiculous. But the plain fact was that he could be extremely irritating,

even to the most loyal supporters. In his diary Boland recorded numerous instances of challenging behaviour by the Chief.

> 3 Dec. Wed. New York. De V talks all night, no one else.
> 16 Dec. Tues. Washington. Chief entertains filing expert for 2 hours to dissertation on correct filing system.
> . . .
> 26 Jan. Mon. New York. Very, very busy packing ten bags for Washington. Chief is a 'terrible man' for bags, books and notes. Each trip we take, no matter how short travel, enough books etc. to fill a room. As usual, nearly miss the train.[79]

In January 1920, when de Valera finally decided that Boland would be better employed on other duties, he sought a personal assistant from Ireland. Boland described the duties to Collins.

> Unless the man is an expert shorthand writer and typist he need not come – he would be useless to us, and further that he be prepared to be with the President all the time and give the little personal attentions necessary (believe me it is a hell of a job!).[80]

The team supporting de Valera kept expanding. Liam Pedlar became his private secretary for a time, accompanying him on his southern tour, as well as being involved in arms purchases.[81] Joseph Begley later fulfilled the same dual function.[82] The Chicago journalist Charles N. Wheeler became press spokesman. A more permanent addition was Kathleen O'Connell. A native of Caherdaniel in Co. Kerry, she had been in America since 1904. She had worked for the Gaelic League and the FOIF before becoming a full-time personal secretary to de Valera in October 1919.[83] She was one of his closest, and most loyal, collaborators until her death in 1956.

Even from the other side of the Atlantic, de Valera's nit-picking could irritate colleagues. He objected to a suggestion in a letter from Collins that he had been 'converted' to the idea of the Dáil Ministry assuming liability for Fenian bonds, insisting that he had never opposed acknowledging it as a national debt.[84] In reply, Collins pointed out that de Valera had insisted on removing a paragraph relating to this issue from the prospectus for the new Dáil bond, before wearily adding, 'For God's sake de V don't start an argument . . . Don't please. It's quite alright.'[85] However, de Valera seemed intent on arguing, though on a different issue: the date from which interest on the bonds would be calculated. He

complained in September that the loan certificates promised interest from the day on which the certificate was paid for, rather
than from the date of the recognition of the Republic and the evacuation
of British troops. 'The accumulated debt interest might be a very serious
handicap . . . We must look to the future.'[86] Collins was astonished: he
said that he knew exactly what they had promised, that Griffith agreed
and that in any event it was too late to change the terms now.[87] This view
was confirmed by the Ministry a few days later[88] – a sign of independence
their Chief may not have found congenial.

His colleagues were certainly in no hurry to have him back. In
December 1919 the Dáil Ministry 'unanimously decided to request you
to remain for the present in the United States and consolidate the great
work you are performing'. Griffith said de Valera's continued presence in
America 'is essential to our success. So long as you hold Irish America
what they can do to us here is non-effective'.[89]

But, as de Valera explained in a letter to Griffith, 'the great difficulty is
to get Americans to put Irish interests above their own politics'.[90] In
public, all appeared reasonably well. On 17 January 1920 de Valera
received the Freedom of New York City. It was, according to a typically
ebullient entry in Harry Boland's diary, a 'great day for New York . . . 69th
in full uniform, wild enthusiasm, cheers, band, songs . . .'[91] And then de
Valera gave his enemies their opportunity to pounce.

De Valera's infamous 'interview' with the *Westminster Gazette* was actually
material he had prepared for a speech, which he allowed the journalist W. J.
Hernan to quote from. Hernan's story was published in the *New York Globe*
on 6 February and on the following day in the *Westminster Gazette*. The
Globe in particular exaggerated the significance in it of an alleged concession,
seeing it as 'the withdrawal by the official head of the Irish Republic of the
demand that Ireland be set free to decide her own international relations'.
This was certainly not de Valera's intention: he merely wanted to scotch the
argument that Britain denied Ireland independence out of fear for her own
security. He had suggested four methods by which those security worries
could be allayed: a treaty obligation not to allow Irish territory to be used as a
base of attack against Britain (similar to an article of the Platt Amendment
relating to Cuba); a ban on foreign powers intervening in Ireland, similar to
the 'Monroe Doctrine'; an international treaty safeguarding Irish neutrality,
similar to Belgium; or a guarantee by the League of Nations. His comments
didn't suggest subservience but neutrality; however, in the *Gaelic American*,
Devoy immediately accused him of compromise: 'It will be hailed in England
as an offer of surrender'.[92]

De Valera and his team tried to limit the damage, insisting that the *New York Globe* had used 'a misleading headline', and that there was nothing in the interview 'but a statement of what Ireland had always been willing to concede – equality of rights between nations'.[93]

Liam Mellows assured a supporter that 'the President did not in the least lower the flag – if it were so I would be the first to protest'. All he had done, Mellows insisted, was demonstrate that concern over security was no reason to deny Ireland the independence it sought.[94] Boland wrote to 'Field' (the codename Collins used when dealing with IRB affairs) deploring the 'dastardly' attack on de Valera after the interview, claiming that Cohalan and his allies had used it to

> knife us, and to knife Ireland. If de Valera did happen to make a mistake, which I don't believe he did, would not one think that the duty of any friend of Ireland would be to come to him and if a mistake had been made it could have been rectified by an addition or subtraction to the interview, but Cohalan thought that this was an opportune moment, and by taking this stand that de Valera had lowered the flag he could dishonour and discredit him.'[95]

In his diary Boland recorded that de Valera was 'on edge' and that Devoy

> is causing Chief grave concern. I can see what is to come. I prophesy here that we will win out. Chief very sad. 'Poor Sinéad, 'twill break her heart' . . .

By the 23rd the only topic de Valera could talk about was Devoy and Cohalan; on the 24th, he was 'in a rage'; on the 25th, he was 'not in good form. Nervous indigestion'. Two days later he was 'in bed sick for two days, looks bad, this Devoy business has done him no good'. Finally, on the 28th, de Valera rose from his sick bed to deliver a speech and he was 'cured of his gall'.[96]

While Collins was in private critical of the remarks, Griffith as usual defended de Valera.

> We know the President better than we know the men who are opposed to him in America. It is our business to be perfectly loyal to him.[97]

The interview did not go down well with some of his allies in America. The mention of Cuba was particularly damaging in American eyes, as they were well aware of the island's dependence on the United States. Patrick McCartan compared the incident to 'a thunderbolt'. McGarrity, he recalled, thought it might do some good if it taught de Valera 'to put his feet under the table', that is, to consult more closely with those who understood America better than he did. But, like their colleagues at home, there was little they could do but stand by their man.

> We had either to stand by and see de Valera destroyed, and with him our cause, and our hope of international aid for Ireland, or we had to defend him and to explain away that fatal interview.[98]

De Valera was sufficiently worried to send McCartan back to Ireland to brief the leadership. He also wrote to Griffith asking to be informed immediately if the Ministry or the Dáil 'feel the slightest want of confidence in me', and assuring him that 'I *never* in public or private say or do anything here which is not thoroughly consistent with my attitude at home as you have known it'. He claimed to be the victim of 'a deadly attempt to ruin our chances', but admitted that the trouble arose from personalities. 'I cannot feel confidence enough in a certain man [Cohalan] to let him have implicit control of tactics here without consultation and agreement with me'.[99]

When McCartan personally explained the situation at a specially convened meeting of the Ministry, he reported hostility from Plunkett, Brugha and Markievicz to the Cuban interview. 'But Collins and Griffith shut down the discussion and led in the acceptance of de Valera's explanation,' Griffith's support having evidently overcome Collins's doubts.[100] De Valera's wish for backing from home was handsomely fulfilled in an official commendation from Griffith – the Ministry assuring him of the 'unshakeable loyalty' of the Irish people.[101]

Crucially, the IRB also backed de Valera, Collins sending Boland a new authorisation from the Supreme Council fully backing all de Valera's actions in the United States.[102] With the home front secure, de Valera could now turn to his tormentors in America.

A decision was made to confront Cohalan, and Boland was sent to him with a letter from de Valera, which was received in 'painful silence'.[103] De Valera wrote that he could no longer ignore critical articles in the *Gaelic American,* which he believed were written with Cohalan's 'consent and approval'. He insisted that he alone was responsible to the Irish people for the task with which he had been entrusted, and therefore he was not in a position to 'blindly delegate these duties'. Cohalan, he said, was the officer of the Friends of Irish Freedom who, de facto, wields unchallenged the executive power of that organisation . . . It is vital that I know exactly how you stand in this matter.[104]

Claiming to be 'amazed' at the contents of the letter, Cohalan replied that Devoy was responsible for what was printed in the *Gaelic American*, and that he was entitled to 'comment upon or discuss your public utterances' as he saw fit. And he warned de Valera against interference in internal American matters.

Do you really think for a moment that American public opinion will permit any citizen of another country to interfere as you suggest in American affairs?[105]

De Valera decided not to answer this letter, as

the only reply I could make would be a broadside of a kind which would make it absolutely impossible for me to work with the Judge in any way.

He rather undermined the purity of his own stand by adding:

I realised early that . . . big as this country is it was not big enough to hold the Judge and myself.

He had expected that supporters would

read what I had said carefully and take from it its obvious meaning. I had never dreamt that those who professed themselves friends would dream of going out of their way to pick a quarrel on an obvious mis-representation. However, one lives and learns![106]

Cohalan attempted to assert his dominance over de Valera at a meeting at the Park Avenue Hotel in New York on 19 March, when de Valera was supposed to be out of the city. McGarrity heard of the supposedly secret gathering and managed to get in. The meeting heard severe criticism of de Valera, especially over the Cuban interview. Devoy said they were willing to allow the President of the Republic to be the leader in Ireland, but 'they were not willing to take dictation from him here'. But McGarrity then derailed proceedings by standing up to demand that de Valera be allowed a hearing. When de Valera was summoned from the Waldorf-Astoria Hotel, the chairman of the meeting asked him to wait outside until the present speaker had finished, 'but Mr Boland brushed the man at the door aside and . . . the President entered; all arose and applauded for a considerable time'. De Valera, according to McGarrity, 'was apparently under a great strain; his teeth were set and he looked over the crowd, anxious, apparently, to see the makeup of the same'. He sought clarification on what was being discussed so that he could answer any charges against him. He then denounced the interpretations put on his interview and criticised what he called the 'politicians' in the movement, insisting that he and his colleagues in Ireland were not politicians, and that as soon as Ireland was free many of them would return to their previous professions.[107]

A moment of drama came when de Valera accused Devoy of having written letters saying it was time to drive him from America. According to an extract McCartan would later include in his book *With de Valera in America* (1932), Devoy had written that de Valera had always wanted a fight, that he was attempting to drive Devoy and Cohalan out of the movement, and that

his judgment is very poor, but he is filled with the idea that the great ovations he got here were for him personally and practically gave him a mandate to do as he pleases. His head is turned to a greater extent than any man I have met in more than half a century.[108]

Calm was restored by Bishop William Turner of Buffalo, who called for peace. Everyone knelt to pray, and the meeting broke up with three cheers each for de Valera, Cohalan and Devoy.[109] In his diary Boland recorded the emotional climax.

Dirty attempt to break Chief fails miserably . . . Jas. O'Mara cool and calm. Boland crying. DeV shaken. Devoy and Cohalan licked.[110]

After this conflict de Valera was 'full of pep' and had to be prevailed upon not to cancel a planned holiday in Atlantic City.

Nunan and Boland raise hell of a row. DeV surrenders. Chief can only secure rest by working. Works day and night, his mind never rests.[111]

In his own diary de Valera recorded continuing troubles with O'Mara, who was threatening resignation and had sent de Valera a letter he intended sending to the Dáil. In his diary de Valera wrote:

Why I wonder! There is a big streak of vanity in us all . . . I have my own idea why he is resigning – that without him some end of this mission would have gone to pot. If I could only acquire his habit of doing things on the spot. I trust I am not too old to improve.[112]

On 25 March 1920, as he prepared to head off on a speaking tour of the southern states, de Valera wrote to Griffith about his plans. His own wish was to come home, although he would regret not continuing work that could help Ireland. He wanted to avoid an open rupture with Devoy and Cohalan until the bond drive was complete, but he was convinced they would be no help in any effort to influence the American presidential election in November. The best Ireland could hope for from the coming election was a friendly president – but not even a friendly president 'would go the length of giving us formal recognition'. And without the co-operation of the Irish-American leaders there was a limit to how much they could influence the election.

Unless the Dáil were to vote me secretly the right to use from one-quarter to one-half Million Dollars, I do not think we will be able to get anywhere during the election campaign in impressing the distinctly Irish point of view on any of the parties . . .[113]

With almost indecent haste the Ministry gave de Valera full discretion to spend between $250,000 and $500,000.[114] It was almost as if they didn't want him back.

In the meantime, President Wilson's dream of having the Treaty of Versailles ratified and of America becoming a founder-member of the League of Nations, which had been bitterly opposed by Cohalan and de Valera, ended in failure. Republican Senators attached reservations to the treaty, knowing that Wilson would not accept them. One additional reservation was attached by the Democrat Peter Gerry, affirming self-determination for Ireland. With Wilson stubbornly refusing to accept the reservations, the amended treaty couldn't get the necessary two-thirds majority for ratification, and therefore died in the Senate in March 1920.[115]

De Valera's tour of the south went ahead in April 1920; it did not go very well. In Alabama the governor pointedly said that, although the expulsion of a foreigner was a matter for the State Department, if he were in charge he would order de Valera's deportation 'without delay'.[116] The opposition to de Valera was due not only to his wartime activities but to his religion – the Alabama Ku Klux Klan had been directing its attentions against Catholics. At a mass meeting in the Jefferson Theatre, de Valera tried to overcome his pro-German image by having uniformed soldiers from the First World War on stage with him – as well as four Confederate veterans. In a further appeal to local prejudice, he stressed that Ireland was 'the only white nation on earth still in the bonds of political slavery'.[117] While de Valera was a genuine admirer of Abraham Lincoln, and while in New York there were close links between the Sinn Féin delegation and black civil rights activists, he clearly felt the need to tailor his message for his audience in the south.[118]

In May, it was Harry Boland's turn to come home to Ireland, where he was reunited with his close friend Michael Collins, who took him to Greystones to visit Sinéad de Valera, 'a very wonderful and very brave woman . . . trusting to see her husband soon'.[119] The main business of his visit was, of course, to explain her husband's immediate plans. The Ministry agreed to most of de Valera's proposals. While a delegation to Russia was approved, it was thought wiser not to seek formal recognition there before similar requests had been made of other countries, particularly the United States. The Dáil would be asked to approve the spending of $1 million on the campaign to secure recognition in America; the allocation of the same amount to the Department of Defence was approved immediately. De Valera's colleagues were once again insistent that 'you should not return home just now'.[120]

The Dáil later ratified the spending decisions: $500,000 to be spent 'in connection with the election campaign for the Presidency of the United States of America', and $1 million for the campaign for recognition there.[121] The British viewed the allocation of money for the election campaign as an attempt to bring about a quarrel between them and the American government, and they promptly publicised the story.[122] When asked about it, de Valera temporised, claiming that he had not yet received the Dáil minutes and therefore didn't know if the story was accurate (which he certainly did, as he had been advised months before by Collins that the spending had been approved).[123]

By this time, British intelligence was happily forecasting that the split between de Valera and the Devoy-Cohalan camp 'seems likely to develop materially', and they reported that Devoy's agents were attempting to have de Valera 'repudiated from Ireland so that his downfall cannot be attributed to the Irish agitators in America'.[124]

They were right to focus on the constant rows that were sapping faith in de Valera – even among some supporters. James K. Maguire, former chairman of the Clan na Gael Executive, thought him 'unexcelled' in his devotion to principle but 'a most lamentable failure' as a negotiator, 'lacking in decision, changeable, unsteady'.[125] Patrick McCartan had similar concerns.

> My experience of him and Harry [Boland] is that they come to a conference not knowing what they want; have an unconscious contempt or seem to have such for opinions of others.[126]

The British constantly speculated that de Valera was about to leave the United States – for Australia,[127] or Ireland.[128] They were also hopeful that de Valera's somewhat indiscreet contacts with radical elements, both domestic and foreign, would alienate the American public, as his 'alleged relations with Bolshevik extremists identify him with the disruptive elements which Americans hate'.[129] The British believed he was attempting to construct 'some kind of Sinn Féin/Bolshevik nexus'.[130] As well as sending McCartan to Moscow,[131] he agreed to lend money to the Russian mission in the United States, receiving some jewels as security – an exchange which would provoke controversy during the 1948 general election.

De Valera also had contact with Indian nationalists, having being presented with a sword by the radical Ghadar ('Rebellion') party in San Francisco in July 1919. He told them 'the Irish People recognise the justice of your fight and are heartily with you'. He also addressed a dinner of the Friends of the Freedom of India in New York in February 1920, with more than 500 in attendance and hundreds more crowding in to hear his speech.[132] He said their causes were identical and spoke of the need for physical force.

> If ever the sword was legitimate it is in a case such as ours . . . We of Ireland and you of India must each of us endeavour, both as separate peoples and in combination, to rid ourselves of the vampire that is battening on our blood . . .[133]

Strong words, but not backed up by action: de Valera turned down a request for $75,000 to fund an Indian rebellion.[134]

For months, de Valera had known that the best hope of securing recognition for Ireland in America was to get the two main parties to pledge their support before the presidential election.[135] This meant getting recognition of the Irish Republic adopted as policy at the party conventions – as 'a plank in the platform', in the American jargon. So de Valera and his entourage trooped off to the Republican Convention in

Chicago at the beginning of June, and to the Democratic Convention in San Francisco later in the month. In Chicago the Irish delegation opened an office opposite the convention centre, published a daily newsletter and organised a 5,000-strong torchlight parade on the evening before the convention. De Valera was self-righteously oblivious of the effect this might have on Americans, later claiming he had been 'very careful . . . Nobody (officials of the parties) raised any questions about my being present'.[136] McCartan had a more realistic view: 'There was no chance of offending America that we did not take'.[137]

The Cohalan side appointed a committee to meet de Valera and appeal to him to desist from his overt intervention – what John P. Grace, former Mayor of Charleston, described as 'an injurious and spectacular descent upon Chicago'. Grace suggested that the request for a 'plank' should come from 'an American committee with links to the Republican Party'. De Valera rejected this advice, saying he would rather have a definite rejection from the Republicans than any more postponement.[138]

Cohalan and his allies believed there was no chance of a bald commitment to recognise the Irish Republic, and they were right: de Valera's proposed plank was defeated in the Resolutions Committee by 11 votes to 1. Cohalan's alternative was passed by 7 votes to 6, but de Valera publicly objected to it, and the Republican Party gladly dropped any reference to Ireland from its election platform. Cohalan's resolution was later misrepresented by de Valera's supporters as one of 'sympathy', much weaker than de Valera's own demand for 'recognition'.[139] This was nonsense. Cohalan's proposed plank said that

> the people of Ireland have the right to determine freely, without dictation from outside, their own governmental institutions and their international relations with other States and peoples.[140]

It was arguably a stronger position than the one set out by de Valera in his *Westminster Gazette* interview.

So if it wasn't really about policy, why did he sabotage the Cohalan plank? The answer lies in their power struggle, and particularly in de Valera's fear of being seen as subordinate. In a public statement after his Chicago performance had been criticised by the *Gaelic American*, de Valera said

> it would be inconsistent with my duty to become a puppet to be manipulated by anybody. It would injure our cause even to allow it to appear that I was a puppet.[141]

After the disappointment in Chicago, de Valera travelled on to San Francisco for the Democratic Convention, where he again failed to have recognition adopted as party policy.[142] In July he returned to Chicago for the convention of the Farmer-Labor Party, where after much work he succeeded in having a plank calling for recognition of the Republic adopted. This was a complete waste of time – the party's candidate won just one per cent of the vote in November. Boland, who returned from Ireland to find de Valera 'looking very tired after his strenuous months in Chicago and San Francisco'[143] later indirectly conceded that Cohalan had been right all along: 'I can plainly see that if we get deep into American politics we will be skinned, so keep clear'.[144]

De Valera was increasingly eager to return to Ireland; he was, in Boland's words, 'very lonely for home' and 'longing to get back to wife and children'.[145] In Washington on New Year's Eve, Boland had been woken from an early night by the bells and bugles signalling the arrival of 1920. He found de Valera writing to Sinéad – what he referred to as 'his first duty' in the new year.[146] His letter was more sad than dutiful.

> Another New Year's night away from you and the children – I hope you are not as lonely as I am. This separation is the great sacrifice and I know it is hard on you. When playing with the youngsters at McGarrity's, I felt more lonely than ever.[147]

Her letters similarly indicate loneliness. In February 1920 she recalled that it was a year since he had escaped from Lincoln Prison.

> How I wish you could escape home to us again. Everyone tells me there is little hope of your return for about a year yet. Well, Dev dear, I know it is my part to bear your absence for Ireland. But for every reason I wish that things would develop so as to ensure your coming sooner.

She chided him for sending presents only to the two older children, Vivion and Máirín, and urged him to send

> some little books or something addressed to Éamon, Brian and Ruaidhrí. They talk so much about you, Brian said to me the other day 'Daddy is thinking of me.'

She closed with another gentle exhortation.

Remember, Dev dear, I don't expect long letters nor do I expect them frequently but oh! I love to hear from you.[148]

Michael Collins kept a close eye on Sinéad, sending regular financial support and visiting her in Greystones.[149] His letters to de Valera in America frequently mention a visit to the family, with news of the children and of Sinéad's own spirits.[150] Boland, while at home in Ireland in June, apparently raised the possibility of Sinéad's going to America. He had mentioned the idea to de Valera before he left, and de Valera, thinking it highly unlikely said, 'Do, if you can.'[151] Collins thought 'you were all mad to have put the idea in her head' but felt that 'the journey will do her good and she badly wanted some change. She has had a very hard time'.[152]

Leaving her sister Bee in charge of the children, Sinéad slipped away from home, the local RIC finding out only two days later. 'I am not able to say yet how she went or where she went . . .'[153] On 18 August 1920 she arrived in New York. De Valera's official biography records that, given the pressure of work, the reunited couple 'had little time together'.[154] This was certainly true of the latter part of her visit – but on the day of her arrival in New York, they went to the Edgewood Inn, in Greenwich, Connecticut, a popular summer resort.[155]

It was just 50 kilometres outside New York, so de Valera was able to visit the office on some of the days they spent there, and then return to his wife at their hotel.[156] The couple later spent time together in Rochester with de Valera's mother,[157] whom Sinéad found less 'severe and strict' than she expected – an indication of what her husband had said about her.[158]

By the time Longford and O'Neill came to write de Valera's biography, he probably wished to stress his austere life in service to the Irish people, so it is perhaps not surprising that he didn't mention this idyll of connubial bliss. But at the time it certainly had an impact on him. Boland told Kitty Kiernan, the young woman he and Collins were pursuing, that Sinéad had made 'a fine impression on everyone, "the Chief" is a new man as a result, and we are all very happy to have her here'.[159]

But of course the work had to go on, and Sinéad found herself with 'nothing really profitable to do and spent a good deal of time in the hotel'.[160] Missing her children, she eventually decided to go home. On her return she concluded that she

must have been half crazy to go such a long journey for such a short visit . . . Somehow I miss him more than before I went to America.[161]

While the children were interested in hearing about her American adventure, they were more interested in having their father home for Christmas, as 'no one can make a Xmas tree like Daddy'.[162] In another letter, to her husband's secretary, Kathleen O'Connell, she admitted that she could

> feel nothing much else but regret that I went to America . . . Since I came home I find it hard to be content or to get along in the old groove.[163]

Mention of Kathleen O'Connell brings us to the persistent rumour that de Valera was having an affair with his secretary, and was therefore annoyed at his wife's arrival.[164] So persistent were the rumours that de Valera addressed them in the Dáil in 1928: 'I myself was told by a lady in Chicago that a Bishop had told her that my wife had to go over to America in order to keep me straight there because I was associating with women'.[165]

It would appear that this was simply a scurrilous rumour circulated by political enemies, as can be seen by the friendly tone of the correspondence between Mrs de Valera and Miss O'Connell.[166]

Throughout Sinéad's visit, de Valera continued his propaganda work, arguably the most important part of his mission. He denounced British actions, dismissed suggestions of compromise and defended the actions of the Volunteers at home – sometimes imperfectly, given the difficulty of securing up-to-date information. He later complained that he had been unable to properly defend their actions on Bloody Sunday, 21 November 1920, when 12 British intelligence agents and two RIC Auxiliaries were killed, some in their beds, in an operation led by members of Collins's 'Squad', set up to eliminate British intelligence operations. De Valera told Robert Brennan that this had been presented as the murder of army officers simply because they were army officers. 'He had had no knowledge of the facts and was compelled, willy-nilly, to let the reports go uncontradicted until it was too late'.[167] In fact, his statement in the *New York Times* on 23 November appears to have been relatively well informed: he denounced the victims as

> enemy spies . . . rightly deserving death if any human beings deserve death, for they provide the alien government with knowledge and the strength to persecute and inflict endless misery upon a whole nation.[168]

He remained a big draw, with extensive newspaper coverage even after many months in the United States as well as mentions in contemporary novels.[169] Two of the more memorable public meetings of his final six

months in America were in New York. On 18 July 1920 he joined Daniel
Mannix, Archbishop of Melbourne, on stage in Madison Square Garden.
Boland captured the excitement in his diary, noting 12 minutes of
cheering for de Valera from the crowd of 15,000. 'DeV makes slashing
speech. His Grace delivers a wonderful speech. Many thousands outside'.[170] It was 'a return to the enthusiasm and the mass meetings that
hallmarked the best days in America'.[171]

Also notable was a massive meeting on 31 October in the Polo
Grounds to commemorate the Lord Mayor of Cork, Terence MacSwiney,
who had died on hunger strike six days before. De Valera of course knew
MacSwiney well from their time in prison together. MacSwiney's
protracted hunger strike of 74 days had drawn the attention of the world.
In his speech de Valera tore into Lloyd George, the 'miserable opportunist'
and 'contemptible demagogue'. He promised that, just as MacSwiney had
taken the place of the murdered Tomás Mac Curtáin, so others would
take the place of MacSwiney.[172]

While all this was going on the business of the bond drive continued.
It had been launched in January 1920, amid the publicity surrounding de
Valera's receiving the Freedom of New York. He told reporters that it
would be understood

> by each subscriber to the loan that he is making a free gift of his
> money. Repayment of the amount subscribed is contingent wholly
> upon the recognition of the Irish Republic as an independent nation.[173]

Such statements, the British hoped, meant that 'the popularity of the loan
is not likely to be excessive'.[174]

There were plenty of takers, though. More than 300,000 people
bought bond certificates, mostly in amounts of $25 or less, making for a
total of $5 million (€55–60 million today).[175] But raising the money was
relatively straightforward compared with the task of getting it back to
Ireland. It was laundered through two banks, then sent by draft from a
New York priest to Bishop Michael Fogarty of Killaloe, one of the trustees
of the Dáil. By the end of 1920 only $1 million had made it back to
Dublin.[176] A rather high-handed reply came back when Collins complained to Boland about this.[177] Boland explained that they had about $3
million to send back but that de Valera was

> particularly anxious that you at home be satisfied that you can safe-
> guard the money . . . He is uneasy lest . . . the enemy may get wise to

the arrangement . . . To allay his fear, will you, in your next despatch, assure him that you can safeguard the funds?[178]

Collins snapped in reply that 'our chief way of safeguarding it up to the present has been by spending it'.[179]

Meanwhile, the battle for control of the Friends of Irish Freedom was played out in public. In August, Bishop Michael Gallagher of Detroit became president of the FOIF, delivering an acceptance speech severely critical of de Valera.[180] De Valera robustly defended his position, noting the need for 'a fresh and more vigorous campaign for the enlightenment of the American people' and condemning the feud that was frittering away 'energies which are so badly needed for the cause'.[181]

It was clear that a confrontation was coming. De Valera had been seeking a special meeting of the National Council of the FOIF for months, ostensibly to co-ordinate campaign efforts but in reality to challenge its leadership. When it was finally held, Cohalan and his allies filibustered to prevent de Valera putting forward his proposals for reorganisation. Finally, taking offence at remarks by John P. Grace, de Valera walked out.[182] Boland called on all those 'who wanted to help the Irish Republic' to meet him in the Waldorf-Astoria the following morning.[183]

There de Valera explained to his followers 'the need for democratic control' of the FOIF. Resolutions calling for a national convention were passed, and duly ignored, leading de Valera to finally decide to form a new organisation.[184]

Before de Valera could turn his attention to these matters, however, he had another task: the submission of a formal request to the US government for recognition of the Irish Republic. The Ministry at home had urged him to stay in the United States until this demand had been presented – with the important caveat that this should not be done before the new President and Congress had come into office.[185] This implied a significant extension of de Valera's stay: the presidential inauguration would not take place until March 1921 and the new Congress would not meet until 11 April.[186]

Patrick McCartan was installed in a hotel in Washington and ordered to prepare the recognition demand. After a few days de Valera arrived to take charge – a copy of Machiavelli in his pocket, according to McCartan.[187] Characteristically, de Valera was 'thoroughly disappointed' with the work that had been done by McCartan and a number of lawyers, so he decided to draw up the demand himself, 'working almost night and day' on it.[188]

In his request for recognition of the Republic, de Valera once again stressed that Ireland was prepared by treaty to ensure England's safety against foreign powers using Ireland as a base of attack. He compared Ulster unionists to the 'loyalists' who opposed George Washington, stressed the democratic backing for independence in the 1918 general election, and asserted that ignoring the principles of self-determination established during the war would be 'immoral and impossible'.[189] The demand for recognition, submitted in the dying days of Wilson's presidency, had little prospect of success. But there was even less chance of a better hearing from his successor, Warren Harding, who, asked during the campaign about the Irish question, had replied, 'I would not care to undertake to say to Great Britain what she must do any more than I would permit her to tell us what we must do with the Philippines.'[190]

De Valera then finally moved to make the decisive break with Cohalan and Devoy, holding a conference in Washington to form his new organisation. He chose the name – the American Association for the Recognition of the Irish Republic – himself. While the name, and the acronym AARIR, didn't quite roll off the tongue, there could at least be no ambiguity about its aims, as there had been with the Friends of Irish Freedom. In his speech at the founding conference, de Valera stressed his central demand. 'Combined, concerted action will be possible only with Ireland herself as the co-ordinating centre for such auxiliary aid as other countries may wish to give her.'[191] There would also be no ambiguity about aims or control in the new organisation. In an effort to avoid further controversy, he removed one inflammatory paragraph from the speech, which referred to

> a few individuals and . . . a certain newspaper, impelled by some insensate fear for their own power and supremacy, restlessly . . . sowing the seeds of distrust that could only crop in a harvest of discord and dissension.[192]

The new organisation quickly grew to an impressive membership of 700,000.[193]

The bond drive was ticking over; a new organisation loyal to the Irish leadership had been established; the recognition demand had been submitted. A new public face of the mission had also arrived in the United States on 5 December: Mary MacSwiney, sister of the martyred Terence. A fiery, passionate guardian of Republicanism, MacSwiney was a powerful draw in America and proved a canny political operator, managing to get on much better with Devoy and Cohalan than de Valera had. While de Valera retained his ambivalence about women in public life, she was 'the best possible candidate available' to take his place in leading the bond drive.[194]

It could be argued that de Valera's work in America was done. It was true that it had been done imperfectly – the Republic was no nearer to being recognised, and Irish-America was split more profoundly, than when he arrived. But no argument could be advanced by his colleagues in Dublin to make him stay. In any case, developments at home seemed to require his presence. Arthur Griffith had been arrested, leaving Michael Collins as Acting President. And there were rumours of peace moves in the air.

At a final meeting in his hotel he gave instructions to his staff.[195] A quasi-legal letter, witnessed by McGarrity and O'Mara, expressed his opinion on what should happen to the bond money 'in case of my death'. If the Irish people were to vote to establish any parliament that was not Republican, part at least should be held in trust to fund the Republican party, or military activity (against the British).[196] Extravagant plans were also made for spending hundreds of thousands of dollars on organisation in the United States[197] – plans he repudiated once back in Ireland, telling O'Mara to cut spending in America, as operations in Ireland 'are much more extensive than you could imagine'.[198] The contrast with his belief while he was there in the value of spending money in America was striking.

As he prepared to leave, emotions ran high. In a letter to Seán Nunan, de Valera said he would 'not write the sentimental things I feel lest I lose your good opinion . . . what I am tempted to write you could count as womanish'.[199] McGarrity recorded the President's final depature. After shaking hands, de Valera theatrically stood to attention and saluted before leaving. Predictably, the emotional Harry Boland 'was much more deeply affected than anyone in the room'.[200]

Once again, Barney Downes smuggled him onto his ship, this time the *Celtic,* which left New York on 11 December 1920, arriving in Liverpool nine days later.[201] Although colourful stories were later told about the perils he faced on the high seas, his main difficulty was as ever his terrible seasickness. 'He looked so ghastly that when he closed his eyes, you could easily imagine he was dead.'[202] In Liverpool, he was kept under wraps until passage could be arranged on the mail boat to Dublin. But these efforts were unnecessary: the British government was no longer attempting to capture him or prevent him returning to Ireland.

CHAPTER 13

FEELERS ARE BEING THROWN OUT IN ALL DIRECTIONS

This policy might necessitate a lightening off of their attacks on the enemy.

Éamon de Valera, January 1921[1]

Feelers are being thrown out in all directions just now.
Éamon de Valera to Michael Collins, March 1921[2]

The more you tighten things up and hurry them the better I will be pleased.
Éamon de Valera to Robert Brennan, April 1921[3]

On 13 December 1920, the British Cabinet had agreed that de Valera, 'who had expressed open approval of the murder campaign', should not be allowed to return to Ireland.[4] But a week later Lloyd George asked his ministers to reconsider, and to read two newspaper articles before making a final decision.[5] One, by Stephen Gwynn, advocated de Valera's return to Ireland, because he had far better judgement than Arthur Griffith.[6] The other, in the *Times,* predicted that 'political developments might be swifter and more satisfactory than most people dare to hope'.[7] Lloyd George pointed out that, while Gwynn was a nationalist, the Ireland correspondent of the *Times* was a unionist, and 'from different points of view they take pretty much the same hopeful view of the situation'. He then suggested that their policy should be to 'crush the murder gang', but that 'whenever there is any opening for peace take it and do not be too rough on the purely political lot'.[8]

So on the very day de Valera arrived in Liverpool, Home Secretary Edward Shortt, ordered that he was not to be prevented from landing anywhere in the United Kingdom.[9] Three days later the ban on his entry was formally lifted,[10] and immigration officers were instructed that he was not even to be searched on arrival.[11] He was to be 'regarded as "political" and no step was to be taken without reference to London'. When one intelligence operative saw de Valera in Dublin he 'looked the other way'.[12]

The day he landed in Dublin, 23 December, was also the day the Government of Ireland Act (1920) came into force. It formally partitioned Ireland and paved the way for elections the following year in the 26-county Southern Ireland and the six-county Northern Ireland. While nationalists would continue to rail against partition, it was now, as far as the British were concerned, an established fact, removing the main barrier to self-government for the rest of Ireland. The only matter still to be decided was exactly how much self-government could be won.

After landing, de Valera was driven to 5 Merrion Square, the home of his friend Robert Farnan.[13] Collins was among his early visitors, as was Cathal Brugha, the Minister for Defence, who arrived with a gun in his pocket.[14] Showing how out of touch he was, de Valera argued that the gun was more likely to get him into trouble than out of it; the implacable Brugha insisted that he would use it if necessary. According to de Valera's subsequent account, Brugha immediately started complaining about Collins, who had become President Substitute on Griffith's arrest. But the President did not then regard these differences 'as being of a dangerous character' and ignored them.[15]

The next morning, he had another important visitor, the chief of staff of the Volunteers, Richard Mulcahy. According to Mulcahy, de Valera was dismissive of guerrilla tactics, telling him that

> you're going too fast. This odd shooting of a policeman here and there is having a very bad effect on us from the propaganda point of view in America. What we want is one good battle about once a month with about five hundred men on each side.[16]

Not surprisingly, this comment did not go down well with Mulcahy, who noted:

You would feel that he disparaged our military efforts – at any rate he had no words of compliment or praise to give to it.[17]

Perhaps as a response, GHQ produced a military assessment of the campaign early in the new year, claiming that 'guerrilla strokes may be laughed at as "flea bites", but those of the Regular Army are blows in the air'.[18] That was as good a definition of, and justification for, guerrilla warfare as one could wish for. However, the debate with de Valera would continue.

Each minister was summoned individually to meet de Valera in Merrion Square to discuss their departments. At least one, Ernest Blythe, also discussed wider questions, arguing that compromise was essential, because there was no chance of winning a Republic; he understood de Valera to be broadly in agreement. On another occasion de Valera remarked that their best hope of a settlement was with the coalition then in power in Britain, and that 'we must endeavour to negotiate and agree with them before they went out of office'. Blythe recorded that 'I was quite positive from that time on that Mr. de Valera was no doctrinaire republican.'[19]

These one-on-one meetings are evidence of de Valera's preferred way of working. At his first Ministry meeting after his return from America, on 9 January, it was decided that meetings should be monthly and that de Valera 'may summon some members for consultation when required'.[20] Issues were to be dealt with either one-to-one or by *ad hoc* groups of ministers, rather than the full Ministry.[21] Of course, this was due in part to British activity,[22] but it also restricted collective decision-making, and concentrated power in de Valera's hands.

Collins had meanwhile been looking for a more suitable home for the President, finding it in a house owned by Margaret MacGarry, a wealthy sympathiser, in Strand Road, Sandymount. The house looked out over Merrion Strand and was secluded enough to allow de Valera to work quietly. He stayed there from 6 January until it was raided by the military in April. The household consisted of MacGarry's daughter Maeve as housekeeper and cook;[23] de Valera's personal secretary, Kathleen O'Connell; and a courier, Seán Harling.[24]

De Valera made himself at home, sending out to Greystones for books (on international law) and clothes.[25] Sinéad was also brought to meet her husband,[26] though even after five weeks back in Ireland he hadn't managed to see their children.[27] (As usual, Sinéad was understanding, sending a message to him 'not to try to come home or bother about us'.[28])

Collins in particular was irritated by de Valera's repetitious American yarns: on one occasion he pointed out that a particular anecdote had already been told two or three times.[29] In a letter to Griffith about the January meeting of the Dáil, Collins observed that 'the President himself went into matters connected with his wanderings at some length, but all the points are well enough known to you'.[30] Griffith too was struck by a change in de Valera's manner after the adulation he had received in the United States, considering him 'a good man who had been ruined by America'.[31]

One of de Valera's apparently more bizarre ideas was to send Collins to the United States. This seemed inopportune to some. Mulcahy, for instance, thought that 'only a person living in fairyland' could think that Collins 'could be spared at such a moment'.[32] Collins himself, as he told Boland, was 'not anxious to leave home, and is making a fight for his view'.[33] One Ministry colleague remembered him being 'rather truculent about the matter' when it was raised at the first meeting after de Valera returned to Ireland.[34] However, the Ministry unanimously backed the suggestion – a less than rousing vote of confidence in the Minister for Finance from his colleagues.

De Valera's attempt to send Collins to America is usually interpreted as a sign of 'his lack of confidence in Collins and his determination to suppress any perceived threat to his own authority',[35] and the remark attributed to Collins – 'The long hoor won't get rid of me as easy as that' – is generally taken as a sign that he was 'outraged and hurt'.[36] However, it may not be as simple as that, and it is important not to read the later animosities over the Treaty back into this disagreement. There was undoubtedly tension as de Valera moved to take over the reins that Collins had held so well. But Mulcahy, no fan of de Valera's, referred to Collins's 'long hoor' remark as 'pungent if laughing'.[37]

And it is arguable that Collins was the very man to achieve the many aims de Valera set for him: to get the American mission's finances under control and prepare for a new loan; to set up an Irish banking institution and a trading company; to establish a boycott of British goods; to improve communications and propaganda; to secure military supplies; to allow Boland to come home; and to secure unity among Irish-Americans. Collins's position in the IRB might help bring Devoy and Cohalan back on board ('I believe you are the only man who can'). De Valera also rightly emphasised the effect Collins could have in America 'if only you will not be too modest to exploit your fame'. And he ended with a final plea in favour of his going.

Of course there is an aspect to your mission which to me is as important as any in the above. It is that we will not have here, so to speak, 'all our eggs in the one basket', and that whatever coup the English may attempt, the line of succession is safe, and the future provided for.[38]

There was another reason for wanting to send Collins out of the country: his presence was a potential block to the tentative peace moves. Before Christmas, Lloyd George had asked the Archbishop of Perth, Patrick Clune, to approach Sinn Féin on his behalf. Clune – whose nephew Conor had been murdered in Dublin Castle on the night of Bloody Sunday, along with two Volunteer officers, Dick McKee and Peadar Clancy – met Griffith, who was in jail, and Collins to pass on Lloyd George's offer of an unofficial truce, under which the British would call off reprisals, arrests and pursuits if the Volunteers ceased operations.[39]

Both Griffith and Collins were enthusiastic, but Lloyd George's position stiffened after a number of indications that Sinn Féin was weakening – an inquorate meeting of Galway County Council called for peace talks, as did Sinn Féin Vice-President Father Michael O'Flanagan, while Wexford TD Roger Sweetman criticised the IRA campaign.[40] Lloyd George now demanded that the IRA should surrender arms before a Truce – a demand which had no prospect of success.

So by the time de Valera arrived back in Ireland, the Clune initiative was dead. However, his 'first official work' in Dublin was to read the file dealing with it,[41] and he would surely have noticed that one of Lloyd George's conditions related to any meeting of the Dáil during a truce. Lloyd George said there were some members 'they could not allow to assemble', naming Collins and Mulcahy in particular, and suggesting that they might leave the country for a time to avoid difficulties. Clune told him that this was impossible,[42] but it may well have occurred to de Valera that this was another reason to send Collins to the United States. If this was in de Valera's mind, he was careful not to say so. In any event, by April he had accepted that it was better for Collins to stay, for the moment at least.

Desultory peace moves continued throughout January 1921, involving a mixed cast of characters: Father O'Flanagan, who was working with Lord Justice James O'Connor (a former Blackrock College pupil); Dublin Castle officials Andy Cope and Mark Sturgis, as well as Margery Greenwood, wife of the Chief Secretary, Hamar Greenwood.

Of more immediate concern to him were the elections for the new Parliament of Northern Ireland, which were to be held in May. De Valera approached the Nationalist leader in the North, Joe Devlin (apparently in the first week of January),[43] and also discussed the forthcoming elections with the Bishop of Down and Connor, Dr Joseph MacRory, who was optimistic that the other nationalist parties would stand down in favour of Sinn Féin.[44] De Valera recognised the danger of contesting if Republicans and Nationalists couldn't be sure of winning at least ten seats. If they couldn't manage that, the British would claim that partition was justified, and it would be better to boycott the elections. But if they could realistically hope to win a quarter or so of the seats, 'the arguments are altogether in favour of vigorously contesting . . . the representatives elected will become members of Dáil Éireann'. Failing to contest would also be taken as an acceptance of partition and would, according to de Valera, drive supporters into the Nationalist Party camp – 'a result which might later have a dangerous reactionary effect, by contagion, on the South'.[45]

The elections to the Northern Parliament, as to the Southern, would be held under proportional representation, a largely unknown quantity as far as de Valera was concerned ('I have not yet studied the PR system in use'[46]). The rationale for its introduction was to protect minorities on both sides of the border; it would also, of course, tend to reduce the dominance of the biggest party in the system and could prevent a landslide similar to 1918. Local elections using PR were held (in the 32 counties) in two stages in 1920, with cities and towns voting in January, and rural areas in June. In the January poll Sinn Féin did relatively poorly, winning only 550 of the 1,806 seats on offer.[47] The elections for rural councils in June were a different story, with many seats uncontested (thanks to 'persuasion' by the IRA in many areas), giving Sinn Féin a landslide.[48] De Valera asked for a statistical study of the results in the area of Northern Ireland, as well as for predictions of the likely outcome in a general election.[49]

The Dáil Ministry decided on 6 February to contest the elections in the North, appointing Austin Stack as Director of Elections. Given his rather mixed record as a minister, this 'did not augur well for the campaign'.[50]

While de Valera had tried to meet as many TDs as possible individually, it was obviously more important to hold a session of the Dáil, and a secret meeting was organised for 21 January, the second anniversary of its inaugural meeting. But while Collins thought the risk worth taking, Brugha strongly opposed de Valera's attending, fearing a British swoop that could leave the entire Ministry and Dáil behind bars.[51] De Valera accepted Brugha's advice, much to the annoyance of the 24 TDs who risked arrest and imprisonment by attending. They were told that de Valera would meet any of them he had not seen individually, and it was suggested that the reports of various ministers could be read and discussed. But the deputies revolted, refusing to discuss matters in the absence of

Collins and Brugha as well as de Valera, and unanimously passed a motion calling for another session at which principal ministers would attend, and with a report from de Valera, 'so that definite decisions on policy can be come to by the Dáil'.[52]

It was an insulting way to treat the TDs, and when the session resumed on 25 January in the home of Alderman Walter Cole in Mountjoy Square, de Valera apologised for his absence on the previous occasion. He began by giving his impression – which he admitted was 'from the outside', given his lengthy absence – of the military situation. The enemy had superior force, while the Irish side had only the 'power of moral resistance'. Not being strong enough to bring the conflict to a decision, their policy must be one of delay. Speaking of the Irish forces, he said that

> their policy should be to stick on, to show no change on the outside as
> far as possible, and at the same time to make the burden on the people
> as light as they could. This policy might necessitate a lightening off of
> their attacks on the enemy.[53]

His view was supported by two TDs, Liam de Róiste and Roger Sweetman. But a succession of speakers disagreed with talk of easing off. Piaras Béaslaí suggested that 'everyone in Ireland must suffer'; Joseph MacDonagh urged that, 'even though houses were burned and people shot, it would be well worth while if they achieved the result they hoped to achieve'; Kevin O'Higgins said 'any slackening in military activities would be a mistake', as the British would assume that 'the Republicans were on the run'; and Austin Stack said 'Ireland could well afford to lose some of the 180,000 young men saved [through the avoidance of conscription] in the last few years'.[54]

De Valera accepted that 'the sense of the meeting was that the policy he suggested was too weak' and dropped his proposal.[55]

De Valera's office was busy, with couriers calling four or five times a day with despatches from other departments. Meetings with ministers, military leaders and officials required the arrangement of safe houses and involved de Valera in perilous journeys around the city (he had no idea he was not in danger of arrest). Maeve MacGarry recalled a trip into Fitzwilliam Square for a meeting with Seán MacEntee and Joseph Devlin. After narrowly avoiding a British checkpoint, they found themselves running down a side street just as an ambush began on Leeson Street Bridge.

The firing was going on as we went down Lad Lane, and when we arrived at the house . . . Joe Devlin was in a panic; so was MacEntee who thought we were caught in the ambush.[56]

If de Valera agreed to give an interview to a journalist, an out-of-the-way location would have to be found, and a guide would have to collect the reporter from their hotel and ensure they were not followed.[57] The correspondent of the Associated Press got the first interview with de Valera since his return to Ireland, in conditions of great secrecy. He was invited to climb into a motorcycle sidecar and put on goggles, which in effect blinded him, before being delivered to 'a well-furnished living room', where a 'tall man dressed in a well-fitting lounge suit entered and held out his hand. He was the President.' The writer declined to comment on 'his present appearance' (probably a reference to the moustache de Valera was wearing) but said he 'looks extremely fit and conveys the impression of being free from any sense of personal danger, debonair and alive with energy'.[58]

De Valera was anxious to oversee the work of all departments. In March he had two forms sent to each minister to complete, one noting staff, salary, rent and other expenses, the other a summary of activities and suggestions for the development of the department.[59] He was quick to take ministers to task, with W. T. Cosgrave, Minister for Local Government, a frequent target. A proposed circular needed to be edited and condensed, de Valera said, as it was 'very obscure in parts'. Two days later Cosgrave was accused of having 'missed the whole point' of a government decision. In April another circular was criticised as 'not nearly as telling as they could be made by proper attention to the wording'. De Valera said he would do his best to redraft it but complained that 'really the Department should have a document like this almost perfect before it is sent along for final sanction'.[60]

His most serious problem was Foreign Affairs, where the incompetence of the minister, Count Plunkett, is evident in de Valera's anxiety 'to set up something that might correspond to a real Department'.[61] His solution was to appoint Robert Brennan Under-Secretary for Foreign Affairs, with instructions to keep the President 'in the closest personal touch with this department',[62] as it was the one 'for which I feel the most immediate personal responsibility'.[63] Plunkett didn't appear to realise he was being side-lined, telling de Valera he was 'glad to have Bob Brennan's assistance'.[64] De Valera's instructions to Brennan were clear: he was to 'deal with the correspondence as if you were the head of the Department'.[65]

When he later asked Brennan to consult Plunkett and 'seek his opinions in advance',[66] Brennan pointed out that such consultation 'would be a useless waste of time on my part and would merely shorten my present period of being at large'.[67] De Valera quickly backtracked.

> Just keep him fairly well informed and do him the courtesy of asking his opinion now and then on important matters. The more you tighten things up and *hurry* them the better I will be pleased.[68]

In April 1921 the Archbishop of Dublin, William Walsh, died, leaving vacant the chancellorship of the National University. A group of academics suggested de Valera as his successor,[69] an idea that greatly appealed to him. Clearly he was chosen for political rather than academic reasons – as Donal McCartney dryly observed, his selection, given his academic record, 'should be a matter of encouragement to all struggling students'.[70] When the matter came before the government, de Valera

> manifested a great deal of coyness and proceeded to argue that somebody who had devoted himself to academic affairs would be more suitable; also that perhaps an active politician might not serve the interests of the University best . . . he, who actually wanted to be Chancellor, was arguing against the proposal, while the rest of us, who fundamentally did not care a damn, were urging him to accept the post. Ultimately, Collins asked de Valera to cut the cackle and not keep us there all night.'[71]

This was symptomatic of his tendency to rehearse every aspect of a matter before a decision was reached – a tendency which would become more marked in later years.

The safe house at Sandymount, from where de Valera was operating, was broken up in April. A raid on the MacGarry house in Fitzwilliam Square had disclosed the address; having been warned, de Valera swiftly decamped back to Robert Farnan's house in Merrion Square. Kathleen O'Connell and Maeve MacGarry stayed behind at Sandymount to burn some papers.[72] When the Black and Tans raided the house, they found a pair of fur-lined gloves with de Valera's name inside, a present from Cumann na mBan in Ennis. The two women were 'severely questioned' but not arrested. O'Connell made her way to Merrion Square, where she resumed her duties. 'The work of the government had to go on. The President had to dictate letters and memoranda to me.'[73]

Once again, Collins made arrangements for a more permanent address, enlisting Margaret MacGarry to purchase a house, Glenvar, in Cross Avenue in Blackrock. De Valera, Maeve MacGarry and Kathleen O'Connell moved in on 18 May.[74]

De Valera, at first at least, was very reliant on Collins. He had taken charge of de Valera's accommodation, family visits and personal safety. To Harry Boland he remarked that 'Mick is as usual doing not two, but a dozen men's work',[75] and he urged Collins to be careful. 'For Heaven's sake don't run more risks than are absolutely necessary!'[76] But when the disagreements between Brugha and Collins developed into accusations of financial impropriety relating to the buying of arms in Scotland, de Valera felt that, as President, he must remain neutral – a decision that didn't go down well with Collins. Robert Barton found that Collins 'bore resentment to de Valera for the impartial attitude he adopted regarding this quarrel'.[77]

Collins vented his exasperation with Brugha in a letter to de Valera in February. He sent him a copy of a letter from Brugha 'as a specimen of what I have to submit to and contend with . . . It is not gentlemanly, it is not dignified and above all it is not organisation.'[78] In response to this, or possibly to another similar complaint, de Valera wrote:

> I would be sorry to think that your feeling discontented and dissatisfied and fed up, was due to anything more than natural physical reaction after the terrible strain you have been subjected to.[79]

With hindsight, de Valera was inclined to stress the difficulty of a situation in which Collins was in military matters Brugha's subordinate while at the same time being his equal in the Ministry. But even many years later, he still resented Collins's increasing independence.

> From April on, Collins did not seem to accept my view of things as he had done before, and was inclined to give public expression to his own views.[80]

The accounts row came at a time of increased danger for senior Volunteer officers. For security reasons, Mulcahy would allow no more than two or three members of the Staff to meet at one time, yet Brugha insisted on gathering the entire staff so he could air his suspicions about the Scottish accounts. Mulcahy went straight afterwards to de Valera to complain about Brugha's attitude. The President mused: 'You know I think Cathal is jealous of Mick.' When Mulcahy agreed, de Valera added: 'Isn't it a terrible thing that a man with the qualities that Cathal undoubtedly has would fall a victim to a dirty little vice like jealousy.'[81]

The details of the disagreement are convoluted, but the root of it was Brugha's insistence on strict accounting for funds spent in the murky underworld of arms deals. If it seems unreasonable to expect accurate accounting for arms deals, it should be noted that Collins was a stickler for such accuracy in others; as Director of Intelligence in the IRA he was being held to the standards he himself imposed as Minister for Finance. This argument blew over, but the dislike between Collins and Brugha would resurface during the Truce – with alarming results.

On de Valera's instructions the Standing Committee of Sinn Féin was convened on 10 February 1921, the first time it had met in three months. He stressed that the organisation needed 'the closest possible care and attention at the present moment'. Care and attention would not be needed in the 26 counties, as Sinn Féin got a free run in the May general election: 124 party candidates were returned unopposed from the 26 geographical constituencies and from the National University of Ireland; four Independent Unionist candidates, also unopposed, were returned from Dublin University (Trinity College). All Sinn Féin's efforts could therefore be put into the election in Northern Ireland. De Valera was particularly keen on aiming propaganda at unionists, urging them 'to do their part to end the present struggle by siding definitely with their fellow-countrymen and take away England's last excuse'.[82] The Dáil and Sinn Féin each put up £1,000 for this purpose.[83]

Despite the arrest of Sinn Féin organisers, the confiscation of literature and the clear hostility of the unionist population, de Valera was upbeat about the party's electoral prospects, claiming that Sinn Féin could win a third of the seats (17 or 18) and that 'with the other Nationalist and non-partitionists we may secure even half'.[84] Others were less sanguine, the party's Northern organiser Éamonn Donnelly warning that 'the only effect that all our literature and leaflets etc. will have upon them is to bring them out to vote against us in great numbers'.[85] The unionist *Belfast Telegraph* agreed, saying that the more Sinn Féin attacked partition, the more they 'got the back of the Ulsterman up'.[86] The results (despite the use of proportional representation) were a resounding victory for Sir James Craig and the Unionists: with 67 per cent of the vote, they won 40 seats, every one of their candidates being elected. Sinn Féin ran more candidates than the Nationalists – 20 to their 12 – and won more votes – 20.5 per cent to 11.8 per cent – but each party got six seats.[87] De Valera was elected for Down, Eoin MacNeill for Derry, Michael Collins for Armagh, and Arthur Griffith, Seán Milroy and Seán O'Mahony for Fermanagh-Tyrone. All six were from the South, and all except O'Mahony were elected for constituencies in the 26-county area as well, so the Second Dáil was made up of the 124 TDs returned unopposed in the South, and O'Mahony.[88]

In the wider struggle, propaganda was crucial, and de Valera worked closely with his successive Directors of Publicity, Desmond FitzGerald and Erskine Childers. He wanted to know how press releases were received by journalists ('We must learn by experience what they are eager to get and give it them'[89]), and insisted on information being fully checked before release ('Anything dealing with Dáil transactions . . . should be countersigned by the Secretary or Speaker of the Dáil and its publication sanctioned by me'[90]). And he kept an eye on how individual journalists reported Irish news ('O'Connell should be approached and his carbon of the wire secured, to find out whether the changes were made here or over . . .'[91]).

While some British officials dismissed his comments to the press as 'the usual bombastic highfalutin stuff that this curious President indulges in',[92] de Valera had a good nose for a story. When the British 'Weekly Summary' described him as coming from 'a race of treacherous murderers' he ordered a copy sent to the Spanish ambassador in London, with the offending passage marked, and protests to be arranged from sympathetic Spaniards.[93]

At the end of February, de Valera wrote to Harry Boland in the United States, arguing that

> our position should be simply that we are insisting on only one right, and that is the right of the people of this country to determine for themselves how they should be governed. That sounds moderate, but includes everything.[94]

It didn't seem to occur to him that this was precisely the position he had condemned Daniel Cohalan for taking at the Republican Convention in Chicago the previous year.

Propaganda considerations also governed the decision to have the Dáil take formal responsibility for the activities of the IRA. Mulcahy was opposed to this, believing that if ministers were caught by the British they would have 'a rope tied round their necks' by assuming responsibility for the war.[95] But the acting Director of Publicity, Erskine Childers, took the view that unless the politicians took formal responsibility they would not be able to counteract the British claim that the IRA was a 'murder gang'.[96] Childers won the argument – by no means the last indication of his influence on de Valera.

When the Dáil met on 11 March, de Valera said he didn't think it was right that the IRA should appear to be 'irresponsible forces'. TDs should 'take full responsibility for all the operations of their Army. That would practically mean a public acceptance of a State of War.' His suggestion was approved unanimously.[97]

His other significant comment came during a discussion on the North, when James Dolan asked if the Ministry had considered offering devolution. De Valera responded that this was not the time to do so but that 'he was not against such a policy'.[98]

As the War of Independence dragged on, there was no shortage of potential peace-makers, as de Valera remarked to Collins: 'Feelers are being thrown out in all directions just now'.[99] All these attempts foundered on de Valera's insistence on direct negotiations. The most significant of these approaches involved a pillar of the British establishment. Edward George Villiers Stanley, the 17th Earl of Derby, was a Conservative grandee who had most recently served as British ambassador to France. Word that he was coming came through Dr Edward Mulhern, Bishop of Dromore, who also informed de Valera that Lord Derby would first meet Cardinal Logue. This worried de Valera, as he believed that Logue would sell the pass. De Valera, through Mulhern, tried to get Logue either to insist that a republic was the only solution or to say that it was a matter for politicians. Logue, however, rejected this advice, at which point de Valera

> knew we were in real danger; that a half loaf offer would be made and that there would be a big move on to take the half loaf as being better, it would be said, than no bread . . . I . . . feared a general election in which all the powerful influences would be used against the Republic.[100]

The President and the peer met on 21 April at James O'Mara's house in Fitzwilliam Place. The two men had tea and discussed the situation for two or three hours. De Valera felt that Derby was trying to find out how far he was prepared to go to meet the British position; partly in response to what he regarded as Logue's unhelpful moderation, de Valera stuck strictly to the position that the Republic had been declared and would have to be recognised.[101] While the discussion did not produce much movement, de Valera regarded it as the first important contact with the

British and as an indication that they 'desired to make peace if satisfactory terms could be arranged'.[102]

Derby seems to have come away with the impression, despite de Valera's insistence, that the Irish leaders *would* accept something less than a republic.[103] He reported back to Lloyd George, and on his behalf sent a message to de Valera explaining that the Prime Minister would be making a speech in the House of Commons on Ireland. Lloyd George wanted to know if he could say

> that those controlling the Irish movement will not consent to meet him or any representatives of the Government unless the principle of complete independence be first conceded.[104]

This, of course, would have put the Irish side in the wrong, making it seem that they were refusing to talk until they were guaranteed the outcome they wanted. This de Valera regarded as 'evidence, if any one wants it, of the trickiness of the gentleman we have to deal with in L.G.'.[105]

De Valera's reply to Derby turned the tables, asking Lloyd George a question of his own.

> Will he not consent to meet me or any representative of the Government of Ireland unless the principle of complete independence be first surrendered by us?[106]

Derby wryly responded that 'although you answer my question by asking another it was really a sufficient answer'. He said that he had spoken to Lloyd George before the speech in the House of Commons, and that his statement there 'would give you the information you ask'.[107]

Lloyd George told the House of Commons that he was willing to meet 'any representative Irishman [MP] . . . not under suspicion of murder', to discuss 'any subject of public importance *without laying down any preliminary conditions* as to the policy which the Member desires to advocate, or the opinion he intends to express'. While this was encouraging, he also intimated that the demand for a republic was one 'that the people of this country cannot accept' and that the British government was determined to 're-establish authority in Ireland, whatever time it takes'.[108]

De Valera was right to be suspicious of Lloyd George, who, the day before his speech, told Cabinet colleagues that the IRA 'are gradually being beaten' and that 'a truce would give them breathing space'.[109] A fortnight later he remained obdurate, insisting that 'these people will come round sooner or later' and joining the majority in Cabinet in voting against a truce.[110]

Andy Cope, Assistant Under-Secretary at Dublin Castle, who was behind many of these peace moves, was convinced that one way of making progress was to bring together de Valera and Sir James Craig, Prime Minister-in-waiting of Northern Ireland. Craig, from a wealthy Presbyterian background, was an accomplished organiser. It was he more than anyone who had organised the resistance to home rule before the First World War, and now he was building up an infant government in Belfast. His motive in meeting de Valera was to try to get his agreement about the border.[111] This was as unrealistic as de Valera's aim of persuading Craig to agree to unity, but, encouraged by Hamar Greenwood ('I am certain V is the one man who can deliver the goods'[112]) and by Cope, Craig agreed to the meeting.

With considerable courage, Craig agreed to be conducted by a number of IRA men to meet de Valera. The party changed cars before arriving at a house on the Howth Road protected by a number of guards disguised as workmen. When they went inside, de Valera was waiting. According to Craig, he had 'very much the look of a hunted man, and has also a nervous habit of licking his lips constantly'.[113] De Valera believed the shoe was on the other foot, being 'amused' that Craig was 'very frightened' during their meeting.[114] In their hour and a half of conversation, de Valera struck Craig as being 'more of a visionary than practical . . . harping on the grievances of Ireland for the last 700 years'.[115] Emmet Dalton, one of the IRA guards, claimed that Craig told him after his meeting that de Valera was 'impossible'.[116] A similar sentiment was expressed to Andy Cope, who was told that

> de Valera was like a hunted hare – obviously speaking like a gramophone – Republic – '98 – the republican mandate from the Irish people which had not been revoked, etc. . . .[117]

De Valera later indignantly denied that he had subjected Craig to a lecture.

> The only historical matter discussed was the circumstances in which the Act of Union was passed, and these merely by way of reply to Sir James Craig's contention that Ireland was morally bound by that Act.[118]

In Dublin Castle the meeting was viewed as

> very near, if not quite, a public sign that Sinn Féin will accept less than
> a Republic – for if they *know* they are absolutely irreconcilable why
> meet at all.[119]

In London it was similarly seen as Sinn Féin's 'tacit abandonment of
republicanism as an immediate policy'.[120]

The well-informed Collins picked up on this sentiment, warning de
Valera that the meeting was being taken as 'an admission of something by
you and by us'.[121] Characteristically, de Valera denied this and insisted that
his willingness to meet Craig had benefited their position.[122] However,
given that Craig denied he had sought the meeting, de Valera correctly
blamed Cope for engineering the whole thing, concluding that he was

> unreliable in matters of this nature. I can really see no evidence
> whatsoever that the other side has any disposition towards peace. It is
> manoeuvring, nothing else. I'm done with it.[123]

In London, the Cabinet agreed that if the Parliament of Southern
Ireland wasn't operating by 12 July, Crown Colony government under a
Governor appointed by London would be introduced, along with martial
law. Seventeen additional infantry battalions would give the military the
power to make use of this change in regime.[124] However, this troop build-
up had its limitations. According to General Sir Nevil Macready, the
military commander in Ireland, if the conflict was still going on in
October the entire force would have to be relieved – and he and his
superiors in London were well aware that there was no alternative force
available to do that, given demands elsewhere in the world.[125] This gave
the British three months to suppress the IRA, a very tall order. Macready
was personally opposed to escalation, and in any case doubted the
Cabinet's resolve. 'Will they begin to howl when they hear of our shooting
a hundred men in one week?'[126]

Meanwhile, de Valera was planning some escalation of his own. Early
in 1921, he had proposed two potential 'spectaculars' to the GHQ staff –
the capture of Beggars Bush Barracks, the headquarters of the Auxiliaries,
or the destruction of the Custom House, along with the tax collection
records it housed. He believed something on this scale, and in Dublin,
was necessary in order to attract international attention.[127] The President
was both right and wrong in his desire for a 'spectacular'. Militarily,

larger engagements were a disaster, but they could be justified on propaganda grounds. But as he explained to the Dáil in January, he also assumed that a change in tactics would reduce the pressure on the people, because there would be fewer reprisals. This would of course be better from a humanitarian point of view; but it would have been a disaster for Irish propaganda. One of the main aims of guerrilla warfare is to provoke the opposing force into over-reaction which will win international sympathy for the cause – de Valera's proposed change in strategy would have removed the most powerful weapon in the Irish publicity campaign.

An attack on Beggars Bush was ruled out after reconnaissance, so the Custom House option was agreed on.[128] De Valera later recalled this decision, without mentioning that it had been his own idea.

> I disliked the idea of destroying such a beautiful building, but I was finally satisfied that the extent to which it would destroy British administration here made the sacrifice worthwhile.[129]

The Custom House was set on fire on May 25 and the records destroyed, but a botched withdrawal meant that British forces arrived before the IRA could get away. Five IRA men were killed and about a hundred arrested, which put the Dublin Brigade out of action for the foreseeable future – a very heavy price to pay.

On 22 June further disaster appeared to strike when de Valera was arrested. The house in Blackrock should have been safe – and it would have been had the local IRA been aware that the President was staying there. But they weren't and so used the neighbouring house as a base for censoring intercepted post. The result was a raid by the military, which led them next-door.[130] De Valera was sitting on a bench in the garden with Dr Farnan's sister-in-law, Margaret Macken, teaching her Irish, when they saw a file of soldiers approaching.[131] With the house full of documents it wasn't long before the officers realised they had caught someone important, though they didn't know who. De Valera gave his name as 'Sankey'[132] – ironically, had he given his real name he might not have been arrested. Among the documents found were an IRA operations report relating to an ambush in Drumcondra, and a draft letter for signature by the Minister for Defence – both highly incriminating.[133] In Portobello Barracks he was accommodated in the officers' quarters and fed from the officers' mess. His captors noted that 'the point which appeared to rankle most with him was the fact that his arrest was effected by a party of troops consisting of only ten men'.[134] He had arranged that, in the event of his arrest, Austin Stack was to take over, as President Substitute,[135] which was odd, given that Collins had taken over when Griffith was arrested.[136]

While de Valera was kicking his heels in British custody, Cope had been busily attempting to set up a meeting with him. When he discovered he had been arrested he ordered his immediate release. Cope's colleague at the Castle, Mark Sturgis, noted that this would be a 'snub to our hero who has boasted of being on the run and who can't look very grand when we pick him up and instantly let him go'.[137] Cope had hoped to keep the arrest and release secret; but de Valera himself instructed the Department of Publicity to issue a press release to avoid suspicions of a secret deal.[138]

De Valera wrote to Diarmuid O'Hegarty, the Secretary to the Ministry, that 'I was released, of course, unconditionally, but for reasons of high British policy I expect.'[139] He initially thought he would be unable to continue running the underground government, and considered joining the flying columns in the South.[140] O'Hegarty warned him not to move about too much – 'there is such a thing as a "murder gang"' – but de Valera decided he could now come more into the open, setting up an office in the Mansion House from Monday 27 June.[141] In the meantime, he had received (through Bishop Mulhern) what he had been waiting for: a direct invitation to talks from Lloyd George.[142]

Why did Lloyd George suddenly change his mind on talking to Sinn Féin? There were a number of explanations: Cabinet pressure for a truce; the military situation; and the election results, north and south. The usually well-informed Tim Healy claimed that, 'when the Cabinet was almost split over Ireland, Winston wobbled, and LG's letter to De V is simply the result of the intrigue'.[143] There was also the military need for an (unlikely) quick victory to avoid the problem of troop rotation in the winter. And the elections had shown Sinn Féin's stranglehold in the South; more importantly, it brought Northern Ireland into being.

This last development was seized on by the Prime Minister of the Union of South Africa, Jan Smuts, who was in Britain for the Imperial Conference. In the middle of June he wrote to Lloyd George pointing out that

> the establishment of the Northern Parliament definitely eliminates the coercion of Ulster, and the road is clear now to deal on the most statesmanlike lines with the rest of Ireland . . .

He suggested that the visit of the King to Belfast to open the new Northern Ireland Parliament could be used to call for peace.[144]

On 22 June, the day of De Valera's arrest, King George V opened the Parliament, and, in words written by Smuts, said,

> I appeal to all Irishmen to pause, to stretch out the hand of forbearance and conciliation, to forgive and forget, and to join in making for the land they love a new era of peace, contentment and goodwill.[145]

Two days later, the British Cabinet agreed with Lloyd George's suggestion that they should follow this appeal by inviting Craig and de Valera to talks. The cessation of hostilities was not to be made a precondition.[146] Lloyd George regarded the invitation as an each-way bet: it might lead to peace, but if de Valera refused to come it would 'strengthen our position when we come to set up Crown Colony Government and martial law'.[147]

Lloyd George's letter invited Craig, as Prime Minister of Northern Ireland, and de Valera, 'as the chosen leader of the great majority in Southern Ireland', to come to London for talks; he could bring with him any colleagues he chose, all of whom would be given safe conduct.[148] Sinn Féin's agent in London, Art O'Brien, remarked that the letter was 'a further and very interesting advance on the part of England,' noting the lack of any exclusion on the colleagues de Valera could bring with him.[149] Michael Collins agreed that the letter was an advance,

> but I waver in my opinion as to whether or not it is genuine – even if genuine, I believe its underlying principle is that our acceptance of the letter would by implication also mean our acceptance of Partition.[150]

For de Valera, the invitation was a vindication of his refusal to entertain suggestions of secret negotiations. He sent a holding reply, laying down a marker that agreement would be impossible 'if you deny Ireland's essential unity and set aside the principle of national self-determination'. He then informed Lloyd George that he was 'seeking a conference with certain representatives of the political minority in this country'.[151] He then wrote to Craig, and to the southern Unionists Lord Midleton, Sir Maurice Dockrell, Sir Robert Woods and Andrew Jameson, inviting them to a meeting on 4 July, where he, as 'spokesman of the nation', could 'learn from you at first hand the views of a certain section of our people of whom you are representative'.[152] Craig considered de Valera's invitation to be 'sheer insolence'[153] – he was, after all, already Prime Minister of an established government, and he intended 'to sit on Ulster like a rock'.[154] The other four, who had no such luxury, accepted.

Cheering crowds thronged Dawson Street as first de Valera and then the southern Unionist leaders arrived. After their three-hour meeting, Midleton acted as an intermediary with Lloyd George, securing from him an agreement to a truce.[155] This was in itself a significant victory for Sinn Féin: there was no demand for the surrender of arms, as there had been during the Clune talks, and by agreeing a truce the British were in effect recognising the IRA as a combatant force, not a 'murder gang'.

Prime Minister Smuts came to Dublin on the 5th to meet de Valera and his colleagues and to continue 'jollying them along the garden path'.[156] He claimed South Africans were better off now as a dominion than they had been under the old Boer republics.[157] Smuts was not impressed by de Valera, who 'spoke like a visionary. He spoke continually of generations of oppression and seemed to live in a world of dreams, visions and shadows'.[158]

After a further meeting on 8 July with de Valera, Midleton and his colleagues went to General Macready's headquarters to discuss a truce; finally, Macready himself went to the Mansion House to speak directly to de Valera, and terms were agreed.[159]

In his memoirs, Macready was dismissive of de Valera – 'a highly strung, vain individual of limited outlook, incapable of a broad view on any subject, but an adept at splitting hairs',[160] sentiments which may have been prompted by his unhappiness at having to negotiate with a man he regarded as a rebel. The Truce was to come into force at noon on the 11th. The terms were almost identical to those proposed in the Clune talks more than six months before.[161]

In a proclamation to the Irish people, de Valera urged them to show discipline and to be ready to resist should force be used. Their representatives, he assured them, would 'do their utmost to secure a just and peaceful termination of this struggle'[162] – there was no mention, interestingly, of the Republic.

Dublin greeted the Truce with joy.

Crowds flooded the streets, and overladen trams took tens of thousands of day trippers to the seaside. Members of the Auxiliary Division commandeered military vehicles to join them. Ice cream vans sold 'Gaelic ice cream', and the city's dealers laid out the fruit and vegetables on their handcarts in patriotic displays.[163]

Charlie Dalton, a young member of Collins's Squad, was almost overcome.

> I saw our tricolour flag waving from every window. I am not going to describe my emotions. I felt like a kid, a lump in my throat, trying not to burst out crying.[164]

Liam Deasy, one of the fighting men of the South, experienced a different reaction.

> The news was received in silence. There was no enthusiasm. The feeling seemed to be that this was the end of an epoch and that things would never be the same again.[165]

Whether these forebodings would come true depended largely on de Valera's next moves.

CHAPTER 14

I BEGGED THEM TO RISK IT

They were leaving their ablest player in reserve . . .
            W. T. Cosgrave on de Valera's decision not to
                            attend peace negotiations[1]

This is the supreme test, if we survive this test we have won.
            Éamon de Valera, October 1921[2]

*They said at the Cabinet meeting that it was a gamble – I begged
them to risk it.*

            Éamon de Valera, December 1921[3]

As Dublin was celebrating the Truce, de Valera and his staff were busy packing for their departure to London to meet Lloyd George. The delegation chosen by de Valera included the ministers Arthur Griffith, Count Plunkett, Austin Stack and Robert Barton (all but Griffith being hard-liners on the issue of the Republic); Erskine Childers; and the Lord Mayor of Dublin, Laurence O'Neill. They were accompanied by de Valera's personal secretary Kathleen O'Connell; and his friend Robert Farnan and his wife, Lora.[4] The delegation did not, however, include Michael Collins, who came out to Blackrock to protest at his exclusion. O'Connell recorded 'hot discussion. President rather upset.'[5] De Valera later claimed he excluded Collins in order to maintain his anonymity, so that if war resumed he could continue to evade British capture[6] – though if this was really in his mind it makes his attempt to send Collins to America, and his insistence on him being one of the plenipotentiaries later in the year, all the stranger.

The Irish delegation arrived in London on 12 July; while the rest of the party stayed at the Grosvenor Hotel, de Valera, O'Connell and the

Farnans went to a private house in West Halkin Street. O'Connell found the time to send a card to Sinéad de Valera with a photo of herself and Lora Farnan; in return, Sinéad suggested that 'by way of a little diversion' they should get de Valera and Robert Farnan to sing 'The Whistling Thief' – 'but be sure Dev takes the part "Mary, Mary"'.[7] The party was unlikely to have had time for such light relief, though it was noticeable that de Valera's secretary was better at keeping in touch with his wife than he was.

Lloyd George was keen to stress to de Valera their shared Celtic background, scoring an early point by claiming that the Celts had no word for 'Republic'.[8] He could equally have stressed their somewhat similar childhoods. The Welshman had also lost his father in infancy, and had been raised in part by his maternal uncle. However, he enjoyed a much closer relationship than did de Valera, adding his uncle's surname, Lloyd, to his own, George, in his honour.[9] As a young MP he had been an outspoken opponent of the Boer War, but he was always ambivalent about the Irish question, believing that whatever its merits, it was 'worth neither the destruction of the Liberal government nor the postponement of other legislation'.[10] He was also, of course, the head of a Coalition with an overwhelming Conservative majority.

Lloyd George was famously untrustworthy. He was always determined in negotiations 'to make a quick bargain rather than find a permanent solution to the underlying problem'.[11] According to John Maynard Keynes, who observed him at close quarters during the Paris Peace Conference, he was 'rooted in nothing; he is void and without content'. And yet, Keynes conceded, his negotiation skills were beyond compare, 'with six or seven senses not available to ordinary men, judging character, motive, and subconscious impulse, perceiving what each was thinking and even what each was going to say next, and compounding with telepathic instinct the argument or appeal best suited to the vanity, weakness, or self-interest of his immediate auditor...'[12]

De Valera, however, was unimpressed by such tactics: 'Mr Lloyd George's play-acting at our first interview . . . was too patent to deceive even a child.'[13] The Prime Minister tried charm, offering his guest a cigar and a drink (both were refused), before attempting to overawe him, pointing out all the red of the British Empire on a map hanging on the wall of the Cabinet Room, contrasting this with Ireland, which he was able to cover with the end of his fountain pen.[14] Then he tried flattery, pointing out the chairs around the Cabinet table, naming the Dominion leader who occupied each, falling silent as he came to the last one.

De Valera studiously avoided taking the bait, so Lloyd George had to explain that the final chair was reserved for Ireland. Recounting the story years later, de Valera was 'well pleased at not having asked the question expected of him'.[15]

Even Lloyd George acknowledged that he had failed to knock de Valera off balance. He was left 'white and exhausted' by the encounter. Comparing negotiating with de Valera to trying to get in front of a man on a merry-go-round, he complained, 'I listened to a long lecture on the wrongs done to Ireland starting with Cromwell, and when I tried to bring him to the present day back he went to Cromwell again.'[16] He later likened talking to him to trying to pick up mercury with a fork (prompting de Valera to suggest he should have used a spoon[17]). He also complained that de Valera 'was very difficult to keep to the point – he kept on going off at a tangent, and talking in formulas and refusing to face facts'. He also claimed that de Valera 'was the man with the most limited vocabulary he has ever met'.[18]

By contrast de Valera was reasonably happy after their first meeting, telling Collins back in Dublin that Lloyd George was drawing up a proposal for consideration by the Irish side. 'The proposal will be theirs – we will be free to consider it without prejudice.'[19] In response to press suggestions that he was offering 'compromise demands', de Valera sent a statement to Harry Boland in Washington clarifying that he had made only one demand, 'that the self-determination of the Irish Nation be recognised'.[20] Again, no mention of the Republic.

Craig, who had also met Lloyd George, left London on the 19th, having left a nasty surprise for de Valera. In a statement to the press he said that, because the recent Northern elections had shown an overwhelming majority in favour of their parliament, the only question to be decided between de Valera and Lloyd George was the relationship between Britain and the 26 counties.[21] De Valera was extremely angry, and the delegation was told to get ready to leave for home.[22] Before storming off, though, de Valera wrote to Lloyd George, insisting on the 'essential unity' of Ireland and warning that there would be no point in further discussion if the British government supported Craig's position. Lloyd George, who had agreed to Craig's statement,[23] sent a conciliatory reply, denying responsibility for it (though not repudiating its contents). It was enough to calm de Valera down.[24]

After three lengthy meetings with Lloyd George, de Valera warned Collins that 'things may burst up here suddenly, so all should be prepared'.[25] Lloyd George, meanwhile, was confessing to his Cabinet colleagues that while de Valera 'had an agreeable personality . . . he found it difficult to say exactly where the Irish leader stood'. However, he was now 'asking questions in regard to such matters as the entry of south Ireland into the Empire, swearing allegiance, the form of the oath, the name of the new State, and so forth'. Lloyd George felt this was progress, but the 'real difficulty', he believed, was 'Ulster'.[26]

Craig had made it clear that he would not accept a single Parliament of Ireland with membership proportionate to population (implying that he might accept one with equal representation between North and South). Lloyd George pointed out to de Valera that if he insisted on proportionate membership, the South would be in the same position towards the North as Britain was towards the South, and that civil war could be the result. De Valera stated that 'Southern Ireland would never allow itself to be implicated in civil war. It would rather let Northern Ireland alone,' to which Lloyd George not unreasonably asked why they wouldn't leave it alone now. Lloyd George also threatened de Valera, telling him that if fighting resumed 'the struggle would bear an entirely different character', with reduced global commitments allowing the British to bring home troops who could be stationed in Ireland.[27]

The British Cabinet approved Lloyd George's offer to de Valera, which would give Ireland dominion status – with power over taxation, finance, justice, home defence, policing and so on – with all the autonomy of the self-governing dominions but subject to certain conditions. These were that the Royal Navy was to control the seas around Ireland and have access to Irish ports; facilities for military and civil aviation were to be granted; limitations would be agreed on the size of an 'Irish Territorial Force'; British military recruitment was to continue, as was free trade between Britain and Ireland; and the Irish people were to take on a share of Britain's war debt. The British side insisted that unity could come only through consent, that the existing powers and privileges of the Parliament of Northern Ireland were to be maintained, and that North and South must determine between themselves whether the powers of the new dominion were to be exercised 'by a single Irish body, or taken over separately by Southern and Northern Ireland, with or without a joint authority to harmonise their common interests'.[28] It was, Sir Henry Wilson fulminated in his diary,

an abject surrender to murderers. It gives complete independence under the guise of Dominion Home Rule . . . In short, Ireland is gone.[29]

The British proposals were delivered at 10 p.m., and the Irish delegation sat up debating them until after 3 a.m.[30] Stack, Plunkett and Barton denounced them, Barton suggesting that it would be 'treason to the Republic' to bring them back to Ireland.[31]

The final meeting between de Valera and Lloyd George, on the 21st, was described by Lloyd George as 'pretty hopeless'. De Valera demanded a united Ireland and dominion status without limitations; the only alternative, he argued, was 'complete independence for Southern Ireland'.[32]

Back in Dublin on Sunday 24 July, de Valera hosted a meeting of what he described as the 'Inner Cabinet' at the safe house in Blackrock. Apart from himself, the group consisted of the ministers Michael Collins, Arthur Griffith, Cathal Brugha, Austin Stack and Eoin MacNeill; also present were Richard Mulcahy and Erskine Childers[33] – an indication of who he saw as important. The meeting was not recorded in the official Ministry minutes, but handwritten notes are in de Valera's papers. Brugha was the most obdurate about the British proposal, insisting that it was 'not credible to consider agreement abandoning republic'. Stack supported him, while de Valera said there would be no better chance 'to try to solve' the question. MacNeill thought the Republic could be retained 'in background' if they claimed dominion status; Griffith insisted that the offer should be referred to the people; Collins thought it was a 'step on the road', though he believed that Lloyd George's document would 'set country against us'.[34]

The full Ministry met the following day. Stack recorded that Brugha would have 'none of it'. Joseph MacDonagh, Sceilg, Art O'Connor and Seán Etchingham 'were all dead against accepting less than absolute Independence'.[35] It is noteworthy that these last four were shortly to be removed from the Ministry by de Valera. But even without them it was clear that his main problem was Brugha, always the most extreme in the leadership. De Valera explained the balancing act he had to perform between Griffith and Brugha.

> I made it my own peculiar function to forestall crises where sharp differences might arise by steering along a line of policy which would be in accord with the aspirations of both . . . My sentiments and associations were mainly with Cathal Brugha and the group he represented, whilst in the majority of cases my reason inclined to the other side.[36]

He had managed to come up with a compromise in 1917 to keep both Brugha and Griffith in Sinn Féin; could he do it again?

The concept he would shortly unveil was his effort to achieve this. He would slowly develop support for

a modified course, relinquishing the naked demand for an isolated Republic (simple international recognition and nothing more) and substituting the idea of a Republic as independent as before but in free external association with Britain.[37]

He did this with great skill, slowly bringing Brugha along with him. The problem was that this time his compromise would have to be accepted not by a Sinn Féin ard-fheis but by the British government, which contained people just as committed to the Crown as Brugha was to the Republic.

De Valera had drafted a reply to Lloyd George describing

the form of association we felt we could enter into with the States of the British Commonwealth. When I presented it to the Ministry meeting, although it was not unfavourably criticised, yet it did not get the type of active support that I felt necessary. I said we could all sleep over it . . .

On the morning of the resumed Ministry meeting on the 27th, de Valera had a happy inspiration. The word 'external' occurred to him – he would propose that Ireland should be in 'external association' with the British Commonwealth. He redrafted his reply to Lloyd George, and his colleagues approved it unanimously.[38]

External association, de Valera later explained to Joe McGarrity, 'would leave us with the Republic unless the people wished to change it'; it would get rid of the King and allegiance to him, and of the Governor-General; it would make the people Irish citizens rather than British subjects; and it would lead to the withdrawal of all British forces of occupation. All they would have to do in return was consult members of the Commonwealth on matters of common concern. 'In entering such an association Ireland would be doing nothing incompatible with her declared independence.'[39]

He developed a way of explaining the concept, drawing a large circle containing five other circles, and then another circle adjoining the large one. The large circle was the Commonwealth, the five circles inside it were the dominions, and Ireland was the adjoining circle, in 'external association' with Britain and the Commonwealth. Collins later complained, 'How could one argue with a man who was always drawing lines and circles to explain his position?'[40] Mary MacSwiney was treated to the same performance but was not convinced, believing that external association was 'insidious and dangerous' and 'inconsistent with the Republican position'.[41] De Valera was still drawing his diagram as an explanation of the concept as late as 1969.[42]

Part of the problem with external association was its very vagueness. As Robert Barton recalled, 'even the Delegates had but a hazy conception of what would be its final form', although they were clear it meant 'no vestige of British authority would remain within Ireland'.[43] But its great virtue lay in its ability to keep committed Republicans on side. Shortly after the negotiations began, Brugha finally gave de Valera confirmation that he would support a settlement along the lines of 'external association'. He wrote:

> All other matters being satisfactorily settled we are prepared to recommend to our people that the accepted head of Great Britain be recognised as the head of the new association. We are prepared to co-operate with and send a representative to whatever council is appointed to conduct the affairs of the group. In matters that do not affect the group we continue to act independently; our form of government remains the same as at present, and can only be altered by the Irish people themselves.[44]

For Brugha, this was quite a concession; for de Valera, it was 'priceless'.[45] Given that it guaranteed the support of the most extreme of the political leaders, and therefore guaranteed a united Ministry, he was right – as long as any settlement reached in London conformed to it.

The reply to Lloyd George, sent on 10 August, didn't explicitly set out external association, because de Valera wanted to keep the idea in reserve for the negotiations. Dominion status was rejected as being likely to make Ireland 'a helpless dependency' of Britain's; it didn't have the advantage of distance, as the other Dominions did.

> The most explicit guarantees, including the Dominions' acknowledged right to secede, would be necessary to secure for Ireland an equal degree of freedom.

This gave at least a hint that some form of dominion status *might* be acceptable to de Valera. He went on to say that he and his colleagues would be prepared to recommend a 'treaty of free association' with the Commonwealth – given a united Ireland.[46]

Lloyd George was in Paris, so this letter was handed to Austen Chamberlain (leader of the Conservative Party in the coalition government), by Art O'Brien, Robert Barton and Joe McGrath. They were taken aback by Chamberlain's reaction: he said it was 'a very grave document, a very serious document', and indicated that it might lead to an immediate breakdown in negotiations.[47] The Sinn Féiners tried to convince Chamberlain that it was 'a friendly reply breathing peaceful aspirations throughout'.[48] Griffith, in charge in Dublin while de Valera was in the south, confirmed to Barton that 'it is certainly not our intention to bolt and bar the door [to further negotiations], and I do not see how the reply can be so construed'.[49]

On his return from Paris, Lloyd George dismissed de Valera's letter as 'a silly answer',[50] and his Cabinet colleagues thought it was 'a clumsy attempt to keep open the discussion'. It was agreed to reply refusing to consider an Ireland outside the Empire.[51] Lloyd George was gung-ho for a resumption of hostilities on a new scale if his offer was rejected. Martial law was on the cards, the division of the country into sections by means of block houses (a policy he had vociferously opposed as a younger man during the Boer War), control of food, and the introduction of identity cards.[52] The potential for a ruinous intensification of violence was very real; de Valera thus needed to avoid a break-down with Lloyd George while also avoiding what he would regard as a surrender of principle.

The first meeting of the Second Dáil took place on 16 August. In advance of a fuller discussion in private session, de Valera gave a brief outline of the negotiations, during which he made his famous comment that 'we are not Republican doctrinaires'; this has been frequently quoted out of context by critics of his later insistence on maintaining the Republic. In fact, it was a reiteration of his compromise formula of 1917. He said the Irish people had given their 'unmistakeable' answer in the 1918 general election to the question of how they wanted to be governed.

> I do not say that that answer was for a form of government so much, because we are not Republican doctrinaires, but it was for Irish freedom and Irish independence, and it was obvious to everyone who considered the question that Irish independence could not be realised at the present time in any other way so suitably as through a Republic.[53]

He may not have been a Republican doctrinaire, but he was making it clear that he remained firmly committed to full independence.

On 22 August the Dáil discussed the peace negotiations in private session. At the outset, de Valera described what was on offer as not Dominion status but a sort of Home Rule for a divided Ireland with more general powers than were offered in the best Home Rule proposals heretofore.[54]

He warned deputies that if they were determined to make peace only on the basis of the recognition of the Republic, they were going to face war.[55] The moderate TD Liam de Róiste suggested that, if the British were not going to improve their offer, the terms should be put to the people before war was renewed. Mary MacSwiney rejected this idea, pointing out that governments didn't give their people a vote on whether or not to go to war; if they did, there would have been no Great War.[56]

The other source of disagreement was the North. De Valera insisted that 'they had not the power, and some of them had not the inclination, to use force with Ulster'. If the Republic was recognised he would be

in favour of giving each county power to vote itself out of the Republic if it so wished. Otherwise they would be compelled to use force.

J. J. Walsh and Eoin O'Duffy objected to this, O'Duffy stating that 'as far as they in Ulster were concerned they thought force should be used against Ulster'.[57] Despite these differences, the Dáil unanimously approved the actions of the Ministry to date.

When the latest reply to Lloyd George was read to deputies the following day, there was a very brief discussion, with some minor changes being suggested (and rejected). De Valera asked if anyone objected to the rejection of the British offer or to his use of the phrase 'government by consent of the governed'; nobody did.[58] He also acknowledged that he was likely to be nominated for re-election; if he was he would retain the freedom to decide issues on their merits:

I have one allegiance only to the people of Ireland and that is to do the best we can for the people of Ireland as we conceive it . . . I keep myself free to consider each question as it arises.[59]

Liam de Róiste noted admiringly in his diary that 'Dev can utter truths plainly and none desire to criticise ever; but one like myself uttering the same truth runs into danger!'[60]

Challenged by Walsh on whether he would be prepared to consider a proposal to exclude any part of the country, de Valera replied that he would not accept office if he was fettered in any way; allowing certain counties to vote themselves out of an independent Ireland would be 'a way in which a certain result could be obtained. I would be ready to consider that.'[61] He also announced that he would not be one of the plenipotentiaries if talks got under way; he would stay at home, where he 'could be more valuable'. He acknowledged that the Ministry might be divided on whatever agreement was reached. 'In such a case the majority would rule. Those who would disagree with me would resign.'[62] Clearly, a situation in which *he* was in the minority was inconceivable.

The other business of note was Constitutional changes proposed by Brugha. It was agreed that the number of Ministers would be reduced to six – Foreign Affairs, Home Affairs, Defence, Finance, Local Government and Economic Affairs. Brugha's other proposal was that the President would be 'President of the Republic'. De Valera acknowledged that up to then the office was President of the Ministry of Dáil Éireann. However, George Gavan Duffy and others objected to the title 'President of the Republic', as they thought that one person should not be President both of the government and of the Republic. An objection was also made that specifying the title now would imply that the office hadn't existed before. In a burst of creative ambiguity, de Valera agreed to change the amendment to refer to the 'President who shall be Prime Minister',[63] though he always claimed that

> the assumption here was that the word 'President' would carry the meaning 'President of the Republic' on account of the common acceptance of it as such, and that the Clause meant the President of the Republic would also be Prime Minister.[64]

And when, back in public session on 26 August, he was nominated for re-election, it was as President of the Republic.

Seán Mac Eoin nominated him on the orders of Collins, president of the IRB, who wanted to clarify that the Brotherhood no longer regarded its own president as President of the Republic.[65] The nomination was seconded by Richard Mulcahy, who also referred to the office as President of the Republic; there were no other candidates. In his reply, de Valera modestly said he had been given credit for the work of

> loyal comrades like Arthur Griffith, Cathal Brugha, Michael Collins, and other heroes working with me. It is as a team that we have worked, and it is as a team that we shall work.[66]

He then carefully waited two minutes until noon, the time set for publication, before reading the latest reply to Lloyd George.

This informed Lloyd George that the Dáil had unanimously rejected his proposals. Ireland wanted peace, but if Britain insisted on 'conditions that involve surrender of our whole national position and make negotiation a mockery', Britain would be responsible for the continuation of the conflict. But de Valera added that peace was possible 'on the basis of the broad guiding principle of government by the consent of the governed'. If that principle was accepted in London, he concluded, the Dáil would appoint representatives to reach agreement with the British government.[67]

The new Cabinet was made up of de Valera and six executive officers. These were Arthur Griffith (Foreign Affairs), Austin Stack (Home Affairs), Cathal Brugha (National Defence), Michael Collins (Finance), W. T. Cosgrave (Local Government) and Robert Barton (Economic Affairs). Outside the Cabinet were Kevin O'Higgins as Assistant Minister in Local Government (the only one of this second string to be invited to attend Cabinet by de Valera[68]); Blythe in Trade and Commerce; Desmond FitzGerald in Publicity; Plunkett in Fine Arts; J. J. O'Kelly ('Sceilg') in Education (the old Department of Irish renamed and enlarged in scope); Constance Markievicz in Labour; Art O'Connor in Agriculture; and Seán Etchingham in Fisheries. The last five were all to oppose the Treaty; the political effect of the changes was to make the Cabinet, the crucial decision-making body, considerably less hard-line.

In private session the Dáil discussed the possible appointment of plenipotentiaries if a favourable reply was received from Lloyd George. De Valera successfully argued that the hands of any plenipotentiaries should not be tied in advance; 'that men sent over to make peace come back and their actions were ratified or not'.[69] With a reply from London reportedly 'on the wire', the Dáil adjourned until the following morning, in the expectation that it might be appointing plenipotentiaries. These hopes were disappointed.

When Lloyd George received de Valera's letter of 24 August he seized on the phrase 'government by the consent of the governed' as the operative one. 'That was the principle of Gladstone's Home Rule campaign – we can accept that,' he told Tom Jones.[70] There was some doubt in the British Cabinet about what de Valera really meant. Was he refusing to recognise the Crown, or just saving face before doing so? It was agreed that an uncompromising reply should be sent.[71]

Lloyd George's reply stressed the generosity of the British offer and warned that the Truce would be in danger if 'definite and immediate progress' was not made.[72] A further uncompromising letter from de Valera reached Lloyd George, on holiday in Scotland. He decided a Cabinet meeting was required, summoning his ministers to meet him in Inverness Town Hall (much to their disgust).[73]

Lloyd George argued strongly against issuing an unconditional invitation to talks which would be a sign of weakness. In particular, he feared the talks breaking down over the position of Cos. Fermanagh and Tyrone, where the Sinn Féin position was strongest, and over which it would be difficult to resume hostilities. 'Men will die for the Throne and Empire. I do not know who will die for Tyrone and Fermanagh.' In relation to de Valera's performance in their initial discussions Lloyd George noted that he was

> greatly relieved to go through the conversations with him without Tyrone and Fermanagh being raised. He was an unskilled negotiator but you cannot always count on his being maladroit.[74]

However, with opinion against a break with de Valera stronger than expected within his Cabinet, Lloyd George was forced to considerably tone down his draft reply.[75] This once again insisted that a conference would be impossible if the Irish side demanded the right to set up a republic and repudiate the Crown; however, it also offered a discussion on any guarantees to ensure 'Irish freedom'. Lloyd George then asked de Valera if he was 'prepared to enter a Conference to ascertain how the association of Ireland with the community of nations known as the British Empire can best be reconciled with Irish national aspirations'.[76]

De Valera's reply, accepting the invitation, was agreed by the Dáil Cabinet on 9 September. It was clear that the Cabinet expected this to be the end of the matter, because it also selected the team to attend the talks: Arthur Griffith, Michael Collins, Robert Barton, Éamonn Duggan and George Gavan Duffy.

Griffith would chair the delegation, but it was Collins that de Valera viewed as indispensable: 'Whenever I did not go on the delegation, Michael Collins had to go. He didn't want to. I had to insist . . . I thought that he had committed himself to the Republic so absolutely that there would be no drawing back for him.'[77] Collins knew that if the talks broke down, he would be blamed for their failure; if agreement was reached, he would be blamed for compromising.

De Valera would have liked Cathal Brugha to go, but he admitted that if he went the delegation would spend most of its time arguing. While

Brugha was honest, 'he is a bit slow at seeing fine differences and rather stubborn'. He felt Collins and Griffith wouldn't work with Austin Stack, or with Mary MacSwiney (because of their attitude to 'women in general'). Therefore, Barton had to be the choice with the added back-up of his cousin, Childers, as Secretary. 'I felt that with these in touch with the delegation, and the Cabinet at home hanging on to their coat-tails, everything was safe for the tug-of-war.' Duggan and Duffy he dismissed as 'mere legal padding'. [78] The Cabinet also arranged the establishment of panels of advisers on finance, commerce and defence relations. (The following day, almost as an afterthought, a further panel on 'the question of Ulster' was added.)[79]

On 14 September the Dáil met to ratify the plenipotentiaries to meet the British side. De Valera explained to deputies his latest letter to Lloyd George, in particular the second paragraph, which read:

> In this final note we deem it our duty to reaffirm that our position is and can only be as we have defined it throughout this correspondence. Our nation has formally declared its independence and recognises itself as a sovereign state. It is only as the representatives of that state and as its chosen guardians that we have any authority or powers to act on behalf of our people.[80]

He told the deputies that, while this could have been phrased more diplomatically, he felt it was 'absolutely necessary at this stage to state definitely and clearly their position'. He warned them before they voted that 'it could mean peace or war, but that the Cabinet intended to stand by that paragraph'.[81] A string of deputies – including Mary MacSwiney, Margaret Pearse, Seán Milroy and Kevin O'Higgins – supported the Cabinet and deplored any suggestion of compromise. No dissenting voices were heard.

De Valera then asked the Dáil to approve the plenipotentiaries and explained once again why he would not be among them.

> To be in the very best position for the possibilities of a break down and to be in the best position to deal with those questions as they would arise and not to be involved in anything that might take place in those negotiations – to be perfectly free . . .

For these reasons he 'asked the Cabinet not to insist' on his going as one of the deputation.

But this united front quickly broke down when Cosgrave proposed that de Valera should in fact go.

He had an extraordinary experience in negotiations . . . This was a team they were sending over and they were leaving their ablest player in reserve.

Some deputies were clearly taken aback by this unusual breach in Cabinet unity and Cosgrave's suggestion was rejected, but there was a further indication of Cabinet disagreement when Collins's name was discussed. Collins said he believed that 'the President should have been part of the delegation'. In addition', he 'did not want to go himself and he would very much prefer not to be chosen'. De Valera, however, insisted that Collins was 'absolutely vital to the delegation'.[82] The delegation was chosen; but would it have a negotiation to go to?

Harry Boland and Joe McGrath had been despatched to hand over the reply, arriving on the day of the Dáil meeting. As soon as Lloyd George read the letter, he declared he couldn't possibly accept it.

It won't do, I can't have it, why did he put in that second paragraph? He, De V., said that on each occasion I saw him; he said it in public, why could he not leave it at that. I am done, I am done.[83]

The letter as written meant that the proposed conference was off. He seemed particularly aggrieved at de Valera's attitude, after he had deliberately used the word 'association' in his invitation – the word de Valera himself had used. The Irishmen left, after it was agreed that Lloyd George would not publish the letter.[84]

In his diary Boland recorded

De V very mad at non-publication, insists on letter as written – more power to you, de Valera. Conference off.[85]

A further exchange ensued between Lloyd George and de Valera, each insisting on his position.[86] Finally, Lloyd George broke the logjam by announcing that he was ignoring the previous correspondence and issuing

a fresh invitation to a conference in London on October 11th. where we can meet your delegates as spokesmen of the people whom you represent, with a view to ascertaining how the association of Ireland with the community of nations known as the British Empire may best be reconciled with Irish national aspirations.[87]

This allowed de Valera to respond that, while their 'respective positions have been stated and are understood', the Irish side agreed to accept the invitation.[88]

This acceptance implied compromise, because it was clear there would not be an isolated republic with no connection to Britian. Critics of de Valera's attitude to the Treaty would make this point many times in the years to come. But while acceptance was incompatible with an isolated republic, it was *not* incompatible with de Valera's concept of external association: Lloyd George's wording left open the possibility of an Ireland outside the Empire but still associated with it.

On 5 October the Dáil Cabinet discussed the draft treaty the Irish side would present – but, crucially, this document was unfinished before the talks began. 'Draft Treaty A' recognised Ireland as a sovereign independent state, with the British renouncing all claims to govern it or to legislate for it, but would also bring Ireland into 'external association' with the Commonwealth. There would be reciprocal citizenship rather than the common citizenship of the Commonwealth – an innovation that would allow Irish citizens to enjoy the rights, without the responsibilities, of being British subjects.[89]

Remaining in Ireland would give de Valera the chance to step in at the last minute if the talks broke down. As Barton put it,

> we could always break off negotiations and threaten war and still have de Valera in the background to come in at the last and find some way of carrying on if the army was not ready.[90]

This was certainly an advantage. On the other hand, if de Valera had gone, he would certainly have been more precise in some of his communications with Lloyd George than Griffith proved to be, and he might have proved more adept at playing for time when the crunch came.

But de Valera believed he had done enough to keep control in his own hands in Dublin. The credentials given to the delegates described them as 'envoys plenipotentiary' with full power

> to negotiate and conclude . . . a Treaty or Treaties of Settlement, Association and Accommodation between Ireland and the community of nations known as the British Commonwealth.[91]

But de Valera attempted to limit these powers with secret instructions from the Cabinet. These, however, were contradictory: the first clause acknowledged that the plenipotentiaries had 'full powers as defined in their credentials', which made any attempt to limit those powers nugatory. The instructions continued that, before decisions were reached on the main questions, the Cabinet would be informed 'and a reply will be awaited by the Plenipotentiaries before the final decision is made'; the same would happen with the complete text of the draft treaty about to be signed, and with the final Irish proposals submitted before a break, and the Cabinet was to be kept regularly informed of the progress of the negotiations.[92] The instructions were sometimes seen as an assurance that nothing would be signed in London that had not been *approved* at home.[93] However, while this might have been de Valera's intention, it was not what the instructions stated: they simply required the delegates to inform the Cabinet and await a reply. All they had to do was get the views of their colleagues before they used their full powers to conclude a treaty.

De Valera regarded these instructions as crucial.

In the light of the specific instructions given I expected to be in the closest touch with it. In fact, it was my intention to be as close almost as if I were in London.[94]

He would also have been aware of the mathematics: there were three members of the Cabinet on the delegation, and four remaining in Dublin. His assumption throughout was that the four at home – himself, Brugha, Stack and Cosgrave – would overrule any temptation by those in London to compromise. He miscalculated how closely he could control the delegation; he also miscalculated the Cabinet mathematics.

While the negotiations got under way, de Valera oversaw the continued operation of the government. Right from the start of the Truce he had been anxious to continue all activities that weren't strictly military in character.[95] And he remained as painstaking as ever, sometimes to the despair of his staff. 'He's an extraordinary man,' complained Gearoid McGann, who was working in his office. 'If he was only ordering a bag of coal he'd write the letter three times.'[96]

The Presidential establishment left Glenvar in October, and after a brief stay in Mountjoy Square moved to 53 Kenilworth Square in Rathgar.[97] It wasn't all work, of course. De Valera began spending more time at Robert Farnan's house in Howth. As would be his practice over the years, he generally went without Sinéad or other members of his family, though Kathleen O'Connell was often there (one Sunday saw some members of the party blackberrying, while de Valera and the Farnans went for a walk over the hills, and 'all [were] disappointed at no tennis playing'[98]). His birthday was celebrated at Glenvar with 'a delightful evening of song' with some friends – again, there is no indication that his wife was there.[99]

Entering negotiations, both the Irish and British sides needed to demonstrate that they were ready for a breakdown in talks and a resumption of hostilities, even if they had no real intention of going back to war. De Valera did his best to emphasise the preparedness of the IRA. Guided by Liam Lynch, commander of the 1st Southern Division, and by Richard Mulcahy, he visited ambush positions and inspected flying columns 'under arms and equipment'.[100] He later visited other units in the south and west, with newsreel cameras on hand to send the desired message to London. Certainly many of the more active IRA men were ready for a resumption of hostilities. Ernie O'Malley complained that the Truce was 'much worse than war; I'm seriously looking forward to war for a slight rest in the line of active service.'[101]

However, the readiness of the IRA was open to question. Views on this issue tended to colour attitudes towards the Treaty, and of course attitudes to the Treaty coloured retrospective views of the ability of the IRA to continue. Another factor was the rancorous split at the very top of the army, partly caused by political divisions, which would in turn be reinforced by the split. Although the argument was at heart between Cathal Brugha and Michael Collins, it soon spread to take in Richard Mulcahy and other senior officers, pitting them against Brugha, as Minister for Defence, and, by extension, against the whole concept of civilian control of the army. Ironically, those who favoured political control of the military – de Valera, Brugha, Stack – were the very people who the following year found themselves following military extremists into civil war, while those who bridled at political supervision in 1921 – Collins, Mulcahy, O'Duffy – were loud in their condemnation of the anti-Treatyite forces in 1922.

The divisions came to a head over the case of W. G. Robbie, the manager of a typewriter company, who had been ordered to leave Ireland on the basis of faulty intelligence. Brugha fumed that the handling of the case 'displays an amateurishness that I thought we had long ago outgrown'. He demanded a full explanation from the Director of Intelligence (Collins).[102] Mulcahy's reply, a month later, was hardly calculated to placate Brugha. He said Collins had taken steps to prevent a recurrence and had offered sufficient explanation. But he then went on to complain that the tone of Brugha's letter

> is very unfortunate . . . Unless something can be done to eliminate the tendency to revert to this tone when differences arise, I cannot be responsible for retaining harmony and discipline among the Staff.[103]

This rather insolent letter provoked an explosion from Brugha, who warned that any further correspondence in the same tone would lead to Mulcahy's removal. He also complained of Mulcahy's 'presumption' in ignoring Stack, the 'duly appointed' deputy chief of staff. (Stack had never actually worked with GHQ despite his nominal appointment some months earlier.) Brugha continued that,

> before you are very much older, my friend, I shall show you that I have as little intention of taking dictation from you as to how I should reprove inefficiency or negligence on the part of yourself or the D/I [Collins] as I have of allowing you to appoint a Deputy Chief of Staff of your own choosing.[104]

Some days later, having given Mulcahy 24 hours to give a satisfactory answer to his concerns, Brugha sacked him, ordering him to hand over his books and accounts to Stack. Once that was done, his salary would be paid up to the date of his dismissal.[105]

The relationship between Brugha and Mulcahy (and, by extension, Collins) appeared to have irretrievably broken down. Mulcahy appealed to de Valera for support, warning that the toxic atmosphere would 'lead to the destruction in a very short time of the vigour and discipline of the Staff'. He said he couldn't usefully discuss any matter with Brugha, and therefore he couldn't allow him to chair or even be present at Staff meetings. Mulcahy urged de Valera to have the position 'estimated and adjusted without delay'.[106] This was an extraordinary letter for Mulcahy to send; the implication was that either he or Brugha would have to go.

Clearly, this was not a situation that de Valera could tolerate: hostilities with the British could break out again at any time, and the army would be thrown into turmoil if the chief of staff resigned. On the other hand, while Brugha's removal would not have any particular effect on the military side of things, it would be politically disastrous. Mulcahy was summoned to a meeting, where he found Brugha and Stack with the President. Stack left the room, and de Valera demanded to know what the argument was all about. According to Mulcahy, Brugha 'just burst out crying', saying that he 'could do no wrong', before leaving the room. De Valera told Mulcahy that, as Assistant Minister for Defence, he should attend Cabinet meetings (an indication that his sacking was cancelled), morosely adding, 'No, you would be as bad as any of them in a fortnight'.[107]

The crisis had been averted, but not for long. The following month Brugha was again complaining that Stack was not being summoned to Staff meetings. The dysfunctional relationship between Brugha and Mulcahy explains the development of a new initiative. In the middle of September the Cabinet took a far-reaching set of decisions aimed at asserting its control over the army. All HQ Staff and division commandants were to be 'ratified' by Cabinet, and all personnel asked to re-enlist. While Mulcahy was to continue to preside at Staff meetings, Brugha could do so if he wished in order to meet the Staff on a particular question. Stack was to attend Staff meetings, and Brugha was 'to get an office of his own' (the fact that he had not had one up to then is evidence of how removed he was from the actual operation of the army).[108] This was a very significant increase in Brugha's potential power, and yet he appears to have done nothing to implement it. The Cabinet decided on 4 November that he was 'to take steps immediately to give effect to a former decision for recommissioning of the Army'.[109]

The 'new army' was to come into being on 25 November 1921, the eighth anniversary of the formation of the Volunteers. De Valera thought that the process was necessary

> in view of the possibility of further fighting, and in order to put the Army of the Republic in an unequivocal position as the national defence force under the control of the civil government.[110]

The GHQ Staff were invited to a meeting with the Cabinet on 25 November. It was decided that 'the supreme body directing the Army is the Cabinet'. While the chief of staff was to be 'the professional or technical Head of the Army' and 'supreme on the field of battle as regards the disposition of his forces', the Minister for Defence was the 'Administrative Head of the Army'; all commissions derived their authority from the Cabinet, and all appointments had to be sanctioned by the minister. Austin Stack and Eoin O'Duffy were to be joint deputy chiefs of staff, but in Mulcahy's absence O'Duffy was to be his 'full representative'.[111]

The Cabinet minutes do not, however, convey the tension of the meeting. De Valera explained that Stack, as deputy chief of staff, would hold a 'watching brief' for Brugha;[112] each member of the Staff in turn objected to Stack's appointment. While the excitable O'Duffy was speaking – he was 'a little bit shrill' and displayed a 'slight touch of hysteria', according to Mulcahy – de Valera lost his temper, declaring,

> in a half-scream, half-shout, 'Ye may mutiny if ye like, but Ireland will give me another army,' and dismissed the whole lot of us from his sight.[113]

This serious disagreement occurred at a time when a breakdown of the talks in London was entirely possible, and the unity of the army was more vital than ever. The new arrangement would undermine the power of the IRB within the army – as well, of course, as undermining Collins personally. It would reduce the autonomy of GHQ and clarify the relationship between the army and the government. On the other hand, Stack was already unpopular with many of the GHQ Staff and was unlikely to have worked in harmony with them; his record as Minister for Home Affairs had not inspired confidence in his efficiency. Above all, his appointment would replicate the very problem that had led to tension between Brugha and Collins: he would be Mulcahy's subordinate as deputy chief of staff but his superior as minister. It was a recipe for further problems.

So why did de Valera do it? Some have seen it as an attempt to put 'his' man at the heart of the military apparatus, but that is to anticipate the Treaty split which was still some weeks off. At the time, in de Valera's eyes, they were *all* 'his' men. A more compelling explanation may simply be that it was part of the price for keeping Brugha on board, which remained de Valera's key political need at this time. Despite all the controversy over his appointment, it appears that Stack never actually attended a meeting of the GHQ Staff.[114]

Meanwhile, the talks were continuing in London. De Valera was kept well informed by Griffith and Childers, and by Collins, who continued to moan about being there ('This place bloody limit. I wish to God I were back home', 'Having a terrible time'[115] and so on). The conference began with a discussion of the proposals sent to de Valera on 20 July – giving the initiative to the British.[116] The Irish side would have been better off submitting their own proposals in order to set the agenda, had they been ready. Griffith reported to de Valera his impression that the British were anxious for peace.[117] In response de Valera observed that Lloyd George is just covering again the ground he covered with me. You will have to pick him up soon, I fear, on this 'further than this we can't go' stunt.[118]

Before the talks opened, the British delegation had agreed on the advisability of

creating a friendly atmosphere . . . What was to be feared was some unexpected explosion which would plunge the conference into the wrong atmosphere.[119]

The explosion wasn't long in coming, and it was detonated by de Valera. His intervention was prompted by an exchange of telegrams between Pope Benedict XV, who expressed the hope that the conference would be successful, and King George V, who responded that he hoped it would

achieve a permanent settlement of the troubles in Ireland and may initiate a new era of peace and happiness for my people.[120]

De Valera was furious and, without warning the delegates in London, fired off his own telegram to the Pope, thanking him on behalf of the Irish people, who

are confident that the ambiguities in the reply sent in the name of King George will not mislead you, as it may the uninformed, into believing that the troubles are 'in' Ireland, or that the people of Ireland owe allegiance to the British King.[121]

This bald restatement of the Irish claim to sovereignty played right into Lloyd George's hands. In public, he took a dim view, describing de Valera's telegram as 'a grave challenge' and reiterating the British rejection of its central claim to independence.[122] In private, however, he gleefully told his Cabinet colleagues that it 'enabled the main matters to be brought to an issue'.[123]

At the sixth session of the conference, the day after de Valera's telegram was published, Lloyd George was able at last to put the Irish delegation where he wanted them, addressing the thorny issue of the Crown.

Can you under no conditions accept the sovereignty of the King in the sense that Canada and Australia accept it? Is the communicating link of the Crown to be snapped for ever?[124]

Alarmed, the delegation sought advice from Dublin. Childers wrote to de Valera explaining that they could either refuse allegiance to the Crown (and thereby collapse the talks) or play for time, saying they would consider the question once they were satisfied on such issues as Ulster, defence and trade. The delegation specifically asked for instructions from Dublin; Childers noted on his copy of the letter that no reply was received.[125] It seems quite extraordinary that on such a vital issue de Valera failed to give instructions when asked. Collins, back in Dublin for the weekend, urged de Valera to join the negotiations. He refused. 'I am loath to go unless the situation imperatively calls for it'.[126]

However, he was not slow to assert his authority when it suited him. On 24 October, pressed by Lloyd George on the question of the Crown, Griffith said: 'If we came to an agreement on all other points I could recommend some form of association with the Crown', stressing that any agreement was contingent on the 'essential unity' of Ireland being assured.[127] On reading this, de Valera was 'very much disturbed'.[128] The ministers remaining in Dublin – Brugha, Stack and Cosgrave – along with Kevin O'Higgins, met each evening to discuss the reports from London. Having read out the latest despatch, de Valera asked each of them whether allegiance could be given to Britain. They all 'replied in the negative, and all seemed to be most serious and determined about it'.[129] A letter was then sent to Griffith.

> We are all here at one that there can be no question of our asking the Irish people to enter an arrangement which would make them subject to the Crown, or demand from them allegiance to the British King. If war is the alternative, we can only face it, and I think that the sooner the other side is made to realise that the better.[130]

The five delegates responded angrily, protesting at his letter, which they regarded as 'tying their hands in discussion and as inconsistent with the powers given them on their appointment'. If their powers were withdrawn they would have to return to Dublin immediately.[131]

De Valera sent a conciliatory reply claiming that there had been a 'misunderstanding' and that there was no question of tying the hands of the plenipotentiaries 'beyond the extent to which they are tied by their original instructions'. He added that the delegates must understand that

> these memos of mine, except I explicitly state otherwise, are nothing more than an attempt to keep you in touch with the views of members of the Cabinet here on the various points as they arise.[132]

However, he didn't withdraw the observation that, if war was the only alternative to coming under the Crown, 'we can only face it'. Neither did the delegation disagree with this statement.[133] De Valera's reply also implied that he *could* give the plenipotentiaries orders if he chose ('except I explicitly state otherwise'). De Valera later told Joe McGarrity he was unhappy about the incident, suspecting that some of the plenipotentiaries were 'looking for an excuse to return and throw the blame for the breakdown of the negotiations on us who were at home'. In other words, he suspected them of trying to make him the scapegoat – exactly the same thing some of them, particularly Collins, accused him of. From that moment on, de Valera said,

> I began to speak on every occasion as strongly as I could against any idea of accepting the Crown . . . Everywhere I spoke my text was the same – continuance of the war rather than allegiance.[134]

In London, progress was slow. At a meeting in Churchill's house on 30 October, Lloyd George 'indicated that if they were certain of real good-will on our side, they would take risks and fight'.[135] In an effort to prove this good will, Griffith agreed to write a personal letter to the Prime Minister stating his position.[136]

In the first draft, Griffith stated that, if he was satisfied on other points, he was 'prepared to recommend a free partnership of Ireland with the British Commonwealth'. However, after further discussion with Lloyd George, he changed this to say he was 'prepared to recommend a free partnership of Ireland with the other States associated within the British Commonwealth'.[137] Griffith wrote to de Valera saying that this formula 'is consistent with external association and external recognition',[138] but the clear implication is that Ireland would be one of the states associated with others *within* the British Commonwealth. Some time later (it is not clear when), de Valera would annotate his copies of these letters. On the first he wrote:

> I would have agreed to every word as faithfully representing my own ideas at that date. It was a most accurate and concise summing up of our attitude.

But on the second he wrote that 'this letter shows the beginning of the fatal slide'.[139]

But at the time this 'slide' wasn't evident, at least not to de Valera: a week after the letter to Lloyd George he was telling Griffith that the delegation had managed the whole question 'admirably'.[140] Childers, unusually, also seemed to miss the significance of the word 'within'. When he complained in his diary about the amended letter, it was in relation to defence issues.[141] Above all, if this letter really was the 'beginning of the fatal slide' the one man who could have been relied on to pay attention to its drafting was de Valera himself; his absence allowed the 'fatal slide' to begin.

Griffith's letter was, according to Lloyd George, to be used 'as a weapon against Craig'. The British leaders insisted that if Craig refused to come under an all-Ireland parliament 'they would resign rather than make war' on Ireland.[142] Their resolution didn't last long. Lloyd George did try to persuade Craig to come under the Dublin parliament, but was rebuffed. Lloyd George's dramatic revelation that he might have to resign failed to stir the phlegmatic Craig, who unsympathetically replied, 'Is it not wonderful how many great men have come to grief over the eternal Irish question?'[143] In a depressed mood, Lloyd George told Jones he would have to resign – unless he could persuade the Irish side to accept an alternative. He sent Jones to sound out Griffith and Collins on the idea of a Boundary Commision – an idea that the Prime Mininster himself had argued against just three weeks before.[144] Jones presented the idea as his own, stressing the alternative: chaos, Crown Colony government and civil war.

The following day Griffith indicated that if Lloyd George put the idea forward 'we will not turn him down on it'.[145] As Frank Pakenham (later Long Longford) observed, this released Lloyd George from his obligation to resign if he couldn't secure an all-Ireland parliament.[146] It also proved fatal to Irish efforts to break on Ulster.

Griffith understood Jones to mean that a Boundary Commission 'would give us most of Tyrone, Fermanagh, and part of Armagh, Down, etc.'.[147] De Valera later claimed that he was unable to understand how Griffith

> allowed himself to be deluded by the Boundary Commission idea . . . The part of his letters dealing with this make pathetic reading.[148]

It was odd, then, that de Valera included the relevant clause unchanged in his initial alternative to the Treaty – presumably he too was 'deluded' by it. Initially, it was proposed that the Boundary Commission would redraw the border in line with the wishes of the inhabitants. To this, though, was added the proviso that the new line should be 'compatible with economic and geographical considerations'. This was designed to meet the case of the Glens of Antrim – where a nationalist majority was stranded far from any possible border – but it was eventually interpreted in such a way as to undermine the original aim of giving large swathes of territory to the South.

De Valera, though, was more worried about the Crown than about partition. In a tactfully worded letter to Griffith, he praised the delegation for the way they had pushed Craig and his government into a corner, but he warned of the danger

> that we should be tempted, in order to put them more hopelessly in the wrong, to make further advances on our side. I think, as far as the 'Crown and Empire connection' is concerned, we should not budge a single inch from the point where the negotiations have now led us.[149]

A week later, Lloyd George sent 'tentative suggestions' for a Treaty. He proposed that Ireland would be a self-governing dominion, with the same relationship to Westminster as Canada; that the British navy would defend the Irish coast, pending an arrangement between Ireland and Britain for an Irish naval force, though the British would get whatever naval and air-force facilities they required; that the dominion would cover the 32 counties but that the Parliament of Northern Ireland could opt out; in that event, a commission would be appointed 'to determine in accordance with the wishes of the inhabitants' the boundary between Northern Ireland and the rest of Ireland.[150] In a letter to de Valera, Griffith again gave priority to unity over status.

> The crucial question – 'Crown and Empire' must be met next week. If 'Ulster' gets us to break on them, she will have re-won the game. The seriousness of the position will be realised by the Members of the Cabinet, and I trust they will give us their best-weighed suggestions.[151]

In response, de Valera sent a 'rough draft of treaty', which was handed to the British on 22 November. The Irish side once again proposed external association, with recognition of the Crown 'as head of the association'.[152] Lloyd George pointed out that this brought them back to where they were six weeks before. Griffith argued that the proposals were 'a great advance on our side towards peace', but advised de Valera that if he couldn't convince Lloyd George of this, the negotiations might be terminated.[153]

A breakdown was avoided, but the two sides were still far apart. On the 25th the Cabinet in Dublin unanimously approved a formula that inched towards the British: 'Ireland shall recognise the British Crown for the purposes of the Association as symbol and accepted head of the combination of Associated States'.[154] This was quite a concession for the likes of Brugha. The Irish delegation pointed out that 'for Ireland freely to accept the Crown in any capacity is a momentous step on her part in view of history and the existing facts'.[155]

But de Valera realised that it was unlikely to be enough for Lloyd George, as recognition fell a long way short of allegiance. De Valera told Harry Boland that

> as things stand today it means war. The British ultimatum is allegiance to their King. We will never recommend that such allegiance be rendered . . . If I appear with those who choose war, it is only because the alternative is impossible without dishonour.

He added that 'it is likely that my view will be that of the Cabinet as a whole'.[156] He had good grounds for believing this: Brugha, Stack and Cosgrave had all agreed on 25 October that war was preferable to swearing allegiance to the King. Barton was a hard-liner, as Collins was assumed to be. As far as de Valera could see, only Griffith was certain to vote for peace at this price.

And yet it was Griffith, not de Valera, who again led the charge in London. He met Lloyd George on 28 November, who said the latest Irish proposals 'brought them further apart'.[157] Lloyd George offered to put any phrase the Irish side liked into the Treaty to ensure that the Crown would have no more power in practice than it did in Canada. He also offered to modify the proposed oath of allegiance. Promising that the Governor-General would be merely a symbol, he said that 'no one would ever be appointed to whom the Irish Ministry offered any objection'.[158] A British draft treaty was given to Griffith on 30 November, including a proposed oath for members of the Dáil, which stated:

> I . . . solemnly swear to bear true faith and allegiance to the Constitution of the Irish Free State; to the Community of Nations known as the British Empire; and to the King as the Head of the State and of the Empire.[159]

The negotiations had been going on for six weeks; the moment of crisis had arrived; and de Valera was in Co. Clare.

He was visiting his constituency for the first time in four years, which was a rather extraordinary gap, even allowing for his time in prison and in

America. But the main purpose of the trip was a military one; accompanied by the Minister for Defence, Brugha, and the chief of staff, Mulcahy, he was to inspect troops in the region. In an address to the Mid-Clare Brigade of the IRA, de Valera said the achievement of Ireland's aim depended on their determination. 'That which we are fighting for can never be beaten as long as there are men ready to die rather than submit.'[160] After staying overnight with Bishop Fogarty he reviewed troops of the West Clare Brigade, before an urgent summons interrupted his schedule.[161]

Griffith wired from London to say a Cabinet meeting was essential to consider the British proposals. It was arranged for 3 December, and de Valera left Clare on the afternoon of the 2nd to meet Griffith in Dublin that night.[162] De Valera arrived back at his office in Kenilworth Square shortly after 11, following a long and tiring drive. Griffith stayed with him until after 1 a.m.[163] When Griffith showed him the British proposals, de Valera was adamant, telling Griffith

> definitely that I would never consent to or sign any such agreement. He said *he* would not break on the Crown. We parted at that.[164]

De Valera later said it was 'unfortunate' that discussion was postponed to the Cabinet meeting, but he was 'very tired'.[165] His fatigue was understandable; what was less understandable was the chaotic nature of the following day's meeting, one of the most crucial ever held by an Irish Government.

There is no single reliable source for the meeting. In Diarmuid O'Hegarty's absence in London, Colm Ó Murchadha acted as secretary and took notes. But these were not formal minutes and do not record all of the discussion; they may, however, be more reliable on the decisions reached. Childers recorded his version of what transpired in his diary, as did, later on, Barton, Stack and de Valera himself. All these accounts must, of necessity, be treated with some caution, as they are naturally partisan. What is beyond doubt is that there was confusion about exactly what had been agreed.

De Valera wasn't the only one who was exhausted: the ship carrying the delegates back from London had collided with a fishing boat, three of whose crew were killed. As a result, the delegation arrived late into Dún Laoghaire at 10:15 a.m. and had to go straight to the Mansion House for the Cabinet meeting at 11. Childers, for one, was 'terribly tired'.[166] Apart from the plenipotentiaries – Griffith, Collins, Barton, Duggan and Gavan Duffy – and their secretary, Childers, the meeting was attended by the

Dublin Cabinet members – de Valera, Cosgrave, Stack and Brugha – as well as the assistant minister Kevin O'Higgins. Griffith told the meeting that he favoured the British draft of the Treaty, as he refused to break on the question of the Crown. Barton did not believe that this was Britain's last word, or that it would resume war on the question of allegiance. Gavan Duffy agreed that the British were bluffing and that the Irish proposals – external association – could be won. Duggan agreed with Griffith: the treaty was 'England's last word' and he wouldn't take the responsibility of turning it down. Collins's view was more confused. The secretary's note records him as being 'in substantial agreement' with Griffith and Duggan, and that rejecting the Treaty would be a gamble, because England could arrange war in Ireland within a week. He believed that further concessions could be gained on trade and defence, and that sacrifices to Ulster were justified in order to gain essential unity. But on the oath he was ambivalent, pointing out that it wouldn't come into force for 12 months, and it might be worth taking that time

> and seeing how it would work. Would recommend that Dáil go to country on Treaty, but would recommend non-acceptance of Oath.[167]

Childers was dismissive of his contribution.

> MC difficult to understand, repeatedly pressed by Dev, but I really don't know what his answer amounted to.[168]

After a break, discussion resumed with only the Cabinet (and O'Higgins) in attendance, which excluded Duggan, Gavan Duffy and Childers. According to Ó Murchadha's note, de Valera said that the Treaty 'could not be accepted in its then form'. He would not take the oath, nor could he agree to a document that allowed 'North East Ulster' to vote itself out of the Irish state. With modifications, however, he said 'it might be accepted honourably', and he would 'like to see the Plenipotentiaries go back and secure peace if possible'. He believed that the delegates had 'done their utmost and that it now remained to them to show that if document not amended that they were prepared to face the consequences – war or no war'.

Griffith said he didn't like the document, but it was not dishonourable; it would 'practically recognise the Republic and the first allegiance would be to Ireland'. The people would not fight on the question of allegiance, and he suggested that the plenipotentiaries should sign it 'and leave it to

President and Dáil to reject'. Brugha declared himself to be 'in perfect agreement with the President', though he was still 'reluctant to recognise the King of England as Head of the Associated States'.[169]

Childers, Duggan and Gavan Duffy rejoined the meeting at 5 p.m. Ó Murchadha recorded the decision that de Valera would not join the negotiations at this stage; but he did not record *why* this decision was made. According to Stack's account (written a year later), Griffith had reiterated that the document should be signed; Brugha replied that signing it 'would split Ireland from top to bottom'. In response, Griffith said:

> I suppose that's so. I'll tell you what I'll do. I'll go back to London. I'll not sign the document but I'll bring it back and submit it to the Dáil and, if necessary, to the people.[170]

Barton had a similar recollection,[171] and de Valera said it was this 'express undertaking' that helped him decide not to go; he was worried the British would interpret his arrival as an attempt to prevent a breakdown, leading them to stiffen their position.[172]

Later, Griffith would maintain in the Dáil that he had promised only not to sign the British draft – the Treaty itself was a different document.[173] However, he did admit that he had tried to get the British to let him take the Treaty back to the Dáil unsigned but had been unsuccessful – an indication that he felt bound by a promise.

Another contentious matter concerns the proposed oath. Ó Murchadha records de Valera suggesting an amended oath.

> I . . . do solemnly swear true faith and allegiance to the constitution of the Irish Free State, to the Treaty of Association, and to recognise the King of Great Britain as Head of the Associated States.[174]

O'Higgins later recalled the scene.

> Mr de Valera sat back in his chair, bit the top of his pencil and pondered, and we sat and waited for five or seven minutes. Two of our plenipotentiaries, Mr Barton and Mr Gavan Duffy, took their notebooks from their pockets and sat waiting with pencils poised, ready to take what would be said. Finally . . . de Valera said to Collins and the others – Here is the formula that would be acceptable to me . . .[175]

Griffith and Collins took this to be a firm proposal to be put to the British; but de Valera and his supporters would later deny this. The suggested wording was 'impromptu', they claimed, and it was spoken rather than written; and, crucially, it was claimed that he had no idea it would be presented to the British as a counter-proposal. He simply thought that if the British were to present an oath in those terms 'it would not be unacceptable'.[176] Quite how the British were expected to come up with such a proposal unprompted was not clear.

It was also denied that he had suggested recognising the King as 'Head of the Associated States', rather than as 'Head of the Association', the latter formula being in line with external association. Unfortunately for de Valera and his apologists, Childers's diary disagrees with them. 'Decided to keep oath but amend it, recognising King [as head] of Associated States.'[177]

Unknown to de Valera, the Cabinet wasn't the only body considering the draft Treaty. Collins had given a copy of the British draft to Seán Ó Murthuile, secretary of the IRB, to put before 'the lads' – the Supreme Council. According to Ó Murthuile, the oath proposed by the British was unacceptable, but a new version was drafted that expressed allegiance to the 'Irish Free State', with fidelity to the British monarch in a subsequent clause.[178] At best, this was an appalling breach of confidentiality by Collins; at worst, it suggests he regarded the views of the Supreme Council as being of greater value than those of the Cabinet: the oath contained in the final treaty was in the IRB's form rather than de Valera's.

The instructions given to the plenipotentiaries as they prepared to return to London were again somewhat contradictory. Ó Murchadha recorded that the delegates were 'to carry out their original instructions with same powers' – which was not particularly helpful in deciding whether their full powers to sign a treaty were outweighed by the requirement to report back to Dublin before doing so. And then there is his record of the decision rejecting the British draft.

(a) Delegation to return and say that Cabinet won't accept Oath of Allegiance if not amended and to face the consequences, assuming that England will declare war. (b) Decided unanimously that present Oath of Allegiance could not be subscribed to. (c) Mr Griffith to inform Mr Lloyd George that the document could not be signed, to state that it is now a matter for the Dáil, and to try and put the blame on Ulster.[179]

Again, this was contradictory: the *present* oath couldn't be accepted *if not amended*; which implies that an amended oath could be accepted. Of course, it may be that Ó Murchadha's record was incorrect, but surely it was incumbent on de Valera as President to ensure that the delegation had clear, precise instructions. In his diary, Childers acknowledged that 'all this amendment business was too hurried', adding that he, Barton and Gavan Duffy understood that 'amendments were not mandatory on Delegation but suggestive'.[180] This, from an unimpeachably anti-Treaty source, again suggests that the plenipotentiaries were entitled to take independent action.

As the delegation travelled back across the Irish Sea, they were, then, entitled to feel some confusion. Was de Valera really prepared to risk a resumption of war over the difference between external association and dominion status? All of his public and private comments then and subsequently suggest that the answer is yes.

> They said at the Cabinet meeting that it was a gamble – I begged them to risk it. A win meant triumph, definite and final. If we lost, the loss would not be as big as it seemed, for we would be no worse than we had been six months ago.

Even 'extreme Republicans, like Cathal Brugha, and Stack', were prepared to accept external association. Therefore, he insisted, it was worth staking everything.[181]

What of Barton's suggestion, mentioned above, that de Valera didn't join the delegation so that he could make a last-minute intervention if the talks collapsed?[182] This theory offers a more logical explanation for de Valera's approach than any other; but it makes his decision to leave Dublin immediately after the Cabinet meeting and return to his tour of the west even more inexplicable.

While the delegates in London have frequently been criticised for failing to get in touch with de Valera before signing the Treaty, he can equally be criticised for choosing to leave Dublin, where there was at least some chance of staying in contact. De Valera and Brugha caught up with Mulcahy on the night of 3 December in the house of the Bishop of Clonfert, Dr Thomas O'Doherty, in Loughrea, Co. Galway. Brugha and de Valera sat by the fire with O'Doherty, discussing what would be acceptable in a final agreement; the curiously incurious Mulcahy went to bed.[183]

The following day the three reviewed troops in Galway, before returning to Ennis to attend a Gaelic League concert. Addressing the crowd, de Valera said he couldn't go into details, but he assured them that their principles were safe.[184]

The following day, 5 December, he told a review of the 1st Western Division that they must be prepared 'to act on orders at a moment's notice'.[185]

That evening the party moved on to Limerick, where de Valera and Kathleen Clarke received the Freedom of the City. In his acceptance speech he recalled the rejection of the proposals of 20 July and said they would have as little hesitation in rejecting any new unacceptable proposals.

> This is no idle talk on my part, because what we say we mean . . . We may have years of terror. We had it before, but when it was all over they [the British] were as far away from achieving their main purpose as when they started . . . They will never – not to the end – get from this nation allegiance to their rulers.[186]

The story of the final, dramatic hours of the negotiations in London has often been told.[187] On 4 December, Griffith duly put forward the counter-proposals 'as suggested by the President'; these were duly rejected by Lloyd George as

> a refusal to enter the Empire and accept the common bond of the Crown. They were but the same proposals which had already been discussed and rejected.

The discussions broke up when Gavan Duffy unwisely stated that the Irish difficulty was 'coming within the Empire'.[188] This was the most explicit statement of the Irish case made during the negotiations, and the British reaction demonstrated why Griffith (and indeed de Valera in his correspondence with Lloyd George) had been careful to avoid mentioning the Republic if at all possible. Had the Irish side explicitly demanded a republic the talks would never have begun, or would have collapsed immediately.[189]

On 5 December the Irish negotiators argued that they could not accept a relationship with the Crown before they had an answer from Craig on 'essential unity'. Lloyd George convinced Griffith that the Boundary Commission, which Griffith had promised not to repudiate, would ensure essential unity – and there ended the attempt to break on Ulster.

The conference then discussed changes to the oath of allegiance, specifically the proposed wording suggested by the IRB and submitted by Collins, and eventually agreement was reached on this and a number of other issues, including trade and defence.[190] At this point Lloyd George added a theatrical gesture, claiming that the final agreement must be sent to Craig in Belfast by 10 o'clock that night by special train and destroyer.[191] He then 'directly threatened war' if there was no agreement.[192] This was pure showmanship, and could surely have been dismissed by the Irish delegation (this was the opinion of Geoffrey Shakespeare, one of Lloyd George's secretaries).[193] Lloyd George demanded that all five pleni-potentiaries must sign the agreement and recommend it to the Dáil – which was enough to persuade Gavan Duffy, and finally Barton, to sign. At 2:20 a.m. on Tuesday 6 December 1921 the Anglo-Irish Treaty was signed at 10 Downing Street.

There is some confusion about exactly when news of the agreement reached de Valera in Limerick. Three weeks later he told McGarrity that he was told over the telephone on Monday night that

> some agreement had been reached, and I felt like throwing my hat in the air. I felt certain, on account of Griffith's undertaking, that *our* proposals had been accepted.[194]

Mulcahy remembered the phone call coming on the morning of the 6th (which seems more likely, given the time at which the Treaty was signed), but de Valera's reported response – 'I didn't think they [the British] would give in so soon'[195] – is similar. Kathleen Clarke, who travelled back to Dublin in the same train compartment as Brugha and de Valera, recorded a similar comment from de Valera: 'If they have signed, they must have got all we demanded.'[196]

The morning papers – though probably not the country editions available in Limerick – had news that agreement had been reached, but no details (although the *Irish Independent* reported that 'important modifications had been made in the British proposals').[197] There is no doubt, then, that by the time de Valera reached Kingsbridge (Heuston) Station in Dublin at 2:30 p.m. he knew an agreement had been reached but did not know the terms. Given the momentous nature of this news, his reaction was astonishing: he apparently made no attempt to find out more about what had been agreed.

According to his diary, he had lunch at his office in Kenilworth Square, then drove out to Greystones to visit his family, before finally heading back into the Mansion House at 7:15 p.m. for a celebration of the 600th anniversary of the death of Dante organised by the new Minister for Fine Arts, Count Plunkett.[198] But when he arrived Austin Stack was waiting for him with copies of the evening papers. Although it had been agreed by the negotiators that the text of the Treaty would not be released until 8 p.m., some details had inevitably leaked. From London the Central News Agency reported: 'It is learned officially that the agreement makes allegiance and association within the British Empire certain.'[199] Stack, having seen these reports, 'felt really sick'.[200] De Valera recorded in his diary (non-contemporaneously): 'Met Stack who showed me copy of *Evening Mail* – incredible.'[201]

Shortly afterwards, Éamonn Duggan and Desmond FitzGerald arrived at the Mansion House from London bearing a copy of the Treaty. Those who believe that de Valera's rejection of the Treaty was the result of pique have plenty of evidence in his reaction to their arrival. According to Stack, the President ignored the envelope Duggan proffered.

'What should I read it for?'

'Oh,' said Duggan, 'it is arranged that the thing be published in London and Dublin simultaneously at 8 o'clock, and it is near that hour now.'

'What,' said the President, 'to be published whether I have seen it or not?'[202]

Desmond FitzGerald later denied that de Valera was in a 'towering rage' when they gave him the Treaty. He thought he was simply 'irritable' and

preoccupied with the question as to whether he should wear his Chancellor's robes at the meeting . . . I persuaded him time and again to turn back to the document, but he seemed never to read beyond the third clause . . .[203]

Of course, the palaver about the robes was one way of avoiding a disagreeable confrontation over the terms of the Treaty. But while his refusal to read the entire text might appear odd, the first three clauses may have been enough: they deal with Ireland's status as a dominion and with the Governor-General.

Perhaps his getting the first intimation of what was in the Treaty from Stack was unfortunate, as it led him to ignore the substantial advances the plenipotentiaries had made. In contrast to the last British draft, the oath no longer required TDs to swear 'true faith and allegiance' to the Crown, only to the 'Constitution of the Irish Free State'. Although there was still a requirement to swear fidelity to the King, he was no longer described as the head of state; the 'Free State' was given the right to have revenue and fishery-protection vessels; the British monopoly on coastal protection was to be reviewed after five, rather than ten, years; and fiscal autonomy – an Irish demand throughout the negotiations – had been granted at the last minute. The delegates had even got rid of the term 'British Empire': for the first time in an official document, the title 'British Commonwealth of Nations' was used instead.[204] These were important improvements which justified the refusal to accept the last British draft.

But de Valera could see no good in what had been done and was gloomily predicting that he would be back teaching within three weeks. Stack recalled that

> he appeared to me to be an almost broken man. Afterwards, Cathal [Brugha] and myself met him in the study but little or nothing was said. We were too full of disappointment.[205]

Given that de Valera was prepared to compromise – external association was, on his own admission, not his ideal solution – why was he so opposed to the compromise reached in London? Some argue that he was motivated by wounded vanity. Ronan Fanning claims that de Valera

> opposed the treaty not because it was *a* compromise, but because it was not *his* compromise – not, that is, a compromise which he had authorised in advance of its conclusion.[206]

There is something in this. But it is far from the whole story. External association had been carefully designed to maintain the unity of the Republican movement, keeping the likes of Brugha and Stack on board. He still believed that if the Treaty was rejected by the Cabinet and the Dáil he could put sufficient pressure on London to get what he wanted. His attitude, then, was justifiable, as long as that scenario remained in play. But it was no longer justifiable on that basis once the Treaty had been accepted by the Dáil.

The full text of the Treaty was published in the newspapers on 7 December, along with reports of congratulations from world leaders and celebrations throughout the country. The *Freeman's Journal* headline is typical: 'Dublin's glad surprise: Citizens resigned to war amazed by news: Story told in happy faces'.[207] There was no mention, however, of de Valera's reaction. Behind closed doors, he was reported to be in an awful state. Oh, what a disappointment to our bright hopes – what a fiasco . . . Partition of our country and British subjects is the 'freedom' we are to have.[208]

The available members of Cabinet – Brugha, Stack and Cosgrave – as well as O'Higgins, were summoned to a meeting in the Mansion House. De Valera proposed issuing a statement repudiating the agreement and announcing that he had

> dismissed, as was my Constitutional right, those Ministers who had violated their pledges to the Cabinet and signed the 'Treaty'.

He was dissuaded from this drastic action by Cosgrave, who suggested that the signatories should be allowed to give an explanation before being sacked.[209] In what turned out to be a monumental error, de Valera agreed; had he replaced the three signatories with 'sound' Republicans, the Cabinet would have rejected the Treaty and the Dáil may well have followed suit. De Valera, however, still regarded Cosgrave as an ally, and didn't realise that he couldn't count on his vote – which was now the crucial swing vote in a seven-member Cabinet divided between three signatories and three bitter opponents of the Treaty.[210]

De Valera contented himself with a public statement.

> In view of the nature of the proposed Treaty with Great Britain, President de Valera has sent an urgent summons to the Members of the Cabinet in London to report at once so that a full Cabinet decision may be taken.[211]

Telegrams were also sent to Griffith, Collins and Barton ordering them home – a superfluous instruction, as they were already on the way. Desmond FitzGerald was surprised at the tone of the announcement: 'It reads as if you were opposed to the settlement,' he pointed out to de Valera. 'And that is the way I intend it to read. Publish it as it is.' Taken aback, FitzGerald whispered to Stack: 'I did not think he was against this kind of settlement before we went over to London.' Stack replied: 'He is dead against it now anyway. That's enough.'[212]

The statement was duly printed in the following day's papers, though its significance does not appear to have sunk in. The *Irish Independent* was happily reporting that the only opposition to the Treaty came from Conservative and Ulster Unionist newspapers, though it did note the surprise of foreign journalists 'at the absence of flags and outward signs of rejoicing' outside the Mansion House.[213]

The plenipotentiaries faced recriminations at the Cabinet meeting in the Mansion House. When Childers walked into the room, he found de Valera 'head in hands' reproaching Collins for having signed. When the meeting began, the President complained that the delegation had broken its instructions by not consulting the Cabinet. Gavan Duffy, Barton and Collins all said they hadn't thought of it. De Valera also pointed out that they were supposed to send draft documents back to Dublin before signing them; the delegates replied that they had discussed the British draft on the 3rd; but de Valera rightly answered that the Treaty as signed had not been seen by the Cabinet. He also reproached Griffith, for breaking his promise not to sign; Griffith said the alternative was war. In turn he reproached de Valera himself for not going to London. De Valera replied he would have gone had it not been for Griffith's promise, and he would have told Lloyd George, 'Go to the devil; I will not sign.'[214] Barton also criticised de Valera for refusing to go to London, saying the crisis was due to de Valera's 'vacillations' from the beginning; de Valera, speaking 'at great length', explained that he had been working all along for an association the Brugha party

> could just accept and which would not give up the Republic. Now all thrown away without an effort and without permission of cabinet or even consultation.[215]

Collins said all they were doing was recommending the Treaty to the Dáil; de Valera replied that it was 'much more than that'.[216] A look at that day's newspapers, exulting in the achievement of peace, would bear him out.

Those inside the room claimed that the debate was relatively even tempered. Stack recalled, 'Strangely enough, we were not unfriendly towards one another,'[217] and Barton said, 'I don't think there were any insults hurled about . . . It was a very tense meeting, with very visible efforts at restraint'.[218] But the efforts at restraint may not have been quite as effective as they remembered: as he briefed journalists outside, Frank Gallagher had to speak loudly in order to drown out the noise of 'angry voices' from the meeting room,[219] while Lord Mayor Laurence O'Neill recalled that 'the fierceness of the language could be heard outside'.[220]

But had anybody's mind been changed? De Valera, Brugha and Stack were clearly voting against the Treaty; Griffith and Collins were in favour; Barton 'thought he was bound to vote for the document, having signed it and undertaken to recommend it'.[221] And that left Cosgrave.

Some years later, Cosgrave observed that de Valera thought he had Cosgrave 'in his pocket'.[222] But the President had every reason to think this. The two men were personally close: de Valera's diaries are full of references to having lunch with his colleague and going to events with him.[223] He also, as Cosgrave acknowledged, defended him when others wanted him dismissed as minister.[224] And, most importantly, de Valera believed him to be against giving allegiance. 'Mr Cosgrave, prior to the signing of the "Treaty", gave no intimation to me . . . that he would favour any such proposals.'[225] Cosgrave had supported the telegram to the Pope and the message of 25 October rejecting allegiance to the Crown. On the other hand, he had shown independence by raising the issue of de Valera's participation in the talks in the Dáil, and by rejecting the plan to sack the plenipotentiaries from Cabinet. Cosgrave was his own man: he had been a member of Sinn Féin and follower of Arthur Griffith for a decade and a half; and he was a pragmatist rather than an ideologue. His vote was decisive, giving the Treaty 4 votes to 3. (O'Higgins was also recorded as supporting the Treaty, though he had no vote.)

When Cosgrave cast his vote in favour of recommending the Treaty to the Dáil, de Valera's control of the Cabinet was destroyed. Against all his expectations, he was in the minority. It was agreed that he would issue a statement defining his position and that of Brugha and Stack. The Dáil would meet the following Wednesday to discuss the Treaty. In the meantime, ministers would remain in control of their departments.[226] A regular Cabinet meeting scheduled for the following day was cancelled;[227] the united Sinn Féin Cabinet would never meet again.

De Valera's statement appeared prominently in the next day's press.

> The terms of this agreement are in violent conflict with the wishes of the majority of this nation as expressed freely in the successive elections during the last three years . . . I cannot recommend the acceptance of this Treaty, either to Dáil Éireann or the country. In this attitude I am supported by the Ministers of Home Affairs and Defence.

After assuring the public that ministers, though divided, would carry on their work as usual, and that the army was not affected by the political situation, he concluded:

> The great test of our people has come. Let us face it worthily without bitterness and above all without recriminations. There is a definite constitutional way of resolving our differences – let us not depart from

it, and let the conduct of the Cabinet in this matter be an example to the whole nation.

The implication of this, of course, was that the vote of the Dáil would be accepted.

But de Valera was uneasily aware – as he had been for some time – that public opinion was not nearly as steadfastly dedicated to the Republic as he liked to suggest and that the mood for peace was strong. That was why he was desperate to avoid a public vote for as long as he possibly could.

On 9 December, as the public digested his repudiation of the Treaty, de Valera was in the Mansion House, rallying resistance for the Dáil battle to come. Apart from his two Cabinet colleagues, he met Mary MacSwiney, Kathleen Clarke and Art O'Brien, among others, all dedicated opponents of the Treaty.[228] To the delight of Erskine Childers he was aiming his plans at the more Republican end of the spectrum, rather than trying to win the middle ground.

> He was thinking more of one which he could get extremist support for than moderate support! His nerve and confidence are amazing. Seems certain of winning.[229]

He also met the GHQ Staff in the Oak Room of the Mansion House for an hour. He claimed that the meeting was to discuss whether they were ready to resume hostilities if necessary; Mulcahy claimed it was to find out if the Staff would support him if he won the vote in the Dáil. De Valera terminated the meeting by assuring them that, if he lost the vote, 'he would not stand for a moment for mutiny in the Army'.[230]

De Valera's stance inevitably encouraged opposition to the Treaty, which up to then had been muted. One paper, the *Donegal Vindicator*, explained that, while it had been unhappy about the oath,

> we thought silence our duty trusting as we do in our leaders. We registered only a little half-hearted regret . . . Now Éamon de Valera has spoken that he cannot counsel acceptance and one may speak the hidden thoughts . . .[231]

De Valera was, as Lynch put it, 'the first to rebel'.[232] His rebellion was prompted by a double failure: he thought he could control the delegation, but he was wrong; he thought he could control the Cabinet, but he was wrong. Was he now correct in thinking he could win a vote in the Dáil?

The photographs of de Valera's parents, Catherine Coll and Vivion de Valera, which he kept in his office. (Reproduced by kind permission of UCD Archives, the Éamon de Valera papers, P150/190 and P150/168.)

A native New Yorker – one of the first known photographs of de Valera. (Reproduced by kind permission of UCD Archives, the Éamon de Valera papers, P150/4(2).)

Wearing his American velvet suit and his aunt's boots, the four-year-old de Valera, before his curls were cut. (Reproduced by kind permission of UCD Archives, the Éamon de Valera papers, P150/5 (4–6).)

'I love study so much ...' Posing for a group photograph in Blackrock, de Valera carefully keeps his place in his book. (Reproduced by kind permission of UCD Archives, the Éamon de Valera papers, P150/21.)

'Edward de Valera, Professor, of Rockwell College.' (Reproduced by kind permission of UCD Archives, the Éamon de Valera papers, P150/41(9–10).)

'I need a kiss, urgently ...' De Valera and Sinéad on their wedding day. (Reproduced by kind permission of UCD Archives, the Éamon de Valera papers, P150/142.)

Sinéad de Valera with her children – baby Terry, Emer, Ruairí, Brian, Eamonn (holding cat), Máirín and Vivion. (Reproduced by kind permission of UCD Archives, the Éamon de Valera papers, P150/151(5).)

The Irish teacher: on the beach on Tamhain island, Co. Galway. (Reproduced by kind permission of UCD Archives, the Éamon de Valera papers, P150/75(1–2).)

On the fringes – the Adjutant of the Dublin Brigade with the O'Donovan Rossa funeral committee. De Valera is fourth from the left in the back row; Thomas MacDonagh is on the extreme left; Tom Clarke is in the centre of the second row. (Courtesy of National Library of Ireland, Ke 175.)

Easter 1916 – after the surrender, de Valera leads the 3rd Battalion into captivity. (Reproduced by kind permission of UCD Archives, the Éamon de Valera papers, P150/503(2, 6).)

De Valera awaits court-martial in Richmond Barracks. (Reproduced by kind permission of UCD Archives, the Éamon de Valera papers, P150/523.)

'Three cheers for Ireland, lustily given ...' The convicted prisoners return home. De Valera is in the left foreground, wearing a light-coloured suit. (Reproduced by kind permission of UCD Archives, the Éamon de Valera papers, P150/533.)

A group photograph of the returned prisoners in the grounds of the Mansion House. In the middle of the second row, Eoin MacNeill has his arm around de Valera. (Courtesy of National Library of Ireland, NPA DEV67.)

'The coming Parnell of Ireland ...' De Valera discovers his talent for electioneering in the East Clare by-election. (Reproduced by kind permission of UCD Archives, the Éamon de Valera papers, P150/556(1).)

'He was I believe unselfishly patriotic ...' De Valera and Arthur Griffith. (Reproduced by kind permission of UCD Archives, the Éamon de Valera papers, P150/1465(2).)

Shortly after they arranged his escape from Lincoln Prison, Harry Boland and Michael Collins are pictured outside the Mansion House with de Valera in April 1919. (Courtesy of National Library of Ireland, INDH54.)

'The largest welcome ever accorded to any individual in the history of America ...'
The crowd at Fenway Park, Boston, for de Valera's first major public meeting.
(Reproduced by kind permission of UCD Archives, the Éamon de Valera papers,
P150/753(4).)

'I spend most of my
time shaking hands ...'
The president on tour.
(Reproduced by kind
permission of UCD
Archives, the Éamon
de Valera papers,
P150/1079(6).)

De Valera's mother listens to a recording of her now-famous son during his American tour. (Reproduced by kind permission of UCD Archives, the Éamon de Valera papers, P150/191.)

De Valera with his half-brother, Father Tom Wheelwright. (Reproduced by kind permission of UCD Archives, the Éamon de Valera papers, P150/206(6).)

July 1921 – the Irish delegation leaves Dublin for a meeting with Lloyd George: Arthur Griffith, Robert Barton, Laurence O'Neill, Count Plunkett, Éamon de Valera. (Courtesy of National Library of Ireland, INDH97.)

The new Chancellor of the National University of Ireland. (Reproduced by kind permission of UCD Archives, the Éamon de Valera papers, P150/93(9).)

6 December, 1921. Hours after the signing of the Truce – but before he knew the terms – de Valera is photographed at Strand House in Limerick. Cathal Brugha is on the far right, Richard Mulcahy stands behind their host, Stephen O'Mara. (Reproduced by kind permission of UCD Archives, the Éamon de Valera papers, P150/1530.)

'Not only was it almost impossible to hear ... it was difficult even to see who was speaking ...' The Treaty debates in UCD. (Reproduced by kind permission of UCD Archives, the Éamon de Valera papers, P150/1365.)

A stern-faced de Valera with his anti-Treaty TDs. (Courtesy of National Library of Ireland, HOG234.)

His lighter side was on display as the photograph was set up – but such levity was not for public consumption. (Courtesy of National Library of Ireland, HOG235.)

15 August, 1923 – de Valera is arrested while making a speech in Ennis.
(Courtesy of National Library of Ireland, INDH554.)

In Arbour Hill military prison, a Free State officer points a gun at de Valera as a
joke, while Austin Stack and 'Keegan' look on. (Reproduced by kind permission
of UCD Archives, the Éamon de Valera papers, P150/1875.)

On one of his voyages to the United States, de Valera signs autographs for fellow passengers. (Reproduced by kind permission of UCD Archives, the Éamon de Valera papers, P150/2129.)

The Fianna Fáil TDs elected in June 1927. De Valera is seated between Constance Markievicz, who had only weeks to live, and Kathleen Clarke. Seán MacEntee is fifth from the left in the back row, with Gerry Boland to his left. Frank Aiken is second from right in the middle row, beside Seán Lemass and P. J. Ruttledge. (Courtesy of National Library of Ireland, NPA DEV64.)

CHAPTER 15

I AM SICK TO THE HEART

I am sick and tired of politics . . . no matter what happens I would go back to private life.
Éamon de Valera, January 1922[1]

'Twas like whistling jigs to milestones . . .
T. M. Healy on urging de Valera to moderate his position in March 1922[2]

Young men and young women of Ireland . . . Ireland is yours for the taking. Take it.
Éamon de Valera, April 1922[3]

De Valera began the crucial Dáil debate on the Treaty in December 1921 with a piece of verbal trickery. Speaking in Irish, he said his grasp of the language wasn't good enough for the purposes of the discussion, and so he would continue in English. He then said in English that he was using that language because 'some of the members do not know Irish, I think'.[4] His opponents would argue that this set the tone for his participation in the debate, which in turn set the tone for the rest of his political career. Certainly, the self-righteousness and inability to admit the other side's point of view displayed in these tense debates would be a recurring theme in his political career; and of course the division that opened up during the Dáil's deliberations would define Irish politics for generations to come. But those who ascribe de Valera's position solely to wounded vanity and stubbornness miss the essential point: he was desperately trying to find a compromise that would preserve unity. That doing so would also preserve his own leadership he chose to regard as a happy accident.

Throughout his career he would pretend that he was reluctant to take on the mantle of leadership, that he would prefer to go back to teaching his beloved mathematics. Occasionally, he was honest enough in private to admit the truth. As he put it in a revealing conversation with Dorothy Macardle:

> It is extraordinary the change that occurs once people are in office. I see it in myself. I watch it. Once you are satisfied that the welfare of the country is served by your retaining power you get impatient of all opposition – inclined to think it is all factions.[5]

In December 1921 de Valera certainly believed that the welfare of Ireland would be served by his retention of power. His impatience of opposition was evident, and he accused the other side of introducing 'party politics' into the Dáil.

Before the debate, de Valera gathered some trusted colleagues, including Erskine Childers and Frank Gallagher, to help him draw up his alternative to the Treaty.[6] His pencilled notes on the text of the Treaty show his main concerns: the prescribed mention of the King in the oath meant that 'Irish become British subjects'; the clause relating to defence appeared to be 'for *ever*'; article 12 'permitted' partition; and article 17, relating to transitional arrangements before a constitution was established, gave power to a provisional government of 'Southern Ireland' rather than to the Dáil.[7] De Valera's plan was to secure unanimity in the Dáil on removing these objectionable features, and then to offer to the British this alternative. As drafting continued, his downcast mood improved, according to Gallagher. 'All of us around him noticed the new energy and . . . hope in the already lined face'.[8]

There were, however, a number of serious flaws with this tactic. The first was that the drafting was done at speed – never de Valera's strong suit. The second was that it offered a tempting target for his opponents while not appealing to doctrinaire Republicans. Thirdly, his alternative was very close to the proposals already put to the British negotiators, and already rejected.

He planned to keep as closely as possible to the language used in the Treaty, so that 'the average person who would not read closely would be inclined to say that there was only a "shadow" of difference between them'. But, as he later realised, the more he succeeded in making the difference *appear* a mere shadow, the more the public would believe it *was* a mere shadow. He felt his biggest mistake was on the clauses dealing with

'Ulster'. He claimed he planned to speak against them in the Dáil, even though he left them intact in his alternative; after all, he thought, he was only preparing a draft.[9]

There was no 'Crown' in Document no. 2; neither was there a 'Republic'. But it explicitly stated that all power in Ireland derived 'solely from the people of Ireland' – a rejection of the Treaty's implicit acceptance that the British Crown was the source of authority. If this principle was recognised in the Constitution, Republicans could have no qualms about swearing allegiance to it. Instead of referring to the 'Republic' or the 'Free State', de Valera simply referred to 'Ireland'.[10] In line with his theory of external association, he included a provision for acting in matters of common concern with the states of the Commonwealth; but the King was recognised as 'head of the association', not as 'head of the associated states'.[11]

These two changes would have brought the Treaty into line with the form of oath he had suggested at the Cabinet meeting on 3 December – though he did not include an oath in Document no. 2, contrary to popular belief. He made a number of changes to the defence clauses, which limited British use of Irish facilities in peace time to five years, and restricted their use in time of war to naval facilities. He specified that British requirements must be 'reasonable' – which implied that the Irish government would have to agree to what was considered reasonable.[12] This policy would prove acceptable to Britain in 1938; there is no reason to suppose it would have been accepted in 1921. Five of the six clauses dealing with the North were unchanged, covering its right to opt out of the new state, and the Boundary Commission. He added an introductory clause denying 'the right of any part of Ireland to be excluded from the supreme authority of the national Parliament and Government', but agreeing to the opt-out clause in the interests of peace and rejecting the use of force or coercion. He also deleted the clause prohibiting the endowment of religion, North or South.[13]

The Dáil met to debate the Treaty on 14 December in the Council Chamber of University College, Dublin, in Earlsfort Terrace. The room was

immensely long and narrow . . . The deputies sat on folding chairs interspersed with tables all higgledy-piggledy down the long room. . . . Because the ceiling of the Chamber was so low its acoustics were nearly non-existent. Not only was it almost impossible for members in the back of the hall to hear what the orators were saying, it was difficult even to see who was speaking.[14]

The usual venue, the Round Room of the Mansion House, was occupied by the annual Aonach, or Christmas fair. The change of location meant very severe restrictions on access for the public, which was no bad thing in some eyes. When a move back to the Mansion House was suggested after the Aonach concluded, both de Valera and Griffith opposed it, on the grounds that there would be a tendency for partisan crowds to cheer speeches.[15]

According to one observer, de Valera, 'looked grave'.[16] To another, he was 'terribly gaunt and stern, and immensely tall in his dead black overcoat'. He sat with Stack and Brugha, facing Griffith, Collins and Cosgrave on the other side of the room. 'Thus were the lines drawn.'[17]

The first business of the public session of the Dáil was to discuss whether they should go into private session, which led to a lengthy wrangle that cut across divisions over the Treaty: both Collins and Brugha wanted the sitting to be public. Eventually it was agreed to have what was expected to be a brief discussion in private, de Valera saying that the private session would require an afternoon, and that they would meet in public the following morning 'for the sole question of ratification'.[18]

Before the press left they were treated to an indication of the tensions in Cabinet, with de Valera reading out the instructions given to the plenipotentiaries and complaining that they had not submitted the final Treaty to Cabinet before signing it, though he admitted that they were 'acting in accordance with their rights' in doing so.[19] This relatively limited complaint provoked Collins, who demanded that the plenipotentiaries' powers should also be read out, his fury evident. 'From slow, measured tones his speech mounted until it reached a crescendo of anger and indignation'.[20] But that was the only indication that the public would get of the passions involved for some days, as the Dáil resumed its deliberations behind closed doors.

De Valera began his contribution to the private session with a complaint: that the Treaty had been signed without consulting him. He claimed this development undermined his ability to 'keep the two groups together' – an ability he considered to be his main use to the country. His principal concern was to secure peace if that could be done honourably, and he believed this could be done with external association. In order to make that possible, he said, he had 'battered down the wall of the isolated Republic . . .'[21]

Although TDs hadn't yet got copies of his alternative, he tried to explain it. He believed that the distance between it and the Treaty was 'so small that the British would not wage war on account of it', but that this small difference 'makes all the difference'; it would 'satisfy the aspirations of the country', though he acknowledged that it would not satisfy those who wanted an isolated Republic.[22]

In response, Griffith defended the plenipotentiaries, pointing out that they were sent to negotiate a settlement and that recognition of the Republic had not been a precondition for the talks. They had, through the Treaty, 'brought back the name of the State, the army, the flag, and it is for Dáil Éireann to say whether they believe that is dishonourable to Ireland and whether they will declare war'.[23] Both he and Collins insisted that what de Valera was suggesting was exactly what had been put to Lloyd George and rejected twice already. The Treaty had to be taken as it stood and either accepted or rejected.[24] In private, Griffith claimed to be bewildered by the President's attitude. 'I can't understand de Valera; he is a changed man,' he told Richard Mulcahy's wife, Min. 'He has become an absolute wall against the whole thing.'[25]

Copies of de Valera's alternative document were distributed that evening, and the following morning he laboriously explained it. The main difference, he claimed, was that there was nothing in his document that was inconsistent with the Republic. In order to 'eliminate the Ulster question out of it' he would leave the relevant clauses 'practically the same, with an odd verbal change'.[26]

The following day, in yet another lengthy (and somewhat rambling) contribution, he told the Dáil that if the Treaty was adopted he 'would have no interest in continuing in public life'. He acknowledged that 'every true Irishman' was 'bound to obey the majority of this House whatever way it goes', though the Republic could be disestablished only by the will of the people. He then discussed his own standing with the public.

> I believe I have got a certain reputation. I don't deserve it. I don't know that I do. But the reputation for honesty, I want to preserve that for the benefit of the nation.[27]

That reputation might have been questioned had the public known of an exchange between the President and Deputy Kathleen Clarke the following day; she said de Valera had said of the plenipotentiaries, before they went to London, that 'We must have scapegoats'. He denied this at first, but then added: 'I forget what particular idea was in my mind at the time' – an admission that that was exactly what he had said.[28]

Over the next few days the alternatives were debated in private. Seán Milroy argued against going sideways into the British Empire. If we are going to go in let us go in with our heads erect and not try to get in dodging around a corner when no one is looking.[29]

Kevin O'Higgins admitted that the signature by the five plenipotentiaries had changed his attitude. 'I would have gone back to war rather than recommend a settlement involving allegiance if the Treaty had not been signed.'[30] Margaret Pearse said she could not accept the Treaty, as if she did 'I would be haunted by the ghosts of my sons'.[31] Childers insisted that Document no. 2 removed the King from Ireland, and Ireland from the Empire.[32] Seán T. O'Kelly claimed that de Valera's document was the only way to avoid a split, and the only way to keep de Valera in charge, 'for if this thing is turned down he goes down'. This observation didn't appeal to the man himself, who interjected, 'That has not any bearing on it.'[33]

There was bad temper and intolerance on both sides; but there were light moments, too. Gearoid O'Sullivan, talking about the difference between 'allegiance' and 'fidelity' in the proposed oath, observed that a man getting married 'promises to be faithful to his wife which is a very different thing from owning allegiance to her'. One of his colleagues advised him: 'Wait until you get married'.[34]

The Dáil resumed its public session on 19 December – with de Valera immediately seizing the initiative. The Chairman, Eoin MacNeill, announced that the President had withdrawn the document introduced during the private sessions, and it 'must be regarded as confidential until he brings his own proposal forward formally'. Griffith was understandably furious. 'Are my hands to be tied by this document being withheld after we were discussing it for two days?' Collins said he couldn't, as a public representative, agree to withhold from the Irish people his knowledge of what the alternative to the Treaty was. De Valera insisted that he wasn't withholding anything from the Irish people – the document would be published in due course – but he didn't want to distract attention from the debate on the merits of the Treaty. Griffith grumpily concluded, 'While I shall so far as I can respect President de Valera's wish, I am not going to hide from the Irish people what the alternative is that is proposed.' He then moved the motion that the Dáil should approve the Treaty.[35]

Griffith was obviously handicapped by the failure to publish de Valera's alternative. He complained that it was being asserted that the President 'stood uncompromisingly on the rock of the Republic', when in fact the difference between them was 'merely a quibble of words'.[36] The oath – of allegiance to the Constitution and of faithfulness to the King, in his capacity as head of the Commonwealth – could be taken by any Irishman with honour. As it did for de Valera, their oath to the Republic bound them to do the best they could for Ireland, and they had done that.[37]

De Valera said he was opposed to the Treaty because it would not end the centuries of conflict between Great Britain and Ireland. The Constitution to which deputies would be required to swear allegiance would have the King as head of Ireland, which would subvert the Republic. He also, rather bizarrely, defended his alternative, which he had withheld from the public, claiming that he had been trying to bring forward a document that would bring 'real peace' between the two countries. And he hit back at the suggestion that the differences were 'a quibble of words'.

> You may sneer at words, but I say . . . in a Treaty words do mean something, else why should they be put down? They have meanings and they have facts, great realities that you cannot close your eyes to.[38]

On paper, this speech is not particularly impressive. It reads as if de Valera was rambling and poorly prepared, perhaps suffering the strain of the private sessions. But it was much more effective in delivery. According to journalistic accounts, de Valera was

> in magnificent form – mentally and physically. Unquestionably his speech electrified the assembly. His blinding sincerity so impresses you that you find yourself listening dazzled and profoundly moved. Every word came with rugged clearness.

He concluded by quoting Parnell – 'No man has the right to fix a boundary to the march of a nation; no man has the right to say to his country, Thus far shalt thou go and no further' – after which there was:

> a prolonged outburst of applause as his last words were slowly and impressively uttered. It was a great speech, spoken straight from the heart of the man.[39]

The Dáil briefly adjourned to allow de Valera to attend his induction as chancellor of the National University – a glittering acknowledgement of his status, at the same time as that status was ebbing away in Earlsfort Terrace. On the resumption, Collins delivered a lengthy and passionate speech defending the Treaty.

In my opinion it gives us freedom, not the ultimate freedom that all nations desire and develop to, but the freedom to achieve it.[40]

The following days of debate, before the Christmas break, were repetitious, long-winded and not very illuminating. As one observer recalled, the atmosphere was 'sombre, gloomy, not to say sad, as harder and harder words were exchanged'.[41] When Griffith objected to going into another private session in order to discuss military matters, de Valera snapped, 'I think something else besides the Treaty has come from Downing Street.'[42] After a break he apologised and withdrew the comment, explaining that it had been prompted by accusations that he was trying to keep things from the public.[43] Some humour was provided by W. T. Cosgrave, who gently poked fun at de Valera over two of his favourite subjects, maths and rugby.

If x be absolute independence and y be independence . . . x, in my opinion, would equal y if you put *minus* £42,000,000 per annum and 60,000 English troops and a foreign judiciary . . .

Referring to comments by Collins about English penetration of Irish life, Cosgrave said, 'The best colleges play the foreign games. The President can bear me out in that.'[44] Even de Valera had to laugh.

Mary MacSwiney then gave a speech that lasted an extraordinary three hours. Nobody could doubt her commitment, or the passion with which she attacked the Treaty and its signatories. De Valera, however, doubted her wisdom, later claiming that she had affected the final result.[45] MacSwiney had strongly objected to any suggestion of preventing a TD from speaking for as long as they liked; this was prompted by de Valera and Griffith saying they were anxious to have the vote before Christmas.[46] De Valera wanted to continue discussions all night if necessary in order to have the vote on the 23rd. 'We should not leave this question hanging over; we ought to be able to make up our minds on the matter.' But he received little support: the pro-Treaty side were not going to allow their speakers to be curtailed after MacSwiney had spoken for so long. In any case, as Collins observed, 'it would be more convenient for the country members and for the country – and I see very great national advantages in it – to adjourn over the Christmas'. Accordingly, it was decided to adjourn until 3 January.[47]

De Valera told Joe McGarrity that had the vote been taken on the 22nd, it was thought we might have got a majority of one or two against the treaty. But the press is hard at work throughout the country trying to get the local public bodies, County Councils, etc. to pass resolutions in favour of the treaty – and the Church is also hard at work.[48]

At least two TDs – Daniel O'Rourke and P. J. Ward – later said they had been opposed to the Treaty, but had changed their mind after talking to constituents over the Christmas break.[49]

De Valera's tactical approach was coming under fire, at least in private. Kathleen Clarke thought that de Valera

> to a large extent is to blame, for one thing his lack of experience which I always feared, and another, his habit of trying to work things out alone in his own way taking no one entirely into his confidence, and also trusting too much in the goodness of other people.[50]

Clarke was not entirely fair in suggesting that de Valera was not taking colleagues into his confidence. He proudly told McGarrity that his revised Document no. 2, on which he had been working over Christmas, was being supported by 'all the Republicans like Brugha, Stack, Miss MacSwiney etc. . . . proof that it is quite orthodox'.[51]

This document added a wordy introduction claiming that the Treaty would not be the basis for an enduring peace between Britain and Ireland, and offering the British an alternative which could achieve peace. Apart from a few tweaks to the language, it closely followed his first draft. Again, there was no form of oath. However, evidently stung by criticism of the original, which included the Treaty clauses dealing with the North largely unchanged, de Valera now removed them. Instead of having what he regarded as an internal matter dealt with in an international treaty, he included an addendum, which was to be passed by the Dáil. This denied the right of any part of Ireland to be excluded from the authority of the Dáil, but 'in sincere regard for internal peace, and in order to make manifest our desire not to bring force or coercion to bear', it agreed to grant 'privileges and safeguards not less substantial than those provided for' in the Treaty.[52] What exactly this might mean was not clear. It could, for instance, be held to allow Northern Ireland to remain under the control of Westminster. Whether it would provide for the Boundary Commission was not at all evident, and it wasn't clarified during the debate.

In later years, Republicans would pretend that partition was a core issue in the Treaty debates; it was not.[53] The reason was simple: both sides thought the Boundary Commission would make Northern Ireland unsustainable. Collins believed that the Boundary Commission would give the South at least two counties, Fermanagh and Tyrone, and probably large parts of Down, Derry and Armagh.[54] Strong opponents of the Treaty, such as Máire Comerford, agreed. 'Even to the most intransigent of us the Boundary clause seemed to be one of the least objectionable sections of the Treaty'.[55] The only TD to devote an extensive part of his speech to partition was Seán MacEntee, a Belfast man representing Monaghan in the Dáil. But even he claimed that the Treaty would copper-fasten partition, not because the Boundary Commission wouldn't work, but because it *would* work. He said the effect would be to remove nationalist-majority areas from the North, thereby making unity less likely. In a reference to the former Ulster Unionist leader Edward Carson, he said, 'That is being done in order that Carsonia shall secure a homogeneous population.'[56]

Far from the Treaty's having 'made Partition possible', it attempted to undermine a political entity that already existed – an entity, in fact, whose existence had made the Treaty possible in the first place. Quite apart from the Boundary Commission, the Southern leaders (including de Valera) thought that the financial provisions of the Government of Ireland Act (1920), which would subject Northern Ireland to British tax rates, would strangle Craig's government.[57] De Valera made the mistake of thinking that partition would prove temporary, while the status of the Free State would prove permanent – the exact opposite of what transpired.

As far as de Valera was concerned, the opposition to him was the result of sinister machinations, not of his own mistakes. He complained that Dáil Éireann was

> no longer the united patriotic body it had been. The spirit of party had entered, and party spirit, not patriotism, became the ruling sentiment.[58]

He was more explicit about who was to blame in a letter to McGarrity.

> M.C. [Collins] had got the IRB machine working . . . It was a case of [Daniel] Cohalan and his machine over again . . . Curse secret societies![59]

Although the reference to Cohalan – his American nemesis – may have been designed to appeal to McGarrity, it also suggests a more worrying element of de Valera's attitude: to him, all opposition was the result of ill-will, bad faith and the workings of cabals. Therefore no compromise was possible; allies must be found to defeat the conspiracy; the good fight had to be fought until victory. It was a dangerous approach in a combustible situation.

When the Dáil resumed on 3 January 1922 there was little new that could be added to what had gone before – but still the debate went on. When de Valera said he would introduce his amendment the following day, Griffith observed that the document that was being distributed to deputies – the revised Document no. 2 – had been changed significantly. This was quibbling, de Valera claimed. He then

> uttered the words authoritatively. 'I am responsible for the proposals, and the House will have to decide upon them. I am going to choose my own procedure.' Arthur Griffith spoke coldly, but intently: 'The President has said he is going to choose his own procedure. This is either a constitutional body or it is not. If it is an autocracy let us know and we will leave it.'[60]

De Valera's supposed autocratic tendencies were severely criticised in the following morning's *Freeman's Journal,* which also carried an editorial attacking his 'criminal attempt to divide the nation' and the influence over him of Childers, 'an Englishman who has achieved fame in the British Intelligence Service'.[61] The paper was roundly condemned by TDs on all sides, some of whom wanted to expel its journalists from the Dáil; but de Valera, Griffith and Collins all supported freedom of the press.[62] De Valera also denied that his comment about choosing his own procedure was an attempt at dictation; he had meant only that he did not require the agreement of the other side before introducing his amendment.

He was more worried about the publication of his original draft of Document no. 2. The only difference, he claimed, was 'a slight change of form', and 'I think it is an absolute abuse of confidence to publish that document, not that I am ashamed of it'. Griffith admitted that he had given the original to representatives of the *Freeman's Journal* and the *Irish Independent* the previous evening.

> I called attention to the fact that it was not Document No. 2 and the President stood up and accused me of quibbling. I therefore handed it to the Press to let the Irish people judge whether I was quibbling or not. I made no abuse of confidence.[63]

De Valera regarded Griffith's action as a grievous breach of trust; and Griffith believed De Valera to have been guilty of sharp practice himself.

Meanwhile, a serious attempt at averting a breach was being made behind the scenes, but it foundered on de Valera's obduracy. An unofficial backbench committee representing both sides agreed on a document proposing that, if the Treaty was accepted, 'the active services of President de Valera should be preserved for the nation. In this way every ounce can be got out of the Treaty'. It called on de Valera to advise opponents of the Treaty to abstain; he would continue as President of Dáil Éireann; a provisional government, deriving its powers from the Dáil, would be permitted to function; and the army would be responsible to that government.[64]

Griffith and Collins accepted this proposal, but de Valera rejected it outright, urging the committee to accept Document no. 2 instead.[65] De Valera later claimed that the proposed agreement 'simply meant that we would let the Free State take existence and take root, and then try to pull it up again'.[66] The last hope of compromise in order to avoid a devastating split was gone.

De Valera said he was going to settle the matter by resigning at the public session in the afternoon.

> I am not going to be a party to manoeuvres of this kind at all . . . The whole of Ireland will not get me to be a national apostate and I am not going to connive at setting up in Ireland another government for England.[67]

The *Irish Independent* journalist Pádraig de Búrca described the scene as the public session began.

> De Valera, looking more haggard than I have ever seen him before, was sitting at his table with his heavy overcoat closely buttoned. He seemed – as indeed the event proved – to be assuring himself that some weighty decision he had taken would for ever stand the test of conscience . . . At most times he speaks with a rapidity unusual in a statesman. Today he spoke with that slowness and deliberation which are the mark of a man who has weighed well the meaning of the consequences. Not a sound broke the stillness save the clear, one might almost say musical, voice of the Irish Chief. Every ear was strained to catch every sentence, every syllable. We had reached a crisis in the long drawn-out debate.[68]

De Valera said the Cabinet was split 'irrevocably, not on personalities or anything of that kind or matter, but on absolute fundamentals', and that this could continue no longer. If he was to remain as President, he had to have the power to do the job – and he had to have a united Cabinet. This was the occasion of his now-famous claim that he knew what the Irish people were thinking.

> I have been brought up amongst the Irish people. I was reared in a labourer's cottage here in Ireland [applause]. I have not lived solely amongst the intellectuals. The first fifteen years of my life that formed my character were lived amongst the Irish people down in Limerick; therefore, I know what I am talking about; and whenever I wanted to know what the Irish people wanted I had only to examine my own heart and it told me straight off what the Irish people wanted.

This was not, as is sometimes suggested, a claim of omniscience, but an attempt to portray himself as an ordinary and down-to-earth Irishman, despite his exotic name and cerebral career. He added that if he was re-elected, Document no. 2 would be put to the Dáil by a united Cabinet; the Dáil had to decide, he said, between two policies, not between personalities.[69]

But his opponents thought it was *precisely* a question of personalities. The character of the President was the strongest card in the anti-Treaty hand; and by staging such a vote before the vote on the Treaty, they might win. Griffith described the resignation as 'an unfair attempt to bring in another discussion, and to close discussion on the motion before the House', and Collins said it was drawing 'a red herring across our path here'.[70]

Faced with this opposition, de Valera backed down – after a performance described by the *New York Times* as 'like a hysterical schoolgirl'.[71] De Valera said

> I am sick and tired of politics – so sick that no matter what happens I would go back to private life . . . What has sickened me most is that I got in this House the same sort of dealing that I was accustomed to over in America . . . I am straight with everybody and I am not a person for political trickery . . . If there is a straight vote in this House I will be quite satisfied if it is within forty-eight hours.[72]

In fact, the decision would come not in 48 hours but in 24.

Surprisingly, the final speaker on the anti-Treaty side the following day was not de Valera but Cathal Brugha. This turned out to be a colossal error, as Brugha launched a bitter personal attack on Collins, all the envy de Valera had detected the previous year spilling out in a diatribe that probably cost his side votes. Patrick McCartan claimed that the Treaty was in danger until Brugha 'made his silly attack on Collins'.[73] C. S. 'Todd' Andrews, an anti-Treaty observer, said everyone, including de Valera, 'was shocked and embarrassed by it'.[74] Brugha's ire was provoked by an earlier reference by Griffith to Collins as 'the man who won the war'. This, Brugha said, was nonsense.

> He is merely a subordinate in the Department of Defence . . . He was made a romantic figure, a mystical character such as this person certainly is not.

Anti-Treaty deputies tried to interrupt him; the pro-Treatyites gleefully said he should be allowed to continue. 'He is making a good speech for the Treaty'.[75]

Griffith was due to deliver the closing speech, but de Valera, 'with characteristic gallantry, urged that it would not be fair to Griffith to continue without an interval'.[76] No doubt the gallantry was genuine, although the break also diluted the effect of Brugha's disastrous intervention. Griffith's hour-long speech was described as 'powerful'.

> Never for a moment did he become personal, never for a moment lose his coolness or depart from the solid rock of argument.[77]

Griffith said they had been sent to London 'to make some compromise, bargain or arrangement'. They were not sent to demand a republic – if they had been, their talks in Downing Street would have been over in five minutes. The Treaty could of course be better, but 'it has no more finality than that we are the final generation on the face of the earth'. The Treaty gave the Irish people 'a chance to live their lives in their own country and take their place amongst the nations of Europe'.[78]

De Valera, of course, could not allow that to be the last word before the vote. He interjected with a 'last protest', claiming that if the Treaty was passed the Irish people would judge them for what they got out of it, compared with 'an explicit document where there is nothing implied but everything on the face of it'.[79] This last, almost incoherent, plea for Document no. 2 was the final word before the roll-call vote.

The Chairman, Eoin MacNeill, had already ruled that each TD would have only one vote, meaning that the northern constituencies represented on the double by de Valera, Griffith, Collins, Milroy and MacNeill himself would in effect be disenfranchised – and the Treaty side would be three votes worse off.[80] (MacNeill, on the Treaty side, announced that, as Chairman, he would vote only in the event of a tie.) The pro-Treaty Tom Kelly, absent through illness, and the anti-Treaty Laurence Ginnell, on government business in South America, had unsuccessfully asked for their votes to be recorded.[81] The Tipperary TD Frank Drohan, unable to reconcile his own opposition to the Treaty with his constituents' support, had resigned his seat two days earlier,[82] and Patrick McCartan, who had said he would abstain, decided to vote for the Treaty, as he felt the result would be close. There were therefore 121 votes to be counted.

The roll was called. As the results were being checked, 'suddenly a mighty cheer was heard outside. The waiting crowd had got the result even before the Speaker had had the totals placed in his hand.'[83] The Treaty had been approved, by 64 votes to 57. De Valera, 'whose features now wore a deadly pallor',[84] rose to address the Dáil.

> It will, of course, be my duty to resign my office as Chief Executive. I do not know that I should do it now.

Collins said he shouldn't. De Valera then said the vote meant

> simply the approval of a certain resolution. The Republic can only be disestablished by the Irish people . . . This Republic goes on.

Collins followed him, calling for unity, and suggesting some form of joint committee to ensure it, finishing with a tribute to de Valera. 'He has exactly the same position in my heart now as he always had.'[85] De Valera seemed receptive to Collins's approach, but any hope of unity evaporated when MacSwiney spoke.

> I, for one, will have neither hand, act, nor part in helping the Irish Free State to carry this nation of ours, this glorious nation that has been betrayed here tonight, into the British Empire . . . there can be no union between the representatives of the Irish Republic and the so-called Free State.[86]

Not for the last time, de Valera's options had been closed off by hard-liners.

The minutes of the Dáil convey de Valera's feeling as he made his closing remarks.

I would like my last word here to be this: we have had a glorious record for four years; it has been four years of magnificent discipline in our nation. The world is looking at us now . . . (The President here breaks down).[87]

The flinty Ernest Blythe later denied that de Valera had actually wept. 'I noted that he put his hand over his eyes for a moment, but no tears were visible to me.'[88] Others were not so sure. Kathleen O'Connell recorded 'an awful moment . . . He sits down and buries his face in his hands. Will I ever forget!'[89] He had certainly suffered a shattering blow. Since the signing of the Treaty, the unquestioning deference to which he had become accustomed over the previous four years had ebbed away.

However, despite his frequent references to leaving politics, de Valera had no intention of retiring. Before his emotional closing statement he had suggested a meeting the following day of 'all those who have voted on the side of the established Republic'.[90] These deputies duly met on 8 January in the Mansion House and agreed to form a new organisation, Cumann na Poblachta.[91] De Valera also briefly met unidentified army officers in the afternoon before returning to his office for another meeting of his new inner circle: MacSwiney, Boland, Mellows, Childers, Brugha and Stack.[92] This group was distinctly more hard-line than de Valera himself: four of them would die in the Civil War, and the two survivors would remain in Sinn Féin when de Valera left to form Fianna Fáil.

Some republicans argued that the Treaty vote was illegitimate because it was carried out under the threat of British coercion, and therefore they were not obliged to accept the will of the majority.[93] This attitude was taken to extremes by Count Plunkett, who argued that those who voted for the Treaty were 'traitors' who had exceeded their powers, and that 'the powers of the Dáil remain vested in the elected persons who have been faithful to these institutions'.[94] In later years, Republicans made a fetish of the Second Dáil, arguing it was the only legitimate parliament in Ireland; but they meant, of course, only the anti-Treaty members of the Second Dáil – the minority. In any event, it was not immediately clear to many why, if the Dáil had declared a Republic, it could not decide to disestablish it. In the heat of the moment de Valera allowed himself to be caught up in the dubious approach of the 'doctrinaires' to the legitimacy of the Dáil; it would take him half a decade to extract himself.

The following morning, back in Earlsfort Terrace for the Dáil session, de Valera 'presented clear traces of the great emotional strain through which he has passed'.[95] As he tendered his resignation, Collins proposed once again that a joint committee should be set up to ensure public safety, as 'no one here in this assembly or in Ireland wants to be put in the position of opposing President de Valera'. However, de Valera insisted they would have to proceed constitutionally and elect an executive.[96] In reply to Gavan Duffy, de Valera said that, if re-elected, he would carry on the executive work of the Republic, and would not 'actively oppose' the implementation of the Treaty.[97] In reply to Professor Joseph Whelehan, he confirmed that either a Cabinet of the pro-Treaty majority or a Combined Cabinet would be 'out of the question': he would form 'a Cabinet that would be composed for the time being of those who stood definitely by the Republic'.[98] This rather bizarre notion was roundly condemned by pro-Treaty deputies: it was tyranny and dictatorship, according to Patrick Hogan; the President would dictate policy regardless of the decision of the Dáil, W. T. Cosgrave claimed; Seán Milroy said it was an attempt to undo Saturday's vote on the Treaty.[99] De Valera unconvincingly denied all this.

> I do not ask you to elect me. Therefore I am not seeking to get any power whatever in this nation. I am quite glad and anxious to get back to private life . . .[100]

This vote has received much less attention than the vote on the Treaty two days before, though it was potentially just as significant. Had de Valera secured re-election he would have appointed a solidly anti-Treaty Cabinet. Although pledged not to 'actively interfere' in the implementation of the Treaty, it would, by its very existence, have made the creation of the Irish Free State almost impossible. Griffith and Collins would still have had a mandate from the Dáil to implement the Treaty, but the Provisional Government would have been set up in competition with the Dáil Cabinet, rather than working in tandem with it. And their opponents would have had control of all the resources of the Dáil – most importantly, of course, the IRA. Given how difficult the Free State would find it to establish its legitimacy with Griffith as President of the Dáil Cabinet, it would surely have been next to impossible with de Valera in that office.

There were five changes from Saturday in how TDs voted. De Valera himself ostentatiously abstained, a high-minded gesture that might have proved very costly, given how close the result was. Two TDs who had voted for the Treaty voted for de Valera's reappointment: Robert Barton (who voted for the Treaty only because he had signed it) and Paul

Galligan. Two more TDs who had supported the Treaty abstained: Liam de Róiste and Tom O'Donnell, de Valera's former teaching colleague in Rockwell (who is frequently and incorrectly said to have voted for de Valera[101]). A seven-vote margin of defeat on the Treaty thus became a two-vote defeat on re-election, 58 votes to 60. It was an extraordinarily close-run thing; had he succeeded in having this vote before the vote on the Treaty, he would surely have won.

Griffith was immediately on his feet:

> I want to say now that there is scarcely a man I have ever met in my life that I have more love and respect for than President de Valera. I am thoroughly sorry to see him placed in such a position. We want him with us.

This sentiment was echoed by Collins.[102] Then de Valera replied. Speaking 'with smiling friendliness, with relief', he 'accepted the thunders of applause that greeted his rising with graceful, almost boyish delight'.[103] While they could not co-operate on the Treaty, he said, they would be there against 'any outside enemy' and he repeated the phrase he had used at the time of the split of the Volunteers in 1914: 'You will want us yet.' According to O'Connell, de Valera was surprisingly positive about his defeat. 'President in great form. Felt a heavy load had been lifted.'[104]

When the Dáil met on 10 January to elect a new President, de Valera harried Griffith over his status. Would he be President of the Republic? Would the Republic be kept in existence? He acknowledged that the Dáil had given them a mandate to carry out the Treaty, and his side would not interfere in their work if they acted as the government of the Republic. But if they *didn't* act as the government of the Republic, 'we would have to take action to prevent you from doing anything counter to it, as we would against Dublin Castle'.[105] Given that the servants of Dublin Castle had been considered legitimate targets only months before, this was a potentially threatening observation. Griffith pointed out, correctly, that under the Constitution the office in question was 'President of Dáil Éireann', but de Valera insisted, 'I was President of the Republic of Ireland.' On the point of exasperation, Griffith said that he didn't care 'a single rap about words' and that he would occupy the same position as de Valera had, whatever it was called. He also assured de Valera that he would 'keep the Republic in being until such times as the establishment of the Free State is put to the people, to decide for or against'.[106]

These assurances seemed to satisfy his opponent.

I feel that I can sit down in this assembly while such an election is going on, because it is quite constitutional that Mr. Griffith, if elected, is going to be in the same position which I held . . .[107]

But de Valera's position changed after some of his supporters took a harder line, particularly MacSwiney. After her contribution, de Valera urged Griffith not to take office as President while attempting to implement the Treaty.[108] And then, just before the vote, he said he would leave the chamber as

> a protest against the election as President of the Irish Republic of the Chairman of the Delegation, who is bound by the Treaty conditions to set up a State which is to subvert the Republic.

All his supporters followed him, amid angry exchanges which are captured in the minutes:

> *Michael Collins:* Deserters all! We will now call on the Irish people to rally to us. Deserters all!
> *Dáithí Ceannt:* Up the Republic!
> *Michael Collins:* Deserters all to the Irish nation in her hour of trial. We will stand by her.
> *Countess Markievicz:* Oath breakers and cowards.
> *Michael Collins:* Foreigners – Americans – English.
> *Countess Markievicz:* Lloyd Georgeites.[109]

It was an appalling demonstration of the animosity that was building, and one that reflected little credit on anyone. In the absence of the anti-Treaty deputies, Griffith was elected with 61 votes recorded in his favour, and none against. He named a new Cabinet: Collins (Finance), Gavan Duffy (Foreign Affairs), Mulcahy (Defence), Duggan (Home Affairs), Cosgrave (Local Government) and O'Higgins (Economic Affairs).[110]

The anti-Treaty deputies, meanwhile, were meeting in another room. De Valera again talked about resigning and returning to his teaching, saying that, while he was prepared to be the leader of the Irish people, he didn't want to be leader of a party. He was – without too much difficulty – persuaded to stay.[111] He led his followers back into the Dáil when it resumed after lunch. He promised Griffith support in his role as President of the Republic, though not in any actions taken on behalf of the Provisional Government.[112] Griffith continued his conciliatory tone, saying he would not have asked de Valera to resign: 'He is an individual whom I esteem and love, although, in the interests of the nation, I had to oppose him'. However, Griffith lost his temper when Childers persistently questioned him, snapping 'I will not reply to any damned Englishman in this Assembly'.[113]

After this ugly moment, things returned to a more even keel. De Valera agreed to Griffith's suggestion of a month's adjournment, to allow the new government to find its feet, despite objections from a number of anti-Treaty deputies. And he secured an assurance from the new Minister for Defence, Mulcahy, that 'the Army will remain the Army of the Irish Republic'.[114]

A cynic might wonder how sincere the pro-Treaty side were in their expressions of devotion to de Valera. But they did try to soften the financial blow of loss of office. The new Cabinet instructed Cosgrave to approach de Valera about possible payments to former ministers.[115] Cosgrave made his approach gingerly.

> You are so touchy about these matters that I find it difficult to say anything fearing to offend you, which I hope and think by this you know would be the last thing I would dream of doing.[116]

De Valera refused to accept any salary for himself, though to his credit he did successfully seek holiday pay and a bonus for Kathleen O'Connell, who declined to work for the new government.[117] Sinéad returned her husband's £50 salary cheque for January,[118] telling Collins that 'we should not get money now, since Éamon is no longer President.' She added her thanks to Collins for all he had done for her, signing herself 'your friend always'.[119] De Valera also offered to surrender his office at Kenilworth Square – an offer Griffith rejected, saying he didn't need it and 'it is entirely at your service'.[120]

The Sinn Féin Ard-Chomhairle met in the Mansion House on 12 January to elect a new Standing Committee; the result was a disaster for the anti-Treatyites. 'We were heavily defeated,' Childers recorded in his diary. Apart from himself, the list of unsuccessful Republicans included Robert Barton, Kathleen Clarke, Mary MacSwiney, Constance Markievicz, Margaret Pearse and Hanna Sheehy-Skeffington.[121] Of the 15 members of the new Standing Committee, 11 were supporters of the Treaty, one (Father Pat Gaynor) was neutral, and only three were anti-Treatyites.[122] De Valera suggested to the Ard-Chomhairle that they were hopelessly divided, and it was better to face that fact than to try to work together 'in an impossible combination'. After some discussion it was decided to call an extraordinary ard-fheis to discuss the future.

Given the results of the Standing Committee vote, de Valera's eagerness to form a new political organisation is understandable. As soon as the Sinn Féin meeting was over, he was busy at a meeting of the new Republican party, Cumann na Poblachta, deciding an outline of policy.[123] That policy concentrated on the Treaty, to the exclusion of socio-economic matters.

Meanwhile, de Valera had other matters to attend to, which took him to Paris, where a long-planned Irish Race Convention was to be held. It would become the latest battleground between the two sides. Although de Valera wasn't a fugitive, he still had qualms about getting a British passport and feared difficulties in getting to France, so in London a false passport was secured in the name of a priest, 'Father Walsh'. He crossed the Channel in the company of Seán Nunan, Seán MacBride and Father Tim Shanley, a friend from New York.[124]

MacBride found de Valera 'very pleasant to travel with,' even though 'one always had to keep an eye on his not missing trains.' De Valera nearly blew his cover when he went to buy a fountain pen in London, signing his real name on a piece of paper to try it out. MacBride 'gave him a strong kick' and removed the offending signature.[125]

In Paris, both sides of the Treaty split manoeuvred for advantage; but de Valera and his colleagues were much better at it. Griffith's government had decided to send a delegation representing both pro-Treaty and anti-Treaty factions, with Eoin MacNeill heading the former and de Valera the latter. But it banned Robert Brennan, Under-Secretary for Foreign Affairs, from attending.[126] Brennan promptly resigned, and by the time the government's Director of Publicity, Desmond FitzGerald, arrived in Paris, he found Brennan and Harry Boland firmly in charge of the arrangements for the conference. FitzGerald complained about the 'quite unscrupulous' methods of his opponents;[127] but the reality was that they were just better at politics than he was.

The ineptitude of the pro-Treatyites was further disclosed when it came to nominating a president for Fine Gaedheal, a new international organisation to be established by the convention. When de Valera was nominated, the pro-Treatyites nominated Griffith, who wasn't there and hadn't given written agreement to being a candidate. He was therefore disqualified and de Valera was elected unopposed.[128] Later, Seán T. O'Kelly, the Dáil's representative in Paris, hosted a banquet at which de Valera was the main speaker; none of the pro-Treaty delegates was asked to speak. As MacNeill noted, this banquet was paid for by the same government that was being ignored. When he confronted O'Kelly about it, O'Kelly 'threw the whole blame on De V'.[129]

During a debate on a motion calling for the new organisation to help the people of Ireland attain 'their full political, cultural and economic ideals', there was debate around the word 'full', which was seen as pro-Republican. When the proposer of the motion said he hadn't used the word 'full' in his text, de Valera, who was chairing, cheerfully admitted that he had inserted the word himself, claiming unconvincingly that he had done so 'to enable the two parties to work together'.[130]

The final successful stroke by the anti-Treatyites was to have Brennan appointed organising secretary of Fine Gaedheal.[131] This was despite the best efforts of MacNeill, who threatened to canvass all the delegates against the appointment. In his diary de Valera claimed to be 'disgusted with MacNeill's tactics'.[132] Disgusting or not, those tactics were utterly ineffective: the anti-Treatyites had managed to gain complete control of the new organisation. MacNeill believed that de Valera's aim was to have Fine Gaedheal as an alternative source of power in case he ran into difficulties 'with his diehard friends'.[133] But the organisation's controversial birth alienated many of the international delegates, and it never amounted to anything.

Back in Dublin, on 12 February, de Valera's new Republican party, Cumann na Poblachta, held its first major event, a public meeting in O'Connell Street, with three platforms, several detachments of the Dublin Brigade of the IRA, and the Foresters' brass band.[134] Rosamund Jacob thought he spoke 'much as usual . . . tremendously in earnest and good in spots, but not very exhilarating'; she was much more impressed by the fiery Liam Mellows.[135] De Valera in his speech listed his problems with the Treaty: it was signed under duress, there was an oath to the King, and the British would continue to hold Irish ports. But now he stressed partition 'above all'.

> This ancient nation that has been one from the dawn of history is now to suit the exigencies of British politicians . . . to be broken up into two warring States.[136]

He wouldn't have admitted it, but this emphasis on partition was entirely new and not particularly deeply held. When a correspondent from the Hearst news agency asked him about how 'Irish unity' could be established, evidently thinking of the North, de Valera began talking about the unity of Sinn Féin and of Dáil Éireann – he was automatically thinking in terms of the 26 Counties.[137]

On 21 February the extraordinary ard-fheis of Sinn Féin met.[138] De
Valera proposed a characteristically verbose motion that would in essence
re-commit the party to securing the recognition of Ireland as an
independent Republic. It also stipulated that in the coming election Sinn
Féin would endorse only those candidates who promised 'not to take an
oath of fidelity to or own allegiance to the British King'. Griffith's
counter-motion endorsed the Dáil's approval of the Treaty, which it
claimed was in accordance with the aims of Sinn Féin.

In his speech, de Valera said that if the ard-fheis couldn't agree to abide
by its constitutional aims (in other words, by his motion) it would be
better for the party to split.

> An army can only march as fast as its slowest unit. If we can get a swift
> moving force and a force that will not move so quickly, let us divide
> provided we do not turn one upon the other.

Collins urged unity, saying they would be weaker if they divided. In
response, de Valera said unity could be maintained only by delaying
elections. He acknowledged that the pro-Treatyites 'do for the moment
represent the majority', because of the British threat of war, but he argued
that the country should not be asked to pronounce on the Treaty until the
new Constitution was ready.

The following day the ard-fheis accepted by acclamation an agreement
worked out between de Valera, Stack, Griffith and Collins over the course
of more than four hours of talks.[139] The ard-fheis was to be adjourned for
three months; the election was to be postponed until the Constitution was
ready; the Dáil would continue to meet, but 'no vote in Dáil Éireann shall
be regarded as a party vote requiring the resignation of the President and
Cabinet'; and the Officer Board (split 50-50 on the Treaty issue) was to
act as a Standing Committee, in place of the pro-Treaty body elected in
January. This all seemed like a victory for de Valera: he had avoided an
early election he was bound to lose, and he had a much better chance of
controlling the party machinery. On the other hand, Griffith and Collins
had secured assurances that the work of both the Dáil Cabinet and the
Provisional Government would be allowed to continue unimpeded; there
was a better chance when the election came of it being fought in peaceful
conditions; and a split in the party was avoided. Some of de Valera's
staunchest supporters thought he had missed a trick. Kathleen O'Connell
wrote of the ard-fheis that

the vast majority were Republicans. What a pity a division wasn't taken. We could start a new Republican party clean. Delays are dangerous. Many may change before the Ard Fheis meets again.[140]

Under the terms of the Treaty, the British government was to hand over administration to a Provisional Government elected by the Parliament of Southern Ireland. The pro-Treaty deputies – as well as the four Unionists elected for Trinity College – duly met and formally elected a Provisional Government, with Collins as Chairman. When the Dáil met on 28 February, Griffith informed deputies of this development, carefully avoiding the use of the term 'Parliament of Southern Ireland'. Dublin Castle had been taken over, British troops were being evacuated and the Dáil departments were continuing to function, he said.[141] Red post boxes in Dublin were also being painted green[142] – cynics would claim that this was the only real difference between the British and Free State regimes.

De Valera was prominent in asking awkward questions about the relationship between the Dáil Cabinet and the Provisional Government.

> Dáil Éireann is supreme in Ireland. It is only on that basis that I feel justified in remaining here . . . If there is some other sovereign body I, for one, do not want to come here.

Griffith assured him that the Dáil ministers would 'see that the Provisional Government works in harmony with Dáil Éireann until we have an election'.[143]

The following day, during a discussion on land division, de Valera stated, 'Dáil Éireann is supreme.' Collins snapped back, 'The people are supreme . . .'[144] This was to be a frequent theme in the months ahead: did sovereignty reside in the people, or in an assembly elected by the people? De Valera certainly felt there were limits to the sovereignty of the people, frequently stating that 'the majority have no right to do wrong'.[145] Years later, he stuck to this line, observing that, if the people voted unanimously that you should shoot your neighbour, it wouldn't make it right. 'Therefore the majority rule does not give to anybody the right to do anything wrong, and I stand by the statement'.[146] But in the context of the time, the phrase clearly meant that opponents of the Treaty had the right to ignore the wishes of the majority of the Irish people. And there was worse rhetoric to come.

His speech in Thurles on St Patrick's Day is the most infamous of his inflammatory utterances at this time. He pointed out that Irish people seeking independence had, up to then, been fighting a foreign government, but this would change if the Treaty was accepted.

> If the Volunteers of the future tried to complete the work the Volunteers of the last four years had been attempting, they would have to complete it, not over the bodies of foreign soldiers, but over the dead bodies of their own countrymen. They would have to wade through Irish blood, through the blood of the soldiers of the Irish Government, and through, perhaps, the blood of some of the members of the Government in order to get Irish freedom.

It is, of course, possible that he was misquoted but, at the time, he complained not of misquotation but of misinterpretation.[147]

He spent the night in Rockwell College in Cashel, along with Brugha and Seán MacBride, and was reported to be 'dreadfully hoarse and haggard looking', though he perked up sufficiently the next morning to take some exercise vaulting, to practice firing his automatic and to sign autographs for the boys.[148] Then he headed to Killarney, where he delivered another inflammatory speech, this time with a direct encouragement to action.

> If our Volunteers continue, and I hope they will continue until the goal is reached . . . and we suppose this Treaty is ratified by our votes, then these men, in order to achieve freedom, will have, I said yesterday, to march over the dead bodies of their own brothers. They will have to wade through Irish blood. If you don't want that, don't put up that barrier . . .[149]

His opponents, naturally, noted the phrase 'and I hope they will continue'. In a speech in Wexford, Collins pleaded:

> Can he not cease his incitements? They are incitements whatever may be his personal intention. Can he not strive to create a good atmosphere instead of seeking to create a bad one?[150]

De Valera's speech is not even mentioned in Dorothy Macardle's exhaustive history *The Irish Republic* (1937). De Valera and his supporters always claimed that his words were a warning, not an incitement. Peadar O'Donnell later said: 'You may as well blame a rainy day on the weather forecaster as blame de Valera for the Civil War.'[151] The difference, of course, is that a forecast will not affect the weather, but a speech can change the political climate.

And it should be remembered that neither the use of inflammatory language nor the subsequent denials were isolated incidents. In the Dáil on 1 March, during a heated exchange with the Minister for Agriculture, Patrick Hogan, de Valera denounced his claim that the Provisional Government was the body that was capable of conducting land division.

> But for the majority of Dáil Éireann you would not be talking as a member of the Provisional Government, because you would be swept out of the country by the Army.

A few minutes later he repeated his incendiary remark more directly.

> Only that it is a sovereign assembly I would be the very first to ask the Army to sweep you and the like of you out.[152]

The following day, when the *Irish Independent* reported his remarks, he denied them; and when Desmond FitzGerald asked him what he had said, he replied, 'I do not deliver what I say from notes. I know definitely what I said was not this'.[153] But what was reported was close enough, according to the official report.

During another Dáil exchange, in April, Hogan referred to de Valera's statement in January that if he was re-elected he would form his government from the minority of the Dáil. This is precisely what de Valera did say; but now he refused to admit it. 'I deny it. I did not do anything of the kind . . . It is a lie.'[154] Most of those in the chamber must have known that he was wrong.

De Valera's rhetoric may have been prompted by the increasing militancy of the anti-Treaty section of the army. As early as January an Acting Military Council had been set up, with Rory O'Connor as chairman, to counteract the pro-Treaty GHQ.[155] After Richard Mulcahy, as Minister for Defence, banned a planned army convention, O'Connor held a press conference to announce that it would proceed anyway, admitting that this meant they were 'repudiating the Dáil'.

> If a Government goes wrong it must take the consequences . . . If the Dáil is the government of the country we are in revolt against it.

Asked by journalists if they were to understand that they were going to have a military dictatorship, O'Connor replied that they could take it that way if they liked. He also acknowledged that de Valera had asked them to obey the existing GHQ but that they couldn't do so, because the Minister for Defence had broken his agreement with them.[156]

This distancing of the radicals from de Valera was rather undermined by the fact that the press conference was held in de Valera's office in Suffolk Street. Griffith picked up on this fact, and on O'Connor's threat of revolt against the Dáil. He asked de Valera 'to state categorically whether you repudiate that threat, or whether you repudiate the Dáil'.[157] De Valera avoided a simple answer to this question, asserting that the Dáil was entitled to the respect and obedience of every citizen, 'so long as it upheld the Republic established by the people and functioned as the Government of that Republic'.[158]

On 23 March, Tim Healy visited de Valera and spent more than an hour with him,[159] urging him to do what he could to prevent the banned army convention going ahead. Healy told him he would be a sorry man within a year if he approved the use of force; de Valera brusquely replied, 'I don't think so.'[160] Healy later recalled the futility of his appeal.

> Twas like whistling jigs to milestones . . . Ingredients of blame belong, it is true, elsewhere, but on him the guilt is blackest . . .[161]

The anti-Treaty army convention met at the Mansion House on 26 March and elected an Army Executive to take control of the IRA, or of that section of the IRA prepared to follow it. The civilian control that Brugha and de Valera had insisted on only months before had been destroyed. Liam Lynch of the 1st Southern Division was elected chief of staff. Though more moderate than Rory O'Connor and Liam Mellows, Lynch's position gradually hardened, especially after the Army Executive forces seized the Four Courts in Dublin in the early hours of Good Friday, 14 April.

> I am absolutely convinced that the Free State was sent to its doom by our action last week and come what may the Republic must now live.[162]

How much influence did de Valera really have on the militants? This is a crucial question, because those who blame him for the Civil War assume that he could have restrained them if he had wished to. But it wasn't as easy as all that. As Mary MacSwiney told Richard Mulcahy, 'If de Valera were on your side we should still fight on. We do not stand for men but for principles'[163] The IRA commander in Scotland, Joseph Robinson, was reported as saying that Rory O'Connor 'has set up a military dictatorship in Ireland and that in these operations de Valera does not count'.[164]

Decades later, de Valera claimed to have 'no definite recollection of meeting Rory O'Connor at this time . . . I think they did not wish to involve me in any way. They wished to be independent'.[165] It came as a complete surprise to him, his official biography claims, when they seized the Four Courts.[166] This seems odd, because he had had three lengthy meetings with the Army Executive leaders in the fortnight leading up to their occupation of the Four Courts. On 1 April he met Seán Moylan, Liam Mellows, Rory O'Connor, Liam Lynch and Joe McKelvey in Kenilworth Square; eight days later Lynch, O'Connor and Moylan followed him out to Greystones for a meeting; and on the 12th, O'Connor and Brugha called to see him; all this at a time when even such an illustrious person as W. B. Yeats was unable to make an appointment to see him.[167]

De Valera's tone became if anything more bellicose after the controversial speech in Thurles. An Easter message to the young men and women of Ireland, issued the day after the seizure of the Four Courts, was practically an incitement to the anti-democratic use of violence.

> Yours is the faith that moves mountains – the faith that confounds cowardly reason and its thousand misgivings. Yours is the faith and love that begot the enterprise of Easter, 1916. Young men and young women of Ireland, the goal is at last in sight. Steady all together, forward. Ireland is yours for the taking. Take it.[168]

It is true that he later regretted his support for O'Connor, writing of 'his unfortunate repudiation of the Dáil, which I was so foolish as to defend even to a straining of my own views in order to avoid the appearance of a split'.[169] But his second thoughts were too late to make any difference. When it mattered, his public statements contributed to the rise of extremism. In the words of Michael Hayes, 'he put his political cloak around all the people who wanted to use force'.[170]

However, he did play a moderating role in private. When fighting nearly broke out in Limerick between pro- and anti-Treaty forces seeking to take over from the departing British, de Valera wrote to Mulcahy urging him to avoid violence that 'may well be the beginning of a civil war and a general break-up of the army'.[171] A peaceful solution was found in Limerick – largely because Mulcahy felt that the pro-Treaty forces were not yet ready to fight.[172]

At a conference in the Mansion House on 26 April (organised by Archbishop Byrne, the trade unionist William O'Brien and the Lord Mayor, Laurence O'Neill), Brugha accused Griffith and Collins of being

British agents, assuring them that they were two of the ministers whose blood would have to be waded through. De Valera was considerably milder in his tone, agreeing that there was a 'background of truth' to Griffith's claim that de Valera had asked him to escape the 'strait-jacket' of the Republic.[173]

However, he rejected a suggestion by Collins for a head-count at church gates on the question of the Treaty, deriding it as 'a plebiscite with Stone Age machinery' that would deliver a questionable verdict. De Valera claimed that Griffith's insistence on an election in June would involve the acceptance of partition, because it would be held only in the 26 Counties; it would also be run on an inaccurate register and would breach the ard-fheis agreement, as the Constitution would not be ready. De Valera then quoted the views of 'Republicans', without saying whether he agreed with them.

> They maintain . . . that there are rights which a minority may justly uphold, even by arms, against a majority, and that such a right is that of defending and preserving for themselves and for those who come after them the precious heritage of belonging to a nation that can never be said to have voluntarily surrendered its territory or independence.[174]

These remarks seem to show de Valera attempting to walk a thin line, co-opting extremist support to bolster his own arguments for a delay, and talking about 'rights' that could be defended in arms against a majority, without actually stating his own position. It was of a piece with his 'wading through blood' speeches, as it could be interpreted as merely a warning. It was unsurprising that the pro-Treatyites took such comments to be threats. Of course, he was circumscribed by his uncompromising supporters. Brugha's truculence in the Mansion House was a demonstration of how difficult it was for de Valera to compromise. Joe McGarrity, who visited Ireland in February and March 1922, did his best to bring de Valera and Collins together, no easy task as 'one or the other of them' would 'get up in anger to walk out'.[175] McGarrity wanted them to agree on a constitution. If they could, the movement could present a united front to the British. De Valera was sceptical.

> Honestly, I am afraid that this is a dream pure and simple. I don't believe the other side will make any advance beyond the strict terms of the 'Treaty', which, of course precludes a Constitution which we could agree to.[176]

Eventually, at McGarrity's insistence, de Valera drew up three points for the guidance of Collins and his colleagues. They should avoid committing the country to the Treaty (it was not clear how); they should try to frame a constitution that did not recognise British sovereignty or authority in Ireland (he later added, as an afterthought, 'or partition in Ireland'); and they should try to get the British to simply 'register' that constitution, rather than implement it through British legislation.[177]

During this period his visits home were infrequent. More often than not, he stayed in town, working late writing speeches, drafting articles and meeting his cronies.[178] As usual, Sinéad held the fort at home. She was pregnant with their seventh child, who would be born on 4 June 1922 and named Terry, after Terence MacSwiney. She was also looking for a new house and had enlisted the aid of Kathleen O'Connell, as 'Dev is always so terribly rushed when he gets home that there is no time to discuss things properly'.[179] Eventually the family moved to 18 Claremont Road in Sandymount in November 1922, where they stayed until 1925. The man of the house wouldn't spend much time there. Even before that he was distracted: when Sinéad drew his attention to the wave in the baby's hair, he snapped, 'How can I mind about the wave in Terry's hair when they are fighting in the Four Courts?'[180]

At about this time, Harry Boland indiscreetly told Kitty Kiernan that de Valera didn't like Michael Collins because Collins was 'too anxious for power'. She promptly told Collins, who replied:

> I know that about de V well. I have known it all along. That's what he says of everyone who opposes him. He has done it in America similarly. It's just typical of him.[181]

The deterioration in relationships was further evident in the Dáil. There were no more expressions of love for de Valera. Griffith tore into his predecessor, accusing him of intimidating the people, and claiming (correctly) that, on his return from America, de Valera had suggested easing off the war. Griffith added:

> When I was going to London Mr. de Valera said to me, 'There may have to be scapegoats' . . . I said I was willing to be a scape-goat to save him from some of his present supporters' criticism . . .[182]

De Valera's reaction was indignant.

I deny that I have treated the members of the delegation in the manner that has been suggested. I say it is an infamous suggestion and I would not be fit to be alive if I had done that.[183]

But his most effective thrust hit de Valera in an old wound – one that was clearly still raw. When de Valera said one of his statements was on the record, Griffith responded that so was his 'Cuban statement' – a remark that prompted an almost hysterical response.

Oh! You are mean! You are vilely mean! You know you said those who attacked me on that occasion were mainly responsible for the record of terror in Ireland.[184]

These exchanges were no credit to either side; that was certainly the view of one observer, the anti-Treaty commandant of Cork no. 1 Brigade, Seán O'Hegarty (brother of the fiercely pro-Treaty P. S. O'Hegarty). He established a committee of officers drawn from the IRB but representing both sides, which presented a plan to the Dáil the following week, suggesting an agreed election that would maintain the present strength of the two parties.[185]

Although Liam Mellows dismissed the officers' statement as a 'political dodge', it was agreed to establish a committee of TDs representing both sides to consider it.[186] When it was suggested that a truce should be called while the committee sat – there had been reports of 18 deaths in fighting in Kilkenny – de Valera urged the government to order its forces to cease fighting, 'and so far as we are able to affect the Army Executive they also will get a similar order'. When challenged to give an assurance that the fighting would stop, de Valera had to admit to his impotence. 'The Army has taken up an independent position in this matter. All we can do is what I stated.'[187]

The commitee agreed that a coalition government should be formed after an agreed election – but their opening positions showed they had very different ideas of what that meant. The pro-Treatyites wanted a competitive election, with both sides putting up an extra candidate in each constituency to ensure voters would have a choice. The anti-Treatyites wanted the existing TDs to form the Third Dáil, without the need for any election at all. They also wanted it 'accepted and understood that no issue is being determined by the election', and they objected to the draft preamble by the pro-Treaty side, which said it was acknowledged that the Treaty 'would be accepted by the majority of the people'.[188]

The final proposals from the pro-Treaty side stipulated that the 'panel' of Sinn Féin candidates should be nominated on a basis of 5 to 3 in favour of the pro-Treaty side; that the coalition government formed after the election should have a President and ten ministers (six pro-Treaty and four anti-Treaty); and that any interest was free to contest the election against the national panel.[189] The anti-Treatyites wanted the proportion of candidates to be roughly equal to the outgoing Dáil, and the coalition government to be made up of the President (elected by the Dáil), the Minister for Defence ('representing the Army') and nine other ministers (five from the majority party and four from the minority).[190] Given that the army was certain to elect an anti-Treaty minister, with de Valera having been mentioned as acceptable, this would give the anti-Treatyites five of the 11 seats at Cabinet.

The real crux was the proportion of candidates to be placed on the panel. The pro-Treaty party naturally wanted to be sure of a working majority; the anti-Treaty side didn't want to abandon any of their members (apart from anything else, it would in effect penalise them for voting against the Treaty). A breakthrough seemed to have arrived when Harry Boland stated he would agree to the pro-Treaty demand. According to Kathleen Clarke, Boland told her that de Valera had agreed to this concession. Liam Mellows, however, remained obdurate, and a recess was called so the anti-Treatyites could confer.

At a party meeting, de Valera denied that he had agreed to give in to the pro-Treaty side. Clarke claimed she later overheard Boland angrily saying to de Valera, 'It's all right, Chief, you let me down, but I won't give you away.'[191] It may be, as de Valera claimed, that Boland misunderstood him; or it may be that de Valera backtracked when faced with the militancy of Mellows.

In any event, when the Dáil debated the committee's deliberations, de Valera insisted the only basis for allocating places on the panel was the existing strength of the parties in the Dáil. 'In one case, you base it on no principle and in the other case you have a definite thing to go upon.' Griffith said they could not agree to the Irish people being 'muzzled to prevent them expressing their view on this Treaty'.[192] With the committee deadlocked, Griffith moved to call an election on 16 June, and the Dáil reverted to bitter mud-slinging.[193]

Separately, Collins had been discussing matters directly with de Valera, and thought he had secured an agreement that the anti-Treaty side would not defeat the Government on vital issues; but de Valera came back to inform him that his party refused to give such a guarantee.[194]

Had de Valera really been overruled by his party? It is possible that this concession, like the one offered by Boland, was rejected by the likes of Mellows. But it is also possible that de Valera, sensing that Collins was eager for a deal, was playing hardball. If so, it worked, because Collins sought another meeting, at which agreement was reached after three hours of heated argument.

De Valera had won on all the issues. The preamble acknowledging popular support for the Treaty was gone. The panel would be filled by candidates from each side in proportion to their present strength in the Dáil. The post-election coalition government would be as de Valera proposed. If the coalition had to dissolve, an election would be held as soon as possible on adult suffrage. Clause 5 of the agreement could even be interpreted as undermining partition: 'Constituencies where an election is not held shall continue to be represented by their present Deputies.'[195] This could be taken (as it was by writers sympathetic to de Valera[196]) to refer to Northern Ireland; although it may simply have been a recognition that there would not be a contest in some constituencies.[197] Overall, it was a good result for de Valera, but he later came to regard the pact as a defeat for the Republicans, precisely because it meant 'acceptance of the people's decision as the final court' – and the people favoured the Treaty.[198]

For Collins, the great benefit of the pact was that an election would be held. Given that the only authority in many areas was the IRA, an election would be impossible without its cooperation. The benefit of the agreement was shown when electoral registers seized by anti-Treatyites were returned.[199] He also secured agreement that other interests were free to contest the election against the Panel, a key demand that had been resisted by the anti-Treatyites. This meant there would be a real contest and a real choice for voters. Though Griffith was distinctly unhappy about the Pact,[200] it was accepted by acclamation by the Dáil.[201]

The Sinn Féin ard-fheis, adjourned from February, met in the Mansion House on 23 May in the warm glow of agreement. De Valera presented the pact for the approval of delegates, saying there would be no speeches, to avoid controversy. He said they looked on the agreement 'not as a triumph for one section or for the other section but as a great triumph for the Irish Nation'.[202]

When an Irish delegation went to London to discuss the proposed Free State Constitution of the Irish Free State they met with a furious reception. Of particular concern to the British was the proposal for a coalition government following the election. Would the anti-Treaty ministers state in writing their acceptance of the Treaty, as was required under article 17 of the articles of agreement? Arthur Griffith and Éamonn Duggan explained that they would be 'extern' ministers rather than members of the government and would therefore not have to sign.[203] This did not satisfy the British side; nor were they pleased with the draft Constitution itself. Lloyd George said it 'was purely republican in character'. He objected in particular to the fact that the King 'was not part of the Legislature'; therefore the King would not summon or dissolve the Dáil, nor would he appoint ministers, and his representative would be reduced 'to a sort of Commissioner'. He objected to the Irish claim of the right to make their own treaties, to the exclusion of the Privy Council as a court of appeal, and to the omission of the oath from the Constitution itself.[204]

Collins believed that British resistance was stiffened by the unsettled conditions in Ireland. 'It's really awful – to think of what I have to endure here owing to the way things are done by the opponents at home.'[205] But in fact it was the pact itself that convinced the British to stand firm, according to Churchill.

> Had the proposed election been a bona fide one, they could have put pressure on us to stretch the Constitution to suit them . . . As no election of value is contemplated we are in a position to be much more searching in our examination of the Constitution.[206]

The British Cabinet discussed contingencies if agreement was not reached, including a resumption of hostilities. Churchill was full of plans to seize Dublin, Cork and Limerick, and to use air power to subdue other areas. It is not clear how seriously Lloyd George took him: he compared his Colonial Secretary to a chauffeur 'who apparently is perfectly sane and drives with great skill for months, then suddenly he takes you over a precipice'.[207]

However, faced with implacable British pressure, the Irish side yielded, and the agreed Constitution lost its Republican tone. True, it still stated, in its second article, that all powers of government and all authority in Ireland – legislative, executive and judicial – 'derived from the people of Ireland'. But article 51 stated that the Executive Authority 'is hereby declared to be vested in the King' and exercised by the Governor-General, who had the power to summon and dissolve the Oireachtas and to withhold assent to any bill.[208] And the Treaty was attached to the Constitution as a schedule: any article of the Constitution or any law that was repugnant to the Treaty would be void. The Governor-General was required to exercise his powers in accordance with the practices in Canada.

If the Constitution was bad from a Republican viewpoint, even worse was the fact that it was published only on the morning of 16 June – polling day. It could not, therefore, be subjected to the kind of scrutiny that had been expected. It also sounded the death-knell for any coalition arrangement after the election: no Republican could have taken office under its terms. Some on the anti-Treaty side didn't appear to realise this fact – or at least they pretended they didn't. On 22 June, Boland observed that the Constitution 'ends our hopes in Mr Collins's desire to see an independent Ireland'.[209] But he was claiming a fortnight later to have been expecting a phone call 'from Mick as to the men on our side who would be required to fill the posts in the Cabinet, in accordance with the agreement'.[210] This was almost certainly written for propaganda purposes, in order to accuse the Free State side of bad faith. Neither Boland nor de Valera can seriously have expected that the coalition could go ahead under the Constitution agreed in London.

However, the election campaign continued as agreed. Of the 124 Sinn Féin TDs elected in 1921 (excluding John O'Mahony), 118 were renominated; there were only 54 non-Sinn Féin candidates, so the panel was sure of at least 74 seats – a comfortable working majority if the coalition was formed.[211] De Valera loyally called for support for panel candidates. He had plenty of time to campaign nationally, as his own constituency of Clare was one of eight (out of 28) in which there was no contest, as only the panel candidates were nominated. In the case of Clare, this was the result of intense pressure being put on Patrick Hogan of the Labour Party in the minutes before the deadline for nominations. Once he withdrew his name, two farmer candidates and an independent did likewise.[212] This may have been no bad thing for de Valera. He was in no danger of losing his seat and might have had the satisfaction of being the only anti-Treatyite to head the poll if there had been a contest, but this was by no means assured – constituency executives in both East and West Clare had voted to support the Treaty.[213]

Doubt about the loyalty of the pro-Treaty side to the pact appeared to be cast by a now famous – or infamous – speech by Collins in Cork on 14 June, two days before polling.

I am not hampered now by being on a platform where there are Coalitionists. I can make a straight appeal to you citizens of Cork to vote for the candidates you think best of ... You understand fully what you have to do and I will depend on you to do it.[214]

This 'breaking of the pact' by Collins gave Republicans a convenient excuse for their dismal performance. Dorothy Macardle, for instance, claimed that the *Freeman's Journal* 'printed headlines in large type to call the attention of the electorate to Collins's speech'.[215] M. J. MacManus said that Collins's pronouncement was 'printed with flaming headlines . . . The Pact was no longer worth the paper on which it was printed.'[216] This was simply untrue. In fact, the speech got relatively little attention, and was reported without comment by the newspapers.[217] Pro-Treaty voters largely abided by the terms of the pact. While 71 per cent of anti-Treaty votes transferred to pro-Treaty candidates, 68 per cent went in the other direction. The big difference was in what happened to the remainder of the votes: 25 per cent of anti-Treaty votes were non-transferable, while only 8.6 per cent of pro-Treaty votes were. Pro-Treaty voters were far more likely to transfer to other candidates (all of whom were, broadly speaking, pro-Treaty), with 23 per cent of their votes doing so.[218]

Only 18 members of the Second Dáil managed to vote against the Treaty and then hold onto their seats in a contested election.[219] Erskine Childers got the second-lowest vote in the whole election; Liam Mellows was also beaten – the only outgoing TD west of the Shannon to lose his seat.[220] In the 20 contested seats, 19 anti-Treatyites were elected, while 22 were defeated; 41 pro-Treaty candidates won, while only 7 were beaten. But not a single seat was lost by the anti-Treatyites because of poor transfers from the pro-Treaty candidates.[221]

In later years, Republicans tried to put a gloss on the results. If seen as a vote on the merits of coalition rather than on the Treaty, it was suggested, the national panel had secured a thumping victory, with 94 of the 128 seats in the new Dáil and 73 per cent of the vote[222] – though this interpretation obviously undermines the claim that Collins had negated the pact with his speech in Cork. But at the time, there was no doubt in the minds of de Valera and his followers of what the results meant. Boland noted in his diary: 'Early results bad for Republicans', 'Treatyists winning', 'Labour and Treaty sweep country'.[223] In a press statement, de Valera said that the people, under threat of war, 'have in a majority voted as England wanted', and that the defeated Republican candidates 'have gone down with their flag flying'.[224] He informed a visiting American that 'we are hopelessly beaten, and if it weren't for the Pact it would have been much worse'.[225]

The anti-Treaty Army Executive had become increasingly intransigent during the election campaign anyway; the result merely heightened this. On 18 June the army convention resumed its deliberations, debating a motion from Tom Barry calling for war to be declared on Britain. After some procedural wrangling, the motion was declared lost, whereupon the more extreme elements withdrew from the convention, planning to hold a rival meeting in the Four Courts the following day.[226] With the elections out of the way, talks broken down, and the anti-Treatyites badly split, the temptation for the Provisional Government to tackle them increased.

The pressure to do so intensified on 22 June, when Sir Henry Wilson, former Chief of the Imperial General Staff, latterly an MP and military adviser to the Northern Ireland government, was assassinated by two IRA men on his doorstep in London. General Nevil Macready, who still had troops in Dublin, was ordered to attack the Four Courts but managed to persuade his political superiors that this would simply reunite the Republican movement against the British.[227] Instead, Lloyd George wrote to Collins demanding action against the anti-Treatyites.[228]

The Provisional Government was reluctant to be seen to bow to British pressure, but the Army Executive at the Four Courts relieved them of their dilemma by taking action that couldn't be ignored. In a reprisal for the arrest of the anti-Treaty officer Leo Henderson, they kidnapped the assistant chief of staff of the pro-Treaty forces, Ginger O'Connell. This gave the Provisional Government a reason to attack the Four Courts, which no-one in the army could dispute, and on 27 June the decision was taken to deliver an ultimatum to Rory O'Connor and his men to surrender or else face military action.[229] The pro-Treaty forces assured the government that any fighting would be short-lived; the adjutant-general, Gearóid O'Sullivan, said the irregulars all over the country would be dealt with in a week, or at most a fortnight. George Gavan Duffy later claimed he would not have agreed to taking action if he had realised how destructive and lengthy the struggle would be.[230]

The bombardment of the Four Courts, using borrowed British artillery, began at 4 a.m. on 28 June. Driving into town from Greystones later that morning, de Valera was stopped at an army checkpoint and warned to turn back, as there was trouble in the city centre, but he insisted on going on.[231] In Suffolk Street he met Austin Stack and Cathal Brugha, who confirmed the attack on the Four Courts. He suggested an attempt to arrange peace moves through the Lord Mayor, Laurence O'Neill, but Brugha told him it was no use. 'These fellows have gone over to the British. We're going to fight back.'[232] De Valera issued a statement saying that the pact, 'if faithfully observed', would have given internal peace and the chance to 'make this nation strong against the only enemy it has to fear – the enemy from outside'. Now, 'at the bidding of the English this agreement was broken, and at the bidding of the English, Irishmen are today shooting down on the streets of our capital brother Irishmen'.[233]

After spending the night at Robert Farnan's, he rejoined his old unit, the 3rd Battalion, at York Street, later transferring to Dublin Brigade Headquarters at the Hammam Hotel, in Upper O'Connell Street. Kathleen O'Connell and her sister brought him his guns from Greystones.[234] After five years as a politician, he was a soldier again.

CHAPTER 16

THE MOST HATEFUL OF CONFLICTS

There is . . . a civil war going on in the minds of most of us, as well as in the country.

Éamon de Valera, September 1922[1]

Victory for the Republic, or utter defeat and extermination, are now the alternatives.

Éamon de Valera, November 1922[2]

The phase begun in 1916 has run its course.

Éamon de Valera, April 1923[3]

The Civil War was the most miserable time of de Valera's life, as he was swept along by the course of events, side-lined and deprived of the power to shape his own and the country's destiny. He later complained that 'I have been condemned to view the tragedy here for the last year as through a wall of glass, powerless to intervene effectively.'[4] He was in this position, of course, largely because of his own tactical ineptitude in becoming a captive of the extremists. However, it was not true to say that he lacked influence: his advice was sought and sometimes acted on. What he lacked was *control*, the final power of decision to which he was accustomed. The Civil War would blacken his reputation, as many argued that it would not have been as extensive or as lengthy without his influence. Certainly he must bear his share of responsibility for giving political respectability to those prepared to use force to assert their views. And while he did at various points of the conflict urge that it should be ended, he was by no means consistent in this.

The assumption by the pro-Treaty military authorities that any fighting would be short-lived turned out to be wrong, mainly because the more moderate wing of the anti-Treatyite forces swung in behind their comrades in the Four Courts.

De Valera was an example, joining the Dublin Brigade under Oscar Traynor, who had occupied a block of buildings on the east side of Upper O'Connell Street. The seized buildings ran from Cathedral Street to Findlater Place (now part of Cathal Brugha Street). As well as the Dublin United Tramway Company offices, the 'Block' contained several hotels, including the Gresham and the Hammam, the latter of which became Traynor's headquarters.[5] Traynor was rightly contemptuous of the Four Courts position, and of 'locking within this walled fortress nearly two hundred of the best fighting men in Dublin', with no prospect of escape.[6] But his own strategic position was no better, as it was equally vulnerable to being surrounded and then reduced by artillery fire. De Valera was critical of 'the very foolish type of battle' into which the Dublin Brigade had been drawn.[7]

In the Hammam, de Valera used some of his time to do the work at which he was most effective: propaganda. A statement (typed by Kathleen O'Connell, who risked sniper fire in getting into the hotel) insisted that the Dáil, not the Provisional Government, was the legitimate government of Ireland, that the Republic had not been disestablished, and that the soldiers 'fighting to uphold the Republic' were acting in accordance with their oath. A further statement, addressed to the people of the United States, said that the danger which he feared 'and which I warned our people of' – a reference to his 'wading through blood' speeches – had come: civil war. The pact that ensured peaceful elections had been 'torn up', the Dáil was not allowed to meet, and the Provisional Government 'has unconstitutionally assumed a military dictatorship'.[8] He might not have been doing much fighting, but he was certainly providing encouragement to those who were.

Traynor's original plan was to wait for reinforcements, which he confidently expected to flood in to Dublin from around the country. On 30 June he ordered the Four Courts garrison to surrender in order to help him continue the fight outside.[9] How this surrender, which freed up the pro-Treaty troops and guns surrounding the Four Courts, would actually help him is not entirely clear. As the Free State cordon tightened, Traynor began to realise that the anticipated reinforcements were not coming, and he planned a gradual evacuation of the buildings under his control.[10]

Traynor had intended to stay in command in O'Connell Street, but Brugha persuaded him that he should not allow himself to be captured.

According to Traynor, Brugha offered to take command, promising to surrender if defeat was unavoidable.[11] It seems that his promise was accepted at face value by his colleagues. Traynor, de Valera and Stack were guided to safe lodgings at 11 Upper Mount Street,[12] on the other side of Merrion Square from where the Provisional Government was being established. Word was then sent back to the Hammam Hotel for Brugha to come next, but he refused.[13]

Brugha ordered the remaining members of the garrison to leave in small groups, eventually leaving him alone in the ruins of the hotel with Linda Kearns of Cumann na mBan. Kearns recognised that Brugha had no intention of being taken alive. He went out the rear of the hotel into Thomas's Lane, his two pistols drawn, and began blazing away at the pro-Treaty troops. Kearns believed that their return fire was aimed deliberately low in order to avoid killing him, but one of the bullets severed his femoral artery.[14]

At first, it appeared that he would survive. De Valera sent him a mildly reproving letter:

had you gone down and been lost to us the cause would have suffered a blow from which it would have hardly recovered. You were scarcely justified therefore in taking the risk you ran . . . But all's well that ends well.[15]

All did not end well for Brugha, however. On 7 July he died of his injuries in the Mater Hospital. 'Our lion heart is gone,' de Valera noted in his diary.[16] His death meant

we are all robbed of the one man who could have made victory possible . . . Oh cruel, cruel that it is by Irish men he should be killed.[17]

The shelling of the Four Courts had begun on 28 June, two days before the second Dáil had been due to meet. Republicans were to make a great deal of capital out of the supposed failure to properly dissolve the Second Dáil. The First Dáil had met after the election of its successor, in order to be formally dissolved, in a procedure devised by de Valera to ensure there would be no break in continuity – a reasonable precaution in the summer of 1921, when the War of Independence was in full swing. He therefore condemned the failure to summon the Second Dáil after the 1922 elections as 'a breach of faith and a distinct breach of the constitution as understood'.[18] De Valera's complaint had some validity: in the absence of any decision to the contrary by the outgoing Dáil, precedent should have been followed. However, it was not quite as clear-cut as de Valera liked to imply. In 1921 the First Dáil agreed that it would automatically dissolve as soon as the Second Dáil was called to order. So there was no need for the old Dáil to meet at all; it would simply cease to exist once the new Dáil met.[19]

Far more serious was the failure to summon the Third Dáil to meet for the first time – a failure that, in effect, gave the Provisional Government dictatorial powers.[20] Had the Third Dáil met, it would have at the very least given de Valera and his followers the option of pursuing non-violent resistance, though once the Four Courts was shelled it was unlikely this route would have been taken. Even at the height of the War of Independence, the Dáil managed to meet and to retain a veneer of legitimacy; now the Provisional Government simply ignored the new Dáil, in which its supporters were in a minority, and appointed W. T. Cosgrave as President, replacing Arthur Griffith, without even attempting to consult TDs. De Valera claimed the government had 'acted irregularly, unconstitutionally, *illegally* and in an arbitrary manner'.[21] While he had a point, it could be argued that it was the armed resistance of the anti-Treaty forces that led to these actions, not the other way around.

In his hideaway in Upper Mount Street, de Valera attempted to keep political work going, instructing Seán T. O'Kelly to keep the office in Suffolk Street open.[22] He also had a more ambitious instruction for O'Kelly. He was to tell the 57 Republican members of the Second Dáil to get out of Dublin so that they could form a government if requested to do so by the anti-Treaty IRA:

> Unfortunately the Army Executive . . . do not seem to realise that they should either set themselves up as a Government or better get the Republican TDs to do it.[23]

In fact, the situation was worse than that. It wasn't that the military leaders didn't *realise* that there was a need for a government – they had resolutely set their faces against establishing one. Liam Lynch curtly informed Ernie O'Malley that

> we have no notion of setting up a Government, but await until such time as An Dáil will carry on as Government of the Republic without any fear of compromise; in the meantime no other Government will be allowed function.[24]

This refusal to entertain politics meant a refusal to appeal to the general public – whose support was absolutely vital to any successful military campaign.

Lynch was oblivious to such subtleties; de Valera most certainly was not. He was able to see the potential political advantages in the fact that the pro-Treaty side started the conflict by shelling the Four Courts, which 'gave a definite beginning . . . otherwise not to be dreamt of by us'. But he also recognised that the anti-Treatyites faced an uphill battle to get their message through to the public. 'The newspapers are as usual more deadly to our cause than the machine guns.'[25] With resistance in Dublin crumbling, and increasingly conscious that he was away from the centre of power in the anti-Treaty movement, de Valera began to get uneasy and restless, anxious to get 'down to the boys in the country'.[26]

On 11 July he left for the south. His party got a few hours' sleep in a hotel in Callan in Co. Kilkenny, 150 kilometres from Dublin. Ominously enough, it was the first place they passed through to be held by anti-Treaty forces.[27] He arrived in Clonmel, the site of Lynch's Field Headquarters, on the afternoon of the 12th, where he was appointed to the not particularly glamorous role of adjutant to the Director of Operations, Seán Moylan.[28] Despite this military appointment, he immediately began assembling an essentially political team, sending to Dublin for Kathleen O'Connell, and for Robert Brennan and Erskine Childers, as he thought Clonmel was 'an ideal place for Publicity HQ'.[29]

In Clonmel, the ebullient Harry Boland found 'the Chief . . . hale and well, the same gentle, honest, straightforward, unpurchaseable man'.[30] However, despite Boland's description, de Valera was not confident about the military prospects facing the anti-Treaty forces. Even before arriving in Clonmel, Childers heard reports that 'Dev says we should surrender while we are strong . . . Dev, I think, has collapsed'.[31]

When Childers and Brennan got to Clonmel some days later, they found Lynch putting the finishing touches to a flagged map showing the positions of the rival forces; the Republicans held a line from Waterford to Limerick, controlling the territory to the south (sometimes known as the 'Munster Republic'), while the pro-Treaty forces held the rest of the country. De Valera drew his two propagandists into another room and suggested that now, while they still had some territory to bargain with, was the time to sue for peace.[32] He got an unenthusiastic response, though Brennan quickly realised that de Valera had a point: as they moved through such towns as Mallow and Fermoy, the people looked at us sullenly, as if we had belonged to a hostile invading army. Dev had seen all this . . . and that was one of the reasons he was so desperately trying for peace while he had still some bargaining power.[33]

De Valera was also conflicted about the legitimacy of the struggle. Some months after the Civil War began, he wrote to Joe McGarrity that it was the

> most hateful of conflicts . . . a war in which there can be no glory and no enthusiasm . . . Worst of all, there seems to be no way out of it.

The other side, he claimed, was responsible, by breaking their word at the dictation of England, by reneging on the pact, by attacking the Four Courts. 'Still, the fundamental question is "the Treaty or not the Treaty" – and we are in a minority on that'. If Republicans stood aside, it meant the surrender of the ideals for which they had fought; if they did not, it meant civil war and the flouting of the will of the majority. 'Is it any wonder that there is, so to speak, a civil war going on in the minds of most of us, as well as in the country?'[34]

The precarious nature of the Republican position was brought home to O'Connell on her first night in Clonmel, when she was woken at 2 a.m. to be told the pro-Treaty forces were on their way and the garrison was being evacuated.[35] This undignified early-morning retreat was, according to Dan Breen, 'due to something like panic'.[36] De Valera went to Fermoy with the rest, but then sought, and received, permission to return to Clonmel to assist Séamus Robinson, commander of the 2nd Southern Division, who was facing the brunt of the pro-Treaty advance.[37] De Valera arrived at the Headquarters of the 2nd Southern Division, 'dressed in cap, trench coat and leggings, with a rifle slung loosely on his shoulder'.[38] His first act was to persuade Robinson that

> the burning of the barracks would be an indication that we had left those areas, and it would mean an enemy advance . . . to take these towns.

A good part of the Clonmel barracks was saved, but it was too late for those in Tipperary and Carrick. He also managed to get troops forward to establish posts in Golden, Cashel and Fethard.[39] His diary for these weeks reveals constant movement as he shuttled between the outposts of the 2nd Southern Division: Fermoy, Clonmel, Carrick-on-Suir, Kilmacthomas,

Cahir, Tipperary and Cashel. Evidence of the fluidity of the situation is that Divisional HQ moved to Carrick on 19 July and then back to Clonmel ten days later.[40]

The anti-Treaty cause was doomed in this 'line fighting' period, partly due to the superior numbers and resources of the Free State forces, partly due to the inability of the Republican troops, trained for guerrilla warfare, to adapt to conventional warfare.[41] The new National Army, by contrast, had a leavening of former British servicemen, including senior officers who had fought on the Western Front. The other difficulty facing the anti-Treaty forces, according to Breen, was lack of will: 'at this opening stage of the war they had no heart for the fight'.[42] This was evident in Limerick, where Liam Lynch was hesitant to see battle joined – in stark contrast to Eoin O'Duffy, who captured the city two days after taking command of the Free State troops there.[43] The same day, July 21st, Waterford was captured by Commandant General John Prout, who then pushed on towards de Valera's positions in Tipperary.[44] The anchors at either end of 'the line' were gone – it was only a matter of time before it was rolled up.

Séamus Robinson paid a handsome tribute to de Valera's work 'during the hottest part of the fighting', claiming that 'had he had charge of the whole Army he would have turned the scales'.[45] This was, no doubt, an exaggeration, though de Valera appears to have been an efficient and hard-working staff officer. He directed operations fairly closely, giving instructions to the column commandants Dan Breen, Dinny Lacey and James Hurley.[46] He helped prepare the defences of Clonmel, studying the lie of the land and advising on the siting of strong points.[47] He also attempted to form a 'striking force' – a mobile reserve that would allow the Republicans to go on the offensive.[48]

On 2 August he visited the different fronts: Fermoy, Cashel, Fethard, Carrick and Slievenamon – a mountain to the north of Carrick and Clonmel, where he witnessed an attack by pro-Treaty forces. 'The enemy advanced in overwhelming force from Mullinahone over the passage of Slievenamon . . .' Breen suffered a leg injury, and his column was forced to retreat. De Valera wrote of the need for more petrol supplies, and for a new line of defence to be established.[49] But he also heard even more disturbing news. Another close colleague had been wounded. This time, it was Harry Boland.[50]

Boland had been surprised at the Grand Hotel in Skerries, Co. Dublin, by pro-Treaty troops; rather than surrender, he grabbed a gun and was mortally wounded. Though some Republicans later accused Collins of ordering Boland's murder, de Valera did not believe this, putting the blame on Boland for behaving 'impetuously' and on the inexperience of the pro-Treaty soldiers.[51] On hearing of his death, Kathleen O'Connell wrote: 'Poor old Har. What an end. It was a fearful shock.' She fretted about how she would break the news to de Valera, but when she met him the following day she could see that he had already heard.

> He was broken hearted and sad. On that long journey [from Fermoy back to Clonmel] we never spoke a word.[52]

She recorded that de Valera 'felt it terribly – crushed and broken. He lost his most faithful friend'.[53]

Boland's death was only one of the depressing developments facing de Valera as the inexorable advance of pro-Treaty forces continued. Grasping at straws, he went to Mitchelstown, Co. Cork, where 90 men of the Mid-Limerick Brigade were stationed. He intended to find out if they had transport 'which will enable them to be thrown into battle-line north of Clonmel . . . It might change the whole battle'.[54] But a trip to the 2nd Southern Division revealed that such reinforcements would be of little use, with 400 pro-Treaty troops reported to be in Clonmel.

Kathleen O'Connell found him 'awfully tired and depressed' when he returned to Fermoy. As he was having a cup of tea in the mess with O'Connell, Liam Lynch and Katherine Barry (who ran communications between Cork and the anti-Treaty forces in Dublin), he learnt that the situation was so dire that the barracks in Fermoy had been cleared in preparation for burning at a 'moment's notice'.[55] This drastic move had been necessitated by recent advances by pro-Treaty forces. On 2 August, pro-Treaty troops had landed at Fenit and subsequently captured Tralee; six days later Emmet Dalton led a landing at Passage West, Co. Cork; and on the 10th the anti-Treatyites evacuated Cork, burning the barracks as they went. Now Fermoy – the last town held by Republicans in the entire country – would have to be abandoned.

As the barracks went up in flames, Dan Mulvihill, intelligence officer of the Kerry Brigade, burst into the aria 'Home to Our Mountains' from *Il Trovatore* by Verdi – a suitable choice given that this was where the Republicans were heading, to resume guerrilla warfare.[56] There was no danger of de Valera singing. He recorded his mood in his diary.

> Waiting in F barracks to leave. One of the most if not the most miserable days I ever spent. Thoughts! Thoughts![57]

His depression didn't lift. That evening, at Kilpadder, near Mallow, he walked around a field pondering the prospects of victory.

> If there was any chance[,] duty to hold on to secure it. If none[,] duty to try to get the men to quit – for the present. The people must be won to the cause – before any successful fighting can be done. The men dead and gloomy – just holding on. How long will it last?

That evening there came a rumour that Arthur Griffith had died. In his diary de Valera showed traces both of his affection for, and his resentment of, the man who was his deputy and then his successor.

> He was I believe unselfishly patriotic – and courageously. If only he had not stooped to the methods he employed to win.

The following day, when the news was confirmed, de Valera wrote of him:

> I wish I could know his ideas when he signed that treaty – did he think when it was signed I'd accept the fait accompli?[58]

On 12 August, de Valera visited the former MP William O'Brien at his home. There de Valera stressed his own role in 'keeping the peace' between Brugha and Griffith, insisting that he had wanted peace with England all along and denying responsibility for the oath to the Republic taken by TDs and Volunteers (which he had in fact been kept fully informed about).[59] O'Brien then raised the question of the destruction by Republicans of the railway viaduct over the Blackwater at Mallow (known locally as the Ten Arches), claiming that few people in the area were against the anti-Treatyites until it was blown up. O'Brien recorded de Valera as agreeing and saying that if that sort of thing went on much longer 'the public would begin to regard the anti-Treatyites as "bandits".'[60]

De Valera's remark about 'bandits' rings true, as he was increasingly disenchanted with the war. But he was still caught in Liam Lynch's slipstream. At two o'clock in the morning of the 15th, de Valera left Kilpadder in a rush – 'had to move off with HQ Staff, Liam Lynch, etc.'[61] Pro-Treaty forces had been reported in Buttevant, 20 kilometres away on the far side of Mallow, so the entire party had to pack up and depart at speed.[62] Their destination was the valley of Gougane Barra, 70 kilometres away on the far side of Macroom, Co. Cork.

By this time de Valera was a somewhat unwelcome guest at Lynch's headquarters – a point little understood by the pro-Treaty side. O'Duffy, for instance, regarded Lynch as merely a 'tool of de Valera',[63] which was a complete misunderstanding of the relationship. Lynch was increasingly irritated at de Valera's attempts to have the fighting stopped, later reporting that de Valera 'was most pessimistic and regarded our position as hopeless. He even at that time contemplated taking public action which would ruin us.'[64] Lynch warned Liam Deasy, now in command of the 1st Southern Division, that de Valera was on his way to see him and asked him 'not to give Dev any encouragement'. When he turned up on the evening of 21 August, de Valera argued that they had made their protest in arms but couldn't hope to achieve a military victory, so the honourable course was to withdraw. Deasy, though agreeing with much of what he said, pointed out that there were a thousand men under arms in the 1st Southern Division, and that there was no way they would agree to an unconditional ceasefire.[65]

The following day, de Valera left for Dublin. Deasy accompanied him as far as the crossroads at Beal na Bláth, Co. Cork. There they heard from a scout that Michael Collins had passed through a couple of hours before on a tour of west Co. Cork. According to Deasy, de Valera expressed unease at the idea that an ambush might be laid for Collins, pointing out that if he was killed he might be succeeded by a 'weaker' man.[66] De Valera later said he had no recollection of making this remark, and denied that he regarded Collins as being in any serious danger, as he believed Collins knew the area and would know which routes were safe.[67] Long after de Valera had left – and after most of the ambush party had withdrawn – a small rearguard engaged Collins and his party, killing him when he unwisely stood up from behind cover.[68]

Several accounts report de Valera as being deeply shocked by the news of Collins's death. One witness said he put his hands to his head and said, 'This cannot go on, the best men [or "brains"] of Ireland are going, it must be stopped'.[69] Later, before a number of other people, he said, 'What a pity and shame poor Mick is gone – he was the only man we could make peace with.'[70] These were natural reactions to the death of a man who had been a close colleague. But there had been very serious disagreements between them, and it was natural that de Valera in later life would have ambivalent feelings towards Collins. In 1934 he would tell Dorothy Macardle, 'Thinking back over the different groups of colleagues I have had, I would say that Michael Collins was the most intelligent.' However, he obviously thought better of such an unqualified tribute, because it is crossed out in her notes, to be replaced with a more restrained mention of Collins's intelligence and energy, and the slightly condescending observation that 'when a piece of work had to be done he was the one who went and did it. He used to get good workers under him.'[71]

Perhaps his best-known comment on the subject, thanks to its prominent use in Neil Jordan's biopic of Collins, was that 'in the fullness of time history will record the greatness of Collins, and it will be recorded at my expense'. There is, however, some doubt about whether de Valera ever actually said this. Tim Pat Coogan claims that de Valera made the remark in 1966. Coogan further claimed, when challenged on its accuracy, that de Valera also said, in relation to Collins's death, that he 'had it coming to him'. Both of these quotes were third-hand by the time they got to Coogan, so there is at least a question mark over them.[72]

On de Valera's trek back to Dublin, the difficulties he faced are further evidence of how far his position had sunk. By taxi, private car and pony and trap, and on foot, he was transferred from one guide to the next, making painfully slow progress, as a hunted man. Back roads were the order of the day, and when a checkpoint was seen up ahead, de Valera got out of the car and made his way through the fields, to save the other occupants of the vehicle from arrest. He wore a beard as a disguise, and for at least part of the journey he dressed as a priest.[73]

De Valera arrived back in Dublin on 2 September, a full 11 days after leaving Beal na mBláth, returning to his bolt-hole in Upper Mount Street.[74] He had already sent Kathleen O'Connell back to Dublin after realising that there was no chance of arranging a proper office at the front. 'A typewriter even will be a luxury,' he wrote. 'In Dublin only will you be able to do any real work.'[75] He was quickly placing demands on her services: making copies of a letter from Liam Lynch ('You must hold up the paper between you and the light in order to read it'), gathering material for a series he wanted to write on the peace negotiations, typing copies of press clippings – one for him, one for the 'library' he asked her to keep.[76]

Soon after de Valera's return, he gave an interview to the journalist and Irish-language activist Shán Ó Cuív (father of his future son-in-law, Brian)[77]. Ó Cuív began his report for the *Manchester Evening News* by pointing out that de Valera

is not dead . . . neither is he dying from cancer or pneumonia, single or double, as rumour has it. Nor is he a prisoner in the hands of the Provisional Government troops. Nor has he left the country . . .'[78]

But he was very much peripheral to events, as was made clear in a letter to Joe McGarrity, in which he said the Civil War would continue 'if the Army is determined to hold on'. The only way out that he could see, given the popular support for the Treaty, was a new movement to seek revision of that agreement. 'It will be very difficult to get this cry raised, and still more difficult to get any enthusiasm behind it. But, it is the only hope there is'.[79]

One of the first things he did on his arrival back in Dublin was meet the Minister for Defence, Richard Mulcahy, who was also, since Collins's death, commander-in-chief of the pro-Treaty army. Mulcahy agreed to the meeting on his own initiative – in fact, the Provisional Government had just decided that no negotiations were to be held with the anti-Treatyites.[80] The priest who organised the meeting had told Mulcahy that de Valera and Stack were 'changed men' and that if he saw them he could stop the Civil War. A very brief conversation proved that this was not the case. According to Mulcahy, de Valera told him that 'some men are led by faith, others were led by reason', that he would 'tend to be led by reason', but as long as there were 'men of faith like Rory O'Connor, taking the stand that he was taking,' that he, de Valera, was 'a humble soldier following after'. Mulcahy then said goodnight and went home.[81]

The abortive meeting had significant political consequences for Mulcahy. It convinced him that there could be no peaceful conclusion to the Civil War and encouraged him to seek emergency powers allowing the pro-Treaty army to execute irregulars caught with arms; the Dáil duly passed the legislation later in September.[82] It also increased mistrust in Mulcahy among civilian ministers, particularly Kevin O'Higgins and Ernest Blythe, who 'never had full confidence in him afterwards'.[83] The British government was also deeply suspicious. After the deaths of Griffith and Collins, Churchill worried that their successors might be tempted to make

a sloppy accommodation with a quasi-repentant de Valera. It may well be that he will take advantage of the present situation to try and get back from the position of a hunted rebel to that of a political negotiator.[84]

Andy Cope enquired about newspaper reports of a meeting between de Valera and Mulcahy but was told somewhat disingenuously that 'the Government has no official knowledge of the matter'.[85]

For de Valera the meeting was also significant, because Mulcahy (along with MacNeill) was one of the few pro-Treaty ministers he had any time for. He thought that the members of the Provisional Government in general were 'very weak', that 'Cosgrave is a ninny',[86] and that 'there is no doubt there is a bit of the scoundrel in O'Higgins'.[87] Therefore, if there was to be a political solution it would have to be with someone like Mulcahy. Afterwards, he said he found their meeting

> rather amusing . . . We got nowhere in discussion, however, for I made revision of the Treaty the basis, whilst he insisted on acceptance of the Treaty as the basis. Of course that means 'quit' for the Republicans, and if it has to be done it is much better to do it boldly without any camouflage.[88]

The lack of progress also removed any final doubts de Valera had about how to handle the opening of the Third Dáil the following Saturday, which was still an open question in Republican circles. His inclination had been to boycott it and even have the anti-Treaty forces proclaim it an illegal assembly, but he held his hand pending the meeting with Mulcahy, in case it caused him to change his mind.[89] In the event it didn't, and anti-Treaty TDs were told not to attend, which was probably wise: the Provisional Government had decided that any members who had 'taken up arms against the Government' were to be arrested, and that those in prison were not to be released to attend.[90]

In the light of the later controversy over whether abstention from the Dáil was a matter of principle or of expediency, and over who had committed Sinn Féin to the policy in the first place, it is interesting to note that, before the Third Dáil met, de Valera was quite clear.

> I have considered the matter, and am of the opinion that, both from the point of view of principle and expedience, we as a party should not attend.

On the point of principle, he argued that the Second Dáil was not dissolved and remained the sovereign authority, and that the assembly summoned to meet on 9 September was not the Dáil but the Provisional Parliament. And 'then there is the oath'. As for the argument of expediency, he said that the Republican side would be attacked by all the other groups; that they would not get a fair hearing; and that their own unity would be enhanced by abstention. While the party would not go, he thought Laurence Ginnell should attend if he wanted to, as should John O'Mahony, the TD for Fermanagh. If O'Mahony was refused entry it would confirm that this was not the Dáil but the Provisional Parliament.[91] Ginnell duly attended, and duly got himself thrown out – a procedure he had turned into an art form in his time at Westminster.

As the head of an abstentionist party, and on the run from pro-Treaty forces, de Valera had to decide on a course of action. First he took himself off to a safe house in Stillorgan, Co. Dublin, to work on an exhaustive account of the Treaty negotiations. He stayed there for a fortnight before returning to 11 Upper Mount Street.[92] This, the home of Annie Kane, would become the main headquarters of the Republican government. For long periods it was also the residence of his ministers: Austin Stack, P. J. Ruttledge and Michael Colivet.[93]

Shortly after de Valera's return from the south, his friend the Rev. Pádraig de Brún, who had been tutored in mathematics by de Valera at Rockwell College and Clonliffe, was followed to the house by pro-Treaty troops, and de Valera, Stack and O'Connell evaded capture only by using a secret hideaway under the stairs.[94] The dangers of being on the run were all too evident to de Valera. 'It is very difficult to exist here at the moment. The Free State and the British are both out for my blood'. He reported that two members of Collins's Squad had been sent south to 'get' him. 'Who would have believed such a thing possible even six months ago?'[95] With an air of fatalistic detachment, he even began writing his memoirs (a publisher had offered to purchase them while he was in London the previous year[96]), at the request of several people.

> I suppose it is because sudden death is around that they are so anxious about the matter. It does indeed look as if most of the actors who occupied the stage in the political life of the country for the past five or six years are likely to go down in this struggle.[97]

It seems strange that the Provisional Government wasn't able to find him, given that he had used many of the same haunts during the War of Independence. W. T. Cosgrave airily told the British government that de Valera 'was not worth arresting as the Irregulars no longer took orders from him'.[98] But many years later Mulcahy explained that, while they did in fact do their best to catch de Valera,

> we couldn't find him. He was all around the place in hiding. If we had found him then we would have found it very difficult not to have shot him . . .

He added (with perhaps a trace of regret) that after the ceasefire order it became very difficult to consider executing him.[99]

De Valera's repeated references to Document no. 2 in this period went down like a lead balloon with those on his own side. Count Plunkett urged him to make no further reference to it in public. 'The use, dishonest and malicious, made of it throughout the country, has turned our own people against it.'[100] Joe McGarrity told him that any suggestion of its acceptance should come from the other side, not from him.

> That *cannot* be made your starting point. As a united Ireland is essential, your minimum must include that – a united Ireland. By that I mean all of Ulster in with the same rights and privileges as any other part – nothing more, nothing less . . .[101]

In response, de Valera said he would make peace on the basis of the document, 'and I do not want the young fellows who are fighting for the Republic to think otherwise'.[102]

Some months later, Liam Lynch was even more scathing.

> Your publicity as to sponsoring Document No. 2 has had a very bad effect on army and should have been avoided. Generally they do not understand such documents . . .[103]

De Valera replied indignantly that he had been dealing with political questions for a number of years – the implication being that his critics had not – and suggesting that the army should either leave political matters to the politicians or 'think intelligently along political lines' when dealing with those matters.

> If an opportunity for making peace with England on the lines of the proposals I put forward in Dáil Éireann, January 1922, should present itself, I would unhesitatingly recommend that such a peace be made and would regard it almost as a miraculous victory.[104]

De Valera was well aware the radicals didn't like Document no. 2; the point was that they wouldn't go to war against it.

> I am confident that the proposals I put forward would not be resisted in arms, although some Republicans might not be satisfied with them . . .[105]

Mary MacSwiney tackled de Valera after hearing 'rumours of compromise and secret interviews'. She was certain of victory 'if we only hold together and have faith now'. She had heard he was depressed and without hope, and she advised him that

> we are going to win out. You must have the faith that moves mountains – with that, well we shall soon move the mountain of the Free State out of our path forever . . .[106]

In a revealing reply, de Valera said he was guided by reason, not by faith.

> I do not believe we have any right to expect the Almighty to work miracles for our special benefit . . . I have felt for some time that this doctrine of mine unfitted me to be leader of the Republican Party . . . For the sake of the cause I allowed myself to be put into a position which it is impossible for one of my outlook and personal bias to fill with effect for the party. I must be the heir to generations of con- servatism. Every instinct of mine would indicate that I was meant to be a dyed-in-the-wool Tory or even a Bishop, rather than the leader of a Revolution . . . As soon as I can do it without injuring the cause, I intended to claim my own personal freedom again.[107]

He voiced similar sentiments to McGarrity. Referring to rumours that Daniel Cohalan and John Devoy, his American enemies, had offered financial support to the anti-Treaty party if he was removed as leader, de Valera wrote:

> I am almost wishing I were deposed, for the present position places upon me the responsibility for carrying out a programme which was not mine.

Almost – but not quite. His policy, he said, would be to revive the Sinn Féin idea in a new form by ignoring England and acting in Ireland as if

> there was no such person as the English King, no Governor-General, no Treaty, no Oath of Allegiance. In fact, acting as if Document 2 were the Treaty. Later we could act more independently still.[108]

The question of establishing a Republican government arose again in October. While he acknowledged 'grave difficulties', he told McGarrity that he was willing to head such a government – on certain conditions.[109] These were spelt out in a memorandum he sent to Liam Lynch and the members of the Army Executive. The need for a Republican government had become 'imperative' in order to provide a rallying point, to preserve the continuity of the Republic (and therefore deny the legitimacy of the Free State), and, importantly, to 'establish a claim to the funds and other resources of the Republic'.

As the 'faithful' members of the Dáil were prevented from meeting, it was up to the army to act. He suggested that the Army Executive should request the Republican members of the Dáil to establish a government, with the personnel and the broad outline of policy to be agreed in advance. The maintenance of the Republic would be the only public policy necessary, but he suggested there should be agreement between the army and the politicians on 'the right of the people to determine freely their own government and the relations of the State with foreign states'; on 'the terms on which the present armed opposition to the Free State might be desisted from'; and on 'the terms short of a simple recognition of the Republic on which . . . we might make peace with England and with the Northern Unionists'. Regarding the last point, he believed that the best they could hope to get from the British government was something along the lines of Document no. 2. As regards the right of the people to decide, he told the Army Executive that this was a fundamental principle he could not possibly oppose, were it not for 'the most exceptional circumstances'. He added, 'The fact that we are seemingly acting in opposition to this principle is by far the greatest weakness of our cause at the moment'. If this observation was likely to prove unpalatable to the militarists, he concluded on an optimistic note.

> I am convinced that now is the right time for a vigorous constructive drive. The others have shot their last bolts. The worst is over.[110]

He told McGarrity that

> I do not care what Republican government is set up so long as some one is – only I will not take responsibility if I do not get the corresponding authority to act in accordance with my best judgement. If the Army think I am too moderate, well, let them get a better President and go ahead.[111]

The Army Executive duly approved the appointment of a government; but its allegiance was far from unqualified. The exact terms of the motion stated that this Executive calls upon the former President of Dáil Éireann to form a Government, which will preserve the continuity of the Republic. We pledge this Government our wholehearted support, and allegiance, while it functions as the Government of the Republic; and we empower it to make an arrangement with the Free State Government, or with the British Government, provided such arrangement does not bring the Country into the British Empire. Final decision on this question to be submitted for ratification to the Executive.[112]

In other words, the final say on any peace deal rested with the Executive, obviously anxious to avoid a repeat of the Treaty negotiations; allegiance was promised only 'while it functions as the Government of the Republic', so any backsliding would give the IRA an excuse to withdraw support; and de Valera was referred to by his correct title – President of Dáil Éireann – not the more common President of the Republic (which he used himself).

Once de Valera was notified of the Army Executive's decision, he quickly wrote to Lynch, saying he was anxious to meet the Army Council (which ran the army day to day) to get a government set up at once. 'Every moment is precious now.'[113] Two days later he wrote again, with a proposed Cabinet of Austin Stack (Finance); P. J. Ruttledge (Home Affairs); the imprisoned Liam Mellows (Defence), with Liam Lynch as Acting Minister; the imprisoned Seán T. O'Kelly (Local Government), with Dónal O'Callaghan acting in his place; the imprisoned Robert Barton (Economic Affairs), with Michael Colivet acting in his place; and Erskine Childers (Director of Publicity and government secretary).[114]

If de Valera expected unquestioning acceptance of his suggestions, he was to be disappointed. Lynch declined to become acting Minister for Defence, because he didn't think GHQ officers should be ministers, and in any case he wasn't a TD. De Valera said he understood his position, but added, 'Look through the list of re-elected TDs, and see how limited our choice is'.[115] Lynch and de Valera agreed to co-sign any necessary documents while Mellows was in prison. The army felt that Colivet 'would not carry sufficient weight especially in the South', and suggested Seán Moylan instead (even though he was due to go to the United States); de Valera agreed.[116] But the most serious disagreement was over the nomination of Barton, who was, after all, a signatory of the Treaty. Despite this, de Valera had a fondness for him.

Since the beginning of hostilities, I think his views have been more in accord with my own than any others who have explained their views to me. It is so hard to get people to talk frankly.[117]

There was no difficulty in getting Lynch to talk frankly on this subject: he could not recommend Barton for office because he held him 'part responsible for present loss of life of our Officers and men, I could not do so and bear any responsibility to them afterwards'.[118] De Valera eventually got his way; but the fact that he had to fight so hard to get what he wanted demonstrated the limits to his power.

De Valera began a flurry of activity. He was no longer pushing for an end to the fighting, and a proclamation denied rumours of peace talks.

The principles which Republicans are defending are by their nature irreducible and not open to compromise. Victory for the Republic, or utter defeat and extermination, are now the alternatives.[119]

All debts contracted and appointments made by the Provisional Government were declared 'illegal, null and void'.[120] Another proclamation revoked the Dáil's approval of the Treaty and declared the Provisional Government an 'illegal body'.[121] He wrote to Timothy Smiddy, the Provisional Government representative in Washington, ordering him to hand over his office, funds and staff to the Republican representative, Laurence Ginnell (cheekily demanding that a financial report be sent to Stack).[122] He also displayed his usual rigorous (or pedantic) approach to office work, insisting on punctuality by messengers,[123] and specifying the lay-out of official notepaper.[124] Just before Christmas, Lynch wrote with satisfaction to McGarrity that 'the situation has immensely improved' since the formation of the Republican government. 'Departments are functioning as heretofore, and the people of the country are now in the same position as in late war'.[125] If Lynch believed this, he was as delusional about the political situation as he was about the military.

One way for a government to prove its existence is, of course, to levy taxes. As de Valera observed in December 1922,

the man who can devise a system by which revenue will be paid to us, and not to the Free State, will save the Republic . . . not merely because without funds we cannot carry on, but because the very payment of revenue to us is an act of recognition of the Government.[126]

He told Stack, who was dubious, that

> the machinery for collecting revenue must be set up . . . We must quit
> or go ahead. Dragging on this war unless we are able to make definite
> progress in functioning as a Government is altogether unjustifiable.[127]

When Stack continued to express doubts, de Valera curtly instructed him,
'We can spend no further time in discussing it. Draw up a Decree . . .' He
wanted to make the payment of rents, annuities and taxes to the Free
State a crime, and to replace income tax with 'a general property or
valuation tax', a duty on spirits and a licence fee for publicans.[128] He
acknowledged that the taxes might not be fair, but they were not
permanent. He would prefer some unconventional measure,

> even if we had to go back to a hearth tax or a window tax. By the time
> they would have made arrangements for evasions the war will be
> over.[129]

Towards the end of October, de Valera received a letter from Erskine
Childers, who had just arrived at the Barton family home in Glendalough.
After reading it, de Valera burnt it, saying to Kathleen O'Connell that
'Childers realises things at last'[130] – an indication that he had accepted de
Valera's view of their prospects in the Civil War. How far this conversion
went was never to be known, because on 10 November, Childers was
captured. O'Connell recorded that de Valera was 'frightfully upset and
unhappy about it. Fears he will be given an awful time of it.'[131] On his
arrest, Childers had had a gun in his possession, ironically given to him by
Collins. De Valera described it as 'a tiny automatic, little better than a toy
and in no sense a war weapon',[132] but it was enough to get Childers a
death sentence. The first executions carried out under the new emergency
legislation were of four unknown young anti-Treaty soldiers; a week later
Childers shared their fate.

De Valera was devastated by Childers's execution, describing it as 'one
of the blackest crimes in Irish history'.[133] When Lynch wrote to him a day
later, informing him that he had given orders for the execution of
members of the Provisional Government, de Valera replied:

> The efficacy of reprisals is open to doubt, but as I see no other way to
> stop these others and protect our men, I cannot disapprove.

This is in line with the image he later tried to project of reluctant agreement to extreme measures. But in this letter to Lynch he went further than merely not disapproving: he drafted a suggested message to the Ceann Comhairle, warning that every TD who supported the emergency legislation was as guilty as members of the Provisional Government.

> We therefore give you notice that we have given orders that for each soldier of the Republic whom you execute or deport in accordance with these regulations an equal number of your body are to be shot at sight.[134]

This draft message puts de Valera's fingerprints on the most drastic action taken by the anti-Treaty forces, the murder of TDs.

On 7 December 1922, a day after the Irish Free State legally came into existence, Deputies Seán Hales and Pádraig Ó Máille were shot by Republicans, Hales fatally, as they were returning to the Dáil after lunch in the Ormond Hotel. In response, the Executive Council of the Free State approved the execution without trial of four prisoners in Mountjoy – Rory O'Connor, Liam Mellows, Joe McKelvey and Dick Barrett – who had been captured when the Four Courts fell, and who could therefore have had no role in the shooting of the TDs. Kathleen O'Connell's diary captures the shock felt at this reprisal.

> Another Stop Press!! Who is it now we wonder – we hold our breaths . . . Courier arrives. We can hardly wait until she tells us – the news is told very simply. We are stunned – Rory & Liam, Joe McKelvey & Dick Barrett were taken out this morning and executed.[135]

This shocking act was effective in that no more TDs were assassinated – but their houses were still being burnt down, with one of Seán McGarry's children being killed in one such incident and Kevin O'Higgins's father murdered in another.[136] De Valera told Lynch these burnings were 'puerile and futile'. Despite his earlier approval for the shooting of TDs, he now advised Lynch that 'the policy of an eye for an eye is not going to win the people to us, and without the people we can never win'.[137] Lynch disagreed: the other side was using 'barbarous methods', and TDs who voted for the emergency legislation could not 'be allowed visit restaurants and places of amusements while they sanction murder of our Prisoners of War'. De Valera said he understood Lynch's reasoning but was concerned about the effectiveness of his policy. 'The ultimate results are what I am concerned about'.[138] He told P. J. Ruttledge he was in favour of the burning of offices but not of houses – particularly that involving the death of McGarry's son, which

> looks mean and petty . . . Terroristic methods may silence those of our opponents who are cowards, but many of them are very far from being cowards and attempts at terrorism will only stiffen the bold men amongst them.[139]

De Valera remained convinced that the anti-Treaty forces should adopt 'civilised' tactics. 'We must not let them justify the name "irregulars" which they have christened us with'.[140] When Lynch trenchantly defended the policy of reprisals, de Valera clarified his view.

> Those who are directly responsible on the other side, e.g. those who voted for the Army Bill, and those who are particularly active and aggressive, have deliberately taken their side as we have ours, and must abide by the consequences if we are to carry on at all. I shall be satisfied if you confine yourself to these. I do not think a systematic persistent effort to get at the principals is being made.[141]

If this was moderation, it was only moderate in comparison with Lynch. If any further executions were carried out, Lynch proposed the shooting of all TDs and senators, all army officers, 'aggressive civilian supporters of enemy', senior civil servants, 'all legal officials including Justices, Judges, etc.' and 'senior enemy Press officials' (though he didn't want to shoot ordinary soldiers).[142] De Valera agreed that orders might have to be issued regarding TDs and senators, army officers and judges.[143] He did not regard this as definite approval for Lynch's policy; but Lynch did, and he issued Operation Order 17, sanctioning, if further executions were carried out, the shooting on sight of pro-Government TDs, army officers, certain senators, civilian officials who ordered prisoners to be fired on, torturers, legal advisers connected with courts-martial, members of firing parties, 'aggressive civilian supporters of the Free State Government policy of executions of POWs', and the owners, managers and editorial staff of hostile newspapers.[144]

Lynch asked that the Republican government

take responsibility and clearly state consequences of further executions. As terrible action must and will be taken, it would be well that such, if possible, be averted . . .[145]

It was, de Valera felt, 'a frightfully drastic business',[146] and he baulked at supporting it, denying that he had agreed to the order's being issued and pointing out that no member of his government would agree to certain parts of it; they would agree to others only if their implementation was strictly controlled by GHQ.[147] He added that, knowing the views of some ministers, 'which partially coincided with my own, I would never have consented to letting that Order out in its entirety'.[148]

Of course the use of such tactics – indeed, the continuation of the war at all – could be justified only if there was some chance of success. De Valera had his doubts about this from the start, though he blew hot and cold on the prospects for victory, depending on the circumstances of the moment and the audience he was addressing. But scepticism was his default position. De Valera grumbled that Lynch had

> far too low an estimate of the strength of our opponent's position and his determination, and far too high an estimate of our own . . . Unless a large section of the Free State Army can be won over, or the people turn overwhelmingly to support us rather than the Free State, there is little prospect of that type of victory which would enable us to *dictate* terms . . . which is unfortunately what we require.[149]

Lynch did not anticipate outright victory, but he was confident they could

> bring the enemy to the position of bankruptcy, and make it impossible for a single Department of his Government to function. He will then realise his general position and have to stand with us in upholding our independence.

De Valera conceded that this was the only objective that promised any hope of success, 'and the only one that justifies our fight under the circumstances', but he did not share Lynch's optimism that it could be achieved.[150]

On 31 January 1923, de Valera was 'stunned' to receive a plea from Liam Deasy to surrender.[151] Deasy had been captured on 19 January, and court-martialled and sentenced to death the following day. Convinced of the futility of continued fighting, and with a troubled conscience over his own role in conducting the Civil War, he sought permission to write to the other members of the Army Executive urging them to call off the war. He was told that a stay of execution would be granted only if he signed an unconditional surrender.

> If I were to agree there might be some hope of ending the war. If not then I had to face that I was leaving behind me a terrible mess for which I had much responsibility . . .[152]

He signed the surrender and then wrote to each member of the Army Executive, as well as to de Valera, urging them to surrender themselves, all those associated with them, and all arms and equipment.[153] A covering letter attempted to explain his position, saying that the fight could not go on indefinitely, that the position was getting worse rather than better, and that, because the war would inevitably end in negotiations anyway, it was better to stop now.[154]

De Valera considered this 'the most serious blow that has been aimed at the Republic since the Government was formed'.[155] Had de Valera been anxious for peace, as he certainly was some months later, he might have used this development to move in that direction. Instead, he took a hard line, telling Lynch that a peace that allowed the Free State to function unhindered could not be considered

> now that they have resorted to terrorism pure and simple . . . Were we to abandon the Republic now it would be a greater blow to our ideals and to the prestige of the nation than even the abandonment of December 6th, 1921 [the signing of the Treaty]. In taking upon ourselves to be champions of this cause we have incurred obligations which we must fulfil even to death.[156]

In the wake of the Deasy debacle, and with further executions due, pressure mounted from senior anti-Treaty officers to clarify the situation. Even Lynch suggested to de Valera, on 7 February 1923, that

> we should know if possible first if there is a way out by which peace can be attained. At least we should give the enemy our minimum terms and receive his . . .

Within two hours, de Valera responded, an indication that at last he saw a chance to influence events.

If we made a decent peace offer which will command the support of reasonable people, the others can't proceed and we shall have a victory.[157]

The following day, de Valera sent a lengthy memorandum to Lynch and to each of his ministers, stressing the need to state publicly that they accepted certain principles 'which the press has made it appear we deny'. He proposed six principles: that the sovereign rights of the nation were 'indefeasible and inalienable' and that any attempt to surrender them was void (a reference to the Treaty); that governmental authority in Ireland derived exclusively from the people, and any instrument purporting the contrary was invalid (also a reference to the Treaty); that, once these principles were not breached, the ultimate arbiters of policy were the people; that no-one who accepted these principles could be excluded from political activity by any political oath or test; that, subject to these principles, the military must be controlled by parliament; and that freedom of expression, of assembly and of the press could not be abrogated.[158]

When circulated, this document was severely criticised by some Republicans, including Mary MacSwiney, who pointed out that

if it is right now to submit to majority rule on this point, it was equally right last July. What have all the lives been lost for?[159]

Somewhat defensively, de Valera told her he had already decided not to publish it, even before her criticism. 'The document was another case of "thinking aloud" from one aspect of the question,' he told her, but he added that it was along the lines he would have followed

if the whole conduct of affairs on our side had been a matter solely of my *personal* will and judgement. It would not be the heroic course. It would probably have been misunderstood, but it would have avoided the terrible immediate risks into which the nation was being run by the course that has actually been followed . . .[160]

After further correspondence, de Valera wearily told her there was no point continuing the debate on paper, as there was really very little difference between them, 'and what differences there are can never be adjusted as long as you are you and I am I'.[161] He admitted that he tended to overestimate the strength and determination of the enemy, and to underestimate their own.

The personal equation of all you diehards is the reverse of this, and of the two I have no doubt that an omniscient being would rate my error as but a very small fraction of yours . . .[162]

Liam Lynch had two main defects as chief of staff: he didn't know when to start fighting (an earlier and more aggressive policy before the pro-Treaty army was organised could have made a huge difference); and, even worse, he didn't know when to stop. Moss Twomey, one of his staff officers, believed that in no circumstances would Lynch surrender, or order anyone under his command to do so. 'He could not or would not face the thought of defeat and collapse of Republican resistance to the imposition of the Treaty.'[163] Lynch's adjutant, Todd Andrews, found it difficult to understand his blindness to the military situation. 'He had developed some mental blockage which prevented him from believing that we could be beaten'. It was only his 'iron will' that kept the Civil War going, Andrews believed.[164]

De Valera's view on the prospects of victory fluctuated. At the start of February, he told Sceilg that

we are at the critical stage now. If our friends everywhere made one big effort we could win and smash the others. It must be death or glory for us now.[165]

But at the end of the month he wrote to Lynch, saying that

many good men have come to the conclusion that we have long ago passed the point at which we should have regarded ourselves as beaten so far as actually securing our objective is concerned. And if you were to hold that the objective was the 'isolated' Republic, I would say they were right . . .[166]

A fortnight later de Valera told MacSwiney that 'a military victory in the proper sense is not possible for us', and he advocated massing 'the public opinion of all who want peace against them [the Free State], and the more moderate our statements are, the better'.[167] Cosgrave observed that de Valera was attempting 'to make a dignified escape from his present position, but we are not going to help anybody in that way'.[168] Cosgrave insisted at the beginning of the Civil War that 'the only terms which the Government would accept from the Irregulars were unconditional surrender', and he informed a correspondent in October that 'the laying down of arms by those who are not properly authorised to bear them is an absolute essential of peace'.[169] Kevin O'Higgins stated the Government's position most succinctly. 'This is not going to be a draw with a replay in the autumn.'[170]

One potential ally in the search for peace was the Vatican. The Irish bishops had taken a distinctly unhelpful approach, from de Valera's point of view. On 10 October 1922, following a request from the Provisional Government, the Catholic Hierarchy had condemned the activities of the anti-Treaty forces and banned them from receiving Communion 'if they propose to persevere in such evil courses'.[171] Cardinal Logue insisted that the Hierarchy had not denied the sacraments to Republicans as such; they had simply said that 'those who persisted in committing crimes which we enumerated were not fit for sacraments which is the plain doctrine of the Church'.[172]

De Valera complained about the Hierarchy to his most prominent ecclesiastical supporter, Daniel Mannix, Archbishop of Melbourne.

Never was charity of judgment so necessary, and apparently so disastrously absent. Ireland and the Church will, I fear, suffer in consequence.[173]

Even many years later, the mention of the Hierarchy's actions in 1922 was enough to drive de Valera into such excitement that his secretary had to change the subject to calm him down.[174] However, de Valera denied that he or any other Republican had been excommunicated, claiming that he had raised the issue in the Vatican and that the Pope had agreed with him. Asked by his biographer Lord Longford what he would have done had the Pope affirmed that he had in fact been excommunicated, de Valera dryly replied, 'I should have considered that His Holiness was misinformed.'[175]

On 19 March 1923 Monsignor Salvatore Luzio arrived in Ireland,[176] sent by the Pope to investigate whether there was anything to be done to bring peace. Luzio had been professor of canon law at Maynooth from 1897 to 1910.[177] Some reports claimed that he knew de Valera personally,[178] though in fact their time at Maynooth did not overlap. Luzio's proposal was for the cessation of hostilities and the destruction of arms by the anti-Treaty forces, to the satisfaction of the Free State (thus getting over the objection to surrender of weapons). In return, Luzio would attempt to get the prisoners released, or at a minimum those required to organise Sinn Féin for the elections.[179] When he met Luzio himself, de Valera rejected these terms.

I liked him personally, but nothing important transpired. Peace can only be made by the sword, or along lines such as that I indicated in the memo I circulated some time ago.[180]

The Free State Executive Council, meanwhile, was most put out that Luzio was attempting to mediate, and it sent a letter of complaint to the Vatican, which led to his recall.[181] He and de Valera exchanged letters regretting that they couldn't meet again before his departure, with de Valera flattering him about the importance of his intervention.

Please give to the Holy Father my dutiful homage. Though nominally cut away from the body of Holy Church, we are still spiritually and mystically of it, and we refuse to regard ourselves except as His children.[182]

At the end of March, the anti-Treaty Army Executive finally met to discuss the war, at the Nire Valley in the Comeragh Mountains, Co. Waterford. The meeting was constantly interrupted by Free State search parties, causing the participants to move several times. In his diary de Valera recorded this disruption.

Meeting continued. Broken off by Free State raid towards evening . . . Free State reported in the neighbourhood. Had to proceed up the valley to the mountains. Meeting held in the open. I had a half loaf of dry bread . . . I was just lying down for a nap when alarm sounded and we had to leave again . . .[183]

Eleven of the 16 members of the Army Executive were there; de Valera attended in a non-voting capacity. Liam Lynch reported on the general military situation, including a recent meeting of the 1st Southern Division Council, at which 'nearly all the officers present declared that their units could only hold out for a very short time longer'. There was also a long discussion of the Deasy affair, and of various other peace moves. Also debated was de Valera's memorandum of 8 February, with Frank Aiken proposing that de Valera should be empowered to open peace discussions on the basis of three of his principles (that Irish independence was inalienable; that the final court of appeal in questions of policy was the people of Ireland; and that no test or oath could be used to exclude people from public life, if they accepted the other principles). With Lynch abstaining, the remaining members split 5-5 on this motion, which therefore failed to be carried.

Lynch did vote on the next motion, proposed by Tom Barry, that 'further armed resistance . . . against Free State Government will not further the cause of independence of the country'; it was defeated by 6 votes to 5.[184] It was agreed to resume the meeting on 10 April. In the meantime de Valera should 'try and find out what the chances were of securing peace on the basis of the principles outlined in his memo'.[185]

De Valera's four-day return journey was a nightmare. On his first night he

> got drenched to the skin through overcoat, leather jerkin, etc. Wettest night I ever experienced. Falling at every step. Misled by the guide. Ignored 'stepping stones' and walked through the streams. Stuck my left leg into a boghole up to the groin. Arrived in the morning, clothes and leather jacket all ruined. Rain soaked through. Had to go to bed naked.[186]

The party was held up by Free State troops in Paulstown, Co. Kilkenny, but evidently he wasn't recognised, as they were allowed through.[187]

Some Republicans had still not had enough of the war. P. J. Ruttledge, Minister for Home Affairs in the Republican government, told de Valera at the beginning of April that a satisfactory peace was impossible; that simply quitting the war would not save lives (presumably because the Free State would continue executions); and that 'peace mongers' should be expelled and the anti-Treaty forces reorganised. Ruttledge was 'convinced that it is only a question of holding out; that something must and will happen to swing public opinion solidly to our side'.[188] This elicited from de Valera perhaps the clearest expression of his views at this stage of the Civil War.

> To me our duty seems plain – to end the conflict without delay . . . The hope of success alone would justify our continuing the fight, and, frankly, I see no such hope . . . The time has definitely come, I think, when a new policy for the prosecution of the cause of national Independence will have to be adopted. The phase begun in 1916 has run its course.[189]

Two days later, he repeated his belief that the war should be stopped.

> My heart and my desires make almost an agonising appeal to hold on and defy them as long as a rifle and a cartridge remains, but my head and my conscience tell me it would not be justifiable. I am afraid we shall have to face the inevitable sooner or later, bow to force, and resort to other methods . . .[190]

On 6 April, the IRA Adjutant General, Tom Derrig, was wounded and captured, along with secret documents relating to the Executive meeting which was due to resume on the 10th.[191] On the same day, Lynch and a number of senior officers were forced to make a run for it across the Knockmealdown Mountains. Caught on a bare mountain top by converging Free State columns, Lynch was shot, and was dead by evening.[192] De Valera was very upset at the 'terrible blow'.[193] He would keep the last message he received from the chief of staff in an envelope on which he wrote 'Very precious. General Liam Lynch's last despatches. National treasures.'[194] Nonetheless, de Valera must have been aware that the main impediment to peace had now been removed.

Meanwhile, another disaster had unfolded. Austin Stack, who had been in the same area in preparation for the Army Executive meeting, had been trying to drum up support for a move to end the fighting. He called a meeting attended by the available senior figures from the Tipperary Brigade. While most agreed with him, they felt that the decision should be left to the Army Executive, so the document he had prepared urging a stop to the war, which he carried in his wallet, remained unsigned.[195] Later, he and some companions built a hiding-place in a haystack. After resting for a while, Stack, who was armed, went outside. Shortly afterwards he was found by a Free State patrol, 'alone and unarmed and lying in a ditch'.[196] The document found on him was given full publicity in the following day's newspapers.[197]

The long-delayed Army Executive meeting resumed on 20 April, in 'Kathmandu', a small room hidden in a cow-shed on the Whelan farm in Mullinahone, Co. Tipperary.[198] Frank Aiken, Lynch's deputy, was unanimously elected chief of staff. The meeting then approved his motion empowering the Republican government and the Army Council to make peace on the basis of two of the principles stated by de Valera in February: that Irish sovereignty was inalienable, and that any instrument that contravened that principle was void. This reiteration of the rejection of the Treaty was accepted by 9 votes to 2. It was unanimously agreed that, if these terms were accepted by the Free State government, 'majority rule would be accepted as a rule of order'. A motion by Tom Barry to call off the war, in view of the condition of the army, was rejected, with only two votes in favour; and there was a tied vote on another motion calling for the war to continue if the terms stated by Aiken were rejected.[199] In effect, the Army Executive was opting for peace if, and only if, the Executive Council of the Free State agreed to reject the Treaty – which was hardly likely.

Three members of the Army Executive – Frank Aiken, Tom Barry and Liam Pilkington – were appointed to the Army Council. They were to decide, in conjunction with the Republican government, on peace or war. A joint meeting on 26 April decided that Aiken should issue an order suspending offensive actions and that de Valera should issue a proclamation setting out their terms for negotiating peace.[200] Aiken ordered all units to cease operations from noon on 30 April but to remain on the defensive in order to 'take adequate measures to protect themselves and their munitions'.[201] The anti-Treaty forces would remain in being, ready to act if the peace moves failed.

De Valera's proclamation listed six principles on which they were prepared to negotiate peace. These were the same as those in his February memorandum – with the important difference that he didn't explicitly state that any instrument (or Treaty) contravening the 'indefeasible and inalienable' sovereign rights of the nation, or the source of all power deriving from the people, would be void.[202] Presumably he felt that this was implicit in the principles, and that he was more likely to get a hearing from the Free State if he left it that way.

De Valera had already chosen the intermediaries he hoped would persuade the Free State government to open negotiations: James Douglas, a Quaker businessman prominent in the White Cross relief organisation during the War of Independence; and Andrew Jameson, the whiskey magnate who helped broker the Truce of 1921.[203] Both were now members of the Free State Senate. Douglas met de Valera first, a few days before the proclamation was issued, and was shocked by the change in him. 'The whole bearing of de Valera was that of a defeated man and his attitude towards me was the reverse of that when I had met him in the old days when he was President.'[204] After publication of his proclamation, de Valera invited Douglas and Jameson to meet him to discuss it. He told them that 'peace is now definitely obtainable if I can only secure cooperation from men of good-will on your side'.[205]

When he met the two senators, de Valera acknowledged that there might be people on his side that the Free State government would not want to meet; equally, there were some members of it he would not be keen on meeting. Pressed on this question by Jameson, he said he was thinking of O'Higgins, 'suggesting that he could not trust him'. Douglas and Jameson formed the opinion that de Valera would agree to any reasonable terms that would allow him to save face.

He was very anxious to explain how much worse things would have been if he had not been with them [the anti-Treatyites] and seemed extra anxious to apologise for himself . . . We were both much impressed by the evident fact that he was a beaten man and that he knows it . . .[206]

After Douglas and Jameson reported to Cosgrave, the Free State government drew up proposals for de Valera to sign. All political issues were to be decided by the majority vote of the elected representatives of the people. As a corollary to that, all lethal weapons were to be in the effective custody of the government. Prisoners would be released, once arms were surrendered and they had each subscribed to these two points.[207] De Valera objected to the prisoners being asked to sign any such document, and he also claimed that he would not be able to secure the surrender of arms.[208] But Cosgrave and his colleagues were adamant: arms must be given up (not necessarily directly to the government); prisoners must agree to the principles of majority rule and non-violence before release; and the oath could not be altered (at least at present).[209] However, they did authorise the two senators to tell de Valera that military action against Republicans would cease once arms were given up, and that Republicans would be given 'a clear field' in the elections, provided they undertook to use solely constitutional methods.[210]

Despite the cessation of offensive operations by the anti-Treaty forces, executions continued – including two men shot in Ennis on 2 May. De Valera's secretary recorded that he 'was very optimistic about situation in general for peace until he heard of executions. He was very upset.'[211]

After consulting his colleagues, principally Ruttledge and Aiken, de Valera formulated final proposals for submission to Cosgrave, and was, according to his secretary, 'confident they would be accepted'.[212] The basis for this confidence is not clear: the proposals differed little from his proclamation of 27 April, apart from a rewording and reordering, to take account of the principles advanced by Cosgrave. The acceptance of majority rule was still subject to the proviso that national sovereignty and the derivation of power from the people be 'fundamental', which in de Valera's view meant that the Treaty and the Free State Constitution were null and void; there was still a demand that the oath should be scrapped. And rather than agreeing to hand over arms, de Valera suggested the provision in each province of a suitable building to be used as an arsenal for Republicans, where their arms shall be stored, sealed up, and defended by a specially pledged Republican guard – these arms to be disposed of after the elections by re-issue to their present holders, or in such other manner as may secure the consent of the Government then elected.

He also wanted American funds released to Republicans for electoral use, all seized property restored, compensation to Republicans for war damage, the release of prisoners and an end to censorship.[213] One wonders what he would have looked for had the Republicans been winning the Civil War.

Cosgrave regarded his proposals as a

long and wordy document inviting debate where none is possible . . . No further communication with Mr de Valera can be entertained save only a communication indicating his definite acceptance of the terms stated in writing and handed to you for his signature.[214]

According to his secretary, de Valera was

very disappointed. How earnestly & anxiously he worked for peace only God alone knows. As he said himself, the voice of the gladiator rings through Cosgrave's reply.[215]

De Valera reported back to a joint meeting of the Republican government and the anti-Treaty Army Council on 13 May 1923. Cosgrave's response, he believed, demonstrated that the Free State 'wanted submission pure and simple'. It was unanimously decided that, rather than trying to engage in negotiations, Frank Aiken should order the Republican forces to 'cease fire' and 'dump arms'.[216] This of course meant that the arms would remain available if required. De Valera wrote to an old Carmelite friend from New York days, Peter Magennis, that the move was inevitable. 'Since I ordered my own Battalion to lay down their arms in 1916, I have not felt such anguish.'[217]

Aiken's order was issued on 24 May. The dumping of arms was to be completed within four days.[218] In an accompanying message to the Republican troops, he stated:

Our enemies have demanded our arms. Our answer is: 'We took up arms to free our country, and we'll keep them until we see an honourable way of reaching our objective without arms.'[219]

De Valera also issued a message to all ranks.

> The republic can no longer be defended successfully by your arms.
> Further sacrifice of life would now be vain ... Military victory must be
> allowed to rest for the moment with those who have destroyed the
> Republic.[220]

He was, according to his secretary, 'very, very upset – heartbroken,
really'.[221] Characteristically, he tried to amend his draft, believing it to be

> psychologically bad. I was more or less in the dumps when I wrote it. I
> have brightened up the second paragraph by pointing out what has
> been achieved ...

His addition would have claimed that the anti-Treaty forces had 'saved
the nation's honour and kept open the road to Independence'.[222] But it
was too late: Aiken had already sent out the original.[223]

In any case, his amended version still included the most controversial
line: the claim that the Republic had been 'destroyed'. This did not go
down well with many Republicans, Ruttledge telling him frankly that he
did not like the use of the word.[224] De Valera later claimed that he had
used it, not in the sense of 'utter ruin', but in 'the secondary meaning of
spoiling, e.g. "I destroyed my coat with the ink".'[225] This was, to say the
least, rather unconvincing. To another correspondent he claimed that the
word came to him 'as a Munsterism perhaps' and that he decided to leave
it, even though people objected,

> for the fact is that the body of the Republic is at this moment paralysed
> and dead as far as its ability to function as living organism is concerned.
> It is as well that we should be all shocked into a realisation of that fact
> as soon as possible.[226]

According to himself, he both did and didn't mean what he had written.

His use of language aside, there were plenty of complaints about the
decision itself. His most formidable opponent – as usual – was Mary
MacSwiney, who claimed that members of the Republican forces were
angry at the ceasefire. De Valera replied that he was angry too,

> because your criticism, like the others, was in the air without reference
> to, or knowledge of, the real situation we have to face ... We have to

shepherd the remnant of our forces out of this fight so as not to destroy whatever hope remains in the future by allowing the right to peter out ignominiously . . .[227]

He also laid out his future programme. The Republican government could remain, he said, but only as a symbol. 'It has not been functioning and cannot function'.[228] More controversially, in a further letter he mentioned the possibility of ending abstention from the Dáil, changing the view he had held the previous September.

> If the oath were removed, to my mind the question of going in or remaining out [of the Dáil] would be a matter purely of tactics and expediency, and had best be left to be decided either by a convention or by the elected members. Circumstances will have them in a sufficiently strait jacket without our adding unnecessarily to its straitness.[229]

The endless arguments over the Civil War – causes, justification and responsibility – contributed to de Valera's growing obsession with his own reputation. He had always been assiduous in retaining documents he regarded as important; he felt it particularly vital to maintain a record of the Treaty negotiations and of the events that followed, in an effort to justify his own position. In June 1923, after the order to dump arms, at a time when he still felt his life could be in danger, he made arrangements for the safeguarding of his papers by an unidentified priest. He hoped to be in a position to catalogue and annotate them some day. If not, the only person who could do so was his secretary, Kathleen O'Connell. De Valera wrote that he had

> endeavoured to save these in order that there may be some documentary material for the history of this period and for a proper appreciation of the motives and actions of the Republican Government and Army Executive.[230]

The bitter dispute over the Treaty, and the Civil War that followed, was to remain the primary cleavage in Irish politics for the next half-century. While pro-Treatyites would, in 1948, form a coalition with a Republican party, Clann na Poblachta (many of whose senior figures had been active in the Civil War), their co-operation with de Valera would be extremely limited. To them, such Republicans as Seán MacBride, who founded the Clann, were sincere people who opposed the Treaty on principle; de Valera, they felt, had done so because of personal ambition.[231] They simply could not see any point of principle in his criticism of the Treaty that would justify supporting an armed conflict. They believed that his support gave the anti-Treaty side a political stature and respectability it would never have attained otherwise, that some were persuaded to oppose the Treaty because of de Valera, and that the Civil War would have been a smaller and a shorter affair without his participation.

Of course, it wasn't only the pro-Treaty side that would have cause for complaint. Republicans would bitterly resent de Valera's later break with Sinn Féin in order to form Fianna Fáil, his entry into the Dáil and his taking of the oath of allegiance. They regarded this as a betrayal of everything that had been fought for in the Civil War, and again he was accused of giving priority to power over principle. De Valera himself acknowledged that he was a reluctant leader of the extremists, describing himself as a 'fish out of water' in the role.

> I urged them to choose someone whose manner of thought and general character was more in consonance with their own. I believe they would have done better had they taken my advice, but they neither did that nor did they really go in the direction I would have taken them . . .[232]

Meanwhile, in the wake of the ceasefire, de Valera wrote to supporters in America, explaining the inevitability of ending the war and looking, as usual, for funds. He told Joe McGarrity on 4 June that

> we shall be in greater need . . . for money than ever before. There are thousands and thousands of the dependants of the prisoners and the men fighting who are on the verge of starvation.[233]

On 20 June he wrote to Monsignor Denis O'Connor, of the Carmelite community in New York, that they would be unable to contest the election, partly because of Free State harassment but also because they would be unable to raise the money necessary.[234] A fortnight later his position was changing: the priority for available funds must be prisoners, the wounded and the bereaved. Nonetheless, 'it is only by political means that we can hope for any measure of success in the near future'. He was not being over-ambitious and was talking of contesting only one seat in each constituency; but that would require money. Though he detested 'starting to send round the hat again', he was asking for $100,000, 'which I think is the smallest sum on which we could hope to put up anything like a decent fight'. He promised that Republicans would be able to stand on their own feet financially after this.[235] In this he was mistaken.

Meanwhile, he had to try and combat the inevitable despair gripping Republicans. Frank Aiken almost succumbed to it, telling de Valera he intended to allow himself to be captured and then refuse to recognise the Free State government's right to imprison him (which would mean a hunger strike). 'I think I can, with the help of God, carry it through in a manner becoming to an officer of the IRA.'[236] De Valera managed to persuade him that his duty was on the outside.

> We must use the Army organisation to build up at once an employment and relief bureau, otherwise our men will be tempted to form into bands roving about and commandeering what they require.[237]

Now that the fighting was over, de Valera was full of schemes.

> Our next project must be to get a daily newspaper. In meeting them in arms we were fighting them on their own chosen ground . . . If we develop properly the line of peaceful political attack, building upon the undoubted desire of the people for complete independence, it is we who are invincible.[238]

There was, he fretted, 'no hope in the future without a paper',[239] and subscriptions were solicited for a fund to establish 'an Irish Daily Republican Press'.[240]

But who was to lead the Republican movement now that the war was over? De Valera had unhappily played second fiddle to Liam Lynch; he had no intention of doing so to Frank Aiken.

> I do not think the combination Army Council and Government should continue in its present form. The Army could be represented on the Ministry by the Chief of Staff, the Adjutant-General and, if necessary, the Assistant Chief of Staff?[241]

The Republican focus must now turn to politics; fortunately for de Valera, he had been preparing for this for some months.

As far back as October 1922 he had made efforts to gain control of the Sinn Féin organisation and to keep the old head office at Harcourt Street operating. Vera McDonnell, one of the stenographers there, was instructed to keep the office open, but continual raids and harassment by Free State soldiers made this impossible.[242] When the treasurers (Jennie Wyse Power and Éamonn Duggan) summoned a meeting of the Standing Committee for 26 October, de Valera moved to fight them, arranging for substitutes to be nominated for himself and Austin Stack (who couldn't appear in public), and insisting that he, as sole trustee, should have control of the party's funds.[243] The Republican members of the Standing Committee appeared doubtful about the value of the party organisation, asking him what, apart from the money, the point was.[244] He explained that the Sinn Féin organisation was an existing, all-Ireland body, 'with a constitution exactly suited to Republican purposes and policy'. He wanted Republican committees established throughout the country, which could infiltrate and take over the Sinn Féin cumainn while also being available to work separately and independently for Republican election candidates.[245] If the other side blocked them, they could always work out of the Cumann na Poblachta head office in Suffolk Street, but he felt it was worth trying to work under the Sinn Féin banner. 'We can make far more rapid progress through Sinn Féin than through new Republican clubs, and there will be less danger of having organisers arrested.'[246]

In December he told P. J. Ruttledge that 'the time is ripe and suitable' for organisation work, that the army must help and that it was vital to 'make the new Sinn Féin thoroughly Republican and *labour* if possible'.[247] With civilians reluctant to work for Sinn Féin after the executions, the IRA was crucial to reorganisation efforts, and organisers were directed to concentrate their efforts on the IRA's divisional areas.[248] In a letter to Mary MacSwiney in December, asking her to take charge of the office at Suffolk Street, de Valera confessed that the Republican government and political organisation had no funds; the only money available was army money. 'I am more afraid of the money question than any other,' he told her. He wanted her to keep the Suffolk Street office open as a point of contact with the public, and with journalists. 'We do not want to allow ourselves to be driven altogether underground.'[249] He would come to regret giving the implacable MacSwiney such a role, but in those difficult times there were not many options.

He remained convinced of the need to control Sinn Féin, worrying that if the other side had a majority, 'as they are likely to have, they would be able to select their candidates, etc. etc. in case of an election and we would have no organisation at all'.[250] But many Republicans doubted the value of the party. Count Plunkett felt that Sinn Féin was dead 'and held in contempt pretty generally . . . The name does not define or indicate a positive belief in the Republic'.[251] But, for de Valera, that was part of the attraction of the old name: it could help to bring back supporters who were not extreme Republicans.

> Our aim is not to make a close preserve for ourselves, but to win the majority of the people again. I understand the difficulties but we must teach our people to be broad in this matter.[252]

To help him achieve this aim he brought on board Joseph Connolly, a Belfast businessman and Sinn Féin activist. 'I do not know Connolly very well, but I believe him sincere, patriotic, wise and able, if not perhaps inspiring'.[253] Connolly agreed to chair the committee of 'Sinn Féin Reorganised', on the promise that there would be a ceasefire at an early date, which would allow Republicans to devote all their energies to political work.[254] A week before the ceasefire, de Valera told a confidant that 'it may be necessary very soon to change the defence of our national Independence from the plane of arms to that of unarmed effort'. Sectional interests were springing up – farmers, labour – that would distract from the purely national issue. 'It is vital, therefore, that the reorganisation of Sinn Féin as *the* national organisation should be pushed forwards with all speed.'[255]

De Valera wrote to Molly Childers, widow of Erskine, that

> the hope for the future lies in again reorganising the main body of nationalist opinion . . . The formation by the others of Cumann na nGaedheal has left the way for Sinn Féin clear . . . Very many who opposed the *method* of arms are with us heart and soul as far as our objective is concerned and would be delighted to work through Sinn Féin.[256]

But a preliminary meeting of the reorganising committee demonstrated the difficulty de Valera faced in trying to direct it by remote control. A number of members – particularly Áine Ceannt and Kathleen Lynn – objected to the name 'Sinn Féin'. It wasn't popular, it wouldn't attract uncompromising Republicans and it could be infiltrated by supporters of the Free State. Alternative names were suggested: the 'Irish Republican Organisation' or 'Irish Independence Organisation'.[257] Asked for his opinion, de Valera wrote that they should consider themselves the 'Committee for the Reorganisation of Sinn Féin as the Irish Independence Organisation'.[258] But the committee was having none of it, passing a resolution that the new party should be called the 'Irish Republican

Political Organisation'.[259] De Valera's supporter Michael Comyn warned him that if the word 'republic' wasn't in the title 'it is quite probable that an independent republican party would be started'.[260]

De Valera wrote a strongly worded letter to the organising committee, stressing the need to gather not just Republican opinion but also 'what might be called "Nationalist" or "Independence" opinion in general. If we do not do it, the other side will and the loss will be immense'. He urged them to accept his recommendation (backed as it was by his government and by the Army Executive) that Sinn Féin should be reorganised.[261] Eventually, he had his way: the new, or reorganised, party would be called Sinn Féin.

The agreed aims of the party, as approved by de Valera, did not mention the Republic and instead stressed the need to oppose every form of foreign interference.

> Ireland is an independent State, and that whilst the form of Government may be changed by the free vote of the people, Ireland's Independence cannot be signed away, or voted away.

In a further effort to give himself the maximum freedom of manoeuvre, he stated that 'questions of *method* are open, provided there is no formal recognition of the legality of the Free State regime'.[262]

He also rediscovered the importance of partition, which he now thought was 'a far more real and serious matter than the Crown'. He could not, however, see what the solution would be. He correctly predicted that the Free State would end up making a 'miserable bargain' with James Craig over the boundary. He claimed that he had warned Arthur Griffith that he would be 'euchred' (cheated) on the Boundary Commission, and he 'wouldn't have, myself, placed a particle of dependence on it'.[263] He seemed to have forgotten that he had not objected to the proposal when it was mooted during the Treaty negotiations, and that he had included it verbatim in his original Document no. 2. His own proposal was to give the North a local parliament, with the area covered to be decided by plebiscite. If the North remained determined to keep its parliament, he would then propose

> the formation of three or four other such local areas with subordinate Parliaments of equal powers, the whole to be grouped into the single Federal State of the Republic of Ireland.[264]

The remaining question was whether, and to what extent, Sinn Féin should contest the coming general elections. De Valera strongly favoured contesting, as refusing to stand 'lets the case go by default'. He was not, however, wedded to abstention.

> Our presence as a compact, organised body may get rid of the oath. If we fail in this and have to withdraw and abstain from Parliament, there will have been no harm done that I can see.[265]

But he became gripped by indecision about the election. On 25 July, a month before polling, he pointed out to his Sinn Féin colleagues that there were four options: to abstain completely, on the grounds that the elections would not be free or fair; to put forward only one candidate per constituency, as he had suggested; to put forward a few candidates in selected places ('My own case in Clare, on account of the O'Connell precedent as regards the oath, is an example'); or to put forward as many candidates as they could hope to get elected. In the absence of comprehensive information from each constituency on which to base the decision, he thought abstention to be, 'undoubtedly, the safest ground'.[266]

Luckily for Sinn Féin, the organising committee disagreed, insisting that the party should contest the elections 'to the full limit of our hopes'.[267] Within a couple of weeks, de Valera's doubts had been dispelled; if anything, he became over-confident, telling the director of elections that he heard his own constituency of Clare was 'magnificent', and wondering if they could 'put up sufficient candidates in the constituencies so as to secure a majority or near it?'[268]

After the Free State's Minister for Foreign Affairs, Desmond FitzGerald, said de Valera would be 'kept on the run', he issued a defiant statement. 'If the people of Clare select me as their candidate again, I will be with them and nothing but a bullet will stop me.'[269] He nominated P. J. Ruttledge as his replacement should anything happen to him – 'because P. J. said yes to everything that Dev suggested,' according to a close observer.[270] To Molly Childers, who knew more than most about the risks involved, he wrote that 'there is, of course, danger, but I think it is wise nevertheless . . . I do not err as a rule on the rash side – but I can face the inevitable.'[271]

The danger of a bullet actually stopping him appeared very real. The IRA's Director of Intelligence, Michael Carolan, warned him on 8 August that he had heard from an absolutely reliable source 'that some of the Free State murder gang have sworn to shoot you in revenge for M. Collins' death . . . Please take this as definitely authoritative.'[272] Six days later Carolan named the instigator of the plot as Diarmuid O'Hegarty, the government secretary, who he claimed was trying to persuade former members of Collins's Squad that he had 'definite information that President de Valera took part in the ambush in which Mick Collins was shot'. Carolan advised de Valera that an assassination attempt in Ennis was unlikely, because of the publicity it would attract, but he warned that precautions must be taken, including posting scouts around the platform, keeping all surrounding houses under scrutiny and, if possible, holding the meeting in an open place rather than in the town square.[273]

Shortly before de Valera's departure for Co. Clare, Sinéad spent the night at his hiding-place. Clearly worried about his safety, she was 'heartbroken and awfully anxious' leaving him.[274] On 12 August 1923, de Valera departed for Ennis, with every expectation that he would be killed or arrested.[275] His secretary, Kathleen O'Connell, was distraught. 'I am afraid of this journey.'[276] Her fear was justified.

CHAPTER 17

MASTER OF MY OWN SOUL

They will seal me in the tomb as well as they can.
> Éamon de Valera, Arbour Hill Military Prison,
> January 1924[1]

*I am going to be master of my own soul from the Ard Fheis
out . . .*
> Éamon de Valera, November 1925[2]

*I wish to face boldly the facts of the present situation, because
I know that it is only by facing them that we can hope to
overcome them.*
> Éamon de Valera, launching Fianna Fáil, May 1926[3]

De Valera faced his public appearance in Ennis, and his probable arrest and possible death, with resignation. 'As regards Clare, and my recent commitment, enemy action will settle that. Either way, the effect will be good,' he told the Sinn Féin organising committee.[4] His fatalistic attitude is clear in notes claiming the defeated Republicans would not emigrate.

> The men of the IRA will die in Ireland if they cannot live in it. It may be necessary for some of the leaders to come out and sacrifice themselves in order to assert that right to live. If it should become necessary they will not be found wanting.[5]

The Free State government was rightly worried that arresting de Valera in public would 'make good propaganda for him both at home and abroad'.[6] The army was instructed: 'It is absolutely essential that de Valera should be arrested before he appears in public.'[7] However, according to the officer in charge, de Valera had got to the stage before they recognised him.[8] Nobody else in Ennis failed to recognise him. The speeches were already under way as de Valera's car arrived, but when some of the 3,000 people in the square realised it was him, cheering broke out for 'two or three minutes'.[9] Kathleen O'Connell recorded that 'people cheer madly and frantically when the P appears' and 'simply go wild when he stands up. He looks wan and tired but supremely happy and pleased.'[10]

He spoke for several minutes before Free State troops arrived, marching towards the platform with fixed bayonets, firing volleys in the air as they neared. The officer in charge claimed that this was in response to shots being fired from the platform and from the crowd – no other account mentions shots before the army opened fire – though he admitted he had not given the order to fire and did not know who did.[11] The firing led to a stampede among the crowd in the square. At least 20 people were injured, four of whom suffered bullet wounds, despite the soldiers supposedly firing into the air.[12] On the platform, Peg and Pauline Barrett threw themselves in front of de Valera to protect him. Pauline suffered splinter wounds;[13] de Valera was hit in the leg.[14]

Whether because of his wound, because of the crush of people trying to escape the platform, or because he threw himself down to avoid being shot, de Valera disappeared from view.

> When he managed to struggle to his feet his clothes were covered in dust, and his dishevelled appearance momentarily made him unrecognisable. And then he went down the steps of the platform to where the soldiers were waiting for him.[15]

De Valera made no attempt to evade arrest; he was taken through the crowd who jeered the file of soldiers on either side of him. An armoured car following on behind shepherded him to the barracks. He was later transferred to Arbour Hill Military Prison in Dublin, held as a danger to public safety.[16]

The arrest did the Republican election campaign no harm; it might even have helped. On polling day, 27 August, the Republican share of the vote was 27.6 per cent, up from 21.5 the year before (partly because this time seven strongly Republican constituencies in the west were contested).[17] It was a remarkable performance, given the undoubted un-popularity of the Civil War, the imprisonment of so many Republican activists and leaders, and harassment by the Free State authorities (though, of course, it was still a defeat). Had they followed de Valera's original plan of putting up only one candidate per constituency, they would have won only 25 seats; instead, they ended up with 44. As Peadar O'Donnell (one of the first-time Republican TDs) noted, it was a huge boost to their confidence. 'The road back was going to be shorter than we dared hope.'[18]

The new government party, Cumann na nGaedheal, won 39 per cent of the vote, and 63 seats; the remaining TDs were 17 independents, 15 Farmers and 14 Labour. In Clare, in his first contested election since his by-election victory in 1917, de Valera secured 17,762 votes (45 per cent of the poll and more than two quotas).[19] He dragged in a running-mate, Brian O'Higgins, whose own first-preference vote was only 114 (0.29 per cent).

Eoin MacNeill was also elected on the first count, with 20.8 per cent of the vote, the final seats being taken by Conor Hogan (Farmers) and Patrick Hogan (Labour).[20] The result must have been a particularly unpleasant shock for MacNeill: two weeks before polling he had told his wife 'we are confident of a big majority' in the constituency.[21]

Meanwhile, de Valera was languishing in Arbour Hill. Given the continuing (though reduced) violence on the outside – the anti-Treaty officer Noel Lemass was abducted on 3 July 1923 and murdered, presumably by Free State forces – it might be argued that de Valera was safer in prison than outside it. Indeed, on at least one occasion Cosgrave claimed that this was the reason for his continued imprisonment.[22] However, given what had happened to Liam Mellows and Rory O'Connor, there could be no guarantee of his safety in the custody of the Free State.

The Executive Council had their man; but what were they to do with him? The day after de Valera's arrest they decided 'that a charge should be brought against him with the least possible delay', and Richard Mulcahy was asked to have all the available evidence examined and given to the Attorney-General, Hugh Kennedy.[23] But there arose a surprising and rather embarrassing problem: there were very few incriminating documents on which a prosecution could be based. In fact, the only real 'evidence' that could be used appeared to be a letter from de Valera to the honorary secretaries of Cumann na mBan.[24] Given all that had been said about de Valera's war guilt, a prosecution on the basis of this letter might well have seemed ridiculous, and the idea was quietly dropped.

A mass hunger strike by Republican prisoners began in Mountjoy on 13 October and quickly spread to other prisons and prison camps; ten days later an estimated 8,000 prisoners were refusing food.[25] De Valera was suddenly transferred to Kilmainham Jail, where some of the original hunger-strikers had also been moved. The authorities claimed that this was done because of fears of a rescue from Arbour Hill; but some of his fellow prisoners were convinced it was an attempt to encourage him to join the hunger strike in Kilmainham.[26] This was unlikely, as de Valera was kept separate from the other prisoners. He exercised alone, and was kept in a special wing on his own where no-one without a permit was allowed enter, and no-one other than the officer on duty was to converse with him.[27] He found Kilmainham 'an awful place at first'. The guards were 'scrupulous in obeying their orders – rigid they must be to judge from their conduct – but they are decent otherwise.'[28]

In November, Mulcahy approved a visit to the prison by a Dr Moore, who attempted to mediate with the hunger-strikers. He found Tomás Derrig 'clear enough' but Austin Stack 'very difficult to deal with, not because he wants to be difficult but because he cannot keep his mind on things'. They told the doctor that they were in no condition to discuss details and that 'de Valera is the man to see'.

Mulcahy approved a visit to the special wing, where de Valera was 'astounded to know that there was a hunger-strike on and thought it a disastrous line of policy'. However, according to Moore, he was uncertain of his own authority. 'He seemed to think that his views would not be worth speaking.'[29] After the deaths of two prisoners, one in Newbridge Camp and the other in Mountjoy, the strike was called off at the end of November.[30]

Early in 1924 de Valera was moved back to Arbour Hill, in part so he could prepare his case for a legal action in the United States relating to Republican bond money. Facilities were granted for his American lawyer, John F. Finerty, to discuss the case with de Valera and Austin Stack (the only time the two prisoners were allowed to meet).[31] Finerty's visits allowed messages to be smuggled out. De Valera complained of the restrictions. 'I can keep nothing here. The cell . . . is likely to be searched at any time'.[32] However, he managed to send P. J. Ruttledge a very lengthy memorandum on policy, covering such issues as agricultural education, temperance, the need to contest the local elections ('Dublin would be particularly important and Seán T. a splendid candidate for Lord Mayor') and the importance of using the spoken rather than the written word ('beware of *documents*'). He finished on a personal note.

As for me – immediately Finerty leaves, they will seal me in the tomb as well as they can . . . they will neither be able to provoke me nor make me really unhappy, no matter what they do . . .[33]

A later memorandum went into detail about organisation, including a suggestion that the 'well-to-do' should be recruited to the cause, as they 'have leisure, there is a void in many of their lives – the younger especially; they are ready made enthusiasts; all that is necessary is the initial enlisting of their sympathies.'[34] He was also 'very anxious about the economic programme'. The old Sinn Féin represented all classes, but

labour as such will be so absorbed with its own programme and organisation that it is unlikely we could win them to our side by any kind of bid no matter how far in their direction we went. We must stand for fair play and justice between all classes.[35]

He also expressed mildly heretical thoughts about the reduced role of the Republican government. 'My opinion strongly is we shouldn't play into our opponents' hands by harping too much on the governmental aspect of our activities'.[36] He suggested the use of the term 'director' for the heads of departments, rather than 'minister'. 'Such names always convey the impression of stage play, unreality, insincerity even, which would be damning to our chances of again winning the people completely to our side.'[37]

De Valera also suggested that his secretary, Kathleen O'Connell, should put together a documentary history of the period from the Rising to the end of the Civil War, conceding that the final work could run to several volumes. With all the leisure of a convict, he wrote 25 pages of instructions on how and where to get the information she would need, concluding patronisingly: 'Now Daddy can tell you no more. You must launch out on your own . . .'[38]

In a later letter he was uncharacteristically expansive in his kind words to her.

I want you to know also that I realise that no cause has had a more loyal adherent than the Republic has had in you and no public man has ever had a more faithful assistant & friend – and now lest you should imagine Jail has in some way affected me that I write like this I turn to business.

He then instructed her to go through his mathematical notebooks, numbering them and noting their contents, and then sending them to him along with a long list of textbooks.

> It will be like making the acquaintance of old friends again and what I have forgotten will come back through them more quickly than in any other way . . . I am afraid Sinéad has grown cynical about my relation to books – and will think this only another of my whims . . . The privilege of being in jail is that one can ask to be indulged in whims of this sort – I'll be shut off as completely as if I were on another planet and these books, old or new, the only friends at hand.[39]

His old pupil the Rev. Pádraig de Brún also sent him several books on the theory of relativity. Vivion de Valera later noted that his father had 'tried to master' them,[40] which suggests that he failed.

Such distractions were badly needed. On St Patrick's Day, 1924, he noted in the shorthand he was practising: 'Very sad and lonely.' At the end of March, a welcome visitor returned.

> Sun entered cell 113 after six months absence – last here Sep. . . . Today it crossed 6.23 (my watch) and sank in clouds at clump trees 6.45.

Sunlight became a preoccupation: he had one-and-a-half hours of it on 16 April, and four days later he noted: 'Just 2 hours . . . Will not be able to see it reach horizon henceforth.'[41]

In an Easter message to his mother, he reflected on his situation.

> I sometimes smile as I think how nearly your wishes as regards my vocation have been met. I have spent a fair number of years now in a very 'enclosed order' – where the world's distractions cannot reach me! Love, Ed.[42]

But all that was about to change.

Following a discussion with Cosgrave, Eoin O'Duffy (now commander of the Free State army as well as Garda Commissioner) agreed to allow de Valera and Stack to associate freely from 10 a.m. to noon and from 2 to 5 p.m., and in a locked cell between 7 and 9 p.m.[43] De Valera laconically recorded in his diary: 'Stack and I were allowed meet.'[44] Stack was considerably more enthusiastic.

Another wonder! Who should walk into my cell, between 7 and 8 o'clock but de Valera. He has just departed from me after a good chat. Evidently we are to be allowed to 'associate' at long last.[45]

They quickly made the most of their new-found privileges, playing game after game of handball against each other, against another prisoner called Keegan, and against Lieutenant Hugh Maguire, one of their captors.[46] There were also games of tennis and chess.[47]

De Valera was told he could see Sinéad, who was allowed to visit on 27 June – their first meeting since before his arrest.[48]

On 16 July, at 7 o'clock in the evening, de Valera and Stack were informed that they were to be released immediately. About an hour later, after packing and arranging for a car to collect them, they passed through the prison gates and were free men once again. Their first call was to the Sinn Féin head office in Suffolk Street (Sinéad and the children were on holiday in Galway).[49]

While he was in prison, the work of organising Sinn Féin had continued, with Mary MacSwiney playing a central role, standing in for him at the ard-fheis in October. The mere mention of the absent President's name led to prolonged cheering. MacSwiney, covering up the doubts she felt about him, told delegates that 'there is nobody but Éamon de Valera himself who can fill the place of Éamon de Valera'.[50] MacSwiney was undoubtedly loyal to de Valera as the figurehead of the Republican movement.

> The Free State stole our regalia, our flag, our uniform, but they were not able to take our president, even though they tried to kill him, and our president is the most valuable asset that we have, the last piece of our regalia.[51]

But she was to remain suspicious of what she saw as his political revisionism.[52] The Sinn Féin Standing Committee organised a reception in the Mansion House on 21 July 1924 to mark his release.[53] Afterwards he went down to Roundstone, Co. Galway, for a reunion with Sinéad and the children, staying for nine days.[54] After he left, Sinéad found the house 'desperately lonely', writing to Kathleen O'Connell in an effort to write off 'the blues'. Typically, she was concerned for her husband, fretting that he would not eat and sleep properly.

> Tell Dev not to bother writing to me. I know what his life will be now. I'll try and build up the children's and my own health and Irish and then I'll be glad when August is over . . .[55]

On 7 August, de Valera presided at a meeting of Comhairle na dTeachtaí, an alternative parliament attended by 55 former or current TDs – the 'faithful' members of the Second Dáil (whether or not they had subsequently lost their seats) and Republicans elected at later elections. Despite the doubts he had expressed in prison, de Valera now believed that the Republican government should remain in existence.

> It will be there to take over the government of the country at any time when the people will make it impossible for the other crowd to carry on as a government.

While the Republican government was, in his view, the *de jure* government, it was not the *de facto* government – but that would change as soon as the people gave them a majority. De Valera was later to distance himself from the Republican fixation with the Second Dáil, but at this point he appears to have been fully in tune with it.

At the meeting of Comhairle na dTeachtaí he gave a lengthy account of the background to the Civil War. He accused the Provisional Government of carrying out a coup d'état by refusing to allow the Second Dáil to meet; it was this that persuaded him 'that I could consistently and constitutionally take up arms and fight for the constitution'. This, of course, ignored the fact that he had enlisted in the anti-Treaty forces *before* the Dáil had been due to meet. He then stressed the importance of economic policy and of trying to help the country become more prosperous – though not so much that it would consolidate 'the very power we are trying to destroy and which must be destroyed before we can get anywhere'. There were some discordant voices. Mary MacSwiney raised the abstention issue. 'It should go out from this body that no speaker should be allowed to say that if the oath were removed we would go into the Free State parliament.' There was no response from de Valera, who was not then endeavouring to change that particular policy.

The following day, when the rump Second Dáil met, Constance Markievicz criticised his proposal that Robert Barton should become a minister without portfolio. De Valera once again defended him. The other members of the Republican government were to be P. J. Ruttledge, also a minister without portfolio; Austin Stack (Home Affairs and Finance); Art O'Connor (Economic Affairs and Local Government); and Frank Aiken (Defence). De Valera himself retained External Affairs.[56]

The anniversary of his arrest, 15 August, was a perfect opportunity for de Valera to make his reappearance in Ennis. Never being able to see a good joke without attempting to smother it in redundant clauses, he began his speech by strangling his obvious opening line: 'I am afraid I would disappoint a number here if I were not to start by saying: "Well as I was saying to you when we were interrupted".'[57] This ponderous attempt at humour pleased the crowd, while maintaining de Valera's image as a man who would not stoop to crowd pleasing.

In the office in Suffolk Street in Dublin he was once again 'the central personality . . . a truly Olympian figure, remote and self-contained but also good-humoured and affable'.[58] He also took up the reins at the National University, becoming an assiduous attender at meetings of the Senate, missing none in 1925 and only one in 1926. He had, of course, been absent for the first three years of his chancellorship, and was following Archbishop William Walsh, who had been at only one meeting in the last six years of his life due to illness. The inevitable result was that the chancellor had become only a figurehead, and de Valera appeared satisfied with this role, 'quite content to play the role of Chairman of the Board, rather than Managing Director'.[59]

If Sinn Féin was going to mount an electoral challenge, it was going to need money. While funds for election work could be sought abroad, de Valera at first thought that it would be better to raise the money for purely organisational work at home.[60] He appealed for financial support, reminding Republicans that 'we must not leave it to our friends abroad. Their generosity has already been overtaxed.'[61] But this attitude didn't last long. He was soon writing to an old San Francisco ally, Father Peter Yorke.

> I hate to admit it, but I am compelled to face the fact that we must for some time longer rely largely upon our friends over there for the means necessary to rebuild our organization and to meet the heavy expenses of contesting election after election.[62]

In May 1925 the de Valera family moved again, to Serpentine Avenue, Sandymount, just around the corner from their previous home in Claremont Road.[63] The house was run down and damp, causing health problems for the children, who also had to adjust to the presence of their father. Eamonn later admitted: 'As a child, I feared my father, and resented his intrusion into our lives . . . I found it hard to accept the stricter discipline he enforced . . .'[64] So did Terry, the youngest, who later recalled being forced by his father to take an unpleasant medicine, and then stomping off up the stairs shouting, 'Dirty fellow, filthy fellow, I wish he would go back to jail again!' De Valera was fond of repeating the story.[65]

Not that there was much time for home life: de Valera was constantly on the move around the country, reorganising Sinn Féin and trying to drum up enthusiasm for the Republican cause. One of his close companions on these trips was the writer Dorothy Macardle, who covered his speeches for anti-Treaty papers. She was, as she admitted, 'zealous to the point of fanaticism' in her devotion to the Republic and to its President.[66] It was Macardle who would fulfil de Valera's ambition of a comprehensive (and sympathetic) account of the revolutionary years, in her mammoth *The Irish Republic*, begun at his request in 1925 and finally finished 11 years later.[67]

De Valera's obsession with the press continued, particularly with the need for a Republican daily paper. 'I fear we shall never be able to make real headway until we have this established.'[68] Robert Brennan was keen on a plan, by an independent group of Republicans, to purchase the defunct *Freeman's Journal*; de Valera worried that a failure to raise the required funds would reflect badly on the movement.[69] The project fizzled out. It would take de Valera's direct and unrelenting involvement to finally get a paper going.

Since his release, he had been beating the anti-partition drum. In a speech in Dundalk in August he claimed that he would never have signed the Treaty 'until the boundary question was settled'[70] – a gross distortion of his position in 1921. In a speech in Carlow he insisted that Republicans 'will never consent to the abandonment of the National sovereignty over a single inch of Irish territory'.[71]

The fall of Ramsay MacDonald's minority Labour government in the autumn of 1924 meant Westminster elections in the North, with Unionists hopeful they could 'considerably… reduce the majority against them'[72] in the two-seat constituency of Fermanagh and Tyrone, where the outgoing MPs were the only Nationalists returned for Northern Ireland constituencies.

However, de Valera decided that Sinn Féin should contest the Westminster election, with two candidates in Fermanagh-Tyrone and six in other constituencies.[73] In response, the Nationalist Party, fearing a split vote, boycotted the elections.[74] De Valera accused them of neglecting an opportunity to register a vote against partition,[75] but, in reality, in a non-PR election Sinn Féin's intervention would ensure a Unionist victory. With many Nationalist voters staying away, the Unionists duly won both seats in Fermanagh-Tyrone, contributing to a clean sweep of Northern Ireland's Westminster seats – and this as the Boundary Commission was at work. As Lady Carson, wife of Sir Edward, noted in her diary: 'Now no one will dare touch these counties'.[76] None of the eight Sinn Féin candidates was in contention for a seat; three of them lost their deposits. It was a reverse for Sinn Féin but a disaster for Northern nationalists.

De Valera, meanwhile, had used the election campaign to get himself imprisoned – eventually. On 24 October 1924 he was arrested by the Royal Ulster Constabulary (successor to the RIC) as he tried to get into Newry Town Hall to address an election meeting. He was served with an exclusion order, which he refused to accept. The following morning, he was put on a train south; he said to the arresting officer, with evident disappointment, that 'he thought it would be internment'. As he boarded the train, he told the officers that he would return.[77] The following night he attempted to address another election meeting, this time at St Columb's Hall in Derry. There was a crowd of 5,000 people inside, and at least as many outside. De Valera, his clothes wet and muddy after being brought to the city cross-country from Co. Donegal, was stopped some distance from the meeting and brought to the RUC barracks before the crowd were any the wiser. When they found out, a cordon of police with fixed bayonets was required to keep them under control.[78]

He was taken to Belfast and sentenced to a month in prison[79] after refusing to recognise the court.[80] Though his arrest didn't help Sinn Féin north of the border, it may well have helped in the Free State, where five by-elections were held on 18–20 November. All five seats had been held by Cumann na nGaedheal, the sitting TDs having died or resigned. Republicans won two of the by-elections, through John Madden in Mayo North and, far more significantly, Seán Lemass in Dublin South. Even more striking, the average Republican vote in the five constituencies was 15.8 percentage points higher than in the general election the previous year.[81] On his release from prison, de Valera told his RUC escort that this result showed that 'Ireland is Republican at heart.'

As they drove from Belfast to the border, de Valera kept up a continuous stream of conversation, assuring the RUC men that he had nothing against them as servants of their government, but complaining that as a (Stormont) MP for South Down, he should have been allowed to address the meeting in Newry. De Valera may have thought he was winning friends and influencing his RUC escort; he was not. 'Without interruption he continued to talk all the way and never seemed to tire . . . he was self-opinionated and domineering.'[82] He probably felt his time behind bars was justified by the election results, though he confessed that of all the prisons he had been in, 'Belfast was the worst, and also it was depressing and disheartening'.[83]

In November 1924 the Executive Council agreed to an amnesty for all acts committed by either side, from the date of the signing of the Treaty to 12 May 1923.[84] Though this might be seen as a conciliatory gesture towards Republicans, it was more likely the only way to protect members of the Free State forces from prosecution. A better indication of the Cosgrave government's attitude was that applicants for civil service entrance examinations were required to give an undertaking that they had not taken part in, or helped, 'the forces in revolt against the Irish Free State government', and they had to promise 'to be faithful to that government and to give no aid or support of any kind to those who are or may in future be engaged in conflict against the authority of that government'.[85] De Valera stated that 'none of our people would sign such a document'.[86] This oath of allegiance was later extended to local government employees.[87] These measures had a serious economic effect on Republicans, many of whom were unable to work in their chosen professions. It also, of course, allowed the Free State government to reward its supporters with jobs.[88] De Valera sourly noted that 'one has to become a national apostate first before one can enter the public service under the new conditions'.[89]

A further electoral test arose in March 1925, in a series of by-elections caused by the resignation of nine former Cumann na nGaedheal TDs, led by Joe McGrath, over the Army Crisis, in which a section of the Free State army issued an ultimatum to the government to suspend demobilisation and the preferential treatment of British ex-officers. While the disarray in the government ranks following the resignations of the TDs was welcome, there was dissension too amongst Republicans over the selection of candidates. Oscar Traynor, former commander of the Dublin Brigade, had been released from prison after signing the Free State undertaking, for which he was court-martialled by the IRA.[90] When Traynor was selected as a Sinn Féin candidate in the by-election in Dublin North, the IRA's adjutant-general, Patrick 'Pa' Murray, complained to Aiken that the Republican government had become subsumed by Sinn Féin.[91]

Instead of heeding this indication of growing mistrust, Aiken doubled down on his relationship with de Valera, agreeing with him that the 'the Government is accepted as controlling authority for the Army'. The offices of chief of staff and Minister for Defence were to be separated, meaning that the head of the IRA would no longer be theoretically in control.[92] Seán Lemass was appointed Minister for Defence in succession to Aiken.[93]

De Valera threw himself energetically into the by-election campaigns, addressing meetings in Cos. Sligo, Roscommon, Mayo, Cavan, Westmeath, Carlow, Kilkenny and Dublin.[94] He also appealed to Seán T. O'Kelly, who was in America to get election contributions.

> Our opponents are throwing all their weight into this election ... If we are to stand up to them our expenses will be exceptionally heavy, and our treasury is practically empty.[95]

De Valera was optimistic. 'Unless there is trickery our chances are good'. So was O'Kelly. 'If we don't win five of the nine I will be desperately disappointed'.[96] Given these expectations, the results were a disaster. The Republicans won only two seats – Traynor in Dublin North and Samuel Holt in Leitrim-Sligo – both of them in constituencies with two vacancies, where the quota was a third of the electorate rather than half. Even worse, the Republican vote was only 9.8 percentage points higher than in 1923, compared with the advance of 15.8 recorded the previous November.[97] The Republican advance was stalling.

De Valera tried to put on a brave face in a letter to O'Kelly as the results were coming in.

> I am not at all disheartened. I have never been one of those who expected miracles, and it would be a miracle if people returned suddenly to their allegiance again ... The very difficulty we experience in getting back to the former position is the best justification for our stubborn resistance to the 'Treaty'.[98]

A month later he was taking a more clear-eyed view, admitting to Joe McGarrity that

> before the elections the cause was gaining ground so rapidly that the Free State was tottering. The elections have given it a stability which promises to last for a considerable time.[99]

And he would later date his conviction that policy had to change to these defeats.

> Since the nine by-elections, I have been convinced that the programme on which we were working would not win the people in the present conditions.[100]

De Valera had demonstrated some ambivalence about abstentionism. At a meeting of Comhairle na dTeachtaí in December 1924 he was asked whether Sinn Féin should enter Leinster House if they won a majority at the next election. He replied that the oath of allegiance to the King 'was a barrier to entering those buildings' – though he stressed it wasn't the sole difficulty. He declined to give a personal view on what they should do.[101] In January, before the by-elections, Sinn Féin's Standing Committee reaffirmed that its candidates were 'pledged against Allegiance to a foreign king'.[102] During the by-election campaign, de Valera angrily rejected a suggestion by Professor Alfred O'Rahilly of University College, Cork, that the oath was 'theologically not an Oath at all'. De Valera told a meeting in Dublin that he regarded it 'as the worst form of blasphemy to take an Oath, not meaning to keep it'.[103] And he told another meeting in Cavan that

> no decent republican would ever enter the present Dáil. No man who stood for the independence of the country, or who had any sense of personal or national self-respect, would take an oath to a foreign king.[104]

That, though, was before the by-election reverses, and views began to change. On 7 May a meeting of the Sinn Féin Standing Committee chaired by de Valera unanimously adopted a resolution proposed by Art O'Connor (a Republican hard-liner) and Gerry Boland. It stated that

> the President may act on the assumption that the question of Republicans entering the Free State 'parliament', if the Oath were removed, is an open question, to be decided on its merits when the question arises on a practical issue.[105]

However, this motion was not made public,[106] and, in any event, at a meeting of Comhairle na dTeachtaí on the 18th, a majority, including de Valera, declared in favour of the principle of abstention.[107] A further subtle hint was given in his oration at the annual parade to Wolfe Tone's grave in Bodenstown, Co. Kildare. While their objective remained unaltered, he told the faithful, the means to be used to reach it was a more open question.[108]

At the beginning of November the Sinn Féin Standing Committee agreed to lay off four members of staff, because of the party's parlous financial situation.[109] At a special meeting four days later, de Valera explained that the Republican government had decided that the best way forward was to dissolve itself and create in its place a council directly representing the main republican organisations: Sinn Féin, the IRA and Comhairle na dTeachtaí itself. The President would be the sole executive officer, and funds from abroad would be channelled through the council (thereby giving de Valera direct control of them).[110]

Although Sinn Féin had agreed to do away with the Republican government, it was in any case repudiated by the IRA soon afterwards. On 14 and 15 November its first Army Convention since the Civil War was held. The socialist Peadar O'Donnell, disillusioned with Sinn Féin's failure to pursue a radical social policy, proposed that the IRA should withdraw its allegiance from the Republican government and resume an independent course. He did not, of course, couch his demand in socialist terms, instead basing it on the failure of the politicians to properly support the military. His motion appeared destined for defeat until Frank Aiken admitted that some in the leadership had discussed a possible end to abstention. The motion was passed, Aiken was replaced as chief of staff, and the IRA returned to being an autonomous organisation.[111]

Meanwhile, the debate on future policy continued within the political side of the movement. From America, MacSwiney urged de Valera and Comhairle na dTeachtaí that 'we can no longer stay as we are'. She wanted a positive economic and social programme spelt out to appeal to voters; but she insisted 'We cannot emphasize too often that we shall never recognise a British-controlled Parliament.'[112]

In a series of articles in *An Phoblacht* (the IRA paper), Seán Lemass was calling for a reappraisal of Sinn Féin's policy.

> There are some who would have us sit by the roadside and debate abstruse points about a de jure this or a de facto that, but the reality we want is away in the distance – and we cannot get there unless we move.[113]

De Valera was also receiving political and theological advice from Monsignor John Hagan of the Irish College in Rome and from Archbishop Daniel Mannix. They suggested that the best way to undermine the Treaty was from within the Free State Dáil and that the oath could be treated as a mere formality.[114] De Valera travelled secretly to Rome with Seán MacBride to hear this advice in person, using a forged British passport.[115] Whether he was convinced by their arguments, as MacBride believed,[116] or whether he was already planning to enter the Dáil,[117] he now had a theological smokescreen should he need it.

The issue came to a head at a meeting of Comhairle na dTeachtaí on 15 November 1925. De Valera pointed out that the IRA's withdrawal of allegiance 'takes away the last shred of authority' from the Republican government. The Cahersiveen cumann had put down a resolution for the Sinn Féin ardfheis invoking the names of Cathal Brugha, Erskine Childers 'and their fellow martyrs' and ruling out entering the 'Free State Parliament' under any circumstances.[118] De Valera did not believe this should be accepted.

> We ought to go out definitely to the country and try to organise the people who don't want that oath but do want stability to organise them to smash the oath and make it clear that Republican representatives . . . would be prepared to participate in that assembly.

He wanted the matter debated, and he would not allow himself to be re-elected president of the party if he was not allowed to give his views. 'I am going to be master of my own soul from the ard-fheis out'.[119]

The ard-fheis had been postponed because de Valera was seriously ill, his doctors being consulted before it was rearranged for 17 November.[120] Held in the Town Hall in Rathmines over three days, it saw lengthy and heated debate. MacSwiney believed that if a vote had been taken on the Cahersiveen resolution there would have been a bitter split.[121] In his address, de Valera flatly denied that TDs would contemplate 'walking into the Free State parliament if the oath were removed tomorrow'. However, he admitted that he had tried to have discussed a different question: whether, if they got the Irish people to 'smash' the oath, they would enter the Dáil following an election. It wasn't enough to want the Republic: 'we must use every honourable means to achieve it'. If the party was going to ban mere discussion of this option, he would resign and 'go into the wilderness'. He concluded by stressing his own personal probity.

> If there is a fear in your minds that a fait accompli might be presented to you, I pledge you my word of honour that I will not have any part of it. But that is quite a different question from telling me that I mustn't think or discuss, or even advocate such views, if I think them good.[122]

A compromise motion postponed a final decision; it agreed that Sinn Féin policy would not be changed, but it allowed discussion of any policy except 'the acceptance of allegiance to a foreign King and the Partition of Ireland'. It added that 'if at any time a change of policy is proposed an ard-fheis must be summoned to deal with the proposal'.[123]

De Valera was happy with the outcome. As he explained to Seán T. O'Kelly,

> entering that Assembly, if the oath be removed, is *not* 'my policy', but I am ready to consider it as a *possible* policy . . . I must insist on keeping the door open.

He still hadn't made up his mind; but a dramatic postscript to this letter indicated that the situation was about to change.

> VERY LATEST! The news boys here are shouting 'Stop Press' announcing MacNeill's resignation from the Boundary Commission. A General Election in the New Year is almost a certainty.[124]

MacNeill's resignation was prompted by a leak of the Boundary Commission's final report to the *Morning Post,* which revealed that the Free State would be awarded far less territory than it expected and that some portions of Co. Donegal would go in the other direction. The Boundary Commission held that 'economic and geographical considerations' trumped the wishes of the inhabitants. Even though de Valera's opposition to the Treaty had not been due to the Boundary Commission, he benefited politically, because many people were under the mistaken impression that it was.[125]

In a series of discussions with the British government, the Free State representatives said the implementation of the Boundary Commission report would lead to their being 'swept out of office', and that no possible alternative government would be prepared to work the Treaty. The only viable course, they argued, was for the border to be left where it was and for the British to give the Free State some financial concessions. De Valera was the cause of this demand. Kevin O'Higgins told the Prime Minister, Stanley Baldwin, that they needed

> something – some life-buoy – when the first great wave of opposition rolled over them. The wiping out of Article 5 [committing the Free State to pay a share of the British national debt] would do this. De Valera was proclaiming that we had tricked the Irish on Article 12 [on partition] and that we would trick them again on Article 5, and that we were out to demand £19,000,000 a year of tribute from Ireland.[126]

A deal was duly struck: the Boundary Commission report would be binned, and the Free State would be relieved of its financial obligations under article 5 of the Treaty. Cosgrave told the British side that their only safeguard was 'de Valera's lack of political foresight', because if he came into the Dáil he could put them in a 'tight corner'.[127]

But was Cosgrave as safe as he assumed? On 1 December, de Valera gave 'an emphatic denial' that the Republican deputies were contemplating entering the Dáil to stop the agreement. 'Such action on our part would be a direct violation of the pledges given by us when we were elected.'[128] But others were not so sure; even the die-hard Austin Stack.

> Could we do it? I mean would there be sufficient opposition to enable us to turn the scale? Oath and all I would be inclined to favour the idea . . . if our going in would defeat the proposal. Would it not be the end of the Free State? And what better issue than Irish territorial integrity?[129]

Stack was undoubtedly right: there would never be a better opportunity to enter the Dáil. De Valera was not convinced, but when he addressed a crowd in O'Connell Street on 6 December he admitted that 'one feels how futile merely verbal protest is'.[130]

De Valera felt that the party was still bound by the decision that only a special ard-fheis could decide the issue, so he proposed that one should be called. For now, though, he declined to support the idea of attending Leinster House – a decision Gerry Boland regarded as a mistake.[131] 'Much as I loved Dev – and to know him closely was to love him – there were times when he could not just make up his mind.'[132] In fairness, it was not clear that the 48 Sinn Féin TDs could have actually defeated the legislation embodying the agreement: the second stage was passed by 71 votes to 20,[133] the committee stage by 56 to 16,[134] and the bill finally passed by 55 to 14.[135] While the committee and final stages would have been defeated if Sinn Féin had voted against, de Valera argued in later life that some of those who opposed the agreement in their absence 'would have been whipped up and induced to vote for it had we entered'.[136]

On 6 January 1926, de Valera addressed a meeting at the Town Hall in Rathmines. Having condemned the oath once again, he stated that he 'would be satisfied to go into any assembly of representatives of the Irish people and work there if there were no formulae of that kind'.[137] While this was a significant public exposition of the policy he had been pushing in private, some journalists missed the significance – there is no mention of this aspect of his address in the *Irish Times*, for instance. The message was heard loud and clear by the *Irish Independent*, which provided the headline: 'Would go in without the Oath: Mr de Valera on the Dáil.'[138]

De Valera's sentiment was repeated in a press statement announcing an extraordinary ard-fheis to debate the issue. De Valera stressed there was no question of immediate entry. 'The oath of allegiance to a foreign power is now, as it has always been, a barrier which no one may cross and remain a representative of, or even a member of, the Sinn Féin Organisation.' The only issue was whether Sinn Féin should agree to enter if that barrier was removed.[139] In private correspondence, de Valera was optimistic. 'I am hopeful that the common sense of the Organisation will assert itself and distinguish between what is mere policy, and what is principle.'[140] He complained that there was 'a good deal of canvassing going on in the Clubs against my proposal',[141] but he still seemed to believe he could win; more importantly, he still seemed to *want* to win, despite some later claims to the contrary.

Meanwhile, two by-elections were pending, in Laois-Offaly and Dublin County. Although the Standing Committee was keen to contest both, the organisation in Dublin County refused, because of outstanding debts and divisions over a possible candidate.[142] Laois-Offaly was a different matter. The vacancy there was caused by the disqualification of the Republican TD John McGuinness (imprisoned for assaulting a garda), and the party had secured 27 per cent of the vote and two seats out of five in 1923. De Valera spent more than a week in the constituency, 'working like a Trojan' for the candidate, Art O'Connor. It was to no avail – O'Connor lost by slightly more than 800 votes.[143]

The special ard-fheis of Sinn Féin convened in Rathmines on 9 March. The nub of de Valera's lengthy motion was in its first line, which declared that, once the admission oaths of the Free State and Northern Ireland assemblies were removed, 'it becomes a question not of principle but of policy whether or not Republican representatives should attend these assemblies'. There were a number of opposing resolutions, the most important being that of Fr O'Flanagan, that it was

> incompatible with the fundamental principles of Sinn Féin, as it is injurious to the honour of Ireland, to send representatives into any usurping legislature set up by English law in Ireland.[144]

During the debate a number of delegates who had been mandated to vote for O'Flanagan's motion were swayed and wished to switch sides. Gerry Boland, who was one of the tellers on de Valera's side, claimed he persuaded them not to, apparently on his own initiative.

> I personally hoped we would lose the majority and let Miss MacSwiney, Sceilg and others keep the moribund organisation, assets and all, and let us make a fresh start.[145]

O'Flanagan's resolution was passed as an amendment to de Valera's by 223 votes to 218; however, when put as a substantive motion, the amended resolution was narrowly defeated, 179 to 177.[146]

The party was therefore very evenly divided: while it had not accepted de Valera's policy, neither had it endorsed O'Flanagan's. However, de Valera chose to interpret the result as a definite indication 'that my policy would not be accepted by the organisation'. In a relatively brief speech the next day, he explained that the people of Ireland would not be won back by their attitude, that the 'Free State junta is solidifying itself as an institution', and that he would not be serving the cause by remaining in an ambiguous position.

> I am now from this moment a free man . . . I therefore formally tender my resignation as President of the Sinn Féin Organisation.

He concluded with the advice that 'if you do break into two groups . . . try to arrange for co-operation'.[147]

He was speaking like a man who was leaving politics. However, when he expressed that intention to Seán Lemass on their way out of the ard-fheis, Lemass immediately remonstrated with him and persuaded him that they must start a new party to implement the policy he had just stated. 'I could not but agree with his logic . . .'[148] It is highly unlikely that de Valera needed much persuasion, but the widely propagated story further burnished his image as a reluctant politician. It is more likely that de Valera was suffering from indecision, rather than sincerely contemplating retirement; not for the last time, his lieutenants forced the pace.

The day after his resignation de Valera made it abundantly clear in a flood of messages to supporters, particularly in America, that he was not done with politics. He cabled to the *Boston Post* that

> this step the necessary prelude to uniting the nation in new advance to secure complete independence. Economic needs of the people urgently pressing and must have attention.

Another telegram, sent via the International News Service, clarified that he had not left Sinn Féin and that he intended to continue asserting the right of the Irish people to complete freedom. He told the Associated Press that his resignation was necessary to allow him to express his views. 'It does not imply any change in my attitude on fundamentals, or any break with Republicanism'.[149] He can't seriously have contemplated pursuing his new policy within Sinn Féin; these statements were probably aimed at avoiding a denunciation from America before he had a chance to explain his position.

A letter to Joe McGarrity on 13 March talked of a new electoral departure, which implied a new political organisation.

> It is vital that the Free State be shaken at the *next* general election, for if an opportunity be given it to consolidate itself further as an institution – if the present Free State members are replaced by Farmers and Labourers and other class interests, the national interest as a whole will be submerged in the clashing of the rival economic groups. It seems to me a case of now or never – at least in our time.

The Sinn Féin programme was too 'high and too sweeping' to win the people; but smashing the oath

> is a definite objective within reasonable striking distance. If I can mass the people to smash it, I shall have put them *on the march* again, and once moving, and having tasted victory, further advances will be possible.[150]

Certainly, some of his supporters were under the impression from the beginning that a new organisation was to be formed, and they welcomed the 'separating of the sheep from the goats' involved in leaving Sinn Féin.[151] Lemass was dismissive of the 'galaxy of cranks' surrounding Sinn Féin and not unhappy at leaving them behind.[152] But de Valera was intent on feeling his way carefully, writing to a number of sympathetic priests and stressing that he was 'prepared to go to the country with these proposals, and would like to know how Republicans in your district feel about them'.[153]

Sinn Féin would, therefore, split. But what about Comhairle na dTeachtaí? A total of 46 members attended a meeting on 28 March to debate a motion proposed by MacSwiney stating that

> the entry of any member of Dáil Éireann into the 'Free State' Parliament or any other Parliament established by English law is incompatible with membership of the de jure Government of the

Republic and inconsistent with the principles and policy advocated by
Republican Teachtaí and candidates since 1922.[154]

The motion was carried by 25 votes to 15, but de Valera declined to
accept this as a definite vote against his policy. MacSwiney therefore
proposed a second motion, stating that 'this assembly does not approve of
the policy as outlined by the President'.[155] She pointed out that if de
Valera and his followers went into the Dáil in a minority, they couldn't get
the oath removed; if they were in a majority, they would not need to go in.
De Valera claimed that, had he not been arrested in Ennis in 1923, he
would have said he was willing to enter the Free State Dáil. MacSwiney's
motion disapproving of the President's policy was carried by 19 votes to
18, and he therefore resigned.[156]

De Valera's supporters – who had already been meeting in secret to
plan the new party[157] – now resigned from the Sinn Féin Standing
Committee and prepared to come into the open.[158] Following de Valera
were 17 of the 37 members of the Standing Committee, and 21 of the 47
Sinn Féin TDs, with others, including Oscar Traynor, joining him later.[159]

De Valera confirmed to the *Irish Independent* on 12 April 1926 that he
was forming a new organisation. A committee had been formed – chaired
by P. J. Ruttledge, with Seán Lemass and Gerry Boland as secretaries, and
Dr James Ryan and Seán MacEntee as treasurers – and they intended to
see if the people could be brought together to pursue the ideal of 'an
Ireland united, free and Irish'.[160]

The following day de Valera and Kathleen O'Connell started work in a
new office at 33 Lower O'Connell Street. It was a spartan beginning, de
Valera noting 'no furniture, no light, no money'. The first meeting of the
organising committee was held by candlelight, and there wasn't even a
table until one was brought over from Suffolk Street on the Friday. But
more important was the 'great enthusiasm and energy displayed by all'.[161]

On 14 April a statement confirmed the name of the new organisation
– Fianna Fáil (the Republican Party) – and made an explicit pitch for a
wider membership than Sinn Féin had attracted. 'There is a place in the
new Organisation for all who, with Pádraig Pearse, believe in one Irish
nation and that free.'[162] In an interview with the United Press, de Valera
stated five aims for his new party.

1. Securing the political independence of a united Ireland as a Republic.
2. The restoration of the Irish language, and the development of a
native Irish culture.

3. The development of a social system in which, as far as possible, equal opportunity will be afforded to every Irish citizen to live a noble and useful Christian life.

4. The distribution of the land of Ireland so as to get the greatest number possible of Irish families rooted in the soil of Ireland.

5. The making of Ireland an economic unit, as self-contained and self-sufficient as possible – with a proper balance between agriculture and the other essential industries.[163]

De Valera was firmly convinced that his new party was of the left. 'We might be regarded as a labour party as we were also trying to improve social conditions'.[164] But, naturally, attention was on the new party's attitude to constitutional issues. Despite leaving Sinn Féin in order to allow more flexibility, de Valera continued giving hostages to fortune on the subject of the oath, telling a meeting in Galway in June that 'to accept the Oath now would be as bad as accepting it four or five years ago', and saying in Cork in October that 'to accept it honestly was to accept England as a master and to accept it dishonestly made one a perjurer'.[165] Such commitments would turn out to be most unwise, but they do counter the claim that he had already decided to take the oath.

The name 'Fianna Fáil' means 'Warrior bands of Ireland' (or, in a popular but erroneous version, 'Soldiers of destiny'). It had been suggested by Father Peadar Ua Laoghaire as a more poetic alternative to 'Óglaigh na hÉireann' as the Irish translation of 'Irish Volunteers', and the initials *FF* were incorporated in the cap badge of the Volunteers.[166] De Valera felt the name would link his new party to the Irish Volunteers. He was also attracted by the fact that it was nearly impossible to translate, telling a journalist many years later, with a smile, that 'there was some advantage in that also'. Lemass wanted the new organisation to be called simply the 'Republican Party' to make its aims crystal clear. The compromise was to use de Valera's choice, with Lemass's in parentheses.[167] The name also appears, of course, in the Irish version of the National Anthem, 'Amhrán na bhFiann', and Richard Mulcahy sourly accused him of 'dipping his dirty fingers' in the Anthem.[168]

Fianna Fáil was from the start regarded by its followers as a movement rather than a party, representing a tradition that went back much further than its own establishment. One supporter claimed that his family had been Fianna Fáil 'since the Rising'. Asked if he meant 1916, he indignantly replied that he was referring to 1798.[169] Several generations later, a prominent minister claimed (only half in jest) that

Fionn Mac Cumhaill definitely was a member of a Fianna Fáil cumann, and Brian Boru, he would have been chairman of the Comhairle Dáil Ceanntair. All great people were always Fianna Fáil, even though the party wasn't founded until 1926![170]

Central to this was de Valera, who was seen by many as the embodiment of the independence struggle, and who consciously created an aura of dignified but somewhat exotic glamour about himself. This was lampooned as his ability to win elections 'by putting on a big black cloak, appearing on platforms at twilight illuminated by blazing sods of turf, and casting spells on people in bad Irish'.[171] While his lieutenants did much of the work in building up the party organisation and had an important input into policy (particularly on economic matters, which did not greatly interest 'the Chief'),[172] there was never any doubt about who was in charge. In his time on the National Executive, Todd Andrews found that 'for all practical purposes Dev *was* the executive because his rulings were never questioned'.[173]

Those who did question him had been left behind. Mary MacSwiney claimed that the whole episode had been

> a tremendous lesson to the country that de Valera, in spite of his great personality and the love we all have for him, was not able to gain the majority for this compromise . . .[174]

Still, she was disappointed that he had decided to actively pursue his new policy:

> We are feeling sore that de Valera has split our forces on a mere hypothesis, and that he and his followers are taking a course, to our minds, incompatible with practical allegiance to the existing Republic . . . I hope and believe that Dev will not send people out to America to preach his policy or to collect for it . . .[175]

She was to be disappointed.

De Valera and MacSwiney had always had a difficult relationship, with frequent disagreements, and the parting of the ways was perhaps inevitable. De Valera's attitude towards her was frequently one of bare toleration. But despite their differences MacSwiney was concerned about de Valera's financial situation: 'those of us, who felt bound to insist on his resignation for the sake of the Republic as we see it, are worried over the undeserved trouble that may fall on him on this account . . .'[176] It is striking that, just as after his previous resignation, in January 1922, his bitter political opponents worried about his personal circumstances; he evidently retained a hold on their sympathies. However, as with Cosgrave four years before, this sympathy would soon dissipate.

The new organisation was busily cannibalising the old. Dáithí Ó Donnchadha, Sinn Féin's honorary secretary, forecast that Sinn Féin would retain only half its membership – at most. He cuttingly observed that their opponents were 'most active. It is surprising that they were not able to show any energy or activity during the past year or two.' Sinn Féin's own records had evidently been copied, because direct contact was being made with cumainn and comhairlí ceanntair (branches and constituency organisations). 'I feel very much tempted to give the ex-President my opinion about the conduct of his supporters. They are deliberately trying to smash our Organisation.'[177]

Eventually, Sinn Féin accepted that co-operation was impossible and called on all TDs who accepted the new policy to resign their seats.[178] This set the scene for a fractious meeting of Comhairle na dTeachtaí on 22 and 23 May, at which the formal election of de Valera's replacement as President of the Republic was discussed. In an apparent effort to prevent Art O'Connor's being elected to this important symbolic office, de Valera came up with the stratagem of denying that he had been President of the Republic since his resignation in January 1922. Given that he had been issuing statements using that title, including the ceasefire order of 1923, his claim left deputies dumbfounded. The Cork TD David Kent angrily pointed out all the times the title had been used in the previous four years, particularly in the business of the Second Dáil. 'Are we now going to be told that all the time we were wrong in calling it Dáil Éireann, and that Mr de Valera was not President of the Republic at all?' De Valera's reply was breathtaking.

I was not President of the Republic from the time I resigned that position when the Treaty was passed . . . I was elected Head of the Emergency Government and I have always maintained that position as such . . . I would not have accepted the position as President of the Republic . . .

However, he was prepared to support Art O'Connor's appointment as 'Chief Executive', so long as Fianna Fáil was given some role in running the Comhairle. His opponents would accept a coalition arrangement if

Fianna Fáil guaranteed not to enter the Dáil. De Valera rejected these terms, and O'Connor was duly elected 'President of the Republic'.[179]

MacSwiney was disgusted by the debate:

> Listening to the arguments and the sneers of some people there one was back in the thick of the Treaty debate. It was horrible . . . Even Dev was as nasty as he could be. He has given me some surprises in these past months I can tell you . . .[180]

Despite his defeat, and despite the bitter rhetoric, de Valera did not yet sever his connections with Comhairle na dTeachtaí. The reason appears to have been money. He had already raised the issue of the American funds, asking if they were 'going to be distributed to Sinn Féin and the Army and was his organisation going to be cut off?'[181] He would remain in Comhairle na dTeachtaí until that question was resolved.

Meanwhile, the IRA had made it clear that it would not be backing Fianna Fáil,[182] though Frank Aiken appealed to IRA members to support it. 'People who desire to see our cause succeed should, in my opinion, support both the Irish Republican Army and the Fianna Fáil organisation.'[183] And the IRA was to prove crucial to the success of Fianna Fáil, which depended far more on the military side of the Republican movement than it did on Sinn Féin.

The tactic adopted by Fianna Fáil organisers was to identify one significant person in each parish – normally the leading IRA officer – and win them over, in the hope that they would persuade others to follow.[184] In some cases, former IRA companies converted *en masse* to become cumainn of Fianna Fáil; many of these IRA members had not been involved in politics at all[185] – despite de Valera's previous appeals for them to join Sinn Féin. Gerry Boland spent many hours convincing Oscar Traynor to come over to the new party, and he had to go to Co. Cork at least three times before Seán Moylan succumbed to his persuasion. Boland's great disappointment was his failure to win over Austin Stack (though he believed he would have succeeded eventually if Stack had not died in 1929).[186] Second-hand cars were purchased to speed the organisational effort,[187] and for the next five years 'hardly any of us were at home for a single night or any week-end . . . We toured every parish in the country founding Fianna Fáil branches'.[188]

While the work of de Valera's lieutenants was crucial, so too was the power of his personality and reputation. Frank Barrett, former commanding officer of the 1st Western Division, speculated on the new party's chances if de Valera were not at its head.

If Ruttledge initiated this matter, and Dev opposed it, what would be its chances? Or even if Dev remained neutral, what would be the hopes of the new departure?

But given that de Valera *was* at the head of Fianna Fáil, Barrett thought he was entitled

to a fair chance on his new scheme, so long as he can guarantee that there is no danger in it to Republicanism. He feels he can guarantee this, but personally I have fears . . .[189]

The new party was not going to be based only on those who fought against the Treaty in the Civil War; de Valera was well aware that this would not be enough. He confidently told a correspondent in America that Fianna Fáil was winning the support of 'at least nine-tenths of the Republican rank and file', but the party also had

those who were 'neutral' since 1923, because they did not believe in armed conflict between Irishmen, and also those who took the 'Treaty' as a stepping-stone – but realise now that none of the official Treaty party will ever step beyond the present position . . . Altogether these three should be a majority of the electorate . . .[190]

The party was a welcoming place for women – at least initially. The first executive included Constance Markievicz, Margaret Pearse, Kathleen Clarke, Dorothy Macardle, Linda Kearns and Hanna Sheehy-Skeffington.[191]

De Valera gave an outline of his programme in a speech at the La Scala cinema in Prince's Street, off O'Connell Street, on 16 May, in 'an atmosphere of delirious enthusiasm'.[192] He was, as usual, dressed 'in a dead black suit, but his sombre clothes did nothing to conceal the fierce light of his leadership'.[193] He asserted that he remained a Republican – but wanted to save Republicanism from 'empty formalism' and restore it to its former strength. Presumably in an attempt to appeal to IRA members, he used strikingly military language, comparing himself to a commander who must judge the situation and plan wisely, just like 'the boys who rescued Jack Keogh the other day' (a reference to the rescue by the IRA of a prominent Volunteer from Dundrum mental hospital).[194] It was, he said, the duty of Republicans to attack the oath 'as being the most vital and at the same time the part most easily destroyed of the entire entrenchments of the foreign enemy.' Once there was 'a united sovereign 26 Counties', they could turn their attention to the North.

> We shall at all times be morally free to use any means that God gives us to reunite the country and win back the part of our Ulster province that has been taken away from us.

He stressed that freedom was not an end in itself, but must be used to improve the condition of the people, and he invoked the name of James Connolly, an appropriation that should have worried the Labour Party. Explaining that he did not have time to go into every aspect of the Fianna Fáil programme, and that he had kept them longer than he intended (a situation party members would get used to in the coming years), he concluded, 'I wish to face boldly the facts of the present situation, because I know that it is only by facing them that we can hope to overcome them.'[195]

Fianna Fáil's first ard-fheis was held at the Rotunda in Dublin on 24 and 25 November. There were by then 435 cumainn registered, and the party had an income of £1,231 and an expenditure of £1,224 in its first six months.[196] In his opening address, de Valera defended the use of force if necessary.

> If the road of peaceful progress and natural evolution be barred, then the road of revolution will beckon, and will be taken.

But that threat could be avoided by 'the opening of the road to free constitutional action'.[197] Responding to the debates in his closing speech, de Valera stressed the need for loyalty in the new party. 'We must have, in the first place, absolute loyalty to our cause, and, next to that, loyalty to one another.'[198] Not to mention, of course, loyalty to himself.

However, loyalty was not top of the agenda for one Republican TD. On 20 January 1927, de Valera's diary records an appointment with Dan Breen, who didn't turn up.[199] Breen had decided that

> it was pure waste of time and energy to sit outside [the Dáil], do nothing and make bellicose speeches and the best of our youth leaving the country. I thought it was time to go in and take part in whatever was there.[200]

Breen duly took his seat on 25 January, his arrival in the Dáil being hailed by the *Irish Times* as 'the first breach in the ranks of the abstentionists'.[201] Breen later recalled that he never saw an Oath. There was an Oath somewhere but no one asked me about it. I just signed a book. I never read any formula.[202]

In response to his action, de Valera nailed his colours ever more firmly to the mast.

If there are any people who think that I, or any of those associated with me will be brought to take the oath, they are deceiving themselves. Neither I, nor any member of Fianna Fáil will ever take that oath. That is final, and I hope it is clear.[203]

Breen's subsequent electoral history certainly wouldn't have encouraged de Valera to follow his example: in the June election he lost his seat in Tipperary, winning just 1,480 votes, or 2.5 per cent of the first preferences, compared with the 16.5 per cent he had received in 1923.

Meanwhile, there were developments in de Valera's relationship with his former comrades in Sinn Féin. At a meeting of Comhairle na dTeachtaí on 18 December 1926, the two opposing parties agreed to co-operate in the Republican bond case to be heard in New York, where they were challenging the Free State government for control of the funds that had not been sent back to Ireland after the bond drive. The Republican members of the Second Dáil could claim, however tenuously, to be the body to which the money was due; and de Valera was the original trustee. It was decided that de Valera would represent the Second Dáil, and he told his erstwhile colleagues, 'I will safeguard the Republican position'.[204] This was a far more nuanced commitment than the members of the Second Dáil seemed to realise at the time. After all, de Valera was firmly convinced that the success of Fianna Fáil would 'safeguard the Republican position'.

This became evident as soon as he landed in New York in March 1927, where he took up residence once again in the Waldorf-Astoria Hotel,[205] and announced that he would be raising election funds for Fianna Fáil. He spent a fortnight attending the court case, before reprising the great days of 1919/20, travelling to the major centres of the Irish diaspora – Chicago, Seattle, Portland, San Francisco, St Louis and Boston, even managing to fit in another trip to the Grand Canyon.[206] The Free State minister to Washington, Timothy Smiddy, reported that he might raise as much as $100,000, 'mainly from the servant class' as he had few wealthy backers.[207]

The court case was decided on 11 May, the day after de Valera arrived back in Ireland. The judge directed that the money be returned to the original bond-holders. De Valera immediately called on them to transfer their cash to Fianna Fáil. Sinn Féin, the Second Dáil and Comhairle na dTeachtaí didn't get a mention.[208]

This trip was significant for another reason: although de Valera had a fake British passport,[209] he now applied for and received an Irish Free State passport on which to travel.[210] Such passports were issued to 'Citizens of the Irish Free State and of the British Commonwealth of Nations' – a description that did not satisfy the British government, as it didn't include the phrase 'British subject'.[211] But it went considerably further than de Valera would have liked. In some eyes, this application, not his later entry into the Dáil, represented his first recognition of the Irish Free State.[212]

The developing political fortunes of Fianna Fáil and Sinn Féin were demonstrated in their changing attitudes to a possible electoral pact. In his ard-fheis speech in November 1926, de Valera regretted that Sinn Féin had decided against a pact, but he expressed the hope that their voters would support each other.[213] Now Mary MacSwiney tried to interest him in a formal arrangement, but she was rebuffed. While she believed that the two parties could between them win a majority, she wouldn't enter a pact unless Fianna Fáil clarified that it would not enter an oath-bound Dáil while it was in a minority.[214] This was the same argument she had been making for more than a year, and de Valera was clearly in no mood to humour her.

> What you call the 'minority' position of FF is an essential part of the whole programme, and to give it up would be to cripple the policy as a whole . . . I feel that we can only agree to differ.[215]

The IRA also made proposals for co-operation between Republicans, but they too were rejected by de Valera.[216] He issued a statement advising all members of Fianna Fáil to give their next preference to other Republican candidates,[217] but there would be no formal co-operation. Soon enough there would be no need for it in any case.

The Fianna Fáil organisation had been put on an election footing from the start of 1927.

> There must be no slackening of activity. The canvass of voters, the holding of meetings, the distribution of literature must be continued without interruption . . . A Cumann which is not already working at full pressure is of little use to the movement.[218]

Candidates were instructed to concentrate on the 'economic aspects' of the campaign and to call for the combination of all parties in an effort to unseat the government, using the slogan 'Sack the lot'.[219]

As de Valera noted, Fianna Fáil was putting forward enough candidates 'to be a majority over all other parties if elected and to form a Government pledged to the programme decided upon by the organisation'.[220] The party had 86 candidates – a sign of ambition and confidence; by contrast, Sinn Féin was only able to field 15.[221] Each of the Fianna Fáil candidates was required to sign a pledge to support the party 'in every action it takes to secure the Independence of a United Ireland under a Republican form of government'; in accordance with its constitution, they were not to 'take any position involving an oath to a foreign power'. The candidates also agreed to surrender their seat if called upon to do so by a two-thirds majority of the National Executive.[222]

The reference to the oath was reinforced in de Valera's election address. 'Fianna Fáil candidates . . . will not of course take an oath of allegiance to the English King or to any dictated constitution'.[223] However, some confusion might have been caused by a front-page ad in the *Irish Independent* a week before polling day, headed 'Fianna Fáil is going in. The next Government will be a Fianna Fáil Government.' The only mention of the oath was a claim that Fianna Fáil was the only party that would provide stable government, 'because it will not shut any party out of the National Assembly'.[224] If there was confusion about the party's intentions, its own advertising was partly to blame.

At its first outing Fianna Fáil won 44 seats, with 26.1 per cent of the first-preference vote; Sinn Féin took only 5 seats, with 3.6 per cent. One of the defeated Sinn Féin candidates was Mary MacSwiney, who had no doubt who to blame. 'What the Free Staters were not able to do in 1922 or 1923 . . . has been accomplished by Fianna Fáil in Cork city.'[225] The Fianna Fáil result very closely mirrored that of Sinn Féin in 1923, and it was frequently with the same personnel, though Fianna Fáil did manage to win seats in constituencies that had no Republican representative four years before, in Kildare, Meath and Wicklow. In Clare, de Valera once again pulled in a huge vote, though it was significantly down on 1923. He received 13,029 votes (33.8 per cent of the first-preference vote). He again dragged in a running-mate, and the other seats again went to Cumann na nGaedheal, Labour and Farmers.

Although Sinn Féin had been neatly supplanted by Fianna Fáil, de Valera was keen to point out that the combined Republican total in seats and votes was greater than that of Cumann na nGaedheal, which won 47 seats (a loss of 16), with 27.5 per cent of the vote. Even without Fianna Fáil and Sinn Féin in Leinster House, Cosgrave was in a parliamentary minority and would require support from smaller parties or independents. Labour took a very healthy 22 seats, with 13.8 per cent of the vote; Farmers took 11 seats, the new National League Party, led by Captain William Redmond, had 8, and there were 16 independents. As John Hagan observed in a letter to de Valera, Fianna Fáil had not won as many seats as might have been hoped; but, while 'it may not have been a positive victory for you . . . it is a positive defeat for the enemy'.[226] De Valera himself was similarly restrained.

> A good foundation has been laid, and the future is surely with us. The immediate task, however, of smashing down the oath barrier will be by no means easy . . .

He was buoyed by the news that the independent Republican TD for Cork North, Daniel Corkery, decided to join Fianna Fáil, giving the party a total of 45 seats.[227]

De Valera later claimed that the election campaign had convinced him that 'the Fianna Fail policy which involved abstention so long as the oath was demanded would be unlikely to secure a majority vote of the people in its favour'.[228] This chimes with the suspicions of the doctrinaire Republicans that he had been planning to enter the Dáil all along, oath or no oath. However, it seems like *post facto* rationalisation. At the time, he firmly stated, 'I want it to be known definitely and finally that under no circumstances whatever will Fianna Fáil deputies take any such oath.'[229] He would hardly have been so downright if he was planning to reverse course in the near future.

Before the first meeting of the fifth Dáil on 23 June 1927, de Valera announced that the Fianna Fáil deputies intended to claim their seats without 'submitting to any oath of allegiance to any foreign power'. If they were excluded by force, 'it will be at the instance of a party whose strength is less than one-third of the whole elected body'.[230] He was armed with legal advice that there was no authority under the Treaty, the Free State Constitution or the Dáil's standing orders to exclude any member of the Dáil before the Ceann Comhairle was elected, and that any member could be proposed and elected as Ceann Comhairle without taking an oath of any kind.[231]

De Valera led his colleagues into Leinster House on 23 June, where they were met by Colonel Paddy Brennan, the superintendent. Brennan asked de Valera to identify his TDs so that they would not be forced to produce identification, then they were shepherded into a committee room.[232] The Clerk of the Dáil, Colm Ó Murchadha, asked them to sign the book, signifying acceptance of the oath, which they refused to do. Newspaper reports claimed that de Valera and a number of others attempted to push their way past a line of gardaí to gain entry to the chamber but were prevented.[233] But, according to Brennan, it was all rather more restrained. By his account de Valera agreed that nothing further could be done and did not attempt to enter the chamber, and the Fianna Fáil TDs 'all walked out peaceable'.[234] Whichever version is correct, it is certainly a fact that the door to the chamber was locked on Brennan's orders and that there was a cordon of gardaí positioned in front of the Fianna Fáil TDs.[235]

In any event, de Valera had got what he wanted: a great deal of publicity. He and his 44 colleagues returned to their head office in Abbey Street, where de Valera told a waiting crowd that 'the platform that had been denied them that day would be found at every crossroads in the country'.[236] A statement in the name of all the TDs asserted that they had been 'wrongfully debarred from taking their seats because they refused to take an Oath to a foreign King'. They repeated their election pledge 'that under no circumstances whatever will they subscribe to any such oath'.[237] De Valera advised supporters in America that he planned a legal challenge to their exclusion; he added that it was 'too much to hope for success there, but there is a possibility, for undoubtedly the action was illegal'.[238]

The party had another shot in its locker: an attempt to gather the 75,000 signatures required to trigger a referendum on the issue.[239] Though de Valera expected the Free State to try to block this, he believed that his side would win a referendum if one was held.[240] A petition calling for the deletion of article 17 of the Constitution, which contained the oath, was duly published in the newspapers of 2 July.[241] Because 350,000 people had voted for Fianna Fáil in the general election, Lemass and Boland suggested that 500,000 signatures 'is not too much to expect'.[242] As it turned out, it was, but all seemed set for a legal and constitutional battle outside the gates of Leinster House, which might yet see Fianna Fáil TDs able to enter the Dáil without taking an oath. And then, a week later, Kevin O'Higgins walked to Mass.

CHAPTER 18

EMPTY FORMULA

I am not going to take an oath. I am prepared to put my name down in this book in order to get permission to go into the Dáil, but it has no other significance.

Éamon de Valera, 11 August 1927[1]

I grant that what we did was contrary . . . to everything we stood for . . . It was a step painful and humiliating for us . . .

Éamon de Valera, 21 August 1927[2]

I hold it is the primary duty of a modern state to ensure that every man who is able and willing to work will have work . . .

Éamon de Valera, 22 August 1927[3]

On the morning of Sunday 10 July 1927, Kevin O'Higgins, the vice-president of the Executive Council, who had just returned from a League of Nations meeting in Geneva, left his house in Booterstown Avenue to walk to Mass. He was both Minister for Justice and Minister for External Affairs. Widely regarded as the strongman of the government, he was detested by Republicans – including de Valera. Having sent his garda detective on an errand, O'Higgins was alone when he was shot by a group of IRA men at the junction of Cross Avenue. Mortally wounded, he was carried back to his house, where he lay dying for some hours, forgiving his attackers – but not de Valera. 'Tell my colleagues that they must be wary of him in public life; he will play down to the weaknesses of the people.'[4]

De Valera was in his constituency in Co. Clare on the day of the assassination. The following day he issued a forthright statement describing it as 'murder' and 'inexcusable from any standpoint . . . It is a crime that cuts at the root of representative Government'.[5] However, Fianna Fáil's commitment to peaceful means was conditional. On the same day, Seán T. O'Kelly, de Valera's second in command, explained to a supporter in America that it was 'out of the question' to consider using force – because public opinion was against it.

> When opportunity offers for any other means to be adopted which have within them the seeds of earlier and better success for the restoration of the Republic which it stands for, those who are responsible for Fianna Fáil will not hesitate to use them.[6]

This may have been an attempt to keep militant Republicans on side; or it may have reflected an ambivalence within Fianna Fáil about extra-constitutional methods.

Another major figure passed from the scene on 15 July with the death of Constance Markievicz. At her funeral two days later, gravediggers refused to bury her as it was contrary to union rules to do so on a Sunday – an ironic end to a career devoted to workers' rights. Her coffin was deposited in a vault until the following day; de Valera delivered his oration anyway, expressing the hope that everything Markievicz had 'longed and worked for may one day be achieved'.[7]

The day after the funeral Fianna Fáil TDs met in the party's head office in Abbey Street. Rumours were flying about that some of them wanted to take the oath and enter the Dáil; but when de Valera asked if any were prepared to do so, no-one replied. One Fianna Fáil TD, Patrick Belton, said he had no moral qualms about taking the oath but would keep his pledge not to do so. But he qualified this statement: if the party's strategy did not succeed (the phrase 'in three or four years' was recorded in the minutes but later crossed out) he would have to review his position.[8]

Making Fianna Fáil review its position was exactly what Cosgrave had in mind. There were two facets to the government's response to O'Higgins's murder: legal and political. On the legal front, it brought forward tough new public order legislation, suspending *habeas corpus*, establishing non-jury courts and reintroducing internment. Though seen as draconian, only four people had been arrested under its terms by the following May, nobody was then detained under it, and nobody had been convicted under it for any offence.[9]

Of more lasting significance was the political aspect. The Executive Council decided 'to make a sworn declaration of intention to comply with Article 17 [the section of the Constitution requiring the oath] . . . a condition precedent to valid nomination for all future elections.'[10] This measure was due to come into effect on 1 February 1928.[11]

This 'oath to take the oath' was lampooned by Fianna Fáil as a 'farce' and 'absurd'. But the party recognised that this measure – along with plans to do away with the popular initiative and referendum,[12] which was the route the party had chosen for removing the oath – would be 'a sentence of political outlawry on Republicanism'.[13] Lemass and Boland wrote to each cumann warning them that the government was trying 'to drive us back to the use of physical force in a manner in which we would be certain of defeat'. They urged members to collect signatures for the attempt to abolish the oath by referendum, setting a one-month deadline.[14]

Cosgrave's move gave de Valera a stark choice: take the oath, or face political extinction.[15] Republican critics assumed de Valera had been planning to enter the Dáil for months if not years; his inability to later admit that he had changed his mind tended to reinforce this interpretation. His own account implies an immediate realisation that Fianna Fáil would have to take the oath,[16] and his official biographers portrayed his manoeuvres in these weeks as efforts to bring his party aong with him.[17] In fact, they were due to dithering as he was torn between the competing factions within Fianna Fáil before finally making a distasteful decision.

The first in Fianna Fáil to act on the iron logic created by the government's initiative was Patrick Belton. A 1916 veteran and a business-man, he was formerly an independent TD and in later years became a Cumann na nGaedheal and Fine Gael TD, before establishing his own anti-communist and anti-Semitic group, the Irish Christian Front, in 1937.[18] He was not, to put it mildly, a team player. Following Cosgrave's initiative in 1927 he wrote to the papers announcing that he was entering the Dáil to fight the new legislation. 'I will not stand idly by while the country is being plunged into chaos and bloodshed without at least casting a vote against such insane proposals.'[19]

With speculation rife that as many as 30 other Fianna Fáil TDs might follow him,[20] de Valera expelled Belton from the party – and further painted himself into a corner. Fianna Fáil TDs had been elected on the understanding that they would not take the oath, and had reiterated that pledge after their unsuccessful attempt to enter the Dáil in June. In a statement following Belton's expulsion, the party said that

the fact that the Free State now propose to block up every avenue by which the oath could be removed by political action will not alter the attitude of Republicans towards the taking of that oath.[21]

This seemed conclusive – so much so that Robert Brennan, who had planned to propose at a meeting of the National Executive that the TDs should take their seats, accepted that 'of course the Chief's statement was final'. De Valera again assured the National Executive that 'definitely he would *never take it*'.[22] If he was planning to take the oath, he was going about it in a very odd way.

Despite his firm stance, he was also talking to the Labour Party and had promised that, if a new coalition government was formed that got rid of the oath, Fianna Fáil 'will not press any issues involving the Treaty to the point of overthrowing such Government during the normal lifetime of the present Assembly'.[23] This was unanimously approved by the parliamentary party. But what did it mean? On the face of it, it referred to a situation in which Fianna Fáil entered the Dáil *after* the oath was removed. But the reality was that, without their votes, there was no way the Dáil would vote to scrap it. De Valera remained trapped in his very own catch-22: the only way to remove the oath was to take the oath.

The party whip Gerry Boland was the intermediary with the Labour Party; while he was ostensibly acting on de Valera's instructions, his un-published memoir strongly suggests that he went further in discussions than authorised. Having already discussed with the IRA the TDs' possible entry to Leinster House (he said they agreed not to criticise such a move), and discussed the same issue with the National League Party,[24] he now pursued the Labour Party, securing a written pledge from party leader Thomas Johnson that a Labour government would seek to remove the oath.[25]

De Valera's opposition to taking the oath was beginning to waver. On 3 August he advised Frank Walsh and William Lydon in America that the political situation had been

> completely changed by the projected Free State legislation . . . The Fianna Fáil way of removing the oath from outside is being made definitely impossible, and will I expect have to be abandoned . . . A new movement will now be required.[26]

At about the same time he suggested to the National Executive that a change of policy might be on the cards. According to Linda Kearns,

> the Chief seemed to be the Devil's advocate – he was all the time putting before us the need to take it [the oath]. Again we parted, but nothing seemed definite.[27]

On 4 August the final stages of Cosgrave's legislation passed the Dáil – the Public Safety Bill by a margin of 28 votes, the Electoral Amendment Bill by only 25.[28] Other things being equal, the votes of the Fianna Fáil TDs could have defeated both. As Thomas Johnson rather testily pointed out when de Valera sought a meeting to discuss joint action against the legislation, the place to stop it was the Dáil, where 'our numerical strength . . . was insufficient – by a not very wide margin – to achieve its defeat.[29]

At a meeting of Fianna Fáil TDs the following day, the attitude towards the oath was significantly changed. It wasn't even referred to as such but as 'the Free State formula for entry into the Free State parliament'.[30] Although 6 of the 27 TDs present were doubtful, the general view was that 'if the question were put to Constituency Conventions they would release the Party from their pledges [not to take the oath] at the present time'.[31]

It was agreed that a committee of de Valera, O'Kelly, Lemass, Boland, MacEntee and Aiken would explore the options for defeating the government's proposals. If this committee was satisfied that it could succeed, Fianna Fáil would 'take the steps which it considers essential to defeat such measures and save the country from their consequences by taking their seats in the Free State Assembly'.[32] The National Executive was summoned to meet on 9 August 'to consider the present political situation and the action which the FF teachtaí should take in relation to it'.[33]

On the face of it, the party's course was set. But de Valera remained paralysed by indecision. MacEntee later recalled that he and his colleagues were 'never quite certain, until the last moment, whether Dev would agree' to enter the Dáil.[34] Boland claimed that, before he arranged a meeting with the Labour Party, he went back no less than three times to get de Valera's confirmation that he wanted to proceed. But on his way out of head office, Boland says, he saw Dorothy Macardle going in. 'I had an instinctive fear that she was going to upset everything.' Sure enough, the following day he found that de Valera had changed his mind. 'He said that he had given Miss Macardle a solemn promise not to enter the Dáil while the Oath was there and he was reminded of this and was going to keep his promise. I asked him what about his promise to me, Seán MacEntee and others, and his appointment that day with the Labour Party. He said that if he had to put on sackcloth and ashes he would do so but would keep his pledged word.'[35]

This account, written four decades later by a man who had become more than a little disenchanted with de Valera, might be taken with a pinch of salt, except that it is borne out by the testimony of Thomas

Johnson. When the Labour Party leaders met de Valera, Boland and O'Kelly on 6 August they were 'confused' by de Valera's attitude. He said taking the oath would be 'an act of national apostasy which would never be forgotten or forgiven'; but he expressed a wish to enter the Dáil. Boland and O'Kelly told them that their Chief's fulminations against the oath need not be taken too seriously.[36]

The special National Executive meeting on the 9th was attended by 57 delegates. Robert Brennan proposed that deputies should be given a free hand to decide the best course of action. Linda Kearns told them some home truths. 'I told the Chief that he would lose the world's opinion of him', which was that 'he was *not* a brilliant leader, but that he was an honest man.' A total of 44 Executive members supported Brennan's proposal; 7 were against. De Valera asked the opponents (including Linda Kearns, Dorothy Macardle and Con Murphy) to remain behind, where he explained his idea that complying with the formality did not mean taking the oath. Kearns thought this a 'rotten weak argument' and a 'ridiculous idea'.[37]

Meanwhile, the back and forth with Labour and the National League continued. Fianna Fáil wanted assurances that any coalition government formed by the two parties would withdraw Cosgrave's Public Safety and Electoral Amendment Acts. They were also to remove the threat to the referendum; abolish political tests for public servants; allow TDs to take their seats without taking the oath; abolish article 17 (containing the oath) or hold a referendum on it; and pay the holders of Republican bonds.[38] Most of this was acceptable, though both Johnson and Redmond insisted that the removal of the oath would have to be negotiated with the British government. If that proved impossible, a referendum would be held; and if the British refused to accept the result, the two parties would resign and support a government committed to implementing the referendum verdict.[39] The British government would thus be faced with a choice: accept the result of a referendum abolishing the oath or face a government led by de Valera.

Backed by these assurances, the Fianna Fáil TDs met on 10 August. Newspapers reported the vast majority were in favour of entering the Dáil, the lengthy meeting being 'directed towards securing unanimity in the party'.[40] A statement on the oath drafted by de Valera underwent minor changes (he had originally called the formula 'meaningless' rather than 'empty') and was signed by all the party's TDs.[41] It tried to explain how entering the Dáil did not contravene the party's previous position; new legislation would block Republicans from political activity, but it was still not possible for them 'to transfer their allegiance' from the Republic. But 'the required declaration is not an oath', being 'merely an empty political formula which Deputies could conscientiously sign without becoming involved, or without involving their nation, in obligations of loyalty to the English Crown'. Therefore, not wanting to be blocked by an empty formula, they would attend Leinster House and sign the Clerk's book, all the while asserting that 'their only allegiance is to the Irish nation'.[42]

Fianna Fáil's entry into the Dáil was deliberately low key. Two months before, when their entry was blocked, its TDs had marched as a body to Leinster House, where crowds of supporters waited for them. This time they arrived in twos and threes, their supporters conspicuously absent.[43] Lemass, Boland and Aiken, the party whips, arrived at 11 o'clock. They were greeted by Johnson and Redmond, who escorted them to the Clerk's office, where they signed the roll. De Valera was the last to arrive, at 1:40 p.m., accompanied by James Ryan and Martin Corry. He put on a suitably theatrical performance in the office of the Clerk, Colm Ó Murchadha. In Irish, he told Ó Murchadha of the statement signed by the Fianna Fáil deputies the previous night; Ó Murchadha not unreasonably said this was nothing to do with him, but de Valera 'insisted on showing it to him, and explaining exactly what it was'.[44] He then read out a statement in Irish, which translates as:

> I am not prepared to take an oath. I am not going to take an oath. I am prepared to put my name down in this book in order to get permission to go into the Dáil, but it has no other significance.[45]

He then took the Bible off the table and left it on a couch by the door, covered the text of the oath with papers he was carrying, and signed the book, stating that one day he would see that the book was burnt.[46]

> I signed it in the same way as I would sign an autograph in a newspaper . . . It [the oath] was neither read to me nor was I asked to read it.[47]

Meanwhile, his deputies were being shown around Leinster House by ushers, supplied with copies of the standing orders and assigned seats in the chamber. All was being readied for a seemingly inevitable change of government. The *Irish Independent* forecast that Cosgrave would lose a vote of confidence by 74 votes to 70, even taking account of the defection from the National League of Vincent Rice, who refused to have anything to do with de Valera.[48] It seemed the gamble of entering the Dáil was about to pay off, though Cosgrave told journalists he was 'very pleased to see them coming into the Dáil, and I think it is the best thing that has happened during the last five years.'[49]

Boland believed that entering the Dáil 'was a tremendous decision for de Valera, and I doubt if he would ever have taken it, if O'Higgins had not been murdered'.[50] This was, however, only one factor. The *Irish Independent* identified three prompts for Fianna Fáil's decision: Cosgrave's legislation; internal party pressure; and the agreement with Labour and the National League, which offered immediate benefits for entering the Dáil.[51] None of these factors on their own would have been enough; together they made the argument for taking their seats unanswerable.

There was also a fourth factor: changes to the procedure for taking the oath, which helped make it an 'empty formula'. De Valera's use of this phrase has often been ridiculed, but taking the oath in 1927 was very different from doing so in 1922. Then, on 6 December, the day the Free State Constitution came into force, TDs were called individually before the Ceann Comhairle, who was acting for the Governor-General. One by one they repeated the oath before signing the roll, the entire process carried out 'in a very formal and official manner'.[52] But by 1927 there was no requirement on the deputies to read out the oath: they simply had to sign their name in the book.[53]

Fianna Fáil's taking of the oath did a number of things. It helped consolidate the Free State political system; it directed the bulk of opposition to the Treaty into constitutional channels; and it secured de Valera's position as leader of that opposition. It therefore gave the 26-county state, Fianna Fáil and Éamon de Valera their political futures, and removed the danger of a return to violence over the Treaty settlement. While it consolidated that settlement, it also planted the seeds of its destruction, because once de Valera and Fianna Fáil were inside the system it was only a matter of time before they would win control of it.

On Friday 12 August 1927 the 43 Fianna Fáil TDs took their seats in the Dáil chamber. The only one of them to address the Dáil that day was Seán T. O'Kelly, who spoke briefly in Irish on the Currency Bill, saying they had not had time to study its provisions, and should not be taken as approving of it. Of more significance was Johnson's announcement that he would propose a motion of no confidence in the Executive Council the following Tuesday.[54]

While there was some uncertainty about the intentions of some of the National League TDs, an internal party motion to support a new government was proposed by one of the 'doubtful' deputies, James Coburn, and seconded by another, John Jinks.[55] Johnson was so confident of victory that he went to a hotel in Enniskerry with two colleagues to sketch out a Cabinet; they were spotted by the *Irish Times* journalist R. M. 'Bertie' Smyllie, who rifled through a wastepaper basket in the hotel and pieced together their list, publishing the details in the following day's paper.[56] Johnson's government was to be made up of Labour, National League and independent members; there would be no Fianna Fáil ministers.

The Dáil met to debate Johnson's motion of no confidence on 16 August, amid excitement not seen since the Treaty debates five-and-a-half years before.[57] There were confident predictions in that morning's papers that the government would be defeated.[58] Leinster House was packed, so much so that the sketch writer in the *Independent* feared for the stability, not of the government, but 'of the gallery, in which four hundred visitors swayed back and fro and craned their necks to catch every word'. The Dáil chamber, too, was packed, containing as it did more TDs than ever before, thanks to the arrival of the Fianna Fáil deputies. The party's only contribution was again from O'Kelly, who, 'after a hurried consultation with Mr de Valera', arose to announce, in Irish, that his party had 'no desire to intervene in the debate, but would vote for the motion'.[59]

The result was in doubt as the deputies filed up the stairs to vote, with observers believing at first that the motion had been carried.[60] The 43 Fianna Fáil TDs voted for the motion, as did their former comrade Patrick Belton. But there were only 21 Labour Party votes, because the deputy leader, T. J. O'Connell, was in Canada; and the National League could muster only 6 votes, after Jinks left the chamber rather than vote with Fianna Fáil (he later denied reports that he had been kidnapped or waylaid with drink). Cumann na nGaedheal had 45 votes, one more than expected, thanks to the return of the recuperating Desmond FitzGerald; the 11 Farmers' Party TDs supported the government, as did 15 independents (including John O'Hanlon, who told the Dáil he couldn't vote for an Englishman – Thomas Johnson – as head of the government, despite having been listed by that Englishman as prospective Minister for Agriculture[61]).

The two sides were therefore evenly divided, with 71 votes each; the decision rested with Ceann Comhairle Michael Hayes. He explained that his casting vote should be influenced by two principles: allowing the Dáil to review its decision later, and preserving the status quo. On both grounds he would vote against the motion. The result, then, was the narrowest of escapes for Cosgrave and his colleagues.[62] After this announcement, Johnson was pale, but unperturbed. Mr de Valera still sat, grim and pallid of countenance, with his head resting on his left hand, studying his order paper.[63]

The Dáil then adjourned until 11 October.[64]

The gamble of entering the Dáil in an effort to topple the government had not paid off. This may have been a blessing in disguise: Boland later felt that Fianna Fáil 'knew nothing about Parliamentary procedure or the science of government. The next five years . . . was an apprenticeship for government.'[65] Lemass also thought the five years in opposition provided 'a very valuable training for us'.[66] At a meeting of the Fianna Fáil parliamentary party immediately after the vote, TDs agreed to push ahead with the effort to collect signatures supporting a referendum on the oath. They were also 'instructed to familiarise themselves with the local needs of their Constituencies, so that they could press them on the reopening of the Free State Assembly'.[67] Unlike Cumann na nGaedheal, Fianna Fáil would assiduously attend to the parish pump in order to garner votes. It would pay off handsomely.

Meanwhile, Fianna Fáil faced the by-elections for the seats of O'Higgins and Markievicz. Robert Brennan was chosen to run in the former contest, in Dublin County, which was viewed as unwinnable; Dublin South, however, was a different story: Seán Lemass had won a by-election there for Sinn Féin in 1924, so the Fianna Fáil candidate should have been in with a shout. But who would that candidate be? According to Linda Kearns, who had opposed entering the Dáil, at least two similarly minded potential candidates were mentioned: Hanna Sheehy-Skeffington and Con Murphy. Sheehy-Skeffington was out of the country, though, and Murphy stood down in favour of the former TD Joe O'Doherty. But then, apparently without sanction from the National Executive, the suitably loyal Bob Briscoe emerged as the candidate. Kearns told Sheehy-Skeffington that his appearance was due to Lemass.

They will lose both seats, and maybe it will be a lesson, but nothing seems to teach them. The Chief is hopeless as you always said . . . Lemass is the very limit.[68]

De Valera felt the need to justify himself in a public speech at the Queen's Theatre in Pearse Street on 21 August, three days before the by-elections. He rejected rumours that he had opposed the decision to enter the Dáil. They were faced with the alternative of taking the oath or abandoning the political field.

I grant that what we did was contrary to all our former actions, and to everything we stood for – contrary to our declared policy, and to the explicit pledges we gave at the time of our election. It was a step painful and humiliating for us who had to take it, and for those who had supported us . . . Still, that it was our duty to take the step became increasingly clear as the situation was examined . . .[69]

Reaction to de Valera's decision was mixed. Hard-line Republicans were predictably outraged. Mary MacSwiney suggested he had 'committed treason . . . It was as much a national surrender the day he took it as it was in 1922.'[70] The IRA Army Council reiterated its policy that no IRA member could swear or pledge allegiance to the Free State or Northern parliaments or their constitutions.[71] In America the implacable Joe McGarrity had 'no doubt of the sincerity of the Chief . . . but his party have adopted a policy contrary to the ideals of the army and we must either stand with them or against them'.[72] On the other hand there were a lot of Republicans who thought de Valera 'was going slowly, but he was going somewhere – and they were happy with it'.[73]

Sheehy-Skeffington, who was in France, resigned immediately from Fianna Fáil and its National Executive, because of its 'compete reversal of policy'.[74] She reminded de Valera that she had considered resignation before but had deferred it at his request, 'in order to support, if need be, those opposed to taking the oath. At that time no one contemplated the possibility of all the deputies doing so . . . I wish that you and a few others of the old guard had stood out together to the end.'[75] These remarks suggest that she believed that de Valera had agreed to take the oath only reluctantly. Another feminist member of the National Executive, Dorothy Macardle, was slower to move. On the 14th, two days before Sheehy-Skeffington resigned, Macardle defended the TDs, maintaining that 'they took no oath and saved their honour, and that the only alternative was civil war'.[76] A fortnight later, however, she decided, 'very reluctantly', to resign from the National Executive. Though she understood the reasons for the decision, she could 'have nothing to do with asking Irish men and women to take that oath'.[77]

Such resignations were, however, very much the exception; though disliking the move, most party members were prepared to accept it. De Valera had, of course, not summoned an ard-fheis to make the decision, leaving it to the presumably more malleable National Executive. This contrasted with his earlier insistence on calling an extraordinary Sinn Féin ard-fheis to decide the hypothetical question of whether that party would enter the Dáil if the oath was removed.[78] When the Fianna Fáil grass roots finally had their say, at the party's second ard-fheis, in November, they unanimously supported a motion approving entry to the Dáil – but added that 'the furthermost limits in compromise have been reached'.[79]

On 24 August, Cumann na nGaedheal won both Dublin County and Dublin South with massive swings, partly because of sympathy for Kevin O'Higgins, partly because of the absence of independents and Labour Party candidates. Winning Markievicz's seat from Fianna Fáil slightly improved Cosgrave's Dáil position, but a snap general election offered the prospect of a far more stable majority. Cosgrave called an election for 15 September.

De Valera accused him of 'sharp practice' and of 'rushing the country into an unnecessary election during the harvest season', adding that 'Fianna Fáil is not quite as unprepared as they think . . . We call on our friends everywhere to come to our aid with the old enthusiasm'.[80] His immediate need was for money, and he fired off a telegram to William Lyndon, secretary of the American Association for the Recognition of the Irish Republic.

> To catch us with resources exhausted Cosgrave has sprung another General Election. We ask all friends of Irish Ireland to unite and to come to our aid in this final battle against English Imperialism.[81]

De Valera must have worried that the new policy would affect subscriptions, but the plea was successful: a cash book shows election contributions of relatively small sums from Irish sources but much larger ones from overseas, including £1,000 from Archbishop Daniel Mannix in Australia, £3,000 from Frank Walsh, £2,000 from the AARIR in Chicago, and £1,645 from Boston.[82] By contrast, Sinn Féin, now cut off from its supply of American cash, was unable to contest the election.

Cosgrave's hope of catching de Valera with his party coffers empty was therefore dashed; but he believed de Valera's support would be hit by his reversal on the oath. Indeed, the *Irish Times* believed that the by-election results showed that the country was 'disgusted with Mr de Valera'.[83] Cumann na nGaedheal's election ads made much of this, pointing out that Fianna Fáil 'took the Oath to save their party – they would not take it in 1922 to save the country from Civil War'.[84]

The election came at a time when de Valera was trying to broaden the appeal of Fianna Fáil by stressing the economic virtues of protection. In a speech in Blackrock Town Hall during the by-election campaigns he committed the party to a policy of full employment. 'I hold it is the primary duty of a modern state to ensure that every man who is able and willing to work will have work, so that he may earn his daily bread'. The way to provide this work was to start 'building up the industries necessary to meet our own requirements in food, clothing and shelter'.[85]

The Blackrock speech also contained a significant commitment to constitutional methods: 'I want to reply to the suggestion now being put forward that our purpose in entering the Free State Dáil is to destroy it. That is a falsehood. We are entering in the hope of helping to make it develop to be what it should be ultimately – the sovereign assembly of the Irish nation.'[86] By entering the Dáil, by committing to using constitutional means, and by outlining an activist economic programme, Fianna Fáil could hope to do what it had not done in June: appeal beyond the republican constituency that had voted Sinn Féin in 1923.

In the general election campaign, de Valera was critical of the government's budgetary policy, claiming that England ran the whole of Ireland for £14.5 million but that it was now costing £30 million to run the 26 counties.[87] He said £25 million of imported goods could be produced at home, if there was 'a patriotic lead by a Government and a change in public spirit. A free people would do things that a subject people would not'.[88] The country could 'support three or four times the present population in comfort if industries were set up and there was a proper government to give the right lead'.[89] The only prosperity he could see 'was among officials paid high salaries, and if this were allowed to continue national bankruptcy was almost inevitable'.[90] However, he promised that Fianna Fáil in power 'would have no policy of revenge. Their eyes were on the future not on the past . . .'[91]

He was enthusiastically recieved. His car was stopped on the outskirts of Waterford by a crowd who 'carried him shoulder high from Ferrybank to Waterford North station'.[92] Even the hostile *Irish Independent* reported his 'great reception' in Scariff, Co. Clare, and paid tribute to his stamina, with his speeches not finishing until one o'clock in the morning on two nights running.[93] There was a 'big display' put on by his supporters in Westport, with bonfires blazing and the Town Hall 'densely crowded' for his two-hour speech.[94]

In the main, though, the newspapers were bitterly hostile to de Valera and to Fianna Fáil, and made much of his somersault on the oath and of his personal responsibility for the Civil War, the 'result of his tragic folly', as the *Irish Times* put it.[95] De Valera responded in kind with a 'violent attack on the Irish press' in a speech in Grand Parade in Cork after the election, in which he claimed that the newspapers were 'the biggest enemy of peace in this country'. He 'dramatically turned and pointed at the press representatives sitting on the platform. His gesture was greeted with mingled cheers and hisses by his audience'. De Valera complained that no party had ever suffered as much vituperation in the press as Fianna Fáil.[96] Clearly, a sympathetic newspaper would have to be a priority if the party was to prosper.

The Cumann na nGaedheal vote was up by 11.2 percentage points, to 38.7 per cent, and it won an extra 15 seats, taking 62 – just one seat and 0.1 per cent of the vote off its triumphant performance in 1923. Fianna Fáil's vote, at 35.2 per cent, had increased by 9.1 percentage points, and it won 13 more seats than in June, giving it 57 TDs. In Clare, de Valera managed to bring home a third Fianna Fáil candidate at the expense of the Farmers' Party. Labour's vote slumped from 13.8 to 9.5 per cent, and it lost 9 of its 22 seats, including party leader Thomas Johnson. Outside the three (or two and a half) main parties, it was a rout: from 40, the number of Independents and minor party TDs dropped to just 21. The snap election had paid off for Cosgrave – though he was still well short of a majority in the 153-seat Dáil.

Immediately after the results were announced, de Valera told the *Daily Express* that

> it is true that Mr Cosgrave's party have gained a slight majority over that of Fianna Fáil but that is not a certain indication that they will form the Government. We must wait and see.[97]

Asked if there was any prospect of an alliance with Labour and the National League, which together had co-operated in the attempt to unseat Cosgrave, de Valera was cautious.

> There had been no 'alliance' before the dissolution, and . . . it was not likely that there would be any.[98]

Whatever faint prospect there might have been of an anti-Cosgrave alliance was scotched by predictions that he would be supported by the six Farmers TDs and all 12 independents, giving him a comfortable majority.[99]

De Valera quickly turned his attention to the future, suggesting to Seán T. O'Kelly that 'we must now consolidate our gains and prepare at once for the final advance. Another election cannot be far off.'[100] And that election, he confidently predicted, would 'give us a majority great enough to put into operation our full national and economic programme'.[101]

When the Sixth Dáil met, on 11 October 1927, de Valera made his first contribution as a Fianna Fáil TD (he had not spoken at all on the two sitting days after the party entered the Dáil in August). When Michael Hayes was nominated for reappointment as Ceann Comhairle by Cosgrave, and seconded by the new Labour Party leader, T. J. O'Connell, de Valera spoke in Irish, saying he did not object to the nomination but did object to his salary, as his party did not believe anyone should be paid more than £1,000 a year.[102] O'Kelly was again Fianna Fáil's main speaker in the debate on the election of President, which Cosgrave won by 76 votes to 70.

Addressing Fianna Fáil's second ard-fheis, in November 1927, de Valera again defended the decision to enter the Dáil.

> When circumstances change, methods must change; but the thing that has not changed is the aim, and that aim is to secure the complete freedom of this country . . .

He referred to his famous statement that he was not a doctrinaire Republican.

> I meant that I was a realist, and I hold that I have always been a realist in politics. And these men opposed to us are not realists any more than the English were in dealing with this country, because they close their eyes to the real factor in the whole situation, and that is that the Irish people want to be free and will never rest until they are free . . .[103]

But whether they would vote for him to lead them to freedom largely depended on his performance in the coming years as leader of the opposition – and on whether he could achieve his aim of establishing a newspaper that would back him and his party in the next election contest.

CHAPTER 19

A PRACTICAL RULE

As a practical rule . . . I am prepared to accept majority rule as settling matters of national policy . . .

Éamon de Valera, 1929[1]

We look beyond political independence to social justice.

Éamon de Valera, 1931[2]

Our central purpose . . . is to provide the Irish people with a paper which will give them the truth in news . . .

Éamon de Valera, 1929[3]

De Valera was now the leader of the opposition – which meant frequent confrontations across the Dáil chamber with W. T. Cosgrave, his former protégé and now bitter enemy. One British writer described them.

> Trim little Cosgrave managing his ministerial papers with an air of competence and a neat reply to every Opposition argument, and there confronting him a lean figure with a pinched mouth and two solemn horn-rimmed eyes. That was de Valera . . . He looked as solemn as any public man that I had ever seen . . . I never caught a gleam of anything that could have been mistaken for a smile . . . The pinched mouth was tightly closed, and the unsmiling eyes persisted in their mournful vigil though his enormous spectacles.[4]

According to the historian T. Desmond Williams, who knew both men, Cosgrave 'was more contemptuous of Dev than Dev was of him.'[5]

Cosgrave's contempt was mainly expressed in private. In 1927 he told the Earl of Granard, a member of the Senate, that he wished de Valera 'were as strong as he is unfortunately weak'; in 1931 he complained to Diarmuid O'Hegarty that de Valera had

> a type of arrested mental development . . . This man who wants to have himself regarded as a pacificator, as a great man, with great ideals who, when he uses one sentence follows it with another which makes it impossible for anybody to understand what he means; this man who, pretending to show respect for me, dislikes me more and has greater hatred for me than any other man in this country has for another.[6]

De Valera's dislike spilled out during a Dáil debate when a Cumann na nGaedheal TD accused him of staying in America to avoid danger during the War of Independence. De Valera responded by accusing Cosgrave of running away to England, claiming that he summoned him back. 'I saved him from the Cabinet that would have kicked him out'.[7]

Fianna Fáil was keen to present itself as a government in waiting; special committees shadowed various ministers – in most cases the chairmen of the committees would go on to occupy the relevant portfolio in government. Lemass chaired the Industry and Commerce committee, Aiken was in Defence, O'Kelly in Local Government. Jim Ryan was initially given the chair of Finance, but the following February was moved to Agriculture, with Seán MacEntee taking over Finance, the portfolio he would occupy in 1932. The most important difference was in Justice. P. J. Ruttledge was appointed to chair the Justice Committee in 1927, but he was not to become Minister when Fianna Fáil took office – de Valera would choose the more conciliatory figure of James Geoghegan for that position.

What sort of a man was the party leader? The British writer Philip Guedella was subjected to the full blast of de Valeran charm: 'Nothing could have been more gracious than his reception of an unimportant stranger . . . It was a fascinating experience, from which no hearer could emerge without a strong conviction of his sincerity. His exposition was a shade impersonal; and much of it bore a strong resemblance to remembered fragments of old platform speeches. But though the familiar records spun round, his needle was not blunted and the instrument was charming. Indeed, the tune belies the stories I had been told about him . . .'[8]

Another English journalist, R. Stephen Williams, was puzzled about the source of de Valera's 'mysterious magnetism'.

He is not a man you would pick out of a crowd . . . He does not wear his clothes; he just suffers them. He does not walk; he just gets from one place to another . . . His face is slightly tanned, but thin and intense – the face of an ascetic. He wears light horn-rimmed spectacles and his eyes are small and brilliant. Wonderfully expressive, those eyes: they pink you like rapiers, they challenge you like dangerous fires; then suddenly they melt into the most gracious friendliness, they sparkle with the most delicious and most mischievous humour . . . When I left him I knew that I had been in the presence of an immensely powerful and significant personality . . . One gets an impression of quiet but inflexible force, indomitable purpose . . [9]

His asceticism was shown in his attitude to alcohol. He told delegates to the October 1927 Ard Fheis that drink

has been a greater curse to our people than perhaps anything else . . . If we want to get back to the spirit of 1917, we will have to get back to the temperate habits that prevailed from 1914 . . . to 1921.[10]

Getting his TDs back to these habits was a constant battle. In October 1927, he urged them 'not to take any drink whatsoever in the bar of Leinster House'. This injunction was disobeyed – in February 1929 it was agreed to name any party member who was 'visibly under the influence of drink in the Dáil', with the first case reported to a parliamentary party meeting in April; the member involved, who wasn't named in the minutes, apologised and said it wouldn't happen again. In May, it was agreed that the Leinster House bar would be 'definitely out of bounds for members of the party'.[11]

Also 'out of bounds' were members of the Government party, particularly ministers. In November 1928 the Fianna Fáil parliamentary party agreed that members should not have contact with government ministers except in committee meetings or at public functions.[12] In July 1929 Margaret Pearse, mother of Patrick and William, was advised by the National Executive not to accept an invitation to the official reopening of the GPO.[13] The following year leading figures in the party boycotted the state banquet to welcome the new papal nuncio.[14] The Ceann Comhairle, Michael Hayes, recalled that while de Valera would discuss business with him in his office, 'he never saluted me in the corridor'. Others, like Lemass and MacEntee, 'were quite cordial, but when in company with de Valera they looked away, which is one of the most disgusting things that I remember . . .'[15]

On a financial matter, Fianna Fáil took an approach that showed how different its ethos was from that of Cumann na nGaedheal. In the government party, TDs were expected to pay for their own campaigns, fully or in part;[16] in Fianna Fáil, TDs were expressly forbidden from doing so, under threat of disciplinary action. 'If this practice was permitted to become established, it would result in only those being selected as Candidates who could afford to pay their own expenses.'[17]

The party's continuing reliance on foreign income was a concern: according to accounts published at the October 1928 ard-fheis, out of receipts of £12,500 only a quarter – £3,700 – had been raised in the national collection.[18] This was a dangerous situation: the flow of funds across the Atlantic could stop at any time, and in any event de Valera had other plans for whatever dollars could be raised from Irish-America.[19]

The following June, Lemass came up with a new scheme to improve the party machinery. The existing organisers were paid off, to be replaced by a permanent organiser in each constituency (with two in those covering two counties, and in Donegal and Galway). They would be paid £5 per month in expenses, but their main income would be tied to results: they could keep a tenth of the national collection raised in their constituency, as well as up to a fifth of the funds raised for the local organisation. It was envisaged that they would be part time, perhaps 'a farmer's son, a small shopkeeper, or an Insurance Agent'.[20] The figures published at the ard-fheis in October 1930 show that the scheme was a success: domestic income came to £6,813, while expenditure was £6,819.

> In other words we have paid 99.9 per cent of our expenses for the year ... out of Cash received through the Organisation and the Party.[21]

There was no doubt about Lemass's energy and work rate. It was claimed that he was then giving six speeches to every one by de Valera, and that he was 'the brains of the Fianna Fáil party'.[22] His value to it is evident in a decision taken in 1928 to pay him £10 a month so he could work for the party full time.[23] His efficiency was noted by de Valera, who urged the chairmen of other policy committees to follow Lemass's example in typing reports rather than writing them by hand.[24]

Such praise from the Chief probably did little for Lemass's popularity with his colleagues, and when he occasionally overstepped the mark in his public comments they were quick to rein him in. In January 1930, while de Valera was in America, O'Kelly criticised Lemass over comments in the *Irish Independent*, which were 'a breach of the understanding arrived at last month'.[25] At the National Executive, Robert Brennan raised comments Lemass had made on policy and asked how far the party was committed by such statements.[26] Particular objection was taken to his statement in 1931 that Fianna Fáil 'could not be accurately described either as pro-Treaty or anti-Treaty'. The National Executive firmly stated that Fianna Fáil was necessarily anti-Treaty, as it stood for 'the independence and the unity of Ireland, both of which are incompatible with the terms of the "Treaty"'.[27]

While ham-fisted, Lemass's statement was part of an effort, spearheaded by de Valera, to widen Fianna Fáil's appeal. De Valera had told the ard-fheis in 1928 that they wanted 'an open organisation' that could contain all those

> who sincerely wished to see Ireland free and united as one Nation . . . We will never be able to work in a political movement until we have the majority of the people behind us, and how are we going to get the majority if, when anybody who was not with us before wants to come to us, we try to push them off.[28]

Among those targeted for recruitment by de Valera was James Dillon, son of the last leader of the Irish Party. They had a 'most amicable' meeting in 1929, but Dillon 'had no intention of joining any party that was a section of Sinn Féin . . . and we parted on that understanding'.[29]

More significant was the choice of candidate in a by-election in Longford-Westmeath, caused by the death of the Fianna Fáil TD James Killane. His seat had been lost in the June 1927 general election to his party colleague James Victory, but he had won it back in September. Victory expected to be the Fianna Fáil by-election candidate, but he lost the nomination to the barrister James Geoghegan, a former Cumann na nGaedheal supporter who had provided legal advice for Fianna Fáil on the land annuities question. During the campaign, Geoghegan caused consternation by stating that he would favour keeping the Treaty if the alternative was war with Britain. As *An Phoblacht* dolefully pointed out, 'Fianna Fáil headquarters, and not Geoghegan, have changed . . .'[30]

Geoghegan won the seat, with 53.6 per cent of the vote, though, given that Fianna Fáil outpolled Cumann na nGaedheal in the constituency in the September 1927 general election, his victory was anticipated. Geoghegan was to be de Valera's choice for the sensitive Justice portfolio in 1932, his pro-Treaty background making him a less controversial choice than P. J. Ruttledge, who had a colourful Civil War record.

Decades later, de Valera observed that 'in those days I believe we could be called Socialists, but not Communists',[31] an important distinction at a time when being described as the latter was the electoral kiss of death. He told a French journalist that any tendency to communism in Ireland existed only because of 'grave social evils', and Fianna Fáil in office would remove those evils.[32] However, because of its reputation as a Republican and anti-British party, Fianna Fáil occasionally found itself in suspect company. In 1929 de Valera decided not to attend a meeting in Paris of the International League against Imperialism, though Fianna Fáil did contribute £20 to it.[33] This support for a Comintern front organisation could have been risky had it become widely known, because the Free State government was constantly trying to tar Fianna Fáil with the Bolshevik brush.[34]

Given such attacks, it is scarcely surprising that de Valera displayed ostentatious piety in public. He played a prominent role in the celebrations of the centenary in 1929 of Catholic Emancipation, acting as a canopy-bearer, along with the Minister for Justice, James Fitzgerald-Kenney.[35] There was, though, given the experience of the Civil War, a strain of anti-clericalism within the party; the leadership was quick to stifle this strain. A motion before the National Executive advising party members not to join the Knights of Columbanus was withdrawn after discussion.[36] The following month the same happened with a motion calling for the establishment of a committee 'to collect information regarding all cases of improper interference in political matters by Catholic Priests, with a view to bringing such cases to the notice of the Papal Nuncio'.[37]

The attempt to collect enough signatures to force a referendum on the oath continued – fitfully. Lemass and Boland, as honorary secretaries, stressed the importance of this collection at the ard-fheis in November 1927, following this with a letter to each cumann secretary bemoaning the failure to secure enough names. 'This is a serious reflection on the efficiency of our Organisation in many areas ... *We must not fail in it.*'[38]

When the petition, signed by 96,000 voters (a far cry from the initial target of 500,000), was finally presented to the Dáil in May 1928, the government introduced long-promised legislation to abolish the referendum and the initiative.[39] In protest, Fianna Fáil adopted a policy of obstruction. De Valera urged his party whips 'to organise the campaign carefully ... New forms of obstruction should be constantly thought out.'[40]

Despite this, the Constitution (Amendment No. 10) Bill was passed at the end of June. The day before the Dáil was to resume after the summer recess, the Fianna Fáil parliamentary party's Standing Committee agreed that 'while determined opposition should be continued, purely dilatory obstruction should be allowed to lapse'.[41]

The problem, of course, was that such obstruction was rather popular with the grass roots. The ard-fheis at the end of the month urged TDs 'to continue their fighting and militant policy in conducting their opposition in the Free State Parliament'.[42] This motion prompted de Valera to remind delegates that they were not in the same position as Parnell was in Westminster; measures going through the Dáil had a large and immediate effect on the people of Ireland. Therefore, he argued,

> it would be very ridiculous to obstruct for obstruction's sake . . . I have only one view in my mind therefore . . . to make good things better, and, if they bring forward bad things, to try to prevent them.[43]

Almost despite itself, Fianna Fáil was becoming a conventional party.

While de Valera wanted to reach beyond the core Republican constituency, he also wanted to keep as much of that constituency on board as possible. This led to vocal Fianna Fáil criticism of the Garda Special Branch, and opposition to anti-IRA legislation. De Valera's own distaste for the forces of law and order in the Free State was demonstrated when the Gardaí told him they had information that he was to be shot and insisted on placing an armed guard outside his house despite his objections. Shortly after this police protection began, he observed, his house was burgled.[44]

These attitudes, as the historian Donnacha Ó Beacháin has pointed out, reflected an ambivalence within Fianna Fáil about the institutions of the Free State. While the party's political culture was entirely opposed to those institutions, its programme depended on gaining control of them.[45] This duality would throw up all sorts of interesting problems for Fianna Fáil in power; in opposition, it was evident in Lemass's famous characterisation of the party as 'slightly constitutional'.[46] An editorial in the party's weekly paper, the *Nation,* made a similar point – the party would follow constitutional means, but only so long as they were effective.

> If Fianna Fáil's programme of peaceful penetration into our own land is in any way blocked or interfered with by an outsider, then, if the occasion should arise, it will no more fear the cry of Revolutionary than it does today of Constitutionalist.[47]

De Valera's view on the legitimacy of the Free State was given in the Dáil in March 1929.

> You have secured a de facto position. Very well. There must be some body in charge to keep order in the community and by virtue of your de facto position you are the only people who are in a position to do it. But as to whether you have come by that position legitimately or not, I say you have not . . . You brought off a coup d'état in the summer of 1922 . . . As long as there was a hope of maintaining that Republic, either by force against those who were bringing off that coup d'état or afterwards, as long as there was an opportunity of getting the people of this country to vote again for the Republic, I stood for it . . . As we were not able to get a majority to meet outside this House, we had to come here . . . As a practical rule, and not because there is anything sacred in it, I am prepared to accept majority rule as settling matters of national policy, and therefore as deciding who it is that shall be in charge of order.

And he had this to say about Sinn Féin: 'Those who continued on in that organisation which we have left can claim exactly the same continuity that we claimed up to 1925.'[48] The last comment could be taken – as it was by the Labour Party leader, T. J. O'Connell, who spoke next in the debate – as an indication that de Valera believed the rump Second Dáil to still be the 'legitimate' government of Ireland. Although de Valera later claimed that this was a misinterpretation, he did not object to it at the time.[49]

These comments about the legitimacy of the Dáil came back to haunt him the following year, after the government suffered a surprise defeat on a Fianna Fáil private member's bill. The Old Age Pensions Bill was designed to reverse in part the government's infamous pension cut; the second stage was passed by only two votes, 66 to 64, because several government TDs were absent.[50] The following day, claiming that the Bill would cost £300,000 a year, Cosgrave said the government was not prepared to implement it and announced his resignation, with a vote to be held the following week to choose a President. Seán T. O'Kelly immediately announced that Fianna Fáil would be proposing de Valera, who was then in the United States arranging finances for a Fianna Fáil newspaper.[51] A special meeting of the parliamentary party agreed to vote for the Labour Party nominee if de Valera was defeated.[52] On the morning of the vote the parliamentary party adopted a more cautious approach: they would abstain on O'Connell's nomination unless Labour voted for de Valera, or unless their votes were likely to actually elect him in place of Cosgrave.[53] The caution turned out to be justified, because after the absent de Valera was nominated by O'Kelly, O'Connell severely criticised de Valera on the basis of his lukewarm attitude towards the Dáil.

> Any person who denies or questions or even doubts the sovereignty of this Parliament, who denies or questions or even doubts its moral right to make and administer the laws of this State, and to insist on the strict observance of these laws, is not . . . a suitable person to be entrusted with the control of the powers which are inherent in this Parliament.[54]

This led to a withering (if not entirely relevant) attack by Seán Lemass on Labour: 'The members of that Party desire to be respectable above everything else. So long as they cannot be accused of being even pale pink in politics they seem to think they have fulfilled their function towards the Irish people.'[55] Lemass was already contemptuous of Labour, claiming in private that any time the government was in potential difficulty on a tight vote, 'members of the Labour Party left the house so as not to defeat the Government . . . They have saved the Government repeatedly in this way.'[56]

After de Valera's nomination was defeated, 54 votes to 93, O'Connell was nominated. Lemass said they couldn't take the proposal seriously, as attempting to form a government with only 13 TDs was 'ridiculous',[57] and O'Connell was duly defeated, 13 votes to 78, with Fianna Fáil abstaining. Cosgrave was then re-elected, 80 votes to 65.

The episode strained relations between Fianna Fáil and Labour. The smaller party's attitude was criticised at the next meeting of the Fianna Fáil National Executive, with suggestions that supporters should be advised not to transfer to Labour in the next election.[58] No action was taken, presumably because such advice could prove a double-edged sword, and because the support of Labour Party TDs could be required to elect de Valera – as in fact it would be in 1932.

In January 1930, Lemass warned de Valera that they 'must emphasise the Republican basis of our policy this year to a greater extent than heretofore' to prevent younger members being attracted to more militant groups. He blamed the progress being made by these groups on anti-police sentiment.[59] Special Branch men were in violent conflict with the IRA at this time – and there was no doubt which side Fianna Fáil was on.

Among the worst affected areas was de Valera's own constituency of Clare, where the IRA was led by T. J. Ryan of Kilrush.[60] After the murder of two Gardaí and a suspected informer, Special Branch officers planned to retaliate by drowning Ryan, but the plot was discovered and foiled by the head of Special Branch, David Neligan.[61] One of Ryan's most audacious acts was framing a local Garda Superintendent, William Geary, for bribery and collaboration with the IRA; Geary was summarily dismissed from the force in June 1928. Luckily, he was both persistent in his campaign for justice, and lived to a great age – he was finally cleared of the charges in April 1999, at the age of 100.[62]

In July 1929, after visiting Ryan in his home, de Valera wrote to Cosgrave, citing Ryan's claims of assault and describing his own encounter with a detective outside the house.

> He accosted me as I was about to enter, asking my name, which I gave. When I entered he followed; and when Mr. Ryan invited me into his bedroom, he accompanied us and was present in the bedroom whilst I took notes of Mr. Ryan's statements.

De Valera concluded:

> May I ask why Mr. Ryan is kept virtually a prisoner in his own home; what legal authority there is for it; and whether you will have an enquiry held into the conduct of the Guards who have assaulted Mr. Ryan?

The Minister for Justice, James Fitzgerald-Kenney, replied to the letter, claiming that Ryan's injuries were sustained when he was kicked by one of his cattle (which led to the Special Branch being referred to as 'Fitzgerald-Kenney's cows'). He suggested that Ryan had brought the surveillance on himself by his leadership of 'those people in West Clare who desire to upset the established form of Government by violence . . . it is essential for the preservation of public peace that Mr. Ryan's movements should be watched by the police'. Not surprisingly, this answer didn't satisfy de Valera, who told the Dáil that 'certain members of the Detective Division are trying to create a reign of terror down in Clare', and that the suggestion that the injuries had been caused by a cow 'is absolutely absurd'.[63]

At about the same time, de Valera airily dismissed the need for new legislation to protect jury members, telling the Dáil that

> I am not to be taken as sympathising with attacks on or intimidation of jurors . . . [but] if you want to have the law respected you will have to have the law people can respect.[64]

The source of this observation was rather unexpected. In one of his diaries he had written: 'Drastic laws bring law into contempt. Machiavelli.'[65]

Further IRA activity late in 1930 and early in 1931 guaranteed a backlash from the Free State government. A number of alleged informers were murdered; even worse was the killing of Garda Superintendent John Curtin outside his house near Tipperary. The Department of Justice had two main concerns about the situation. The first was that IRA intimidation was making trial by jury impossible. The second was the threat of communism.

> There are a number of Associations, many members of which are also members of the IRA, whose object is the bringing about in this country of a revolution on the lines of the Russian Revolution.[66]

While this concern was certainly overblown, the intimidation of jury members was not, and there was increasing pressure from Garda Commissioner Eoin O'Duffy for strong action to be taken. 'There is no good reason why an Organisation making war on the State should be afforded the protection which the State affords its loyal citizens.'[67]

Cosgrave's government eventually agreed drastic legislation to counter the IRA, to be introduced as an amendment to the Constitution, and therefore known as article 2A. But Cosgrave also sought to secure the support of the Catholic Hierarchy, preparing a dossier for distribution to the bishops and arranging a number of meetings with Cardinal Joseph MacRory to explain the situation.[68]

> Doctrines are being taught and practised which were never before countenanced amongst us and I feel that the influence of the Church alone will be able to prevail in the struggle against them.[69]

Here lay potential danger for de Valera and his party. Military Intelligence believed that the 'left wing' of the Fianna Fáil party – including Frank Aiken, Oscar Traynor, Séamus Robinson and 'Briscoe the Jew' – sympathised with the views of 'the Militant National plus Communist section' of the IRA and various associated groups.[70] Concerns that Fianna Fáil could be included in a denunciation by the bishops were raised at its National Executive on 13 October 1931, the day before the emergency legislation was introduced. It was suggested that the party should issue 'a declaration of policy to forestall a pronouncement expected from the Irish Hierarchy'. However, it was decided that such a declaration was not required.[71] The reason was that de Valera had already dealt with the situation. After being given a copy of the government memorandum to the Hierarchy by a friendly bishop, he met MacRory to state Fianna Fáil's opposition to communism.[72]

Having secured his ecclesiastical flank, de Valera used his Dáil speech on the measure to question the need for it, to stress his opposition to communism and to burnish his Catholic credentials. If there were a real emergency, he wondered, why had the Dáil not been recalled from its summer recess? He also restated his case that communism could make progress only if social conditions were difficult, and that therefore the best way to prevent its spread was to improve those conditions. He stressed that Fianna Fáil supported the Catholic social principles mentioned by Cosgrave. But by far the most important part of his speech related to the legitimacy of the Dáil and of the Free State government.

> We here on these benches have never been slow to point out that we do not stand for crime . . . I said long before we came into the Dáil that . . . there was no authority outside this House that was entitled to take human life . . . if there is no authority in this House to rule, then there is no authority in any part of the country to rule . . .

Though he characteristically claimed that his position had not changed, this went considerably further than his acceptance two years previously that the government had achieved a 'de facto position'. Fitzgerald-Kenney welcomed this 'remarkable statement'.[73]

The following day, de Valera rowed back slightly, explicitly comparing the IRA of 1931 to the men of the Rising. The IRA men

> are misguided, if you will, but they were brave men, anyhow; let us at least have for them the decent respect that we have for the brave. They have done terrible things recently I admit, if they are responsible for them, and I suppose they are. Let us appeal to them and ask them in God's name not to do them . . . Social order must be maintained, even if there were nothing but a de facto Government.

This was certainly a less ringing endorsement of the legitimacy of the Dáil, but he added that the only way to ensure progress was 'through the leadership of the Government that will be elected here . . . Any other way means first of all that you will have to face civil conflict.'[74] Fianna Fáil may have been 'slightly constitutional', but it was constitutional nonetheless.

Three days later the Catholic Hierarchy issued a pastoral condemning the left-wing Republican organisation Saor Éire, led by Peadar O'Donnell, as well as communist activities. In a statement to a news agency, de Valera was careful to avoid criticising the Church.

The priests and bishops, in genuine anxiety as pastors lest their flocks should be misled into immoral paths or lend an ear to doctrines subversive of religion, would feel bound in duty to condemn crime and to issue warnings.

His criticism was reserved for the government, which he accused of trying to turn the Hierarchy's warnings to its own advantage by claiming that it was the only party that could stop communism. He again dismissed the threat of communism – 'It passes my comprehension why anybody should feel that Communism has the slightest likelihood of winning any measure of acceptance here'[75] – which rather undermined the free pass he had just given the bishops.

When article 2A was brought into force on 20 October 1931, 12 Republican and socialist organisations were banned (though not Sinn Féin – evidence of its impotence), while the establishment of non-jury military courts did away with the intimidation of jurors and curbed political violence, at least for the time being.[76]

De Valera's attitude towards the treatment of minorities was revealed in the case of Letitia Dunbar Harrison, who was recommended for the post of County Librarian of Mayo by the Local Appointments Commission, but rejected by the County Council because she was a Protestant and a graduate of Trinity College. In the Dáil in June, 1931, de Valera defended the Council. Catholics had a right, he insisted, to have a Catholic in charge of choosing their books, just as they had a right to a Catholic doctor and a Catholic teacher: 'if I had a vote on a local body, and if there were two qualified people who had to deal with a Catholic community, and if one was a Catholic and the other a Protestant, I would unhesitatingly vote for the Catholic'.[77] Protestants were entitled to their share of public appointments, but not at the expense of upsetting Catholics. The Minister for Local Government, Richard Mulcahy, observed that de Valera had in effect ruled out the appointment of Protestant librarians to any county library in the country.[78] And yet, de Valera in office proved to be sensitive to the needs of the minority community, and helpful to Trinity College; it is difficult to avoid the conclusion that his position in this case was driven entirely by electoral considerations.

De Valera had been talking about the importance of economic issues before Fianna Fáil entered the Dáil, and he had made the economy a central plank of the September 1927 election campaign. In the new Dáil, he repeated the policy he had first outlined in his Blackrock speech. 'We stand firmly on the principle that it is the duty of a modern state under modern conditions to see that work is available for those willing to work'.[79] But how was the state to achieve this aim? Not through an expansionary fiscal policy: Fianna Fáil was firmly committed to reducing state spending, proposing in 1928 that the Budget should be trimmed by £2.8 million, including £500,000 off both the civil service and the Gardaí, £800,000 off the army, and a smaller but politically significant saving of £78,475 off the Oireachtas and the Governor-General.[80] The party also wanted to increase taxation of what it saw as frivolous spending: cosmetics, greyhound-racing and dances – though 'wholly Irish dances' were to be exempt.[81]

Nor was redemption to be found in state-led investment: de Valera was a consistent critic of the Shannon hydroelectric scheme, the most impressive example of government capital investment under Cosgrave. Completed in October 1929, the Ardnacrusha hydro-electric power station would by 1937 meet 87 per cent of the demand for electricity in the State.[82] But de Valera – the deputy, it should be remembered, for Clare, where the project was located – thought it was too ambitious, as it would supply more power than was immediately required. 'We think that it would have been far more economic to start with the Liffey scheme and work it where you are going to have an immediate demand for the supply, and link it up afterwards.'[83] To de Valera, its £8.7 million price tag marked it out as a 'white elephant',[84] a cost 'so high as to preclude the possibility of selling really cheap power and light except at financial loss'.[85] He was wrong, and his opposition to State-led economic development would be reversed when he entered Government.

For de Valera, the solution to the Free State's problems lay not in big government but in high tariffs. 'We know that the interests of our country, and its very existence as a nation, demand a policy of rigorous protection, and we shall not flinch in applying it', he told an audience in Limerick in January 1929.[86] At about the same time, Seán Lemass was committing similar thoughts to paper. He acknowledged that the case for unlimited free trade 'is unanswerable' if 'the welfare of mankind as a whole, irrespective of local or national interests', was the aim; however, when the problem was examined from the point of view of an individual nation, the answer was different. Ireland had discovered during the Union that free trade might increase overall wealth, but not all parts would benefit equally. Therefore, to avoid continued emigration

> and the destruction of our Nation, we must take steps to preserve and develop here the industries which mean employment for our people in their own country.[87]

Lemass's position on protection was, then, the same as his Chief's. Where de Valera went further than some of his colleagues was in his emphasis on frugality. In the same Limerick speech he said:

> If we mean to retain our population and provide employment for those at present unemployed, we must be prepared to make sacrifices in certain directions for a time. We may, for example, have to wear somewhat less fashionable – though by no means less serviceable – shoes, or hats or hosiery.[88]

It is an outlook he would famously state in his St Patrick's Day broadcast, 1943.[89] He also stated it in the Dáil in July 1928, when he pointed out that Ireland simply couldn't afford to match the services provided in Britain. He used the analogy of a servant, unhappy at his treatment, deciding to leave the mansion of his employer for humbler lodgings.

> If a man makes up his mind to go out into a cottage, he must remember that he cannot have in the cottage the luxuries around him which he had when he was bearing the kicks of the master . . . If he goes into the cottage, he has to make up his mind to put up with the frugal fare of that cottage . . . If I had that choice to make, I would make it quite willingly.[90]

In October 1929 he told the Fianna Fáil ard-fheis that, 'leaving aside the main political issues . . . the most important single topic to which we can address ourselves is the unemployment problem'. Given the amount of attention that would be devoted in government to such questions as the abolition of the oath, this was a rather large caveat; nevertheless, de Valera outlined a programme for tackling unemployment, including the growing of wheat, the protection of industries, the improvement of technical education and the creation of an Economic Council of experts, 'which in the economic struggle would serve the State as a Headquarters Staff serves it in war'. He breezily suggested that more than £34 million in imported goods could be produced at home, creating 90,000 jobs, 'or nearly twice our estimate of the number at present out of work in the Free State'.[91]

This speech was delivered just days before the Wall Street Crash, and the following year de Valera's ard-fheis speech acknowledged the 'new situation', with emigration closed off as a result of the global depression.

> We must either absorb in industry the natural increase in our working population, or face the prospect of an appalling increase in unemployment . . . A fundamental change is necessary.

He acknowledged that people might not like bread made with Irish wheat, but they would have to develop a taste for it, as they would have to become accustomed to other changes.

> Some of us may find it a hardship to give up Paris or London fashions and fabrics for our own. But greater sacrifices have been made for the preservation of the Irish nation, and we shall surely not permit them to be in vain because of any preference of taste or fashion . . . As we stand today, the nation cannot survive without Protection . . .[92]

While such economic issues as emigration, unemployment and protection were central to Fianna Fáil's appeal in urban Ireland, one issue above all defined its appeal in rural areas. Land annuities were the £3 million a year repayments by Irish farmers of money advanced by the British Government, under various Land Acts, to purchase their farms. Resistence to them was led by the socialist Peadar O'Donnell, who saw opposition to the annuities as a way of building a broad anti-imperialist front, which would revive the Republican movement and drag it to the left. De Valera could see the potential for such a development – which explains his extreme wariness in dealing with it. O'Donnell opposed the annuities on the basis of historical justice. Why, he argued, should Irish farmers be forced to pay for land that was stolen from their ancestors? De Valera's approach was more legalistic, based on an interpretation of British legislation and various agreements between Dublin and London. O'Donnell urged farmers to refuse to pay the annuities; de Valera, pointing out that the annuities proved title to the land, wanted them to keep paying the money, which would be retained in the Irish exchequer instead of being sent to Britain.[93] O'Donnell succeeded in forcing Fianna Fáil to take up the issue, but it was de Valera's solution that was followed. As he watched de Valera address an anti-annuities meeting in Ennis in 1928, O'Donnell realised that he 'was handing away a trump card'.[94]

De Valera's legal argument was a strong one. Under the Government of Ireland Act (1920), land annuities were to be retained by the two new governments in Dublin and Belfast. Article 5 of the Treaty was held by the British to supersede this and to require the payment to Britain, but this was debatable: Michael Collins was confident that a review of all such matters would leave the Free State a net beneficiary, because of previous over-taxation. In any event, the Boundary Commission agreement of 1925 released the Irish government from the provisions of article 5 of the Treaty, and although the Ultimate Financial Settlement of the following year committed the Free State to pay the annuities, this agreement was never ratified by the Dáil.[95] The validity of de Valera's case was demonstrated by British reluctance in later years to accept independent arbitration on the issue.

In an interview in 1929 de Valera portrayed himself as a 'workaholic'.

> When the Dáil is in session I arrive in town about eleven in the morning, and seldom get home much before midnight . . . I might take a day off, but what would be the use? People would only be ringing me up at every hour of the day, and I hate doing business at home. Any official transactions or official interviews I like to conduct at the office . . .[96]

Helping him were his personal secretary, Kathleen O'Connell, and his political secretary, a role filled first by Frank Gallagher and then, from January 1929, by Seán Moynihan,[97] a Kerry republican who would later serve as secretary to the Executive Council. But, as always, it was O'Connell who was indispensable; when she went on holidays de Valera complained that Moynihan couldn't find anything he wanted.[98]

Although he claimed to have no interest in holidays, he did have one trip in this period that might qualify, to a meeting of the Inter-Parliamentary Congress in Berlin in August 1928. He stopped in Paris for nearly a week, seeing the sights (Versailles, Les Invalides, Chartres and Montmartre), taking in a couple of plays, and exploring the book shops.[99] In Berlin, outside conference hours, he hit the tourist trail again, visiting Potsdam and the opera, and taking a stroll down Siegesallee, Kaiser Wilhelm's 'Victory Avenue', lined with historical statues. In an unusually vivid letter to Frank Gallagher he described the street 'where German princes and poets and bishops in stone try to remind the whispering swains and swainesses in the alcoves that Germany had a past as well as the future they are interested in'.[100]

At home, the de Valera family was growing up. Terry, the youngest, started school in August 1928.[101] Vivion, Eamonn and Máirín were all in UCD by the end of 1931, studying chemistry and physics, medicine and maths respectively.[102] Máirín had been 'pressurised' by her father to study maths, but she later dropped the subject and turned to botany, in which she would have a distinguished career.[103]

There was no doubt about who was in charge at home: Sinéad had full command of the domestic arrangements, including finding a new house, in Cross Avenue, Blackrock, where they moved in March 1930. As Terry recalled, 'Father always had complete confidence in her and left such arrangements in her capable hands'.[104]

It was just as well that Sinéad was a good household manager, because money was always tight. Until September 1929 her husband's Dáil salary was paid into party funds. In that month it was decided that he could keep it and that his annual allowance from the party should be increased to £364.[105] In February 1931 the party agreed to buy him a new car.[106] But it stuck to the policy of having a maximum salary in the public service of £1,000, despite a suggestion by O'Kelly that the President of the Executive Council should receive £1,500 (though once de Valera actually got the job a different attitude was taken[107]).

Now well into middle age, he was also feeling the advancing years. On his 46th birthday, he wrote in his diary: 'My birthday what a different sound . . .'[108] a reference to a line from Thomas Moore: 'My birthday! What a different sound that word had in my youthful ears; and how each time the day comes round, less and less white its mark appears.' His eyesight was also starting to trouble him more. In 1929 he complained to his consultant that, when he stood at his place in the Dáil, he found it 'difficult to read notes laid on my desk in front of me. The reading lenses are out of focus, and the distance lenses . . . are difficult to bring into play'.[109] It was an ominous portent of a problem that would increasingly affect him.

Once Fianna Fáil entered Leinster House, there was naturally speculation about whether de Valera and Éamonn Donnelly, the party's two Stormont MPs, would enter the Northern Ireland Parliament as well. The *Irish Times* 'confidently expected' such a move,[110] while the Northern Prime Minister, James Craig, asked his colleagues to consider lifting the exclusion order against de Valera if he took his seat.[111] However, the question was moot, as de Valera ruled out entering Stormont. The position there was 'quite different' from that in the Dáil.

In the latter, those who stood for an Irish Ireland were in the majority. All that was necessary was to get them to agree upon a policy for the attainment of their ideals. In the Six County area they were in a minority, and could not hope to secure control.[112]

De Valera and Donnelly had both been elected as members of Sinn Féin in 1925; but Fianna Fáil decided well in advance that it would serve 'no useful national purpose' to contest the next Stormont elections in May 1929.[113] The problem was how to explain this to the party faithful, who tended to think that partition demanded more than lip-service. In their report to the third Fianna Fáil ard-fheis, in October 1928, Lemass and Boland advanced a frankly partitionist rationale.

> The general view among Republicans is that an essential step to the realisation of national Unity will be a political victory by Republicans in the South and that it will be wise policy not to divert our energies from that object until it has been attained.[114]

The policy was to remain even when Fianna Fáil did achieve power in the South; despite anti-partition rhetoric, elections across the border were regarded as a distraction.[115]

This didn't mean, however, that the North couldn't be useful to Fianna Fáil's onward march in the 26 counties. In 1929 de Valera was invited to Belfast to open a fair organised by the Gaelic League and the Gaelic Athletic Association. He accepted, despite being well aware that, because of the exclusion order, he risked imprisonment. The RUC, aware of his plans from the newspapers, sought government approval to arrest him if he crossed the border.[116] On 5 February, de Valera caught the afternoon train to Belfast, accompanied by Frank Fahy, a Galway TD and Gaelic League activist.[117] At Goraghwood Station, outside Newry, RUC men boarded the train and arrested him. According to the RUC,

> he said 'all right' and putting on his hat took hold of his attaché case and accompanied me to the Station Master's Office, where we awaited the arrival of a motor car by which I had him removed to Bessbrook RUC Barracks.[118]

He was then driven to Belfast, and two days later he was sentenced to a month in prison.[119]

There were calls within Fianna Fáil for a comprehensive boycott of Belfast goods, but these suggestions were twice rejected by the National Executive.[120] Fianna Fáil's response to the arrest of its leader was entirely propagandist, which of course was the point: de Valera's arrest didn't engender any change in the North, but did improve Fianna Fáil's political position in the South.[121]

Cosgrave, well aware of the political impact, appealed to Craig to release de Valera 'purely as an act of grace'. The Stormont Government agreed, provided he promised not to re-enter the North without per-mission.[122] There was no danger of de Valera accepting these conditions, and in the Dáil, Seán T. O'Kelly condemned Cosgrave's 'crawling, creeping, begging letter' to Craig, and said neither Griffith nor Collins would have stood for a citizen on a peaceful visit being arrested. He added, theatrically, 'Is that what the Black and Tan war was fought for? Is that what honest men in Ireland of all shades of opinion died for?'[123] Cosgrave was unmoved. 'I should be sorry to believe that this whole thing was planned with a view to getting political kudos. But it has very much that appearance'.[124]

De Valera was released from his last spell in prison on 6 March. His month as a guest of His Majesty does not appear to have taken too much out of him: later that year he told an English journalist that the only exercise he took was while in jail. 'I should have to go to prison again if I wanted a really bracing holiday!'[125] The reason he was so busy was that, apart from being leader of the opposition, he was also establishing a newspaper.

For Éamon de Valera, the publication of the first edition of the *Irish Press* was 'probably the most notable date in his diary next to Easter Monday 1916'.[126] Establishing the paper took up a staggering amount of his time – far more than politics. But he firmly believed, probably correctly, that without a supportive newspaper Fianna Fáil would not have won the 1932 election. More controversial was the scheme he designed to control the paper. While the *Press* was identified with Fianna Fáil, it was not controlled by the party, but by de Valera personally, and he would keep control within his own family: having lost the support of close colleagues in 1921 and 1926, he was not certain he could always rely on Fianna Fáil (the same aim could have been achieved by vesting control in an independent trust, of course).

De Valera had always been conscious of the power of the press, even before he was the victim of it during the Civil War. In November 1918, from Lincoln Prison, he wrote to his mother about the press.

> What a power for evil it is, setting classes and nations at each other's throats. To me it seems that its powers for evil are those always used – its powers for good seldom.[127]

In the words of a colleague, he 'had suffered from misrepresentation and misinterpretation and, what was of greater importance to him, he had realised the power of the press to mould and guide the people for good or ill'.[128] As was seen in Chapter 17, he had made desultory efforts to start a newspaper when released from jail in 1924. Now those efforts were renewed.

De Valera hoped to raise £100,000 in Ireland to fund the project, and another $500,000 (£100,000) in the United States. After a New York court had ruled that republican-bond money should be returned to the original subscribers, de Valera urged them to assign the money to him for use by Fianna Fáil. Now he wanted to return to this well, sweeping up as much of the remaining bond money as he could for the newspaper project. His old nemesis Mary MacSwiney, naturally, disapproved. 'It is flagrantly wrong to ask for the Dáil money for his new paper, but he is doing so many wrong things that – well, I can't spare time to write about him'.[129]

In December 1927 de Valera went to America to raise funds for the project. Once again he travelled in style, accompanied by the faithful Frank Gallagher on the *Leviathan*. After their 'stormy passage', Gallagher ruefully noted that 'if you think big boats are harder to get seasick in than small boats you had better change your mind. The Chief had a bad time'.[130] However, once they were in New York and safely installed again in the Waldorf-Astoria, things began to look up. Christmas for de Valera was spent in Rochester, New York, with his mother, 'in a foot of snow'.[131]

De Valera's time in America happened to coincide with a visit there by Cosgrave in January 1928. While admitting that 'the people of Chicago are all agog about Cosgrave's coming', de Valera dismissed his visit as 'a matter of little consequence to us'.[132] Asked at a news conference if he would pay de Valera a visit, Cosgrave was similarly dismissive. 'I see no reason why the head of the government should call on one of his citizens'.[133] The two men at one point ended up in the same hotel but apparently did not meet.[134]

The business of de Valera's trip was conducted mainly in private, with groups of supporters in various cities summoned to meetings at which he gave 'a complete explanation of all the details in connection with the establishment of the paper'. It was stressed that he would be joined on the board of the new venture by 'six of Ireland's most prominent business men'.[135] His old ally Joe McGarrity suggested he should try to interest the newspaper magnate William Randolph Hearst in setting up a paper in Ireland instead.[136] A Hearst newspaper would be sympathetic to de Valera's politics – but it would also be out of his control. No more was heard of this idea.

The trip saw the establishment of promotion committees in various centres to run the campaign,[137] and of a national committee to promote the

'Irish Daily Newspaper Company', with two stalwarts of the bond campaign on board, Frank Walsh (chairman) and Garth Healy (secretary).[138]

De Valera and Gallagher left New York on 11 February 1928, reaching home on the 18th.[139] With the work in America under way, it was now time to get Ireland organised. At the first meeting of the parliamentary party after his return he urged TDs and senators 'to do their best to get subscriptions for the proposed daily newspaper'.[140] He followed this with a ten-day blitz of the country, with conferences in Wexford, Waterford, Carlow, Kilkenny, Cork, Tipperary and Thurles.[141] The strain took its toll: in March de Valera fell ill and was out of action for a month.[142]

When he got back to work, the newspaper remained his top priority. Ten thousand leaflets were printed and circulated to the Fianna Fáil cumainn, and deputies were again urged 'to energetically push forward collection for daily paper'. In June, six deputies were 'relieved of their parliamentary duties in order to canvass for subscriptions for the new daily paper'.[143]

Finally, on 5 September 1928, the Irish Press Company was registered – though there would be three more years of relentless work before the first edition would roll off the presses.[144] The *Irish Independent* rejected the first advertisement seeking funds from the public, but it appeared in the *Nation* on 15 September 1928. 'Today the Irish people are given the opportunity to break the stranglehold of an alien Press'.[145] Writing to McGarrity, de Valera said he was sure he would understand the need for the project.[146] While impressed that his old friend had raised a significant amount of money in Ireland, McGarrity was not encouraging about the prospects in the United States, at least among supporters of Clan na Gael.

> The Clan as an organisation . . . are cold to the proposition which they consider a part of the Political effort in which they have no faith whatever and I must say I am in hearty agreement with their opinion . . .[147]

While Ireland produced the £100,000 it had been asked for, America had provided only $135,000 of the $500,000 sought. De Valera despatched Frank Aiken to America to try to drum up support, warning that if they didn't fill the American quota they 'will have received the biggest blow we have got since the Cease Fire'. Part of the American target was to be met by subscriptions, part by the reassignment of Republican bonds. The money released by the New York court case in 1927 (58 cents in the dollar) was still being slowly paid out, and de Valera was anxious to get as much as possible redirected to the newspaper. He also knew there would be a bonus: the Free State government was committed to refunding bond-holders the remaining 42 cents in the dollar once the distribution was complete.[148] If the newspaper had the bonds by then, it would be the beneficiary.

De Valera was determined to keep control of the new company, and had come up with a cunning plan to do so. As he explained to Frank Aiken, all American subscriptions would be pooled and the money used to buy shares in de Valera's name. 'This will give me the voting strength of the whole of the American shares.'[149]

Most American subscribers would get shares in the Irish Press Corporation, registered in Delaware, which would hold 43 per cent of the shares in Irish Press Ltd in Dublin. The corporation's own shares would be made up of 60,000 non-voting A shares and 200 B shares, carrying the voting rights – and de Valera would own these crucial B shares.[150] As de Valera made clear, the American subscribers would retain the financial rights to their shares, but he would retain their legal ownership.[151]

He also made sure he would have full operational control of the newspaper by appointing himself controlling director, editor-in-chief and managing director. This gave him the power to appoint all the staff of the paper (from the editor down to the reporters and sub-editors), to dictate editorial policy and to direct the company in every detail. The controlling director was not elected: once appointed, they could stay in office as long as they saw fit and could transfer their powers to any one of the other directors.[152] When the time came, de Valera chose to confer his powers on his son Vivion, who in turn passed them on to his son Éamon. This retention within the family of what was a valuable asset paid for by others would generate controversy and bitterness for many years to come.[153] This all, though, lay in the future – he still had to find the money to establish the newspaper in the first place.

By September 1929 de Valera could report the acquisition of a site at Burgh Quay in Dublin and the preparation of the architect's plans for its alteration and reconstruction. 'Without another day's delay we could now place the various contracts and get on with the work, full steam ahead if we had capital in hands to justify our doing so.' He believed that the money could be secured from the former subscribers to the Republican loan who were about to get their money back, 'if only they are properly approached on the matter'.[154] And the proper approach could only come from him, which meant another trip to America. While it was, he told McGarrity, 'very inconvenient from every point of view for me to go, I feel the circumstances being what they are there is hardly any choice left'.[155] He told the Fianna Fáil National Executive that he would be away for about six weeks[156] – in fact the trip would take six months, from the end of November 1929 to the end of May 1930.

Arriving in New York six weeks after the Wall Street Crash, de Valera reported that, 'although conditions financially are worse than when I was here last I have hopes that we will succeed'.[157] He still got plenty of attention from journalists, but 'they are not giving so much publicity because I am on a business mission'.[158] He missed O'Connell's help and wished he had been able to bring Liam Pedlar (who was ill) with him rather than Seán Moynihan.[159]

De Valera set to work immediately, tapping his faithful supporters. 'The Newspaper is of such fundamental importance, and you have given such devoted service in the past, that I feel I can rely on you to come.'[160]

He explained that the money already raised would cover the cost of premises and machinery, but not running costs, 'and we will not endanger our independence by seeking bank credits . . .' He also used a phrase that would become the motto of the *Irish Press*.

Our central purpose . . . is to provide the Irish people with a paper which will give them the truth in news, without attempting to colour it for party purposes.[161]

De Valera's hopes of concluding his mission quickly and getting home were frustrated by legal challenges that delayed the distribution of the bond money. In January 1930 Lemass advised him to take the time he needed to finish his task. 'It is the most important thing we have on hands, no work done here would compensate for failure there.'[162] Two months later Lemass again stressed the importance of establishing a paper – without it they were 'only beating the air . . . Our success at the next Election will be measured by your success now'.[163]

In a circular to bond-holders, de Valera argued that 'no more useful service can be rendered to Ireland at the present time' than the establishment of a daily newspaper. This theme was expanded on by Frank Walsh in an accompanying leaflet: the project could go ahead if the directors of the company had an assurance that the bond money was coming. This could be achieved by the bond-holders assigning their interest to de Valera.

Whilst these funds are being solicited by way of donations, Mr de Valera will, of course, not derive personally any monetary profit from them. He intends to make the necessary and proper arrangements to ensure that if any profits accrue from the enterprise . . . such profits . . . will be made available for the donors.[164]

The form of assignment stated that the bond-holder agreed to

sell, assign, transfer and set over unto Éamon de Valera, his executors, administrators, and assigns, all my right, title and interest in and to Bond Certificate No. . . . in the sum of $ . . . of the Republic of Ireland Loan . . .[165]

As Desmond FitzGerald pointed out in the Dáil, the American subscribers were not getting shares in the newspaper, and they were signing over to de Valera not just the proportion of their bond money they would receive arising from the court case but also the right to secure the rest from the Irish government. And de Valera would be able to use the money for any purpose he liked, not just the paper.

It means that he will, if elected here, take an action against himself to get out of the State funds here money which . . . will actually be handed over to himself . . .[166]

FitzGerald's prediction was entirely accurate.

There were also demands from home for money for Fianna Fáil. Lemass warned that

we cannot see how we are going to meet the estimated expenditure until May next when the 1930 Collection is due. Our estimated revenue is about £250 short . . . If we could get a windfall of about £500 now it would help us over the most difficult period.[167]

But as de Valera explained, the American economy was so bad that 'it will be *almost impossible* to raise the money we require' for the paper – there would be nothing for the party.[168]

Apart from New York and Rochester, he visited Boston, Philadelphia, Detroit, Chicago, Seattle and other cities.[169] Everywhere he went, he visited the local newspaper office, noting the type of machinery used, as well as the names of the editors. But more than equipment, he was interested in editorial structures, enquiring on at least one occasion: 'How do you control the thing?'[170] The trip, having proved educational as well as financially rewarding, came to an end in May 1930, when de Valera and Moynihan crossed the Atlantic once again, reaching home on the 30th.[171]

It was not until as late as 9 March 1931 that it was finally confirmed that the new paper would be called the *Irish Press*, and that it would be a morning rather than an evening paper.[172] This choice was significant, given that de Valera had told shareholders that an evening paper was 'the more profitable branch of a daily newspaper enterprise'.[173] A morning paper, however, is regarded as being more influential, and its political effect greater.[174] If there was a choice to be made between making money and influencing the public, de Valera would unhesitatingly choose the latter. It was planned to produce an evening paper and a Sunday paper, 'to render in full the national service we require', once the company had 'proved itself capable of successfully handling the morning edition'.[175]

Although de Valera toyed with the idea of appointing an American to the editor's chair, Frank Gallagher was the obvious choice. He certainly thought so himself, applying to the company secretary, Robert Brennan, for the job, giving his experience and stating his expected salary: £1,000 a year, with annual increments of £50, to a maximum of £1,200. He also suggested a contract 'over a period of years'.[176] De Valera baulked at this sum (understandably, given the party policy that no one was worth more than £1,000 a year), and Gallagher offered to come down to £800 for the first year, on the understanding that he 'was doing so in pursuance of a principle rather than as an estimate either of the requirements of the position or its worth'.[177] In the end, the board was slightly more generous, giving Gallagher £850, with a salary review after a year; but the contract was only for one year.[178] The penny-pinching attitude should have served as a warning to Gallagher: despite his ability, loyalty and huge contribution to the establishment of the *Irish Press,* he was to be treated shamefully by the company – which meant by de Valera.

Gallagher was an experienced journalist and offered wise advice to his staff – starting with the obvious but important point that 'Ireland matters most to the *Irish Press*'. He told them to

> write simple English . . . Verify all quotations. Acknowledge everything of importance taken from other papers. When in doubt *find* out . . . If you don't understand your copy the public won't.

The *Irish Press* would not be a Dublin paper, and it would remember that there are O'Connell Streets in other cities. He warned against being sucked into the 'imperialist' world view of the British and foreign news agencies.

> Do not pass the word 'bandits' as a description of South American revolutionaries. Pirates and robbers in China are not necessarily Communists and therefore should not be described as such . . . These agency stories show ignorance of Catholic practice . . . Check all doubtful references in such copy . . .[179]

De Valera kept a close, almost obsessive, eye on developments at Burgh Quay, intervening to smooth out problems with the builders, overseeing conferences about the laying of electrical cables, and organising a priest to bless the premises as the presses were being tested.[180] His pocket diary contains notes on printers' measures, sizes of paper and potential employees, including the future President of Ireland, Cearbhall Ó Dálaigh, as Irish Editor. He also kept notes on what he thought should be in the paper: financial and foreign news, a women's column covering fashion and cookery, and efforts to promote Irish goods. He also wanted the paper to refer to 'Ireland' rather than the 'Free State' (a precursor of his new constitution six years later).[181]

As 5 September 1931, the date for the publication of the first issue, approached, pressure on the staff, and on de Valera, increased. The builders 'had almost to be forcibly thrown out' so that the paper could be produced – they were still putting the roof on the despatch department, preventing a dry run in that crucial area.[182] De Valera stayed all night in Burgh Quay on 30 August, and until 5 a.m. the following day, as dummy papers were produced. The first full trial of the presses took place on 3 September, with Margaret Pearse pressing the button to set them rolling – a task she performed again when the paper was published on the morning of 5 September. Production delays meant that only about half the parcels made the 3:55 a.m. special train, which delivered the papers throughout the country. De Valera recorded in his diary that the

> tension as the minutes sped by after 2 a.m. was nerve-racking. It was the excellent work of the despatch department that enabled the train to be caught at all.[183]

The new paper looked different from its rivals. Most obviously, it had news on its front page, as opposed to the advertising on the front pages of the *Irish Times* and the *Irish Independent*. The *Irish Press* had a much greater emphasis on sport, particularly Gaelic games, with the first issue timed to coincide with the all-Ireland hurling final in Croke Park the following day.[184] In the *Round Table*, J. J. Horgan (de Valera's former sponsor for a post in UCC) sniffily described it as 'a cross between the *Daily Express* and a parish magazine. Its sporting news is given the abnormal space common to most modern newspapers'.[185] A back-handed compliment came from the *Irish Independent* and *Irish Times*, who after some time managed to have the new paper excluded from the 3:55 delivery train. The *Press* applied to the Railway Tribunal to have the Great Southern Railway's arrangement with the other papers set aside, but its application was rejected, which was both 'a psychological and financial blow'.[186]

But, for the time being, it was self-inflicted problems which bothered de Valera. The second edition, of Monday 7 September,

> failed utterly to catch the train, 3.55. Rotten organisation in the case room. Type misplaced – the chief offender causing the delay was the Advertising manager with his late adverts . . . Have found it very hard to keep my temper.

De Valera managed to get home to sleep for an hour and a half, before having to attend a board meeting and then return to Burgh Quay. 'Got assurances that all would be right tonight. Let us hope so.' For the next week he spent every night at the *Irish Press* building.[187] He was critical of the first issue, believing it to be 'far from satisfactory', and he feared that 'many who bought it out of curiosity were not impressed as we should like'.[188]

These teething problems could be expected in any new publication, and by and large the paper was a success. Circulation for October and November was more than 54,000, rising to 61,000 in December, before falling back to 54,000 in January 1932. But the excitement of the election and of Fianna Fáil's entry into office raised sales, to 81,000 in February and 97,000 in March – a figure it would not surpass for a year.[189] Lemass and Boland urged delegates to the ard-fheis in October 1931 to support it in every way, 'particularly by giving preference to those firms which use its columns for advertising purposes'.

But if the party supported the paper, how closely did the paper support the party? According to Lemass and Boland, the *Irish Press* was 'guided in national and economic matters by the same general principles as Fianna Fáil'.[190] A similar message was propounded by de Valera, who told the ard-fheis that the *Irish Press* should not be 'tied to any party'. The paper was allied to the paper, but would not necessarily support it on every detail.

The party's public representatives expected a rather more supportive attitude. Gallagher and Brennan attended a meeting of the parliamentary party, where they heard criticism of 'the treatment in the paper of public meetings, Dáil reports, racing, etc.'. Gallagher defended his staff but must have felt some pressure to keep the party happy (what exactly the criticism of the racing coverage was, and how it related to Fianna Fáil, is not clear).[191]

In a letter to his mother, de Valera complained that he had been extremely busy, and he told her that 'the paper is doing fairly well – but we must do better'.[192] This pursuit of excellence was taken out on the unfortunate Gallagher. De Valera took exception to articles on Spain and Russia on 15 September. The paper's lead story was an interview with Victoria Kent, Director of Prisons of the Republican Government of Spain, and a distant relative of Thomas Kent, executed in Cork after the Rising. Gallagher followed this with an editorial that, while raising concerns about the treatment of the Church, was broadly sympathetic to the Spanish Republicans. The article dealing with Russia was a report of a garden party held in Maude Gonne MacBride's house in aid of the Friends of Soviet Russia; again, it could be seen as broadly sympathetic to the communist regime.[193] De Valera recorded his having a 'long chat' with Gallagher about these articles.

> He was nettled a bit. Said some blunt things. Danger of our attitude being misunderstood[,] must avoid this whilst being fearless in giving the 'truth in the news' . . .[194]

Evidently, de Valera wanted his editor to be fearless – but not too fearless. While such close attention was probably irksome, de Valera at least continued to keep the cash coming, urging members of the parliamentary party to collect arrears from subscribers, and to seek further capital of £45,000 to meet the paper's running costs.[195] He also urged greater efforts in America on Garth Healy. 'We *must* get the full nominal capital to be on safe ground.' He complained to Healy that he was 'overwhelmed with different types of work' – especially as the general election was now looming, and he had to worry about finding the money for the campaign as well.[196]

Many of the themes of the years in opposition were summed up in de Valera's speech to the Fianna Fáil ard-fheis in October 1931, five months before entering government. On the crucial question of the legitimacy of the state he said that the pillars on which the policy of the organisation rests are: the acceptance of the vote of the majority of the people's elected representatives as deciding national policy, and the abolition of the oath which at present prevents a section of our people from having representation in the representative assembly.

Once the oath was removed, 'there will be no shadow of excuse for anyone resisting the authority of the elected representatives of the people sitting in parliament'. This, of course, implied that there *was* an excuse for doing so while the oath was in force. But it also implied that once the oath was gone, the IRA would have to come to heel – a warning it did not heed. He also said that, after the abolition of the oath, another general election must be held within a year, or at most two, 'so as to give to the section that will be excluded at the coming election an opportunity for securing representation'. The Governor-General might have to be retained for the time being to avoid legal difficulties, but the 'ultimate aim would be to assimilate the office to that of President of the Republic'. On partition, he was vague.

> I see no immediate solution of that problem. Force is out of the question. Were it feasible, it would not be desirable. The only hope that I can see now for the reunion of our people is good government in the 26 counties and such social and economic conditions here as will attract the majority in the six counties to throw in their lot with us.

While they desired to live in peace with the North, 'our attitude would be one of non-cooperation so long as Britain persisted in any attempt to force the terms of the imposed treaty upon us'.[197]

There was some doubt about when the general election would be. There had been speculation about an election in the summer or autumn of 1931; de Valera felt that if Cosgrave didn't go to the country before the *Irish Press* began publication he would be likely to wait until after the Eucharistic Congress in June 1932. De Valera was not too confident of the result.

> It is very difficult to forecast what the result will be. It will require tremendous effort to win. The moment the campaign is on the threats which have been so effective in the past will all be made again . . . The majority of the people are not prepared to risk any change that might involve conflict with Britain.[198]

This caution was justified by the record of the seven by-elections during the Sixth Dáil, which did not show Fianna Fáil's rise to be inexorable. Cumann na nGaedheal won five of them, winning a seat off Fianna Fáil in Leitrim-Sligo in June 1929. Fianna Fáil's two victories – in Longford-Westmeath in June 1930 and Kildare in June 1931 – were in constituencies where it had out-polled the government party in 1927. The vacancy in the first constituency was caused by the death of a Fianna Fáil member, and Kildare had been a Labour Party seat. In other words, Fianna Fáil, the main opposition party, didn't win a single seat off the government in seven by-elections. While the Fianna Fáil vote increased on its general election poll in each of the seven, so did Cumann na nGaedheal's; both parties benefited from the absence of smaller parties and independents.[199]

The election was called on 29 January 1932, with polling set for 16 February and with the new Dáil to meet on 9 March.[200] The Fianna Fáil message to electors promised to remove the oath; to retain the land annuities, using the money to abolish agricultural rates and reduce taxation; to seek legal advice on whether other payments should be made to Britain; to introduce protection for industries in order to meet the country's needs in manufactured goods; to preserve the home market for agriculture; to negotiate trade agreements; to eliminate waste and extravagance in public administration; and to endeavour to preserve Irish and make it the spoken language of the people. To these policies were added a vague pledge to 'strive' to bring partition to an end by peaceful means, and a promise not to

> use our majority to pursue a vindictive course against any minority . . . Ordinarily such promises would not be necessary. Apprehensions, however, have been aroused and it is necessary to allay them. We may add that we have no leaning towards Communism and no belief in Communistic doctrines . . .

The manifesto also promised that the party would not exceed its mandate in the field of international relations 'without again consulting the people' – a pledge not to pick any further fights with Britain.[201]

This programme was carefully designed to neutralise the attacks of Cumann na nGaedheal. And the government party *was* obsessed with attacking its opponent: more than a quarter of the Cumann na nGaedheal election statement was devoted to the opposition.[202] Just in case the government wasn't already seen as heavy-handed, it further helped the Fianna Fáil cause by prosecuting Frank Gallagher, editor of the *Irish Press,* at the Military Tribunal for publishing articles critical of the treatment of prisoners. The trial began four days before the election was called.[203]

A constant theme of government propaganda was that 'the gunmen are voting for Fianna Fáil'; they were correct. On 12 January 1932 the IRA Army Council revoked the order prohibiting IRA members working at or voting in elections, and it recommended that they 'vote against the candidates of the Cumann na nGaedheal party and other candidates who actively support the policy of that party'. Republican purity was retained by stating that the IRA did not 'accept or approve of the policy of any of the parties contesting the Elections', nor did they believe that elections could achieve the IRA's aims.[204]

Fianna Fáil ran an energetic campaign. The *New York Times* said de Valera was 'arousing emotions and enthusiasms strangely like those Adolf Hitler is spreading through Germany', though it acknowledged that he was 'anything but a firebrand, this mild academic, lean and tight-lipped, who lectures his audience and leaves it to his lieutenants to revive emotions of more troubled times'.[205] De Valera had been too ill in early January to attend a number of selection conventions.[206] But once the Dáil was dissolved he had little option but to throw himself into the fray. In Co. Kerry he was welcomed by marching bands, with men on horseback and dozens of torch-bearers. In Cork he was met by an estimated 12,000 people, the greatest reception he had ever received in the city.[207]

A week before polling, de Valera adopted a conciliatory tone towards Britain in an interview with an American journalist. Asked if he would insist on establishing a Republic outside the Commonwealth, he replied mildly, 'That will come in its own good time. Meanwhile our mandate does not extend so far.' Asked if he would try to open negotiations with Britain and Northern Ireland on Irish unity, he said he would be happy to do so 'if occasion presents itself'.[208]

King George certainly knew who he wanted to win the election. When the Free State's representative in London, John Dulanty, called on him in January, the King 'hoped that there might be no doubt about the return of the present Government', expressing regret that 'the Fianna Fáil party should be led by somebody who was, as far as he could discover, not an Irishman at all'. Dulanty took the opportunity to pass on to him a warning from Cosgrave that

it would be most unwise for the British Government to adopt too aggressive an attitude or iron hand methods towards a Government made up of the Fianna Fáil party. Such action might bring about the destruction of the constructive work that had been done by the Government in the past ten years.[209]

The King agreed with this sentiment; but would his government feel the same way?

The Secretary of State for the Dominions, J. H. Thomas, warned colleagues some days before the election that a de Valera government would produce 'a difficult situation'.[210] He advised that, if the Free State was to leave the Commonwealth, it should do so on its own responsibility. 'In other words we must not take action which would enable Mr. de Valera to say that we were forcing him out of the British Commonwealth'. And they must insist that 'the compulsory taking of the Oath is an essential part of the Settlement of 1921'. If the oath was abolished, or if the annuities were withheld, sanctions of some sort would have to be considered.[211]

On polling day the Fianna Fáil machine outclassed Cumann na nGaedheal. In Co. Waterford one government supporter reported 'strong supporters of Fianna Fáil' acting as presiding officer and clerk in several polling stations. There were fleets of cars for transporting voters – 'mostly illiterate, all well tutored how to vote' – to the polls, and he noted their precise instructions on how to vote in each area in order to elect as many candidates as possible.[212]

The result of the general election saw Fianna Fáil become the most popular party – a position it would retain for an astonishing 79 years. Its 44.5 per cent share of the first-preference vote (up more than nine points since September 1927) provided 15 more seats, for a total of 72 – the highest won to date by a single party and only five short of an absolute majority. Cumann na nGaedheal dropped five seats, returning 57 TDs, Labour won seven seats, down six, while there were four Farmers and 13 Independents.

The Labour Party held the balance of power and could secure the election of either de Valera or Cosgrave, though the party was highly unlikely to vote for the latter, who in any case made it clear he would not be seeking Labour's support.[213] Cumann na nGaedheal had come to the conclusion that if Fianna Fáil formed a government it would soon collapse. 'They will fail and that will finish them', as one party supporter put it.[214] This was a disastrous misjudgement, but the initiative clearly lay with Fianna Fáil anyway.

De Valera cautiously told a journalist that, as Fianna Fáil was the largest party,

> I expect the task of forming a Government will be given to us. From
> its attitude during the elections I conclude that we shall have the
> cooperation of Labour in working out our programme . . .[215]

In fact he was wary of the Labour Party, and had been for some time. The
previous summer he had told John T. Ryan that he feared being dependent
on Labour Party votes.

> They are opposed to us on all the fundamental political issues and
> would probably throw their weight against us when questions involving
> the treaty would come up. For our programme it is essential that we
> have a substantial majority over all other parties . . .[216]

Luckily, Labour proved more co-operative than de Valera feared. On 26
February it confirmed that, while it would neither seek nor accept office, it
would support a Fianna Fáil government, as long as its proposals did not
conflict with Labour Party policy.[217] The decision made sense, given that
the Labour Party had urged its voters to transfer to Fianna Fáil in the
election campaign; 73 per cent of Labour voters complied, compared with
the 14 per cent who gave their lower preferences to Cumann na
nGaedheal.[218] Another factor was the party leader – T. J. O'Connell had
lost his seat and been replaced by William Norton, who was far more in
tune with de Valera.

On the same day that newspapers reported the Labour Party's decision,
they published a statement by Cosgrave denying claims that some
members of his government were planning to obstruct the transfer of
power.[219] The claim had been aired in the *Irish Press*. While Cosgrave
flatly rejected the idea, the fact is that elements in the Free State army –
and more particularly Eoin O'Duffy, commissioner of the Garda Síochána
– had at the very least considered the possibility. In the event, O'Duffy
found to his surprise that his former colleagues in the army were not
willing to go along with his plans: the chief of staff, Michael Brennan,
transferred suspect officers and made it clear that the army must serve the
elected government, whatever its complexion might be.[220]

Now that a change of government seemed certain, de Valera was
invited to broadcast to America, which he did in the early hours of 4
March (he had spent several days sick in bed,[221] probably a reaction to the
strain of the campaign). He said that all friends of Ireland would be
overjoyed at 'the reunion of the national forces' after ten years of division.
The oath would be removed

and every section of our people will at last without coercion of conscience or sacrifice of principle be able to send their representatives to the people's assembly . . . Thus we shall have internal peace without coercive legislation and with that peace the conditions which will make it possible to devote the energies of our people to the task of economic reorganisation and reconstruction . . . The drain of the millions of pounds which Mr Cosgrave's government has been sending to England yearly without justification must also stop.[222]

On the morning of 8 March, the day before the Seventh Dáil assembled, de Valera, accompanied by Seán T. O'Kelly and Gerry Boland, met the Labour Party leader William Norton (together with William Davin and Thomas Johnson).[223] He promised to tackle unemployment and housing, and to introduce a pension scheme for widows and orphans. The Labour Party representatives pledged their support for the abolition of the oath and for an attempt to reach a new financial settlement with Britain.[224] All was ready for a change of government the following day.

Exactly ten years and two months had passed since de Valera resigned the Presidency after the Treaty vote. It was a stunning recovery from apparent political oblivion that would leave other Lazarus acts – Winston Churchill, Richard Nixon, Charles Haughey – in the shade. In his decade in the wilderness he had been a reluctant soldier, a defeated rebel, a despised prisoner; he had rebuilt a political party and then split it when he failed to get his way; he had founded another political movement, as well as a national newspaper; he had led his followers from the margins to the centre of the Free State political system, by taking an oath he had sworn never to take; and he had repeatedly defied predictions that he was finished. It was an even more astonishing achievement considering that it was his second rise against seemingly insurmountable odds. His first, from obscurity to national leadership in 1917; his second, from the disaster and ignominy of the Civil War to government in 1932. Supporters and critics alike must have wondered what gave him the determination and strength of character to defeat those odds – and how that character would define his coming rule of Ireland.

CHAPTER 20

THE DISARMING FRIENDLINESS OF HIS EYES

In March 1922 – between the vote on the Treaty and the outbreak of the Civil War – the writer Susan Mitchell delivered a lecture titled 'Hints for historians', in which she discussed the personalities of various literary and political figures. 'How', she asked, 'could the historians of the future ever understand from anything he had said the influence of Mr de Valera over his past and present colleagues, unless someone had noted the disarming friendliness of his eyes?'[1] How indeed.

De Valera's personal charm was a vital ingredient in his success. It is striking how many people – even, or perhaps especially, those who had just fallen out with him – spoke of their love for him. They included Arthur Griffith ('He is an individual whom I esteem and love, although, in the interests of the nation, I had to oppose him'[2]); Batt O'Connor ('I loved de Valera and love him still . . . I found it hard to take sides against such a charming personality as brave de Valera'[3]); and Mary MacSwiney ('De Valera, in spite of his great personality and the love we all have for him, was not able to gain the majority for this compromise'[4]). The love he inspired in his followers was generally less qualified, though even his loyal lieutenant Gerry Boland could add a caveat. 'Much as I loved Dev – and to know him closely was to love him – there were times when he could not just make up his mind.'[5] James Dillon also recognised the power of his personality, which he claimed was irresistible. He told the journalist Douglas Gageby, about to meet de Valera for the first time, that 'you cannot remain the same. You will have been in the presence of the enchanter.'[6]

This ability to inspire devotion, and even love, helps explain his rise, and his retention of power. His personality marked him out for advancement by his superiors in the Volunteers – Bulmer Hobson, Patrick Pearse and Thomas MacDonagh; it helped him dominate the prisoners in Lewes, and to impress Griffith among others on his release, therefore allowing him to secure the leadership of Sinn Féin; and, once he was in a position of authority, the relatively small leadership groups at the top of Sinn Féin and, later, Fianna Fáil came under his sway, and were as a result prepared to follow his lead, and to accept his sometimes irritating behaviour. What other leader would have got away with the interminable monologues he mistook for discussion, for instance? Of course, his hold on others was not absolute – as the examples of Griffith, O'Connor and MacSwiney demonstrate – but it was strong enough to keep enough of his followers loyal for him to maintain his position for an extraordinary length of time.

And he could project his charisma beyond the level of individuals or small groups and hold a large crowd – a vital skill at a time when rallies were the primary means of political campaigning. Seán Lemass recognised this quality the first time he saw de Valera, the newly appointed commandant of the 3rd Battalion, with his 'enormous personal magnetism' outweighing his 'rather queer-looking appearance'.

> It was this capacity to talk to audiences in simple terms that gave him the tremendous influence he had. I have seen crowds of people standing in bitter cold and heavy rain while he talked for an hour and a half or two hours about political matters in simple terms they could understand.[7]

'Sincerity' is one of the words often used by witnesses to his speeches; another is 'dignity' – a quality identified by his early biographer Seán Ó Faoláin, who suggested it 'contributes greatly to his influence'.[8]

Sincerity, dignity, charm – all useful qualities for a political career. And all pointless if not harnessed to drive, determination and self-belief. These too were an important part of de Valera's personality and were vital to his rise – a more important part, in fact, because while charm can be acquired, dignity adopted and sincerity faked, there is no substitute for the burning goad of ambition. While de Valera went to considerable lengths to deny this ambition, and made frequent references to his desire to lay down the burden of leadership and return to his maths books, he never quite seemed to get around to it. He had enough self-knowledge to recognise the effect power had on him.

It is extraordinary the change that occurs once people are in office. I
see it in myself. I watch it. Once you are satisfied that the welfare of
the country is served by your retaining power you get impatient of all
opposition – inclined to think it is all factions.[9]

And, of course, inclined not to give up leadership.

This is an important factor in de Valera's rise: he found that he liked
leadership, and that he was good at it. On the trivial level of sport, it is
striking that his reminiscences of his rugby career concentrate almost
entirely on his captaincy of the Blackrock Second team, barely mentioning
his frequent appearances for the Firsts. Status appeared to be more
important to him than the quality of rugby he played. His leadership in
the Volunteers was of a far more important character, but there was a
similar ambition for promotion, and a somewhat prickly insistence on the
recognition of his status – as his second in command, Seán Fitzgibbon,
found, when he was unwise enough to challenge it on St Patrick's Day,
1916. So where did de Valera's drive and ambition come from?

In recent years he has been variously described as an English spy, a
Catholic visionary and an Asperger's genius.[10] The first suggestion is
ridiculous, the second overstated, the third misconstrued. In fact, his
character can more satisfactorily be explained by the circumstances of his
life. He never knew his father and appears to have had some doubts about
what he was told about him; he barely knew his mother and resented her
decision to send him across the Atlantic; he had a relatively harsh
upbringing in rural Ireland; and even when he managed to escape this
background, to the sanctuary of Blackrock College, he worried about his
status – a worry that was accentuated by his failure to live up to his own
expectations about his academic performance.

He found some solace for these difficulties in reinventing himself, first
as a gentleman student, then as an Irish-language enthusiast, then as a
Volunteer, then as a Republican. Each new stage carried him further away
from his unsatisfactory background. Baptised George De Valero in
Manhattan, known as Naddy Cull in Bruree National School, he became
Eddie de Valera at Blackrock College, then Professor de Valera of
Rockwell College, then (briefly) Éamon de Bailéara of the Gaelic League,
before achieving the recognition and status he craved: commandant of the
Volunteers, President of the Republic, and finally, simply, the Chief.

While this was emotionally satisfying, it might be wondered if it was
emotionally healthy. When de Valera was elected president of Sinn Féin,
Kathleen Clarke confided her concerns to her diary. 'He is getting enough

adulation to turn an older and more experienced man's head'.[11] In the United States, John Devoy grumpily noted the 'great ovations' de Valera was receiving and claimed that 'his head is turned to a greater extent than any man I have met'.[12] Griffith was similarly struck by the changes wrought by his trans-Atlantic odyssey, describing him as 'a good man who had been ruined by America'.[13] And despite the adulation, the admiration, even the love, he attracted, his insecurity never really left him.

Of course, the higher he rose, the further he had to potentially fall – a fear he had expressed as far back as 1903. 'It is heartless cruelty . . . to bring a youth up from a low station . . . then only to disillusion him and place him . . . where to advance is impossible and to go back out of the question'.[14] The setbacks he received during his rise heightened this insecurity: the hostility of Daniel Cohalan and John Devoy in America, the perceived betrayal by Michael Collins and Arthur Griffith over the Treaty, the refusal of his colleagues in Sinn Féin to accept his proposed change of direction in 1926. Whenever he was challenged he assumed cheating: he (wrongly) blamed Sinn Féin for a failed election bid in the Gaelic League, suspected 'wrangling' in an election for officers in the Volunteers, was convinced of a conspiracy against him in America, and blamed Collins's IRB network for the defeat in the Dáil vote on the Treaty. Because even the closest of colleagues might prove untrustworthy, he must, in the final analysis, rely on himself. As a result, he convinced himself that he needed to fashion a new political party in which his decisions would be unchallenged, to establish a newspaper in which his views would be uncontested, and to build a new relationship with the Irish people in which his ideas would be accepted.

As a result of his insecurity he could rarely admit he was wrong, or even that he had changed his mind. Father Pat Gaynor recalled that, at Sinn Féin ard-fheiseanna, de Valera was

> constantly on his feet to explain and justify his ideas, and to prove his consistency . . . Always he was courteous, but a reflection on his consistency roused his ire. He was human and normal, if over-sensitive, in his reaction to criticism.[15]

In later life, de Valera displayed extreme sensitivity about his reputation and was prepared to go to extraordinary lengths to persuade historians that he had been right, especially on the Treaty and the Civil War. Lord Longford, a great admirer, believed that he had been wrong not to go to London for the Treaty negotiations, but recalled that de Valera used to go on arguing about it to the end of his life . . . He would never admit it was an error, but he was always ready to argue it at great length.[16]

Of course, a very good argument could be made that de Valera *was* right about 'external association': a very similar arrangement would, a quarter of a century later, reconcile Indian national aspirations with an association with Britain. The point, however, was that in 1921 external association didn't satisfy anyone other than Éamon de Valera – not the British, not the Republicans, not the moderates. Perhaps his mathematical mind convinced him that, if the correct formula is followed, the right result will be reached. But this didn't take account of the human factor or the political realities of the day, and so the concept was doomed to failure.

His self-sufficiency was pronounced ('I had only to examine my own heart and it told me straight off what the Irish people wanted'[17]), but not perhaps surprising in a boy whose favourite book was *Robinson Crusoe*, and whose solitary game as a child was ruling his own little island near his house. Despite his unseemly haste in escaping from the place, Bruree remained important to his self-image throughout his life. Whatever might be said of his obscure background, no-one could deny that he had been shaped by the rural Ireland in which he grew up.

After the Treaty debates the *Irish Times* journalist Bertie Smyllie referred to de Valera's

curious character . . . single minded, terribly sincere, but a slave to his own convictions. A politician, however firm may be his principles, must be prepared to yield before the pressures of irresistible facts. Mr de Valera, like Woodrow Wilson, allowed his sincerity to make him an autocrat.[18]

But de Valera was no dictator, at least by the time he entered government. Badly scarred by his experiences in America and during the Treaty negotiations, he placed a high value on consensus – too high for some of his colleagues, as government meetings dragged on for hours as he attempted to secure, not acquiescence, but acceptance of his views. It is also true that his mind *could* be changed, on occasion, by his colleagues – most notably over entry to the Dáil in 1927. The trick, as Lemass was to discover 30 years later when trying to chart a new course on the economy, was to convince de Valera that the new approach was consistent with previous policy. Once this had been achieved, de Valera was happy to go along with it.

By 1932 his character had both shaped his career and been shaped by it; he entered office with certain skills, and certain limitations. He was, in the words of his colleague Jim Ryan, 'pliable but unbreakable'[19] – a mixture of determination and flexibility that would serve him well in his political career. He was also pedantic, convinced that he was always right and over-sensitive to criticism. After coming to power in 1932 he would spend 21 of the following 27 years in government, before serving another 14 years as the country's elected head of state. It was an extraordinary political achievement, which will hardly be matched by any successor. Against all the odds, de Valera had risen again to regain power – the question now was how he would use it.

ENDNOTES

ABBREVIATIONS USED IN NOTES

— BMH – Bureau of Military History
— CE – *Cork Examiner*
— DED – Dáil Éireann Debates – references give date, volume and column numbers
— DIB – Dictionary of Irish Biography
— DIFP – Documents on Irish Foreign Policy – references give volume and document numbers
— EDV – Éamon de Valera
— EH – *Evening Herald*
— EP – *Evening Press*
— ET – *Evening Telegraph*
— FJ – *Freeman's Journal*
— II – *Irish Independent*
— IT – *Irish Times*
— IP – *Irish Press*
— IPC – Irish Press Corporation documents (private source)
— IV – *Irish Volunteer*
— KOC – Kathleen O'Connell
— MSP – Military Service Pensions collection, BMH
— NLI – National Library of Ireland
— P150 – Éamon de Valera papers, UCD Archives
— SDV – Sinéad de Valera
— SED – Seanad Éireann Debates – references give date, volume and column numbers
— SI – *Sunday Independent*
— SP – *Sunday Press*
— UCDA – UCD Archives
— WIT – *Weekly Irish Times*
— WS – Witness Statements, BMH

CHAPTER 01: SLÁN LEAT, DEV

1 This account is based on reports in the *Irish Press*, the *Irish Independent* and the *Irish Times* on 25 June 1973, as well as on the RTÉ film of the event, in the 'News Review' of 1973.

2 *IP*, 22/6/1973.

3 The original building had been replaced in 1951: http://archiseek.
   com/2014/bolands-mill. It has since been redeveloped into Treasury
   Building, home of the National Treasury Management Agency.

CHAPTER 02: THE QUESTION OF FAMILY HISTORY

1 Undated [1916], EDV to Catherine Wheelwright, P150/172.

2 15/3/1950, EDV to Miss Sol de Valera, P150/220.

3 19/12/1962, EDV to Msgr James Hamilton, P150/227.

4 BMH, WS 767, Patrick Moylett, quoting his father-in-law; Oliver St John
   Gogarty to Lady Londonderry, PRONI D3099/3/16.

5 Undated letter, P150/171.

6 New York passenger lists, 1820–1957. Database at www.ancestry.com.

7 United States Census Bureau, '1880 Fast facts 1880', https://www.census.
   gov/history/www/through_the_decades/fast_facts/1880_fast_facts.html.

8 EDV, typescript recollections, P150/1; 1880 Brooklyn Directory, online at
   http://www.bklynlibrary.org/sites/default/files/files/pdf/bc/citydir/1880%20
   A%20-%20H.pdf.

9 Silinonte, Joseph M, 'Vivion de Valera: The Search Continues, part 2', p. 8.

10 Find a Grave, Frank S. Girard (Giraud), http://www.findagrave.com/
    cgi-bin/fg.cgi?page=gr&GRid=61305545&ref=acom.

11 Silinonte, Joseph M, 'Vivion de Valera: The Search Continues, part 2', p. 8.

12 FitzGibbon and Morrison, *The Life and Times of Éamon de Valera*, p. 11.

13 The two versions can be found in separate accounts of his mother's story in
    de Valera's papers, P150/228. The inconsistency doesn't seem to have struck
    him.

14 Bromage, *De Valera and the March of a Nation*, p. 15.

15 Dwane, *Early Life of Éamon de Valera*, loc. 163–4. De Valera later described
    the book as containing 'fundamental inaccuracies'. 2/6/1922, EDV's
    secretary to publishers Sealy, Bryers and Walker, P150/1609.

16 Undated, Kate to EDV, P150/171.

17 9/4/1931, Catherine Wheelwright deposition, P150/184.

18 EDV, notes on his mother's recollections, P150/228.

19 6/9/1935, Fr M. A. Magnier, St Patrick's, Jersey City, to Father Edward
    Harnett, P150/229.

20 13/9/1956, Judge Peter Artaserse to EDV, P150/187.

21 17/9/1956, EDV to Artaserse, Ibid.

22 13/9/1956, Artaserse to EDV, Ibid.

23 10/1/1957, Hamilton to Artaserse, Ibid.

24 21/1/1961, Hamilton to Furniss, P150/227.

25 19/12/1962, EDV to Hamilton, Ibid.

26 8/1/1963, Hamilton to EDV, Ibid.

27 15/1/1963, EDV to Hamilton, Ibid.

28 Terry de Valera, *A Memoir*, p. 161.

29 Silinonte, Joseph M., 'Vivion de Valera: The Search Continues, part 1'.

30 Silinonte also searched civil marriage records for New York and Brooklyn between 1875 and 1885, with no result. Silinonte, Joseph M, 'The Search for Vivion de Valera, part 1', p. 23.

31 Silinonte, Joseph M., 'The Search for Vivion de Valera, part 1' and 'Vivion de Valera: The Search Continues, part 1'.

32 9/4/1931, Catherine Wheelwright deposition, P150/184.

33 11/6/1931, depositions of Patrick J. Hennessy and Catherine Daly, P150/184. Both these depositions, and that of Catherine Wheelwright, also incorrectly use a capital D in the surname.

34 Typed notes of his mother's recollections, P150/228.

35 Silinonte, Joseph M., 'The Search for Vivion de Valera, part 2'.

36 Ibid.

37 Ibid.

38 Terry de Valera, *A Memoir*, p. 169.

39 Unsigned affidavit by Kate Wheelwright, P150/528.

40 See several versions of the baptismal certificate in P150/3.

41 *IT*, 31/1/2005, Tim Pat Coogan's response to criticisms of him by Martin Mansergh.

42 EDV, notes from conversation with mother, and notes taken from flyleaf of bible, P150/228.

43 17/6/1944, EDV to Tom Wheelwright, P150/200.

44 See correspondence in P150/200.

45 12/10/1963, EDV to Ed Coll, P150/216.

46 26/3/1935, M. Ó Flannagáin to EDV, P150/221.

47 23/4/1938, KOC to Leopold Kerney, P150/224.

48 28/4/1938, Leopold Kerney to KOC, Ibid.

49 13/12/1961, M. Ó Flathartaigh (secretary to President de Valera) to Mayor of Cabra, Spain, P150/221.

50 31/9/1930, EDV to Sr Emilia Laguna Valera, P150/220.

51 'The President is very doubtful however of the correctness of this story, or that he is descended from the Antonio de Valera in question.' Draft memorandum on the de Valera family, P150/228

52 See correspondence in P150/220.

53 See correspondence between Michael Rynne (Irish embassy, Madrid) and the Marqués de Ciadoncha (Archivo Heráldico de los Señores de Rújula, Madrid), 1960, in P150/226.

54 10/9/1961, John G. Furniss to EDV, P150/227.

55 14/6/1961, Sr Villarreal de Álava, letter and family tree, P150/227.

56 24/12/1965, note from Spanish embassy, NAI, 98/1/70.

57 19/8/1924, T. M. Healy to his sister, quoting John Devoy, Healy-Sullivan Papers, UCDA, P6/A/103.

58 24/7/1933, memorandum of discussion between John Hearne and EDV, *DIFP*, IV:204.

59 2/7/1921, Plunkett to EDV, P150/1388. Plunkett blamed Jews for directing the First World War, attempting to 'injure, if not destroy, the Papacy' and of being 'sweaters' of British workers.

60 20/7/1921, Plunkett to EDV, P150/1388.

61 Silinonte, Joseph M., 'Vivion de Valera: The Search Continues, part 2', p. 9.

CHAPTER 03: MORE OR LESS AN ORPHAN

1 21/12/1905, EDV to Catherine Wheelwright, P150/170.

2 DED, 6/1/1922, vol. T/14, col. 274.

3 EDV, reminiscences in Macardle's hand, P150/3662.

4 EDV, reminiscences, begun 4/7/1954, P150/87.

5 EDV, typescript recollections, P150/1; 19/9/1955, reminiscences dictated by EDV, P150/228.

6 Montague, 'The Unpartitioned Intellect: Dante, Savanarola, and an Old Sign', p. 6.

7 Coll, 'My cousin Ed'.

8 See EDV to his brother Tom (31/5/1943), and reply (12/8/1943), P150/200. De Valera posed a series of questions to be put to Edward Coll, mainly about the Coll side of the family but also relating to his father. The reply gives his uncle's replies to the Coll questions, with no mention of his knowing anything at all about Vivion. It seems strange that Coll would have no observations to make about his brother-in-law, assuming he ever met him.

9 Coll, 'My cousin Ed'.

10 List of personal dates, P150/435.

11 Coll Millson, 'My cousin Éamon de Valera'.

12 Coll, 'My cousin Ed'.

13 The date is sometimes given as 20 April, but the correct date was found in Lloyd's records. 11/3/1955, R. J. O'Halloran (Irish Shipping) to P. Hanrahan, P150/439.

14 EDV, dictated reminiscences, begun 4/7/1954, P150/87.

15 EDV, 'Some events in Mother's life', P150/228.

16 EDV, reminiscences, in Dorothy Macardle's hand, P150/3662.

17 Questionnaire completed by Elisabeth Coll Millson for journalist Kees Van Hoek, NLI, Ms 33/688/A.

18 Marriage certificate, P150/228.

19 See 1900 and 1910 US Census entries, www.ancestry.com. This point is made by Joseph Silinonte in *Irish Roots*. Kate was also prone to shaving a few years off her age in her census entries.

20 26/12/1889, EDV to Hannie, P150/170.

21 2/3/1896, EDV to Hannie, Ibid.

22 6/10/1902, EDV to Tom, P150/200.

23 21/12/1905, EDV to Catherine Wheelwright, P150/170.

24 16/12/1909, Tom to EDV, P150/200.

25 As Owen Dudley Edwards points out, this meant that 'in strict terms de Valera had but one Irish grandparent'. Dudley Edwards, *Éamon de Valera*, p. 25.

26 19/9/1955, EDV, notes on the Carroll family, P150/228.

27 Handwritten notes from school register, P150/231.

28 The dates of her emigration, and of her son's birth, disprove the persistent rumour that he was the son of a local landlord.

29 9/11/1955, letter from Custom House to EDV, P150/231.

30 EDV, reminiscences begun 4/7/1954, P150/87

31 Ibid.

32 Ibid.

33 Ibid.

34 Ó Dúlaing, *Voices of Ireland*, pp. 14, 29.

35 EDV, reminiscences begun 4/7/1954, P150/87.

36 EDV, partial scheme for an autobiography, c. 1949, Kathleen O'Connell Papers, UCDA, P155/86.

37 Seoighe, *From Bruree to Corcomohide*, p. 239.

38 EDV, reminiscences in Dorothy Macardle's hand, P150/3662.

39 *IP*, 9/10/1972, article by Seán Cryan on EDV's visit to Bruree.

40 Ó Dúlaing, *Voices of Ireland*, p. 14

41 EDV, reminiscences begun 4/7/1954, P150/87

42 Farragher, *Dev and His Alma Mater*, p. 12.

43 Bromage, *De Valera and the March of a Nation*, pp. 19–20.

44 EDV, reminiscences, in Dorothy Macardle's hand, P150/3662.

45 Lewis, *A Topographic Dictionary of Ireland*, Vol. 1, p. 228.

46 EDV, notes on the distinctive sounds of Bruree, P150/3408.

47 2/1/1957, draft of lecture to Bruree Fianna Fáil cumann, P150/89.

48 Seoighe, *From Bruree to Corcomohide*, p. 26.

49 Ó Dúlaing, *Voices of Ireland*, p. 17.

50 'Various Incidents and Recollections of Bruree. Dictated by Chief 20/8/56', P150/87.

51 DED, 2/7/1943, vol. 91, cols 205–6.

52 Fanning, *Éamon de Valera*, p. 6.

53 Ó Dúlaing, *Voices of Ireland*, pp. 22–3.

54 Drafts of articles regarding the career of EDV, Frank Gallagher Papers, NLI, Ms 21,261.

55 Ó Dúlaing, *Voices of Ireland*, p. 28.

56 EDV, early recollections, P150/380.

57 Ó Dúlaing, *Voices of Ireland*, p. 29.

58 Seoighe, *From Bruree to Corcomohide*, p. 142.

59 See *DIB* entries on James MacGeoghegan, and the translator Patrick O'Kelly.

60 EDV, undated recollections, P150/87.

61 *IT*, 26/5/1938, obituary. These councils were created by the Local Government Act (1898), which did away with the old Poor Law Unions and brought democracy to local affairs.

62 Ó Dúlaing, *Voices of Ireland*, p. 29.

63 O'Connor, *A Labour History of Ireland*, pp. 53, 62.

64 Census (1901), http://www.census.nationalarchives.ie/pages/1901/ Limerick/Bruree/Knockmore/1490204. Ten years later he described himself as a 'general carter'.

65 Cronin, *The McGarrity Papers*, p. 36.

66 Seoighe, *From Bruree to Corcomohide*, pp. 144–5.

67 Ó Dúlaing, *Voices of Ireland*, p. 30.

68 Ibid, p. 28

69 2/1/57, draft of lecture to Bruree Fianna Fáil cumann, P150/89.

70 EDV, reminiscences begun 4/7/1954, P150/87.

71 EDV, reminiscences recorded 6/8/1955, P150/13.

72 19/9/1955, Appendix to reminiscences, 'The Coll Family', P150/228.

73 EDV, reminiscences, P150/87.

74 EDV, reminiscences in Dorothy Macardle's hand, P150/3662.

75 EDV, outline of autobiography, P150/380.

76 EDV, reminiscences, P150/87.

77 Silinonte, Joseph M., 'The Search for Vivion de Valera, part 2', p. 27.

78 Undated letter, P150/211. EDV describes himself as 'Professor of Mathematics', so it must have been written after he started at Rockwell College in 1904.

79 This point is made in Dudley Edwards, *Éamon de Valera*, p. 27.

80 28/9/64, note dictated by EDV, P150/170.

81 *IP*, 9/10/72, article by Sean Cryan on EDV's visit to Bruree.

82 Ó Dúlaing, *Voices of Ireland*, p. 20.

83 EDV, reminiscences in Macardle's hand, P150/3662.

84 Ibid.

85 EDV, outline of autobiography, P150/380.

86 2/3/1896, EDV to Aunt Hannie, P150/170.

87 15/1/1898, EDV to Catherine Wheelwright, P150/170. In other words, whatever financial support she gave was not enough to pay all the costs of going to Charleville.

88 EDV, reminiscences recorded 6/8/1955, P150/13.

89 Quote from EDV, reminiscences in Dorothy Macardle's hand, P150/3662; other details from Ó Dúlaing, *Voices of Ireland*, pp. 18/9, and EDV, outline of autobiography, P150/380.

90 *IT*, 14/10/1950, article by Kees van Hoek on 'Young Dev'.

91 McCullagh, *The Reluctant Taoiseach: A biography of John A. Costello*, p. 11.

92 Examination certificates, P150/11.

93 15/1/1898, EDV to Catherine Wheelwright, P150/170.

94 Examination certificates, P150/11.

95 1898, Charleville school results, P150/12.

96 EDV, reminiscences 6/8/1955, P150/13.

97 *IT*, 5/9/1898, p. 7.

98 EDV, reminiscences 6/8/1955, P150/13.

99 Ibid.

100 31/8/1898, Healy to Liston, quoted in Farragher, *Dev and His Alma Mater*, p. 13.

101 Ibid, pp. 13–14.

102 EDV, reminiscences of going to Blackrock recorded 24/4/1956, P150/22.

103 EDV, reminiscences 6/8/1955, P150/13.

104 EDV, reminiscences of going to Blackrock recorded 24/4/1956, P150/22.

CHAPTER 04: I HOPE TO DO SOMETHING

1 2/3/1901, EDV to Catherine Wheelwright, P150/170.

2 6/10/1902, EDV to Thomas Wheelwright, P150/200.

3 EDV, paper on the Irish university question, read 18/2/1903, P150/49.

4 EDV, reminiscences of going to Blackrock 24/4/1956, P150/22.

5 Blackrock College, 'About us', http://www.blackrockcollege.com/about-us/history.

6 Farragher, 'Éamon de Valera and Blackrock', in Doherty and Keogh (eds), *De Valera's Irelands*, p. 30.

7 Foster, *Vivid Faces: The Revolutionary Generation in Ireland 1890–1923*, p. 39.

8 Farragher, *Dev and His Alma Mater*, p. 33.

9 EDV, reminiscences recorded 24/4/1956, P150/22.

10 EDV, reminiscences in Dorothy Macardle's hand, P150/3662.

11 Farragher, 'Éamon de Valera and Blackrock', in Doherty and Keogh (eds), *De Valera's Irelands*, p. 30.

12 Recollection of Cardinal John D'Alton, quoted in Farragher, *Dev and His Alma Mater*, pp. 34–5.

13 Farragher, *Dev and His Alma Mater*, p. 15; also 5/7/1966, Marie O'Kelly to Patrick Harrold, P150/27.

14 Fr Patrick Walsh article on EDV's schooldays, *Missionary Annals*, July 1966, copy in P150/31.

15 EDV, 'My going to Blackrock College', recorded 24/4/1956, P150/22.

16 Farragher, *Dev and His Alma Mater*, p. 16.

17 Memo by Marie O'Kelly of EDV, reminiscences, P150/24.

18 Transcript of 'Downfall of Poland', P150/24.

19 Farragher, *Dev and His Alma Mater*, pp. 6, 19.

20 Ibid, pp. 23–4.

21 EDV, partial scheme for an autobiography, Kathleen O'Connell Papers, UCDA, P155/86.

22 Farragher, *Dev and His Alma Mater*, p. 35. The cardinal must have forgotten that de Valera beat him in religious instruction.

23 Ibid, p. 19.

24 Ibid, pp. 23–4.

25 He scored 82% in arithmetic, 80% in Euclid, 66.6% in algebra, 58% for Greek, 57% for Latin, 46% for English and 23% for French. Calculated from marks in P150/25.

26 Middle grade results, Ibid.

27 EDV, 'My going to Blackrock College', recorded 24/4/1956, P150/22.

28 Farragher, *Dev and His Alma Mater*, p. 27.

29 EDV, reminiscences in Dorothy Macardle's hand, P150/3662.

30 EDV, 'My going to Blackrock College', recorded 24/4/1956, P150/22.

31 26/12/1899, EDV to Thomas Wheelwright, P150/199.

32 6/3/1900, EDV to Catherine Wheelwright, P150/170.

33 EDV, 'My going to Blackrock College', recorded 24/4/1956, P150/22.

34 Results, P150/25.

35 6/3/1900, EDV to Catherine Wheelwright, P150/170.

36 1/6/1966, Fr John Ryan, Blackrock College, to EDV, P150/26.

37 Farragher, *Dev and His Alma Mater*, p. 39.

38 These ranged in age from 15 to 23. Curiously, the form, signed by the college president, John T. Murphy, gives de Valera's place of birth as Co. Limerick. Evidently his New York origins were not widely known. Census (1901), http://www.census.nationalarchives.ie/pages/1901/Dublin/Blackrock/Williamstown_Avenue/1313563.

39 Farragher, *Dev and His Alma Mater*, p. 42.

40 Ibid, p. 46

41 2/3/1901, EDV to Catherine Wheelwright, P150/170.

42 12/6/1947, registrar, NUI, to EDV, P150/35. According to the list published in *WIT*, 3/8/1901, p. 20, his was tenth of the ten first-class exhibitions; his old rival John D'Alton, now at Clonliffe College, was fourth. EDV got 67% in natural philosophy, 63% in English, 58% in Latin, 55% in Greek and 32% in maths. Percentage marks calculated by the author.

43 1/6/1966, Fr John Ryan, Blackrock College, to EDV, P150/26.

44 Farragher, *Dev and His Alma Mater*, p. 49.

45 Ibid, pp. 43–4.

46 Ibid, pp. 64.

47 EDV, 'Some recollections of the Castle', recorded 30/6/1956, P150/23

48 Now in the de Valera Museum in Bruree.

49 Short biography of EDV by Frank Gallagher, p.2 NLI, Ms 21, 273.

50 Farragher, *Dev and His Alma Mater*, pp. 55–6.

51 Ibid, p. 56.

52 Quoted in Ibid, p. 54.

53 Ibid, pp. 53–4.

54 EDV, 'Some recollections of the Castle', recorded 30/6/1956, P150/23.

55 See Marie O'Kelly note, P150/24, and Farragher, 'Éamon de Valera and Blackrock', *College Annual* 1975, in P150/3561, which refers to him being 'almost "sent to Coventry" for his pains'.

56 Extracts from University College Debating Society, P150/25.

57 Paper on the Irish university question, read 18/2/1903, P150/49.

58 12/6/1947, registrar, NUI, to EDV, P150/35, and Farragher, *Dev and His Alma Mater*, p. 49. There were ten first-class exhibitions, and his was the first of the second-class exhibitions, so he presumably came 11th in Ireland; *WIT*, 2/8/1902, p. 20. He got 49% in Latin, 44% in English, 41% in natural philosophy, 39% in Greek and only 23% in maths. Percentage marks calculated by the author.

59 1/6/1966, Fr John Ryan, Blackrock, to EDV, P150/26.

60 6/10/1902, EDV to Tom Wheelwright, P150/200.

61 13/6/1903, EDV to St Wilfred's College, England, P150/49.

62 Farragher, 'Éamon de Valera and Blackrock', in Doherty and Keogh (eds), *De Valera's Irelands*, p. 37.

63 6/10/1902, EDV to Tom Wheelwright, P150/200.

64 13/6/1903, EDV to St Wilfred's College, England, P150/49.

65 McCartney, *The National University of Ireland and Éamon de Valera*, pp. 17–19. His marks were maths 38%, Greek 36%, Latin 34%, French 28% and mathematical physics 17%. 12/6/1947, registrar, NUI, to EDV, P150/35. Percentage marks calculated by the author.

66 Farragher, 'Éamon de Valera and Blackrock', *College Annual* 1975, in P150/3561.

67 Ibid.

CHAPTER 05: A HARD BATTLE TO FIGHT

1 EDV, reminiscences in Dorothy Macardle's hand, P150/3662.

2 21/12/1905, EDV to Catherine Wheelwright, P150/170.

3 3/4/1912, Whitaker to EDV, P150/57.

4 Farragher, *Dev and His Alma Mater*, p. 71.

5 Account drawn up by Fr Cotter, bursar, P150/40.

6 Typed partial scheme by EDV for an autobiography, c. 1949, P150/86.

7 EDV, reminiscences in Dorothy Macardle's hand, P150/3662.

8 Farragher, *Dev and His Alma Mater*, p. 73.

9 31/10/1958, EDV to Mrs Margaret Barrett, P150/539.

10 Farragher, *Dev and His Alma Mater*, p. 73.

11 *DIB*, entry on Michael and John Ryan.

12 12/11/1904, gun licence, P150/40

13 30/1/1965, Patrick Ryan, New York, to EDV and reply (6/2/1965), P150/44.

14 Farragher, *Dev and His Alma Mater*, pp. 77–8.

15 Poem, 'What's the Sigh-for?', by Fr McGrath, dated 28/1/1904, P150/40 – there are three more stanzas.

16 *DIB*, entry on Michael Ryan.

17 Mellett, *If Any Man Dare*, p. 2.

18 Ibid, p. 4.

19 See *DIB* entry on Mossie Landers.

20 See extract from *The Nationalist*, 30/3/1904, describing the try he scored against Cork County, in P150/45.

21 EDV, recollections dictated 13/9/1956, P150/8.

22 *Limerick Leader*, 13/3/1905, p. 3.

23 Mellett, *If Any Man Dare*, p. 3. Mellett wrongly described the game as the final of the Munster Senior Cup; it was actually a first-round match, the final that year saw Cork Constitution beating Queen's College.

24 EDV, 'Some incidents in Rockwell', dictated 30/6/1956, P150/13.

25 Quoted in Coogan *De Valera: Long Fellow, Long Shadow*, pp. 31–2, based on notes in the Frank Gallagher Papers, NLI.

26 Ibid, p. 32, based on notes in the Frank Gallagher papers, NLI.

27 Farragher, *Dev and His Alma Mater*, p. 83.

28 *IT*, 29/10/1904, p. 6. He got 262 marks out of 1200 (22%) in Mathematics, and 183 out of 1200 (15%) in Mathematical Physics; 12/6/47, registrar, NUI, to EDV, P150/35.

29 31/3/1912, Conway testimonial, 'Qualifications and Testimonials of Edward de Valera', P150/58.

30 Results in P150/25.

31 12/6/1947, registrar, NUI, to EDV, P150/35.

32 2/11/1904, Bromwich to EDV, P150/40.

33 17/12/1904, Prof. G. Chrystal, University of Edinburgh, to 'Reverend' EDV, P150/40.

34 EDV, outline of autobiography, P150/380.

35 15/8/1902, Louis C. Purser to EDV, P150/42.

36 23/2/1904, Louis C. Purser to EDV, Ibid.

37 21/1/1905, receipt, Ibid.

38 Fitzpatrick, 'Éamon de Valera at Trinity College', p. 11.

39 16/1/1905, S. B. Kelleher to EDV, P150/42.

40 Out of 125 marks for each paper, he was awarded 20 in pure mathematics by two examiners, 16 in applied mathematics by another – and only 1 by a fourth. Fitzpatrick, 'Éamon de Valera at Trinity College', p. 12.

41 Farragher, *Dev and His Alma Mater*, p. 87.

42 Coogan, *De Valera: Long Fellow, Long Shadow*, pp. 30, 33.

43 Brennan testimonial, April 1912, P150/58.

44 EDV, outline of autobiography, P150/380.

45 EDV, 'List of residences', P150/438.

46 31/10/1958, EDV to Mrs Margaret Barrett, P150/539.

47 21/12/1905, EDV to Catherine Wheelwright, P150/170.

48 Undated, EDV to Catherine Wheelwright from prison after the Rising, referring to his brother Tom's ordination, P150/172. 'One son at least [has] gone the path you would desire . . .'

49 1/10/1905, Keogh to EDV, P150/50.

50 President's diary, 7 and 10/1/1906, original in Dublin Diocesan Archives, quoted in Coogan, *De Valera: Long Fellow, Long Shadow*, pp. 37–8.

51 Fanning, *Éamon de Valera: A Will to Power*, p. 13.

52 He got 66 out of 125 from one examiner in applied mathematics and 40 from another, and 33 for pure mathematics, but only 9 out of 75 for geometry and 0 for algebra.

53 Fitzpatrick, 'Éamon de Valera at Trinity College', pp. 12–13.

54 Farragher, *Dev and His Alma Mater*, p. 89.

55 Ibid, p. 90.

56 EDV, partial scheme for an autobiography, c. 1949, Kathleen O'Connell Papers, UCDA, P155/86.

57 19/9/1906, agreement between EDV and Sr Alice Kennan, principal, P150/53. This isn't a very mathematical formula, but that is the agreement de Valera signed.

58 Farragher, *Dev and His Alma Mater*, p. 90.

59 18/4/1912, Sr M. L. Keenan, principal, Carysfort, 'Qualifications and Testimonials of Edward de Valera', P150/58.

60 19/9/1906, agreement between EDV and Sr Alice Keenan, principal, with addendum dated 1/7/1910, P150/53.

61 Copy in P150/53.

62 19/10/1965, personal secretary to Mrs Mona Campbell, P150/438.

63 Farragher, *Dev and His Alma Mater*, p. 90.

64 EDV, partial scheme for autobiography, c. 1949, Kathleen O'Connell Papers, UCDA, P155/86.

65 The Irish Universities Act (1908) foreshadowed partition, establishing the National University of Ireland with colleges in Dublin, Cork and Galway, and the separate Queen's University, Belfast.

66 Farragher, *Dev and His Alma Mater*, p. 97.

67 EDV, 'Lists of personal dates', P150/435.

68 3/4/1912, Whittaker to EDV, P150/58. The letter explains that he couldn't support de Valera for a post at UCG, as he had already promised his support to another former pupil.

69 'Qualifications and Testimonials of Edward de Valera', P150/58.

70 Quoted in *DIB*, entry on Sir William Rowan Hamilton.

71 *EP*, 15/11/1958.

72 31/3/1912, Arthur Conway testimonial, 'Qualifications and Testimonials of Edward de Valera', P150/58.

73 Synge, 'Éamon de Valera', pp. 640–1.

74 Abbey Theatre, 'A Christmas Hamper' (production information), http://www.abbeytheatre.ie/archives/play_detail/10285.

75 *IT*, 4/9/1963, report of EDV's remarks at an Abbey Theatre function.

76 28/9/1905, extract from diary of Joseph Holloway, P150/52.

77 For example, EDV, 'Some recollections of the Castle', recorded 30/6/1956, P150/23.

78 *IT*, 23/3/08, p. 7.

79 Farragher, *Dev and His Alma Mater*, p. 91. He incorrectly names Wesley as the opposing team.

80 22/3/08, anonymous postcard to EDV, P150/15.

81 See *SI*, 22/3/08, p. 10; *II*, 23/3/08, p. 3; *IT*, 23/3/08, p. 7.

82 McCartney, *The National University of Ireland and Éamon de Valera*, pp. 19–20. The standard must have been high, as his marks were very respectable in the four papers – 60%, 55%, 50%, 68% – with 62½% in the oral exam and 60% in the practical. NUI, Diploma in Education examination (1910), P150/62.

83 EDV, partial scheme for an autobiography, c. 1949, Kathleen O'Connell Papers, UCDA, P155/86.

84 McCartney, *The National University of Ireland and Éamon de Valera*, p. 20.

85 2/10/1912, Mannix to EDV, P150/64.

86 18/10/1913, J. F. Hogan to EDV, P150/66.

87 21/5/1913, EDV to secretary, UCC, P150/65.

88 April 1912, testimonial of Prof. William Magennis, 'Qualifications and Testimonials of Edward de Valera', P150/58.

89 J. J. Horgan, quoted in McCartney, *The National University of Ireland and Éamon de Valera*, pp. 21–2.

90 Ibid, pp. 22–4.

91 13/7/1912, Horgan telegram to EDV, P150/65.

92 McCartney, *The National University of Ireland and Éamon de Valera*, pp. 22–4.

CHAPTER 06: I NEED A KISS, URGENTLY

1 SDV, reminiscences in Terry de Valera, *A Memoir*, p. 118.

2 *IT*, 25/11/2000, p. 40, Cian Ó hÉigeartaigh, 'Dev's days of sensual longing'.

3 Ernest Blythe, 'Notes on Sinéad', Ernest Blythe Papers, UCDA, P24/2017.

4 EDV, 'Joining Gaelic League and later the Volunteers', dictated 29/10/1956, P150/445.

5 4/11/1925, notice of meeting, P150/78; copy book with questions for students, P150/53.

6 29/11/1922, EDV to editor, *An Reult*, P150/1609.

7 Undated draft letter, NAI, Taoiseach's Private Office, 97/9/415.

8 EDV draft of speech, June 1938, P150/3157.

9 EDV, 'Joining Gaelic League and later the Volunteers', dictated 29/10/1956, P150/445.

10 Kissane, *Explaining Irish Democracy*, p. 105.

11 Ó Fearaíl, *The Story of Conradh na Gaeilge*, p. 39.

12 EDV, 'Joining Gaelic League and later the Volunteers', dictated 29/10/1956, P150/445.

13 Ibid.

14 *DIB*, entry on Sinéad de Valera.

15 Biographical details, P150/129.

16 SDV, reminiscences in Terry de Valera, *A Memoir*, p. 115.

17 Ibid, pp. 115–16.

18 Biographical details, P150/129.

19 O'Neill, *From Parnell to de Valera*, p. 48.

20 SDV, reminiscences in Terry de Valera, *A Memoir*, p. 112.

21 Undated, Máirtin MacDhomhnáil to Sinéad de Valera, P150/132.

22 Central Branch handbook for 1907/8, P150/78.

23 Ó Broin, *Revolutionary Underground*, pp. 146–7. Both of them were younger than herself – O'Casey by two years, Blythe by eleven.

24 SDV, reminiscences in Terry de Valera, *A Memoir*, p. 118.

25 EDV, outline of a biography, P150/380.

26 SDV, reminiscences in Terry de Valera, *A Memoir*, p. 118.

27 Ernest Blythe, 'Notes on Sinéad', Ernest Blythe Papers, UCDA, P24/2017.

28 Dudley Edwards, *Éamon de Valera*, footnote 9, p. 150, based on 'private information'.

29 Farragher, *Dev and His Alma Mater*, p. 101.

30 Terry de Valera, *A Memoir*, p. 119.

31 EDV, poem [c. 1910], P150/59.

32 20/12/1909, Kate Wheelwright to EDV, P150/171. He must have waited quite some time after the engagement before informing his mother.

33 SDV, reminiscences in Terry De Valera, *A Memoir*, p. 119.

34 EDV, partial scheme for an autobiography, c. 1949, UCDA, P155/86. Nora Ashe had written 'Go raibh ort i gconaí', a wish for every good luck in the future; de Valera translated it as 'Good luck in your dwelling'. Sinéad's phrase was 'Is deacair rud olc a mharú' to which her fiancé replied 'tar go deimhin'.

35 Terry de Valera, *A Memoir*, p. 119.

36 EDV, list of schools, etc., P150/36.

37 14/6/1910, Seoirse Ó Muanáin, Leinster College, to EDV, P150/71.

38 Bromage, *De Valera and the March of a Nation*, pp. 30–31.

39 Mitchell, *Roger Casement*, pp. 157–8.

40 15/8/1912, Casement to EDV, NLI, Ms 14,100 (21).

41 1/9/1912, Casement to EDV, NLI, Ms 14,100 (22).

42 EDV, undated draft report, P150/75.

43 *IP*, 19/8/1953.

44 *IT*, 25/11/2000, Cian Ó hÉigeartaigh, 'Dev's days of sensual longing', p. 40.

45 Quoted in Coogan, *De Valera: Long Fellow Long Shadow*, pp. 41–2.

46 EDV, partial scheme for an autobiography, c. 1949, Kathleen O'Connell Papers, UCDA, P155/86. More likely it was one of those tedious jobs others were reluctant to take on.

47 EDV, 'Joining Gaelic League and later the Volunteers', dictated 29/10/1956, P150/445.

48 BMH, WS 4, Diarmuid Lynch.

49 Ó Broin, *Revolutionary Underground*, pp. 140–1.

50 Professor Liam O Briain, quoted in Ó Lúing, *I Die in a Good Cause*, p. 55.

51 Dwyer, *De Valera: The Man and the Myths*, p. 12; Yeates, *A City in Wartime*, p. 39.

52 Ó Fearaíl, *The Story of Conradh na Gaeilge*, p. 44.

53 Eoin MacNeill, biographical memoir, pp. 53, 69, Eoin MacNeill Papers, UCDA, LA1/S.

54 7/8/1917, Rosamond Jacob diary, quoted in Lane, *Rosamond Jacob*, p. 116.

55 See an interesting discussion of this issue in Lewis, *Frank Aiken's War*, pp. 13–15.

56 BMH, WS 99, Patrick McCartan; also *DIB*, entry on McCartan.

57 Ernest Blythe, 'Notes on Sinéad', Ernest Blythe Papers, UCDA, P24/2017. Blythe had absolutely no reason to speak well of Éamon de Valera, so his report of Hobson's comment is likely to be accurate.

CHAPTER 07: THOSE WHO SIDE WITH IRELAND

1 Irish Volunteers, manifesto, P150/448.

2 BMH, WS 242, Liam Tannam, p. 3.

3 14/3/1916, report on the Command of the Dublin Brigade, J. J. O'Connell, Chief of Inspection, Thomas MacDonagh Papers, NLI, Ms 20,643/2/10.

4 EDV notes, dictated 15/2/1962, P150/445.

5 Jones, *History of the Sinn Fein Movement*, p. 86.

6 Author's copy, signed by his great-grandfather William McCullagh, in Keady, Co. Armagh.

7 Quoted in Horgan, *The Complete Grammar of Anarchy*.

8 Eoin MacNeill, 'The North began', text at http://historyhub.ie/assets/The-North-Began.pdf.

9 Eoin MacNeill biographical memoir, Eoin MacNeill Papers, UCDA, LA1/S, pp. 69–70.

10 Martin, 'MacNeill and the Irish Volunteers', in Martin and Byrne (eds), *The Scholar Revolutionary*, p. 156.

11 *FJ*, 26/11/1913, quoted in Ibid, p. 109.

12 EDV, 'Joining Gaelic League and later the Volunteers', dictated 29/10/1956, P150/445.

13 Martin, 'MacNeill and the Irish Volunteers', in Martin and Byrne (eds), *The Scholar Revolutionary*, p. 174.

14 BMH, WS 139, Michael Walker, p. 1.

15 Martin, 'MacNeill and the Irish Volunteers', in Martin and Byrne (eds), *The Scholar Revolutionary*, p. 171.

16 Hobson, 'Foundation and growth of the Irish Volunteers', in Martin (ed.), *The Irish Volunteers*, p. 28.

17 EDV, reminiscences in Dorothy Macardle's hand, P150/3662; see also EDV, 'Joining Gaelic League and later the Volunteers', dictated 29/10/1956, P150/445.

18 Photocopy in P150/449 from original in NLI. While some excuse might be made for the mistake with his Spanish surname, it is bizarre that a common Irish first name like 'Éamon' was so badly mangled, particularly in a nationalist organisation.

19 EDV, 'Notes as basis of account of my connection with Volunteers', begun 12/3/1949, P150/447; and 'Joining Gaelic League and later the Volunteers', dictated 29/10/1956, P150/445.

20 'Military Instructions for Units, 1914', in Martin (ed.), *The Irish Volunteers*, p. 129.

21 21 EDV, 'Joining Gaelic League and later the Volunteers', P150/445; EDV, 'Notes as basis of account of my connection with the Volunteers', 12/3/1949, P150/447; EDV, correspondence with William Condron, P150/453.

22 EDV, 'Joining Gaelic League and later the Volunteers', P150/445.

23 BMH, WS 4, Diarmuid Lynch, p. 2.

24 EDV, 'Joining Gaelic League and later the Volunteers', P150/445.

25 John Swift, quoted in Lee and Ó Tuathaigh, *The Age of de Valera*, pp. 207–8.

26 *FJ*, 30/5/1914, in P150/449.

27 *Irish Volunteer*, 22/8/1914.

28 'A brief chronicle of E Company, 3rd Battalion, 1st Dublin Brigade, Irish Republican Army', P150/508.

29 Hobson, 'Foundation and growth of the Irish Volunteers', in Martin (ed.), *The Irish Volunteers*, pp. 48–9.

30 Laffan, *The Resurrection of Ireland*, p. 34.

31 Foy and Barton, *The Easter Rising*, p. 7.

32 Townshend, *Easter 1916*, p. 53.

33 Macardle, *The Irish Republic*, p. 98.

34 EDV, recollections, dictated 23/8/1961, P150/452.

35 Ibid; also EDV, reminiscences in Macardle's hand, P150/3662.

36 Turtle Bunbury, 'Death on Bachelor's Walk', http://www.turtlebunbury. com/history/history_irish/history_irish_bachelors_walk.htm.

37 Boyne, *Emmet Dalton*, p. 14.

38 EDV, reminiscences in Macardle's hand, P150/3662.

39 12/8/1914, Pearse to McGarrity, quoted in Cronin, *The McGarrity Papers*, p. 48.

40 EDV, recollections, dictated 23/8/1961, P150/452.

41 Ferriter, *A Nation and Not a Rabble*, p. 135. The German guns bought by both sides were purchased privately, but couldn't have been exported without the approval of the German government.

42 Clarke, *The Sleepwalkers*, p. 529. Wilson, from Co. Longford, was a bitterly partisan supporter of the Unionist cause, so he may well have been exaggerating. No government, however, could take the risk that he was bluffing.

43 Meleady, *John Redmond*, p. 307. Meleady makes the point that the unscripted Woodenbridge speech didn't go any further in substance than Redmond had already gone in the House of Commons on the Amending Bill, but it became much better known.

44 Handwritten notes on the split, Thomas MacDonagh Papers, NLI, Ms 20,643/1/1.

45 24/9/1914, Statement from Provisional Committee, Thomas MacDonagh Papers, NLI, Ms 20/643/1/10.

46 Meleady, *John Redmond*, p. 308.

47 Sister paper of the Redmondite *Freeman's Journal*.

48 *ET*, 30/9/1914, in P150/508.

49 Undated, handwritten letter for publication by *ET*, 3/10/1914, in P150/449.

50 BMH, WS 242, Liam Tannam, p. 3.

51 Undated, handwritten letter for publication by *ET*, 3/10/1914, in P150/449.

52 EDV, 'Notes as basis of account of my connection with Volunteers', 12/3/1949, P150/447.

53 BMH, WS 130, Seán Fitzgibbon, p. 12. Fitzgibbon, who had voted against accepting Redmond's ultimatum, pointed out that they could not have anticipated the course of events that allowed them to have the split on their own terms and at the right time.

54 7/10/1914, EDV to Joseph Mary Plunkett, Joseph Mary Plunkett Papers, NLI, Ms 36,114.

55 BMH, WS 242, Liam Tannam, p. 4.

56 16/1/1963, note by Michael Hayes, Richard Mulcahy Papers, UCDA, P7b/188.

57 23/1/1948, George Lalor to KOC, P150/508.

58 BMH, WS 242, Liam Tannam, pp. 5–6.

59 'Scheme of Military Organisation for the Volunteers, December 1914', in Martin (ed.), *The Irish Volunteers*, pp. 175–8.

60 *Irish Volunteer*, 20/3/1915, in P150/449.

61 Longford and O'Neill, *Éamon de Valera*, p. 24.

62 11/3/1915, P. H. Pearse to EDV, P150/450.

63 EDV, 'Notes as basis of account of my connection with Volunteers', 12/3/1949, P150/447.

64 Ibid.

65 *IP*, 20/1/1969, 'Seán Lemass looks back' (interview with Michael Mills), part 1, p. 9.

66 Ó Broin, *Revolutionary Underground*, pp. 156, 177.

67 As recorded by William O'Brien; quoted in Morrissey, *William O'Brien*, p. 103.

68 Foy and Barton, *The Easter Rising*, pp. 14–18.

69 Fitzpatrick, *The Two Irelands*, p. 58; McGarry, *The Rising*, pp. 98, 101.

70 Irish Volunteers, manifesto, P150/448.

71 *Irish Volunteer*, 22/5/1915, P. H. Pearse, 'Why we want recruits', in Martin (ed.), *The Irish Volunteers*, p. 192.

72 BMH, WS 433, Simon Donnelly, p9.

73 BMH, WS 251, Richard Balfe, p.3.

74 BMH, WS 328, Gearoid Ua h-Uallachain, p. 33.

75 BMH, WS 198, joint statement of Thomas and James Walsh, pp. 4–6.

76 BMH, WS 433, Simon Donnelly, p. 8.

77 15/12/1915, Syllabus of Training, Thomas MacDonagh Papers, NLI, Ms 20,643/2/8.

78 BMH, WS 1670, Séamus Kavanagh, p. 23.

79 BMH, WS 433, Simon Donnelly, p. 7.

80 Lar Joye, 'Weapons of the 1916 Rising', Century Ireland, http://www.RTÉ. ie/centuryireland/index.php/articles/weapons-of-the-1916-rising.

81 EDV, 'Notes as basis of account of my connection with Volunteers', 12/3/1949, P150/447.

82 Ibid.

83 BMH, WS 249, Frank Henderson, p. 16.

84 BMH, WS 1700, Alphonsus O'Halloran, p. 16.

85 EDV, 'Notes as basis of account of my connection with Volunteers', 12/3/49, P150/447; BMH, WS 249, Frank Henderson, p. 16; WS 157, Joseph O'Connor, pp. 14–5; WS 175, John Styles, pp. 7–8.

86 BMH, WS 157, Joseph O'Connor, p. 16.

87 Quoted in Longford and O'Neill, *Éamon de Valera*, p. 26.

88 See 'Scheme of military organisation for the Volunteers, December 1914', in Martin (ed.), *The Irish Volunteers*, p. 182.

89 17/9/1915, EDV to MacDonagh, and 7/9/1915, EDV to MacDonagh, Thomas MacDonagh Papers, NLI, Ms 20,643/10/9–10; February 1916, EDV to Patrick O'Byrne, Seán O'Mahony Papers, NLI, Ms 44,120/1.

90 11/11/1917, Rosamond Jacob diary, NLI, Ms 32,582/32. MacDonagh's papers in the National Library show that de Valera was not exaggerating: his writing was appalling.

91 EDV, 'The Volunteers and the IRB', dictated 7/7/1961, P150/472. De Valera wrongly dates the incident at the convention to the first Volunteer convention in October 1914, at which he was also a delegate, but it is clear from the context that it was actually the second convention, in 1915. The conversation at the tram has sometimes been characterised as an invitation by MacDonagh to de Valera to join the Military Council planning the Rising (see *IT*, 12/8/2016, 'End of line for chestnut tree where de Valera had fateful conversation', p. 5), which is highly improbable, given that MacDonagh himself did not join it until the beginning of April 1916.

92 De Valera, as brigade adjutant, may have worked out the ceremonial details of this parade; 3/3/1916, MacDonagh to EDV, notebook, Thomas MacDonagh Papers, NLI, Ms 44,337/4.

93 BMH, WS 157, Joseph O'Connor, pp. 16–17.

94 Yeates, *A City in Wartime*, pp. 82–3.

95 EDV, 'Notes as basis of account of my connection with Volunteers', 12/3/1949, P150/447; EDV, note dictated 15/2/1962, P150/445.

96 See for example, BMH, WS 139, Michael Walker, p. 2; WS 157, Joseph O'Connor, pp. 16–17; WS 175, John J. Styles, p. 5; WS 249, Frank Henderson, pp. 16–17; WS 360, Seamus Daly, p. 21; WS 734, Thomas Meldon, pp. 14–15.

97 EDV, 'Notes as basis of account of my connection with Volunteers', 12/3/1949, P150/447; EDV, note dictated 15/2/1962, P150/445.

98 Gaughan, *Austin Stack*, p. 53.

99 BMH, WS 157, Joseph O'Connor, p. 17.

100 BMH, WS 242, Liam Tannam, pp. 5, 7.

101 EDV, note dictated 7/7/1961, P150/472.

102 EDV, 'Notes as basis of account of my connection with Volunteers', 12/3/1949, P150/447.

103 Ibid.

104 EDV, typed questions and answers on Rising, P150/409.

105 BMH, WS 340, Oscar Traynor, p. 5.

106 Carden, *The Alderman*, pp. 100–1.

107 10/4/1916, intelligence report, in P150/512.

108 EDV, copy of manuscript notes, 12/3/1949, P150/447.

109 EDV, instructions to company commanders, P150/463.

110 BMH, WS 157, Joseph O'Connor, p. 19.

111 SDV, reminiscences in Terry de Valera, *A Memoir*, p. 121.

112 EDV, notes, 12/3/1949, P150/447.

113 BMH, WS 157, Joseph O'Connor, p. 19.

114 BMH, WS 160, Joseph O'Byrne, pp. 3–4.

115 BMH, WS 157, Joseph O'Connor, pp. 19–23.

116 14/3/1916, Commandant J. J. O'Connell, 'Report on the command of the Dublin Brigade', Thomas MacDonagh Papers, NLI, MS 20/643/2/10.

117 SDV, quoted in Terry de Valera, *A Memoir*, p. 122.

118 EDV, typed questions and answers on Rising, P150/409.

119 EDV, 'Notes as basis of account of my connection with Volunteers,' 12/3/1949, P150/447.

120 BMH, WS 157, Joseph O'Connor, p. 23.

121 SDV, quoted in Terry de Valera, *A Memoir*, p. 122.

122 Eoin MacNeill notes on weeks leading up to Rising, Thomas MacDonagh Papers, NLI, Ms 43,228.

123 Simon Donnelly manuscript, 'Easter Week, 1916', P150/504.

124 BMH, WS 157, Joseph O'Connor, p. 24.

125 Litton, *16 Lives: Thomas Clarke*, pp. 166–7; Johnston, *Home or Away*, p. 141.

126 BMH, WS 284, Michael Staines, p. 9.

127 MacNeill to EDV, Easter Sunday, 1:20 p.m., P150/462.

128 BMH, WS 215, Michael Hayes, p. 3.

129 Brennan-Whitmore, *Dublin Burning*, pp. 34–6.

130 EDV to MacNeill, NLI, Ms 41,711.

131 BMH, WS 215, Michael Hayes, p. 3.

132 BMH, WS 157, Joseph O'Connor, p. 25; WS 377, Peadar O'Mara, p. 12.

133 Simon Donnelly manuscript, 'Easter Week 1916', P150/504.

134 BMH, WS 157, Joseph O'Connor, p. 25.

CHAPTER 08: IRISHMEN WHO DARE

1 EDV, note to Sinéad from Boland's Bakery, P150/131.

2 Simon Donnelly manuscript, 'Easter Week 1916', P150/504.

3 'Easter Week diary by Miss L. Stokes', *Nonplus*, No. 4, Winter 1960, in P150/522.

4 BMH, WS 242, Liam Tannam, p. 17.

5 BMH, WS 160, Joseph O'Byrne.

6 BMH, WS 157 Joseph O'Connor.

7 BMH, WS 377, Peadar O'Mara.

8 EDV, typed questions and answers on Rising, P150/409.

9 1/3/1951, Simon Donnelly to KOC, P150/504.

10 EDV, note from Boland's Bakery, P150/131. In fact, it would have only been four times stronger.

11 BMH, WS 480, Eileen Walsh (Mrs Martin Murphy), p. 5.

12 McCarthy, *Cumann na mBan and the Irish Revolution*, p. 55.

13 BMH, WS 157, Joseph O'Connor, p. 26.

14 *An tÓglach*, 10/4/1926, George A. Lyons, 'Occupation of Ringsend area in 1916', part 1, p. 8.

15 BMH, WS 160, Joseph O'Byrne, p. 5.

16 BMH, WS 188, Seán O'Keeffe.

17 Even some reputable historians make this mistake. They know who they are.

18 BMH, WS 188, Seán O'Keeffe.

19 BMH, WS 157, Joseph O'Connor, p. 30.

20 BMH, WS 277, Peadar O'Mara, pp. 13–14.

21 Foy and Barton, *The Easter Rising*, p. 76.

22 Townshend, *Easter 1916*, pp. 177–8. At least one Volunteer who fired on them insisted that he had observed them on previous occasions and that they were in fact armed and carried ammunition: BMH, WS 310, James Grace, pp. 7–8.

23 WS 348, Captain E. Gerrard, p. 4.

24 *An tÓglach*, 10/4/1926, George A. Lyons, 'Occupation of Ringsend area in 1916', part 1, p. 5.

25 *Irish Life*, 12/5/16, 'The Week of Fools', P150/514.

26 BMH, WS 188, Seán O'Keeffe, p. 8.

27 Ibid.

28 Simon Donnelly manuscript, 'Easter Week 1916', P150/504.

29 BMH, WS 188, Seán O'Keeffe, pp. 8–9.

30 BMH, WS 1768, Andrew McDonnell, pp. 9–10.

31 EDV, typed answers to questions on Rising, P150/409.

32 Ibid.

33 BMH, WS 1768, Andrew McDonnell, p. 12.

34 *An tÓglach*, 17/4/1926, George A. Lyons, 'Occupation of Ringsend area in 1916', part 2, p. 4.

35 MacManus, *Éamon de Valera*, loc. 504.

36 BMH, WS 1768, Andrew McDonnell, p. 13.

37 The rebels had themselves occupied both the South Dublin Union and the Mendicity Institute.

38 BMH, WS 433, Seán Byrne, p. 14; 27/6/1959, Lt-Col G.F. Mackay to EDV, P150/506.

39 *SP*, 15/8/1954.

40 BMH, WS 208, Séamus Kavanagh, p. 9.

41 'Memoirs of Brigadier Ernest Maconchy', p. 451, National Army Museum (London), online at http://www.nam.ac.uk/online-collection/detail.php?acc=1979-08-62-2, pp. 446, 449

42 Townshend, *Easter 1916*, p. 197

43 BMH, WS 310, James Grace, pp. 10–14.

44 BMH, WS 198, joint statement of Thomas and James Walsh, p. 22

45 Maconchy, p. 450.

46 Maconchy, p. 451.

47 Molyneux and Kelly, *When the Clock Struck in 1916*, p. 202.

48 *IT*, 4/5/1966, letter from Joseph O'Byrne.

49 Undated letter, Simon Donnelly, P150/504.

50 BMH, WS 208, Séamus Kavanagh, pp. 12–13.

51 Townshend, *Easter 1916*, p. 210.

52 *An tÓglach*, 17/4/1926, George A. Lyons, 'Occupation of Ringsend area in 1916', part 2, p. 3.

53 *IP*, 29/4/1964, Seán J. White interview with Andy McDonnell, part 2.

54 BMH, WS 160, Joseph O'Byrne, p. 7.

55 EDV, typed questions and answers on Rising, P150/409.

56 Simon Donnelly manuscript, 'Easter Week 1916', P150/504.

57 Terry de Valera, *A Memoir*, p. 132.

58 Longford and O'Neill, *Éamon de Valera*, p. 43.

59 7/4/1964, EDV to Simon Donnelly, P150/507.

60 *An tÓglach*, 17/4/1926, George A. Lyons, 'Occupation of Ringsend area in 1916', part 2, p. 5

61 Ibid, p. 5

62 Ibid, p. 4.

63 *An tÓglach*, 24/4/1926, George A. Lyons, 'Occupation of Ringsend area in 1916', part 3, p. 3.

64 *An tÓglach*, 10/4/1926, George A. Lyons, 'Occupation of Ringsend area in 1916', part 1, p. 7.

65 3/1/1952, Donnelly to KOC, P150/504.

66 Obviously all readers look at the notes; why else would they be written?

67 18/4/1964, Caulfield to Dick Humphreys, P150/3661.

68 *SP*, 5/4/1964, letter from Simon Donnelly.

69 Simon Donnelly manuscript, 'Easter Week 1916', P150/504.

70 BMH, WS 157, Joseph O'Connor, p. 41. Emphasis added.

71 Ibid, pp. 36–7; Simon Donnelly manuscript, 'Easter Week 1916', P150/504.

72 One might ask whether Donnelly was in fact justified in obeying apparently irrational orders from a man suffering from exhaustion.

73 Simon Donnelly manuscript, 'Easter Week 1916', P150/504.

74 *An tÓglach*, 24/4/1926, George A. Lyons, 'Occupation of Ringsend area in 1916', part 3, p. 3.

75 BMH, WS 377, Peadar O'Mara, p. 18.

76 Copy of order, counter-signed by EDV, NLI MS 10,605.

77 BMH, WS 157, Joseph O'Connor, p. 39.

78 EDV, memo, 7/12/1965, P150/503.

79 29/4/1949, Major H. E. de Courcy-Wheeler to EDV, NAI, PRES/2002/7/17.

80 EDV, memo, 7/12/1965, P150/503.

81 EDV note to Sinéad, P150/131.

82 EDV to O'Connor, undated, NLI, MS 48,173.

83 EDV letter to 'The Intelligence Officer', NLI, MS 49,174

84 BMH, WS 422, Seán Byrne, pp. 15–16.

85 BMH, MSP34REF2281, John Byrne, sworn statement, 24/1/1936.

86 BMH, WS 377, Peadar O'Mara, pp. 18/9.

87 Simon Donnelly manuscript, 'Easter Week 1916', P150/504.

88 Dr A. D. Courtney, 'Reminiscences of the Easter Rising, 1916', copy in P150/522.

89 BMH, WS 160, Joseph O'Byrne, p. 14; WS 1768, Andrew McDonnell, p. 16.

90 BMH, WS 208, Seamus Kavanagh, p. 14.

91 Longford and O'Neill, *Éamon de Valera*, p. 46; this is sometimes rendered as the rather unlikely 'knives and forks'; see *An tÓglach*, 24/4/1926, George A. Lyons, 'Occupation of Ringsend area in 1916', part 3, p. 4.

92 27/6/1959, Lt-Col G.F. Mackay to EDV, P150/506.

93 BMH, WS 1768, Andrew McDonnell, p. 16.

94 'Easter Week diary by Miss L. Stokes', *Nonplus*, No. 4, Winter 1960, in P150/522.

95 BMH, WS 1768, Andrew McDonnell, p. 16.

96 Proposed address by Redmond J. Murphy at Boland's Jubilee Celebrations, Friday 15/4/1966, P150/506.

CHAPTER 09: Q95

1 4/5/1916, EDV to Mick Ryan, P150/3375. The date on this letter must be wrong.

2 20/10/1916, Reade to Dryhurst, NAUK, HO 144/10309.

3 EDV, Hunter and Ashe, 'Final Order – Whit Monday', 28/5/1917, P150/529.

4 BMH, WS 422, Seán Byrne, p. 19.

5 BMH, WS 1768, Andrew McDonnell, p. 16.

6 Bromage, *De Valera and the March of a Nation*, p. 56.

7 EDV, recollections, dictated 15/2/1962, P150/445.

8 BMH, WS 1768, Andrew McDonnell, pp. 17–18. The Volunteers assumed they had relatives in the British Army.

9 BMH, WS 920, Father Augustine, p. 21.

10 BMH, WS 248, Liam O'Flaherty, p. 6.

11 Enright, *Easter Rising 1916: The Trials*, p. 202.

12 EDV diary for 1916, written into an adapted 1933 diary, P150/261.

13 BMH, WS 1379, Peter Howley, p. 16.

14 BMH, WS 1766, William O'Brien, p. 20.

15 Bew, *A Yankee in de Valera's Ireland*, p. 75. Gray heard this story from O'Kelly at a reception in Dublin Castle; it was confirmed by de Valera. Gray characteristically decided that his hosts had been pulling his leg.

16 Bromage, *De Valera and the March of a Nation*, pp. 57–8.

17 Enright, *Easter Rising 1916*, p. 63. All four trials were held in public, with defence counsel for the accused; these included Capt. John Bowen-Colthurst, who murdered Francis Sheehy-Skeffington and a number of others.

18 Ibid, p. 74. Enright points out that Brig.-Gen. Byrne, sometimes referred to as Maxwell's 'advocate-general' was in fact his adjutant-general, an administrative rather than a legal post. Ibid, pp. 19–20.

19 BMH, WS 1019, Sir Alfred Bucknill, pp. 26, 30.

20 Enright, *Easter Rising 1916*, p. 30.

21 Quoted in Ibid, p. 30.

22 5/2/1953, F. H. Boland to Seán Nunan, recounting conversation with Bucknill, P150/521.

23 Wylie memoir, NAUK, PRO 30/89/2.

24 Note by Wylie of conversation with President de Valera, 29/4/1964, NAUK, PRO 30/89/10/18.

25 Enright, *Easter Rising 1916*, p. 201. Enright points out that the register was drawn up by the Judge Advocate General's office in London, based on the case papers; it was, therefore, 'a contemporaneous document compiled by a disinterested party'.

26 Nicholas Mansergh, 'Conversation with President de Valera, 21/9/1965', in Mansergh (ed.), *Nationalism and Independence*, p. 192.

27 5/2/1953, F. H. Boland to Seán Nunan, recounting conversation with Bucknill, P150/521.

28 Longford and O'Neill, *Éamon de Valera*, p. 48.

29 EDV, diary for 1916, written into an adapted 1933 diary, P150/261.

30 Clarke became a US citizen on 2 November 1905. Litton, *16 Lives: Thomas Clarke*, p. 82.

31 SDV, reminiscences in Terry de Valera, *A Memoir*, pp. 122–4.

32 Whelan, 'The Wilson administration and the 1916 Rising', in O'Donnell (ed.), *The Impact of the 1916 Rising among the Nations*, p. 93.

33 Whelan, *United States Foreign Policy and Ireland*, p. 103.

34 Whelan, 'The Wilson Administration and the 1916 Rising', in O'Donnell (ed.), *The Impact of the 1916 Rising among the Nations*, pp. 105–6.

35 Ibid, p. 102.

36 Farragher, *Dev and His Alma Mater*, p. 112.

37 24/7/1916, SDV to Kate Wheelwright, P150/172.

38 5/2/1953, F. H. Boland to Seán Nunan, reporting conversation with Bucknill, P150/521.

39 3/7/1969, EDV, memo, P150/524.

40 Thomas Kent, court-martialled on 4 May, was executed in Cork on the 9th; Roger Casement was tried in London and executed on 3 August.

41 Court-martialled on 9 May, the day after de Valera, Connolly and Mac Diarmada were executed on 12 May.

42 30/4/1916, Dillon to Redmond, quoted in Meleady, *John Redmond*, p. 370.

43 3/5/1916, Redmond to Dillon, quoted in Ibid, p. 371.

44 9/5/1916, Asquith to Redmond, quoted in Meleady, *John Redmond*, p. 372.

45 9/5/1916, Maxwell to Asquith, P150/512.

46 11/5/1916, Maxwell to Kitchener, Ibid.

47 BMH, WS 189, Michael Soughley, p. 2.

48 4/5/1916, EDV to Mick Ryan, P150/3375. The date on this letter must be wrong.

49 9/5/1916, EDV to Mother Gonzaga, P150/3375.

50 9/5/1916, EDV to Jack Barrett, P150/539.

51 11/5/1916, EDV to SDV, quoted in *IT*, 25/11/2000, Cian O hÉigeartaigh, 'Dev's days of sensual longing', p. 40.

52 SDV, reminiscences, quoted in Terry de Valera, *A Memoir*, pp. 124–5.

53 Ibid, p. 125.

54 Mansergh, 'Conversation with President de Valera, 21/9/1965', in Mansergh (ed.), *Nationalism and Independence*, p. 192.

55 Brennan, *Allegiance*, p. 95.

56 BMH, WS 679, Jack Shouldice, p. 4.

57 Brennan, *Allegiance*, p. 98.

58 Ibid, p. 99.

59 EDV cap badge, P150/526.

60 BMH, WS 170, Peter Paul Galligan, pp. 16–17.

61 BMH, WS 679, Jack Shouldice, p. 6.

62 Brennan, *Ireland Standing Firm*, pp. 98–9.

63 Quoted in Fitzpatrick, '"Decidedly a personality"', p. 41.

64 1/6/1916, Eoin MacNeill to his wife, Eoin MacNeill Papers, UCDA, LA1/K/142(1).

65 EDV, recollections, dictated 15/2/1962.

66 This was Kathleen Clarke's interpretation of de Valera's gesture. Clarke, *Revolutionary Woman*, pp. 148–9.

67 EDV, recollections, dictated 1/6/1959, P150/526.

68 Brennan, *Allegiance*, p. 103.

69 Eoin MacNeill, biographical memoir, Eoin MacNeill Papers, UCDA, LA1/S, p. 135. His memoir was written in the 1930s, when he had absolutely no reason to exaggerate de Valera's success (though of course he had every reason to exaggerate the warmth of his own reception).

70 18/1/1928, Frank Gallagher diary, quoted in Coogan, *De Valera*, p. 80.

71 Eardley-Wilmot's report of the account of Reade quoted in Fitzpatrick, 'Decidedly a Personality', p. 41.

72 EDV, dictated 1/6/1959, P150/526.

73 Fitzpatrick, 'Decidedly a Personality', p. 41.

74 Seán MacEntee, 'De Valera: The Man I Knew', *Iris*, Winter 1975, copy in P150/3557.

75 23/8/1916, letter from the Rev. Thomas Roche, Plymouth, seeking permission to visit de Valera and Tom Hunter – he had been taught by the former and came from the same town as the latter; 30/8/1916, Reade note of visit on 25 August; both in NAUK, 144/10309.

76 14/6/1916, EDV petition, and response (23/9/1916), in NAUK HO 144/10309.

77 McConville, *Irish Political Prisoners*, p. 516.

78 28/7/1916, Reade to Home Office, NAUK HO 144/10309.

79 19/10/1916, Frederick Dryhurst, Prison Commissioner, to Major Reade, NAUK, HO 144/10309.

80 22/5/1960, EDV to Prof. W. B. Stanford, P150/526.

81 18/9/1916, EDV to Catherine Wheelwright, P150/172.

82 See the extensive correspondence in P150/528.

83 See 28/6/1916, Edward Bell (US embassy) to Maj. Frank Hall (War Office), and reply (29/6/1916), NAUK KV 2/514; 1/7/1916, Bell to J. F. Moylan (Home Office), NAUK, HO 144/10309.

84 16/7/1916, Senator James Wadsworth to Tom Wheelwright, P150/528.

85 23/6/1916, Kate Wheelwright to Tom, P150/201.

86 Undated, EDV to Catherine Wheelwright, P150/172.

87 9/8/1916, Maj. Reade (governor of Dartmoor), to Prison Commission, Home Office, NAUK, HO 144/10309.

88 18/9/1916, EDV to Catherine Wheelwright, P150/172.

89 Brennan, *Allegiance*, p. 112.

90 He was getting extra bread after complaining about the diet.

91 16/10/1916, statement of offences and punishments, NAUK, HO 144/10309.

92 The untwisting of old rope into fibres, an unpleasant job that was hard on the hands.

93 18/10/1916, governor's report on EDV, NAUK, HO 144/10309.

94 Ibid.

95 19/10/1916, Dryhurst to Reade, NAUK, HO 144/10309.

96 20/10/1916, Reade to Dryhurst, Ibid.

97 20/10/1916, Battiscombe report to Reade, Ibid.

98 Brennan, *Allegiance*, pp. 76; 78.

99 20/10/1916, Battiscombe report to Reade, NAUK, HO 144/10309.

100 27/10/1916, Dryhurst to Reade, Ibid.

101 9/11/1916, EDV petition to Home Secretary, Ibid.

102 EDV note, dictated 18/9/1964, P150/530.

103 7/3/1917, EDV to Charles Murphy, NLI, Ms 46,062.

104 30/10/1916, Maidstone, memo on EDV, NAUK, HO 144/10309.

105 20/11/1916, Maidstone memo on EDV, Ibid.

106 24/11/1916, E. Cavendish (governor of Maidstone) to Prison Commission, Ibid.

107 SDV, reminiscences in Terry de Valera, *A Memoir*, p. 130.

108 McConville, *Irish Political Prisoners*, p. 522.

109 14/11/1916, Home Office comments on EDV's petition, NAUK, 144/10309.

110 14/11/1916, note by commissioners, Ibid.

111 29/11/1916, minute to chair of Prison Commission, Ibid.

112 27/11/1916, note by Sir Evelyn Ruggles-Brise, Ibid.

113 Brennan, *Allegiance*, p. 115.

114 20/6/1917, questionnaire for Penal Reform League completed by Eoin MacNeill, Eoin MacNeill Papers, UCDA, LA1/G/158.

115 22/12/1916, EDV to Catherine Wheelwright, P150/172.

116 26/3/1917, Eoin MacNeill to his sister Margaret, Eoin MacNeill Papers, UCDA, LA1/G/150.

117 12/2/1917, Eoin MacNeill to his wife, Eoin MacNeill Papers, UCDA, LA1/K/142.

118 See notebook for Irish, dated 2/4/1917, P150/530.

119 EDV, detailed outline of topics for autobiography, P150/380.

120 Brennan, *Allegiance*, p. 128.

121 See William O'Brien notes on Macardle's *Irish Republic*, p. 209, William O'Brien Papers, NLI, Ms 13,972.

122 WS 1043, Joseph Lawless, pp. 432/3.

123 Brennan, *Allegiance*, p. 129.

124 Béaslaí, *Michael Collins*, quoted in McConville, *Irish Political Prisoners*, p. 525.

125 Ó Lúing, *I Die in a Good Cause*, p. 126.

126 EDV, undated order to fellow prisoners, P150/529.

127 Brennan, *Allegiance*, pp. 129–30.

128 Brennan, *Ireland Standing Firm*, p. 103.

129 EDV, reminiscences in Macardle's hand, P150/3662.

130 Hart, *Mick*, p. 128.

131 21/4/1917, Seán T. O'Kelly to Kate Ryan, Seán T. O'Kelly Papers, NLI, Ms 47,974/1.

132 BMH, WS 1766, William O'Brien, pp. 107–111.

133 23/4/1917, EDV to Simon Donnelly, P150/529.

134 8 and 9/4/1917 (Easter Sunday and Monday), EDV to Simon Donnelly, P150/529.

135 Reply suggested by Ashe, P150/529.

136 Townshend, *Easter 1916*, p. 328.

137 Laffan, *The Resurrection of Ireland*, p. 98.

138 8/4/1917 (Easter Sunday), McGuinness to Plunkett, P150/529.

139 EDV, 'Reasons for reply to Count Plunkett's request', P150/529.

140 23/4/1917, EDV to Simon Donnelly, P150/529.

141 BMH, WS 679, John Shouldice, p. 13.

142 Fitzpatrick, 'Decidedly a personality', p. 44.

143 BMH, WS 1399, Thomas Peppard, p. 8.

144 17/3/1917, EDV to Charles Murphy, NLI, Ms 46,062.

145 Fitzpatrick, 'Decidedly a personality', p. 44.

146 23/3/1917, EDV to Charlie Murphy, NLI, Ms 46,062.

147 22/3/1917, EDV petition to Home Secretary, NAUK, HO 144/10309.

148 23/3/1917, EDV order, P150/529.

149 Fitzpatrick, 'Decidedly a personality', p. 45.

150 23/4/1917, EDV to Simon Donnelly, P150/529.

151 BMH, WS 155, P. S. Doyle, p. 30.

152 Ó Lúing, *I Die in a Good Cause*, p. 126.

153 28/5/1917, EDV, Hunter and Ashe, 'Final Order – Whit Monday', P150/529.

154 BMH, WS 679, John Shouldice, p. 14.

155 Quoted in Fitzpatrick, 'Decidedly a personality', p. 45.

156 Brennan, *Allegiance*, p. 132.

157 BMH, WS 679, John Shouldice, p. 14.

158 BMH, WS 244, John McGallogly, p. 18.

159 Brennan, *Allegiance*, p. 132.

160 BMH, WS 510, Frank Thornton, p. 37.

161 BMH, WS 510, Frank Thornton, p. 37.

162 McConville, *Irish Political Prisoners*, p. 536.

163 Fitzpatrick, *Harry Boland's Irish Revolution*, p. 58.

164 EDV, note dictated 9/8/1964, P150/538.

165 BMH, WS 315, Seamus Doyle, p. 19.

166 *IT*, 16/6/1916, p. 5.

167 EDV, detailed outline of topics for autobiography, P150/380.

168 Eoin MacNeill, biographical memoir, p. 143, Eoin MacNeill Papers, UCDA, LA1/S.

169 BMH, WS 244, John McGallogly, p. 18.

170 Tierney, *Eoin MacNeill*, p. 254.

171 17/1/1959, EDV to Mrs King, P150/536.

172 BMH, WS 345, Brian Molloy, p. 17.

173 *IT*, 19/6/1917, p. 5.

174 BMH, WS 264, Áine Ceannt, p. 52.

175 BMH, WS 1511, Gerald Doyle, pp. 94–5.

176 BMH, WS 1770, section 5, Kevin O'Shiel, p. 49.

177 BMH, WS 1511, Gerald Doyle, p. 95.

178 *IT*, 19/6/1917, p. 5.

179 BMH, WS 1770, section 5, Kevin O'Shiel, pp. 49–50.

180 *IT*, 19/6/1917, p. 6.

181 Ibid, p. 5.

182 Handwritten notes on SDV, P150/129.

183 SDV, reminiscences in Terry de Valera, *A Memoir*, p. 130.

184 4/7/1917, SDV to Tom Wheelwright, P150/203.

185 9/9/1906, John Keogh to 'Dear Michael', P150/50.

186 BMH, WS 487, Joseph O'Connor, p. 5.

CHAPTER 10: THE COMING PARNELL OF IRELAND

1 25/7/1917, resolution by Corofin rural district council, P150/555.

2 *II*, 24/10/1917, p. 4.

3 Notes compiled by Kathleen Clarke following Sinn Féin convention, 25-6/10/1917, Kathleen Clarke Papers, NLI, Ms 49,356/2.

4 This committee included Plunkett, Griffith, Alderman Tom Kelly, Father Michael O'Flanagan, Michael Collins, Laurence Ginnell, Rory O'Connor, Darrell Figgis, Sceilg, Michael O'Callaghan (Limerick), George Murnaghan (Omagh), F. J. O'Connor (Omagh), Thomas Farren and William O'Brien (the trade unionist). O'Brien, *Forth the Banners Go*, p. 145.

5 BMH, WS 1766, William O'Brien, pp. 134–5.

6 He was later vice-commandant of the Dublin Brigade during the War of Independence and was shot dead in Dublin Castle by Auxiliaries on the night of Bloody Sunday, 1920; *DIB*.

7 *IT*, 14/6/1917, p. 5.

8 17/4/1963, Joe Barrett account of convention, P150/548.

9 Father Alfred Moloney is credited with nominating de Valera in BMH, WS 1322, Art O'Donnell, p. 25; WS 683 Hugh Hehir, p. 9; and 6/4/1963, Seán O'Keeffe, Ennis, to Seán O'Grady, P150/548.

10 *IT*, 15/6/1917, p. 4.

11 Browne, *Éamon de Valera and the Banner County*, p. 16.

12 BMH, WS 1766, William O'Brien, pp. 134–5.

13 Telegram in P150/548, sent to EDV c/o Sinn Féin head office at 6 Harcourt Street, Dublin, with a copy sent also to a sympathiser in London.

14 December 1957, memorandum by Páidín O'Keeffe on reorganisation of Sinn Féin, Michael Hayes Papers, UCDA, P53/315.

15 McCartan, *With de Valera in America*, p. 9.

16 Ó Lúing, *I Die in a Good Cause*, p. 129, quoting interview with Pádraig Ashe, cousin of Thomas.

17 Ibid, p. 130.

18 BMH, WS 687, Msgr Michael Curran, p. 156, quoting diary entry, 23/6/1917.

19 Eoin MacNeill, biographical memoir, p. 145, Eoin MacNeill Papers, UCDA, LA1/S.

20 EDV in conversation with Eibhlín Tierney, quoted in Tierney, *Eoin MacNeill*, p. 260.

21 *CE*, 25/6/1917, p. 8.

22 BMH, WS 929, Daniel O'Shaughnessy, p. 34.

23 BMH, WS 1103, Denis Madden, p. 11.

24 BMH, WS 659, Justin McCarthy, p. 2.

25 BMH, WS 1048, Seán Murnane, p. 5.

26 Fr Pat Gaynor, in Gaynor, *Memoirs of a Tipperary Family*, p. 74.

27 *II*, 25/6/1917, p. 1.

28 Moynihan (ed.), *Speeches and Statements by Éamon de Valera*, p. 6.

29 *CE*, 29/6/1917, p. 4.

30 EDV election handbill, in possession of author.

31 Handbill with song, P150/550.

32 Notes for speeches in East Clare, P150/551.

33 BMH, WS 1322 Art O'Donnell, p. 26.

34 19/6/1917, Annie O'Brien to John Redmond, quoted in Meleady, *John Redmond*, p. 431.

35 *DIB*, entry on Paddy Lynch. Lynch was a sincere nationalist, a former Parnellite who went on to join Sinn Féin, take the anti-Treaty side in the Civil War and eventually become de Valera's Attorney-General.

36 Meleady, *John Redmond*, p. 426.

37 June 1917, extract from inspector-general, RIC, in NAUK, KV 2/514.

38 See, for example, BMH, WS 1047, Seán McNamara, p. 14; WS 1048, Seán Murnane, p. 6.

39 BMH, WS 1068, Michael Brennan, pp. 22–3.

40 RIC confidential reports, June 1917, quoted in Townshend, *Easter 1916*, p. 332.

41 BMH, WS 1048, Sean Murnane, p. 6; WS 258, Mrs Maeve Cavanagh MacDowell, p. 18; WS Liam de Róiste, p. 171

42 Typed extract from *Clare Champion*, 13/11/1971, NAI, 2007/125/38.

43 BMH, MSP34REF17155, Thomas Pugh.

44 Eoin MacNeill, biographical memoir, p. 147, Eoin MacNeill Papers, UCDA, LA1/S; Laffan, *The Resurrection of Ireland*, pp. 108–9.

45 BMH, WS 707, Michael Noyk, p. 23.

46 10/7/1917, Liam de Róiste diary; BMH, WS 1698, Liam de Róiste, p. 172.

47 Magennis, 'Frank Aiken', in Evans and Kelly (eds), *Frank Aiken*, p. 63.

48 See Browne, *Éamon de Valera and the Banner County*, pp. 49, 53.

49 BMH, WS 722, Dan McCarthy, p. 16.

50 Browne, *Éamon de Valera and the Banner County*, p. 25.

51 BMH, WS 907, Laurence Nugent, p. 116.

52 Extract from report by intelligence officer, Southern District, in NAUK, KV 2/514.

53 Notes for speeches in East Clare, P150/551.

54 Lynch handbill on conscription, P150/550.

55 Lynch circular to voters, Ibid.

56 Handbill with speech by Fr Hayes, Ibid.

57 'The Angelus', copy in NLI, Ms 18,464.

58 *II*, 25/6/1917, reporting speech at Tulla the previous day.

59 Browne, *Éamon de Valera and the Banner County*, pp. 34–45.

60 BMH, WS 707, Michael Noyk, p. 23.

61 *CE*, 4/7/1917, p. 6.

62 EDV, Notes for speeches in East Clare, P150/551.

63 BMH, WS 907, Laurence Nugent, p. 110.

64 *II*, 11/7/1917, p. 3.

65 11/7/1917, Liam de Róiste diary, BMH, WS 1698, p. 172.

66 *CE*, 12/7/1917, editorial, p. 4.

67 *IT*, 12/7/1917, editorial, p. 4.

68 Quoted in Welles and Marlowe, *The Irish Convention and Sinn Fein*, loc. 772.

69 *IT*, 12/7/1917, p. 5. Direct speech restored.

70 *IT*, 13/7/1917, p. 6.

71 De Valera Sinn Féin club, Bruree, to EDV, P150/554; Castlehaven Sinn Féiners to EDV, P150/554; 25/7/1917, resolution by Corofin Rural District Council, P150/555.

72 12/8/1917, 'De Valera Irish Dancing Class', 41 York Street, to EDV, P150/546.

73 18/7/1917, Brennan-Whitmore to EDV, P150/546.

74 16/7/17, Stack to EDV, P150/562.

75 31/7/1917, extract from report by intelligence officer (Southern District), NAUK, K 2/514.

76 Augusteijn, *From Public Defiance to Guerrilla Warfare*, p. 63.

77 Valiulis, *Portrait of a Revolutionary*, p. 23.

78 13/7/1917, Collins to EDV, P150/565.

79 21/7/1917, P. Ó Caoimh to EDV, P150/575.

80 17/7/1917, P. S. O'Hegarty to EDV, P150/457.

81 25/7/1917, Collins to EDV, P150/563. Ashe and Hunter attended the meeting; it appears EDV did not.

82 Register of American Grants, INA & VDF Papers, NLI, Ms 23494, and Special Grants Committee, minutes, 21/11/1916; INA & VDF Papers, NLI, MS 23473, quoted in Fitzpatrick, *Harry Boland's Irish Revolution*, pp. 96–7. By contrast, Peter Hart claimed that EDV was one of very few to turn down the offer of money, though no citation is given. Hart, *Mick*, p. 122.

83 22/8/17, C. Cullen, house painter, to EDV, P150/564.

84 SDV, reminiscences in Terry de Valera, *A Memoir*, p. 137

85 Handwritten SDV reminiscences, P150/129.

86 *IT*, 25/11/00, Cian O hÉigeartaigh, 'Dev's days of sensual longing', p. 40.

87 McConville, *Irish Political Prisoners*, p. 613.

88 Valiulis, *Portrait of a Revolutionary*, p. 24.

89 Browne, *Éamon de Valera and the Banner County*, pp. 78, 83.

90 28/9/1917, O'Kennedy (Ennis), telegram to Griffith, P150/546.

91 14/7/1917, meeting of War Cabinet, NAUK, CAB/23/2, document 34.

92 31/7/1917, Mahon to Duke, NAUK, CO 904/198/105.

93 10/8/1917, Duke to Under-Secretary (Sir William Byrne), NAUK, CO 904/198/105.

94 14/8/1917, Crime Department (RIC) to chief commissioner (DMP), NAUK, CO 904/199.

95 BMH, WS 1280, Éamonn Broy, pp. 54–5.

96 15/8/1917, Supt Brien to chief commissioner (DMP), NAUK, CO 904/199.

97 BMH, WS 1280, Éamonn Broy, p. 56.

98 16/8/1917, Under-Secretary to Duke, NAUK, CO 904/108/105.

99 16/8/1917, Duke to Under-Secretary, NAUK, CO 904/108/105.

100 19/8/1917, Sgt W. Horgan report on Tipperary Feis, NAUK, CO 904/199.

101 All quotes from 20/10/1917, Duke memorandum for Cabinet, NAUK, CAB 24/29.

102 Ibid.

103 23/10/1917, minutes of War Cabinet 255, NAUK, CAB/23/13, document 24.

104 *II*, 24/10/1917, p. 4.

105 *IT*, 24/10/1917, p. 4.

106 Prof. Thomas Dillon, 'Events of 1916–17', P150/576.

107 *IT*, 24/9/1917, p. 5.

108 24/9/1953, Prof. Thomas Dillon, 'Arthur Griffith and the reorganisation of Sinn Féin', P150/575.

109 December 1957, Paídín O'Keeffe, 'Memorandum on reorganisation of SF', UCDA, Hayes Papers, P53/315.

110 BMH, WS 4, Diarmuid Lynch, p. 13.

111 BMH, WS 104, George Lyons, pp. 7–8.

112 2/5/1917, Michael Collins to Tom Ashe, quoted in Ó Lúing, *I Die in a Good Cause*, p. 122. How Collins reached this conclusion while EDV was still in Lewes, and before they came to know each other well, is not clear.

113 25/9/1964, Richard Mulcahy, note of conversation with Paddy O'Keeffe, Richard Mulcahy Papers, UCDA, P7/D/5.

114 BMH, WS 279, Séamus Dobbyn, p. 15; WS 1004 Daniel Kelly, p. 36.

115 Brennan, *Allegiance*, p. 154.

116 BMH, WS 391, Helena Molony, pp. 50–1.

117 Thomas Dillon, 'Events of 1916–17', P150/576.

118 8/4/1963, Richard Mulcahy, note of talk with P. Ó Caoimh, Richard Mulcahy Papers, UCDA, P7/D/1.

119 EDV, typewritten comments, P150/1584.

120 *II*, 26/10/1917, p. 3.

121 *IT*, 26/10/1917, p. 5.

122 21/10/1917 and 25/10/1917, Rosamund Jacob diary, NLI, Ms 32,582/32.

123 Notes compiled by Kathleen Clarke following Sinn Féin convention, 25-6/10/17, NLI, Ms 49,356/2.

124 Typescript record of ard-fheis proceedings, P150/575.

125 BMH, WS 1770, Kevin O'Shiel, section 5, p. 87.

126 Typescript record of ard-fheis proceedings, P150/575.

127 Ibid.

128 Hart, *Mick*, p. 155.

129 25/10/1917, Rosamund Jacob diary, NLI, Ms 32,582/32.

130 In Gaynor, *Memoirs of a Tipperary Family*, p. 79.

131 Typescript record of ard-fheis proceedings, P150/575.

132 Ibid.

133 Brennan, *Allegiance*, p. 153.

134 Farrell, 'MacNeill in Politics', in Martin and Byrne, *The Scholar Revolutionary*, p. 193.

135 Typescript record of ard-fheis proceedings, P150/575.

136 Notes compiled by Kathleen Clarke following Sinn Féin convention, 25-6/10/1917, Kathleen Clarke Papers, NLI, Ms 49,356/2.

137 Typescript record of ard-fheis proceedings, P150/575.

138 Notes compiled by Kathleen Clarke following Sinn Féin convention, 25-6/10/1917, Kathleen Clarke Papers, NLI, Ms 49,356/2.

139 BMH, WS 465, Mary O'Sullivan, p. 7.

140 Hart, *Mick*, suggests their reticence 'was probably not cowardice so much as better judgement', p. 155.

141 BMH, WS 767, Patrick Moylett, p. 14.

142 25/10/1917, carbon text of EDV's speech, P150/575.

143 See, for instance, Fitzpatrick, *The Two Irelands*, pp. 66–7.

144 25/10/1917, carbon text of EDV's speech, P150/575.

145 Shouldice, *Sniper*, p. 251

146 Jacob Diary, 26/10/17, NLI, Ms 32,582/32.

147 Typescript record of Ard Fheis proceedings, P150/575.

148 26/10/17, Duke memorandum, 'Sinn Féin Convention in Dublin', NAUK, CAB 24/30/1.

149 BMH, WS 400 Richard Walsh, pp. 32–3.

150 22/11/1917, McGarry to MacNeill, Eoin MacNeill Papers, UCDA, LA1/H/6.

151 22/10/1917, MacNeill to EDV, P150/458.

152 BMH, WS 81, Bulmer Hobson, p. 18.

153 BMH, WS 487, Joseph O'Connor, p. 8.

154 BMH, WS 1337, David Daly, p. 3.

155 BMH, WS 400, Richard Walsh, p. 33.

156 Fanning, *Éamon de Valera*, p. 62.

157 In Gaynor, *Memoirs of a Tipperary Family*, p. 75.

158 Quoted in Akenson, 'Was de Valera a Republican?', p. 235.

159 O'Hegarty, *The Victory of Sinn Féin*, p. 12.

160 Ibid, p. 14.

161 16/11/1917, O'Brien to Healy, William O'Brien Papers, NLI, Ms 8556/16.

162 Notes compiled by Kathleen Clarke following Sinn Féin convention, 25-6/10/1917, Kathleen Clarke Papers, NLI, Ms 49,356/2.

CHAPTER 11: THE MOST EFFECTIVE MEANS AT OUR DISPOSAL

1 6/4/1918, note of EDV speech, NAUK, CO 904/198/105.

2 EDV, handwritten notes, P150/626.

3 28/5/1919, 'Report on Revolutionary Organisations in the United Kingdom', NAUK, CAB 24/80/68.

4 *IP*, 24/7/1961, 'Memoirs of Seán T', part 18, p. 9.

5 Brennan, *Allegiance*, pp. 162–4.

6 DMP Special War 'B' List, December 1917, RIC Papers, UCDA, P59, 6(2).

7 14/3/1918, Rosamund Jacob diary, NLI, Ms 32,582/33.

8 1/11/1917, Duke memo, 'The Situation in Ireland', NAUK, CAB 24/30, document 67.

9 O'Malley, *On Another Man's Wound*, p. 86.

10 Liam Deasy, quoted in Ryan, *Tom Barry*, p. 14.

11 12/11/1917, Liam Lynch to his brother Tom, Liam Lynch Papers, NLI, Ms 36,251/4.

12 See correspondence relating to a pension claim by T. J. Vaughan, the driver of the car, in BMH, MSP 28925.

13 5/1/1918, Duke memorandum, 'The Situation in Ireland', NAUK, CAB 24/38/33.

14 Meleady, *John Redmond*, pp. 447–8.

15 12/11/17, *Waterford Star*, in P150/568.

16 Jacob diary, 11/11/1917, NLI, Ms 32,582/32.

17 Brennan, *Allegiance*, p. 164.

18 Quoted in Laffan, *The Resurrection of Ireland*, p. 123.

19 Lewis, *Frank Aiken's War*, p. 35.

20 BMH, WS 487, Joseph O'Connor, pp. 8–9.

21 BMH, WS 511, Michael Lynch, p. 39.

22 Lewis, *Frank Aiken's War*, p. 34.

23 Quoted in Ferriter, *A Nation and Not a Rabble*, p. 177.

24 Quoted in Meleady, *John Redmond*, p. 462.

25 EDV, notes on Imperial Hotel paper, P150/598.

26 27/1/1918, quoted in Bowman, *De Valera and the Ulster Question*, p. 35.

27 Meleady, *John Redmond*, p. 453.

28 7/2/1918, EDV to McCartan, John Devoy Papers, NLI, Ms 18,003/4B/9.

29 BMH, WS 353, James McGuill, p. 33.

30 Feeney, *Seán MacEntee*, p. 42.

31 The incident is recounted in strikingly similar terms in BMH, WS 1485, Liam O'Duffy, p. 3; WS 1516, P. H. Doherty, pp. 3–4; WS 1546, Anthony Dawson, p. 3; WS 1582, Thomas McGlynn, p. 4; WS 1583, Michael Doherty, pp. 3–4.

32 Chief Inspector, Derry, Monthly Report, February 1918, quoted in Augusteijn, *Defiance*, p. 192.

33 Anecdote related by Fionán Lynch, in 13/4/1918, Rosamund Jacob diary, NLI, Ms 32,582/33.

34 Laffan, *The Resurrection of Ireland*, p. 125.

35 BMH, WS 707, Michael Noyk, p. 26.

36 BMH, WS 1105, Nicholas Whittle (Director of Elections), pp. 10–12.

37 Ibid, pp. 16–24.

38 14/3/1918, Rosamund Jacob diary, NLI, Ms 32,582/33.

39 Laffan, *The Resurrection of Ireland*, p. 128.

40 Ward, 'Lloyd George and the 1918 Irish conscription crisis', p. 109.

41 Ibid, p. 110.

42 See *WIT*, 6/4/1918, p. 2.

43 6/4/1918, note of EDV speech, NAUK, CO 904/198/105.

44   Morrissey, *William J. Walsh, Archbishop of Dublin*, pp. 307–8.

45 War Cabinet 388, NAUK, 10/4/1, CAB/23/6, document 10.

46 10/4/1918, Tom Jones diary, in Middlemas (ed.), *Whitehall Diary*, p. 2.

47 Ward, 'Lloyd George and the 1918 Irish conscription crisis', p. 112.

48 *IT*, 11/10/1918.

49 13/4/1918, memorandum by Chief Secretary, 'Grave Crisis in Ireland', NAUK, CAB 24/48, document 18, Appendix GT 4218.

50 BMH, WS 687, Msgr Michael Curran, pp. 270–2.

51 Ibid, pp. 272–4.

52 Morrissey, *William O'Brien*, p. 147.

53 O'Brien, *The Irish Revolution*, loc. 5289.

54 Townshend, *The Republic*, p. 13.

55 O'Brien, *Forth the Banners Go*, p. 166.

56 Morrissey, *William O'Brien*, p. 148.

57 Wheeler, *The Irish Republic*, loc. 2750.

58 2/5/1918, O'Brien to Healy, William O'Brien Papers, NLI, Ms 8556/19.

59 Valiulis, *Portrait of a Revolutionary*, p. 29.

60 18/4/1918, Lord French to Lloyd George, quoted in Townshend, *The Republic*, p. 11.

61 Ward, 'Lloyd George and the 1918 Irish conscription Crisis', pp. 125–6.

62 Quoted in Fanning, *Fatal Path*, p. 177.

63 EDV, notes, 1922, P150/3691.

64 Tom Jones minute, quoted in Fanning, *Fatal Path*, p. 183.

65 Joseph Dowling was later sentenced to penal servitude for life but was released after six years. Macardle, *The Irish Republic*, p. 253.

66 Dudley Edwards, *Éamon de Valera*, p. 75.

67 BMH, WS 1280, Éamonn Broy, pp. 72–4.

68 BMH, WS 1765, Seán T. O'Kelly, part 2, pp. 109–110.

69 Brennan, *Allegiance*, p. 167.

70 18/5/1918, Liam de Róiste diary; BMH, WS 1698, Liam de Róiste, p. 177.

71 BMH, WS 1280, Éamonn Broy, p. 73.

72 BMH, WS 1765, Seán T. O'Kelly, part 2, p. 111.

73 Richard Mulcahy, 'Notes on Piaras Béaslaí's *Michael Collins*', Richard Mulcahy Papers, UCDA, P7/D/67, p. 5.

74 The Prisoners' Book can be viewed online: https://digital.ucd.ie/view/ucdlib:43949.

75 22/5/1918, War Cabinet 414 (a), NAUK, CAB/23/14/19.

76 23/5/1918, War Cabinet 416, with appendix GT 4621, NAUK, CAB 23/6/38.

77 EDV, memorandum on Irish Army organisation, reprinted in memorandum for Cabinet, 31/12/1920, NAUK, CAB 24/117/92. It was being considered for inclusion in a further press statement aimed at discrediting EDV during the War of Independence.

78 30/5/1918, Price to MI5D (War Office), NAUK, KV 2/514.

79 EDV's memorandum continued to be quoted by ministers; in a memorandum for the Cabinet in June 1918, arguing for the abandonment of plans to introduce home rule, the Colonial Secretary, Walter Long, said it showed 'that his preparations for the formation of an Irish Army were complete and thorough in every detail'. 19/6/1918, Long memorandum, NAUK, CAB/24/54/82.

80 25/5/1918, Healy to William O'Brien, William O'Brien Papers, NLI, Ms 8556(19).

81 20/8/18, EDV letter, P150/612

82 Ferriter, *A Nation and not a Rabble*, pp. 220–1.

83 SDV, reminiscences in Terry de Valera, *A Memoir*, pp. 137–8.

84 2/10/1918, Terence MacSwiney to Connolly, enclosed with letter to Muriel MacSwiney, Terence MacSwiney Papers, UCDA, P48b/88.

85 Dunne, *Peter's Key*, p. 105.

86 25/10/1918, Standing Committee to EDV, P150/626.

87 Macardle, *The Irish Republic*, p. 265.

88 2/11/1918, EDV to Standing Committee, P150/626.

89 EDV, handwritten notes, P150/626.

90 Brennan, *Allegiance*, p. 168.

91 29/11/1918, EDV to James O'Mara, NLI, Ms 21,546.

92 DED, 17/12/1921, vol. T, col. 251.

93 O'Hegarty, *The Victory of Sinn Féin*, p. 21.

94 Fanning, *Éamon de Valera*, p. 71.

95 Laffan, *The Resurrection of Ireland*, pp. 151–2.

96 Gaughan, *Thomas Johnson*, p. 120.

97 Figures from http://www.ark.ac.uk/elections/h1918.htm.

98 Uncontested seats were not of course uncommon under the first-past-the-post system; in December 1910, 53 of the Irish Party's 84 seats were won without a contest. Ferriter, *A Nation and Not a Rabble*, p. 119.

99 Bowman, *De Valera and the Ulster Question*, p. 40.

100 Matthews, *Fatal Influence*, pp. 14–15.

101 BMH, WS 1047, Seán McNamara, pp. 16–17. McNamara went to Co. Mayo with 300 Volunteers from Co. Clare.

102 Manning, *James Dillon*, p. 24

103 Gallagher, *The Four Glorious Years*, pp. 52, 55.

104 EDV, account of escape, P150/620.

105 28/11/1918, EDV to Catherine Wheelwright, P150/173.

106 EDV, 'Story of Lincoln escape', P150/620.

107 Card in P150/615.

108 Dunne, *Peter's Key*, p. 154.

109 Longford and O'Neill, *Éamon de Valera*, pp. 81–5.

110 Macardle, *Republic*, p. 283

111 Longford and O'Neill, *Éamon de Valera*, p. 84.

112 BMH, WS 274, Liam McMahon, p. 8.

113 Shouldice, *Grandpa the Sniper*, p. 293.

114 Hart, *Mick*, p. 188.

115 25/3/1919, Sgt John Harrington (Glasgow) to officer in charge (Crime Special Branch), NAUK, CO 904/199.

116 15/2/1919, Sir H. Rumbold (Berne) to London, NAUK, KV2/515.

117 4/3/19, British Embassy Madrid to MI5, London, NAUK, KV2/515.

118 *WIT*, 22/2/19, p. 2

119 Fitzpatrick, *Harry Boland's Irish Revolution*, p. 116.

120 Longford and O'Neill, *Éamon de Valera*, p. 87.

121 BMH, WS 384, J. J. O'Kelly (Sceilg), p. 59.

122 EDV, diary for 1919, written into adapted 1930 diary, P150/263.

123 *IP*, 24/7/1961, 'Memoirs of Seán T', part 20, p. 9.

124 DED, 21–22/1/1919, vol. F, nos 1 and 2.

125 BMH, WS 1739, Dan Breen, p. 21.

126 Yeates, *A City in Turmoil*, p. 7.

127 15/1/1964, Richard Mulcahy conversation with Seán Mac Eoin, Richard Mulcahy Papers, UCDA, P7/3.

128 *IT*, 14/3/1919, p. 6, quoting statement by Boland.

129 BMH, WS 687, Msgr Michael Curran, pp. 353–7.

130 EDV, diary for 1919, written into adapted 1930 diary, P150/263.

131 7/2/1919, Lord French, memo, 'Release of Sinn Féin prisoners', NAUK, CAB 24/76/13.

132 Shouldice, *Grandpa the Sniper*, p. 297

133 Terry de Valera, *Memoir*, p. 142

134 *IT*, 15/4/1919, p. 7.

135 22/3/1919 Sinn Féin Executive circular, quoted in Townshend, *The Republic*, pp. 82–3.

136 31/3/1919, Chief Secretary to Laurence O'Neill, NAUK CO 904/169, quoted in Ibid, pp. 82–3.

137 24/3/1919, War Cabinet meeting, NAUK CAB/23/9/37.

138 25/3/1919, O'Hegarty to Harry Boland, P150/617.

139 26/3/1919, Collins to Austin Stack, NLI, Ms 17,090.

140 27/3/1919, EDV to Laurence O' Neill, NLI, William O' Brien Papers, Ms 20,765.

141 *IT*, 28/3/1919, p. 6.

142 29/3/1919, report by Sgt M. Turnbull (Greystones), NAUK, CO 904/199.

143 Brennan, *Ireland Standing Firm*, p. 120. There is a less pointed version of this anecdote in Brennan, *Allegiance*, pp. 238–9.

144 Richard Mulcany, 'Notes on Piaras Béaslaí's Michael Collins', p. 5, Richard Mulcahy Papers, UCDA, P7/D/67.

145 6/9/1963, Richard Mulcahy, 'Reaction note', Richard Mulcahy Papers, UCDA, P7/D/3.

146 DED, 1, 2 and 4/4/1919, Vol. F, cols 30–42.

147 Alexandra Kollontai was a minister in 1917 in Soviet Russia. *II*, 13/12/2015.

148 *IT*, 9/4/1919, p. 6.

149 9/4/1919, cutting from *Daily Mail*, in NAUK, KV2/515.

150 Feeney, *Sinn Féin*, pp. 121–2.

151 *IT*, 10/4/1919, p. 7.

152 DED, 10/4/1919, Vol. F, cols 46–7. Emphasis added.

153 DED, 20/8/1919, Vol. F, cols 152–3.

154 DED, 10/4/1919, Vol. F, cols 67–9.

155 McGarry, *Eoin O'Duffy*, p. 42.

156 DED, 4/4/1919, Vol. F, col 42.

157 28/5/19, 'Report on Revolutionary Organisations in the United Kingdom', NAUK, CAB 24/80/68.

158 Dwyer, *De Valera: The Man and the Myths*, p. 30.

159 25/6/1919, Clemenceau to US Secretary of State (Robert Lansing), quoted in Fitzpatrick, *Harry Boland's Irish Revolution*, p. 136.

160 9/6/1919, Wilson to Tumulty, quoted in Carroll, 'The American Commission on Irish Independence', p. 114.

161 24/5/1919, O'Kelly to Dublin, *DIFP*, I:11.

162 EDV, 'Recollections of American Mission', dictated to Marie O'Kelly, November 1962, P150/1100.

163 Terry de Valera, *A Memoir*, p. 144.

164 23/6/1919, report by Sgt W. McFeely (DMP), NAUK, CO 904/199.

CHAPTER 12: REACHING FOR THE STARS

1 Edward Patrick Coll, 'My cousin Ed'.

2 13/8/1919, EDV to Collins, P150/726.

3 McCartan, *With de Valera in America*, p. 165.

4 Fitzpatrick, *Harry Boland's Irish Revolution*, p. 122.

5 5/3/1918, Rosamund Jacob diary, NLI, Ms 32,582/33.

6 4/6/1919, Boland to EDV, P150/1132.

7 11/6/1919, EDV to Boland, Ibid.

8 BMH, WS 797, Mícheál Ó Laoghaire (Liverpool Volunteers), p. 41.

9 Barney Downes, account of voyage, P150/668.

10 Ibid.

11 Fitzpatrick, *Harry Boland's Irish Revolution*, p. 124, and footnote 12, p. 366.

12 Barney Downes, account of voyage, P150/668.

13 Fitzpatrick, *Harry Boland's Irish Revolution*, p. 151.

14 Ibid, p. 124.

15 11/6/1919, EDV to Boland, P150/1132.

16 A point strongly argued by Dudley Edwards, *Éamon de Valera*, p. 94.

17 Boland addendum to 11/6/1919, EDV to Boland, P150/1132.

18 14/1/1958, note by Nicholas Nolan, P150/1311.

19 Hannigan, *De Valera in America*, pp. 16–17.

20 19/11/1963, note dictated by EDV, 'What position did I hold from 1/4/1919 until my resignation on 9/1/1922', P150/1311.

21 EDV, 'Recollections of American Mission', dictated to Marie O'Kelly, November 1962, P150/1100.

22 Doorley, 'The Friends of Irish Freedom'.

23 9/3/1938, Diarmuid Lynch to Military Services Pensions Board, and 19/10/1944, letter by EDV, both in BMH MSP34REF497.

24 Doorley, 'The Friends of Irish Freedom'.

25 McCartan, *With de Valera in America*, p. 71.

26 Ibid, p. 71.

27 30/1/1920, Boland to Collins, P150/1125.

28 Gonne MacBride, *A Servant of the Queen*, p. 233.

29 Ward, *Hanna Sheehy-Skeffington*, pp. 187–8.

30 A later Irish politician on a mission to the US got short shrift when making a similar argument – Dick Spring was roundly lambasted for staying in the Waldorf while in New York. See, for example, *IT*, 13/11/1993, 'Drapier', p. 12.

31 Moynihan (ed.), *Speeches and Statements by Éamon de Valera*, pp. 29–31.

32 Quoted in Carroll, 'De Valera and the Americans', p. 42.

33 12/7/1919, Lord Lieutenant's secretary to Irish Command, NAUK, KV2/515; 28/9/1919, Foreign Office cypher telegram to Mr Lindsay (Washington), NAUK, HO 144/10309.

34 See 16/7/1919, R. H. Brade (War Office) to Director of Military Intelligence, NAUK, KV2/515.

35 21/10/1919, I. MacMahon (Chief Secretary's office, Dublin Castle) to the Secretary (War Office), Ibid.

36 11/11/19, Collins to EDV, P150/726.

37 25/6/1919, Edward Coll to EDV, P150/208.

38 Coll Millson, 'Cousin'

39 Edward Patrick Coll, 'My cousin Ed'.

40 20/1/1921, Devoy to Jeremiah Lynch (Butte, Montana), NLI, Devoy Papers, MS 49,353/8 I.iii.8.

41 9/7/1919, Boland to Griffith, *DIFP*, I:19.

42 29/7/19, 'A friend of the Irish suffering people' to EDV, P150/669; given de Valera's unavailability, the manager of the Waldorf tried to interest Harry Boland in the offer instead.

43 *Boston Post*, 30/6/1919, copy in NAI, 97/9/1023.

44 Quoted in Hannigan, *De Valera in America*, pp. 45; 48–9.

45 17/7/19, New York Report No. 107, NAUK, KV2/515.

46 12/9/1919, Andrew J. Gallagher (San Francisco) to Seán Nunan, with details of EDV's visit to San Francisco and Oakland, 17–22/7/1919, P150/792.

47 13/8/19, EDV to Collins, P150/726.

48 18/8/1919, EDV to Walsh, P150/965.

49 EDV, 'Recollections of American mission', dictated to Marie O'Kelly, November 1962, P150/1100.

50 Memorandum by OLM (Division of Western European Affairs, US State Department), c. Feb. 1920, NAW, ROC, 841.D/51/2, quoted in Fitzpatrick, *Harry Boland's Irish Revolution*, p. 145.

51 McCartan, *With de Valera in America*, p. 143.

52 BMH, WS 690, Mrs M. A. O'Mara, p. 5.

53 EDV, 'Observations with respect to Tour', P150/965.

54 EDV, 'Account of American Mission', dictated in Utrecht, 13–14/12/52, P150/380.

55 Townshend, *Easter 1916*, p. 227.

56 Briscoe, *For the Life of Me*, p. 44.

57 Fitzpatrick, *Harry Boland's Irish Revolution*, p. 133.

58 EDV, diary for 1919, in adapted 1930 diary, P150/263.

59 3/10/1919, Harry Boland diary, P150/1170.

60 21/10/1919, J. M. Cooney report on EDV's visit to Notre Dame (Indiana), NLI, Ms 17,439/10.

61 5/10/1919, Harry Boland diary, P150/1170.

62 10/10/19, Ibid.

63 16/10/19, Boland circular letter, P150/869.

64 EDV, reminiscences in Dorothy Macardle's hand, P150/3662.

65 22/10/1919, EDV, 1919 diary, written into adapted 1930 diary, P150/263.

66 Sarbaugh, 'Irish Republicanism vs "Pure Americanism"', p. 179.

67 Ibid, p. 183.
68 EDV, 'Recollections of American mission', dictated to Marie O'Kelly, November 1962, P150/1100.
69 O'Hegarty, *The Victory of Sinn Féin*, p. 26.
70 Yeates, *A City in Turmoil*, p. 51.
71 Mulcahy, *My Father, the General*, p. 49.
72 Letter from EDV to Dáil, DED, 17/6/1919, vol. F, col. 112.
73 29/3/1920, Collins to Nunan, P150/1125.
74 30/11/1919, Harry Boland diary, P150/1170.
75 19/12/1919, EDV to McGarrity, NLI, Ms 17/439/6.
76 Mellows to Nora Connolly, quoted in Dudley Edwards, *Éamon de Valera*, p. 91.
77 See Davis, 'Éamon de Valera's political education', pp. 65–78, for an interesting discussion of this.
78 21/8/1919, EDV to Griffith, NAI, DE/2/245.
79 Fitzpatrick, *Harry Boland's Irish Revolution*, pp. 125–6.
80 30/1/1920, Boland to Collins, P150/1125.
81 9/4/1937, Seán Nunan to Pedlar, BMH, MSP34REF21572 (Liam Pedlar).
82 22/3/1938, Liam Pedlar to Begley, BMH, MSP34REF983 (Joseph Begley).
83 *DIB*; see also BMH MSP34REF60286, KOC statement, 16/6/1945.
84 13/8/1919, EDV to Collins, P150/726.
85 19/8/1919, Collins to EDV, Ibid.
86 6/9/1919, EDV to Collins, Ibid.
87 6/10/1919, Collins to EDV, Ibid.
88 14/10/1919, Collins to EDV, Ibid.
89 8/12/1919, Griffith to EDV, Ibid.
90 2/1/1920, EDV to Griffith (incomplete), P150/727.
91 17/1/20, Boland diary, P150/1170. The '69th', of course, was the 69th Infantry Regiment, an Irish-dominated National Guard unit.
92 Quoted in Longford and O'Neill, *Éamon de Valera*, p. 105.
93 Undated official statement, NAI, DE/2/239.
94 9/3/1920, Liam Mellows to Mrs John J. Hearn, NLI, Ms 15,986.
95 26/2/1920, Boland to 'Field' [Michael Collins], P150/1125.
96 Typed copy of Harry Boland diary entries, P150/1170.
97 BMH, WS 767, Patrick Moylett, p. 64.
98 McCartan, *With de Valera in America*, pp. 150–2.
99 17/2/1920, EDV to Griffith, *DIFP*, I:30.
100 McCartan, *With de Valera in America*, p. 153.
101 19/3/1920, Griffith to EDV, NAI, DE/2/245.
102 26/4/20, 'Field' [Collins] to 'James Wood' [Boland], with enclosures, P150/1125.
103 16 and 20–22/2/1920, Harry Boland diary, quoted in Fitzpatrick, *Harry Boland's Irish Revolution*, p. 154.
104 20/2/1920, EDV to Cohalan, P150/1134.

105 22/2/1920, Cohalan to EDV, Ibid.

106 EDV, undated commentary on Cohalan letter, Ibid.

107 25/3/1920, McGarrity's account of meeting, P150/1191.

108 McCartan, *With de Valera in America*, p. 165.

109 25/3/1920, McGarrity's account of meeting, P150/1191.

110 20/3/1920, Harry Boland diary, P150/1170.

111 25/3/1920, Ibid.

112 30/3/20, EDV diary for 1920, P150/264.

113 25/3/1920, EDV to Griffith (for Cabinet), NAI, DE/2/245.

114 19/4/1920, Collins to Boland, Ibid.

115 Cooper, *Woodrow Wilson*, pp. 558–9.

116 O'Neill, 'Towards American recognition of the Republic of Ireland', pp. 302; 307.

117 Franklin, 'Bigotry in 'Bama'.

118 Walsh, *Bitter Freedom*, pp. 215–16.

119 2/6/1920, Harry Boland diary, quoted in Fitzpatrick, *Harry Boland's Irish Revolution*, p. 169.

120 8/6/1920, O'Hegarty to EDV, *DIFP*, I:39.

121 20/7/1920, O'Hegarty to EDV, P150/729.

122 August 1920, 'Monthly Report on Revolutionary Movements in the British Dominions and Foreign Countries', NAUK, CAB 24/112/42.

123 9/8/1920, copy of EDV interview with Frederick William of the *Public Ledger*, P150/716.

124 17/3/1920, Irish Intelligence Summary, NAUK, KV2/515.

125 16/11/1920, Maguire to Boland, quoted in Fitzpatrick, *Harry Boland's Irish Revolution*, p. 188.

126 12/7/1920, McCartan to McGarrity, in Cronin, *The McGarrity Papers*, p. 83.

127 21/6/20, Director of Military Intelligence to Melbourne, NAUK, KV2/515.

128 4/8/20, Political report from America, Ibid.

129 September 1920, 'Monthly Review of Revolutionary Movements in the British Dominions and Foreign Countries', NAUK, CAB 24/112/100.

130 O'Halpin, 'Long fellow, long story', p. 187.

131 20/7/1920, McCartan to EDV, NLI, Ms 17,677/10.

132 Silvestri, '315 million of India with Ireland to the last', in Foley and O'Connor (eds), *Ireland and India*, pp. 249–50.

133 28/2/1920, EDV speech to Friends of Freedom of India, P150/1056.

134 Silvestri, '315 million of India with Ireland to the last', in Foley and O'Connor (eds), *Ireland and India*, p. 250.

135 6/3/1920, EDV to Griffith, *DIFP*, I:31.

136 EDV, 'Recollections of American Mission', dictated November 1962, P150/1100.

137 Dwyer, *De Valera: The Man and the Myths*, p. 42.

138 8/6/1920, draft minutes of meeting, P150/1000.

139 See for example Macardle, *The Irish Republic*, p. 370, and Gallagher, *The Four Glorious Years*, pp. 257–8.

140 19/11/1920, FOIF circular letter to members, P150/976.

141 19/6/1920, EDV, statement, P150/703.

142 EDV, 'Recollections of American Mission', dictated November 1962, P150/1100. Other nationalities did better, with supportive planks adopted in favour of Armenia, the Philippines, China, Persia, Finland, Poland, Czechoslovakia and Yugoslavia. Hannigan, *De Valera in America*, p. 222.

143 9/7/20, Boland Diary, P150/1170

144 4/8/20, quoted in Fitzpatrick, *Harry Boland's Irish Revolution*, p. 178

145 5/5/1920 and 9/7/1920, Harry Boland diary, P150/1170.

146 31/12/1919, Ibid.

147 *IT*, 25/11/2000, Cian O hÉigeartaigh, 'Dev's days of sensual longing', p. 40.

148 1/2/1920, SDV to EDV, P150/159.

149 BMH, WS 644, Joseph Hyland (IRA driver), p. 13.

150 See, for example, 12/7/1919, 1/8/1919 and 15/12/1919, Collins to EDV, P150/726.

151 13/12/1952, EDV, 'Account of American mission', dictated in Utrecht, P150/380.

152 14/8/1920, Collins to EDV, P150/726.

153 10/8/1920, Greystones RIC report, NAUK, CO 904/199.

154 Longford and O'Neill, *Éamon de Valera*, p. 113.

155 http://www.greenwichhistory.org/LS_witherell

156 21/8/20, EDV diary, P150/264

157 2/10/1920, EDV diary, P150/264.

158 2/11/1920, SDV to Tom Wheelwright, P190/203.

159 18/9/20, Boland to Kiernan, quoted in Fitzpatrick, *Harry Boland's Irish Revolution*, pp. 191–2.

160 Terry de Valera, *A Memoir*, p. 145.

161 26/11/1920, SDV to Mrs John Hearn, NLI, Ms 15,987.

162 2/11/1920, SDV to Tom Wheelwright, P190/203.

163 SDV to KOC, Kathleen O'Connell Papers, UCDA, P155/4(2).

164 Coogan, *De Valera*, pp. 184–7 gives details.

165 DED, 22/11/28, Vol. 27, col 606.

166 See, for example, 23/9/20, SDV to Kathleen O'Connell, P150/236.

167 Brennan, *Allegiance*, p. 297.

168 Quoted in Hannigan, *De Valera in America*, pp. 267–8.

169 Sinclair Lewis in *Babbitt* (1922) refers to the demand for 'this Mick agitator' de Valera to be deported; F. Scott Fitzgerald refers to his visit to Boston in *This Side of Paradise* (1920). Both quoted in Carroll, 'De Valera and the Americans', pp. 43, 46.

170 Harry Boland diary, quoted in Fitzpatrick, *Harry Boland's Irish Revolution*, p. 177.

171 Hannigan, *De Valera in America*, p. 227

172 31/10/1920, EDV speech, Polo Grounds (New York), P150/1045.

173 Hannigan, *De Valera in America*, pp. 144, 147.

174 December 1919, 'Review of Revolutionary Movements in Foreign Countries', NAUK, CAB 24/95/8.

175 Ferriter, *A Nation and Not a Rabble*, p. 216.

176 Fitzpatrick, *Harry Boland's Irish Revolution*, pp. 145–6.

177 14/8/1920, Collins to Boland, quoted in Hart, *Mick*, p. 191.

178 22/9/1920, Boland to Collins, P150/1125.

179 15/10/1920, Collins to Boland, quoted in Fitzpatrick, *Harry Boland's Irish Revolution*, p. 183.

180 Quoted in Jordan, *Éamon de Valera*, p. 69.

181 6/8/1920, EDV to Gallagher, P150/987.

182 EDV, 'Recollections of American Mission', dictated November 1962, P150/1100.

183 Fitzpatrick, *Harry Boland's Irish Revolution*, p. 190.

184 EDV, 'Recollections of American Mission', dictated November 1962, P150/1100.

185 9/10/1920, Cabinet minutes, NAI, DE/1/3. A later meeting agreed that he could present it to the old administration as well if he wished, but the primary aim was to influence the new one. 23/10/1921, Cabinet conclusions, NAI, DE/1/3.

186 US House of Representatives, session dates, http://history.house.gov/Institution/Session-Dates/60–69.

187 McCartan, *With de Valera in America*, p. 212

188 10/10/1920, EDV to James O'Mara, quoted in Lavelle, *James O'Mara*, p. 190.

189 27/10/1920, EDV, 'Ireland's request: An open letter to President Wilson', in Moynihan (ed.), *Speeches and Statements by Éamon de Valera*, pp. 41–6.

190 Quoted in Dwyer, *De Valera; The Man and the Myths*, p. 45.

191 16/11/1920, EDV speech at founding conference of AARIR, Washington, P150/1033.

192 16/11/1920, EDV, draft speech and excised paragraph, P150/1034.

193 Ferriter, *The Transformation of Ireland*, p. 198.

194 Fallon, *Soul of Fire*, pp. 53, 62, 70.

195 6/12/1920, EDV, 'Points Discussed at Meeting in Waldorf', P150/1073.

196 9/12/1920, EDV letter, quoted in Cronin, *The McGarrity Papers*, p. 92.

197 Fitzpatrick, *Harry Boland's Irish Revolution*, p. 184. These included $50,000 each for Boland's office in Washington, Diarmuid Fawsitt's consulate in New York, and the Committee for Relief in Ireland; $100,000 for the AARIR; and $200,000 to raise a second loan.

198 3/2/1921, EDV to O'Mara, quoted in Lavelle, *James O'Mara*, p. 236.

199 10/12/1920, EDV to Nunan, P150/954.

200 9/12/1920, McGarrity memorandum on departure of EDV, Joseph

McGarrity Papers, NLI, Ms 17,439/4.
201 11/3/1955, R. J. O'Halloran (Irish Shipping), to P. Hanrahan, P150/439.
202 Barney Downes account of voyage, P150/668.

CHAPTER 13: FEELERS ARE BEING THROWN OUT IN ALL DIRECTIONS

1 DED, 25/1/1921, Vol. F, col. 241.
2 18/3/1921, EDV to Collins, NAI, DE/2/244.
3 5/4/1921, EDV to Brennan, DIFP, I:74.
4 13/12/1920, extract from Cabinet conclusions, NAUK, KV2/515.
5 20/12/1920, Cabinet conclusions, NAUK, CAB/23/23/19.
6 *Observer*, 19/12/1920, Stephen Gwynn, 'Will de Valera come to Ireland?'
7 *Times*, 20/12/1920, Our Own Correspondent, 'Towards Irish peace'.
8 Jones Diary, 20/12/20, in Middlemas (ed.), *Whitehall Diary*, pp. 46–7.
9 20/12/1920, note by Home Office official, NAUK, HO 144/10309.
10 23/12/1920, Home Office to Under-Secretary (Dublin Castle), NAUK, KV2/515.
11 31/12/1920, W. Haldane Porter (chief inspector, Aliens Branch, Home Office) to immigration officers, NAUK, HO 144/10309.
12 21/12/1920 and 5/1/1921, Mark Sturgis diary, in Hopkinson (ed.), *The Last Days of Dublin Castle*, pp. 96 and 106.
13 EDV, 'Recollections of arrival', dictated February 1962, P150/1415.
14 BMH WSBMH, WS 475, Julia O'Donovan, p. 5.
15 EDV, 'Recollections of arrival', dictated February 1962, P150/1415.
16 28/11/1962, transcript of conversation between Richard Mulcahy, Mrs Mulcahy, Maj.-Gen. Paddy Daly, Joe Leonard and Senator Hayes, Richard Mulcahy Papers, UCDA, P7/D/1.
17 Richard Mulcahy, 'Notes on Piaras Béaslaí's *Michael Collins*', p. 74, Richard Mulchay Papers, UCDA, P7/D/67.
18 Townshend, *The Republic*, p. 230.
19 BMH, WS 939, Ernest Blythe, pp. 124–5, 129.
20 9/1/1921, Ministry and Cabinet minutes, NAI, DE/1/3.
21 See, for example, 26/2/1921, EDV to O'Hegarty, NAI, DE/2/3, requesting a meeting with a number of named ministers to discuss local government.
22 See Laffan, *The Resurrection of Ireland*, p. 287, for a similar curtailment of meetings of the Sinn Féin Standing Committee.
23 27/4/1945, EDV reference for Maeve MacGarry, P150/437.
24 BMH, WS 935, Seán Harling, p. 4.
25 6/1/1921, O'Hegarty to R. MacCoitir, and 10/1/1921, O'Hegarty to Joe O'Reilly, NAI, DE/2/3.
26 7/1/1921, Collins to EDV, NAI, DE/2/244.
27 3/2/1921, EDV to O'Mara, quoted in Lavelle, *James O'Mara*, p. 236.

28 Undated, SDV to KOC, Kathleen O'Connell Papers, UCDA, P155/4(3).

29 BMH, WS 939, Ernest Blythe, p. 129.

30 26/1/1921, Collins to Griffith, NAI, DE/2/242.

31 Michael Hayes, review of vol. 1 of Ó Néill and Ó Fiannachta's biography of de Valera, UCDA, Hayes Papers, P53/389.

32 Richard Mulcahy, 'Notes on Piaras Béaslaí's *Michael Collins*', p. 73, Richard Mulcahy Papers, UCDA, P7/D/67.

33 Fitzpatrick, *Harry Boland's Irish Revolution*, p. 218

34 BMH, WS 939, Ernest Blythe, p. 129.

35 Fanning, *Éamon de Valera*, p. 95.

36 Coogan, *De Valera*, p. 202.

37 Richard Mulcahy, 'Notes on Piaras Béaslaí's *Michael Collins*', p. 72, Richard Mulcahy Papers, UCDA, P7/D/67. The phrase is more a term of endearment than a deadly insult among many Cork people. There's no accounting for them.

38 18/1/1921, EDV to Collins, NAI, DE/2/448.

39 BMH, WS 362, Msgr J. T. McMahon (secretary to Archbishop Clune), pp. 3–4.

40 Extract from *FJ*, 4/12/20, and *II*, 6/12/20, in NAI, DE/2/234A; also 14/12/20, Collins to Art O'Brian, P150/1413.

41 11/9/1922, EDV, 'Negotiations with England', P150/1649.

42 9/12/1920, Art O'Brien to Collins, P150/1413.

43 Laffan, *The Resurrection of Ireland*, p. 334.

44 26/1/21, Collins to Griffith, NAI, DE/2/242.

45 17/1/1921, EDV to all members of the Dáil Ministry, P150/1380.

46 17/1/1921, EDV to all members of Ministry, *DIFP*, I:56.

47 Laffan, *The Resurrection of Ireland*, pp. 326–7.

48 Ibid, pp. 328–9.

49 Ibid, p. 334.

50 Ibid, p. 335.

51 EDV, 'Recollections of arrival', dictated February 1962, P150/1415.

52 DED, 21/1/1921, Vol. F, cols 236–7.

53 DED, 25/1/1921, Vol. F, col. 241.

54 Ibid, cols 242, 244–7.

55 Ibid, col. 249.

56 BMH, WS 826, Maeve MacGarry p. 17.

57 BMH, WS 935, Seán Harling, pp. 4–5.

58 16/3/1921, text of interview with representative of the Associated Press, P150/1438.

59 5/3/21, EDV to O'Hegarty, NAI, DE/2/14

60 17/1/1921, 19/1/1921 and 4/4/1921, EDV to Cosgrave, P150/1376.

61 15/1/1921, O'Hegarty to Gavan Duffy, *DIFP*, I:54.

62 6/2/1921, EDV to Brennan, Ibid, I:59.

63 28/2/1921, EDV to Brennan, Ibid, I:62.

64 12/2/1921, Plunkett to EDV, and 12/2/1921, Plunkett to Brennan, NAI, DE/2/526.

65 10/3/1921, EDV to Brennan, NAI, DE/2/526.

66 1/4/1921, EDV to Brennan, *DIFP*, I:71.

67 2/4/1921, Brennan to EDV, Ibid, I:72.

68 5/4/1921, EDV to Brennan, Ibid, I:74.

69 McCartney, *The National University of Ireland and Éamon de Valera*, p. 26.

70 Ibid, p. 28.

71 BMH, WS 939, Ernest Blythe, p. 135.

72 BMH, WS 356, Milo MacGarry, p. 11.

73 28/6/1945, transcript of KOC's evidence to Pensions Tribunal, P150/245.

74 BMH MSP34REF60286, KOC.

75 7/3/1921, EDV to Boland, P150/1132.

76 29/5/1921, EDV to Collins, P150.

77 Undated [1922], Barton to Archbishop Mannix, P150/1568.

78 10/2/1921, Collins to EDV, P150/1377.

79 Undated, EDV to Collins, P150/1377.

80 EDV, note on Collins, August 1969, P150/3483.

81 Richard Mulcahy, 'Talk with Lt-Gen. Costello', 23/5/1963, Richard Mulcahy Papers, UCDA, P7/D/3.

82 9/5/1921, EDV to Director of Publicity, P150/1379.

83 Inoue, 'Sinn Féin and the "Partition Election", 1921', p. 52.

84 Ibid, p. 53.

85 24/5/1921, Donnelly to EDV, quoted in Laffan, *The Resurrection of Ireland*, p. 339.

86 *BT*, 25/5/1921, quoted in Inoue, 'Sinn Féin and the "Partition Election", 1921', p. 61.

87 Northern Ireland parliamentary election results, http://www.election. demon.co.uk/stormont/totals.html.

88 Hayes, 'Dáil Éireann and the Irish Civil War', p. 3. Hayes incorrectly states that Sinn Féin won 5, rather than 6, of the seats in the North.

89 12/1/1921, EDV to FitzGerald, P150/1379.

90 2/4/1921, EDV to Childers, Ibid.

91 15/4/1921, EDV to staff attaché, publicity department, Ibid.

92 20/3/1921, Mark Sturgis diary, in Hopkinson (ed.), *The Last Days of Dublin Castle*, p. 143.

93 21/2/1921, EDV to Art O'Brien (London), P150/1422.

94 28/2/1921, EDV to Boland, P150/1132.

95 25/1/1925, Mulcahy to Bishop Fogarty, Richard Mulcahy Papers, UCDA, P7/C/100.

96 Townshend, *The Republic*, p. 96.

97 DED, 11/3/1921, vol. F, col. 264.

98 Ibid, vol. F, col. 266.

99 18/3/21, EDV to Collins, NAI, DE/2/244.

100 21/1/1963, EDV, typescript statement on Dr Mulhern's role in Derby visit, P150/1440.

101 15/1/1954, Nicholas Nolan, note of EDV's recollection of meeting, P150/1439.

102 15/2/1954, EDV to Randolph Churchill, Ibid.

103 25/4/1921 and 27/4/1921, Mark Sturgis diary, in Hopkinson (ed.), *The Last Days of Dublin Castle*, pp. 163, 165.

104 29/4/1921, EDV to Boland, giving text of message, P150/1132.

105 26/4/1921, EDV to Fogarty, P150/1331.

106 26/4/1921, EDV to Derby, NAI, DE/2/528.

107 28/4/1921, Lord Derby to EDV, NAI, DE/2/528.

108 *IT*, 29/4/1921, p. 6. Emphasis added.

109 27/4/1921, Tom Jones diary, in Middlemas (ed.), *Whitehall Diary*, p. 61.

110 12/5/1921, Tom Jones diary, in Ibid, pp. 69–70.

111 Buckland, *James Craig*, pp. 1–2, 55.

112 3/5/1921, Greenwood to Craig, PRONI, T3775/14.

113 5/5/1921, memo by Lady Craig, PRONI, D1415/B/32.

114 5/5/1921, EDV diary, note by KOC, P150/265.

115 5/5/1921, memo by Lady Craig, PRONI, D1415/B/32.

116 Boyne, *Emmet Dalton*, p. 211.

117 5/5/1921, Mark Sturgis diary, in Hopkinson (ed.), *The Last Days of Dublin Castle*, p. 171.

118 9/3/1929, EDV reply to Churchill account of meeting, P150/1567.

119 5/5/1921, Mark Sturgis diary, in Hopkinson (ed.), *The Last Days of Dublin Castle*, p. 171.

120 23/5/1921, 'Survey of the state of Ireland', NAUK, CAB 24/123/84.

121 7/5/1921, Collins to EDV, NAI, DE/2/244.

122 7/5/1921, EDV to Collins, P150/1377.

123 7/5/1921, EDV to Fr O'Flanagan, P150/1414.

124 24/5/1921, Cabinet conclusions, NAUK, CAB/23/25/25.

125 Wilson diary, quoted in Pakenham, *Peace by Ordeal*, p. 64.

126 Quoted in Fanning, *Fatal Path*, p. 259.

127 Oscar Traynor memoir, P150/3297.

128 BMH, WS 1410, Michael O'Kelly, pp. 2–3.

129 28/9/1945, EDV statement, P150/245.

130 Farragher, '1916: Rockmen and the Rising', *College Annual*, 1966, copy in P150/31. Eoin MacNeill's sons Niall and Brian were responsible.

131 BMH, WS 455, Margaret Keady (nee Macken), p. 4.

132 BMH, WS 826, Maeve MacGarry, p. 24.

133 30/6/1921, 'Report on Revolutionary Organisations in the United Kingdom', NAUK, CAB 24/125/104.

134 25/6/1921, report by Macready, NAUK, CAB 24/125/99.

135 Gaughan, *Austin Stack*, p. 149.

136 Brennan, *Allegiance*, pp. 313–14.

137 23/6/1921, Mark Sturgis diary, in Hopkinson (ed.), *The Last Days of Dublin Castle*, p. 190.

138 Gallagher, *The Four Glorious Years*, p. 300.

139 Undated, EDV to O'Hegarty, P150/1380.

140 3/2/1955, EDV, 'Recollections of events in 1921', P150/1575.

141 24/6/1921, O'Hegarty to EDV, and reply (29/6/1921), NAI, DE/2/2.

142 3/2/1955, EDV, Typescript typescript recollections of 1921, P150/1575.

143 28/6/1921, Healy to O'Brien, William O'Brien Papers, NLI, Ms 8556(26).

144 14/6/1921, Smuts to Lloyd George, in Middlemas (ed.), *Whitehall Diary*, p. 75.

145 22/6/1921, King's speech to the Parliament of Northern Ireland, NAUK, CAB 24/128/30.

146 24/6/1921, Cabinet conclusions, NAUK, CAB 23/26/8.

147 24/6/1921, Tom Jones diary, Middlemas (ed.), *Whitehall Diary*, p. 80.

148 24/6/1921, Lloyd George to EDV, NAI, DE/2/302/2.

149 1/7/1921, O'Brien to Collins, NAI, DE/2/262.

150 6/7/1921, Collins to O'Brien, NAI, DE/2/302/2.

151 28/6/1921, EDV to Lloyd George, NAUK, CAB/24/128/30.

152 29/6/1921, EDV to Unionist leaders, P150/1456.

153 Buckland, *James Craig*, p. 64.

154 11/7/1921, Mark Sturgis diary, in Hopkinson (ed.), *The Last Days of Dublin Castle*, p. 202.

155 7/7/1921, Lloyd George to Midleton, P150/1456.

156 5/7/1921, Mark Sturgis diary, in Hopkinson (ed.), *The Last Days of Dublin Castle*, p. 200.

157 15/9/1936, EDV to Dorothy Macardle, P150/3662.

158 6/7/1921, Tom Jones diary, Middlemas (ed.), *Whitehall Diary*, p. 83.

159 9/7/1921, Report by the GOC on the situation in Ireland, NAUK, CAB/24/126/35.

160 Quoted in Dudley Edwards, *Éamon de Valera*, p. 24.

161 Terms are in NAUK, 24/128/30.

162 Quoted in Macardle, *The Irish Republic*, p. 478.

163 Yeates, *A City in Turmoil*, p. 285.

164 Dalton, *With the Dublin Brigade*, p. 196.

165 Deasy, *Brother against Brother*, p. 21.

CHAPTER 14: I BEGGED THEM TO RISK IT

1 DED, 14/9/1921, vol. S, col. 95.

2 28/10/1921, EDV speech to ard-fheis, P150/579.

3 27/12/1921, EDV to McGarrity, P150/1560.

4 12/7/1921, KOC diary, P150/237.

5 11/7/1921, KOC diary, Ibid.

6 5/11/1969, Marie O'Kelly to T. Ryle Dwyer, P150/1582.

7 Undated, SDV to KOC, Kathleen O'Connell Papers, UCDA, P155/4(4).

8 Jones to Churchill, 1929, in Middlemas (ed.), *Whitehall Diary*, p. 89.

9 See Hattersley, *David Lloyd George: The Great Outsider*, passim.

10 Ibid, loc 2987.

11 Ibid, loc 4145.

12 Quoted in Berg, *Wilson*, p. 525.

13 9/3/29, EDV response to Churchill memoirs, P150/1567.

14 As told by EDV to Joseph O'Connor in BMH WS 544, Joseph O'Connor, p. 14.

15 Nicholas Mansergh, 'The prelude to Partition', in Mansergh (ed.), *Nationalism and Independence*, p. 54.

16 Shakespeare, *Let Candles Be Brought In*, p. 76.

17 15/8/1924, speech in Ennis, quoted in Browne, *Éamon de Valera and the Banner County*, p. 203.

18 Stevenson diary, quoted in Ged Martin, 'De Valera imagined and observed', in Doherty and Keogh (eds), *De Valera's Irelands*, p. 91.

19 15/7/1921, EDV to Collins, NAI, DE/2/244.

20 18/7/1921, Childers to Boland, with statement from EDV, P150/1469.

21 19/7/1921, Craig statement, P150/1470.

22 Austin Stack's account in BMH, WS 418, Mrs Austin Stack, p. 37.

23 Bowman, *De Valera and the Ulster Question*, p. 51.

24 19/7/1921, EDV to Lloyd George, and reply of same date, P150/1470.

25 19/7/1921, EDV to Collins, NAI, DE/2/244.

26 20/7/1921, Cabinet conclusions, NAUK, CAB/23/26/15.

27 Ibid.

28 20/7/1921, 'Proposals of the British government for an Irish settlement', NAUK, CAB/23/26/15, Appendix.

29 Callwell, *Field Marshal Sir Henry Wilson*, pp. 300–1.

30 20/7/1921, Erskine Childers diary, P150/1489.

31 Stack account in BMH, WS 418, Mrs Austin Stack, p. 38.

32 Lloyd George to King George V, quoted in Fanning, *Fatal Path*, p. 265.

33 23/7/1921, EDV to O'Hegarty, NAI, DE/2/2.

34 24/7/1921, handwritten notes of meeting of 'Inner Cabinet', *DIFP*, I:143.

35 Stack's account in BMH, WS 418, Mrs Austin Stack, pp. 38–9.

36 16/3/1923, EDV to William O'Brien (former MP), P150/1622.

37 Erskine Childers, Irish notebooks, quoted in Boyle, *The Riddle of Erskine Childers*, p. 300.

38 5/2/1964, EDV note dictated to Marie O'Kelly, P150/1471.

39 27/12/1921, EDV to McGarrity, P150/1560.

40 To Michael Hayes, quoted in Garvin, *1922*, p. 51.

41 Fallon, *Soul of Fire*, pp. 77–8.

42 FitzGibbon and Morrision, *The Life and Times of Éamon de Valera*, pp. 94–5.

43 Undated [1922], Barton to Mannix, P150/1568.

44 Cathal Brugha, note, written between 20 and 25/10/1921, P150/3618.

45 Bromage, *De Valera and the March of a Nation*, p. 135.

46 10/8/1921, EDV to Lloyd George, NAUK, CAB/23/26/21, Appendix 2.

47 11/8/1921, Barton to EDV, P150/1474.

48 11/8/1921, Jones to Lloyd George, in Middlemas (ed.), *Whitehall Diary*, pp. 95–6.

49 12/8/1921, Griffith to Barton, P150/1474.

50 12/9/1921, Tom Jones diary, in Middlemas (ed.), *Whitehall Diary*, p. 97.

51 13/8/1921, Cabinet conclusions, NAUK, CAB /23/26/21.

52 17/8/1921, Tom Jones diary, in Middlemas (ed.), *Whitehall Diary*, pp. 99/100.

53 DED, 16/8/1921, vol. S, col. 9.

54 DED, 22/8/1921, vol. S, col. 27.

55 Ibid, col. 33.

56 Ibid, col. 34. Of course, many people might think that was a very strong argument for allowing them to vote on such issues.

57 Ibid, col. 29.

58 DED, 23/8/1921, vol. S, col. 44.

59 Ibid, cols 57–8.

60 Liam de Róiste diary, quoted in Regan, *The Irish Counter-Revolution, 1921–1936*, p. 10.

61 DED, 23/8/1921, vol. S, col. 58.

62 Ibid, col. 59.

63 Ibid, col. 56.

64 19/11/1963, EDV, note dictated to Marie O'Kelly, P150/1311. The 'common acceptance' was of course due to his own use of the title in America.

65 BMH, WS 1716, Gen. Seán Mac Eoin, part 2, pp. 32–4.

66 DED, 23/8/1921, vol. S, col. 79.

67 24/8/1921, EDV to Lloyd George, NAUK, CAB/23/26/27, Appendix.

68 DED, 3/1/22, vol. T, col. 198, for O'Higgins' account of being invited to attend, but not vote, at Cabinet meetings by de Valera.

69 DED, 26/8/1921, vol. S, cols 81–3.

70 25/8/1921, Tom Jones diary, in Middlemas (ed.), *Whitehall Diary*, p. 102.

71 25/8/1921, Cabinet conclusions, NAUK, CAB/23/26/27.

72 26/8/1921, Lloyd George to EDV, NAUK, CAB/23/26/28.

73 Hattersley, *David Lloyd George*, loc. 10097.

74 7/9/1921, Tom Jones diary, in Middlemas (ed.), *Whitehall Diary*, pp. 109–11.

75 8/9/1921, Tom Jones diary, Ibid, pp. 112–13.

76 7/9/1921, Lloyd George to EDV, NAUK, CAB/23/27/1.

77 EDV, reminiscences in Dorothy Macardle's hand, (apparently from July 1934), P150/3662.

78 27/12/1921, EDV to McGarrity, P150/1560.

79 Cabinet minutes, 9/9/1921 and 10/9/1921, P150/1371.

80 12/10/1921, EDV to Lloyd George, NAUK, CAB/24/128/1.

81 DED, 14/9/1921, vol. S, col. 90.

82 Ibid, col. 95.

83 14/9/1921, Boland and McGrath, report for EDV, *DIFP*, I:154,.

84 Ibid.

85 Fitzpatrick, *Harry Boland's Irish Revolution*, pp. 233–4.

86 See 15/9/1921, Lloyd George to EDV, NAUK, CAB/24/128/11; 16/9/1921, EDV to Lloyd George, NAUK, CAB24/128/12; 16/9/1921, Lloyd George to EDV, NAUK, CAB/24/128/30; 17/9/1921, EDV to Lloyd George, NAUK, CAB/24/128/18; 18/9/1921, Lloyd George to EDV, NAUK, CAB/24/128/30.

87 29/9/1921, Lloyd George to EDV, NAUK, CAB/24/128/47.

88 30/9/1921, EDV to LG, NAUK, CAB/24/128/52.

89 5/10/1921, Cabinet minutes, NAI, DE/1/1/3.

90 Undated [1922], Barton to Mannix, P150/1568.

91 Copy of Griffith's credentials, NAI, DE/2/351. This implied an Ireland outside the Commonwealth.

92 7/10/1921, instructions to plenipotentiaries from Cabinet, *DIFP*, I:160.

93 See, for instance, Gallagher, *The Four Glorious Years*, p. 322.

94 25/2/1963, EDV to Lord Longford, P150/3620.

95 12/10/1921, EDV to Collins, P150/1377.

96 Gearoid McGann quoted in Ó Broin, *Just Like Yesterday*, p. 44.

97 KOC diary, 28/10/1921 and 15/11/1921, P150/237.

98 KOC Diary, 2/10/1921, Ibid.

99 KOC Diary, 5 and 14/10/1921, Ibid.

100 22/8/1921, Lynch to his brother, NLI, Ms 36,251/18.

101 25/8/1921, Ernie O'Malley to Mabel FitzGerald, in O'Malley and Dolan (eds), *'No Surrender Here!'*, p. 7.

102 30/7/1921, Brugha to adjutant-general, Richard Mulcahy Papers, UCDA, P7a/1.

103 2/9/1921, Mulcahy to Brugha, Richard Mulcahy Papers, UCDA, P7a/1.

104 6/9/1921, Brugha to Mulcahy, Ibid.

105 12–13/9/1921, Brugha to Mulcahy, Ibid.

106 Undated, Mulcahy to EDV, Ibid.

107 23/5/1963, Mulcahy, 'Talk with Lt-Gen. Costello', Richard Mulcahy Papers, UCDA, P7/D/3.

108 15/9/1921, Cabinet conclusions, P150/1371.

109 4/11/1921, Cabinet conclusions, Ibid.

110 EDV, notes, P150/350.

111 25/11/1921, Cabinet conclusions, NAI, DE/1/3.

112 Mulcahy, *A Family Memoir*, p. 85.

113 Richard Mulcahy account quoted in Townshend, *The Republic*, p. 330.

114 Gaughan, *Austin Stack*, p. 143

115 12 and 13/10/1921, Collins to EDV, P150/1377.

116 11/10/1921, Tom Jones diary, Middlemas (ed.), *Whitehall Diary*, pp. 119–20.

117 11/10/1921, Griffith to EDV, *DIFP*, I:163.

118 12/10/1921, EDV to Griffith, P150/1498.

119 10/10/1921, Tom Jones diary, in Middlemas (ed.), *Whitehall Diary*, p. 118.

120 Quoted in Dwyer, *De Valera: The Man and the Myths*, p. 74.

121 20/10/1921, EDV to Pope Benedict, *DIFP*, I:171.

122 24/10/1921, extract from Hansard, P150/1364.

123 10/11/1921, Tom Jones diary, Middlemas (ed.), *Whitehall Diary*, p. 160.

124 21/10/1921, Tom Jones diary, Ibid, p. 139.

125 21/10/1921, Erskine Childers to EDV, P150/1503.

126 25/10/1921, EDV to Griffith, P150/1498.

127 24/10/1921, Griffith to EDV, *DIFP*, I:176.

128 25/10/1921, KOC diary, P150/237.

129 Austin Stack's account, in BMH, WS 418, Mrs Austin Stack, p. 47.

130 25/10/1921, EDV to Griffith, P150/1498.

131 26/10/1921, combined Irish delegation to EDV, *DIFP*, I:179.

132 27/10/1921, EDV to Griffith, *DIFP*, I:181.

133 Pakenham, *Peace by Ordeal*, p. 183.

134 27/12/1921, EDV to McGarrity, P150/1560.

135 31/10/1921, Griffith to EDV, P150/1499.

136 2/11/1921, Erskine Childers diary, P150/1489.

137 Text of both letters in P150/1499.

138 3/11/1921, Griffith to EDV, *DIFP*, I:188.

139 Annotations on letters in P150/1499.

140 9/11/1921, EDV to Griffith, P150/1498.

141 2/11/1921, Erskine Childers diary, P150/1489.

142 3/11/1921, Ibid.

143 Buckland, *James Craig*, p. 68.

144 He had argued it would create a more homogenous Northern Ireland and therefore decrease the chances of reunification. 14/10/21, Tom Jones diary, in Middlemas (ed.), *Whitehall Diary*, pp. 130–1.

145 7, 8 and 9/11/1921, Tom Jones diary, Ibid, pp. 154–7.

146 Pakenham, *Peace by Ordeal*, p. 209.

147 8/11/1921, Griffith to EDV, *DIFP*, I:191.

148 Quoted in Bromage, *De Valera and the March of a Nation*, p. 138.

149 9/11/1921, EDV to Griffith, P150/1499.

150 16/11/1921, 'Tentative suggestions', *DIFP*, I:197.

151 18/11/1921, Griffith to EDV, *DIFP*, I:198.

152 22/11/1921, 'Memorandum by the Irish representatives', P150/1511.

153 22/11/1921, Griffith to EDV, *DIFP*, I:200.

154 25/11/1921, Cabinet conclusion, NAI, DE/1/3.

155 28/11/1921, 'Memorandum by the Irish delegation on their proposal for the association of Ireland with the British Commonwealth', P150/1511.

156 29/11/1921, EDV to Boland, P150/1560.

157 29/11/1921, Erskine Childers diary, P150/1489.

158 29/11/1921, Griffith to EDV, *DIFP*, I:206.

159 30/11/1921, British draft of Treaty, *DIFP*, I:207.

160 Browne, *Éamon de Valera and the Banner County*, p. 127.

161 Ibid, p. 133.

162 30/11/1921, O'Hegarty to McGann, NAI, DE/2/2.

163 2/12/1921, KOC diary, P150/237.

164 27/12/1921, EDV to McGarrity, P150/1560.

165 13–14/12/1952, EDV account of period between return from USA and Treaty, P150/380.

166 3/12/1921, Erskine Childers diary, P150/1489.

167 3/12/1921, Ó Murchadha, note of meeting, P150/1371.

168 3/12/1921, Erskine Childers diary, P150/1489.

169 3/12/1921, Ó Murchadha, note of meeting, P150/1371.

170 Stack's account in BMH, WS 418, Mrs Austin Stack, p. 54.

171 Note by Barton, P150/1521.

172 27/12/1921, EDV to McGarrity, P150/1560.

173 DED, 14/12/1921, vol. T, col. 126; see also Collins, DED, 15/12/1921, vol. T, col. 177.

174 3/12/1921, Ó Murchadha, note of meeting, P150/1371.

175 *IT*, 17/5/1927, p. 5; report of O'Higgins's election speech, Rathmines Town Hall.

176 Undated typed notes on oath issue, P150/1533.

177 3/12/1921, Erskine Childers diary, P150/1489.

178 Ó Broin, *Revolutionary Underground*, p. 196; McGarry, *Eoin O'Duffy*, p. 89.

179 3/12/1921, Ó Murchadha, note of meeting, P150/1371.

180 3/12/1921, Erskine Childers diary, P150/1489.

181 27/12/1921, EDV to McGarrity, P150/1560.

182 John M. Regan cogently argues a similar interpretation. Regan, *The Irish Counter-Revolution, 1921–1936*, pp. 15–16.

183 Richard Mulcahy, 'Notes on Piaras Béaslaí's *Michael Collins*', p. 167, Richard Mulcahy Papers, UCDA, P7/D/67.

184 Quoted in Browne, *Éamon de Valera and the Banner County*, p. 135.

185 Quoted in Ibid, p. 139.

186 Limerick speech, 5/12/1921, in Moynihan (ed.), *Speeches and Statements by*

Éamon de Valera, pp. 79–80.

187 Despite its age and lack of access to official records, Frank Pakenham's *Peace by Ordeal* (1935) is particularly vivid; the contemporary documents in *DIFP*, vol. 1, provide a fascinating account.

188 4/12/1921, Griffith to EDV, *DIFP*, I:211.

189 Pakenham, *Peace by Ordeal*, pp. 313–14.

190 5 and 6/12/1921, notes by Robert Barton, *DIFP*, I:213.

191 This was, in fact, how the news was sent – Lloyd George's secretary, Geoffrey Shakespeare, left Euston Station in London at 2:50 a.m., reaching Holyhead in just under five hours, where the destroyer HMS *Salmon* was waiting to take him to Belfast; his trip was only about two hours shorter than the 12 hours the quickest mail boat service took. *EH*, 6/12/21, p. 3.

192 5/12/21, Childers Diary, P150/1489.

193 Shakespeare, Geoffrey, *Let Candles be Brought In*, pp.87–88.

194 27/12/1921, EDV to McGarrity, P150/1560.

195 Richard Mulcahy, 'Notes on Piaras Béaslaí's *Michael Collins*', p. 168, Richard Mulcahy Papers, UCDA, P7/D/67.

196 Clarke, *Revolutionary Woman*, pp. 189–90.

197 *II*, 6/12/1921, p. 5; *FJ*, 6/12/1921, p. 5.

198 See 10/10/1921, Plunkett to EDV, and reply 11/10/21, P150/1388.

199 *EH*, 6/12/1921, p. 3.

200 Stack's account in BMH, WS 418, Mrs Austin Stack, p. 57.

201 6/12/1921, EDV Diary, P150/265.

202 Stack's account in BMH, WS 418, Mrs Austin Stack, p. 57.

203 1/11/1937, Desmond FitzGerald, 'Notes on Piaras Béaslaí's *Michael Collins*', Michael Hayes Papers, UCDA, P53/314. The 'towering rage' claim was made by Béaslaí.

204 Mansergh, 'Ireland and the British Commonwealth', in Mansergh (ed.), *Nationalism and Independence*, p. 98.

205 Stack's account in BMH, WS 418, Mrs Austin Stack, p. 58.

206 Fanning, *Independent Ireland*, p. 3.

207 *FJ*, 7/12/1921, p. 5.

208 7/12/1921, KOC diary, P150/237.

209 3/3/1925, EDV statement, P150/1922.

210 Laffan, *Judging W. T. Cosgrave*, p. 103.

211 7/12/1921, Cabinet conclusions, NAI, DE/1/3.

212 Stack's account in WS 418, Mrs Austin Stack, p. 59.

213 *II*, 8/12/1921, p. 5.

214 8/12/1921, Erskine Childers diary, P150/1489; also *DIFP*, I:216.

215 Bowman, '"Entre Nous": some notes by Erskine Childers on the making of the Anglo-Irish Treaty, 1921', in Fox (ed.), *Treasures of the Library*, p. 228.

216 8/12/1921, Erskine Childers diary, P150/1489; also *DIFP*, I:216.

217 Stack's account in BMH, WS 418, Mrs Austin Stack, p. 60.

218 BMH, WS 979 Robert Barton, p. 41.

219 Gallagher, *The Four Glorious Years*, p. 364.

220 Quoted in Yeates, *A City in Civil War*, p. 25.

221 Stack's account in BMH, WS 418, Mrs Austin Stack, p. 61.

222 *Boston Sunday Post*, 22/1/1928, quoted in Laffan, *Judging W. T. Cosgrave*, p. 104.

223 See for example, 27/10/1921, President's desk diary, Kathleen O'Connell Papers, UCDA, P155/138. 'P. [President] went to Gresham with Cosgrave to K. O'H. [Kevin O'Higgins] wedding'.

224 Laffan, *Judging W. T. Cosgrave*, p. 104.

225 3/3/1925, EDV statement, P150/1922.

226 8/12/1921, Cabinet conclusions, P150/1371.

227 9/12/1921, secretariat to each minister, NAI, DE/2/2.

228 9 and 13/12/1921, KOC diary, P150/237.

229 9/12/1921, Erskine Childers diary, quoted in Laffan, *The Resurrection of Ireland*, p. 353.

230 3/5/1968, Mulcahy letter to *II*, Richard Mulcahy Papers, UCDA, P7/D/80.

231 *Donegal Vindicator*, 9/12/1921, editorial, quoted in Laffan, *The Resurrection of Ireland*, p. 358.

232 12/12/1921, Lynch to his brother Tom, NLI, Ms 36,251/22.

CHAPTER 15: I AM SICK TO THE HEART

1 DED, 6/1/1922, vol. T, col. 281.

2 2/3/1926, Healy to O'Brien, William O'Brien Papers, NLI, Ms 8556/31.

3 EDV, Easter message, P150/1588.

4 DED, 14/12/1921, vol. T, col. 7.

5 Undated EDV reminiscences in Macardle's hand, P150/3662.

6 13/12/1921, EDV diary, P150/265.

7 14/12/1921, EDV copy of Treaty, P150/1538.

8 Gallagher, *The Four Glorious Years*, p. 366.

9 18/2/1923, EDV, 'Memo on Oath and Document No. 2', P150/1549.

10 Lee, 'De Valera's use of words', pp. 77–8.

11 18/2/1923, EDV, 'Memo on oath and Document no. 2', P150/1549.

12 Lee, 'De Valera's use of words', pp. 80–1.

13 DED, 10/1/1922, vol. T, Appendix 17.

14 Briscoe, *For the Life of Me*, pp. 130–1.

15 DED, 17/12/1921, vol. T, col. 256.

16 De Búrca and Boyle, *Free State or Republic?*, p. 4.

17 Briscoe, *For the Life of Me*, p. 131.

18 DED, 14/12/1921, vol. T, col. 16.

19 Ibid, cols 7–8.

20 De Búrca and Boyle, *Free State or Republic?*, pp. 4, 7.

21 DED, 14/12/1921, vol. T, col. 101.

22 Ibid, col. 137.

23 Ibid, col. 108.

24 Ibid, col. 138.

25 23/12/1961, discussion between Richard, Min and Risteárd Mulcahy, Richard Mulcahy Papers, UCDA, P7b/183.

26 DED, 15/12/1921, vol. T, cols 150–1, 153.

27 DED, 16/12/1921, vol. T, col. 216.

28 DED, 17/12/21, vol. T, cols 262–3.

29 DED, 15/12/1921, vol. T, col. 155.

30 Ibid, col. 173.

31 DED, 17/12/1921, vol. T, col. 271.

32 Ibid, cols 161–2.

33 DED, 15/12/1921, vol. T, cols 157–8.

34 DED, 17/12/21, vol. T, col. 243.

35 DED, 19/12/1921, vol. T, cols 19–20.

36 Ibid, cols 20–1.

37 Ibid, cols 22–3.

38 Ibid, cols 24–7.

39 De Búrca and Boyle, *Free State or Republic?*, pp. 11–12.

40 DED, 19/12/1921, vol. T, cols 30–6.

41 Andrews, *Dublin Made Me*, p. 221.

42 DED, 20/12/1921, vol. T, col. 67.

43 Ibid, col. 68.

44 DED, 21/12/1921, vol. T, cols 103; 106.

45 Undated, EDV, typewritten comments on Treaty, P150/1584.

46 DED, 20/12/1921, vol. T, col. 83.

47 DED, 22/12/1921, vol. T, cols 167–8.

48 27/12/1921, EDV to McGarrity, P150/1560.

49 DED, 7/1/22, vol. T, cols 315 and 320.

50 19/12/1921, Clarke to Madge Daly, quoted in Clarke, *Revolutionary Woman*, note 1, p. 235.

51 27/12/1921, redrafted Document no. 2, sent to McGarrity, P150/1543.

52 Text in DED, 10/1/1922, vol. T, Appendix 18.

53 See, for instance, Seán T. O'Kelly's claim that 'the Treaty inaugurated . . . the partition of Ireland', *IP*, 24/7/1961, 'Memoirs of Seán T', part 30, p. 9.

54 Typed extracts from *II*, 4/2/1922, NAI, S 6920.

55 Máire Comerford memoir, Máire Comerford Papers, UCDA, LA18/35(19).

56 DED, 22/12/1921, vol. T, col. 155.

57 Matthews, *Fatal Influence*, p. 63.

58 EDV, 'History and Genesis of Document no. 2', P150/1549.

59 27/12/1921, EDV to Cohalan, P150/1560.

60 De Búrca and Boyle, *Free State or Republic?*, pp. 49–50.

61 Dwyer, *De Valera: The Man and the Myths*, p. 93.

62 DED, 5/1/1922, vol. T, cols 265–6. De Valera said, 'I think any action of ours which would limit the freedom of the press is a mistake.'

63 DED, 5/1/1922, vol. T, col. 267.

64 4/1/1922, minutes of meeting, Richard Mulcahy Papers, UCDA, P7a/144.

65 Memo on timeline, Ibid.

66 DED, 7/1/1922, vol. T, cols 318–19.

67 DED, 6/1/1922, vol. T, cols 282–3.

68 De Búrca and Boyle, *Free State or Republic?*, pp. 57–8.

69 DED, 6/1/1922, vol. T, cols 271; 274; 275.

70 Ibid, cols 274–5; 277; 279.

71 *NYT*, 7/1/1922, editorial, quoted in Dwyer, *De Valera's Darkest Hour*, p. 94.

72 DED, 6/1/1922, vol. T, col. 281.

73 31/1/1922, McCartan to Maloney, quoted in Foster, *Vivid Faces*, p. 279.

74 Andrews, *Dublin Made Me*, p. 221.

75 DED, 7/1/1922, vol. T, col. 326 (Brugha) and 327 (exchange between Colivet and McCarthy).

76 de Búrca and Boyle, *Free State or Republic?*, p. 65.

77 Ibid, p. 66.

78 DED, 7/1/1922, vol. T, cols 336–7, 342, 344.

79 Ibid, col. 344.

80 DED, 22/12/1921, vol. T, cols 168–9.

81 DED, 20/12/1921, vol. T, col. 68; Carden, *The Alderman*, p. 190. Had they been allowed, of course, their votes would have cancelled each other out.

82 De Búrca and Boyle, *Free State or Republic?*, p. 56.

83 Ibid, p. 69.

84 Ibid, p. 69.

85 DED, 7/1/1922, vol. T, col. 346.

86 Ibid, col. 347.

87 Ibid, col. 347.

88 11/1/1971, Ernest Blythe to Lord Longford, Ernest Blythe Papers, UCDA, P24/1531.

89 7/1/1922, KOC desk diary, Kathleen O'Connell Papers, UCDA, P155/140.

90 DED, 7/1/1922, vol. T, col. 347.

91 8/1/1922, EDV diary, P150/351.

92 8/1/1922, KOC desk diary, Kathleen O'Connell Papers, UCDA, P155/140.

93 Regan, *The Irish Counter-Revolution, 1921–1936*, p. 49.

94 Jan 1922, Plunkett to EDV, quoted in Laffan, *The Resurrection of Ireland*, p. 360.

95 De Búrca and Boyle, *Free State or Republic?*, p. 72.

96 DED, 9/1/1922, vol. T, col. 349.

97 Ibid, col. 352.

98 Ibid, col. 356.

99 Ibid, cols 353, 356, 361.

100 Ibid, col. 356.

101 Farragher, *Dev and His Alma Mater*, p. 73; Coogan, *De Valera*, p. 301.

102 DED, 9/1/1922, vol. T, cols 379–80.

103 De Búrca and Boyle, *Free State or Republic?*, p. 78.

104 9/1/1922, KOC desk diary, Kathleen O'Connell Papers, UCDA, P155/140.
    Like many Republicans, she continued to refer to him as 'President'.

105 DED, 10/1/1922, vol. T, col. 398.

106 Ibid, col. 400.

107 Ibid, col. 399.

108 Ibid, col. 405.

109 Ibid, col. 410.

110 Ibid, col. 411.

111 Clarke, *Revolutionary Woman*, p. 194.

112 DED, 10/1/1922, vol. T, col. 414.

113 Ibid, cols 415–16.

114 Ibid, col. 423.

115 11/1/1922, Cabinet minutes, NAI, DE/1/4.

116 12/1/1922, Cosgrave to EDV, P150/1546.

117 13/1/1922, Cabinet minutes, NAI, DE/1/4.

118 17/2/1922, Cabinet minutes, Ibid.

119 3/2/1922, SDV to Collins, in Ó Broin and Ó hÉigeartaigh (eds), *In Great Haste*, pp. 114–15.

120 14/1/1922, EDV to Griffith, and reply (17/1/1922), P150/1546.

121 Laffan, *The Resurrection of Ireland*, p. 363.

122 Gaughan, *Austin Stack*, p. 189.

123 12/1/1922, KOC desk diary, Kathleen O'Connell Papers, UCDA, P155/140.

124 There is an entertaining, if lengthy, account of how the passport was secured in BMH, WS 593, Éamon Martin, pp. 2–7.

125 MacBride, *That Day's Struggle*, p. 61.

126 11/1/1922, Cabinet minutes, NAI, DE/1/4.

127 FitzGerald, report on Paris Conference, Desmond FitzGerald Papers, UCDA, P80/705.

128 Keown, 'The Irish Race Conference', p. 370.

129 23/1/1922, Eoin MacNeill to his wife, Eoin MacNeill Papers, UCDA, LA1/G/239.

130 Murphy, *John Chartres*, p. 87.

131 Keown, 'The Irish Race Conference', p. 371.

132 29/1/1922, EDV diary, P150/351.

133 MacNeill, notes, Eoin MacNeill Papers, UCDA, LA1/F/317.

134 Fitzpatrick, *Harry Boland's Irish Revolution*, p. 287.

135 12/2/1922, Rosamund Jacob diary, quoted in Carey, *Dublin since 1922*, pp. 11–12.

136 12/2/1922, typed copy of report of speech, P150/1606.

137 10/4/22, EDV interview with representative of Hearst Press, P150/1588.

138 Unless otherwise stated, all details are from the official report of the ard-fheis, P150/580.

139 21/2/1922, Collins to Kitty Kieran. 'I was with de V yesterday from 4 until 8.30.' Ó Broin and Ó hÉigeartaigh (eds), *In Great Haste*, p. 131.

140 22/2/1922, KOC desk diary, Kathleen O'Connell Papers, UCDA, P155/140.

141 See Townshend, *The Republic*, p. 393, for details of the evacuation, which began as early as 20 January.

142 The first to be repainted was in Dame Street, on 14 March. Carey, *Dublin since 1922*, p. 12.

143 DED, 28/2/1922, vol. S2, col. 91.

144 DED, 1/3/1922, vol. S2, col. 147.

145 He used the phrase several times in a meeting with labour leaders on Good Friday, the day of the seizure of the Four Courts. Desmond, *No Workers' Republic!*, p. 57.

146 DED, 14/10/1931, vol. 40, col 56.

147 See 23/3/1922, EDV, letter to the editor, *II*, P150/1547, accusing the paper of 'criminal malice' in distorting his meaning; and diary reference to 'misrepresentation' of speech; 17/3/1922, EDV diary (obviously filled in later), P150/266.

148 Farragher, *Dev and His Alma Mater*, p. 137.

149 18/3/1922, EDV, speech in Killarney, quoted in Moynihan (ed.), *Speeches and Statements by Éamon de Valera*, p. 103.

150 *FJ*, 10/4/1922, quoted in Dwyer, *De Valera's Darkest Hour*, p. 107.

151 Lee and Ó Tuathaigh, *The Age of de Valera*, p. 203.

152 DED, 1/3/1922, vol. S2, cols 156–7.

153 DED, 2/3/1922, vol. S2, cols 177–8.

154 DED, 27/4/1922, vol. S2, col. 301.

155 16/1/1922, O'Connor to chief of staff [Eoin O'Duffy], NAI, S 1233.

156 *IT*, 23/3/1922, p. 5.

157 24/3/1922, Griffith to EDV, Desmond FitzGerald Papers, UCDA, P80/675.

158 25/3/1922, EDV to Griffith, P150/1611.

159 23/3/1922, EDV diary, P150/266.

160 Bromage, *De Valera and the March of a Nation*, pp. 165–6.

161 2/3/1926, Healy to O'Brien, William O'Brien Papers, NLI, Ms 8556/31.

162 18/4/1922, Lynch to his brother Tom, NLI, Ms 36,251/26.

163 24/4/1922, Mary MacSwiney to Richard Mulcahy, MacSwiney Papers, UCDA, P48a/235(11).

164 20/4/1922, 'Revolutionary organisations in the United Kingdom', NAUK, CAB/24/136/45.

165 17/1/1964, EDV, answers to queries, P150/3297.

166 Longford and O'Neill, *Éamon de Valera*, p. 188.

167 1, 9, 12 and 15/4/1922, KOC desk diary, Kathleen O'Connell Papers, UCDA, P155/140.

168 EDV, Easter message, P150/1588.

169 13/8/1922, EDV to Charles Murphy, quoted in Laffan, *The Resurrection of Ireland*, p. 375.

170 26/4/1966, Hayes memorandum, Michael Hayes Papers, UCDA, P53/279.

171 6/3/1922, EDV to Mulcahy, P150/1608.

172 Valiulis, *Portrait of a Revolutionary*, p. 132.

173 O'Brien, *Forth the Banners Go*, p. 155.

174 2/5/1922, typescript copy of EDV remarks on Mansion House Conference, P150/1617.

175 Quoted in Fitzpatrick, *Harry Boland's Irish Revolution*, pp. 276–7.

176 31/3/1922, EDV to Stack (who had apparently made a similar proposal), P150/1272.

177 Undated EDV memorandum, P150/1623.

178 The desk diary kept by his secretary, Kathleen O'Connell, gives an impression of how little time he was able – or willing – to devote to domestic matters at this period. Kathleen O'Connell Papers, UCDA, P155/140.

179 Undated, SDV to KOC, UCDA, P155/4(6).

180 Terry de Valera, *A Memoir*, p. 13.

181 26/4/1922, Kiernan to Collins, and reply of same date, quoted in Ó Broin and Ó hÉigeartaigh (eds), *In Great Haste*, pp. 167–8.

182 DED, 27/4/1922, vol. S2, col. 304.

183 DED, 27/4/1922, vol. S2, col. 308.

184 Ibid, col. 309.

185 DED, 3/5/1922, vol. S2, cols 357–8.

186 Ibid, col. 359.

187 Ibid, cols 367–8.

188 See reports from both sides, read to the Dáil, DED, 11/5/1922, vol. S2, cols 398–403.

189 DED, 17/5/1922, vol. S2, cols 409–411.

190 Ibid, col. 414.

191 Clarke, *Revolutionary Woman*, pp. 194–5.

192 DED, 17/5/1922, vol. S2, cols 427–8.

193 DED, 19/5/1922, vol. S2, cols 460, 462.

194 Collins, notes of meetings, 18–19/5/1922 (agreed to by de Valera as a fair record), Richard Mulcahy Papers, UCDA, P7a/145.

195 20/5/1922, document signed by EDV and Collins, P150/1623.

196 Macardle, *The Irish Republic*, p. 713; MacManus, *Éamon de Valera*, loc. 2713.

197 See Gallagher, 'The Pact General Election of 1922', p. 406.

198 10/9/1922, EDV to McGarrity, in Cronin, *The McGarrity Papers*, pp. 124–5.

199 Laffan, *The Resurrection of Ireland*, p. 389.

200 WS 939, Ernest Blythe, p. 144.

201 DED 20/5/22, vol. S2, col. 479.

202 23/5/22, minutes of adjourned ard fheis, P150/580.

203 Sexton, *Ireland and the Crown*, p. 57.

204 1/6/1922, Cabinet conclusions, NAUK, CAB/23/30/9.

205 30/5/1922, Collins to Kiernan, in Ó Broin and Ó hÉigeartaigh (eds), *In Great Haste*, p. 176.

206 23/5/1922, Churchill memoranum, quoted in Townshend, *The Republic*, pp. 399–400.

207 2 and 8/6/1922, Tom Jones diary, Middlemas (ed.), *Whitehall Diary*, pp. 208–9; 212.

208 Text of Constitution as enacted, http://www.irishstatutebook.ie/eli/1922/act/1/enacted/en/print.

209 22/6/1922, Boland to McGarrity, P150/1171.

210 7/7/1922, Boland to McGarrity, P150/1171.

211 Gallagher, 'The Pact General Election of 1922', pp. 406, 408.

212 Laffan, *The Resurrection of Ireland*, pp. 392–3.

213 Ibid, p. 407.

214 Quoted in Martin, *Freedom to Choose*, pp. 61–4, 69–70.

215 Macardle, *The Irish Republic*, p. 721.

216 MacManus, *Éamon de Valera*, loc. 2768.

217 Gallagher, 'The Pact General Election of 1922', p. 413.

218 Gallagher, 'Party solidarity, Exclusivity and Inter-Party Relationships in Ireland', pp. 13–14.

219 Kissane, *Explaining Irish Democracy*, p. 129.

220 Laffan, *The Resurrection of Ireland*, p. 405

221 Gallagher, 'The Pact General Election of 1922', pp 415, 418.

222 Macardle, *The Irish Republic*, p. 722; MacManus, *Éamon de Valera*, loc. 2807.

223 19, 20 and 22/6/1922, Harry Boland diary, quoted in Fitzpatrick, *Harry Boland's Irish Revolution*, p. 299.

224 21/6/1922, EDV, statement on election results, P150/1588.

225 Fitzpatrick, *Harry Boland's Irish Revolution*, p. 301.

226 See notes by MacBride on the convention, in O'Malley and Dolan (eds), *'No Surrender Here!'*, pp. 26–8.

227 Walsh, *Bitter Freedom*, pp. 351–2.

228 22/6/1922, Lloyd George to Collins, P150/1679.

229 27/6/1922, Provisional Government decision, NAI, S 1322. Mulcahy later said in the Dáil that the decision to attack the Four Courts 'was practically taken, if not formally taken', before O'Connell was arrested, DED, 12/9/22, vol. 1, col. 173. This may have been the case, but the point was that the kidnapping made the decision far more palatable to the Free State army.

230 BMH, WS 939, Ernest Blythe, p. 148; see also 18/1/1936, Gavan Duffy to Macardle, P150/3662: 'The Cabinet did not intend a civil war, despite the propaganda to the contrary; they were led to believe that the taking of the Four Courts would be an affair of a few hours; it was the protracted resistance of the Four Courts that upset all calculations.'
231 28/6/1945, KOC, evidence to Military Pension Tribunal, P150/245.
232 Brennan, *Allegiance*, p. 343.
233 28/6/1922, EDV statement, P150/1588.
234 28/6/1945, KOC evidence to Military Pension Tribunal, P150/245.

CHAPTER 16: THE MOST HATEFUL OF CONFLICTS

1 10/9/1922, EDV to McGarrity, in Cronin, *The McGarrity Papers*, p. 124.
2 5/11/1922, proclamation, P150/1695.
3 9/4/1923, EDV to Ruttledge, P150/1710.
4 26/2/1923, EDV to Miss Ellis, Máire Comerford Papers, UCDA, LA18/45.
5 Yeates, *A City in Civil War*, p. 88.
6 Traynor account, P150/3297, p. 105.
7 6/7/1922, EDV to Brugha, Mary MacSwiney Papers, UCDA, P48a/255(1).
8 2/7/1922, statement on the legitimate government of the country, and 4/7/1922, statement to the people of the United States, P150/1588.
9 30/6/1922, Oscar Traynor to Ernie O'Malley, in O'Malley and Dolan (eds), *'No Surrender Here!'*, p. 31.
10 Traynor account, P150/3297, pp. 110–11.
11 Ibid, p. 111.
12 Statement of Seán Glynn, P150/3631.
13 Ibid.
14 Yeates, *A City in Civil War*, p. 92.
15 6/7/1922, EDV to Brugha, Mary MacSwiney Papers, UCDA, P48a/255(1).
16 7/7/1922, EDV diary, P150/351.
17 8/7/1922, EDV to Kathy Barry, quoted in O'Halpin, *Spying on Ireland*, p. 179.
18 Undated, EDV, memo, P150/1313.
19 5/8/1922, Department of Justice memorandum, 'Creation and source of authority of first 3 Dála', NAI, DE/4/8/7.
20 Regan, *The Irish Counter-Revolution, 1921–1936*, p. 80.
21 8/7/1922, EDV to Laurence O'Neill, P150/1621.
22 5/7/1922, EDV to O'Kelly, Seán T. O'Kelly Papers, NLI, Ms 27,673.
23 6/7/1922, EDV to O'Kelly, P150/1636.
24 25/7/1922, Lynch to O'Malley, quoted in O'Malley and Dolan (eds), *'No Surrender Here!'*, p. 68.

25 6/7/1922, EDV to Brugha, Mary MacSwiney Papers, UCDA, P48a/255(1).

26 Oscar Traynor account, P150/3297.

27 BMH, WS 938, Daniel Mulvihill, p. 17.

28 12/7/1922, EDV diary fragments, P150/351.

29 13/7/1922, Stack to Brennan, in BMH MSP34REF18488 (Robert Brennan); 14/7/1922, KOC desk diary, Kathleen O'Connell Papers, UCDA, P155/140.

30 13/7/1922, Boland to unidentified recipient, P150/1171.

31 Letter from Molly Childers to EDV, quoting from letter her husband sent her, in Boyle, *The Riddle of Erskine Childers*, p. 311. According to Dwyer, *De Valera: The Man and the Myths*, p. 114, which quotes part of the original letter, it is dated 12/7/1922.

32 Brennan, *Allegiance*, p. 349.

33 Ibid, p. 352.

34 10/9/1922, EDV to McGarrity, in Cronin, *The McGarrity Papers*, p. 124.

35 15/7/1922, KOC desk diary, Kathleen O'Connell Papers, UCDA, P155/140; also 28/6/1945, transcript of KOC's evidence to Military Pensions Tribunal, P150/245.

36 BMH, WS 1763, Dan Breen, p. 50.

37 12/1/1963, EDV account of movements, July and August 1922, dictated to Marie O'Kelly, P150/1639.

38 BMH, WS 1262, Phil Fitzgerald, p. 10.

39 12/1/1963, EDV account of movements, July and August 1922, dictated to Marie O'Kelly, P150/1639.

40 EDV diary for 1922, entries for 16–31 July, P150/266; also EDV diary fragments, 1922, P150/351.

41 BMH, WS 1763, Dan Breen, p. 50.

42 Ibid, p. 50.

43 McGarry, *Eoin O'Duffy*, pp. 107–8.

44 *FJ*, 22/7/22, p. 5.

45 BMH, WS 1721, Séamus Robinson, p. 79.

46 30/7/1922, KOC desk diary, Kathleen O'Connell Papers, UCDA, P155/140.

47 Neeson, *The Civil War*, p. 174.

48 EDV diary fragment, 19/7/1922, P150/351.

49 3/8/1922, adjutant-general (operations) to chief of staff, P150/1639.

50 2/8/1922, KOC desk diary, Kathleen O'Connell Papers, UCDA, P155/140.

51 7/12/1962, EDV statement, quoted in Fitzpatrick, *Harry Boland's Irish Revolution*, p. 322.

52 3 and 4/8/1922, KOC desk diary, Kathleen O'Connell Papers, UCDA, P155/140.

53 4/8/1922, KOC pocket diary, Kathleen O'Connell Papers, UCDA, P155/139.

54 9/8/1922, adjutant-general (operations), 2nd Southern Division, to Lynch, P150/1639.

55 10/8/1922, KOC pocket diary, Kathleen O'Connell Papers, UCDA, P155/139.

56 Boyne, *Emmet Dalton*, p. 201.

57 EDV diary fragments, 1922, P150/351.

58 13 and 14/8/1922, EDV diary, P150/351.

59 O'Brien, *The Irish Revolution*, locs 70; 6289; 6304.

60 William O'Brien account quoted in Kissane, *Explaining Irish Democracy*, p. 152.

61 14/8/1922, EDV diary, P150/266.

62 15/8/1922, KOC desk diary, Kathleen O'Connell Papers, UCDA, P155/140.

63 McGarry, *Eoin O'Duffy*, p. 111.

64 5/9/1922, Con Moloney (adjutant-general), on behalf of Lynch, to Ernie O'Malley, in O'Malley and Dolan (eds), *'No Surrender Here!'*, p. 157.

65 Deasy, *Brother against Brother*, pp. 76–7.

66 Ibid, pp. 77–8.

67 16/10/1964, EDV to Deasy, P150/1639.

68 24/8/1922, IRA report on ambush, in Hanley, *The IRA*, pp. 48–9.

69 14/1/1949, B. P. Hickey to 'Seán', with account of 'Peg', who claimed to have broken the news to him, P150/1639.

70 Undated, Mrs Catherine Shanley to EDV and reply (3/11/1972), P150/1639.

71 24/7/1934 EDV reminiscences in Macardle's hand, P150/3662.

72 See the highly entertaining exchange of opinions between Martin Mansergh and Tim Pat Coogan in *IT*, 22/1/2005; 31/1/2005; 9/3/2005.

73 There are numerous notes and accounts of the journey in P150/1639.

74 2/9/1922, EDV diary, P150/266.

75 14/8/1922, EDV to KOC, P150/239.

76 12/9/1922 and 4/10/1922, EDV to KOC, P150/238.

77 *DIB*.

78 10/9/1922, correct text of interview, P150/1588.

79 10/9/1922, EDV to McGarrity, in Cronin, *The McGarrity Papers*, p. 125.

80 BMH, WS 939, Ernest Blythe, p. 183.

81 7/1/1964, Mulcahy note on conversation with Commandant Vincent Byrne, Richard Mulcahy Papers, UCDA, P7/3.

82 Undated, Richard Mulcahy, conversation with Risteárd, Richard Mulcahy Papers, UCDA, P7b/182; Valiulis, *Portrait of a Revolutionary*, pp. 175–6.

83 BMH, WS 939, Ernest Blythe, p. 184.

84 24/8/1922, Churchill to Cope, quoted in Canning, *British Policy towards Ireland*, p. 48.

85 13/9/1922, note, NAI, S 2210.

86 10/9/1922, EDV to McGarrity, in Cronin, *The McGarrity Papers*, p. 125.

87 5/2/1923, EDV to McGarrity, Desmond FitzGerald Papers, UCDA, P80/791.

88 10/9/1922, EDV to McGarrity, in Cronin, *The McGarrity Papers*, pp. 125–6.

89 6/9/1922, EDV to C. O'M., Máire Comerford Papers, UCDA, LA18/45.

90 30/8/1922, Provisional Government decision, NAI, S 1428.

91 7/9/1922, EDV to Charles Murphy, quoted in Neeson, *The Civil War*, p. 268.

92 15/9/1922 and 2/10/1922, EDV diary fragments, P150/351.

93 8/11/1938, EDV, letter supporting military pension application by Annie Kane, BMH, MSP34REF1067.

94 Gaughan, *Austin Stack*, pp. 216–17.

95 10/9/1922, EDV to McGarrity, in Cronin, *The McGarrity Papers*, p. 126. Cosgrave had written to Collins about this rumour in August; the commander-in-chief appeared ignorant of it, writing on Cosgrave's letter 'Who?' 11/8/1922, Cosgrave to Collins with notations, Richard Mulcahy Papers, UCDA, P7/B/29.

96 1922, note to KOC, P150/3691.

97 11/9/1922, EDV memorandum, 'Memoirs', P150/379.

98 24/10/1922, minutes of meeting between Bonar Law and Irish ministers, quoted in Canning, *British Policy towards Ireland*, p. 72.

99 23/12/1961, discussion between Richard, Min and Risteárd Mulcahy, Richard Mulcahy Papers, UCDA, P7b/183.

100 4/9/1922, Plunkett to EDV, P150/1652.

101 27/9/1922, McGarrity to EDV, NLI, Ms 17,440/7.

102 12/10/1922, EDV to McGarrity, P150/1195.

103 28/2/1923, Lynch to EDV, P150/1749.

104 7/3/1923, EDV to Lynch, Ibid.

105 *FJ*, 17/2/1923, p. 5.

106 10/9/1922, Mary MacSwiney to EDV, P150/657.

107 11/9/1922, EDV to MacSwiney, Ibid.

108 10/9/1922, EDV to McGarrity, in Cronin, *The McGarrity Papers*, p. 126.

109 12/10/1922, EDV to McGarrity, P150/1195.

110 12/10/1922, EDV to Liam Lynch and each member of the Army Executive, P150/1695.

111 19/10/1922, EDV to McGarrity, P150/1195.

112 17/10/1922, Executive Meeting minutes, Moss Twomey Papers, UCDA, P69/179(6).

113 21/10/1922, EDV to Lynch, P150/1749.

114 23/10/1922, EDV to Lynch, Ibid.

115 8/11/1922, Lynch to EDV, and reply (9/11/1922), Ibid.

116 9/11/1922, Ruttledge to EDV, and reply (10/11/1922), P150/1710.

117 31/3/1923, EDV to Dulcibella Barton, P150/1802.

118 16/11/1922, Lynch to EDV, P150/1749.

119　5/11/1922, proclamation, P150/1695.

120　3/11/1922, proclamation signed by EDV and Stack, Ibid.

121　17/11/1922, proclamation, Ibid.

122　26/11/1922, EDV to Mellows, Ibid.

123　29/12/22, EDV to O/C Communications, Ibid.

124　9/11/22, EDV to C.O'M, Ibid.

125　21/12/1922, Lynch to McGarrity, NLI, Ms 17,455/1.

126　23/12/1922, EDV to Ruttledge, P150/1710.

127　14/1/1923, EDV to Stack, P150/1695.

128　20/1/1923, EDV to Stack, P150/1710.

129　28/1/1923, EDV to Comyn, Elgin O'Rahilly Papers, UCDA, P200/49(20).

130　29/10/1922, KOC desk diary, Kathleen O'Connell Papers, UCDA, P155/140.

131　10/11/1922, KOC desk diary, Kathleen O'Connell Papers, UCDA, P155/140.

132　28/11/1922, EDV to McGarrity, P150/1195.

133　24/11/1922, EDV to Lynch, P150/1749.

134　25/11/1922, Lynch to EDV, and reply (27/11/1922), Ibid.

135　8/12/1922, KOC desk diary, Kathleen O'Connell Papers, UCDA, P155/140.

136　There is a good account in Yeates, *A City in Civil War*, pp. 202–3.

137　12/12/1922, EDV to Lynch, P150/1749.

138　14/12/1922, Lynch to EDV, and reply (15/12/1922), Ibid.

139　15/12/1922, EDV to Ruttledge, Ibid.

140　7/5/1923, EDV to Aiken, P150/1752.

141　18/1/1923, EDV to Lynch, P150/1749.

142　30/1/1923, Lynch to EDV and all ministers, Ibid.

143　2/2/1923, EDV to Lynch, Ibid.

144　3/2/1923, Operation Order 17, Ibid.

145　28/2/1923, Lynch to EDV, Ibid.

146　9/3/1923, EDV to ministers, P150/1695.

147　14/3/1923, EDV to Moss Twomey, P150/1749.

148　17/3/1923, EDV to Moss Twomey, Ibid.

149　15/12/1922, EDV to Ruttledge, Ibid.

150　28/12/1922, Lynch to EDV, and reply (4/1/1923), Ibid.

151　31/1/1923, EDV diary, P150/268.

152　Deasy, *Brother against Brother*, p. 111.

153　29/1/1923, Deasy to EDV, P150/1697.

154　30/1/1923, Deasy to EDV, Ibid.

155　31/1/1923, EDV to all ministers and chief of staff, Ibid.

156　2/2/1923, EDV to Lynch, Ibid.

157　7/2/1923, Lynch to EDV, timed 11 a.m.; and reply (12:55 p.m.), P150/1749.

158 8/2/1923, EDV to chief of staff and all members of the Ministry, P150/1695.

159 10/2/1923, Mary MacSwiney to EDV, quoted in Dwyer, *De Valera: The Man and the Myths*, p. 124.

160 19/2/1923, EDV to Mary MacSwiney, P150/657.

161 24/2/1923, EDV to Mary MacSwiney, Ibid.

162 14/3/1923, EDV to Mary MacSwiney, Ibid.

163 Quoted in Ryan, *Liam Lynch*, p. 209.

164 Andrews, *Dublin Made Me*, pp. 291, 305.

165 5/2/1923, EDV to J. J. O'Kelly [Sceilg], P150/1276.

166 28/2/1923, Lynch to EDV, and reply (7/3/1923), P150/1749.

167 14/3/1923, EDV to Mary MacSwiney, P150/657.

168 Cosgrave, 8/2/1923, quoted in Dwyer, *De Valera: The Man and the Myths*, p. 123.

169 1/7/1922, Provisional Government decision, and 31/10/1922, Cosgrave to Maj. J. E. V. Loftus, NAI, S 4522.

170 *IT*, 12/3/1923, p. 7.

171 *FJ*, 11/10/1922, p. 5.

172 21/1/1923, Logue to Byrne, quoted in Keogh, *The Vatican, the Bishops and Irish Politics*, p. 106.

173 6/11/1922, EDV to Mannix, P150/2909.

174 Fanning, *Éamon de Valera*, pp. 148–9.

175 Quoted in Dwyer, *De Valera*, p. 311.

176 *IT*, 20/3/1923, p. 5.

177 7/11/1959, Irish ambassador to the Vatican (Seán Ó hÉideáin), reporting Luzio's death, NAI, PRES1/P55570.

178 Extract from undated British report from Curtis to Loughnane, NAI, S 2198.

179 Undated, Luzio peace terms, P150/1809.

180 8/4/1923, EDV to Mary MacSwiney, P150/657.

181 17/4/1923 and 5/5/1923, Cabinet minutes, NAI, S 2198.

182 29/4/1923, Luzio to EDV, and reply (30/4/1923), P150/1809. This wording suggests he did at the time consider himself to be excommunicated.

183 24–25/3/1923, EDV diary, P150/268.

184 23, 24, 25 and 26/3/1923, minutes of Executive Meeting, Moss Twomey Papers, UCDA, P69/179(37–8).

185 Ibid.

186 27/3/1923, EDV diary, P150/268.

187 30/3/1923, Ibid.

188 2/4/1923, Ruttledge to EDV, P150/1710.

189 9/4/1923, EDV to Ruttledge, P150/1710.

190 11/4/1923, EDV to Ruttledge, Ibid.

191 6/4/23, KOC journal, UCDA, P155/141.

192 11/4/23, Aiken to EDV, P150/1752.

193 10 and 11/4/1923, KOC journal, Kathleen O'Connell Papers, UCDA, P155/141.

194 EDV, handwritten envelope, P150/1749.

195 Andrews, *Dublin Made Me*, pp. 305–8.

196 Gaughan, *Austin Stack*, p. 233.

197 15/4/1923, KOC journal, Kathleen O'Connell Papers, UCDA, P155/141.

198 March 1967, Tomás Culliton to Marie O'Kelly, P150/1815.

199 20/4/1923, Executive meeting minutes, P150/1739.

200 26–7/4/1923, government and Army Council meeting minutes, Moss Twomey Papers, UCDA, P69/179(42).

201 27/4/1923, Aiken to OCs [officers commanding] Commands and independent brigades, P150/1819.

202 27/4/1923, EDV, proclamation, P150/1819.

203 Curiously, de Valera later denied that he had done so. In the Dáil in October 1931, in response to Cosgrave, he was recorded as saying, 'I did not send for them.' When Douglas challenged him, he claimed that what he said was 'I did not select them.' The distinction was hardly important: he had done both. 28/10/1931, EDV to Douglas, Michael Hayes Papers, UCDA, P53/70.

204 Douglas, record of meeting, NAI, S 2210.

205 28/4/1923, EDV to Douglas, P150/1816.

206 Douglas, record of meeting, NAI, S 2210.

207 4/5/1923, Executive Council minutes, NAI, S 2210.

208 3/5/1923, Jameson, report of interview with EDV, NAI, S 2210; also EDV, memorandum on negotiations, P150/1816.

209 4/5/1923, Executive Council minutes, NAI, S 2210.

210 9/5/1923, Douglas, statement in Seanad, Ibid.

211 2/5/1923, KOC journal, Kathleen O'Connell Papers, UCDA, P155/141.

212 8/5/1923, Ibid.

213 7/5/1923, EDV proposals, NAI, S 2210.

214 8/5/1923, Cosgrave to Jameson, Ibid.

215 8/5/1923, KOC journal, Kathleen O'Connell Papers, UCDA, P155/141.

216 13 and 14/5/1923, minutes of meeting of government and Army Council, Moss Twomey Papers, UCDA, P69/179(43).

217 23/5/1923, EDV to Magennis, P150/1809.

218 24/5/1923, Aiken order, P150/1827.

219 24/5/1923, Aiken, Order of the Day, Mary MacSwiney Papers, UCDA, P48a/236(2).

220 24/5/1923, EDV message to all ranks, P150/1827.

221 24/5/1923, KOC journal, Kathleen O'Connell Papers, UCDA, P155/141.

222 24/5/1923, EDV to Aiken, P150/1752.

223 25/5/1923, Aiken to EDV, Ibid.

224 1/6/1923, Ruttledge to EDV, P150/1710.

225 30/5/1923, EDV to chief of staff and all ministers, P150/1695.

226 8/6/1923, EDV memorandum to unidentified recipient, P150/1807.

227 22/5/1923, MacSwiney to EDV, and reply (25/5/1923), P150/657.

228 26/7/1923, EDV to Mary MacSwiney, P150/657.

229 7/8/23, EDV to MacSwiney, Ibid.

230 22/6/1923, EDV to 'Rev. Father', P150/1698.

231 Valiulis, 'The man they could never forgive', in O'Carroll and Murphy (eds), *De Valera and his times*, pp. 92–3.

232 8/6/1923, EDV, memo to unidentified recipient, P150/1807.

233 4/6/1923, EDV to McGarrity, P150/1191.

234 20/6/1923, EDV to Msgr O'Connor, P150/1280.

235 6/7/1923, EDV to Luke Dillon, and EDV to McGarrity, P150/1191.

236 1/6/1923, Aiken to EDV, P150/1752.

237 4/6/1923, EDV to Aiken, Ibid.

238 11/7/1923, EDV to Constance Markievicz, P150/1814.

239 26/7/1923, EDV to Ruttledge, P150/1710.

240 10/8/1923, EDV, circular letter, P150/1841.

241 9/7/1923, EDV to Aiken, P150/1752.

242 BMH, WS 1050, Vera McDonnell, pp. 11–12.

243 22/10/1922, EDV to Constance Markievicz; 25/10/22, EDV to Éamon Donnelly, P150/580.

244 25/10/1922, Republican members of Standing Committee to EDV, Ibid.

245 25/10/1922, EDV to Éamon Donnelly, Ibid.

246 31/10/1922, EDV to Éamon Donnelly, Ibid.

247 3/12/1922, EDV to P. J. Ruttledge, P150/1710.

248 23/1/1923, Ruttledge to President and all ministers, 1st report on Sinn Féin reorganisation, P150/582.

249 8/12/1922, EDV to Mary MacSwiney, P150/657.

250 6/1/1923, EDV to Ruttledge, P150/1710.

251 20/1/1923, Plunkett to EDV, P150/1652.

252 15/1/1923, EDV to Ruttledge, quoted in Kissane, *Explaining Irish Democracy*, p. 169.

253 31/7/1923, EDV to Molly Childers, P150/1794.

254 Gaughan (ed.), *Memoirs of Senator Joseph Connolly*, p. 249.

255 16/5/23, EDV to AL, P150/1825.

256 31/5/1923, EDV to Molly Childers, P150/1794.

257 26/5/1922, AL to EDV, P150/1825.

258 29/5/1923, EDV to AL, Ibid.

259 30/5/1923, AL to EDV, P150/1825.

260 30/5/1923, Comyn to EDV, P150/1713.

261 31/5/1923, EDV to organising committee, P150/1818.

262 11/7/1923, EDV to Connolly, Ibid.

263 23/6/1923, EDV to Msgr Hagan, P150/1809.

264 20/11/1922, EDV to Derrig, P150/1758. A later iteration of Sinn Féin advanced a similar policy, 'Éire Nua', in the late 1970s.

265 8/6/1923, EDV memorandum to unidentified recipient, P150/1807.

266 25/7/1923, EDV to organising committee, P150/1818.

267 26/7/1923, Connolly to EDV, Ibid.

268 14/8/1923, EDV to Donnelly, Desmond FitzGerald Papers, UCDA, P80/802.

269 24/7/1923, EDV, election address, P150/1835.

270 Madge Clifford, quoted in Gaughan, *Austin Stack*, note 2, p. 323.

271 31/7/1923, EDV to Molly Childers, P150/1794.

272 4/8/1923, Director of Intelligence [Michael Carolan] to EDV, P150/1849.

273 10/8/1923, Carolan to EDV, Ibid.

274 6 and 7/8/1923, KOC journal, Kathleen O'Connell Papers, UCDA, P155/141.

275 12/8/1923, EDV diary, P150/268.

276 12/8/1923, KOC journal, Kathleen O'Connell Papers, UCDA, P155/141.

CHAPTER 17: MASTER OF MY OWN SOUL

1 3/1/1924, EDV to Ruttledge, Kathleen O'Connell Papers, UCDA, P155/12(20).

2 15/11/1925, Comhairle na dTeachtaí minutes, P150/1946.

3 16/5/1926, EDV speech, La Scala cinema [Dublin], P150/2014.

4 25/7/1923, EDV to organising committee, Mary MacSwiney Papers, UCDA, P48a/236(3).

5 Undated notes, P150/1844.

6 9/8/1923, Seán Lester (Publicity Department) to McGann (President's Department), NAI, S 1369/15.

7 13/8/1923, cypher message, general officer commanding to adjutant, Limerick Command, P150/1849.

8 15/8/1923, report on arrest by Capt. T. Power, P150/1849.

9 *IT*, 16/8/1923, p. 7.

10 15/8/1923, KOC journal, Kathleen O'Connell Papers, UCDA, P155/141.

11 15/8/1923, report on arrest by Capt. T. Power, P150/1849.

12 *IT*, 16/8/1923, p. 7.

13 *EP*, 15/4/1965, interview with Peg Barrett.

14 Thomas P. O'Neill, Foreword, in Browne, *Éamon de Valera and the Banner County*, p. 10.

15 *IT*, 16/8/1923, p. 7.

16 24/8/1923, detention order signed by Mulcahy, P150/1849.

17 Lee, *Ireland, 1912–1985*, p. 94.

18 Quoted in Ó Drisceoil, *Peadar O'Donnell*, p. 34.

19 It was the highest percentage share in the country (though Richard Mulcahy won more votes in Dublin North, with 22,205 – a 40% share).

20 Calculated from figures on Elections Ireland, http://electionsireland.org.
21 14/8/1923, Eoin to Taddie MacNeill, Eoin MacNeill Papers, UCDA, LA1/G/269.
22 13/2/1924, Seán T. O'Kelly to Msgr O'Hagan, reporting Ald. Tom Kelly, conversation with Cosgrave, in Seán T. O'Kelly Papers, NLI, Ms 48,453/1.
23 16/8/1923, secretary to Executive Council to Minister for Defence, NAI, S 1369/15.
24 23/8/1923, secretary, Department of Defence, to Director of Intelligence, Ibid.
25 Ó Drisceoil, *Peadar O'Donnell*, p. 34.
26 Gerry Boland memoir, pp. 8(E) and 9(E).
27 31/10/1923, special instructions, P150/1862.
28 Received 2/12/1923, EDV to Ruttledge, P150/1863.
29 19/11/1923, note of meeting between Mulcahy and Dr Moore, Richard Mulcahy Papers, UCDA, P7/B/284.
30 Yeates, *A City in Civil War*, p. 265.
31 See correspondence in Desmond FitzGerald Papers, UCDA, P80/1039.
32 Undated, EDV to Ruttledge, Kathleen O'Connell Papers, UCDA, P155/12.
33 3/1/1924, EDV to Ruttledge, Ibid.
34 Undated, EDV to Ruttledge, Ibid.
35 Undated, EDV to Ruttledge, P150/1863.
36 12/1/1924, EDV to Ruttledge, P150/1863.
37 Received 2/2/1924, EDV to Ruttledge, Kathleen O'Connell Papers, UCDA, P155/12(7).
38 19/1/24, EDV to KOK, Kathleen O'Connell Papers, UCDA, P155/13.
39 2/2/1924, EDV to KOC, Kathleen O'Connell Papers, UCDA, P155/20.
40 Letter from Vivion de Valera, quoted in Synge, 'Éamon de Valera', p. 640.
41 17/3/1924, 30/3/1924, 16/4/1924 and 20/4/1924, EDV diary, P150/352.
42 20/4/1924, EDV to Catherine Wheelwright, P150/178.
43 25/4/1924, O'Duffy to Cosgrave, NAI, S 1369/15.
44 25/4/1924, EDV diary, P150/352.
45 25/4/1924, Austin Stack diary, NLI, Ms 17,076.
46 See Stack diary for April, May and June, NLI, Ms 17,076; the mysterious Keegan was probably a Free State 'plant'.
47 8/5/24, Aiken to KOC, P150/243; Commandant Hugh Maguire, 'Chess and handball with 'Dev' in prison', IP, 2/11/79, p. 9.
48 23 and 27/6/24, Stack diary, NLI, Ms 17,076.
49 17/7/1924, Austin Stack diary, NLI, Ms 17,076.
50 16/10/23, ard-fheis minutes, P150/582.
51 8/8/1924, second Dáil minutes, in Gaughan, *Austin Stack*, p. 355.
52 Fallon, *Soul of Fire*, p. 106.
53 17/7/1924, Standing Committee minutes, P150/589.
54 22 and 31/7/1924, EDV diary, P150/269.

55 31/7/1924, SDV to KOC, P150/241.

56 7/8/1924, minutes of Comhairle na dTeachtaí; and 8/8/1924, minutes of second Dáil, in Gaughan, *Austin Stack*, pp. 321–53.

57 T. P. O'Neill, Foreword, in Browne, *Éamon de Valera and the Banner County*, p. 11.

58 Andrews, *Man of No Property*, p. 53.

59 McCartney, *The National University of Ireland and Éamon de Valera*, pp. 32–7.

60 8/8/1924, Sinn Féin Standing Committee minutes, P150/589.

61 EDV, 'Appeal to Republicans', P150/1913.

62 27/8/1924, EDV to Fr Yorke, P150/1261.

63 'Houses in which Chief lived', P150/438.

64 Longford and O'Neill, *Éamon de Valera*, p. 422.

65 Terry de Valera, *A Memoir*, pp. 16–17.

66 BMH, WS 457, Dorothy Macardle, p. 2.

67 Ibid, p. 4.

68 11/3/1925, EDV to Seán T. O'Kelly, P150/1777.

69 3/12/1924, Brennan to EDV, and reply (30/12/1924), P150/1841.

70 *IT*, 25/8/1924, p. 6.

71 5/10/1924, EDV speech, Carlow, Records of the Fianna Fáil Party, UCDA, P176/19 (9).

72 *IT*, 10/10/24, p. 6.

73 11/10/1924, Sinn Féin Standing Committee, P150/589.

74 *IT*, 17/10/1924, p. 5.

75 22/10/1924, EDV statement, P150/583.

76 Quoted in Matthews, *Fatal Influence*, p. 195.

77 27/10/1924, RUC inspector-general's office to Ministry of Home Affairs, and report by T. Fletcher, district inspector (Newry), PRONI HA/32/1/156.

78 27/10/1924, H. Connor, city commissioner, RUC (Londonderry), to inspector-general, PRONI HA/32/1/156.

79 1/11/1924, EDV diary, P150/269.

80 Dwyer, *De Valera's Darkest Hour*, p. 152.

81 Calculated from figures on Elections Ireland, http://electionsireland.org/results/general/04dail.cfm.

82 28/11/1924, report by RUC Sergeant Keery, PRONI, HA/32/1/156.

83 Ibid.

84 4/11/1924, Executive Council decision, NAI, S 4120.

85 Quoted in Gaughan, *Austin Stack*, p. 245.

86 13/1/1925, Stack to EDV, with marginal notes, Austin Stack Papers, NLI, Ms 17,092(2).

87 Matthews, *Dissidents*, p. 132.

88 Ward, *Hanna Sheehy-Skeffington*, p. 259.

89 30/3/1925, EDV to editor, Sinn Féin, P150/1925.

90 19/8/1924, Aiken to EDV, P150/1753.

91 19/1/1925, Murray memorandum, P150/1761.

92 20/2/1925, Aiken-de Valera agreement, Moss Twomey Papers, UCDA, P69/181(130).

93 24/2/1925, EDV to Aiken, P150/1755.

94 15/2/1925 to 10/3/1925, EDV diary, P150/353.

95 14/2/1925, EDV to O'Kelly, P150/1777.

96 11/3/1925, EDV to O'Kelly, and reply (14/3/1925), Ibid.

97 Calculated from figures on Elections Ireland, http://electionsireland.org/results/general/04dail.cfm.

98 12/3/1925, EDV to O'Kelly, P150/1777.

99 30/4/1925, EDV to McGarrity, Joseph McGarrity Papers, NLI, Ms 33,364/1/3.

100 13/3/1926, EDV to McGarrity, Joseph McGarrity Papers, NLI, Ms 17,441/3.

101 11/12/1924, quoted in Murphy, *Patrick Pearse and the Lost Republican Ideal*, p. 145.

102 Maher, *The Oath Is Dead and Gone*, p. 82.

103 28/1/1925, meeting in Thomas Street, Dublin, quoted in Ibid, pp. 83–4.

104 25/1/1925, Cavan meeting, quoted in Dunphy, *The Making of Fianna Fáil Power*, p. 64.

105 7/5/1925, Sinn Féin Standing Committee minutes, P150/590.

106 Pyne, 'The third Sinn Féin party', part 1, pp. 42–3.

107 Murphy, *Patrick Pearse and the Lost Republican Ideal*, p. 146.

108 21/6/1925, EDV, Bodenstown speech, P150/1929.

109 2/11/1925, Sinn Féin Standing Committee Minutes, P150/590.

110 6/11/25, Ibid.

111 Ó Drisceoil, *Peadar O'Donnell*, pp. 39–41.

112 19/10/1925, Mary MacSwiney to EDV and Comhairle na dTeachtaí, P150/1946.

113 Quoted in Farrell, 'De Valera', in O'Carroll and Murphy (eds), *De Valera and His Times*, p. 36.

114 *DIB*, entry on Msgr John Hagan.

115 Passport, P150/115, showing that he landed in France on 31/5/1925 and also departed from that country on 7/6/1925.

116 MacBride, *That Day's Struggle*, p. 90.

117 Murphy, *Patrick Pearse and the Lost Republican Ideal*, p. 157.

118 Motion 5, ard-fheis clár, P150/584.

119 15/11/1925, Comhairle na dTeachtaí minutes, P150/1946.

120 5/10/1925 and 12/10/25, Sinn Féin Standing Committee minutes, P150/590.

121 30/12/1925, Mary MacSwiney to O'Kelly, Mary MacSwiney Papers, UCDA, P48a/136(6).

122 17/11/1925, EDV statement to ard-fheis, P150/584.

123 Handwritten note of ard-fheis decision, Ibid.

124 21/11/1925, EDV to O'Kelly, P150/1777.

125 Dwyer, 'Éamon de Valera and the partition question', in O'Carroll and Murphy (eds), *De Valera and His Times*, pp. 77–8.

126 30/11/1924, Cabinet conclusions, NAUK, CAB/23/51/9.

127 25/11/1925, Tom Jones diary, in Middlemas (ed.), *Whitehall Diary*, p. 237.

128 1/12/1925, EDV, telegram to *Morning Post*, P150/1935.

129 4/12/1925, Stack to EDV, P150/1936.

130 6/12/1925, EDV, speech, P150/1937; *IT*, 7/12/1925, p. 3.

131 Gerry Boland memoir, 1(a) and 2(a).

132 *IT*, 10/10/68, 'Gerry Boland's story' by Michael McInerney, part 3, p. 12

133 DED, 10/12/1925, vol. 13, col. 1768.

134 DED, 15/12/1925, vol. 13, col. 1888.

135 Ibid, col. 1956.

136 9/2/1960, EDV to Canon Thomas Maguire, P150/2863.

137 6/1/1926, EDV, text of speech at Rathmines Town Hall, P150/2001.

138 *IT*, 7/1/26, p. 5; *II*, 7/1/1926, p. 7.

139 15/1/1926, EDV, press statement, P150/586.

140 15/1/1926, EDV to O'Kelly, P150/1777.

141 21/1/1926, EDV to O'Kelly, P150/1777.

142 30/1/1926, Sinn Féin Standing Committee minutes, P150/591.

143 Elections Ireland, http://electionsireland.org/counts.cfm?election=1923B&cons=155&ref=

144 Text of both resolutions in P150/586.

145 Gerry Boland memoir, p. 3(a).

146 10/3/1926, EDV diary, P150/271.

147 11/3/1926, text of EDV remarks, P150/586.

148 *IT*, 19/5/1976, Michael McInerney, 'The name and the game', p. 14.

149 12/3/1926, EDV cable to *Boston Post*; EDV cable to America via International News Service; EDV, interview with Associated Press. All in P150/586.

150 13/3/1926, EDV to McGarrity, Joseph McGarrity Papers, NLI, Ms 17,441/3.

151 19/3/1926, Harry O'Hanrahan to EDV, P150/586.

152 *IP*, 23/1/1969, 'Seán Lemass looks back' (interview with Michael Mills), part 4.

153 22/3/1926, EDV to Fr Allman (Ballinskelligs); also 23/3/1926, EDV to Fr Robert O'Reilly. Both in P150/586.

154 19/3/1926, summons to meeting of Comhairle na dTeachtaí, P150/1948.

155 Statement drafted by Mary MacSwiney and redrafted by Art O'Connor in consultation with EDV, P150/586.

156 28 and 29/3/26, Comhairle na dTeachtai minutes, P150/1948. As in the

votes on the Treaty and his re-election as President in 1922, the result was a lot closer when his personality was put in the scales.

157 *IT*, 10/10/1968, 'Gerry Boland's story', part 3, p. 12.

158 29/3/1926, Sinn Féin Standing Committee minutes, P150/591.

159 Whelan, *Fianna Fáil*, p. 26.

160 *II*, 13/4/1926, copy in P150/2008.

161 13–16/4/1926, EDV diary, P150/271.

162 14/4/1926, Fianna Fáil statement, P150/2009.

163 17/4/1926, EDV, statement of aims given to United Press, P150/2011.

164 *IT*, 19/5/1976, p. 14, Michael McInerney 'The name and the game'.

165 Quoted in Maher, *The Oath Is Dead and Gone*, pp. 167–8, 170.

166 13/6/1950, EDV note on name Fianna Fáil, P150/2084.

167 *IT*, 19/5/1976; p. 14, Michael McInerney, 'The name and the game'.

168 Mulcahy, *Richard Mulcahy: A Family Memoir*, p. 188.

169 Walsh, *The Party*, p. 1.

170 Charlie McCreevy in RTÉ documentary by Nick Coffey, 'Soldiers of the Legion of the Rearguard' (2001).

171 Ó hEithir, *The Begrudger's Guide to Irish Politics*, p. 67.

172 Farrell, 'De Valera', in O'Carroll and Murphy (eds), *De Valera and His Times*, pp. 37–8.

173 Andrews, *Man of No Property*, p. 235.

174 16/4/1926, MacSwiney to McGarrity, Joseph McGarrity Papers, NLI, Ms 17,461/6.

175 12/4/26, MacSwiney circular to Irish-American supporters, NLI, McGarrity Papers, Ms 17,461/7.

176 9/4/26, MacSwiney to John J. Hearn, NLI, Hearn Papers, Ms 15,989.

177 28/4/1926, Ó Donnchadha to Mary MacSwiney, Mary MacSwiney Papers, UCDA, P48a/42.

178 26/5/1926, Stack and Ó Donnchadha to EDV, relaying decision of 22/5/1926, P150/586.

179 Murphy, *Patrick Pearse and the Lost Republican Ideal*, pp. 164–7.

180 8/6/26, MacSwiney to O'Kelly, UCDA, MacSwiney Papers, P48a/136(10)

181 Quoted in Murphy, *Patrick Pearse and the Lost Republican Ideal*, p. 168.

182 29/4/1926, Army Council minutes, Moss Twomey Papers, UCDA, P69/181(39–40).

183 Undated, 'Open letter to all Old IRA men', quoted by Hanley, 'Frank Aiken and the IRA', in Evans and Kelly (eds), *Frank Aiken*, p. 111.

184 Ó Beacháin, *Destiny of the Soldiers*, p. 50.

185 Dunphy, *The Making of Fianna Fáil Power in Ireland*, pp. 74–5.

186 Boland, *The Rise and Decline of Fianna Fáil*, pp. 19–20.

187 By contrast it was not until 1942 that the Labour Party supplied its organiser with a mode of transport, in his case a bicycle. Puirséil, *The Irish Labour Party*, p. 20.

188 *IT*, 23/7/1974, interview with Seán MacEntee, p. 12.
189 7/6/1926, Barrett letter, quoted in Ó Beacháin, *Destiny of the Soldiers*, p. 47.
190 9/7/1926, EDV to Pádraig Ó hÉigeartaigh, P150/1222.
191 Ward, *Hanna Sheehy-Skeffington*, p. 280.
192 Andrews, *Man of No Property*, p. 56.
193 Briscoe, *For the Life of Me*, p. 228.
194 *IT*, 15/5/1926, p. 5.
195 16/5/1926, EDV speech, La Scala [Dublin], P150/2014.
196 Reports by honorary secretaries and honorary treasurers, P150/2047.
197 24/11/1926, EDV, speech opening ard fheis, Ibid.
198 25/11/1926, EDV, speech closing ard fheis, Ibid.
199 20/1/1927, EDV diary, P150/272.
200 Maher, *The Oath Is Dead and Gone*, p. 179, quoting his own 1967 interview with Breen.
201 *IT*, 26/1/1927, p. 5.
202 Maher, *The Oath Is Dead and Gone*, p. 179, quoting his own 1967 interview with Breen.
203 EDV, Limerick speech, 15/2/1927, Fianna Fáil Weekly News Bulletin, quoted in Ó Beacháin, *Destiny of the Soldiers*, p. 61.
204 Quoted in Murphy, *Patrick Pearse and the Lost Republican Ideal*, pp. 172–3.
205 11/3/1927, EDV to Art O'Connor, John J. Hearn Papers, NLI, Ms 15,990.
206 16/4/1927, EDV to Mrs Frank Gallagher, Frank Gallagher Papers, NLI, MS 18,333/1/1/1.
207 5/4/1927, Smiddy to FitzGerald, *DIFP*, III:76.
208 Ó Beacháin, *Destiny of the Soldiers*, pp. 39–41; Murphy, *Patrick Pearse and the Lost Republican Ideal*, pp. 173–4.
209 In the name of Arthur Greenman, dated November 1926, P150/116.
210 EDV passport, issued 21/2/1927, P150/117.
211 Harkness, *The Restless Dominion*, p. 70.
212 Dudley Edwards, *Éamon de Valera*, p. 93.
213 25/11/1926, EDV, speech closing ard-fheis, P150/2047.
214 11/5/1927, Mary MacSwiney to EDV, Mary MacSwiney Papers, UCDA, P48a/43(49).
215 14/5/1927, EDV to Mary MacSwiney, Mary MacSwiney Papers, UCDA, P48a/43(50).
216 13/5/1927, EDV to secretary, Army Council, Moss Twomey Papers, UCDA, P69/48(29).
217 13/5/1927, EDV diary, P150/272.
218 6/1/1927, Lemass and Boland to secretary of each cumann, Records of the Fianna Fáil Party, UCDA, P176/351/1.
219 Undated notes for a specimen speech, Records of the Fianna Fáil Party, UCDA, P176/351/65.
220 EDV, draft election address, P150/2094.

221 Calculated from Elections Ireland, http://electionsireland.org/results/general/05dail.cfm.
222 Quoted in Ó Beacháin, *Destiny of the Soldiers*, p. 49.
223 EDV, draft election address, P150/2094.
224 *II*, 3/6/1927, Fianna Fáil election ad, p. 1.
225 16/6/1927, Mary MacSwiney to Hanna Sheehy-Skeffington, quoted in Fallon, *Soul of Fire*, p. 136.
226 7/7/1927, Hagan to EDV, P150/2035.
227 16/6/1927, EDV, circular to supporters in USA, with postscript relating to Corkery, P150/2094.
228 EDV, note dictated 17/1/1963, P150/260.
229 16/6/1927, EDV statement, Frank Gallagher Papers, NLI, MS 18,359/1/4.
230 14/6/1927, EDV statement to Shán Ó Cuív for the *New York Tribune*, P150/2028.
231 21/6/1927, legal opinion by Arthur Meredith, KC; Albert Wood, KC; and George Gavan Duffy, P150/2033.
232 Michael Hayes, notes on an unidentified thesis (1970), Michael Hayes Papers, UCDA, P53/330.
233 See Maher, *The Oath Is Dead and Gone*, pp. 197–9, for an account of the incident.
234 Michael Hayes, notes on an unidentified thesis (1970), Michael Hayes Papers, UCDA, P53/330.
235 24/6/1927, Hewson to EDV, P150/2041.
236 Quoted in Evans, *Seán Lemass*, p. 53.
237 23/6/1927, statement signed by Fianna Fáil TDs, P150/2031.
238 24/6/1927, EDV to William P. Lyndon (national secretary-treasurer, AARIR), P150/2030.
239 It was actually a bit more complicated than that – the constitutional provisions for popular initiative had yet to be provided for in legislation, so the petition called for that to be done so as to allow for a referendum on the Oath.
240 24/6/1927, EDV to William P. Lyndon (national secretary-treasurer, AARIR), P150/2030.
241 2/7/1927, EDV diary, P150/272.
242 Undated circular to each cumann, Records of the Fianna Fáil Party, UCDA, P176/351/12.

CHAPTER 18: EMPTY FORMULA
1 DED, 29/4/1932, vol. 41, col. 1102.
2 21/8/1927, EDV, Queen's Theatre [Dublin] speech, P150/2046.
3 22/8/1927, speech in Blackrock, quoted in Moynihan (ed.), *Speeches and Statements by Éamon de Valera*, pp. 152–3.

4 White, *Kevin O'Higgins*, p. 242.

5 11/7/1927, EDV statement, P150/2036.

6 11/7/1927, O'Kelly to P. J. Tynan (New York), Seán T. O'Kelly Papers, NLI, MS 48,453/4.

7 *II*, 18/7/1927, p. 8.

8 18/7/1927, minutes of parliamentary party, Records of the Fianna Fáil Party, UCDA, P176/442. The minutes state that this meeting took place after Markievicz's funeral but presumably should have referred to her burial, which took place a day later.

9 DED, 24/5/1928, vol. 23, col. 1928, reply to question by EDV.

10 19/7/1927, Cabinet decision, NAI, S 5485.

11 *II*, 11/8/1927, p. 7.

12 This wasn't accomplished until the following year, by the Constitution (Amendment No. 10) Act (1928).

13 25/7/1927, Fianna Fáil statement, P150/2038. EDV scored out 'so-called' before 'constitutional means' in the statement.

14 25/7/1927, Lemass and Boland to each cumann secretary, Records of the Fianna Fáil Party, UCDA, P176/351/26.

15 Munger, *The Legitimacy of Opposition*, p. 21.

16 EDV, 'Synopsis of political developments', dictated 17/1/1963, P150/260.

17 Longford and O'Neill, *Éamon de Valera*, p. 253.

18 *DIB*, entry on Patrick Belton.

19 *II*, 21/7/1927, p. 10.

20 *II*, 22/7/1927, p. 7.

21 *II*, 26/7/1927, p. 9.

22 16/8/1927, Linda Kearns to Hanna Sheehy-Skeffington, Hanna Sheehy-Skeffington Papers, NLI, MS 41,178/54. Emphasis in original.

23 26/7/1927, statement by Chairman of Fianna Fáil party, P150/2041.

24 Gerry Boland memoir, p. 7(a).

25 Gaughan, *Thomas Johnson*, p. 303.

26 3/8/1927, EDV to Walsh and Lydon, P150/970. The quotations are taken from the catalogue, as the letter does not appear to have been microfilmed.

27 16/8/1927, Linda Kearns to Hanna Sheehy-Skeffington, Hanna Sheehy-Skeffington Papers, NLI, MS 41,178/54.

28 DED, 4/8/1927, vol. 20, cols 1602, 1606.

29 4/8/1927, Johnson to EDV, Records of the Fianna Fáil Party, UCDA, P176/31/3.

30 5/8/1927, parliamentary party minutes, and notes of meeting, Records of the Fianna Fáil Party, UCDA, P176/442.

31 5/8/1926, parliamentary party minutes, Ibid.

32 Ibid.

33 5/8/1927, circular to each member of the National Executive, Hanna Sheehy-Skeffington Papers, NLI, MS 41,178/54.

34 *IT*, 23/7/1974, p. 12, Michael McInerney interview with MacEntee.

35 Gerry Boland memoir, pp. 7(a)–11(a)

36 Gaughan, *Thomas Johnson*, p. 304.

37 16/8/1927, Linda Kearns to Hanna Sheehy-Skeffington, Hanna Sheehy-Skeffington Papers, NLI, MS 41,178/54.

38 8/8/1927, draft notes for an informal conference, P150/2041.

39 8/8/1927, Johnson memorandum, and 10/8/1927, document signed by Redmond, both in Ibid.

40 *II*, 11/8/1927, p. 7.

41 EDV, draft of declaration, P150/2042. It was not signed by James Colbert of Limerick, who was unavoidably absent from the meeting but entered the Dáil with the rest.

42 10/8/1927, declaration by Fianna Fáil TDs, P150/2042.

43 Unless otherwise stated, details are from *IT*, 12/8/1927, p. 7, and *II*, 12/8/1927, p. 7.

44 23/9/1927, statement by Aiken and Ryan, P150/2043.

45 EDV later read this statement into the Dáil record. DED, 29/4/1932, vol. 41, col. 1102.

46 23/9/1927, statement by Aiken and Ryan, P150/2043.

47 DED, 29/4/1932, vol. 41, col. 1102.

48 *II*, 12/8/1927, p. 7

49 *IT*, 12/8/1927, p. 7.

50 9/4/1966, Boland to Michael Hayes, Michael Hayes Papers, UCDA, P53/279.

51 *II*, 12/8/1927, p. 7.

52 Maher, *The Oath Is Dead and Gone*, p. 37.

53 As Frank Munger pointed out, Cosgrave could certainly have intervened, had he so wished, to make the process more difficult for Fianna Fáil by insisting on a more formal and public ceremony. Munger, *The Legitimacy of Opposition*, p. 19.

54 DED, 12/8/1927, vol. 20, cols 1660, 1646.

55 13/8/1927, note of meeting of Irish National League, P150/2041.

56 *IT*, 15/8/1927, p. 7; Gaughan, *Thomas Johnson*, p. 310.

57 *II*, 16/8/1927, p. 7.

58 See *IT*, 16/8/1927, p. 7, where the political correspondent predicted a 73–69 vote against the government.

59 *II*, 17/8/1927, sketch by Pádraig de Búrca, p. 6.

60 *IT*, 17/8/1927, p. 3.

61 DED, 16/8/1927, vol. 20, col. 1700; Cabinet list in Gaughan, *Thomas Johnson*, p. 309.

62 DED, 16/8/1927, vol. 20, col. 1750.

63 *II*, 17/8/1927, sketch by Pádraig de Búrca, p. 6.

64 DED, 16/8/1927, vol. 20, col. 1752.

65 *IT*, 10/10/1968, 'Gerry Boland's story', part 3, p. 12.

66 *IP*, 23/1/1969, 'Seán Lemass looks back' (interview with Michael Mills), part 4, p. 9.

67 16/8/1927, parliamentary party minutes, Records of the Fianna Fáil Party, UCDA, P176/442.

68 16/8/1927, Linda Kearns to Hanna Sheehy-Skeffington, Hanna Sheehy-Skeffington Papers, NLI, MS 41,178/54.

69 21/8/1927, EDV, Queen's Theatre speech [Dublin], P150/2046.

70 12/6/1932, MacSwiney to Dr Cotter, Mary MacSwiney Papers, UCDA, P48a/256(8).

71 16/8/1927, Army Council statement, NLI, Ms 48,453/4.

72 5/1/1928, McGarrity to Luke Dillon, NLI, Ms 17,446.

73 Sheila Humphreys, quoted in English, *Armed Struggle*, p. 48.

74 16/8/1927, Hanna Sheehy-Skeffington to EDV, Hanna Sheehy-Skeffington Papers, NLI, Ms 41,178/54.

75 21/9/27, Sheehy-Skeffington to EDV, Ibid.

76 21/8/1927, 'Rose' [Rosamund Jacob?] to Hanna Sheehy-Skeffington, Hanna Sheehy-Skeffington Papers, NLI, Ms 41,178/54.

77 29/8/1927, Dorothy Macardle to EDV, Records of the Fianna Fáil Party, UCDA, P176/27(15).

78 Ó Beacháin, *Destiny of the Soldiers*, pp. 68–9.

79 24 and 25/11/1927, ard-fheis clár, P150/2048.

80 25/8/1927, EDV statement, P150/2106.

81 25/8/1927, EDV to Lyndon, P150/2095.

82 Cash book, Records of the Fianna Fáil Party, UCDA, P176/25.

83 *IT*, 26/8/1927, editorial, p. 6.

84 Election ad quoted in Maher, *The Oath Is Dead and Gone*, p. 231.

85 22/8/1927, EDV, speech in Blackrock, quoted in Moynihan (ed.), *Speeches and Statements by Éamon de Valera*, pp. 152–3.

86 Ibid.

87 *CE*, 5/9/1927, p. 7, EDV, Gorey speech.

88 *II*, 12/9/1927, p. 12, EDV, Kilkee, Co. Clare, speech.

89 *II*, 14/9/1927, p. 10, EDV, Ballyhaunis, Co. Mayo, speech.

90 *II*, 15/9/1927, p. 10, Letterkenny speech.

91 *II*, 15/9/27, p. 10, Donegal Town speech

92 *CE*, 5/9/1927, p. 11 – a distance of 1.3 kilometres.

93 *II*, 12/9/1927, p. 12.

94 *II*, 14/9/1927, p. 10.

95 *IT*, 12/8/1927, editorial, p. 6.

96 *II*, 24/9/1927, p. 9.

97 Undated report by C. J. Ketchum, P150/2095; EDV excised the first sentence from the draft report.

98 20/9/27, EDV, statement in press interview, P150/2095.

99 *IT*, 21/9/1927, p. 6, editorial.

100 21/9/1927, EDV to O'Kelly, Seán T. O'Kelly Papers, NLI, Ms 48,453/4.

101 20/9/1927, EDV statement for *Irish World*, P150/2095.

102 DED, 11/10/1927, vol. 21, col. 17.

103 EDV speech, 1927 ard-fheis, P150/2048.

CHAPTER 19: A PRACTICAL RULE

1 DED, 14/3/1929, vol. 28, cols 1398–1400.

2 14/7/1931, interview with Henri de Kerillis of Echo de Paris, P150/2166.

3 'Interview with EDV' (actually a press release), P150/2151.

4 Philip Guedalla, 'Éamon de Valera', extract from the *Strand*, September 1932, P150/2229.

5 *IT*, 26/5/1984, Deaglán de Bréadún, 'The course of an Irish historian', p. 15.

6 3/10/27, Cosgrave to Granard; 10/1/1931, Cosgrave to O'Hegarty, both quoted in Laffan, *Judging W. T. Cosgrave*, pp. 252–3.

7 DED, 15/10/1931, vol. 40, col. 305.

8 Philip Guedalla, 'Éamon de Valera', extract from the *Strand*, September 1932, P150/2229.

9 *Daily Express*, 20/7/29, article on EDV by Williams, P150/2146.

10 EDV, ard-fheis speech, P150/2048.

11 Parliamentary Party minutes, 20/10/27, 28/2/29, 18/4/29, 16/5/49, Records of the Fianna Fáil Party, UCDA, P176/443.

12 29/11/1928, parliamentary party minutes, Ibid.

13 9/7/1929, National Executive minutes, P150/2118.

14 5/1/1930, O'Kelly to EDV, P150/3161.

15 Michael Hayes notes for draft book, UCDA P53/298, quoted in Garvin, *Judging Lemass*, p.129.

16 Meehan, *The Cosgrave Party*, pp. 11–12.

17 3/1/1928, Lemass and Boland to each TD, Records of the Fianna Fáil Party, UCDA, P176/351(42).

18 Honorary treasurers' report, third ard-fheis, P150/2049.

19 Ó Beacháin, *Destiny of the Soldiers*, p. 52.

20 19/6/1929, Lemass and Boland to each TD, Records of the Fianna Fáil Party, UCDA, P176/351(63).

21 Honorary treasurers' report, fifth ard-fheis, P150/2051.

22 *Connacht Tribune*, 10/3/1928, and *Free Press* (Wexford), 23/5/1931, quoted in Horgan, *Seán Lemass*, p. 51.

23 22/11/1928, parliamentary party minutes, Records of the Fianna Fáil Party, UCDA, P176/443.

24 27/4/1928, minutes of parliamentary party Standing Committee, Records of the Fianna Fáil Party, UCDA, P176/452.

25 9/1/1930, O'Kelly to Lemass, Seán T. O'Kelly Papers, NLI, MS 48,454/3.

26 15/4/1930, National Executive minutes, P150/2119.

27 24/2/1931, National Executive minutes, P150/2120.

28 25/10/1928, EDV statement at session on general policy, 3rd Fianna Fáil ard-fheis, P150/2049.

29 Dillon memoir, quoted in Manning, *James Dillon*, p. 47.

30 *An Phoblacht*, 31/5/1930, quoted in Maher, *The Oath Is Dead and Gone*, p. 258.

31 *IT*, 19/5/1976, Michael McInerney, 'The name and the game', p. 14.

32 14/7/1931, EDV, interview with Henri de Kerillis of *Echo de Paris*, P150/2166.

33 18/6/1929, National Executive minutes, P150/2118.

34 See Petersson, 'Hub of the anti-imperialist movement: The League against Imperialism and Berlin, 1927–1933', http://www.academia.edu/3087708/Hub_of_the_Anti-Imperialist_Movement_The_League_against_Imperialism_and_Berlin_1927–1933.

35 EDV diary entry, 22/6/1929, P150/277. EDV noted that he wore his NUI chancellor's robes for the procession.

36 21/1/1930, National Executive minutes, P150/2119.

37 11 and 25/2/1930, National Executive minutes, P150/2119.

38 Honorary secretaries' report, 1927 ard-fheis, P150/2048; 2/12/1927, Lemass and Boland to each cumann secretary, Records of the Fianna Fáil Party, UCDA, P176/351(39). Emphasis in original.

39 Lyons, *Ireland since the Famine*, p. 478.

40 12/6/1928, minutes of parliamentary party Standing Committee, Records of the Fianna Fáil Party, UCDA, P176/452.

41 9/10/1928, minutes of parliamentary party Standing Committee, Records of the Fianna Fáil Party, UCDA, P176/452.

42 Ard-fheis clár, motion 8, P150/2049.

43 25/10/1928, EDV statement during session on general policy, Fianna Fáil ard-fheis, P150/2049.

44 1927, EDV, draft article, 'Typical Free State meanness', written in response to the claim that he had requested the protection, P150/2125.

45 Ó Beacháin, *Destiny of the Soldiers*, p. 375.

46 DED, 21/3/28, vol. 22, col. 1615

47 *Nation*, 14/4/1928, p. 4, quoted in Ó Beacháin, *Destiny of the Soldiers*, p. 87.

48 DED, 14/3/1929, vol. 28, cols 1398–1400.

49 Ibid, cols 1406–7.

50 DED, 27/3/1930, vol. 34, col. 240.

51 DED, 28/3/1930, vol. 34, cols 276–8.

52 28/3/1930, parliamentary party minutes, Records of the Fianna Fáil Party, UCDA, P176/443.

53 2/4/1930, Ibid.

54 DED, 2/4/1930, vol. 34, col. 285.

55 Ibid, col. 318.

56 16/8/1929, Lemass to Frank Gallagher, NLI, MS 18,339/3.

57 DED, 2/4/1930, vol. 34, col. 366.

58 15/4/1930, National Executive minutes, P150/2119.

59 13/1/30, Lemass to EDV, P150/3497.

60 Bell, *The Secret Army*, p. 64.

61 McGarry, *Eoin O'Duffy*, p. 181.

62 See, *IT,* 23/10/04, obituary.

63 DED, 31/7/1929, vol. 31, cols 102–6, including quotation of both letters.

64 Quoted in Ó Longaigh, *Emergency Law in Independent Ireland*, p. 97.

65 EDV, undated diary fragment, P150/366.

66 August 1931, Department of Justice report, NAI, S 5864 B.

67 27/7/1931, O'Duffy to secretary, Department of Justice, NAI, S 5864 B.

68 30/7/1931, extract from Cabinet minutes, NAI, S 5864 B.

69 10/9/1931, Cosgrave to MacRory, NAI, S 5864 B.

70 1929, Army intelligence report on left wing of Fianna Fáil, Col. Dan Bryan Papers, UCDA, P71/6.

71 13/10/1931, National Executive minutes, P150/2120.

72 Keogh, *Twentieth-Century Ireland*, p. 55

73 DED, 14/10/1931, vol. 40, cols 54–9, 97–8.

74 DED, 15/10/1931, vol. 40, cols 298–300.

75 29/10/1931, EDV statement to United Press, P150/2168.

76 O'Halpin, *Defending Ireland*, pp. 78–9.

77 DED, 17/6/31, vol. 39, cols 516–9.

78 Ibid, col. 536.

79 DED, 26/10/1927, vol. 21, col. 396, quoted in Feeney, *Seán MacEntee*, pp. 51–2.

80 16/4/1928, minutes of parliamentary party Standing Committee, Records of the Fianna Fáil Party, UCDA, P176/452.

81 27/4/1928, Ibid.

82 Meehan, *The Cosgrave Party*, p. 60.

83 DED, 13/7/28, vol. 25, col. 484.

84 EDV note, dated 20/4/32, P150/3688.

85 29/10/31, EDV statement to United Press, P150/2168.

86 19/1/1929, EDV speech, Limerick, P150/2141.

87 Lemass memorandum, written 'some time in 1929 or 1930', Frank Gallagher Papers, NLI, MS 18,339/5.

88 19/1/1929, EDV speech, Limerick, P150/2141.

89 Consistently but erroneously referred to as his 'dancing at the crossroads' speech, an activity he didn't actually mention.

90 EDV, speech on economic policy, 13/7/1928, in Moynihan (ed.), *Speeches and Statements by Éamon de Valera*, pp. 154–5.

91 17 and 18/10/1929, EDV speech, fourth ard-fheis, P150/2050.

92 30 and 31/10/1930, EDV speech, fifth ard-fheis, P150/2051.

93 O'Neill, 'Handing away the trump card?', p. 39.

94 Quoted in Ibid, p. 19. O'Donnell wrongly remembered the incident as having taken place in 1931.

95 Dwyer, *De Valera*, p. 149.

96 *Daily Express*, 20/7/1929, article on EDV by R. Stephen Williams, P150/2146.

97 3/1/1929, National Executive minutes, P150/2118.

98 13/9/1929, Seán Moynihan to KOC, P150/245.

99 14-20/8/28, EDV diary, P150/355.

100 23/8/28, EDV to Gallagher, NLI, MS 18,333/1/4(2).

101 18/8/1928, EDV diary, P150/355.

102 15/12/1931, EDV to Catherine Wheelwright, P150/181.

103 Terry de Valera, *A Memoir*, p. 66.

104 Ibid, p. 37.

105 19/9/1929, National Executive minutes, P150/2118.

106 24/2/1931, National Executive minutes, P150/2120.

107 11/10/1927, parliamentary party minutes, Records of the Fianna Fáil Party, UCDA, P176/443.

108 14/10/1928, EDV diary, P150/355.

109 25/11/1929, EDV to Robert D. Joyce, P150/101.

110 *WIT*, 27/8/1927, p. 8; see also *CE*, 15/8/1927, p. 8.

111 30/9/1927, Cabinet minutes, item 12, PRONI, CAB/4/196.

112 20/9/1927, EDV, draft press release, P150/2095.

113 27/9/1928, National Executive minutes, P150/2117.

114 25 and 6/10/1928, Hon. secretaries' report, third ard-fheis, P150/2049.

115 Ó Beacháin, *Destiny of the Soldiers*, p. 374.

116 29/1/1929, inspector-general's office, RUC, to secretary, Ministry of Home Affairs, PRONI, HA/32/1/156.

117 5/2/1929, EDV diary, P150/277.

118 6/2/1929, statement by Constable Robert Porter, PRONI, HA/32/1/156.

119 5 and 7/2/1929, EDV diary, P150/277.

120 7 and 14/2/1929, National Executive minutes, P150/2118.

121 Ó Beacháin, *Destiny of the Soldiers*, p. 92.

122 11/2/1929, Cosgrave to Craigavon, and undated note on file, PRONI, CAB/9U/1/1.

123 DED, 20/2/1929, vol. 28, cols 132, 134.

124 Ibid, cols 169–72.

125 *Daily Express*, 20/7/1929, article on EDV by R. Stephen Williams, P150/2146.

126 Gaughan (ed.), *Memoirs of Senator Joseph Connolly*, p. 284.

127 28/11/1918, EDV to Catherine Wheelwright, P150/173.

128 Gaughan (ed.), *Memoirs of Senator Joseph Connolly*, p. 284

129 15/12/1927, Mary MacSwiney to John Hearn, NLI, MS 15,989.

130 11/1/1928, Gallagher to KOC, P150/245.

131 Ibid.

132 17/1/1928, EDV to O'Kelly, NLI, MS 47,971.

133 Meehan, *The Cosgrave Party*, p. 153.

134 Laffan, *Judging W. T. Cosgrave*, p. 268.

135 29/1/1929, invitation to meeting in Hotel Tuller, Detroit, NLI, MS 18,359/8/4.

136 10/1/1928, McGarrity to EDV, NLI, MS 17,441/11.

137 27/9/1928, EDV to Frank Aiken, Frank Aiken Papers, UCDA, P104/2636–7.

138 Undated EDV circular, IPC, A011.

139 EDV diary for 1928, P150/355.

140 23/2/1928, parliamentary party minutes, Records of the Fianna Fáil Party, UCDA, P176/443.

141 3–11/3/1928, EDV diary, P150/355.

142 EDV diary for 1928, P150/355. He was absent from the Fianna Fáil parliamentary party from 19 March to 24 April. Records of the Fianna Fáil Party, UCDA, P176/443.

143 14/5/1928, National Executive minutes, P150/2117; 31/5/1928, parliamentary party minutes, Records of the Fianna Fáil Party, UCDA, P176/443; 12/6/1928, minutes of parliamentary party Standing Committee, Records of the Fianna Fáil Party, UCDA, P176/452.

144 5/9/1928, EDV diary, P150/355.

145 Quoted in Ó Beacháin, *Destiny of the Soldiers*, p. 56.

146 8/9/1928, EDV to McGarrity, Joseph McGarrity Papers, NLI, MS 17,441/12.

147 25/9/1928, McGarrity to EDV, Joseph McGarrity Papers, NLI, MS 17,441/13.

148 Undated circular, IPC, A017.

149 27/9/1928, EDV to Frank Aiken, Frank Aiken Papers, UCDA, P104/2636–7.

150 There is an excellent account of this in O'Brien, *De Valera, Fianna Fáil and the Irish Press*, pp. 23–4.

151 19/8/1930, EDV to directors, IPC, A020.

152 O'Brien, *De Valera, Fianna Fáil and the Irish Press*, p. 26.

153 See the exchange of views between Martin Mansergh and Tim Pat Coogan, *IT*, 22 and 31/1/2005 and 9/3/2005.

154 19/9/1929, EDV to William Lyndon, Records of the Fianna Fáil Party, UCDA, P176/27/33.

155 22/11/1929, EDV to McGarrity, P150/1191.

156 26/11/1929, National Executive minutes, P150/2119.

157 17/12/1929, EDV to O'Kelly, Seán T. O'Kelly Papers, NLI, MS 47,971.

158 11/12/1929, EDV to KOC, Kathleen O'Connell Papers, UCDA, P155/33.

159 15/2/1930, EDV to KOC, Kathleen O'Connell Papers, UCDA, P155/41.

160 17/12/1929, EDV, circular letter, P150/2151.

161 'Interview with EDV' (actually a press release), P150/2151.

162 13/1/1930, Lemass to EDV, P150/3497.

163 10/3/1930, Lemass to EDV, Ibid.

164 30/1/1930, circular signed by EDV, with leaflet by Walsh, Patrick McGilligan Papers, UCDA, P35c/167.

165 Form of assignment, Records of the Fianna Fáil Party, UCDA, P176/27.

166 DED, 2/4/1930, vol. 34, col. 309.

167 13/1/1930, Lemass to EDV, P150/3497.

168 15/2/1930, EDV to O'Kelly, NLI, MS 47,971.

169 See newspaper cuttings in P150/2151.

170 According to Cleveland Press reporter Jim McCoy, quoted in Coogan, *De Valera*, p. 419.

171 EDV, 1930 diary, P150/280.

172 9/3/1931, EDV diary, P150/283.

173 EDV, letter to shareholders, quoted in O'Brien, *De Valera, Fianna Fáil and the Irish Press*, p. 27.

174 As a former reporter with the *Evening Press*, I admit this with some reluctance.

175 EDV, letter to shareholders, quoted in O'Brien, *De Valera, Fianna Fáil and the Irish Press*, p. 27. In fact the *Sunday Press* would not appear until 1949 and the *Evening Press* not until 1954.

176 15/11/1930, Gallagher, job application, Frank Gallagher Papers, NLI, MS 18,361/2/1.

177 3/12/1930, Gallagher to EDV, Frank Gallagher Papers, NLI, MS 18,361/3/2.

178 23/12/1930, Brennan to Gallagher, Frank Gallagher Papers, NLI, MS 18,361/2 (Unnumbered).

179 Frank Gallagher, advice to staff, Frank Gallagher Papers, NLI, MS 18,361/3/25. Much of his advice would stand today.

180 15–16/4/1931; 16/6/1931; 2/9/1931; EDV diary, P150/283.

181 EDV diary for 1931, P150/285.

182 13/9/1931, EDV to William Lyndon, IPC, A059.

183 EDV diary for 1931, P150/283.

184 The image of devotion to the GAA was infamously spoiled by a reference (inserted by the English sports editor) to the time of the game's 'kick-off'.

185 *Round Table*, vol. 22, no. 85 (Dec. 1931), pp. 148–9, quoted in Regan, *The Irish Counter-Revolution, 1921–1936*, p. 315.

186 O'Brien, *De Valera, Fianna Fáil and the Irish Press*, pp. 41–5.

187 7/9/1931 and subsequent entries, EDV diary, P150/283.

188 13/9/1931, EDV to William Lyndon, IPC, A059.

189 Handwritten list of circulation figures, Frank Gallagher Papers, NLI, MS 18,361/4/3.

190 27–28/10/1931, honorary secretaries' report, sixth ard-fheis, P150/2052.

191 17/12/1931, parliamentary party minutes, Records of the Fianna Fáil Party, UCDA, P176/443.

192 15/12/1931, EDV to Catherine Wheelwright, P150/181.

193 *IP*, 15/9/1931, pp. 1–2, 6.

194 21/9/1931, EDV diary, P150/283.

195 10/12/1931, parliamentary party minutes, Records of the Fianna Fáil Party, UCDA, P176/443.

196 14/12/1931, EDV to Healy, IPC, A062.

197 27 and 28/10/31, EDV speech, Fianna Fáil ard-fheis, P150/2052.

198 4/5/1931, EDV to John T. Ryan, P150/1293a.

199 Figures calculated from Elections Ireland, http://electionsireland.org/results/general/06dail.cfm.

200 *IT*, 30/1/1932, p. 9.

201 Fianna Fáil message to electors, P150/2096.

202 Meehan, *The Cosgrave Party*, Appendix 1, p. 233

203 12 and 25/1/1932, KOC diary, P150/288.

204 12/1/1932, adjutant-general to commander of each independent unit, NAI, S 5864 C.

205 *NYT*, 15/2/32, quoted in Manning, *James Dillon*, p. 51.

206 6/1/1932, KOC diary, P150/288.

207 Maher, *The Oath Is Dead and Gone*, p. 273.

208 7/2/1932, questionnaire from John Steele, *Chicago Tribune*, P150/2173.

209 18/1/1932, Dulanty to Walshe, *DIFP*, III:625.

210 17/2/1932, Cabinet minutes, NAUK, CAB/23/70, document 14.

211 February 1932, memorandum by Secretary of State for Dominion Affairs, 'Irish Free State: Political situation', NAUK, CAB 24/228.

212 20/2/32, B.M. Prior, Ballyduff, Co Waterford, to Mulcahy, quoted in Regan, *The Irish Counter-Revolution, 1921–1936*, pp. 314–5.

213 *IT*, 22/2/1932, p. 7.

214 Undated, Rev. E. Egan to McGilligan, Patrick McGilligan Papers, UCDA, P35c/130.

215 20/2/1932, replies to questions from Mr Reeves of the *Sunday Dispatch*, P150/2173.

216 15/7/1931, EDV to Ryan, P150/1293a.

217 *IT*, 27/2/1932, p. 9.

218 Puirséil, *The Irish Labour Party*, p. 37; Desmond, *No Workers' Republic!*, p. 108.

219 *IT*, 27/2/1932, p. 9.

220 O'Halpin, *Defending Ireland*, p. 80.

221 KOC diary, P150/288

222 4/3/1932, EDV broadcast to USA and Canada, P150/2209.

223 8/3/1932, KOC diary, P150/288.

224 Gaughan, *Thomas Johnson*, p. 341.

CHAPTER 20: THE DISARMING FRIENDLINESS OF HIS EYES

1 *IT*, 23/3/1922, p. 3; *DIB*, entry on Susan Mitchell.

2 DED, 10/1/1922, vol. T, col. 415.

3 28/1/1922, Batt O'Connor to his sister Máire, Batt O'Connor Papers, UCDA, P68/4.

4 16/4/1926, MacSwiney to McGarrity, Joseph McGarrity Papers, NLI, Ms 17,461/6.

5 *IT*, 10/10/1968, Michael McInerney, 'Gerry Boland's story' part 3, p. 12.

6 Dudley Edwards, *Éamon de Valera*, p. 16.

7 *IP*, 20/1/1969, 'Seán Lemass looks back' (interview with Michael Mills), part 1, p. 9.

8 Quoted in English, *Irish Freedom*, p. 329.

9 Undated, EDV, reminiscences in Macardle's hand, P150/3662.

10 Turi, *England's Greatest Spy*; Jordan, *Éamon de Valera*; Walker and Fitzgerald, *Unstoppable Brilliance*.

11 Notes compiled by Kathleen Clarke following Sinn Féin convention, 25 and 6/10/1917, Kathleen Clarke Papers, NLI, Ms 49,356/2.

12 McCartan, *With de Valera in America*, p. 165.

13 Michael Hayes, review of vol. 1 of Ó Néill and Ó Fiannachta's biography of de Valera, Michael Hayes Papers, UCDA, P53/389.

14 EDV, paper on the Irish university question, read 18/2/1903, P150/49.

15 Gaynor, *Memoirs of a Tipperary Family*, p. 183.

16 Lord Longford interview, 'The Age of de Valera', RTÉ television.

17 DED, 6/1/1922, vol. T, cols 271, 274, 275.

18 *IT*, 14/1/1922, Nichevo, 'Some Dáil personalities', p. 9.

19 *IT*, 15/3/1967, interview with Dr James Ryan, p. 11.

BIBLIOGRAPHY

ONLINE RESOURCES
— Ancestry.com – online genealogical material
— Bureau of Military History – Witness Statements and Military Service —
  Pension files are available online: http://www.militaryarchives.ie/home
— Census returns from 1901 and 1911: http://www.census.nationalarchives.ie
— Century Ireland – online historical newspaper: http://www.rte.ie/
  centuryireland
— Dictionary of Irish Biography (also available in printed form): http://dib.
  cambridge.org/
— Documents on Irish Foreign Policy (also available in printed form): http://
  www.difp.ie/
— Elections Ireland – a database of election results: http://electionsireland.org/
— Memoirs of Brigadier Ernest Maconchy, National Army Museum, London,
  available online: http://www.nam.ac.uk/online-collection/detail.
  php?acc=1979–08–62-
— Oireachtas – Dáil and Seanad debates: http://oireachtasdebates.oireachtas.
  ie/?readform

ARCHIVES
— **National Archives of Ireland:** Dáil Éireann records; Department of the
  Taoiseach; Office of the Secretary of the President; Taoiseach's Private
  Office
— **National Archives of the United Kingdom:** Cabinet records; Colonial
  Office records; Prime Minister's records; Home Office records; Security
  Service records; Wylie memoir
— **National Library of Ireland:** Kathleen Clarke; Liam Deasy; John Devoy;
  Frank Gallagher; John J. Hearn; Rosamund Jacob Diaries; Thomas Johnson;
  Liam Lynch; Patrick McCartan; Thomas MacDonagh; Joseph McGarrity;
  William O'Brien (MP); William O'Brien (TD); Seán T. O'Kelly; Sean
  O'Mahony; James O'Mara; Joseph Plunkett; Hanna Sheehy-Skeffington;
  Austin Stack; Kees Van Hoek
— **Public Records Office of Northern Ireland:**Cabinet records; Home Affairs
  records; Craigavon Personal Papers; Craigavon Political Papers; 7th
  Marquess of Londonderry papers;

University College Dublin Archives:
— LA1: Eoin MacNeill
— LA18: Maire Comerford
— P6: T.M. Healy
— P7: Richard Mulcahy
— P24: Ernest Blythe
— P35: Patrick McGilligan
— P48: Mary and Terence MacSwiney
— P53: Michael Hayes
— P59: Royal Irish Constabulary
— P68: Batt O'Connor
— P69: Maurice 'Moss' Twomey
— P71: Dan Bryan
— P80: Desmond FitzGerald
— P104: Frank Aiken
— P150: Éamon de Valera
— P155: Kathleen O'Connell
— P176: Fianna Fail
— P200: Elgin O'Rahilly

Papers in private possession
— Gerry Boland Memoir: in possession of Dr Stephen Kelly
— Irish Press Corporation Documents: Private Source

Newspapers
— *Cork Examiner*
— *Evening Herald*
— *Evening Press*
— *Evening Telegraph*
— *Freeman's Journal*
— *Irish Independent*
— *Irish Times*
— *Irish Press*
— *Irish Volunteer*
— *Irish Roots*
— *An t-Óglác*
— *Sunday Independent*
— *Sunday Press*
— *Weekly Irish Times*

SECONDARY SOURCES

— Akenson, D. H., 'Was de Valera a Republican?' *The Review of Politics*, Vol. 33, No. 2 (April 1971), pp. 233–53.

— Andrews, C. S., *Dublin Made Me*, The Lilliput Press, Dublin, 2001.

— Andrews, C. S., *Man of No Property*, The Lilliput Press, Dublin, 2001.

— Augusteijn, Joost, *From Public Defiance to Guerrilla Warfare: The Experience of Ordinary Volunteers in the Irish War of Independence 1916–21*, Irish Academic Press, Dublin, 1996.

— Bell, J. Bowyer, *The Secret Army: The IRA, 1916–1979*, Third Edition, Poolbeg, Dublin, 1989.

— Berg, A. Scott, *Wilson*, Simon and Schuster, London, 2013.

— Bew, Paul (ed.), *A Yankee in de Valera's Ireland: The memoir of David Gray*, RIA, Dublin, 2012.

— Boland, Kevin, *The Rise and Decline of Fianna Fáil*, Mercier Press, Cork, 1982.

— Bowman, John, *De Valera and the Ulster Question, 1917–1973*, Clarendon Press, Oxford, 1982.

— Boyle, Andrew, *The Riddle of Erskine Childers*, Hutchinson of London, 1977.

— Boyne, Sean, *Emmet Dalton: Somme soldier, Irish general, Film pioneer*, Merrion Press, Dublin, 2015.

— Brennan, Robert, *Allegiance*, Browne and Nolan, Dublin, 1950.

— Brennan, Robert, *Ireland Standing Firm: My wartime mission in Washington, and Éamon de Valera, a memoir*, UCD, 2002.

— Brennan-Whitmore, W. J., *Dublin Burning: The Easter Rising from Behind the Barricades*, Gill and Macmillan, Dublin, 2013.

— Briscoe, Robert, with Alden Hatch, *For the Life of Me*, Longmans, London, 1958.

— Bromage, Mary C., *De Valera and the March of a Nation*, Noonday Press, NY, 1956.

— Browne, Kevin J., *Éamon de Valera and the Banner County*, Glendale Press, Dun Laoghaire, 1982.

— Buckland, Patrick, *James Craig*, Gill and Macmillan, Dublin, 1980.

— Callwell, C. E., *Field Marshal Sir Henry Wilson, Vol. 2: His Life and Diaries*, Cassell and Co, London, 1927.

— Canning, Paul, *British Policy Towards Ireland 1921–1941*, Clarendon Press, Oxford, 1985.

— Carden, Sheila, *The Alderman: Alderman Tom Kelly and Dublin Corporation*, Dublin City Council, 2007.

— Carey, Tim, *Dublin since 1922*, Hachette Books Ireland, Dublin, 2016.

— Carroll, Francis M., 'De Valera and the Americans: The Early Years, 1916–1922', *The Canadian Journal of Irish Studies*, Vol. 8, No. 1 (June 1982), pp. 36–54

— Carroll, Francis M., 'The American Commission on Irish Independence and the Paris Peace Conference of 1919', *Irish Studies in International Affairs*, Vol. 2, No. 1 (1985), pp 103–18.
— Caulfield, Max, *The Easter Rebellion*, Frederick Muller, London, 1964.
— Clarke, Christopher, *The Sleepwalkers: How Europe Went to War in 1914*, Penguin, Kindle edition.
— Clarke, Kathleen, *Revolutionary Woman: An Autobiography*, edited by Helen Litton, O'Brien Press, Dublin, 1991.
— Coll, Edward Patrick, 'My cousin Ed', *The Rosary*, January 1960.
— Coll Millson, Elizabeth, 'My cousin Éamon de Valera', *Commonweal*, 18/2/38.
— Coogan, Tim Pat, *De Valera: Long Fellow, Long Shadow*, Hutchinson, London, 1993.
— Cooper, John Milton Jr, *Woodrow Wilson*, Kindle edition.
— Cronin, Sean, *The McGarrity Papers*, Anvil Books, Kerry, 1972
— Dalton, Charles, *With the Dublin Brigade: Espionage and Assassination with Michael Collins' Intelligence Unit*, Mercier Press, Cork, 2014.
— Davis, Troy D., 'Éamon de Valera's political education: The American Tour of 1919–20', *New Hibernia Review*, Vol. 10, No. 1 (Spring 2006), pp. 65–78.
— Deasy, Liam, *Brother Against Brother*, Mercier Press, Dublin, 1982.
— de Burca, Padraig, and John F. Boyle, *Free State or Republic?*, UCD Press, 2002.
— Desmond, Barry, *No Workers' Republic! Reflections on Labour and Ireland, 1913–1967*, Watchword, Dublin, 2009.
— De Valera, Terry, *A Memoir,* Currach Press, Dublin, 2005.
— Doherty, Gabriel, and Dermot Keogh (eds), *De Valera's Irelands*, Mercier Press, Cork, 2003.
— Doorley, Michael, 'The Friends of Irish Freedom: a case-study in Irish-American nationalism, 1916–21', *History Ireland,* March-April 2008.
— Dudley Edwards, Owen, *Éamon de Valera*, GPC Books, Cardiff, 1987.
— Dunne, Declan, *Peter's Key: Peter Deloughrey and the Fight for Irish Independence*, Mercier Press, Cork, 2012.
— Dunphy, Richard, *The Making of Fianna Fáil Power in Ireland,* Clarendon Press, Oxford, 1995.
— Dwane, David: *Early Life of Éamon de Valera*, Talbot Press, Dublin, 3rd Edition [no year given]; digitised by the Internet Archive.
— Dwyer, T. Ryle, *De Valera's Darkest Hour: 1919–32*, Mercier Press, Cork and Dublin, 1982.
— Dwyer, T. Ryle, *De Valera: The Man and the Myths*, Poolbeg Press, Dublin, 1991.
— English, Richard, *Armed Struggle: The history of the IRA*, Pan Books, London, 2004.
— English, Richard, *Irish Freedom: the history of Nationalism in Ireland,* Macmillan, London, 2006.

— Enright, Seán, *Easter Rising 1916: The Trials*, Merrion, Dublin, 2014.
— Evans, Bryce, *Seán Lemass: Democratic Dictator*, The Collins Press, Cork, 2011.
— Evans, Bryce, and Stephen Kelly (eds), *Frank Aiken: Nationalist and Internationalist*, Irish Academic Press, Dublin, 2014.
— Fallon, Charlotte H., *Soul of Fire: A Biography of Mary MacSwiney*, Mercier Press, Dublin and Cork, 1986.
— Fanning, Ronan, *Independent Ireland*, Helicon, Dublin, 1983.
— Fanning, Ronan, *Fatal Path: British Government and Irish Revolution, 1910–1922*, Faber and Faber, London, 2013.
— Fanning, Ronan, *Éamon de Valera: A Will to Power*, Faber and Faber, London, 2015.
— Farragher, Sean P., *Dev and his Alma Mater: Éamon de Valera's lifelong association with Blackrock College, 1898–1975*, Paraclete Press, Dublin and London, 1984.
— Feeney, Brian, *Sinn Féin: A hundred turbulent years*, O'Brien Press, Dublin, 2002.
— Feeney, Tom, *Seán MacEntee: A Political Life*, Irish Academic Press, Dublin, 2009.
— Ferriter, Diarmaid, *The Transformation of Ireland, 1900–2000*, Profile Books, London, 2004.
— Ferriter, Diarmaid, *A Nation and not a Rabble: The Irish Revolution 1913–23*, Profile Books, 2015, Kindle edition.
— FitzGibbon, Constantine, and George Morrison, *The Life and Times of Éamon de Valera*, Gill and Macmillan, Dublin, 1973.
— Fitzpatrick, David, 'Éamon de Valera at Trinity College', *Hermathena*, No. 133 (Winter 1982), pp. 7–14.
— Fitzpatrick, David, *The Two Irelands, 1912–1939*, Oxford University Press, 1998.
— Fitzpatrick, David, 'Decidedly a Personality: de Valera's performance as a convict, 1916–17', *History Ireland*, Vol. 10, No. 2 (Summer 2002), pp. 40–6.
— Fitzpatrick, David, *Harry Boland's Irish Revolution*, Cork University Press, 2003.
— Foley, Tadhg, and Maureen O'Connor (eds), *Ireland and India: Colonies, culture and empire*, Irish Academic Press, Dublin, 2006.
— Foster, Roy, *Vivid Faces: The Revolutionary Generation in Ireland 1890–1923*, Allen Lane, London, 2014.
— Fox, Peter (ed.), *Treasures of the Library: Trinity College Dublin*, Royal Irish Academy, Dublin, 1986.
— Foy, Michael, and Brian Barton, *The Easter Rising*, Sutton Publishing, Gloucestershire, 1999.
— Franklin, David B., 'Bigotry in 'Bama: de Valera's visit to Birmingham, Alabama, April 1920', *History Ireland*, Vol. 12, Issue 4 (Winter 2004).

— Gallagher, Frank, *The Four Glorious Years*, 2nd edition, Blackwater Press, Dublin, 2005.
— Gallagher, Michael, 'Party Solidarity, Exclusivity and Inter-Party Relationships in Ireland, 1922–1977: The Evidence of Transfers', *Economic and Social Review*, Vol. 10, No. 1, October 1978, pp. 1–22.
— Gallagher, Michael, 'The Pact General Election of 1922', *Irish Historical Studies*, 21:84 (1981), pp. 404–21.
— Garvin, Tom, *1922: The Birth of Irish Democracy*, Gill and Macmillan, Dublin, (first published 1996) 2005 edition.
— Garvin, Tom, *Judging Lemass*, Royal Irish Academy, Dublin, 2009.
— Gaughan, J. Anthony, *Austin Stack: Portrait of a Separatist*, Kingdom Books, Dublin, 1977.
— Gaughan, J. Anthony, *Thomas Johnson, 1872–1963: First Leader of the Labour Party in Dáil Éireann*, Kingdom Books, Dublin, 1980.
— Gaughan, J. Anthony (ed.), *Memoirs of Senator Joseph Connolly (1885–1961): A founder of modern Ireland*, Irish Academic Press, Dublin, 1996.
— Gaynor, Éamonn, *Memoirs of a Tipperary Family: The Gaynors of Tyone, 1887–2000*, Geography Publications, Dublin, no date given.
— Gonne MacBride, Maude, *A Servant of the Queen*, edited by A. Norman Jeffares and Anna MacBride White, Colin Smythe, Gerrards Cross, 1994.
— Hanley, Brian, *The IRA: A Documentary History, 1916–2005*, Gill and Macmillan, Dublin, 2010.
— Hannigan, Dave, *De Valera in America: The Rebel President's 1919 Campaign*, O'Brien Press, Dublin, 2008.
— Harkness, David, *The Restless Dominion: the Irish Free State and the British Commonwealth of Nations, 1921–31*, Gill and Macmillan, Dublin, 1969.
— Hart, Peter, *Mick: The real Michael Collins*, Macmillan, London, 2005.
— Hattersley, Roy, *David Lloyd George: The Great Outsider*, Kindle edition, Hachette Digital, 2010.
— Hayes, Michael, 'Dáil Éireann and the Irish Civil War', *Studies*, Vol. 58, No. 229 (Spring 1969), pp. 1–23.
— Hopkinson, Michael (ed.), *The Last Days of Dublin Castle: The Diaries of Mark Sturgis*, Irish Academic Press, Dublin, 1999.
— Horgan, J. J., *The Complete Grammar of Anarchy*, Maunsel and Company, Dublin and London, 1918, digitised by the Internet Archive.
— Horgan, John, *Seán Lemass: The Enigmatic Patriot*, Gill and Macmillan, Dublin, 1997.
— Inoue, Keiko, 'Sinn Féin and the "Partition Election", 1921', *Studia Hibernica*, No. 30 (1998/99), pp. 47–61.
— Johnston, Kevin, *Home or Away: The Great War and the Irish Revolution*, Gill and Macmillan, Dublin, 2010.
— Jones, Francis P, *History of the Sinn Fein Movement and the Irish Rebellion of 1916*, PJ Kenedy & sons, New York, 1917, digitised by the Internet Archive.

— Jordan, Anthony J., *Éamon de Valera, 1882–1975. Irish: Catholic: Visionary*, Westport Books, Dublin, 2010.
— Keogh, Dermot, *The Vatican, the Bishops and Irish Politics, 1919–39*, Cambridge University Press, 1986.
— Keogh, Dermot, *Twentieth-Century Ireland: Nation and State*, Gill and Macmillan, Dublin, 1994.
— Keown, Gerard, 'The Irish Race Conference, 1922, Reconsidered', *Irish Historical Studies*, Vol. 32, No. 127 (May 2001), pp. 365–76.
— Kissane, Bill, *Explaining Irish Democracy*, UCD Press, Dublin, 2002.
— Laffan, Michael, *The Resurrection of Ireland: The Sinn Fein Party 1916–1923*, Cambridge University Press, paperback edition, 2005.
— Laffan, Michael, *Judging W. T. Cosgrave*, Royal Irish Academy, Dublin, 2014.
— Lane, Leeann, *Rosamond Jacob: Third Person Singular*, UCD Press, 2010.
— Lavelle, Patricia, *James O'Mara: A Staunch Sinn Feiner 1873–1948*, Clonmore and Reynolds, Dublin, 1961.
— Lee, Joseph, and Gearóid Ó Tuathaigh, *The Age of de Valera: Based on the Television Series*, Ward River Press, Dublin, in association with RTÉ, 1982.
— Lee, J. J., *Ireland 1912–1985: Politics and Society*, Cambridge University Press, 1989.
— Lee, J. J., 'De Valera's Use of Words: Three Case-Studies', *Radharc*, Vol. 2 (Nov 2001), pp. 75–100.
— Lewis, Matthew, *Frank Aiken's War: The Irish Revolution, 1916–23*, UCD Press, 2014.
— Lewis, Samuel, *A Topographic Dictionary of Ireland*, Vol. 1, 2nd edition, S. Lewis and Co, London, 1847, accessed through irishalmanacs.blogspot.ie
— Litton, Helen, *16 Lives: Thomas Clarke*, O'Brien Press, Dublin, 2014.
— Longford, Frank, and Thomas P. O'Neill, *Éamon de Valera*, paperback edition, Arrow Books, London, 1974.
— Lyons, F. S. L., *Ireland Since the Famine*, Paperback Edition, Fontana, 1973.
— Lyons, George A., 'Occupation of Ringsend Area in 1916, part 1', *An t-Óglác*, 10/4/26.
— Lyons, George A., 'Occupation of Ringsend Area in 1916, part 2', *An t-Óglác*, 17/4/26.
— Lyons, George A., 'Occupation of Ringsend Area in 1916, part 3', *An t-Óglác*, 24/4/26.
— Macardle, Dorothy, *The Irish Republic*, Wolfhound Press, Dublin, 1999.
— MacBride, Seán, *That Day's Struggle: A Memoir 1904–1951*, edited by Caitriona Lawlor, Currach Press, Dublin, 2005.
— McCartan, Patrick, *With de Valera in America*, Fitzpatrick Limited, Dublin, 1932.
— McCarthy, Cal, *Cumann na mBan and the Irish Revolution*, The Collins Press, Cork, 2007.

— McCartney, Donal, *The National University of Ireland and Éamon de Valera*, The University Press of Ireland, Dublin, 1983.

— McConville, Seán, *Irish Political Prisoners, 1848–1922: Theatres of War*, Routledge, London, 2003.

— McCullagh, David, *The Reluctant Taoiseach: A biography of John A. Costello*, Gill and Macmillan, Dublin, 2010.

— McGarry, Fearghal, *Eoin O'Duffy: A Self-Made Hero*, Oxford University Press, 2007.

— McGarry, Fearghal, *The Rising: Ireland, Easter 1916*, Oxford University Press, 2010.

— McManus, M. J., *Éamon de Valera*, Ziff David, Chicago and New York, 1946, digitised by Universal Library, ref no 121405.

— Maher, Jim, *The Oath is Dead and Gone*, Londubh Books, Dublin, 2011.

— Manning, Maurice, *James Dillon: A biography*, Wolfhound Press, Dublin, 1999.

— Mansergh, Diana (ed.), *Nationalism and Independence: Selected Irish Papers of Nicholas Mansergh*, Cork University Press, 1997.

— Martin, F. X. (ed), *The Irish Volunteers, 1913–1915*, James Duffy & Co, Dublin, 1963.

— Martin, F. X, and F. J. Byrne (eds), *The Scholar Revolutionary: Eoin MacNeill 1867–1945 and the Making of the New Ireland*, Irish University Press, Shannon, 1973.

— Martin, Micheál, *Freedom to Choose: Cork and Party Politics in Ireland, 1918–1932*, Collins Press, Cork, 2009.

— Matthews, Ann, *Dissidents: Irish Republican Women, 1923–1941*, Mercier Press, Cork, 2012.

— Matthews, Kevin, *Fatal Influence: The Impact of Ireland on British Politics, 1920–1925*, UCD Press, 2004.

— Meehan, Ciara, *The Cosgrave Party: A history of Cumann na nGaedheal, 1923–33*, Royal Irish Academy, Dublin, 2010.

— Meleady, Dermot, *John Redmond: The National Leader*, Merrion, Dublin, 2014.

— Mellett, James, *If Any Man Dare*, Fallons, Dublin, 1963.

— Middlemas, Keith (ed), *Thomas Jones: Whitehall Diary Volume III Ireland 1918–1925*, OUP, 1971.

— Mitchell, Angus, *16 Lives: Roger Casement*, O'Brien Press, Dublin, 2013.

— Molyneux, Derek, and Kelly, Darren, *When the Clock Struck in 1916: close-quarter combat in the Easter Rising*, Collins Press, Cork, 2015.

— Montague, John, 'The Unpartitioned Intellect: Dante, Savanarola, and an Old Sign', *The Canadian Journal of Irish Studies*, Vol. 12, No. 1 (June 1986), pp. 5–9.

— Morrissey, Thomas J., *William J. Walsh, Archbishop of Dublin, 1841–1921*, Four Courts Press, Dublin, 2000.

— Morrissey, Thomas J., *William O'Brien, 1881–1968: Socialist, Republican, Dáil Deputy, Editor and Trade Union Leader*, Four Courts Press, Dublin, 2007.
— Moynihan, Maurice (ed.), *Speeches and Statements by Éamon de Valera, 1917–1973*, Gill and Macmillan, Dublin, 1980.
— Mulcahy, Risteárd, *Richard Mulcahy: A Family Memoir*, Aurelian Press, Dublin, 1999.
— Mulcahy, Risteárd, *My Father, the General: Richard Mulcahy and the Military History of the Revolution*, Liberties Press, Dublin, 2009.
— Munger, Frank, *The Legitimacy of Opposition: The change of government in Ireland in 1932*, SAGE Publications, London/Beverly Hills, 1975.
— Murphy, Brian P., *Patrick Pearse and the Lost Republican Ideal*, James Duffy, Dublin, 1991.
— Murphy, Brian P., *John Chartres: Mystery Man of the Treaty*, Irish Academic Press, Dublin, 1995.
— Neeson, Eoin, *The Civil War 1922–23*, Poolbeg, Dublin, 1989.
— Ó Beacháin, Donnacha, *Destiny of the Soldiers: Fianna Fáil, Irish Republicanism and the IRA, 1926–73*, Gill and Macmillan, Dublin, 2010.
— Ó Broin, Leon, *Revolutionary Underground: The story of the Irish Republican Brotherhood, 1858–1924*, Gill and Macmillan, Dublin, 1976.
— Ó Broin, Leon, *Just Like Yesterday: an autobiography*, Gill and Macmillan, Dublin, 1985.
— Ó Broin, Leon, (ed.), revised and extended by Cian Ó hÉigeartaigh, *In Great Haste: The letters of Michael Collins and Kitty Kiernan*, Gill and Macmillan, Dublin, 1996.
— Ó Drisceoil, Donal, *Peadar O'Donnell*, Cork University Press, 2001.
— O Dulaing, Donncha, *Voices of Ireland*, O'Brien Press, Dublin, 1984.
— Ó Fearaíl, Pádraig, *The Story of Conradh na Gaeilge*, Clódhanna Teo, Baile Átha Cliath, 1975.
— O hEithir, Breandán, *The Begrudger's Guide to Irish Politics*, Poolbeg, Dublin, 1986.
— Ó Longaigh, Seosamh, *Emergency Law in Independent Ireland, 1922–1948*, Four Courts Press, Dublin, 2006.
— O Luing, Sean, *I Die in a Good Cause*, Anvil Books, Tralee, 1970.
— O'Brien, Mark, *De Valera, Fianna Fáil and the Irish Press*, Irish Academic Press, Dublin, 2001.
— O'Brien, William, *The Irish Revolution and how it came about*, Maunsel and Roberts, Dublin, 1923, digitised by the Internet Archive.
— O'Brien, William, *Forth the Banners Go*, Three Candles, Dublin, 1969.
— O'Carroll, J.P, and John A. Murphy (eds), *De Valera and his times*, Cork University Press, 1983.
— O'Connor, Emmet, *A Labour History of Ireland 1842–1960*, Gill and Macmillan, Dublin, 1992.

— O'Donnell, Ruán (ed.), *The Impact of the 1916 Rising: Among the Nations*, Irish Academic Press, 2008.

— O'Halpin, Eunan, *Defending Ireland: The Irish State and its enemies since 1922*, Oxford University Press, 1999.

— O'Halpin, Eunan, 'Long fellow, long story: MI5 and de Valera', *Irish Studies in International Affairs*, Vol. 14 (2003), pp. 185–203.

— O'Halpin, Eunan, *Spying on Ireland: British Intelligence and Irish neutrality during the Second World War*, Oxford University Press, 2008.

— O'Hegarty, P. S., *The Victory of Sinn Féin*, Centenary Classics Edition, UCD Press, 2015 (first published 1924).

— O'Malley, Cormac K. H. and Dolan, Anne, (eds), *'No Surrender Here!' The Civil War Papers of Ernie O'Malley*, Lilliput Press, Dublin, 2007.

— O'Neill, Charles Edwards, 'Towards American recognition of the Republic of Ireland: De Valera's visit to New Orleans in 1920', *Louisiana History: The Journal of the Louisiana Historical Association*, Vol. 34, No. 3 (Summer, 1993), pp. 229–307.

— O'Neill, Marie, *From Parnell to de Valera: A biography of Jennie Wyse Power*, Blackwater Press, Dublin, 1991.

— O'Neill, Timothy M., 'Handing Away the Trump Card? Peadar O'Donnell, Fianna Fáil, and the Non-Payment of Land Annuities Campaign, 1926–32', *New Hibernia Review*, Vol. 12, No. 1, Spring 2008, pp. 19–40.

— Pakenham, Frank, *Peace by Ordeal*, Jonathan Cape, London, 1935.

— Puirséil, Niamh, *The Irish Labour Party 1922–1973*, UCD Press, Dublin, 2007.

— Pyne, Peter, 'The Third Sinn Féin Party: 1923–1926', part one, *Economic and Social Review*, Vol. 1, No. 1, October 1969, pp. 29–50.

— Regan, John M., *The Irish Counter-Revolution, 1921–1936*, Gill and Macmillan, Dublin, paperback edition, 2001.

— Ryan, Meda, *Liam Lynch: The Real Chief*, Mercier Press, Cork, 2012.

— Sarbaugh, Timothy J., 'Irish Republicanism vs "Pure Americanism": California's Reaction to Eamon de Valera's visits', *California History*, Vol. 60, No. 2 (Summer, 1981), pp. 172–185.

— Seoighe, Mainchín, *From Bruree to Corcomohide: the district where world statesman EDV grew up and where the illustrious Mac Eniry family ruled*, Bruree/Rockhill Development Association, Bruree, 2000.

— Sexton, Brendan, *Ireland and the Crown, 1922–36: The Governor-Generalship of the Irish Free State*, Irish Academic Press, Dublin, 1989.

— Shakespeare, Geoffrey, *Let Candles be Brought In*, Macdonald, London, 1949.

— Shouldice, Frank, *Grandpa the Sniper: the Remarkable Story of a 1916 Volunteer*, The Liffey Press, Dublin, 2015.

— Silinonte, Joseph M., 'The Search for Vivion de Valera, part 1', *Irish Roots*, 1999, No. 4.

— Silinonte, Joseph M., 'The Search for Vivion de Valera, part 2', *Irish Roots*, 2000, No. 1.
— Silinonte, Joseph M., 'Vivion de Valera: The Search Continues, part 1', *Irish Roots*, 2004, No. 1.
— Silinonte, Joseph M., 'Vivion de Valera: The Search Continues, part 2', *Irish Roots*, 2004, No. 2.
— Synge, J. L., 'Éamon de Valera, 14 October 1882–29 August 1975', *Biographical Memoirs of Fellows of the Royal Society*, Vol. 22 (Nov. 1976), pp. 634–53.
— Tierney, Michael, *Eoin MacNeill: Scholar and Man of Action, 1867–1945*, edited by F. X. Martin, Clarendon Press, Oxford, 1980.
— Townshend, Charles, *Easter 1916: The Irish Rebellion*, Penguin, London, 2006.
— Townshend, Charles, *The Republic: The Fight for Irish Independence, 1918–1923*, Penguin Books Ltd, Kindle Edition, 2013.
— Turi, John J., *England's Greatest Spy: Éamon de Valera*, Stacey International, London, 2009.
— Valiulis, Maryann Gialanella, *Portrait of a Revolutionary: General Richard Mulcahy and the founding of the Irish Free State*, Irish Academic Press, 1992.
— Walker, Antoinette, and Michael Fitzgerald, *Unstoppable Brilliance: Irish geniuses and Asperger's Syndrome*, Liberties Press, Dublin, 2006.
— Walsh, Dick, *The Party: Inside Fianna Fáil*, Gill and Macmillan, Dublin, 1986.
— Walsh, Maurice, *Bitter Freedom: Ireland in a Revolutionary World, 1918–1923*, Faber and Faber, London, 2015.
— Ward, Alan J., 'Lloyd George and the 1918 Irish Conscription Crisis', *The Historical Journal*, Vol. 17, No. 1 (Mar., 1974), pp. 107–129.
— Ward, Margaret, *Hanna Sheehy-Skeffington: A Life*, Attic Press, Cork, 1997.
— Welles, Warre B., and N. Marlowe, *The Irish Convention and Sinn Fein*, Frederick Stokes, New York, 1918, digitised by the Internet Archive.
— Wheeler, Charles Newton, *The Irish Republic*, Cahill-Igoe Company, Chicago, 1919, digitised by the Internet Archive.
— Whelan, Bernadette, *United States Foreign Policy and Ireland: From Empire to Independence, 1913–29*, Four Courts Press, Dublin, 2006.
— Whelan, Noel, *Fianna Fáil: A Biography of the Party*, Gill and Macmillan, Dublin, 2011.
— White, Terence de Vere, *Kevin O'Higgins*, Anvil Books, 1986.
— Yeates, Pádraig, *A City in Wartime: Dublin 1914–18*, Gill and Macmillan, Dublin, 2011.
— Yeates, Pádraig, *A City in Turmoil: Dublin 1919–21*, Gill and Macmillan, Dublin, 2015.
— Yeates, Pádraig, *A City in Civil War: Dublin 1921–24*, Gill and Macmillan, Dublin, 2015.

INDEX